THE OXFORD HANDBOOK OF

RELIGION AND THE AMERICAN NEWS MEDIA

THE OXFORD HANDBOOK OF

RELIGION AND THE AMERICAN NEWS MEDIA

Edited by

DIANE WINSTON

OXFORD
UNIVERSITY PRESS

OXFORD
UNIVERSITY PRESS

Oxford University Press publishes works that further
Oxford University's objective of excellence
in research, scholarship, and education by publishing worldwide.

Oxford New York
Auckland Cape Town Dar es Salaam Hong Kong Karachi
Kuala Lumpur Madrid Melbourne Mexico City Nairobi
New Delhi Shanghai Taipei Toronto

With offices in
Argentina Austria Brazil Chile Czech Republic France Greece
Guatemala Hungary Italy Japan Poland Portugal Singapore
South Korea Switzerland Thailand Turkey Ukraine Vietnam

Published in the United States of America
by Oxford University Press
198 Madison Avenue, New York, New York 10016

Library of Congress Cataloging-in-Publication Data
The Oxford handbook of religion and the American news media / edited by Diane Winston.
p. cm.
Includes index.
ISBN 978-0-19-539506-8
1. Mass media in religion—United States. 2. Mass media—Religious aspects.
3. Mass media—United States.
4. Religion and the press—United States.
5. Journalism, Religious—United States. 6. Digital media—Religious aspects.
7. Digital media—United States. I. Winston, Diane H.
II. Title: Handbook of religion and the American news media.
BL2525.O95 2012
070.4'49200973—dc23 2012003855

1 3 5 7 9 8 6 4 2

Printed in the United States of America
on acid-free paper

Contents

Section IV. Issues and Beats

Section V. International Coverage

Section VI. The Religious Press

Acknowledgments

I have been fortunate to work with many smart and large-hearted people on this project. Both Theo Calderara and Sheila Davaney have provided invaluable advice, support, and encouragement. Jillian O'Connor, the project manager, sweated all the details and the prose is richer for it. Words cannot cover my gratitude to her.

All thirty-six writers remained gracious and professional even when we lobbed edits, pressed deadlines, and demanded cuts. Many worked outside their comfort zone and the fledgling field of religion and media studies can only benefit from their efforts.

As ever, I appreciate the fortitude of family members—especially Chris Bugbee and Isabelle Winston, as they, too, have lived with this book. I am also grateful for support from Suzanne Winston, Sara Walters-Bugbee, Erin Walters-Bugbee, and Bill Winston.

I especially want to acknowledge Nick Street, who has been my steadfast colleague for the past five years. Nick has been the yin to my yang, and his humor, friendship, and thoughtfulness are gifts that can never be repaid. For his professional commitment to news, his intellectual passion for religion, and his cheerful willingness to explore the margins, Nick embodies the spirit of this collection.

Contributors

Ashraf Alam is a graduate student at the University of Texas at San Antonio. His interests include religion, social movements, and qualitative methods.

Steven Barrie-Anthony is a doctoral student in religious studies at the University of California, Santa Barbara. His work addresses contemporary religious innovation and change in the context of pluralism and shifting styles of solidarity. This includes research on new spirituality, new religious movements, religion and healing, and religion and the media. He has authored or coauthored several scholarly articles and was formerly a staff writer with the *Los Angeles Times*.

John P. Bartkowski is professor of sociology at the University of Texas at San Antonio. He was previously the Beverly B. and Gordon W. Gulmon Dean's Eminent Scholar of Sociology at Mississippi State University. Much of his work examines the connections between religious conservatism, family, gender, and social welfare policy. The author of three books and fifty articles, he is currently completing a monograph that contrasts programming dynamics among faith-based and secular social service agencies.

Annie Blazer is assistant professor of Religious Studies at Centenary College in Shreveport, Louisiana. She spent a year as a research fellow at Princeton University's Center for the Study of Religion and completed her PhD at University of North Carolina at Chapel Hill. Her primary research and teaching interests are American religion and popular culture. Her forthcoming book, *Faith on the Field: Sports and Evangelical Christianity in America,* examines the social structures, practices, and beliefs that stitch together conservative Christianity and America's sporting industries.

Judith M. Buddenbaum is professor emerita in the Department of Journalism and Technical Communication at Colorado State University where she taught courses on religion and media, communication law, media research, and reporting. Her publications include *Religious Scandals* (Greenwood Press, 2009), *Reporting News About Religion: An Introduction for Journalists* (Iowa State University Press, 1998), and, with Debra L. Mason, *Readings on Religion as News* (Iowa State University Press, 2000), as well as many book chapters and scholarly articles in journals such as *Journalism Quarterly, Newspaper Research Journal,* and *Journalism History*. A former religion reporter, she is cofounder and coeditor of the *Journal of Media and Religion*. She holds an AB in chemistry, an MA in journalism, and a PhD in mass communication from Indiana University.

Anthea Butler is associate professor of Religious Studies and graduate chair at the University of Pennsylvania. Her most recent book is *Women in the Church of God in Christ, Making A Sanctified World,* published by the University of North Carolina Press. She is a blogger and contributor for Religion Dispatches, an online daily revolving around religion. Professor Butler's next project is a book on religion and the Tea Party that will be published with The New Press in 2012.

Lynn Schofield Clark is associate professor, director of Graduate Studies, and director of the Estlow International Center for Journalism and New Media at the University of Denver's Department of Media, Film, and Journalism Studies. She is author of *From Angels to Aliens: Teenagers, the Media, & the Supernatural* (Oxford University Press, 2003/2005), editor of *Religion, Media, and the Marketplace* (Rutgers University Press, 2007), and coauthor of *Media, Home and Family* (Routledge, 2004) in addition to several articles and essays. She is an interpretive sociologist who studies the role of popular media in families and in the religious lives of young people in the United States.

David Copeland is the A. J. Fletcher professor and director of Graduate Studies in the School of Communications at Elon University. He is the author of numerous books on the history of media, most of which deal with the press and the nation prior to the Civil War. He has been selected as the Carnegie Foundation Professor of the Year for Virginia and named Distinguished University Scholar at Elon.

Magali do Nascimento Cunha holds a PhD in Communication Sciences at Universidade de Sao Paulo (Sao Paulo University) and an MA in social memory at Universidade do Rio de Janeiro (Rio de Janeiro University) and a BA in journalism (Universidade Federal Fluminense). She is a professor at the Methodist University of São Paulo working in the School of Theology and in the Graduate Program on Social Communication. She coordinates the research group "Discursus—Practical Theology and Language" and teaches courses and lectures on media and religion, as well as church and society. She is the author of *Explosao Gospel. Um olhar das ciências humanas sobre o cenário religioso evangélico contemporâneo [Gospel Explosion: A Human Sciences Overview of the Contemporary Evangelical Religious Scenery]* (Mauad, 2007).

Carole M. Cusack is associate professor in Studies in Religion at the University of Sydney. She trained as a medievalist and her doctorate was published as *Conversion Among the Germanic Peoples* (Cassell, 1998). Since the late 1990s, she has taught in contemporary religious trends, publishing on pilgrimage and tourism, modern Pagan religions, new religious movements, the interface between religion and politics, and religion and popular culture. She is the author of *The Essence of Buddhism* (Lansdowne, 2001), *Invented Religions: Imagination, Fiction and Faith* (Ashgate, 2010), and *The Sacred Tree: Ancient and Medieval Manifestations* (Cambridge Scholars, 2011). With Christopher Hartney (University of Sydney) she is editor of the *Journal of Religious History* (Wiley) and with Liselotte Frisk (Dalarna

University) she is editor of the *International Journal for the Study of New Religions* (Equinox).

Marcia Alesan Dawkins is an award-winning writer and educator interested in politics, religion, diversity, and communication. In addition to her work as a syndicated blogger for the *Huffington Post*, *Truthdig*, and *Transmissions*, she is the author of two forthcoming books. The first, *Things Said in Passing* (Baylor University Press, 2011), is a critical analysis of "passing" and its impact on the discourse of multiracial identities. The second, *Eminem: The Real Slim Shady* (Praeger Press, 2013), is a study of the cultural and economic significances of Eminem's success. She is currently visiting scholar at Brown University and assistant professor at California State University, Fullerton.

Jill Dierberg is a Joint PhD Candidate in Religion and Social Change at the University of Denver and Iliff School of Theology. Her research interests include the mediatization of religion, youth and young adult religious identity, and the sociology of religion. She teaches Religion courses at Carthage College in Kenosha, Wisconsin.

Darren Dochuk is associate professor of History at Purdue University in West Lafayette, Indiana. He is the author of *From Bible Belt to Sunbelt: Plain-folk Religion, Grassroots Politics, and the Rise of Evangelical Conservatism* (Norton, 2011) and coeditor of *Sunbelt Rising: The Politics of Space, Place, and Region* (University of Pennsylvania Press, 2011). His work has appeared in *International Labor and Working-Class History*, *Religion and American Culture*, the *Journal of American History*, and other leading journals. In 2006, Dochuk won the Society of American Historians' Allan Nevins Prize for the best-written PhD dissertation on a major theme in American history. He is currently at work on a new book, titled *Anointed with Oil: God and Black Gold in Modern America.*

Denise P. Ferguson is associate professor of Mediated Communication and director of Graduate Studies in Communication at Pepperdine University. Ferguson's research has been published in *Public Relations Review*, *The Handbook of Public Relations*, and *Sociological Quarterly* and has been presented at annual conferences of the International Communication Association, National Communication Association, Religious Communication Association, and Public Relations Society of America, where she was awarded the 2008 Top Faculty Paper. She earned a PhD at Purdue University and a master's degree in communication at Bowling Green State University.

Richard Flory is associate research professor of Sociology and director of research at the Center for Religion and Civic Culture at the University of Southern California. His research on religion and media, "Promoting a Secular Standard: Secularization and Modern Journalism, 1870–1930" (in C. Smith, ed., *The Secular Revolution*, University of California Press, 2003), was picked up by a broad spectrum of media outlets, ranging from the *Columbia Journalism Review* to *First Things* and *World Magazine*. Most recently, he is the author of *Growing Up in America: The Power of Race in the Lives of Teens* (Stanford University Press, 2010) and *Finding Faith: The Spiritual Quest of the Post-Boomer Generation* (Rutgers University Press, 2008).

John M. Giggie is associate professor and director of Graduate Studies in History at the University of Alabama. He specializes in southern, African American, and religious history in modern America. He is the author of *After Redemption: The Transformation of African American Religion in the Delta, 1875–1915* (Oxford, 2008) and coeditor of *Faith in the Market: Religion and Urban Commercial Culture in Modern North America* (Rutgers, 2002).

Dalia Hashad is a public interest attorney and consultant. She has been host and executive producer of "Law and Disorder," a national talk radio program on human rights and civil rights in the United States; has run programs at Amnesty International and the ACLU; and has served as a human rights legal adviser in the Middle East. At Amnesty International, she was the director of the USA Program, managing portfolios in racial profiling, criminal justice, national security, LGBT rights, immigrant rights, and conscientious objection to war. She also served as AIUSA's policy specialist in global identity discrimination and gender. At the ACLU, she focused on post-9/11 civil liberties and human rights abuses. Hashad writes frequently and is an editor of the forthcoming book *Patriot Acts: Narratives of Post-9/11 Injustice*. She holds a BA in Environmental Policy from UC Berkeley and a JD from NYU School of Law.

Faiza Hirji is assistant professor in the department of Communication Studies and Multimedia at McMaster University. She specializes in research exploring media representation of race, religion, ethnicity, and gender; use of media in the construction of identity, popular culture, and youth; and the importance of media within diasporic/transnational communities. She is the author of *Dreaming in Canadian: South Asian Youth, Bollywood, and Belonging* (UBC Press, 2010), which explores audience readings of nationalism and religion in Bollywood cinema.

Stewart M. Hoover is professor of Media Studies and Religious Studies and director of the Center for Media, Religion, and Culture at the University of Colorado, Boulder. He has conducted research on religion and spirituality in media households, new media, and domestic religious practices and on gender, media, and religion in the domestic sphere. He is author most recently of *Religion in the Media Age* (Routledge, 2006).

Mark Hulsether is professor of Religious Studies at the University of Tennessee, with special interests in the interplay of religion and social issues in recent US history. He has written on the course of the religious Left in the United States since the 1940s, various aspects of US popular religion, and issues of theory and method in the academic study of religion. His most recent book is *Religion, Culture and Politics* *in the Twentieth Century United States*, copublished by Columbia University Press and Edinburgh University Press.

Jane Naomi Iwamura is the author of *Virtual Orientalism: Asian Religions and American Popular Culture* (Oxford University Press, 2011). She also coedited the volume *Revealing the Sacred in Asian and Pacific America* (Routledge 2003) and has published pieces on Asian American religions, religion and visual culture, and religion and cultural production that have appeared in *American Quarterly, Amerasia Journal*, and *Semeia*. She is a founding member of the Asian Pacific American Religions Research Initiative (APARRI).

Karim H. Karim is a professor at Carleton University's School of Journalism and Communication in Ottawa, where he was previously the director. He recently served as codirector of the Institute of Ismaili Studies in London. His major publications include *The Media of Diaspora* (Routledge, 2003) and the critically acclaimed *Islamic Peril: Media and Global Violence* (Black Rose, 2003), for which he received the inaugural Robinson Book Prize. Dr. Karim has also published extensively on issues of cultural pluralism, multiculturalism, Muslims in the West, and social development in Muslim societies and has delivered distinguished lectures in North America, Europe, and Asia.

Lauri Lebo is an award-winning journalist and author of *The Devil in Dover: An Insider's Story of Dogma v. Darwin in Small-Town America* (New Press, 2008), an account of *Kitzmiller v. Dover* detailing events of the 2005 constitutional test case of intelligent design. Her coverage of this internationally watched story delved into scientific, religious, political, and judicial issues that were inextricably part of the case. A featured blogger for *Religion Dispatches* on the subject of creationist attacks on evolution education, she has also written for *Scientific American, Washington Spectator*, and *Public Eye*.

Kathryn Lofton is assistant professor of American Studies and Religious Studies at Yale University. Her research focuses on the intersection of religious innovation, consumer culture, and the modern imaginary. A specialist in nineteenth- and twentieth-century US religious history, she has published on the evangelical preacher, theological modernism, civil rights activist Fannie Lou Hamer, soap advertisements, and the religious meanings of Oprah Winfrey's multimedia empire. She is the author of *Oprah: The Gospel of an Icon* (University of California Press, 2011).

Peter Manseau is an award-winning author of fiction and nonfiction. He has also written for publications including the *New York Times* and the *Washington Post* and can be heard frequently on NPR. A founding editor of online religion magazine KillingTheBuddha.com, he is a lecturer in Journalism at Georgetown University and the Patrick Henry Writing Fellow at Washington College's Starr Center for the Study of the American Experience.

Debra L. Mason is professor of Journalism Studies at the University of Missouri School of Journalism and director of its interdisciplinary Center on Religion & the Professions, where she collaborates on projects to improve the religious literacy of professionals. In addition, she directs the Religion Newswriters Association and manages the largest collection of resources for journalists reporting on religion, including ReligionLink.com and ReligionStylebook.com. She's a former award-winning journalist, editor of "Reporting on Religion: A Primer on Journalism's Best Beat" (Religion Newswriters Association, 2006), and coeditor, with Judith Buddenbaum, of *Readings on Religion as News* (Iowa State University Press, 2000). Mason is also an entrepreneur who was named publisher of Religion News Service (RNS) in 2011 after creating a new nonprofit organization to acquire RNS, converting its business model into a nonprofit, and developing models for local religion news online.

Sarah M. Pike is professor of Religious Studies at California State University, Chico, where she teaches courses on American religions. Pike is the author of *Earthly Bodies, Magical Selves: Contemporary Pagans and the Search for Community* (University of California Press, 2001) and *New Age and Neopagan Religions in America* (Columbia University Press, 2004). She is currently working on a book about religion and youth culture.

Elizabeth Poole is a senior lecturer in Media Studies at Staffordshire University and Award Leader of the MA in Media Management. She has written widely in the area of the representation and reception of Muslims in the news and is author of *Reporting Islam: Media Representations of British Muslims* (I. B. Taurus, 2002) and coeditor, with John Richardson, of *Muslims and the News Media* (I. B. Taurus, 2006). She has been involved in projects with the Arts and Humanities Research Council and the Institute of Strategic Dialogue.

Jana Riess received her PhD in American Religious History from Columbia University and a master of divinity from Princeton Theological Seminary. She is the author or coauthor of nine books, including *Mormonism for Dummies* (Wiley, 2005), *What Would Buffy Do? The Vampire Slayer as Spiritual Guide* (Wiley, 2004), and *Flunking Sainthood* (Paraclete, 2011), a memoir about the lighter side of twelve months living radical spiritual practices. She spent nine years as the religion book review editor for *Publishers Weekly* and is now an acquisitions editor at Westminster John Knox Press.

Michele Rosenthal is lecturer at the Department of Communication in the University of Haifa. She is the author of *American Protestants and Television in the 1950s: A New Medium* (Palgrave, 2007). She is currently working on a research project with Rivka Ribak titled *Unplugged: Media Ambivalence and Avoidance in Everyday Life.*

Nora L. Rubel is assistant professor of Religion and Classics at the University of Rochester, where she teaches courses in American Judaism, religion and ethnicity, and religion and American foodways. Her first book, *Doubting the Devout: The Ultra-Orthodox in the Jewish American Imagination,* was recently published by Columbia University Press, and she is currently at work on a book about *The Settlement Cook Book* and American Jewish identity.

Jonathan D. Sarna is the Joseph H. & Belle R. Braun Professor of American Jewish History and chair of the Hornstein Jewish Professional Leadership Program at Brandeis University. He also chairs the Academic Advisory and Editorial Board of the Jacob Rader Marcus Center of the American Jewish Archives in Cincinnati and is chief historian of the National Museum of American Jewish History in Philadelphia. Author or editor of more than twenty-five books on American Jewish history and life, his most recent book is titled *When General Grant Expelled the Jews* (Schocken/Nextbook, 2012). His *American Judaism: A History* (Yale University Press, 2004) won six awards including the 2004 "Jewish Book of the Year Award" from the Jewish Book Council.

Philip Seib is professor of Journalism and Public Diplomacy and professor of International Relations at the University of Southern California. He is also director of USC's Center on Public Diplomacy. He studies linkages between media and war and terrorism, as well as public diplomacy issues. He is author or editor of numerous books, including *Headline Diplomacy: How News Coverage Affects Foreign Policy (*Praeger, 1997), *The Global Journalist: News and Conscience in a World of Conflict* (Rowman & Littlefield, 2002), *Beyond the Front Lines: How the News Media Cover a World Shaped by War* (Palgrave Macmillan, 2004), *Broadcasts from the Blitz: How Edward R. Murrow Helped Lead America into War* (Potomac, 2006), *New Media and the New Middle East* (Palgrave Macmillan, 2007), *The Al Jazeera Effect: How the New Global Media Are Reshaping World Politics*, and *Toward a New Public Diplomacy: Redirecting U.S. Foreign Policy* (Potomac, 2008). He is the series editor of the Palgrave Macmillan Series in International Political Communication, coeditor of the Palgrave Macmillan Series in Global Public Diplomacy, and coeditor of the journal *Media, War, and Conflict*, published by Sage.

Mark Silk is director of the Leonard E. Greenberg Center for the Study of Religion in Public Life and professor of religion in public life at Trinity College, Hartford. He holds AB and PhD degrees from Harvard University and was formerly a reporter, editorial writer, and columnist at the *Atlanta Journal-Constitution*. He is the author of *Spiritual Politics: Religion and America Since World War II* and *Unsecular Media: Making News of Religion in America*; is coauthor of *The American Establishment*(Avon, 1981) and *One Nation, Divisible: How Regional Religious Differences Shape American Politics* (Rowman & Littlefield, 2008); and blogs at Spiritual-Politics.org.

Nick Street is a freelance writer and a Buddhist priest at the Hazy Moon Zen Center in Los Angeles. His work has appeared in *Search*, the *Jewish Journal*, the *Revealer*, *Los Angeles CityBeat*, *L.A. Weekly*, the *Los Angeles Times*, and Religion Dispatches.

J. Terry Todd is associate professor of American Religious Studies at Drew University. He is the author of many articles on religious life in the United States, most recently "The Temple of Religion and the Politics of Religious Pluralism: Judeo-Christian America at the New York World's Fair, 1939–1940" (in Courtney Bender and Pamela Klassen, eds., *After Pluralism: Reimagining Religious Engagement*, Columbia University Press, 2010). His current research explores the history of Christianity and celebrity culture in the United States.

Doug Underwood is professor of Communication at the University of Washington and the author of *From Yahweh to Yahoo!: The Religious Roots of the Secular Press* (University of Illinois Press, 2002), which won a 2003 Distinguished Book Award from the Society for the Scientific Study of Religion (SSSR). A former journalist for the *Seattle Times* and the Gannett News Service, he has published in scholarly publications on such topics as media ethics, journalists' religious beliefs, media economics and management, technology in the newsroom, and journalism and literature. His most recent books are *Journalism and the Novel: Truth and Fiction, 1700–2000* (Cambridge University Press, 2008) and *Chronicling Trauma: Journalists and Writers on Violence and Loss* (University of Illinois Press, 2011).

Ken Waters is chair of the Communication Division at Pepperdine University in Malibu, California. He teaches journalism, communication ethics, and intercultural communication. He has published extensively on issues related to Protestant magazine publishing and media ethics. Waters received his BA and MA from Pepperdine and his PhD from the University of Southern California.

Diane Winston holds the Knight Chair in Media and Religion at the Annenberg School for Communication at the University of Southern California. A journalist and a scholar, Winston's books include *Red Hot and Righteous: The Urban Religion of the Salvation Army* (Harvard, 1999); *Faith in the Market: Religion and Urban Commercial Culture* (Rutgers, 2003); and *Small Screen, Big Picture: Lived Religion and Television* (Baylor, 2009). Winston covered religion for the *Raleigh News and Observer*, the *Dallas Times Herald*, and the *Baltimore Sun*. She also has written for television, magazines, and print outlets including the *Wall Street Journal*, *Washington Post*, and *Chronicle of Higher Education*.

THE OXFORD HANDBOOK OF

RELIGION AND THE AMERICAN NEWS MEDIA

"MAPPING THE ROYAL ROAD": AN INTRODUCTION TO THE *OXFORD HANDBOOK ON RELIGION AND THE AMERICAN NEWS MEDIA*

DIANE WINSTON

WRITING in the 1993 *Nieman Reports* special issue "God in the Newsroom," theologian Harvey Cox offered two salient observations about religion and religious movements. First, religious movements can never be studied apart from the cultural and political milieu in which they arise, and second, "religion is the royal road to the heart of a civilization, the clearest indicator of its hopes and terrors, the surest index of how it is changing."[1] By arguing that religion is a reliable cultural barometer, Cox hoped to convince journalists to pay more attention to Pentecostalism. Its booming global growth, he said, signaled significant cultural and social changes, but the news media were missing the story.

Were Cox a media scholar, he might have thought differently. According to many academic studies, reporters are just as likely to skew, stop, or accelerate societal changes as they are to elucidate them. In fact, a close study of news writing often yields as much insight into the culture of journalism as it does into the cultures that journalists cover. That is exactly why reporting about religion matters: it not only reveals social arrangements and cultural trends but also illumines, as would reporting on any other subject, contemporary media practices and their underpinning assumptions. Media is to society, as some scholars have observed, what water is to fish: a taken-for-granted yet all-encompassing environment that shapes beliefs, behaviors, and social interactions.

In the current moment of mediatization, the process by which "media in the long run increasingly become relevant for the social construction of everyday life, society and culture as a whole,"[2] journalistic representations of religion can assume a reality distinct from religions' actual, in-the-world existence. The slippage between representation and reality can be relatively benign—apolitical fundamentalists bristling at portrayals of themselves as card-carrying members of the religious Right—or deeply problematic, as in the case of news consumers who "know" Islam as a religion that oppresses women and condones terrorism. What's at stake for journalists, scholars, and an informed public is understanding how mediated representations come to be, what purpose they serve, and what can be learned from them. By querying four domains—religion, religious studies, journalism, and media studies—and mapping their feedback loops, the *Oxford Handbook on Religion and the American News Media* seeks to illuminate how the news media shape and reflect what the public knows about religion.

The Oxford Handbook of Religion and the American News Media falls in the purview of religion and media studies, an emerging field that encompasses research in religion, history, area studies, sociology, and communications, among other disciplines. Researchers in the field have examined topics ranging from audience reception of online religious gaming to the transatlantic circulation of nineteenth-century evangelical tracts to the semiotics of Hindu soap operas. Religion and the news media, a small subfield, has been dominated by communication scholars interested in studying framing, stereotyping, sourcing, frequency and placement of coverage, denominational biases in coverage, quantity and quality of coverage, the impact of religion in political coverage, and reporters' religiosity. Historians of American journalism also study the intersection of religion and the news, the development of the religion beat, religious journalism, and the role of religion in news about sex scandals and sexual sensationalism.

The *Handbook* aims to complement existing research through a comparative and qualitative study of the themes, narratives, and frames that the American news media employ in their coverage of religions at home and abroad. It also examines the entangled history of religion and the news media in the United States from the colonial era to the present and includes chapters on the religious press. Most chapters are case studies that look at coverage over time and in different media outlets. They are intended not to be definitive, but rather to exemplify how coverage is structured and organized, the questions it addresses, and the messages it relates at particular times and in particular places. Moreover, by adding religion to the social history of American news media, the *Handbook* builds on the work of scholars such as Michael Schudson, Gerald J. Baldasty, and Herbert Gans in studying the relationship between politics, the marketplace, and the press.

The only resource of its kind, the *Handbook* is written for scholars and general readers; secularists and believers; students of religious studies, media studies, and American studies; and journalists. The volume's case studies illuminate what Cox calls "the royal road to the heart of a civilization" by teasing out the hopes and fears, questions and concerns, and stated intentions and implicit agendas expressed in depictions of religion in the news media. (News media encompass both legacy media [pre-online print, radio, and television] and new media [digitized forms of communication].) In the background, though unaddressed in most chapters, are questions of agency and authority: How do reporters know what they know, decide what to write, and structure their stories? How does their work reflect, shape, and frame reality? What specific challenges does religion present to journalists? And, most crucially, what do these stories show about contemporary American society?

Before detailing the *Handbook's* structure and content, several background areas must be addressed in this Introduction. These are the entangled history of religion and news in the United States, a working definition of religion and its impact on reporting, and the present state of research on religion coverage.

Religion and the News in Colonial America

News is current and consequential information on matters that affect and interest its consumers. The defining features of American news are impact, timeliness, prominence, proximity, bizarreness, conflict, and currency.[3] Reported in various intervals and by an assortment of media, news can be received instantaneously through digital connections or delivered infrequently by print, broadcast, or online vehicles. A combination of factors determines the influence of news, including ubiquity (the number and distribution of outlets) and audience (quality and quantity). News can order political priorities, shape social concerns, strengthen loyalties, and foster a sense of belonging, as well as distract and entertain.

Religion performs similar functions of defining and ordering identities and worldviews, as well as providing distraction and entertainment. Benedict Anderson has argued that news superseded religion in the modern world,[4] but at other times religion *was* the news; that is, events were newsworthy because they had teleological significance. Centuries before Christians adopted the term *gospel*, or good news, to describe Jesus's message, men and women used oral, pictorial, and architectural media to share news about the seen and unseen worlds. These reports can still be "read" in places such as the Chauvet cave paintings, the Giza pyramid complex, and Stonehenge.

By the seventeenth century, European journals and newsletters, precursors to today's newspapers, provided information on commerce and politics. But European settlers in the New World, especially the Puritans, found their news in God's revelations, establishing a relationship between religion and American news that would be both mutually constitutive and markedly competitive. That relationship has waxed and waned over nearly four centuries, but several factors are constant. In America, religion has always been part of the news and its coverage has reflected and shaped Americans' worldview.

When British colonists settled in what became the Massachusetts Bay Colony, they found the information they needed in the natural world. Indian raids, failed crops, and stillbirths signaled divine displeasure, while good weather and ample harvests meant that God was pleased with their holy commonwealth. Initially, colonists spread such "news" in sermons, almanacs, and broadsheets. But journals and newspapers that sprang up at the end of the seventeenth century gradually detached teleological significance from daily events. Today's secular journalism notwithstanding, the why and how of Puritan reporting have echoed down the generations, influencing the style and substance of American reportage. According to journalism historian David Paul Nord, "characteristics of American news—its subject matter and its method of reporting—are deeply rooted in the religious culture of seventeenth century New England." Specifically, says Nord, the press's "current-event orientation, supported by reportorial empiricism and authoritative interpretation" is its Puritan legacy.[5] These are evidenced in legacy journalism's use of the omniscient narrator, as well as its commitments to balance over partisanship, objectivity rather than analysis, and breaking news rather than continuity.

By the 1730s, a thriving newspaper culture had spread throughout the colonies with weekly newssheets offering a mix of essays, fiction, and information. Religion was pervasive in the mix: religious activities were regularly noted, and hymns, sermons, prayers, and scripture were featured. Political stories had a religious dimension, and reports on laws and governmental decrees noted religious motivations. Religion was a fact of life covered by the press as well as the primary means for interpreting events, whether a rise in taxes or a series of freakish storms. But in 1739, religion became news in a way that was unprecedented in both scope and span. British evangelist George Whitefield arrived for a preaching tour of the colonies, and his ministry was soon enmeshed in controversy. Up and down the Eastern seaboard, colonists debated whether Whitefield was God's man or a cunning huckster.

A provocative figure, Whitefield was a de facto newsmaker, but shrewd marketing made him a celebrity. Press reports reflected changes in colonial journalism: national coverage that transcended local borders and personality-driven coverage that created media stars. By the time Whitefield died in 1770, the content of coverage had changed, too; economics and politics predominated. The growing commercial sector had amplified economic concerns and oppressive taxation underscored the political toll of British rule. Newspapers still printed religious news and cited religion to show that events, including acts of rebellion, were part of God's plan. But the normative understanding of news as religion and religion as news had waned.

Religion and News in the Nineteenth Century

After the Revolutionary War, newspapers played a key role in shaping the new nation. Many were organs of political parties; others specialized in commercial news aimed at a growing mercantile class. Catering to subscribers who paid a hefty price in advance, editors valued partisanship and debate over balance and objectivity. The formula worked: by 1825, the United States had 800-plus newspapers, more than any other country. New technology would soon transform content, delivery, and audiences. Innovations in printing and papermaking had reduced production costs, and enterprising publishers bet that workingmen would pay a penny for news that informed and entertained. The "Penny Press" re-envisioned news reporting, journalistic standards, and industry economics. It also altered coverage of religion.

The Penny Press won mass audiences by reporting sensational narratives. Most frequently, these were stories of crime and punishment that offered a secular teleology for an increasingly heterogeneous population. American institutions dispensed justice through the provision of law and order with lots of blood and gore along the way. Religion was just another beat in the news mix, but when James Gordon Bennett, publisher of the *New York Herald*, treated clerical improprieties, congregational scandals, and denominational crimes as fair game, he was roundly criticized. A lapsed Roman Catholic, Bennett supported religious liberty. But he also relished exposing religious hypocrisy. Envious competitors and outraged clergy tried shutting him down, but Bennett thrived, widening his scope to report on New England abolitionists, frontier revivals, and midwestern anti-Mormonism.

As newspapers grew more secular in tone and content, the religious press played an increasingly important role for churchgoers and other believers. Before the Penny Press, newspapers printed both religious and secular information. Moreover, most religious periodicals were nonsectarian to attract the greatest number of subscribers. But the same innovations that revolutionized secular publishing also affected religious journals, many of which pioneered mass production to better evangelize the continent. After 1830, individual denominations and missionary organizations launched their own distinctive publications. Some sought to reach coreligionists nationwide; others hoped to convert the unchurched. Still others, active in social reform, wanted to publicize their causes.

Thus, while the secular press plumbed human depravity, religious newspapers exhorted believers to work for the Second Coming, reflecting the postmillennial belief that Christians could help to herald Jesus's arrival. They were expected not only to rescue lost souls but also to eradicate slavery, alcoholism, prostitution, and child labor, among other social ills. According to David Paul Nord, socially minded religious publications exemplified Alexis de Tocqueville's vision of the American press. Tocqueville predicted that newspapers would promote a national culture of democratic pluralism.[6] Readers would debate issues and plan actions over geographic distances. But this pluralistic and participatory model found little traction in the secular press, where instead, a commercial logic commodified news, selling sensationalism and entertainment for the profit of owners and advertisers.

Throughout the nineteenth century, the numbers of American newspapers continued to grow: in 1850, there were 3,000; in 1880, there were 7,000. Content also shifted. The Penny Press ushered in an era of easy reading that made newspapers a daily habit. But in 1851, when Henry Jarvis launched the *New York Times*, he hoped to introduce a level of sobriety to New York's pell-mell press. A decade later, reporters nationwide followed suit, inaugurating a new era of responsible coverage during the Civil War. Religion was woven into battlefield stories and provided a strong narrative thread for reports to families back home. However, when the war ended, the constancy of religion news diminished. The press paid deference to established Protestant denominations, cited clergy as authoritative sources, and frequently published ministers' opinions on the issues of the day. But religious activities rarely made the front pages, a coup reserved for the scandalous, the sensational, and the occasional religious miscreant.

During the 1870s, coverage of these three sometimes coincided. Newspapers, along with the rest of society, had been battered by the decade's economic downturn. To boost sales, editors looked for religion stories that appealed to skeptics as well as believers. These stories made the front page, but holidays, church activities, and episcopal meetings were buried deep inside the paper. Even as significant an event as the 1893 Parliament of the World's Religions could not muster many news columns.

Seeing their work as increasingly peripheral to the news, clergy lamented the press's lack of social responsibility and moral leadership. They criticized sensational stories told in purple prose and condemned advertisements that hawked frivolous products. They argued that newspapers had a social and moral obligation to help improve society, which, to their thinking, meant inculcating a Christian worldview. Clergy understood that the power to sway public opinion had migrated from pulpit to press. The loss of cultural authority was bad enough, but they were doubly frustrated that newspapers bowed to Mammon instead of using moral suasion for social good.

Between 1870 and 1930, changes in the news industry, including the growing importance of advertising, the demise of political partisanship, and the rise of objectivity as a reportorial standard, doomed coverage of clergy opining on politics or standards for social behavior. Journalism professionals—editors, reporters, and educators—aligned themselves with the forces of progress and reason as opposed to religion and superstition. The law, medicine, and education had already cut their religious roots; now journalism would, too. Cast as priests and prophets of a new, secular age, reporters would provide authoritative guidance to society. Describing Joseph Pulitzer's turn-of-the-century "mass journalism," sociologist Michael Schudson calls it a response to readers torn between old, familiar ways and societal shifts in education, urbanization, and mobility. "They wanted the moral counsel of stories as much as any people did, but the tales of the Bible and the lives of the saints were not suited to the new cities. The new journalism was."[7]

Religion and News in the Twentieth Century

In 1933, researcher Hornell Hart noted that a significant change in news coverage had been the "shift from Biblical authority and sanctions to scientific and factual authority and sanctions." Not surprisingly, the number of religion stories fell during this period. Between 1905 and 1909, the *Reader's Guide to Periodical Literature* listed 21.4 stories per year on religion. In 1931, the total was 10.7. Religious content suffered a similar declension; stories positively inclined to "traditional Christianity," which had constituted 78 percent of coverage in 1905, fell by more than half to 33 percent in 1931.[8]

As newspapers reduced religion coverage, general interest magazines picked up the slack with in-depth, illustrated features. In the post–Civil War era, *Harper's*, *Munsey's*, and *The Outlook* covered subjects ranging from the Salvation Army's open-air evangelism to the history of Unitarianism in New York. Of special note was *McClure's*, a monthly magazine founded in 1893 by Samuel Sidney McClure. Raised in a pious Presbyterian home, McClure retained his childhood commitment to religious service. His goal as a publisher was to be God's servant, spreading truth and inspiring readers.

McClure's eponymous magazine was the era's moral lodestar. His Progressive-era journalists exposed corruption in business and government. Dubbed "muck-rakers" for their willingness to dig up the nation's dirt, most of the group—which included Ida Tarbell, Lincoln Steffens, Upton Sinclair, William Allen White, and Ray Stannard Baker—saw their work as akin to a religious vocation. They wanted better laws and governance, but they believed that real change required moral and spiritual regeneration. Even after World War I ended muckraking's heyday, magazines continued to cover religion more expansively than newspapers. When Henry Luce, the son of Presbyterian ministers in China, launched a weekly newsmagazine, he mandated regular coverage of religion. Luce was sincerely interested in religion, but he also believed Christianity was a strategic defense against Communism. In its early decades, the newsmagazine ran updates of religion news as well as extensive feature pieces. When he acquired *Life* magazine in 1936, Luce made certain that the weekly's photojournalism spreads featured country clergy, urban congregations, and worshipers worldwide.

During the interwar years, reporters filed on "kooks and spooks," the newspaper terms for religious oddballs and eccentrics. Coverage of the conflict between fundamentalists and liberals, the subtext of several well-publicized heresy trials in earlier decades, faded after the 1925 *Scopes* verdict. Fundamentalists won the court case, but newspapers had so caricatured their cause that secular elites no longer took them seriously. Reporters still found stories on religious scandals and spiritual outliers irresistible, but they also profiled religious leaders. Headline makers might, like Reinhold Niebuhr, confront powerful politicians; or, like Sister Aimee, court scandal; or, like Gandhi, rally thousands. But two of the century's biggest religion stories were lost in the shuffle of events, deadlines, and news judgment. Neither the destruction of European Jewry nor the militarization of atomic power was well reported. Some news managers may have felt that wartime readers were uninterested in the fate of a far-away, non-Christian community, while others calculated that their staffs were already stretched thin covering the conflict. Nor did the press choose to write much about the debate over the morality of using the atomic bomb, an apt topic for religious leaders. The attacks against Hiroshima and Nagasaki were evaluated solely within the context of ending the war, and several years passed before related ethical concerns became a topic of public conversation.

Maybe as a result of these cataclysmic events or perhaps because of a postwar desire for a simpler time, religion surged in the 1950s. American leaders hailed it as a bulwark against Communism, and a religious revival swept the country. Billy Graham softened Fundamentalism's hard edge; the National Council of Churches convened for ecumenical cooperation; Bishop Fulton Sheen utilized the new medium of television to launch a national ministry; and Conservative Jews went on a suburban building spree, erecting synagogues and community centers. Religion already was a staple of many newsmagazines; now newspapers paid attention, too. Some even elevated their coverage to a distinct beat assigned to a designated religion writer. Reporting reflected the era's mores. Stories on white Protestants predominated. Outsiders—whether Hindus, Buddhists, or African American Christians—were covered either as peculiar or problematic.

Popular memory conjures the 1950s as a respite between the world war just concluded and the domestic strife that was to come. Religion, rediscovered as a social, familial, and personal good during the 1950s, careened into an activist, sometimes disruptive force in the 1960s. The era began with the election of John F. Kennedy, the nation's first Roman Catholic president, and continued with additional challenges to the white Protestant establishment. The civil rights movement, germinating for decades, assumed urgency when college students organized sit-ins to integrate lunch counters (1960) and Freedom Riders challenged segregated transportation (1961). Clergy had long been visible in the movement's leadership, but the Reverend Martin Luther King Jr.'s biblically based message became increasingly compelling in his "Letter from the Birmingham Jail" (1963) and "I Have a Dream" sermon (1964). In 1962 and 1963, respectively, the Supreme Court ended school prayer and Bible reading in public schools. When the court overturned a Connecticut state law prohibiting the sale of contraceptives to married couples (1965), the ruling was not widely perceived as a shift in the religious status quo. But it set the precedent for later cases that legalized birth control (1972) and abortion (1973)—both upending received assumptions about marriage, family, and reproduction. Also in 1965, a new immigration law ended quotas for nonwhite immigrants, which, in subsequent decades, would increase the numbers of Buddhist, Hindu, and Muslim citizens. Yet even before the numbers rose, Eastern gurus attracted thousands of American youth to alternative spiritualities. Not long after *Time* asked "Is God Dead?" (1966), teens and young people turned to swamis and New Age cults for answers.

Religion in the 1960s spilled off the church page, changing its focus from denominations and institutional leaders, which tended to be white and Protestant, to encompass a wide swath of people and practices. Writing about religion became part of the politics, education, and court beats. It was central to stories about the nascent youth culture and relevant to coverage of the Great Society and the Vietnam War, both of which stirred strong feelings among people of faith. The 1970s saw the continuation of many of the same trends—especially shifts in median age, mobility, and education, as well as economic restructuring and a redefinition of the family—that affected religious involvement and affiliation. People found religion could help them accept, resist, or transcend change. Nowhere was this more apparent than in the politicization of white conservative Christians. *Newsweek's* declaration that 1976 was "the year of the evangelical" presaged this seemingly "new" group's prominence in the quarter century that followed.

The emergence of white religious conservatives as political players, following two decades of mainline Protestant and black Christian political leadership, echoed earlier evangelical attempts to perfect society through abolition and temperance. Concerned now with social and cultural challenges to the family, a structure that they considered the backbone of American democracy, as well as integral to God's plan, evangelicals organized on many fronts. They stood as candidates for local office and campaigned in national elections; they challenged rulings against school prayer and fought to gain equal access for religious groups on public school property. They picketed birth control clinics and wrote manuals promoting recreational sex within marriage. Religion coverage expanded by necessity, and news—both implicitly and explicitly—explored the mash-up of religion, culture, and politics. Reporting on religiously infused politics, the secular press affirmed two of Alexis de Tocqueville's observations about its role in a democratic society: first, its coverage legitimated and strengthened the work of local associations, including religious ones, in the political process, and second, it cast religion over and against politics as a touchstone for American democratic ideals.

The first goal fell squarely within the press's mission, although some journalists would not have recognized their work as legitimating groups like Christian Voice or Moral Majority, but the second was problematic. How could religion trump journalism in the defense of American democracy? Many late-twentieth-century news executives kept faith with the Journalist's Creed, the 1906 statement that asserted, "the supreme test of good journalism is the measure of its public service."[9] Ever since Walter Lippmann said the press was essential to democracy, journalists defined public service as guaranteeing a free and accountable government. The press accomplished this through its legitimating and authoritative functions, judging and providing the information that Americans needed to be good citizens. Tocqueville's contention that religion was the ultimate arbiter for democracy by applying a higher standard to temporal power challenged journalism's raison d'être, especially since the religion currently in question, conservative Christianity, upheld values that were diametrically opposed to science and secular rationalism.

The disjuncture was reflected in journalism's subsequent subversion of evangelical legitimacy and authority. It was apparent in 1976 when NBC anchor John Chancellor told millions of viewers, "We've checked this out. Being born again is not a bizarre mountaintop experience."[10] And in 1993 when a front-page *Washington Post* story described followers of the Christian Right as "largely poor, uneducated and easy to command."[11] And again in 2011 when an article on *The Atlantic* website about possible presidential contender Mike Huckabee noted, "People are sometimes caught off guard by Huckabee's intellectual competence because of his rural Arkansas habits (he and his wife lived in a trailer while the governor's mansion was being renovated) and his outspoken evangelical views."[12] It also was clear in the news media's cyclical rediscovery of evangelicals between 1976 and 2000. Despite the election of two Southern Baptists (evangelicals by definition) to the presidency and two others who assiduously courted religious conservatives, political reporters seemed routinely surprised that evangelicals were part of the political mix. Only after George W. Bush's election did journalists seem to acknowledge that evangelicals were a mainstay of American politics and that their agenda had become mainstream.

Both journalists and academics agreed that religion coverage improved after the 1980s.[13] More news outlets, including television and radio, assigned reporters to the beat. Large papers often had several journalists covering religion, and some even revitalized religion sections, expanding church news into reporting on faith, values, and spirituality.[14] Religion was covered instrumentally, as a subset of politics, rather than substantively, as a spiritual experience,[15] but there was a growing apprehension that news consumers wanted more on spirituality, the aspect of religion that was experiential rather than institutional, transcendent instead of political, individual more than social.

Coinciding with this interest in religion as an individual, spiritual experience, the migration of news and information online revolutionized religion coverage. Independent reporting and writing broke free from the constraints of objectivity and newsworthiness. By the early 1990s, The Well, one of the earliest virtual communities, functioned for many as a spiritual hub. By the end of the decade, spiritual seekers could share news and information through hundreds of blogs and forums. More traditional kinds of religion news could be found online at denominational sites, news aggregate sites, online 'zines, forums, and legacy news sites. There were sites that found news in the affinities between the visible and the invisible worlds and those that debunked religion. Some sites used religion news to entertain, others offered in-depth coverage of world religions, and still others prophesized. Faced with the sudden proliferation of voices and alternate viewpoints, legacy news outlets asserted the value of expert, objective news gathering and reportage, even as they developed their own blogs and commentaries, such as the *Washington Post's* "On Faith" feature or the *Boston Globe's* "Articles of Faith."

Despite stressing the primacy of their role, legacy media lost their monolithic control of the news agenda. Citizen reporting on the 2007 Burmese Saffron Revolution pushed the story from newspapers' back pages to the top of the day's headlines. Likewise, tweets, Facebook updates, and cell phone data expanded real-time information on events including the 2010 Gaza flotilla and the 2011 Arab Spring uprisings. Competition between legacy journalism and new media, conducted as a war of both information and ideology, reenacted an old debate between John Dewey and Walter Lippmann. Whereas Lippmann argued for a journalism elite that filtered news for a largely ignorant and self-absorbed citizenry, Dewey believed empowered publics could use and generate news to invigorate democracy. Both positions are embodied in the strengths and weaknesses of legacy versus new media.

Among the earliest examples of these differences was the coverage of the World Trade Center cataclysm on September 11, 2001. Even before traditional news outlets could report the story, victims and witnesses used cell phones to capture fateful decisions and tragic choices. The immediacy of loved ones' last words and the horrific images of their deaths made the catastrophe visceral for millions. In the weeks following, legacy media deployed resources to document and investigate events. Religion was central to subsequent reporting on the hijackers' theological motivations, the last minutes of those trapped on the uppermost floors, the heroic efforts of rescuers, and the shattered lives of both the dead and their surviving families.[16] September 11 also exemplified the impact of mediatization, specifically its impact on news as an experiential, as well as an informational, product. The Internet provided ways to encounter and to memorialize victims, as well as to ensure their virtual immortality. Websites about religion also flourished in the tragedy's aftermath. Some sought to explain Islam; others vilified it; still others seized a seemingly opportune moment to reach the unchurched. Online forums, games, and virtual habitats (such as Second Life) also offered ways to know, experience, and come to terms with 9/11 and its religious implications.

Defining, Mediating, and Covering Religion

Just as religion has influenced the definition and production of news, journalism has had an impact on religion in America. In the heyday of the legacy media, the "who, what, why, where, when, and how" of news gathering shaped how religious groups constructed a public presence, since press coverage could make or break them. (Of course, when reporters discovered discrepancies between a religion's public face and private misdeeds, there was little religious groups could do about subsequent stories.) Yet playing the news game also could distort religious teachings. Groups that received good coverage in one instance could not count on similar treatment other times, and even if they had been treated fairly, their message might not be explained as fully as they would want.

Before the Internet, the legacy press was the main avenue for religions to reach beyond their pews. New media enable faith communities to target constituencies with stories that reflect alternate news standards, worldviews, and values. For example, religious groups are more open to reporting change over time and less concerned with impact, prominence, proximity, and conflict. Many take the long view, appreciating small changes, modest gains, and win-win outcomes. Religious news outlets promote in-group norms, focusing on their own leaders, activities, and practices. This translates into articles about mission projects that enact the group's values, profiles of exemplary clergy, and news about ordinary laypeople doing extraordinary work. In addition to embodying collective core beliefs, these stories also promote American civic values as foundational to democracy and, therefore, integral to religion.

Secular journalism likewise encodes civic values, though its estimation of religion's relationship to those values is more equivocal. As in other beats, secular news coverage of religion focuses on the high and mighty, powerful institutions, and important people. That means congregations, denominations, and parachurch associations (these terms are inclusive of non-Christian religions) receive more attention than ad hoc groups, and that larger bodies, such as the Roman Catholic Church, are more newsworthy than smaller ones, such as the Presbyterian Church USA. If minor religions are bizarre, controversial, or engaged in conflict, they can become headline fodder, as seen in the coverage of Raelians, Scientologists, and polygamous Mormons. Likewise, reporting on religious individuals leans to world leaders such as the pope or the Dalai Lama, celebrities such as Tom Cruise and Madonna, or controversial figures including Jerry Falwell, Jim Jones, and David Koresh. Occasionally, unsung heroes are profiled, as are average believers.

News outlets define religion in conventional, institutional terms. Judaism is a religion; extreme surfing is not, despite their shared aspects of community, ritual, and transcendence. Focusing on large institutions and powerful people marginalizes what some adherents and religion scholars say are the most intriguing and dynamic aspects of belief and believing. From an adherent's point of view, the institutional perspective often overlooks facts on the ground. Clergy sex abuse and denominational debates over gay ordination fit the definition of newsworthiness, but they don't illuminate the mystery of prayer or the impact of small group fellowship. Even more marginalized are beliefs and practices that fall outside traditional faiths: Buddhists who find a meditation community on Second Life; a Muslim and Jewish college dorm; evangelical feminists. The growing number of Americans who seek spiritual connection and community through online forums, Facebook, and affinity groups is essentially ignored.

The very practice of news gathering affects what may be known about religion. Decisions about sourcing, reporting, and framing stories do more than simply convey information; they mainstream certain issues, ideas, and personalities while marginalizing others. Other constituencies, whether union members, hedge fund managers, or athletes, make similar complaints, but religious groups, deservedly or not, cite their singularity, straddling the sacred and the secular. How does a reporter interview God or fact check a miracle? Covering the supernatural is an impossibility and mastering a religion's context—history, theology, creeds, dogma, and doctrine—is daunting. Decisions about newsworthiness, in conjunction with issues of time, space, and resources, can skew public perceptions about fundamental religious tenets. In the case of *jihad*, the Islamic word for struggle, particularly one's internal efforts to know God, a multilayered theological term has become a synonym for holy war and terrorism.

In recent years, scholars have enlarged their definition of what constitutes religion to encompass a wide variety of phenomena that display elements of supernaturalism, meaning making, and the search for identity and purpose. Some see religion in popular culture; others find it in practices that provide structure and significance. Some scholars have argued that "religion" is a historically constructed category that served as a classification tool for Western colonialism. Others have subjected religion to economic, psychoanalytic, and anthropological analysis. Yet few of the insights derived from recent scholarship have migrated to coverage of religion. Rather, in spite of evolving perspectives on what, why, and how people believe and therefore behave, most twenty-first-century legacy news outlets still till the same religious ground—scandal, sensation, and conflict—as their nineteenth-century counterparts.

Likewise, media scholars cling to conventional definitions of religion when studying coverage. Not surprisingly, their work often corroborates professional norms, such as the prevalence of conflict narratives and the predominance of "newsworthy" religion stories. But it also reveals the structural dynamics that inform journalistic choices and point to journalism's role in setting social agendas and maintaining cultural hegemony. For example, a survey of *Time* magazine from 1947 to 1976 revealed that Catholics, Jews, and Episcopalians accounted for 60 percent of its religion coverage. Implicit in the newsmagazine's story selection and content was the depiction of religion as "a frenetic contest waged by certain male prelates on the east coast of the United States, a xenophobic personality clash about matters of today." *Time's* coverage, concluded the researchers, reflects the world of its writers (mostly successful white men in New York City), as well as a rhetorical strategy that produces messages "which grow out of, and are aligned to, certain generic (or class-bound) rules. These generic rules not only constrain how one should express one's thoughts; they also dictate what thoughts one might profitably think."[17] Accordingly, coverage of religion was not unlike sports or politics; all of the newsmagazine's reporting emphasized "action, conflict and personality."[18] Implicit, though not stated, was the ways in which the subjects and presentation of coverage reinforce the status quo.

A survey of *New York Times* and *Washington Post* religion reporting in 1977 similarly found that Catholics, Jews, and Episcopalians received the most attention. The distribution made sense for Catholicism, the largest religious group in the country. But why the overrepresentation of Jews and Episcopalians as opposed to a significantly larger group, such as Baptists? The research ascribed the imbalance to news criteria. "The major issues of these three denominations paralleled those of other established organizations. Political relations (church and state), intra-organizational (church services and liturgy) and inter-organizational (unity), and women's rights are easily associated with most community groups. But the Baptists, the only primarily evangelical group of the four, do not fit in well with the establishment, hence the bias against the denomination."[19]

The ensuing politicization of American evangelicals between 1980 and 2000 underscored the study's argument. Within the next decade, conservative Christians' embrace of political causes drove increased coverage of their leaders and institutions. Most did not welcome the attention. Evangelicals doubted that the press corps could fairly represent their concerns, especially after a 1986 survey found the "media elite" tended to be secular cosmopolitans who were less churchgoing than average Americans.[20] Subsequent studies challenged this hypothesis, finding that as many as 72 percent of journalists said religion was important to them and that many "apply religious values to their jobs."[21] The substance of conservatives' charges also was refuted in studies that found newspaper coverage of fundamentalists was balanced, "slightly cool" but not "cold," and steadily growing.[22] Researchers predicted coverage would continue to increase as the group became more politically active, a finding that corroborated earlier studies and anticipated a 2003 survey of television coverage of fundamentalists.[23] This subsequent investigation found that broadcast journalists covered religious conservatives less frequently than their print colleagues, but that their work dovetailed in two significant ways: the characterizations of fundamentalists were slightly negative and most stories were about politics.

After 9/11, Islam experienced a rise in coverage as its news trajectory intersected with domestic and international politics. In the rush to explain and understand the tragedy, as well as the role Islam played, print and broadcast outlets provided news, features, commentaries, profiles, and analyses of Muslims in the United States and abroad. Scores of articles and several books followed, seeking to understand the press's role in fostering, combating, and changing stereotypes. Similarly, when other religions become newsworthy—usually when their concerns entwine with politics or community events such as papal trips, the 2002 Olympics in Salt Lake City, or the Israeli-Palestinian conflict—studies plumb the amount, types, and reasons for heightened coverage.

In addition to studying spiking interest in particular faiths or the role of news values in determining religion coverage, media researchers have looked at narratives and frames as part of a reflexive shaping of social norms. Journalists work within societal frames to build narrative frames for their stories. These narrative frames are constructed by reporters' choice of expert sources, quotes, details, and information. Such choices can never be neutral; they are subjective decisions based on the interplay between what smells like a good story and what a reporter assumes his or her editor and audience find important. Moreover, choices are a mix of self-serving motives, professional standards, and altruistic aims. Various motivations, then, inform the journalist's decision on how to organize and source his or her story. The frame, emphasizing "specific values, facts and other considerations, endowing them with greater relevance to the issue than they might appear to have under an alternate frame,"[24] is the result. According to media scholar Peter Kerr, "Frames are thus the context that is communicated with the text, which can shape the way the text is received. Frames typically diagnose, evaluate and prescribe. Because of this, they are capable of exerting great social power."[25]

Kerr does not elucidate what this social power is, but other researchers do. Analyzing journalistic discourse of Mormons during the 2002 Olympics, Chiung Hwang Chen found a persistent framing of the group as a "model minority," a designation that serves to "other" outsiders.[26] Mormons are industrious, patriotic, and family oriented. But they also are rigid, conformist, and insular. Whether journalists focus on their teetotaling, polygamous past, or odd undergarments, the cumulative effect deploys religion to demonstrate that Mormons are *them* and not *us*.

Religion scholar Sean McCloud documents a similar effect in his study of the coverage of religious movements between the 1950s and the 1990s. McCloud explores the changing construction of the religious fringe, a journalistic frame that connoted "high levels of religious zeal, dogma, and emotion," as opposed to mainstream norms of religious decorum, laxity, and rationalism. Between the 1950s and mid-'60s, journalists portrayed blacks and lower-class whites as religious outsiders devoted to odd and demanding faiths such as Pentecostalism and the Nation of Islam. Articles implied that their religious enthusiasms left them ill equipped to be good citizens. By the late 1970s the fringe shifted, encompassing "cults" that attracted the young and the rebellious. These groups were "un-American" in their emphasis on communalism and spirituality. McCloud notes "the largest news and general interest magazines often labeled religious groups fringe or mainstream in ways that symbolically reproduced and legitimized inequalities of race and class in postwar America. . . . [W]riters and editors in periodicals like *Time, Newsweek* and *Life* frequently offered, under the guise of objective reporting, a spiritual apologetics for a dominant social order."[27]

An Answer to the "So What" Question

If, as Harvey Cox suggests, "religion is the royal road to the heart of a civilization," then news media—in all their forms—are the vehicles that traverse the road, and frames are the maps they follow. Frames situate media in a specific time and place, as well as provide orientation for a particular civilization. Frames, like maps, keep media on the known road rather than veering into unfamiliar territory. Religion, in its ecstatic, transgressive, and subversive forms, seeks those strange and unfamiliar regions, which is why certain kinds of religious practice and experience never make it on the map.

The essays in this volume illumine contemporary America by studying the road, the vehicle, and the map. What do the news media's depictions of religion in the news say about American "hopes and terrors"? What insights on political norms, economic assumptions, and social hierarchies can be gleaned from reading about Catholicism or Wicca? How does coverage of religion in South America further American cultural hegemony?

In **Section One: History**, contributors examine the entangled past, present, and future of American news and religion. Most journalism histories either neglect or minimize the connection between the two, but these six chapters describe a long-standing and complex relationship. Authors in **Section Two: The Media** explore how print, television, radio, and online journalists have represented various religions in their reporting. In addition to asking how particular media shape religious content, the essays look at how religion figures into media history and what conditions lead to or inhibit exemplary media coverage of religion. The focus of **Section Three: Religions** is the narratives that drive coverage of particular religious groups. Contributors consider how framing affects perceptions of particular faiths and use case studies to demonstrate how social agendas may affect reporting on religion. Likewise, **Section Four: Issues and Beats** takes a close look at how religion intersects with eight subject areas, interrogating how narratives enforce, challenge, and shift social norms. **Section Five: International Coverage** examines the impact of American religion and politics on the coverage of religion globally. **Section Six: The Religious Press** provides an implicit contrast to analyses of secular coverage by looking at faith-based news outlets. What do denominational presses consider newsworthy? Do faith commitments shape coverage, and how much does reporting reflect a group's socioeconomic position, where members are, and where they aspire to be?

Read together, the chapters offer insight into how stereotypes are set, norms are assumed, and power relationships are communicated. Moreover, they reflect the dynamism between religion and media at a particular historic juncture, shedding light on the hopes and fears, dreams and demons of contemporary Americans. Religion is often flattened into a subset of politics, frames are deployed circumscribing what we know, and a wide range of beliefs and practices are reduced to a handful of themes, stories, and sources. But religion, politics, media, and culture are separate categories of human existence only in an abstract sense. In the living reality, they overlap, shape, and influence one another in ways that journalists should be well positioned to describe, scholars eager to analyze, and news consumers keen to understand.

NOTES

1. Harvey Cox, "Why God Didn't Die," *Nieman Reports* XLVII (Summer 1993): 49.
2. Friedrich Krotz, "Mediatization: A Concept With Which to Grasp Media and Social Change," in *Mediatization: Concepts, Changes, Consequences*, ed. Knut Lundby (New York: Peter Lang Publishing Inc., 2009), 24.
3. http://www.uncp.edu/home/acurtis/Courses/ResourcesForCourses/NewsValues.html.

4. Benedict Anderson, *Imagined Communities* (London: Verso, 1983), 35.

5. David Paul Nord, *Communities of Journalism: A History of American Newspapers and Their Readers* (Urbana: University of Illinois Press, 2001), 31.

6. Ibid., 92–107.

7. Michael Schudson, *Discovering the News: A Social History of American Newspapers* (New York: Basic Books, 1978), 106.

8. Richard W. Flory, "Promoting a Secular Standard: Secularization and Modern Journalism, 1870–1930," in *The Secular Revolution: Power, Interests and Conflicts in the Secularization of American Public Life*, ed. Christian Smith (Berkeley: University of California Press, 2003), 398.

9. http://journalism.missouri.edu/about/creed.html.

10. William Martin, *With God on Our Side: The Rise of the Religious Right in America* (New York: Broadway Books, 1996), 150.

11. Howard Kurtz, "Evangelical Outrage Hundreds Protest Description in Post Story," *Washington Post*, February 6, 1993.

12. Nicole Allan, "Mike Huckabee, Comeback Kid?" *The Atlantic*, June 21, 2010, http://www.theatlantic.com/politics/archive/2010/06/mike-huckabee-comeback-kid/58463/.

13. John Dart and Jimmy Allen, "Bridging the Gap: Religion and the News Media," First Amendment Center, Freedom Forum, 2000, http://www.freedomforum.org/publications/first/bridgingthegap/Bridgingthegap.pdf.

14. Susan K. Willey, "The Founding of the Dallas Morning News' Religion Section," *Journalism History* 33, no. 4 (Winter 2008): 194–204.

15. http://www.cmpa.com/pdf/Media_Coverage_Religion_2000.pdf, 80–81, July 15, 2011.

16. Christopher Vecsey, *Following 9/11: Religion Coverage in the New York Times* (Syracuse: Syracuse University Press, 2011).

17. Roderick P. Hart, Kathleen J. Turner, and Ralph E. Knupp, "Religion and the Rhetoric of Mass Media," *Review of Religious Research* 21, no. 3 (Summer 1980): 263.

18. Ibid., 273.

19. John P. Ferre, "Denominational Biases in the American Press," *Review of Religious Research* 21, no. 3 (Summer 1980): 282.

20. S. Robert Lichter, Stanley Rothman, and Linda S. Lichter, *The Media Elite: America's New Power-brokers* (Bethesda, MD: Adler and Adler, 1986).

21. Doug Underwood and Keith Stamm, "Are Journalists Really Irreligious: A Multidimensional Analysis," *Journalism and Mass Communication Quarterly* 4 (Winter 2001): 778.

22. Peter A. Kerr and Patricia Moy, "Newspaper Coverage of Fundamentalists, 1980–2000," *Journalism and Mass Communication Quarterly* 79, no. 1 (Spring 2002): 63–64.

23. Peter A. Kerr, "The Framing of Fundamentalist Christians: Network Television News, 1980–2000," *Journal of Media and Religion* 2, no. 4 (2003): 203–35.

24. Thomas E. Nelson, Rosalee A. Clawson, and Zoe M. Oxley, "Media Framing of as Civil Liberties Conflict and Its Effect on Tolerance," *American Political Science Review* 91: 569.

25. Kerr, "Framing of Fundamentalist Christians," 212.

26. Chiung Hwang Chen, "'Molympics?' Journalistic Discourse of Mormons in Relation to the 2002 Winter Olympic Games," *Journal of Media and Religion* 2, no. 1 (2003): 29–47.

27. Scott McCloud, *Making the American Religious Fringe: Exotics, Subversives and Journalists, 1955–1993* (Chapel Hill: University of North Carolina Press, 2004), 4.

REFERENCES

Anderson, Benedict. 1983. *Imagined Communities*. London: Verso.
Lundby, Knut, ed. 2009. *Mediatization: Concepts, Changes, Consequences*. New York: Peter Lang Publishing Inc.
McCloud, Scott. 2004. *Making the American Religious Fringe: Exotics, Subversives and Journalists*, 1955–1993. Chapel Hill: University of North Carolina Press.
Nord, David Paul. 2001. *Communities of Journalism: A History of American Newspapers and Their Readers*. Urbana: University of Illinois Press.
Schudson, Michael. 1978. *Discovering the News: A Social History of American Newspapers*. New York: Basic Books.

SECTION I

HISTORY

CHAPTER 1

RELIGION AND NEWS IN EIGHTEENTH-CENTURY AMERICA

DAVID COPELAND

RELIGION was often the subject of news in colonial America. On April 24, 1704, in the first issue of the *Boston News-Letter*, John Campbell told his readers that the Reverend Pemberton had preached an "Excellent Sermon on 1 Thes. 4.11" the previous Sunday. The *Boston Gazette* weekly informed readers of the number of people baptized in local churches, as did other newspapers. In 1730, Massachusetts Governor Jonathan Belcher decreed that all citizens of the colony must "attend the publick Worship of GOD on every LORD'S DAY."[1] Newspapers regularly informed readers of days of public fasting and prayer. Entire sermons filled front pages. Overt issues of religion were commonplace in the public prints of colonial America.

But this fact is not surprising. Religion, specifically Protestantism, was central to the lives of colonials. In fact, according to Patricia Bonomi, it penetrated all discourse, was the basis of all thought, highlighted all public and private observances, and gave meaning to all crises faced by Americans of the colonial period.[2] In such a society, any information related to such an important life element naturally was passed on.

But when one reads the news that appeared in America's papers throughout the colonial period, news stories and reports that directly addressed the religious components of life are much less obvious. In fact, from a twenty-first-century perspective, Bonomi's observations on the importance of religion to the eighteenth-century citizen become difficult to discern. References to God, to scripture, and to calls for divine intercession in the lives of the people, for example, can easily be lost in pages filled with news of commerce, politics, social issues, and general entertainment.[3] Overtly religious information, of course, fluctuated in importance in terms of news content, but Bonomi's point was that those living in the eighteenth century did not need to make obvious references to scripture or to God for people to apply divine or scriptural guidance to their lives or to the events that made up their world. The religious became the way to understand life, to confront issues, and to deal with problems. Or, as Max Weber explained, religion as a human institution serves as a means for people to make sense of the political, economic, and social aspects of life.[4] These elements are key to almost every society, and British colonial America was no different. Religion in this context, then, acted as a "Rosetta Stone" for almost everything that people faced. It provided a key to decipher and explain any event, issue, or occurrence. And, because almost all people who lived in British colonial America were steeped in the same religious traditions (Protestantism specifically and Christianity generally), their basic religious psyche did not differ greatly, regardless of where they lived in any of the original thirteen British American colonies.

This essay explores the way religious interpretation shaped news and how a theological lens provided a potential interpretation for all information. In many cases, the elements of the religious were not present in the printed text; news was "simply the news," as David Nord has observed.[5] This does not mean, though, that the components of the religious were not well known and accepted by those who wrote, read, listened to, debated, and discussed the issues and events that filled the press of the century. In colonial America, a religious interpretation for most stories would have been obvious for most people and often applied as a means of understanding critical issues and events.

In eighteenth-century America, two important elements of American religious evolution provided the keys to people's understanding of most of the political, economic, and social issues that they faced and read about in their newssheets. First, there was the concept of the covenant people—that America was a new promised land[6] or the "Land of Promise," the words Robert Beverley used to describe Virginia.[7] Nearly all of the first explorers and settlers of what would become British colonial America used this terminology, but the Puritans who settled in New England and their understanding of the relationship between God and their settlement efforts had the greatest and most lasting impact on Americans' understanding of events and issues—those things that would become "the news" of the eighteenth century. The Puritans attempted and failed in establishing government as a theocracy in America, but the rhetoric and ideals of that effort did become core values in America despite the fact that Puritanism was not the universal way that colonial Protestants approached scripture.

Puritanism provided ideas about the New World relative to the covenantal relationship of humankind and God. Religious parallels between those traveling to the New World to settle and the Hebrews of the Old Testament wandering in the wilderness in search of the Promised Land were essential in seventeenth- and eighteenth-century America. Those who came to the New World were a chosen people sent to the wilderness, where they were tested much as Jesus was in the New Testament. Their experiment in the New World became a light on the hill to serve as an example for others. Somehow, this created a special relationship between God and those in the New World. It provided a unique destiny for those who left all to travel to the New World. They became the embodiment of New Testament prophesy. Or, as Sacvan Bercovitch explained, the early New England Puritan rhetoric "provided a ready framework for inverting later secular values—human perfectibility, technological progress, democracy, Christian social, or simply (and comprehensively) the American Way—into the mold of sacred teleology."[8] One sees this ideology as the basis of the nineteenth-century concept of Manifest Destiny, for example, though the idea of a time "when we shall spread Dominion from the north, and south, and west, Far from the Atlantic to Pacific shores"[9] was a part of the American mentality much earlier.

The second religious element that shaped the understanding of news grew out of the Great Awakening and its promotion of an individual's personal relationship with God—the idea of "what must *I* do to be saved?" The Great Awakening was a religious revival that caused denominations to divide and changed the social structure of British colonial America as it helped to elevate the concept of religious liberty. According to Edwin Scott Gausted, "none escaped its influence or avoided its controversy."[10]

The Great Awakening also helped to change the focus of news in the colonies to events that either originated in the colonies or had an immediate impact on the people of the colonies.[11] The religious implications of the Great Awakening were enough to foment change, but the religious revival of the 1740s had a catalyst, a British itinerant preacher named George Whitefield. Like no person in the brief history of news dissemination in the press, Whitefield captured the attention of printers and the readers of newssheets alike. He made seven preaching tours of America, dying in 1770 on the last one. During his first from late 1739 through early 1741, Whitefield proved that controversy spawns interest and news. "All the newspapers were filled with paragraphs of information, respecting him, or with pieces of animated disputation pro or con," America's first media historian Isaiah Thomas wrote of Whitefield.[12] The newspapers were filled in part with news of Whitefield because he saw papers as a tool of change and had his traveling "public relations agent," William Seward, write stories about his revival meetings both before and after they occurred. In this way, discussion of Whitefield was heightened in all parts of America. Richard Bushman said, "The Awakening was more like the civil rights demonstrations, the campus disturbances, and the urban riots of the 1960s combined."[13] While all of these events surely changed the United States while they occurred and arguably forever, their impact would not have been nearly as powerful or lasting without media coverage. The same was true of George Whitefield and the Great Awakening.

On its surface, the Great Awakening separated the salvation of the person from the welfare of the state and would appear to be at odds with the concepts of America espoused by the Puritans. But the rationalists of the revolutionary era simply adapted the concepts of the Puritans with the welfare/salvation of the individual as a means to push for independence. Religious salvation was personal, but it also had societal connotations. The Deists who provided the rhetoric of the last half of the eighteenth century simply adapted religious understanding of the Puritans with the individuality of the Great Awakening to create a new country of individuals. A new covenant was formed with a new governmental concept that was of, for, and by the people. Individuality was maintained as people were expected to look after their own welfare, as well as that collectively of the new nation.

One other religious component figured into the shaping of news in colonial America, and it came from the apocryphal elements of scripture. Writers of the revolutionary age returned to a less subtle way of using the religious beliefs of people as they spoke of the conflict with Great Britain in terminology laden with references to the Book of Revelation and to the end-time struggle between good and evil. This use of overt religious language melded well with the concepts of the covenantal people, the Promised Land, and the ideas about salvation that arose during the Great Awakening.

Looking back from a two-century-plus perspective, however, to discern how religion became the means of interpretation for news is difficult—unless one looks at critical events of the colonial period. Here, writers tended to tap perhaps unconsciously and deeply into their religious heritage, into the Puritan concepts of the New World and the ideas of the individual from the Great Awakening. One also needs to understand how the press operated because the nature of information gathering and dispersal meant that the populace was much more involved in the process than it would be in America for at least two more centuries.

The Press and Colonial America

The press of the eighteenth century operated in ways vastly different from those of the mass media that developed at the end of the nineteenth century and dominated life in the twentieth. No organized reporting staffs existed. Print shops were largely family operations with journeyman printers and apprentices helping with the day-to-day operations. Printers were booksellers, general merchants, and mechanics who produced government documents, as well as news gatherers and the printers of the weekly public newssheet. Generally, printers accepted news from any source, and they would print almost anything so long as those who wanted items printed paid for the insertion or the content did not cause any legal issues. Sometimes, however, the latter did not matter because controversial subjects could sell papers and potentially increase advertising.

In the eighteenth century, printing presses, ink, paper, and lead type were expensive, and producing a newssheet was timely. As a result, newspapers almost always were published weekly. They were sold by subscription only, and the average printer of the era produced about 600 copies per issue. By 1750, a dozen English-language papers located in all major towns existed. Though this number seems to be small in comparison to the population of approximately 1.7 million at the time, the ability to share information greatly exceeded circulation figures. While papers tended to be purchased by the more wealthy portion of the population because of their cost, newspapers were regularly subscribed to by coffeehouses, taverns, and other public places. Here, they were read aloud for all to hear, which meant that even the illiterate had the chance to hear "the freshest advices," which was the term most printers used to describe the content of their papers.

In addition, papers were easily shared within a town and with other areas of the colonies. Publication schedules often coincided with the schedules of ships and post riders so that they could be sent to other parts of the colonies and even to Europe. As a result, information moved about as fast as was physically possible in the eighteenth century. Since the majority of subscriptions were sold to households, the reading of the newspaper to all members of a family was standard practice. Nearly all papers were then passed on to another family. The average paper ended up miles from its origin, and because papers in the eighteenth century existed in an oral culture, their content penetrated into the general population at a far higher percentage than the actual number of papers to people in America.

Since printers openly called for information that could be run in their papers, the public prints developed into the ideal vehicles to share information and to attempt to persuade. It is here that the press of the eighteenth century resembles that of the twenty-first. A multiplicity of voices could be heard. When an essay was printed in a paper, it became public property and was disseminated though the era's multiple venues. Because items were discussed in churches, in coffeehouses, in taverns, and on the streets where newspapers were read aloud, they stimulated not only conversation but also formal responses from those who wrote essays.

The conversation grew as new "threads" of the debate appeared in print, and they did not remain in papers isolated in one region of the colonies. Printers picked up essays from all regions of British colonial America, as well as from Europe, and presented them in their own communities. Much like web logs and other online means of sharing information in the twenty-first century, newspapers of the eighteenth century allowed for numerous people of varied backgrounds to comment on issues. Whereas corporate, capitalist media of twentieth-century America gave voice to those in powerful positions, the eighteenth century press enabled perspectives from all levels of society, although opinion leaders predominated. They did not, though, control the conversations that the newspapers generated.

The multiplicity of voices in newspapers did have a common means of interpretation, and that was via the theological lens. A Bible was the one printed text found in nearly every home.[14] Being able to read was considered essential to have personal access to scripture, so much so that the Society for the Propagation of Christian Knowledge and the Anglican Society for the Propagation of the Gospel agreed to establish libraries throughout the British colonies to promote religious knowledge.[15] Because of religion's significance in life, it maintained a place of importance for people in their understanding of politics and social issues—in short, all aspects of life.

Defining News Through a Religious Lens?

The crisis that the British American colonies faced in 1754 provides an example of how religion defined news. Increasing unrest in the backcountry of Pennsylvania and Virginia (the Ohio Valley) between colonials migrating there and Native Americans and the French set off a series of alarms from Albany to Williamsburg. Since the fall of 1753, the French and Indians had been conducting attacks on the new British settlements in the region. Virginia's leaders appointed a young land surveyor named George Washington as a military officer and emissary to the Native Americans and sent him to the shores of Lake Erie in late 1753, but the trip did not ease tensions. In March 1754, the colony again sent out Washington, this time to the Ohio Valley. In what would become a disastrous series of events, Indians who had aligned themselves in opposition to the French and with Washington helped Washington and his men surround a French patrol. Ignoring Washington's orders, the Indians butchered a number of the French captives. Washington pulled back to a valley called the Great Meadows, where a blockhouse called Fort Necessity was located. Fort Necessity was soon surrounded by the French and Indians, who picked off Washington's hapless forces until they surrendered. Washington signed French terms of surrender, which held him responsible for the execution of French soldiers. Washington and what was left of his company returned to Virginia in late April and news of what had occurred at Fort Necessity spread throughout America during the next two months. War, most realized, was imminent.

Sensing the implications of what was taking place, Benjamin Franklin took action. On May 9, 1754, he published what is considered the first editorial cartoon in American newspapers. Titled "JOIN, or DIE," the now-famous rattlesnake, severed into individual American colonies, really needed no explanation for those who saw it, and most Americans who had access to newspapers in 1754 either saw a reproduction of the cartoon or had it described in detail for them by a news story in their local newspaper.

The simple message that the colonies could survive together or perish individually fit perfectly with the Puritan concepts that had become engrained in the collective understanding of British colonists and with the ideas of preachers like George Whitefield during the early 1740s Great Awakening. Each New England congregation, for example, was its own entity and saw its actions as those of an individual church, but the individual congregations also comprised the collective of God's Kingdom on Earth. When the separate British American colonies that would one day make up the United States were threatened by France and its Catholicism, Franklin evoked this understanding of the Christian covenant and the individualism of the priesthood of all believers. The colonies were individual entities with the ability to interact independently, but they also were elements of something larger. They made up the body politic of British North America, a collective political entity just as the church was a collective spiritual body.

Franklin, who knew Whitefield well, made the personal element of salvation central to his cartoon's meaning. What must each colony do to be saved? It had to join with the other colonies. In the essay that accompanied the cartoon, Franklin added more reasons for the colonies to join together. Similar to the woodcut of the snake, the essay contained information that was open to religious interpretation, but one part would have been most recognizable to all readers: Franklin's reference to "the disunited State of the British Colonies." The expositors of the Great Awakening often referred to the lost and in-turmoil condition of individuals. They would remain in that state until they realized they needed to become a part of the body of Christ—the church.[16] Franklin no doubt hoped each colony would have a similar realization when he called for a congress at Albany that summer.

Other religious elements helped frame news coverage and commentary of the 1750s, as well as the French and Indian War. Sometimes it was implicit, as in the case of Franklin's "JOIN, or DIE." In other cases, the religious elements were explicit, centering on the overt religious differences between the British and French. In Protestant colonial America, any reference to France in times of war or political upheaval would have been considered synonymous to saying *Catholicism*. Since the Protestant Reformation of the 1500s, the two forms of Christianity had been at odds theologically, politically, and socially. So, when the anonymous Philo Hugo wrote to the *Virginia Gazette* in 1754 to remind readers what the French had done in 1686 to Protestants in France, he really did not need to mention that the actions he was about to describe were perpetrated by Catholics. These types of references to Catholicism had been a key component of newspapers from the first issue of the *Boston News-Letter* on April 24, 1704. In the paper's opening essay, postmaster and publisher John Campbell described France's plans to establish a "Universal Monarchy" by gaining control of Great Britain and its territory in America. And like Philo Hugo fifty years later, Campbell did not need to mention that the establishment of a "Universal Monarchy" would mean establishing Catholicism as the religion of the colonies and Great Britain. The religious tensions between the countries had existed long before New World colonization, and the Protestant–Catholic antipathy was one reason the countries remained perpetual enemies, even if they were not officially at war.

The hostility to Catholics was heightened by the events of 1754. When the anonymous Virginia Centinel figuratively screamed at Americans in a newspaper essay, saying, "Countrymen! Fellow-Subjects! Fellow-Protestants! to engage your Attention, I need only repeat, Your Country Is in Danger,"[17] the Centinel was not referring to the dangers that Native Americans posed to colonials. He was referring to the French and warning that colonies they took over would become Catholic bastions.

The French and Indian War essentially eradicated the French presence from North America with the 1763 Treaty of Paris. This meant that news stories no longer needed to make overt references to the dangers of Catholicism, because France and the Catholic Church were no longer direct threats to colonial America. But the "we must all hang together or we hang separately" mentality—and Franklin's severed snake—would become a fixture in the land. From 1765 to 1776, it was repeatedly invoked to remind Americans of the dangers they faced and the strength they possessed. In 1765, for example, just three weeks before the Stamp Act was to go into effect, the anonymous B. W. sent a letter to the *Boston Gazette.*[18] In it, he warned that an evil people were ready to "enslave us." That, B. W. said, could never happen to the chosen people who were "born in a Land of Light, and reared in the Bosom of Liberty." He reminded readers that remaining free was not a choice that was theirs as a chosen people. "This is your duty, your burden, your indispensable Duty. Ages remote, Mortals yet unborn, will bless your generous Efforts, and revere the Memory of the Saviours of their Country." To make sure that his readers did not miss the religious connotations, B. W. plainly stated, "by the Liberty wherewith Christ *has made you free* . . . be faithful Guardians of the Liberties of [your] Country."

The letter immediately recalls biblical elements that the Puritans used to frame themselves as a chosen people. Because British colonial Americans had long understood themselves as a chosen people in a promised land, they knew that they would face many tests of worthiness, just as the chosen people of the Old Testament did.

The letter also is filled with Enlightenment rhetoric, which most eighteenth-century rationalists understood through a theological perspective. In other words, reason, the other term repeatedly cited in B. W.'s letter for resisting the tyranny of the stamp tax, was the way in which humans understood the divine. God was a necessary and logical part of understanding everything.[19] Most Americans had never heard of John Locke or other apologists of the Enlightenment, but that did not matter. People like Samuel Adams (in all probability the anonymous B. W.) and the other educated opinion leaders of the day had. They incorporated rationalism into their revolutionary rhetoric, and it fit well with the biblical understanding that Americans possessed.

Puritan thought had engrained in Americans an understanding of themselves and their purpose in the New World. Overwhelmingly, they believed that they needed not to consider self first but, instead, the commonweal of the community. Writers such as B. W. stressed this concept, harkening back to Puritans of the previous century. John Cotton, the seventeenth-century Puritan divine, said that this was the principal article of faith for all Christians because "it drawes the heart of a Christian to live in some warrantable calling; as soon as ever a man begins to look toward God, and the ways of his grace, he will not rest till he find some warrantable Calling and employment."[20] So, B. W.'s plea to the people began, "Awake!--Awake, my Countrymen, and, by a regular & legal Opposition, defeat the Designs of those who enslave us and our Posterity." He continued by declaring, "This is your Duty, your burden, your indispensable Duty. Ages remote, Mortals yet unborn, will bless your generous Efforts, and revere the Memory of the Saviours of their Country."

Ideas from the Great Awakening's style of preaching were woven in as well. The statement "If any of you have been till this Time insensible of your Danger, awake now out of your Lethargy" was a re-exposition of George Whitefield's altar call, "What must I do to be saved?" So, in an appeal that has only three biblical references, a short letter pleads with Americans to stand up to Britain and its stamp tax by invoking the concepts of the Promised Land, a covenantal people, the placing of self second to the good of the community, and being a light on the hill that can be seen as a guiding principle for others, as it delivers a call to the altar for salvation that comes when those hearing the words of the letter realize that the only way to save themselves is to give selflessly to save all Americans.

Revolution Looms and News Turns Apocryphal

By the 1770s, the covenantal relationship between the chosen people—Americans—and God assumed center stage in the biblical understanding of the conflict with Great Britain. The essayists and commentators who used newspapers to assess the colonies' situation continued to base much of their writings in the elements of Puritanism and the Great Awakening, but writers also increasingly found it acceptable to make their religious analogies more blatant. No longer was there a need to pit Protestantism against Catholicism. The enemy now was, in a way, from within. The covenantal people were being oppressed by those who held the possibility of being a part of God's chosen but had somehow gone astray. As a result, the rhetoric of the Revolutionary era assumed an apocryphal tone, and religious references became predictions, similar to the writings found in the Book of Revelation, the final book of the Protestant New Testament often referred to as the Apocalypse. In Revelation, the biblical message of the redemption of God's chosen people is brought to a conclusion that depicts a great conflict through a combination of prose and poetry. In that conflict the chosen people, with God leading the way, gained the ultimate victory of those who sought to enslave them.

As conflict between Britain and the American colonies grew more inevitable, the tenor of the language by those writing to newspapers very much assumed an end-time focus. "WHEN I take a view of . . . these once dreary wastes blossoming as the rose, and teeming with an ample supply of all the conveniencies of life; in fine, when I attend to the almost incredible rapidity of population in the American colonies, I am struck with astonishment at the bountiful rewards of the industry of our worthy forefathers, and cannot forbear anticipating the future grandeur of this western world," an anonymous writer calling himself A Soldier said. He then spoke of America's glorious population in the year 2000 and of the fact that his efforts as well as all other Americans fighting tyranny would "render this once despicable country the most powerful and August empire which the annals of history can boast." The New World was obviously despicable before its infusion of God's chosen people but would now be the world's most powerful because "Approving Heaven has hitherto smiled upon almost every enterprize"[21] that God's select have undertaken in America, the New Canaan.

Other writings were even more aligned with the language of the Book of Revelation and also with the Old Testament prophets. A letter addressed "To all Nations under HEAVEN," which appeared in the *Boston Gazette* at the beginning of 1774, announced that a battle of cosmic proportions was about to begin. Once it started, America could not be defeated because God stood with her. Virtue and liberty always trumped tyranny because that was how God would have it.

"Know Ye," the letter began, "*THAT the* People *of the* American World, *are Millions strong,—countless Legions compose their united* Army *of* Freemen—*whose intrepid Souls sparkle with Liberty, and their Hearts are steeled with Courage to effect what their Wisdom dictates to be done*—America *now stands with the Scale of* Justice *in one Hand, and the Sword of* Vengeance *in the other, and whatever Nation or People who dares to lift a hostile Hand against her, to invade her serene Region, or sully her Liberty, shal—Let the Britons fear to do any more so wickedly as they have done, for the* Herculean Arm *of this* New World *is lifted up—and Woe be to them on whom it falls!—At the Beat of a Drum, she can call five Hundred Thousand of her* Sons *to* Arms—*before whose blazing Shields none can stand—Therefore,* ye that are Wise, *make Peace with Her, take Shelter under Her Wings, that ye may shine by the Reflection of* Her *Glory.*

"*May the* New Year *shine propitious on the* New World—*and* Virtue, *and* Liberty, *reign here without a Foe, until rolling Years shall measure* Time *no more.*"[22]

Writers in the 1770s no doubt viewed the events affecting them as needing obvious biblical references because they wanted to portray the colonies versus Britain in terms of good versus evil. This was consistent with an understanding of the confrontations of the Hebrews in the Old Testament where prophets spoke of just wars, of redemption for God's chosen people, and of lands that would flourish now and into perpetuity. This was the same idea as that found in Revelation in the establishment of a new heaven and new earth where God, with his chosen people, would reign until the end of days.[23] This concept from Revelation would have synced perfectly for Americans when they read, "*and* Virtue, *and* Liberty, *reign here without a Foe, until rolling Years shall measure* Time *no more.*"

Conclusion

For colonial Americans, religion was a potent means of explaining events. An earthquake might be God's vengeance for evil acts; a life spared when a ship sank, an act of God's grace.[24] Religion for the eighteenth-century citizen was the common frame for understanding almost everything. While anyone reading colonial newspapers today would be hard pressed to discern a religious meaning for all news, eighteenth-century readers understood critical situations and current events through the religious frame of the Bible, Puritan ideals, and Great Awakening concepts. Religion as expressed through all these elements was the common denominator in the lives of virtually all living in British colonial America. Exegesis of the examples from newspapers used in this chapter could be interpreted differently, but a religious foundation for understanding what writers were saying makes sense when one considers the emphasis placed on religion in almost all of the colonies.

Even rationalists and Deists like Benjamin Franklin had lived their entire lives immersed in Protestant theology and the Puritan dogma that equated America to the Promised Land and the citizens of British colonial America to a chosen people. Franklin even confessed, "I never was without some religious Principles; I never doubted, for instance the Existence of the Deity, that he made the World, and govern'd it by his Providence."[25] Franklin may not have created the "JOIN, or DIE" cartoon intentionally with so many religious references, but it was probably impossible for him not to reflect—at least subliminally—Puritan ideals of America, especially when the colonies faced such dire times. Others like Samuel Adams who used newspapers as a venue to shape debate grew up surrounded by Puritan thought, which led Adams to study theology at Harvard.[26]

The events of the Great Awakening would have still been fresh on the minds of most in the colonies as they faced the threats of the 1750s onward. By 1770, nearly all Americans had been afforded the opportunity to hear and see George Whitefield preach at least once.[27] Whitefield's message that focused on the individual provided Americans with a personal power that was then transferred to the assembled multitude who listened to the itinerant's preaching. Whitefield in this way emphasized the power of the chosen as the collective, the light on the hill.[28] Since his revivals were attended by thousands, people could easily see how as a chosen people they had the ability to change the course of the world, another element of the rhetoric that accompanied the news during the 1760s and 1770s as the colonies moved toward separation from Britain.

As the conflict with Britain grew, fiery apologists gravitated toward writing in ways that echoed the apocryphal language of scripture. Some writings, as seen above, were overt in their biblical references. Other writings, like those surrounding the French and Indian War, were more coded. Thomas Paine, writing as Common Sense, saw what was happening in 1776 as a cosmic battle. "Let it be told to the future world," he predicted in "The Crisis," "that in the depth of winter, when nothing but hope and virtue could survive, that the city and the country, alarmed at one common danger, came forth to meet and to repulse it."[29] The "it" was the subjugation of a free people by Great Britain. Paine blatantly noted that this power "can belong only to God." And he strongly suggested the biblical Christian principle that through Jesus the chosen people had been set free.

At other times, news in colonial America focused directly on religious issues because of the importance of them to people. The Great Awakening was no doubt the single most important event that colonials experienced that had a purely religious focus but whose effects went far beyond the walls of America's churches. The Awakening, specifically its mouthpiece—George Whitefield—became "the common topic of conversation from Georgia to New Hampshire," according to eighteenth-century printer and historian Isaiah Thomas.[30] Religious publications increased more than 160 percent from the year before Whitefield came to America to when he departed in 1741, which refocused conversation toward religion in multiple ways.[31]

Other religious issues also captured people's attention, and those people, in turn, used the press to discuss those issues and events. New York papers, for example, from 1753 to 1755, were embroiled in debate about whether the colony, which was about to establish a university through public funds, should allow the Anglican church of the colony to oversee the school's operation. Almost any issue imaginable could end up with someone quoting scripture or applying biblical principle to it before the debate subsided. The inoculation controversy in Boston of 1721 pitted Congregationalists and Anglicans squarely against each other as to whether smallpox could be stopped via a weakened dose of the disease being given to healthy individuals. The list could continue.

For colonial Americans, news about religion and news with religious connotations regularly appeared in the papers. Though the former, when the entire content of papers is considered, might not capture the attention of a reader from today, it would have been noticed by readers of the time. News that was understood through a religious lens, though it might be imperceptible to most readers from later centuries, explains how Americans understood important events. In 1690, Benjamin Harris started *Publick Occurrences* so "That Memorable Occurrents of Divine Providence may not be neglected or forgotten, as they too often are."[32] Harris knew that, if presented with news, people would be able to see God's actions within it. More than eighty years later, a New England writer again noted divine activity in the lives of the people of the British American colonies. "Great and marvelous have been the appearances of his providence in our favour," the anonymous Junius Cato declared, "for which glory be to his name."[33] The town of Lincoln, Massachusetts, affirmed that "under Divine Providence depends the Preservation of all our Rights and Privileges."[34] When it came to discerning how God would react in a situation for his chosen people, colonial Americans, when reading their news, were certain that God would neither forsake nor abandon them because God had chosen them. They had answered the question "What must I do to be saved?" properly. And though times were dark and dismal in the 1770s, people knew that America "will surpass every other Country and Nation under Heaven" because as a chosen people God would ensure that they "shalt prosper," would "persevere therefore unto the End," and "be sure of Success."[35] They knew this because the theological lens through which they read the news was a part of the American psyche.

NOTES

1. *American Weekly Mercury* (Philadelphia), October 22, 1730.
2. Patricia U. Bonomi, *Under the Cope of Heaven: Religion, Society, and Politics in Colonial America* (New York and Oxford: Oxford University Press, 1986), 3.
3. David A. Copeland, *Colonial American Newspapers: Character and Content* (Newark: University of Delaware Press, 1997), 288–99.

4. Max Weber, *The Theory of Social and Economic Organization* (New York: Free Press, 1947), 358–59.

5. David Paul Nord, "Teleology and the News: The Religious Roots of American Journalism, 1630–1730," *Journal of American History* 77 (1990): 36.

6. A number of scholars discuss Puritanism's concepts as being incorporated into the American mindset including the classic studies by Perry Miller, *The New England Mind: The Seventeenth Century* (New York: 1939) and *The New England Mind: From Colony to Province* (Cambridge, MA: Harvard University Press, 1953), and Sacvan Bercovitch, *The Puritan Origins of the American Self* (New London, CT: Yale University Press, 1975).

7. Quoted in Bercovitch, *The Puritan Origins*, 138.

8. Bercovitch, *The Puritan Origins*, 136.

9. Philip Freneau and Hugh Henry Brackenridge, *A Poem, On the Rising Glory of America* (Philadelphia, 1772), reprinted in *Poems of Philip Freneau: Poet of the American Revolution*, ed. Fred Lewis Pattee, 2 vols. (Princeton, NJ: The University Library, 1902), 1:75.

10. Edwin Scott Gausted, *The Great Awakening in New England* (New York: Harper and Brothers, 1957), 42.

11. Charles E. Clark, "The Newspapers of Colonial America," *Proceedings of the American Antiquarian Society* 100 (1990): 382.

12. Isaiah Thomas, *The History of Printing in America* (1810; repr., New York: Weathervane Books, 1970), 568.

13. Richard L. Bushman, *The Great Awakening: Documents on the Revival of Religion, 1740–1745* (New York: Atheneum, 1970; repr., Chapel Hill: University of North Carolina Press, 1989), xi.

14. Richard Beale Davis, *A Colonial Southern Bookshelf: Readings in the Eighteenth Century* (Athens: University of Georgia Press, 1979), 67; Oscar Theodore Barck, Jr. and Hugh Talmage Lefler, *Colonial America* (New York: Macmillan, 1958), 379.

15. Davis, *A Colonial Southern Bookshelf*, 72–73.

16. Harry S. Stout, *The New England Soul: Preaching and Religious Culture in Colonial New England* (New York and Oxford: Oxford University Press, 1986), 194–95.

17. "*From the* VIRGINIA CENTINEL," *Maryland Gazette* (Annapolis), August 12, 1756.

18. *Boston Gazette, and Country Journal*, October 7, 1765.

19. Henry F. May, *The Enlightenment in America* (New York and Oxford: Oxford University Press, 1976), 10.

20. John Cotton, "Christian Calling," in *The Puritans*, ed. Perry Miller and Thomas H. Johnson (New York: American Book Company, 1938), 319.

21. A Soldier, *Virginia Gazette* (Williamsburg, Pinkney), December 20, 1775.

22. *Boston Gazette, and Country Journal*, January 3, 1774, emphasis included.

23. See Revelation 21.

24. See, for example, *Massachusetts Spy* (Boston), October 23, 1770, and *Boston Evening-Post*, October 13, 1755.

25. Benjamin Franklin, *Autobiography*, ed. J. A. Leo LeMay and P. M. Zall (New York: W. W. Norton, 1986), 45, 65.

26. John K. Alexander, *Samuel Adams: America's Revolutionary Politician* (Lanham, MD: Rowman & Littlefield, 2002), 6, 41–42.

27. Harry S. Stout, *The Divine Dramatist: George Whitefield and the Rise of Modern Evangelism* (Grand Rapids, MI: William B. Eerdmans, 1991), xiii–xiv.

28. Stout, *The New England Soul*, 193–94.

29. Common Sense (Thomas Paine), "The Crisis," *Dunlap's Pennsylvania Packet* (Philadelphia), December 27, 1776.

30. Isaiah Thomas, *The History of Printing in America* (1812; repr., New York: Weathervane, 1970), 568.

31. David A. Copeland, *The Enlightenment and Its Unruly Legacy* (Evanston, IL: Northwestern University Press, 2006), 174.

32. *Publick Occurrences Both Forreign and Domestick* (Boston), September 25, 1690.

33. *New-London Gazette*, January 15, 1773; *Massachusetts Spy, or Thomas's Boston Journal*, February, 2, 1773.

34. *Boston Post Boy*, January 3, 1774.

35. Solon, "To the Americans," *Providence Gazette, and Country Journal*, May 14, 1774.

REFERENCES

Bercovitch, Sacvan. 1975. *The Puritan Origins of the American Self.* New London, CT: Yale University Press.

Bonomi, Patricia U. 1986. *Under the Cope of Heaven: Religion, Society, and Politics in Colonial America.* New York and Oxford: Oxford University Press.

Copeland, David A. 1997. *Colonial American Newspapers: Character and Content.* Newark: University of Delaware Press.

CHAPTER 2

THE PENNY PRESS AND THE BIRTH OF MODERN RELIGION REPORTING

JUDITH M. BUDDENBAUM

THE first decades of the nineteenth century were a time of rapid change. Although President John Adams had predicted it would take a millennium for the United States to become an industrial nation, the transformation had taken less than half a century. Industrialization led to urbanization as thousands of people flocked to cities for factory jobs and business opportunities. However, for those whose values were rooted in the kind of community found in their small towns, the change from a rural, agrarian society to an industrial, urban one seemed threatening, especially because cities were now home to Irish Catholic immigrants.

In response to this perceived threat, the period was also one of unusual religious fervor. During the Second Great Awakening, as historians of American religion have labeled it, wave upon wave of revivalism swept through the nation. New denominations and even new religions sprang up; established churches created missionary, Bible, and tract societies in an effort to make the nation a Christian (i.e., Protestant) one by sending out workers charged with placing a Bible and a regular supply of religious reading material in every American home.[1]

Although that strategy did much to create a Protestant Christian culture, ironically, it also created an appetite for reading that could not be satisfied solely through religious literature.[2] Therefore, religious fervor, along with industrialization and urbanization, helped to create a climate in which a new, more modern kind of press, the Penny Press, could develop and flourish. These developments, as well as the work of James Gordon Bennett, Sr., gave rise to a new and more modern journalism.

The Penny Press

In 1830, there were sixty-five newspapers in the United States, at least nine of them in New York City. Most were of two types: partisan political papers that were funded by and served as the mouthpiece and apologist for a political party, or mercantile ones backed by business and financial interests and serving their needs. Instead of engaging in active news gathering, these papers relied on essays and letters supplied by their supporters. They depended on those same supporters and on advertisements targeting them to help pay the bills. As a result, both their content and writing style were unappealing if not unintelligible to the average person. They were also expensive. A single issue cost six cents and could be obtained only at the newspaper's headquarters or by paying eight to ten dollars in advance for a one-year subscription. But except for the religious newspapers and a few specialized periodicals aimed at an ethnic community or group of factory workers, these political and mercantile newspapers were the only papers available until Benjamin Day started his *New York Sun*. In the very first issue, published on September 3, 1833, Day promised New Yorkers a politically independent paper that would "lay before the public, at a price within the means of everyone, ALL THE NEWS OF THE DAY, and at the same time afford an advantageous medium for advertising."

To provide that news, Day pioneered active news gathering, most notably the court reporting of George Wisner, who wrote about drunks, prostitutes, and petty criminals who found themselves in court. To make those stories accessible to readers, Day used newsboys to sell papers for just a penny an issue to pedestrians.

The crime stories in Day's paper were shocking, opening to public scrutiny the seamier side of everyday life in a way that blurred the boundary between appropriate and inappropriate behavior by making criminal activity seem common and acceptable. Equally shocking was the manner of selling the papers on the streets of New York City. However, both the content and delivery system proved popular with readers, as well as with entrepreneurs, who quickly saw the potential of using the paper as a vehicle for hawking their wares to average people.

Day's paper proved to be the first in a new breed of newspapers that collectively are known as the Penny Press. These nineteenth-century papers are important because they were the first to reach out to a mass audience. In content and style they can be seen as the forerunners of modern concepts of news as a subject, a commodity, and a business.

The success of the first penny paper invited competition. On May 7, 1835, James Gordon Bennett, Sr. brought out the *New York Herald*. In his paper, Bennett picked up on the crime reporting that made Day's *Sun* so popular. At the same time, he gave readers his own independent take on the world of finance, politics—and also religion. By treating religion as a topic for news coverage, Bennett became known as the father of modern religion journalism.

The Father of Religion Journalism: James Gordon Bennett, Sr.

Standard journalism histories classify the *New York Herald* as a sensational newspaper; they describe its founder, James Gordon Bennett, Sr., as a "man of little religious feeling."[3] But that description misses the fact that by education and life experience he was well equipped to pioneer modern religion news.

Bennett was both more knowledgeable about religion and personally more religious than his detractors have cared to admit. He was born into a Roman Catholic family in Calvinist, Protestant northern Scotland. There he studied scripture and theology in preparation for the priesthood. As a seminarian, Bennett became disenchanted with the Catholic Church and never entered the ministry, but his disenchantment was with the institutional church, not with Catholicism. After comparing both the dominant Calvinist Protestantism of his native land and the Protestantism he found in the United States to the Catholic faith, he found them both wanting. He considered atheism an absurdity. Therefore, he remained a Catholic, albeit an independent and relatively inactive one, all his life. Both his Catholic religion and his nationality served him well in his professional life.

Bennett was an experienced, talented reporter. Before starting the *Herald*, he had accumulated more than a decade of newspaper experience that included a stint with Colonel James Watson Webb's *New York Enquirer*. As the *Enquirer*'s Washington correspondent, Bennett relied on his power of observation to produce timely stories about what legislators actually did instead of passing along the self-serving accounts they typically provided to newspaper correspondents for party papers. Readers loved his colorful, descriptive writing, laced as it was with his witty and quite pointed commentary. However, politicians and the editors they supported became increasingly less enchanted with his work. After five years with Webb's paper, Bennett found himself without a job.

Less than two years later, without any substantive business experience, Bennett started his *New York Herald*. There, he proved himself to be a savvy businessman. Although he knew that working-class readers were the core audience for a penny paper, he wanted his paper to be a true mass medium like the penny papers in his native Scotland that for more than a century had served both men and women of all classes. Therefore, he quickly raised the price of his paper from a penny to two cents—low enough to be within reach of his core audience, but high enough to assure those higher on the socioeconomic scale that the *Herald* wasn't merely a cheap paper. The ploy increased readership; increased circulation brought in more advertisers. Extra income from circulation and from advertising enabled Bennett to be independent of political and financial special interests. It also made it possible for him to hire reporters and correspondents to provide the kind of timely news he knew people wanted. But even before his strategy of raising the price of his paper had a chance to pay dividends, Bennett had taken steps to provide news that would appeal to the broad audience he craved. In just the second issue of his paper, he published the first of his many "Money" columns that gave middle- and upper-class readers his own take on Wall Street, commerce, and shipping and the facts to support his opinions.

Bennett also recognized that stories of everyday life appealed to readers. Aware that religion was an important part of that life, he included religion news in the reporting mix. As an astute observer of the American scene, Bennett was fascinated by the proliferation of religions and quasi religions he found in America. He was appalled that some churches "huddle[d] up to the self-made men of the middle, and when possible, the upper class [in a way that] exalted persons over property"[4] in response to industrialization and urbanization. As a result:

> The Protestant churches, shaped in a colonial America which had fostered commonwealth concepts, chartered individualism. A tradition which had exalted persons over property converted and justified absolute rights to property on the part of the industrious. The ideal of organismic community was overshadowed by a religion which largely accepted the laissez-faire competitive enterprise system.

And although Bennett found much to admire in the religious commitment that found expression in missionary, Bible, and tract societies, he saw danger in the anti-Catholic and anti-immigrant sentiment that lurked within them. In those trends, he saw religion stories that needed to be told.

In reporting those stories, Bennett used the same observation-based, descriptive writing style he had used as a political reporter with similar results. The spotlight he shone on the world of religion proved popular with readers, but many clergy called his paper scandalous and a threat to true religion. In 1840, they instigated a Moral War against Bennett and his paper. His former employer, Colonel Webb, as well as other newspapermen and Wall Street businessmen, each with his own reason for wanting to see Bennett put out of business, joined in. Together, they called for a boycott of the *Herald* and its advertisers. Bennett's contemporaries said it was his coverage of religious events that "excited the jealousy of the clergy, the religious Press, and the opposition of the old class of inactive journals."[5] Twentieth-century historians cited Bennett's irreverent comments and salacious stories as the cause.[6] But whatever the reason, the boycott failed to put Bennett out of business. Two years before and two years after the Moral War, the *Herald*'s circulation of 20,000 rivaled that of the *Sun*; it surpassed the combined circulation of all of New York's six-penny papers. Nor did it have any real impact on the way Bennett covered religion.[7]

Religion News in the *New York Herald*

During the first few years, religion news in the *Herald* reflected an image of Bennett as the history books portray him—irascible, irreverent, and with a fondness for the sensational. Bennett frequently reminded readers that he was

Catholic and a Scot, not a Protestant American. He routinely inserted jocular comments about his own lack of conventional religiosity into stories that had nothing to do with religion. He filled space with short, irreverent comments about religion, as well as with apocryphal tales, some of them ostensibly about religion.

On January 19, 1836, in the most sensational of those tales, Bennett published "Awful Disclosures by Maria Monk." In the story, the author told of her discovery, upon becoming a full member of a Roman Catholic religious order in Canada, that she, like the other sisters in her order, was expected to engage "in the practice of criminal intercourse" with priests and even with the bishop. While Bennett published only two episodes of the Maria Monk tale and freely admitted in the pages of the *Herald* that it was fiction, not fact, he kept the story alive for years through frequent allusions to it, most likely because it served his purpose. As much as "Awful Disclosures" may have both titillated and played to the anti-Catholic sentiment of the Protestant majority, it also may have reassured them that Bennett was independent of church influence. That perception may have allowed him to cover all facets of American religion.

Over the years, the *Herald* published less satire and irreverent commentary; stories became longer and more varied. As Bennett turned over more of the actual reporting and writing to staff reporters and national and international correspondents, the writing style and subject matter, especially in terms of religion, diversified. To be sure, Bennett's own independent, somewhat idiosyncratic religious beliefs informed both his news judgment and his opinions. For the most part, however, the *Herald* covered news from the perspective of an interested, essentially neutral outside observer.

Critical News and Commentary

In the *Herald*, three themes dominated coverage of the seamy side of religion: sex, money, and politics. Of the three, sexual scandals and financial improprieties were staples from the very beginning. In 1836, the same year that the fictitious Maria Monk story appeared, Bennett published at least twenty stories about illicit sexual behaviors committed by real clergy, whom he named. In those stories, he sometimes reminded readers of the value in covering real sexual affairs, as he did again on January 11, 1842, in a commentary appended to an article about the trial of the Reverend Van Zandt for the seduction of a young lady:

> Is it not our duty and the duty of every one to inquire seriously into these matters? Is the case of the Rev. Mr. Van Zandt an isolated one? (which we hope and trust it is) or is it but a sample of the conduct of the clergymen of that or any other denomination? This is a matter every father, brother, and parent should think seriously and see settled to his satisfaction without loss of time.

Two years later, on August 1, 1844, he published the complete court testimony in the case of the Reverend Joy H. Fairchild, who was on trial for the seduction of Rhoda Davidson.

Even as Bennett published stories with a sex angle, he produced just as many news items, commentaries, and satires that called critical attention to the interplay between religion and money. He took potshots at his competitors in the newspaper business, frequently criticizing them for claiming to be Christian even as they published their papers on the Sabbath. He targeted Colonel Webb, his business allies, and clergy supporters, whom he sometimes named, for attempting to enrich themselves through speculation in Texas lands. He routinely displayed disdain for Mordecai M. Noah, the publisher of the *Courier and Enquirer*, who had sought funds from the New York legislature for a Jewish homeland on Grand Island in the Niagara River.

However, most of Bennett's attention and ire were directed at clergy and at churches that placed more value on money than on mission. Bennett's most frequent target was Trinity Episcopal Church, Wall Street, although neither other Protestant churches nor Catholic ones were spared from his scrutiny. In this vein, Bennett's most important commentary can be found in his December 14, 1838, "Religion and Salvation." In it, he suggested that the Reverend Jonathan Mayhew Wainwright, who was well known for preaching that God intended for some people to be rich while others remained poor, didn't really believe half of what he taught. Bennett's piece ended with one of his frequent reminders to readers that Trinity, the wealthiest church in New York, claimed title to farmland on Manhattan Island at the expense of the heirs of Anneka Jantz[8]:

> Perhaps Dr. Wainwright may think that the Trinity Church Corporation ought to have a monopoly of religion and roast beef, as it has of certain vast estates, which belong to other individuals. . . . Their immense estates have created a similar state of morals which have characterized the loco-focos and sub-treasury men. More of this by and by. Surplus revenue of any kind, is a dangerous thing.

In between, he offered the clearest statement of his own faith, as well as his perspective on covering religion news:

> Religion—true religion—consists not in eating or drinking—not in high salaries—not in hanging round the apron strings of rich old women—not in presuming to judge the opinions of others beyond what their acts will justify. Neither does true religion—or real Christianity consist in believing the dogmas of any church—or the *ipse dixit* of any set of men. The Bible is before me. Have I not a right to read that book—and to draw out from it religious opinions—and to create a belief and a church of my own?

In contrast to the stories of sexual and fiscal improprieties, news of the mixing of religion and politics was a latecomer, first creeping into the paper in late 1838 after Bennett set up a small network of international correspondents. In stories about Catholic involvement in separatist or revolutionary activities in Ireland and Canada or on the persecution of Jews in Turkey, Bennett showed antipathy to those who, in religion's name, attempted to control others. That antipathy became even more pronounced in 1844 when news of religious persecutions at home nearly drove other kinds of news from the paper; it remained a strong theme in the *Herald* throughout Bennett's career.

Early in 1844 the *Herald* criticized Catholic Bishop John Hughes for his attempts to make the Bible and Catholic theology part of the public school curriculum. Bennett also criticized the bishop for his support of political factions in Ireland and for encouraging Catholics in America to form a voting block. However, when Protestants calling themselves "Native Americans" instigated violence against immigrant Irish Catholics in Philadelphia's Kensington district, the *Herald* gave Hughes space to comment on the attacks. For two weeks the paper published extra editions to bring readers breaking news about the Philadelphia riots. In all of its coverage, the paper's sympathies lay with the beleaguered Catholics. When it became clear that the Native Americans were becoming a political force and their religious rhetoric was infesting both the Democratic and Republican parties, Bennett lashed out with some of his strongest commentaries and satires. On May 15, 1844, with one eye on the Bible and the other on the First Amendment, he wrote:

> We regard the clerical demagogues both of the Protestant and Catholic churches as being equally culpable. They have alike violated the precepts of the master whom they profess to serve, and alike put in jeopardy the glorious civil institutions under which they live, and whose privileges and blessings were designed to be, like the dews of heaven, for all men of whatever creed, or lineage, or clime.

Long after the Philadelphia riots ended, Bennett's sympathy for immigrant Catholics colored the *Herald's* politics. Mistrustful of people who would impose their beliefs on others, Bennett was no fan of temperance societies, which he saw as anti-Catholic. Nor was he a supporter of the abolitionists. During the Civil War, the *Herald* opposed President Abraham Lincoln and the Emancipation Proclamation partly out of concern that newly freed slaves would deprive Catholic immigrants of jobs.

Just as the paper generally sided with Catholics in their struggle to find a place in an overwhelmingly Protestant nation, it exhibited some sympathy for the Church of Jesus Christ of Latter-day Saints. Bennett had on occasion poked fun at the upstart Mormon religion and labeled Joseph Smith, its prophet and founder, a charlatan. When news of Smith's murder and the massacre of Mormons in Nauvoo, Illinois, in July 1844 broke, the *Herald* carried an anti-Mormon account of the events, which it attributed to the *Expositor*, a Nauvoo paper started by Mormons who were disenchanted with Joseph Smith and his teachings. However, that story differed markedly from articles supplied to the *Herald* by its own correspondents in the area. Those accounts attributed the massacre to Christian jealousy over Mormon success. In one of his commentaries on the subject, Bennett linked the attack on Nauvoo's Mormons to the anti-Catholic riots in Philadelphia, as well as to an arson at a Massachusetts convent and parochial school, for which Protestants found justification in sermons by the Reverend Lyman Beecher and others. In that July 12, 1844, commentary, Bennett wrote, "The conduct of the people of Illinois and Missouri has been brutal and detestable in the extreme, and discovering the same spirit that burned the witches at Salem and the Convent at Boston."

After the Mormons left Nauvoo for Utah, the *Herald* continued to take potshots at the church, especially for its practice of polygamy. With Bennett in charge, however, the paper was more sympathetic to Mormonism than was typical at the time. Most other papers clearly supported government efforts to combat what was perceived as a serious threat to both Christianity and the United States.

News of Everyday Religious Life

Although Bennett devoted many column inches to the mixing of religion with politics, as well as to the sexual and fiscal improprieties of clergy and churches, religion news in the *Herald* wasn't all scandal and sensation. Balancing "hard news" stories were features that reported and commented on everyday religious events and activities. Although some of these stories contained critiques of leaders and institutions, most provided a neutral to highly favorable image of religion.

During its first year of publication, the *Herald* published occasional listings of religious events in New York City. On May 23, 1836, the paper carried an account of the annual anniversary meeting of the Bible Society. The story began with a descriptive paragraph that led into synopses of sermons and committee reports; it ended with a complete listing of the number of Bibles and testaments distributed in sixteen languages—"Making in all, 221,694 copies, and an aggregate since the formation of the society of 1,989,430." Two years later Bennett started publishing special eight-page issues in May and June to make room for stories about all of the simultaneously occurring annual anniversary meetings. At about the same time he began publishing accounts of sermons from local churches along with occasional round-up columns of religion news sent to the *Herald* by its correspondents.

Interspersed among those regular religion features were church histories and stories about New York City churches and clergy. The paper told readers about evangelists such as Charles Finney, developments within new religions and quasi-religious movements, and rivalries between and among traditional Protestant denominations. Long descriptive stories took readers to the installation of John Hughes as bishop of New York, to a Jewish festival, to a hillside where Millerites gathered to await the end of the world, to Baptist revivals, and to Methodist camp meetings.

Religion News in Other Nineteenth-Century Newspapers

Bennett's *Herald* was not the first nineteenth-century newspaper to publish news of developments within the world of religion. Accounts of meetings of missionary societies appeared as early as 1820 in newspapers in Boston, where many of them were first located, and in smaller cities where their supporters lived. *Niles Weekly Register* carried several lengthy, mildly critical essays on the topic. One account, dated April 14, 1821, is noteworthy for a letter written by Seneca Chief Red Jacket that was appended as a footnote. The Indian leader provided a counterpoint to the generally laudatory chronicle of missionary activity among Native Americans.

In the months before Bennett started the *Herald*, both Day's penny paper and some six-penny papers gave extensive coverage to the case of Robert Matthews. Self-styled as the Prophet Matthias, this New York City carpenter was on trial for embezzlement, adultery, assault, and murder. The charges stemmed from a police investigation into the suspicious death of Elijah Pierson at Matthews's religious community near Sing Sing, New York. As Matthews's first convert, Pierson had spent his fortune supporting his newfound religion.[9]

Before Bennett, papers rarely reported on religion, but his success invited imitation. Recognizing that people wanted timely news about current events, including religious events, newspaper editors replaced contributions from readers, on which they had previously relied, with stories sourced through active news gathering. As part of that news-gathering process, journalists joined Bennett in reporting on the anniversary meetings of Bible, tract, and missionary societies. By the late 1850s, Horace Greeley's *New York Daily Tribune* competed with Bennett's *Herald* to bring readers the most timely, complete, and colorful stories of revivals and other local church events. The *New York Times* sent reporters to cover Sunday sermons for its Monday paper. Toward the end of the century, church pages on Saturday, Monday, or even both days became common.

Although some frontier newspaper editors delighted in making jocular and irreverent comments about clergy,[10] even they reported on and sometimes promoted temperance and other Protestant causes. In the process, editors helped to make celebrities of evangelists such as Dwight L. Moody.[11] Few papers were inclined to follow Bennett's lead in seeking out and reporting the more sordid side of religion. They would, however, happily cover scandals when they came to light. In 1872, for example, after feminist and women's rights advocate Victoria Woodhull used her *Woodhull and Claflin's Weekly* to break the news of the Reverend Henry Ward Beecher's affair with married congregation member Elizabeth Tilton, newspapers around the country picked up and sensationalized the already sensational story beyond anything Bennett ever did. The *New York Times* alone published more than 100 articles on it; newspapers as far away as New Orleans and San Francisco ran with the story.

But whether out of the personal convictions of newspaper owners and editors or out of deference to the sensibilities of their audience, religion news coverage generally assumed and promoted a Protestant perspective. Just as papers generally avoided going out of their way to find news of hypocrisy and scandal, most also were disinclined to raise serious questions of the kind Bennett favored about religion and politics. However, they could no more ignore the anti-Catholicism that infused every nineteenth-century presidential election than they could ignore the perceived Mormon menace. Nor could they disregard the issues of abolition and emancipation that fanned the flames of the Civil War.

Following Bennett's lead, Horace Greeley and his *New York Daily Tribune* became a strong voice in opposition to attempts to impose a de facto Protestantism on Catholics whether by mob violence or by law. On the Mormon question and on the question of emancipation, Greeley was something of an innovator. While traveling in the West, he interviewed Brigham Young; on August 20, 1859, the *Tribune* published "Two Hours with Brigham Young," one of the earliest examples of interview-based reporting. In it, Greeley used the question-answer format to let the Mormon leader explain his religion and its practices in his own words before offering his own critical opinion as a sort of obligatory appendage. During the Civil War, many newspapers in both the North and the South inclined to a form of religious journalism that had been typical before Bennett's innovations. Each side used the Bible to champion the righteousness of its cause, and each published prayers beseeching God for victory. Greeley, however, became a formidable political force by publishing exchanges of letters between those who, like the Reverend Henry Ward Beecher, favored abolition and their critics. Greeley printed the "Prayer of Twenty Million," his own call for emancipation on August 20, 1862; five days later he published Lincoln's response to the "Prayer" along with his reply to the president. That exchange both reflected and helped solidify Northern opinion in favor of freeing the slaves.

Bennett's Legacy

Over time, Horace Greeley's reputation eclipsed that of James Gordon Bennett. But Bennett was an influential, innovative journalist, especially in the field of religion reporting. For that he richly deserves the title of "father of modern religion journalism."

As a religion reporter, Bennett broke away from the earlier practice that used arguments drawn from religious beliefs to promote or defend a particular worldview. Bennett had little interest in the correctness of anyone's religious beliefs; it was their behavior that fascinated him and that he covered and commented upon. His opinions were formed by active news gathering, the results of which he presented with detailed, sometimes vivid description. By working from the standpoint of an interested, outside observer who presumed only to "judge . . . what their acts will justify," he provided even-handed coverage of both conventional and unconventional religions.

Although few journalists cite Bennett as their role model, his active news gathering became standard. His outsider perspective became enshrined in the canons of journalism as objective reporting. News became separated from opinion and commentary, but his attention to stories of everyday religious life and attention to hard news and critical commentary remain integral elements of religion news. However, in creating a template for modern religion journalism, Bennett also laid the groundwork for some of the challenges and problems still faced by those who report religion.

By the end of the nineteenth century, stories of everyday religious life that before Bennett had been the province of religious newspapers found a permanent home on church pages. At first, news on those pages was narrowly defined as stories about local, usually Protestant, churches and their allied organizations. However, by the end of the twentieth century, the old church pages, with their Christian and institutional connotations, had morphed into religion pages devoted more broadly to faith, value, and ethics. On these revamped religion pages, the kind of feature stories of new and alternative religions that Bennett also pioneered found a place alongside ones about more conventional religions. But that kind of even-handed attention to all religions still generates complaints from those who equate "coverage of" with "support for" religions they consider false.

Bennett's stories about sexual scandals and of the mixing of religion with money, politics, and power gave rise to twentieth-century entrepreneurial and investigative stories about all religions, as well as to critical analyses and editorials about them. But hard news coverage of the kind Bennett pioneered also planted the seed for the kind of complaints that are still voiced by those who believe that journalists for secular newspapers should practice religious journalism instead of the kind of religion reporting that fulfills the surveillance and watchdog functions of the press. Like Bennett before them, journalists today who cover all religions from the standpoint of an essentially neutral but interested outside observer, instead of writing to promote and defend a faith, open themselves to charges they are areligious at best, antireligion at worst.

NOTES

1. David Paul Nord, "Systematic Benevolence: Religious Publishing and the Marketplace in Early Nineteenth-Century America," in *Communication and Change in American Religious History*, ed. Leonard I. Sweet (Grand Rapids, MI: William B. Eerdmans Publishing Company, 1993), 239–69.

2. Martin E. Marty, "Protestantism and Capitalism: Print Culture and Individualism," in *Communication and Change in American Religious History*, ed. Leonard I. Sweet (Grand Rapids, MI: William B. Eerdmans Publishing Company, 1993), 91–107.

3. Edwin Emery and Michael Emery, *The Press and America: An Interpretive History of the Mass Media*, 5th ed. (Englewood Cliffs, NJ: Prentice-Hall, 1984), 146. See also Willard G. Bleyer, *History of American Journalism* (New York: Houghton Mifflin, 1927; repr., New York: DeCapo Press, 1977), 197.

4. Martin E. Marty, *Righteous Empire: The Protestant Experience in America* (New York: The Dial Press, 1970), 107–8.

5. Fredrick Hudson, *Journalism in the United States from 1690–1872* (New York: Harper & Brothers, 1873), 467. See also Isaac Pray, *Memoirs of James Gordon Bennett and His Times* (New York: Stringer and Townsend, 1855; repr., New York: Arno, 1970), 474–76.

6. Emery and Emery, *The Press and America*, 97–99; Frank Luther Mott, *American Journalism*, 3rd ed. (New York: The Macmillan Company, 1962), 325; Bleyer, *History of American Journalism*, 146.

7. Judith M. Buddenbaum, "'Judge . . . What Their Acts Will Justify': The Religion Journalism of James Gordon Bennett," *Journalism History* 14 (Summer/Autumn 1987): 63–64.

8. The legal dispute had been in court a number of times, most recently in 1830 and 1834. The heirs based their claim on Dutch title to the land granted in 1636 "to Roeloff Jansen and his wife," whom Bennett consistently identifies as Anneka Jantz even though court records list her as Anneka Jans Bogardus. Trinity's claim to the land, which courts consistently recognized, rested on title given to it by the English government after the Dutch colony of New Amsterdam became the English colony, New York.

9. Judith M. Buddenbaum, *Religious Scandals* (Santa Barbara, CA: Greenwood Press, 2009), 21–26; see also Paul E. Johnson and Sean Wilentz, *The Kingdom of Matthias* (New York: Oxford University Press, 1994).

10. Kyle Huckins, "Religion and Western Newspapers," in *Media and Religion in American History*, ed. Wm. David Sloan (Northport, AL: Vision Press, 2000), 134–48.

11. Bruce J. Evensen, *God's Man for the Gilded Age: Dwight L. Moody and the Rise of Modern Mass Evangelism* (New York: Oxford University Press, 2003), 72–188.

REFERENCES

Buddenbaum, Judith M. 1987. "Judge . . . What Their Acts Will Justify": The Religion Journalism of James Gordon Bennett. *Journalism History* 14 (Summer/Autumn): 54–67.

Buddenbaum, Judith M., and Debra L. Mason, eds. 2000. *Readings on Religion as News*. Ames: Iowa State University Press, 71–148, 161–76.

Hudson, Frederic. 1873. *Journalism in the United States from 1690–1872*. New York: Harper & Brothers, 289–461.

Pray, Isaac. 1855/1970. *Memoirs of James Gordon Bennett and His Times*. New York: Stringer and Townsend; repr. ed., New York: Arno.

Sloan, Wm. David, James G. Stovall, and James D. Startt. 1993. *The Media in America: A History*, 2nd ed. Scottsdale, AZ: Publishing Horizons, 123–46.

CHAPTER 3

AMERICAN JOURNALISM AND RELIGION, 1870–1930[1]

RICHARD FLORY

> *Many churches are nothing more than private clubs, interested in matters which are exclusively the business of their own members. The ministers in their sermons discuss esoteric doctrines, hopelessly out of date, and of no concern to anybody but the converted.*
>
> —*The Journalist*, May 16, 1931

BETWEEN the years 1870 and 1930, there was both a significant decline in the space devoted to religion reporting and a shift in how religion, and its relationship to scientific knowledge, was conceived and presented in journalistic accounts. Hornell Hart, reporting for the President's Research Committee on Recent Social Trends in 1933, found that as a percentage of all periodicals published between 1905 and 1930, religious periodicals declined at almost the same rate that "popular scientific" periodicals increased in number (see Table 3.1). In addition, Hart showed that articles emphasizing religion, as indexed in the *Reader's Guide*, dropped by about 50 percent between the period 1905–1909 and the years 1930–1931.[2] In his analysis of the *New York Times*, Robert Pettit[3] reports a similar pattern of decline in both the frequency and prominence of religion stories from the 1850s to the 1930s. Similar to Hart, Pettit's findings show that as a percentage of total news space, religion coverage declined by more than 50 percent between 1875 and 1935, with front-page religion stories decreasing by nearly 90 percent during that same period (see Table 3.2).

It may, of course, be explained that these declines in the space devoted to religion resulted simply because religion reporting just didn't live up to the old adage

Table 3.1 Trends in Religion Reporting, 1900–1930

Magazine Circulation (Percent of Total Circulation)	1900	1930
Popular Scientific	1.02	3.73
Religious	4.69	0.83
Articles Dealing with Religion (Per 1,000 Indexed in the *Reader's Guide*)	1905–1909	1930–1931
	21.4	10.7
Story Content (Percent Favorable Toward Traditional Religion)	1905	1931
Popular Magazines	78	33
	1912–1914	1930
Intellectual Magazines	57	18

Source: Hart 1933.

Table 3.2 *New York Times*: Decline in Religion Reporting, 1875–1935

Religion Coverage As:	1875	1935
Percent of total news space	6.85	2.13
Percent of all stories	6.07	3.17
Percent of page one stories	20.05	2.8
Mention of religion per 1,000 cm of nonreligion advertising space	38.89	2.41

Source: Pettit 1986.

"if it bleeds it leads" by providing a good conflict story. Or perhaps there were comparatively fewer religion stories because there was an increase in total space available for news, through either increased numbers of pages in newspapers or an increase in the overall number of periodicals published during this time period. That is, as available outlets increased—whether pages or periodicals—religion coverage may have simply been a victim of the increase in stories covering other important aspects of life in America. Indeed, the *Times* expanded from a newspaper of six pages of six columns each in the 1870s to a newspaper of upwards of twenty pages, in addition to a separate Sunday section, by 1930. Yet, Hart's content analysis of magazine articles published during this time period shows that a more significant change was taking place in how religion was reported than religion stories simply getting crowded out by other news items. In 1905, Hart reports 78 percent of stories were favorable to "traditional Christianity" on such measures as "the infallible Bible, traditional creeds, church organization and the propagation of organized Christianity," but by 1931, this percentage had declined to 33 percent. He concluded that during this time period "the most fundamental change in the intellectual life of the United States . . . is the apparent shift from Biblical authority and sanctions to scientific and factual authority and sanctions."[4]

The focus in this chapter is on two different but related developments within journalism. First, editorials from the *New York Times* from 1870 through 1930 are analyzed, first to determine whether the pattern identified by Hart is found in the *Times* during this period, and second to understand the development over time of the change in the way religion was presented and understood by the *Times*. Even during this time period, the *Times* stood as one of the most influential newspapers in the United States, and as such it is an excellent place to pursue this question. The focus is on editorials rather than general news stories about religion, because the editorials show in a more systematic way the paper's general position regarding religion.[5] In addition, the fact that the editorial board of the *Times* maintained an amazing consistency of members between 1870 and 1930 allows for a control on other influences, such as changes in the editorial board, on the content of the editorials.[6]

The second focus is on the different efforts and strategies employed to create a new profession of journalism that would be on the same social plane as the more established medical and legal professions. These efforts include the development of different domains of journalism activity such as journalism schools and professional organizations and publications, and the different framing strategies used to argue for the development of a profession of journalism. Advocates modeled their efforts to promote and develop the profession of journalism on the dominant and higher social status vocations of medicine and law. Advocates for professionalization thus invoked the scientific status of their enterprise and legitimated their efforts by framing journalism as a product of modern, scientific inquiry. In both the *New York Times* editorials and the different ways of framing modern journalism, advocates for professionalization appropriated a modern, scientific view of religion that presented journalism as ideally situated and uniquely qualified to provide the knowledge and moral direction that individuals and society needed in a modern, scientific world.

Religion and the *New York Times*: From Traditional to Modern Religion

Beginning in the 1870s and continuing through the 1920s, an escalating public confrontation between traditional religious authority and scientific authority in American society centered on what role each could, or should, play in the culture. This conflict was captured in the news media of the day, and editorials arguing for one or another religious viewpoint, including often fairly obscure theological references, were regularly published by the *Times*. In the 1870s and 1880s, the *Times* argued for maintaining traditional religious understandings and for religious leaders to resist the move to replace such beliefs with more modern, scientific approaches to religion. By the mid-1920s, however, traditional religion was becoming an embarrassment, particularly as evidenced by the infamous *Scopes* trial. By 1930, the *Times* was calling for a completely new religious understanding that was compatible with modern science. In December 1875, the *Times* expressed concern that science and its practitioners were in reality working to undermine Christianity, rather than to simply expand the range of scientific knowledge:

> Men of unquestionable learning and ability are everywhere striving to destroy the foundation of the Christian religion. They insist that God cannot and does not exist, but that the universe is governed by some unknown laws, which are the result of spontaneous evolution. . . . It almost seems at times as though the present aim of science was not so much to enlarge its own boundaries and fields of knowledge, as to convince the world that Christianity is an imposture [*sic*] and that its founder was merely an amiable enthusiast.[7]

Similarly, in 1880, the paper took on British philosopher Leslie Stephen's idea of a "religion for all sensible men," which it took to mean "the religion which is to be adopted at some future time by men who have had the good sense to abandon Christianity." The *Times* sarcastically concluded its editorial by predicting that this would result in a religion wherein individuals would seek comfort, particularly in times of personal crisis, in the "great and glorious truth of the binomial theorem" or perhaps by reading "comforting extracts from Loomis's Algebra."[8]

Just five years later, however, the *Times* had begun to moderate its views of traditional religious teachings and their relationship to modern scientific theory and empirical methods. Between 1885 and 1905, editorials commented on the variety of "heresy hunting" and "heresy trials" that were pitting conservatives in the Christian churches against progressive forces[9] who were seeking, in various ways, to synthesize insights from evolutionary theory and from the "higher criticism" with Christian theology. In each case, the *Times* framed those on the progressive side as representing advancement in Christian theology and teaching, and those on the conservative side as being an unnecessary impediment to progress.[10]

By 1905, the *Times* wrote in opposition to the "forces of conservatism" in the churches, arguing that they were going too far in their resistance to change, suggesting that they were becoming "merely another name for dogged opposition to progress." The editorial concluded that conservative leaders were thus "no longer fit" to be "leaders of thought and teachers of doctrine," suggesting instead that progressives, as "advanced thinkers," were better suited to determine the future form of church teachings.[11]

The conflict between science and traditional Christianity that began in the final decades of the nineteenth century reached its zenith in the 1910s and 1920s when the public battles between so-called fundamentalist and modernist Protestants captured the country's attention.[12] These issues were not only debated within the Protestant denominations but also regularly reported in the secular press, including the *Times*. In general, the paper's coverage was even-handed, reporting developments on each side, and often publishing articles by representatives from both the fundamentalist and the modernist positions. In fact, just prior to the *Scopes* trial, the

Times published what were intended as clear statements of what each side believed under the banner headline "Both Sides: Fundamentalism, Evolution." This consisted of two separate articles, one by J. Gresham Machen, a professor at Princeton Seminary and an activist within the Presbyterian denomination on the side of the fundamentalists, and the other by Vernon Kellogg, the chairman of Educational Relations of the Natural Research Council.[13]

Yet, the *Times*' editorial position regarding the relationship between science and religion clearly sided with science, distancing itself from any perspective that might be construed as sympathetic to the fundamentalist perspective. At the outset of the *Scopes* trial, the *Times* opined that the spectacle of religion, calling into question the entire modern scientific enterprise, would bring "the whole nation under a reproach in the eyes of the world. We should be an object at once of astonishment and ridicule."[14] As the trial proceeded, the scene in Dayton grew into an ever larger spectacle. This was due in large part to the stories from the many journalists who had descended on the small Tennessee town, including the infamous reports from H. L. Mencken. The *Times*, however, laid the blame for the circus atmosphere not on its fellow journalists, nor even on the presence of Clarence Darrow,[15] one of the nation's most famous trial lawyers who was now defending John Scopes, but rather on Bryan and the fundamentalists:

> No one need be astonished to read of the influx of queer fish at Dayton, Tenn.... No one can yet measure the impulse and encouragement to erratic thinking which the Dayton trial is giving. It is a sort of notice, posted up so that the whole nation can read it, of the breakdown of the reasoning powers.... But the demonstrated immense attraction at Dayton for all sorts of half-baked creatures, is an indication of the mental and moral infection which has been let loose upon the land, with Mr. Bryan as its chief agent....[16]

As the trial drew to a close, the *Times* concluded that two primary characteristics of the human mind had been exposed; on the one hand, the proceedings had "exhibited the tenacity of the mind in clinging to inherited ideas, in holding on to convictions acquired by association, or in defending atavistic inclinations," while on the other, it showed that the "unsatisfied mind," which pushed forward for knowledge, "in spite of all the weight of precedent, the clog of habit, the love of the familiar, the downward pull of passion and the peril of failure," was the reason for the "highest hope" for the future.[17]

By 1930, the *Times* had moved beyond just being embarrassed by fundamentalist religion to presenting a new, more "modern" religious perspective. To this end, the paper used publications, speeches, and personal profiles of scientific and religious leaders such as Albert Einstein, Robert Millikan, Harry Emerson Fosdick, and G. K. Chesterton to support its conception of a religion that was modern, rational, and scientific—in short, a respectable religion in contradistinction to how fundamentalists had presented themselves at the *Scopes* trial.[18] The *Times* believed that scientists were best qualified to speak—and should have the last word—on religion: "Certainly those who make researches into the very sources of existence should be profoundly religious, though it cannot be admitted that they are, as one of Einstein's contemporaries has said, 'the only deeply religious people.'"[19] Not only was science presented as naturally authoritative over religion, but also scientists were presented as being best suited as the authorities for genuine religious insight and knowledge.

Efforts to Professionalize Journalism

At the same time that the *Times* was developing its arguments for this new modern religious sensibility compatible with scientific methods and findings, attempts to professionalize journalism had begun on several fronts. These efforts consistently portrayed journalism as a scientific and rationally organized profession that was central to the well-being and moral structure of society. These efforts were not organized from any single segment within journalism, but were the results of the efforts of educators, newspaper writers and editors, and even college students, all working toward the same ideal. They all, however, in one way or another, stressed two common and related rationales for the need for journalists to professionalize: first, to increase the status of journalists and the field of journalism, particularly in terms of public perception, and second, to increase journalism's influence and power in American society.

Strategies

The strategies employed by advocates of professionalization fall into two general categories, each intended to provide the kind of legitimacy for the professional status of journalism that they sought. First, there were *institutional strategies*, that is, the establishment of professional associations, university programs for journalism education, and publications focused exclusively on the profession of journalism, that provided an organizational base from which advocates could mount their efforts. Second, there were *framing strategies*, which formed the arguments that articulated journalistic ideals and goals, and thus legitimated both the scientific approach of journalism and its educative role in society.

Institutional Strategies

Institutional strategies provided an organizational base for key professionalizing efforts and also implied the same organization for journalism that the culturally dominant professions had developed. The medical and legal professions were repeatedly referenced as models for the journalistic profession, specifically, for educational programs to prepare practitioners and codes of ethics and standards of practice to guide them. For example, Willard Bleyer, a member of the journalism faculty at the University of Wisconsin, argued that journalism, ". . . must establish and maintain standards for admission and standards of practice, not unlike those of the older professions of law and medicine."[20] Bleyer referenced the medical and legal professions as models for journalism to emulate a total of four times. Several other articles from this period used the same comparison to argue for the development of these structures for journalism.[21]

Sociologist Andrew Abbott has argued that, "In the last century, science, with the broader, related phenomenon of formal rationality, has become the fundamental ground for the legitimacy of professional techniques. In the value scheme on which modern professions draw, science stands for logic and rigor in diagnosis. . . . It implies extensive academic research based on the highest standards of rationality."[22] Thus, the development of structures modeled on the medical and legal professions, such as professional associations, schools, and journals, allowed journalism to appeal to the dominant cultural value of science and rationality to legitimate its professional status, and therefore to increase its social influence.

Journals: Beginning in March 1884, a publication called the *Journalist*, billing itself as "A Weekly Publication Devoted to Newspaper Men and Publishers,"[23] began publication. This journal remained in publication through the entire time period covered by this study and, in fact, is still published today under the name *Editor & Publisher*.[24] This journal provided news on a variety of aspects of journalism, ranging from information about small-town to urban newspapers across the country, spotlights on different publishers, developments within journalism, and tips on various aspects of journalistic practice.

Initially calling itself "The Journalists' Journal," the *Quill* was published monthly beginning in 1912 by the national journalism fraternity Sigma Delta Chi. Unlike the *Journalist*, the *Quill*'s articles were either contributions from editors, publishers, and other prominent figures from within journalism who had a membership or connection to Sigma Delta Chi, or speeches that had been presented to meetings of journalism professionals.

Journalism Education: Although several attempts to establish journalism programs in American colleges and universities date from just after the Civil War, it was not until 1905 that the first permanent collegiate journalism program was established at the University of Wisconsin. Within ten years, journalism departments or schools existed at eighteen other universities.[25] The importance placed on journalism education was addressed not only in school publications such as school catalogs, where both course listings and program rationale were routinely published, but also in articles by journalism educators and others advocating for professionalization that were published in the *Quill*. The best education for journalists combined professional training with a broad exposure to other disciplines such as history, literature, philosophy, and the sciences, with the goal being "not merely acquisition of knowledge but independence of mind and an honest quest for the truth, on the assumption that the journalist of the future must more and more assume the position of a leader in society."[26]

Journalism Associations: The first journalistic association to be organized was Sigma Delta Chi, the undergraduate journalism fraternity, at DePauw University (Indiana) in 1909. Although founded as a fraternity, its founding documents reference broad ideals related to the journalism profession:

> 1. To associate college journalists of talent, truth and energy into a more intimately organized unit of good fellowship.
> 2. To assist the members in acquiring the noblest principles of journalism and to co-operate with them in this field.
> 3. To advance the standards of the press by fostering a higher ethical code, thus increasing its value as an uplifting social agency.[27]

By 1913, the American Conference of Teachers of Journalism voted to make Sigma Delta Chi the official national fraternity for journalism, and over time it evolved into the Society for Professional Journalism, the main professional association for journalism. The importance of Sigma Delta Chi was first in its efforts to socialize college students into the norms and ideals of professional journalism. Beyond that, the fraternity provided a type of continuing education for alumni members through the many articles in the *Quill* that promoted professional ideals and education.

Other associations, with goals similar to Sigma Delta Chi, were also founded in this era: the American Association of Teachers of Journalism (AATJ) in 1912; the American Association of Schools and Departments of Journalism (AASDJ), a development from within the ranks of the AATJ, in 1917; and, in 1923, the American Society of Newspaper Editors (ASNE). AATJ and AASDJ, in conjunction with Sigma Delta Chi, developed a standardized journalism course of study for all American colleges and universities. These organizations all called for the professionalization of journalism and for a statement of professional ideals to which journalists should aspire. The *Quill* routinely published resolutions and program developments from each of these organizations.

Constructing Journalism: Large-scale corporate journalism was also developing between the 1870s and 1930, and the construction of big newspaper buildings was regularly announced in the *Journalist* and *Editor & Publisher*. These descriptions all followed the same formula: an artist depiction of the building, a description of the architecture (style, number of floors, and material), where the building was located in its city (centrally), and the high-quality and modern nature of the building (heating, modern printing presses). A typical example: In 1903, *Editor & Publisher* announced the "*St. Louis Star*'s New Home: Handsome Ten-Story Building now in Course of Erection." The story continued, "The new building of the *St. Louis Star*, now in the course of construction, will occupy a corner in what is known as New St. Louis, which is rapidly centering on either side of the site selected for the *Star*'s new home."[28] A similar story accompanied the announcement of the *Houston Post*'s new building in 1915, although this story focused on the capabilities of the new plant: "The present building is one of the most complete newspaper plants in the South, having 50,000 square feet of space exclusively devoted to the production of the *Post*."[29] This type of presentation of new, modern journalism buildings as central to their cities, complete with advanced newspaper presses and other advantages, served not only to support the different institutional strategies but also as a form of framing strategy in the way the edifices were described for readers. New buildings represented a vigorous, modern, and scientifically oriented profession that stood at the center of the life of the cities they covered.

Framing Strategies

Taken together, these institution-building strategies not only served to depict journalism as a rationally organized and scientifically oriented profession but also established a base from which the ideals and goals of the emerging profession could be promoted through different professionalization framing strategies. Advocates for professionalization regularly published articles in journals such as the *Quill* and *Editor & Publisher* arguing that journalism was a modern and viable profession. Advocates argued that because of journalism's privileged position of gathering and disseminating knowledge to the masses, it was society's most important institution. Accurate and truthful knowledge could only be identified and disseminated through proper journalism work and news organizations. Bleyer, of the University of Wisconsin, contended that journalism was a more important profession than either the medical or legal professions. He argued that while the actions of an incompetent doctor or lawyer might only result in "kill[ing] off prematurely more than a few hundred persons" or might cost a client "loss of money, of freedom, or even of life itself," these risks were insignificant compared to the damage that an "ignorant, incompetent reporter" could cause to society. Indeed, the very success of democracy "is dependent on the competency and the character of our newspaper writers and editors, and I submit to you that the success of our democracy is more vital to the welfare of society than is the possible loss of lives, the money, or the freedom of a few of its members"[30]

But simply gathering and disseminating facts to inform public opinion was not the only meaning that advocates like Bleyer had in mind when they framed journalism as the most important profession in society. Professional journalists were given the role of educator in the broadest sense—as the educator for life who would ensure an enlightened and moral public.[31] This moral educative ideal was even memorialized in the official song of Sigma Delta Chi: "Our business is to brighten men, to frighten and enlighten men, To teach them what they should and shouldn't do."[32]

Mark Cohen, editor of the *Evening Star* in Dunedin, New Zealand, wrote of the duty of the press as a "public educator." Herbert Swope, executive editor of the *New York World* and a founder of the American Society of Newspaper Editors, wrote of public opinion being "intelligenced by the Press," which in turn would have a greater effect on the morals of society than would writing new laws.[33] Similarly, James Williams, editor of the *Boston Transcript*, wrote of the "free press" as a "chronicle of the human race . . . [providing] the 'food of opinion.' To adulterate that food with the poison of untruth is a sin against the public."[34]

For those working to promote the professionalization of journalism, and thus elevate its status and influence in society, what better way to frame their efforts as indispensible truth bearers than to position themselves as members of a scientifically oriented profession that in reality functioned as a replacement for, or was at least equivalent to, religion? In this view, only empirically grounded knowledge could lead to good public and private decisions and moral distinctions. Professional journals such as the *Journalist*, *Editor & Publisher*, and the *Quill* had begun publishing articles comparing journalism to religion as early as the 1890s. In an 1892 editorial, the *Journalist* suggested that the newspaper did not differ substantially from "nature or the Bible" in that it reported both the good and the bad in its stories. For the *Journalist*, "the newspaper . . . is necessarily a moral teacher, a preacher, a social critic and reformer. It is so because life and experience teach, admonish, warn and furnish arguments for what is right, true and of good report."[35]

This framing strategy was popular through 1930, becoming even more explicit in its comparison with religion. Eventually journalism professionals said their profession is—or perhaps should be—the modern replacement for religion. For example, in 1915, an *Editor & Publisher* editorial stated, "A newspaper can more nearly realize its mission the nearer it comes to attaining the ideals of the clergymen and priest in their ministrations. Their flocks are numbered by hundreds, ours by millions."[36] Similarly, Walter Williams,[37] the founding dean of the School of Journalism at the University of Missouri,[38] wrote "The Journalists Creed" in 1915,[39] which consisted of eight articles, each beginning with "I believe . . .," the first being, "I believe in the profession of journalism." This creed echoes the historic confessions of the church. The last article reads like the apostle Paul's chapter on the ideals of love, with journalistic ideals what the profession and individual journalists should desire:

> I believe that the journalism which succeeds best—and which deserves success—fears God and honors man; is stoutly independent, unmoved by pride of opinion or greed of power, constructive, tolerant, but never careless, self-controlled, patient; always respectful of its readers, but always unafraid; is quickly indignant at injustice; is unswayed by the appeal of privilege or the clamor of the mob; seeks to give every man a chance and as far as law and honest wage recognition of human brotherhood can make it so, an equal chance; is profoundly patriotic, while sincerely promoting the international good will and cementing world comradeship; is a journalism of humanity, of and for today's world.[40]

Other advocates for professionalization spoke in similarly religious terms of journalist heroes standing against the powers of injustice and corruption; of journalist martyrs who had been punished, even killed in journalistic service to humanity; and even of journalism as a pilgrimage from a lower to a higher ideal. H. F. Harrington, from the journalism program at the University of Illinois, wrote of the heroic reporter who "shivers his lance against corruption high and low. Crime, money-lust, hypocrisy, vice, sin, stand within his confessional." Once these are exposed, the reporter was rewarded by being ". . . dubbed a muckraker, an underworld detective, a Paul Pry of sensations. The epithets bear witness to his thrift and to the sincerity of his purpose."[41]

Similarly, *New York World* editor Herbert Swope wrote of the journalist martyrs who gave their lives and fortunes as the price for liberty. Here, journalism ". . . and its ministers have suffered themselves to be blamed, condemned, imprisoned, suffered themselves even to be hanged, but they have published their opinions and their versions of pivotal facts, regarding it not only as a right, but as a duty."[42] Swope further contended that journalism was always in its ideals "a priestly-mission," and as its practices improved, there had arisen "within its ranks, a divine dissatisfaction with its failure to be of even greater usefulness."[43]

Finally, Edward McKernon, Eastern division superintendant with the Associated Press, stated quite candidly the state of the world, and journalism's role within it:

> The intelligent are beginning to understand that this old world is pretty much what we make it. That if civilization is to endure we must mentally readjust ourselves to rapidly changing conditions . . . and, looking the facts squarely in the face, work out a philosophy of life that will stand up.[44]

In this it was the responsibility of journalism to provide the information (truth) by which an adequate "philosophy of life" could be constructed. Ultimately, he contended, journalism was a "sacred trust."

Conclusion

As journalism developed its professional status, significant changes took place in its relationship with religion, with simultaneous developments within journalism that served to promote the interests of the emerging journalism profession at the expense of traditional religious expressions. As organizational structures gave institutional legitimacy to journalism through schools, journals, and professional associations, advocates for professionalization were able to use these institutions to advance new ideas about religion and science, and journalism's relationship to each. The driving motives were likely the desire to create a professional identity for journalists and the profession and to elevate the status and influence of journalism. The best strategy was to join the scientific revolution and claim the same legitimacy for journalism as staked by medicine and law.

One result was that those working for the professional status of journalism reframed religion as an atavistic belief system that had lost status, power, and cultural authority in modern society. Religion came up short in its efforts to solve problems, improve society, or even present an adequate understanding of its own role in the modern world. The "enlightened" segments of the population realized that the world would improve through the application of knowledge gained from scientifically informed inquiry—not as a result of "otherworldly" claims. Accordingly, journalism was uniquely suited to provide the type of knowledge necessary for a good society. Journalism assumed an almost ministerial role as the intermediary between primary knowledge producers—found mostly within the halls of science—and the mass public. Journalists took as their task determining what knowledge was important and how it might best be applied in personal or public life. Religious authority was thus reframed as subordinate to scientific authority, and in keeping with their claim to scientific legitimacy, advocates for professionalization began to frame journalism as the natural successor to religion for both individuals and society.

As previously noted, Andrew Abbott has argued that science, and its correlate formal rationality, has been the fundamental legitimization for professional activities for more than 100 years. Those working for the professional status of journalism clearly understood this—as did different religious leaders, evidenced by their increasing reliance on science to legitimate their positions, whether fundamentalist or modernist. For journalism, as it moved toward professionalization, such scientific values as empiricism (through fact gathering and reporting), objectivity, rationality, and rigor in method were emphasized as being core elements of the new profession. As a part of this emphasis on scientific ideals, religious authority was presented as an enemy of modern science. In mass publications such as the *New York Times*, and in professional journals such as the *Quill* and the *Journalist*, religious authority was first called into question and then fully displaced by scientific authority.

Those working for the professional status of journalism, however, were not entirely content with emphasizing the scientific rigor of journalism, but went further and began framing professional journalism in religious terms. Influential leaders such as Walter Williams wrote of "the calling of journalism," the "new kingdom of journalism," and the "solidarity and spirit of journalism."[45] Similarly, Herbert Swope wrote of the "sanctity" of facts and of public opinion, once it was "intelligenced by the press." In this, Swope argued that journalism had moral power and authority to write "'ought' in the hearts of men, instead of placing 'must' in the statute books." The modern age was, according to Swope and others, "the age of the reporter," with journalism and news "among the chief factors in the formulation of conduct."[46]

Thus, over the course of the sixty years between 1870 and 1930, journalism came to conceive itself as the new moral voice for society, taking on the task of educating the common person toward developing a moral—and empirically sound—philosophy of life.

NOTES

1. Portions of this chapter have been published in somewhat different form in Richard W. Flory, "Promoting a Secular Standard: Secularization and Modern Journalism, 1870–1930," *The Secular Revolution: Power, Interests, and Conflict in the Secularization of American Public Life*, ed. Christian Smith (Berkeley and Los Angeles: University of California Press, 2003), 395–433.

2. Hornell Hart, "Changing Social Attitudes and Interests," in *Recent Social Trends in the United States: Report of the President's Research Committee on Social Trends* (New York: McGraw-Hill, 1933), 398.

3. Robert B. Pettit, *Religion Through The Times: An Examination of the Secularization Thesis Through Content Analysis of the New York Times, 1855–1975* (doctoral dissertation, Columbia University), 1986.

4. Hart, "Changing Social Attitudes," 390.

5. My examination of the *New York Times* was conducted in the following manner: using the *New York Times Index* for the years 1870–1930, I selected all news articles and editorials listed under the headings "religion," "churches," "Protestantism," "Bible," "Fundamentalism," etc., for each year, in five-year intervals (1870, 1875, 1880, etc., through 1930). For this analysis, I have focused primarily on the editorials, although I have utilized news articles as well, insofar as they provided needed context for the editorials.

6. During this time frame, the editorial board consisted of three primary members: Charles Ransom Miller, Rollo Ogden, and John Huston Finley. Miller began as an editor in 1881, becoming editor-in-chief in 1883 and remaining in that position until 1922. Ogden came to the *Times* in 1920 and succeeded Miller as editor-in-chief in 1922, and Finley came to the *Times* in 1921, succeeding Ogden as editor-in-chief in 1937.

7. *New York Times*, December 26, 1875.

8. *New York Times*, May 2, 1880.

9. The terms *fundamentalists* and *modernists* were not at this point in usage. I have tried to keep the terminology of the *Times* in this regard.

10. See, for example, *New York Times*, April 5, 1885; July 26, 1890; April 24, 1895; April 28, 1895.

11. *New York Times*, May 11, 1905.

12. For analyses of this controversy, see George Marsden, *Fundamentalism and American Culture* (New York: Oxford University Press), 1980; Ronald L. Numbers, *The Creationists: The Evolution of Scientific Creationism* (Berkeley and Los Angeles: University of California Press), 1993; Edward J. Larson, *Summer for the Gods: The Scopes Trial and America's Continuing Debate over Science and Religion* (Cambridge, MA: Harvard University Press), 1997.

13. *New York Times*, June 21, 1925.

14. *New York Times*, July 5, 1925.

15. Darrow had just the previous year defended Leopold and Loeb in another highly public trial.

16. *New York Times*, July 13, 1925.

17. *New York Times*, July 19, 1925.

18. *New York Times*, December 29, 1930.

19. *New York Times*, November 10, 1930.

20. Willard Grosvenor Bleyer, "The Importance of High Editorial Standards," *The Quill*, March (1925): 7.

21. See, for example, Nelson Antrim Crawford, "Professional Preparation for Journalism," *The Quill*, January (1925): 10–11; Carl H. Getz, "Standardization of Instruction in Journalism Proposed," *The Quill*, July (1916): 6, 12; Lawrence W. Murphy, "Schools of Journalism," *The Quill*, April (1922): 17–18.

22. Andrew Abbott, *The System of Professions: An Essay on the Division of Expert Labor* (Chicago: University of Chicago Press, 1988), 189.

23. *The Journalist*, March 22, 1884.

24. *The Journalist* was the earliest to be published (1884–1907). *Editor & Publisher* (founded 1901) had essentially the same look and content of *The Journalist*, and, in fact, both names were on the masthead for several years before *The Journalist* name was dropped from the publication and the numbering of the editions of the journal was changed to reflect the longer history of *The Journalist.*

25. Willard Grosvenor Bleyer, "The Rise of Education for Journalism," *The Quill*, October (1934): 12.

26. H. H. Herbert, "A Standard School of Journalism," *The Quill*, March (1925): 15.

27. "Sigma Delta Chi—Its Aims and its Progress: A Statement by the Executive Council of the Fraternity" (Sigma Delta Chi Archives, DePauw University, Greencastle, IN, May 1926).

28. *Editor & Publisher* 2, no. 41, April 4, 1903.

29. *Editor & Publisher* 14, no. 38, February 27, 1915.

30. Bleyer, "The Importance of High Editorial Standards," 4.

31. For example, see Mark R. Cohen, "Duty of the Press to the Reading Public: a Reply to William J. Bryan," *The Quill*, October (1915): 3; Bleyer, "The Importance of High Editorial Standards"; Herbert Bayard Swope, "Journalism: An Instrument of Civilization," *The Quill*, December (1924): 6–10; Edward McKernon, "Journalism Defined," *The Quill*, December (1925): 18–20; James T. Williams, Jr., "The Responsibility of the Press," *The Quill*, May (1924): 7–9.

32. "Sigma Delta Chi," *The Quill*, January (1925): 20.

33. Swope, "Journalism: An Instrument of Civilization," 7–8.

34. James T. Williams, Jr., "Responsibility of the Press," 8.

35. *The Journalist* XV, no. 21, August 6, 1892, 4.

36. *Editor & Publisher* 48, no. 23, November 13, 1915, 2.

37. Interesting in this regard is that Williams was an active Presbyterian, was president of his local county Sunday school association, and taught a large Sunday school class.

38. Whereas Wisconsin has the distinction of having established the first permanent "course" or department of journalism in the United States, Missouri has the distinction of having established the first professional "school" of journalism. This seems a subtle distinction perhaps, but one that is constantly pointed out in the sources.

39. This is still listed on the school website (http://journalism.missouri.edu/jschool/#creed).

40. Walter Williams, "The Journalists Creed," *The Quill*, October (1915): 12.

41. H. F. Harrington, "The Reporter as Story-Teller," *The Quill*, July (1919): 7–8.

42. Swope, "Journalism: An Instrument of Civilization," 8.

43. Swope, "Journalism: An Instrument of Civilization," 10.

44. McKernon, "Journalism Defined," 19.

45. Walter Williams, "The Barbed Entanglements of the Press," *The Quill*, July (1919): 6.

46. Swope, "Journalism: An Instrument of Civilization," 7–8.

REFERENCES

Abbot, Willis J. 1926. A Force for Clean Journalism. *The Quill*, January: 6.

Abbott, Andrew. 1988. *The System of Professions. An Essay on the Division of Expert Labor.* Chicago: University of Chicago Press.

Allen, Eric W. 1920. Journalism as a Profession. *The Quill*, April: 3–6, 10.

Bleyer, Willard Grosvenor. 1925. The Importance of High Editorial Standards. *The Quill*, March: 3–7.

———. 1927. *Main Currents in the History of American Journalism*. Boston: Houghton Mifflin Co.

———. 1934. The Rise of Education for Journalism. *The Quill*, October: 12.

Cohen, Mark R. 1915. Duty of the Press to the Reading Public: A Reply to William J. Bryan. *The Quill*, October: 3.

Crawford, Nelson Antrim. 1925. Professional Preparation for Journalism. *The Quill*, January: 10–11.

Dennis, Charles H. 1925. What Schools of Journalism Might Do. *The Quill*, January: 20.

Getz, Carl H. 1916. Standardization of Instruction in Journalism Proposed. *The Quill*, July: 6, 12.

Harrington, H. F. 1919. The Reporter as Story-Teller. *The Quill*, July: 7–8.

Kimball, Bruce A. 1992. *The "True Professional Ideal" in America: A History*. Cambridge, MA, and Oxford: Blackwell.

McKernon, Edward. 1925. Journalism Defined. *The Quill*, December: 18–20.

Murphy, Lawrence W. 1922. Schools of Journalism. *The Quill*, April: 17–18.

The Quill. 1917. Applied Ethics. January: 6, 9.

Swope, Herbert Bayard. 1924. Journalism: An Instrument of Civilization. *The Quill*, December: 6–10.

Williams, James T., Jr. 1924. The Responsibility of the Press. *The Quill*, May: 7–9.

Williams, Walter. 1915. The Journalists Creed. *The Quill*, October: 12.

———. 1919. The Barbed Entanglements of the Press. *The Quill*, July: 6.

———. 1925. Are Schools of Religion Getting Anywhere? *The Quill*, January: 7–9, 13.

CHAPTER 4

RELIGION NEWS COVERAGE BETWEEN 1930 AND 1960

DEBRA L. MASON

SOME scholars interpret the professionalization of journalism and the triumph of science in the 1925 *Scopes* trial as triggering religion news' decline in the mainstream media. Evidence, however, suggests a more nuanced interpretation. College-level journalism education, begun in the early 1900s, experienced unprecedented growth between 1930 and 1960. Throughout these three decades, journalistic news values, ethics, and practice were institutionalized. As a result of journalism's professionalization, the purposes of religious public relations and of religion news grew more distinct. The story of religion coverage between 1930 and 1960 reflects these trends. It's a story of increasing differentiation between the secular and faith-based meaning of religion news. It's the story of religion news becoming a true beat, with its own professional identity. Equally, it's a story of the religion beat's need to improve execution of the craft, as evidenced by its homogeneous framing of faith—fixated on mainline Protestant Christians, Roman Catholics, and Jews.

SHARED VALUES FUEL EARLY VISION FOR PROFESSIONAL RELIGION NEWS

By the 1930s, schools of journalism had enshrined the professional journalist's identity as a protector of democratic values and an enabler of social justice—ideals also dear to contemporary Protestant and Catholic social justice movements. At the same time, new waves of immigrant Jews and Roman Catholics reenergized the Ku Klux Klan, stoking religious bigotry. Overt expressions of religious bias, such as the anti-Semitic rants of Father Charles Coughlin, led to the emergence of interfaith coalitions. New coalitions, including the National Conference for Christians and Jews (NCCJ) founded in 1928, sought unity in the battle against religious prejudice.

The nascent interfaith movement's growth and the honing of journalistic values in the same decade were serendipitous. Both groups, it seems, sought clear-eyed reporting on religion as news. Five years after NCCJ was formed, twenty-four-year-old Louis Minsky was a freelance journalist in New York City and recent immigrant from England. This descendent of Russian Jews was reportedly a man of charisma and verve—and driven by a singular vision: to create the Associated Press of religion. Minsky's charm no doubt helped him in 1933, when he convinced NCCJ to establish what is now known as the Religion News Service (RNS). NCCJ leaders, who wanted a news agency that distributed news pertinent to Christians and Jews, hired Minsky as managing editor. As Minsky later noted in a speech delivered at the Religion Newswriters Association's (RNA) 1953 annual conference, NCCJ believed RNS "could help the religious forces by disseminating accurate information about their activities and beliefs, and at the same time create better understanding among them by acting as a sort of journalistic bridge."[1]

Within twelve months, RNS already had 153 clients paying for its once-a-week dispatches, in part thanks to newspaper editors in Cleveland and Pittsburgh promoting the service to their peers. By decade's end, the news service had amassed a network of domestic and foreign correspondents, a radio service, and daily distribution. Minsky also told RNA members at that 1953 meeting in Syracuse why RNS's work resonated with both secular and religious editors in the 1930s and beyond:

> Church papers of the era rarely published stories involving developments in denominations other than their own. The secular press was not very much concerned with religious news except in a local way and on a minor scale. Many editors either didn't believe that religion was news or they thought it was too hot to handle as news. The idea that "religion is dynamite" was widely held among the nation's editorial directors.[2]

Indeed, although religion sections existed in nearly every major metropolitan daily newspaper by the 1930s, few of these included locally written news stories. Rather, the "church" pages, published mostly on Fridays and Saturdays, were filled with announcements: sermon topics, special services, temperance meetings, and the like. Newspapers lacked regular, substantive religion stories, despite a growing number of denominational communication directors and information officers whose job was to encourage more coverage. And although some faith groups were skeptical of the mainstream press, newspapers at this time were viewed more as allies than adversaries of faith communities.

That's not to say people of faith gave flattering reviews of religion in the news. In fact, criticism of how religion was covered in 1930 could just as easily apply today. In 1930, an ex-pastor and twenty-three-year veteran of the *Chicago Tribune* named

William Bernard Norton detailed the relationship between the faith community and media outlets in a 271-page book called *Church and Newspaper*. In his chapter "Viewpoints of the Daily Newspaper," Norton complained of inaccuracies, unbalanced coverage of various faith groups, and a focus on conflict. He also said churches were sometimes inhospitable to journalists and that clergy often did not respect press freedoms. Despite a flawed relationship, Norton still argued that the press should partner with the faith community for the common good. "There is a constant temptation for the newspaper to exploit criticisms of the church, its weaknesses, failure and departures from the highest standards," Norton wrote. "If a speaker lauds the church, he is very apt to get less newspaper space then if he finds fault with it. Let the newspaper take the church seriously and cooperate with it in promoting the welfare of society, family, and national life."[3]

The addition of a rapidly growing national news service dedicated to religion, however, encouraged journalists at US daily newspapers to experiment with new ways to present religion news. Sermon stories from the 1930s were carried in Monday's papers when the preacher was prominent or the topic was politics, but in some cases the sermon reports were nearly transcripts. Perhaps influenced by a growing professionalization, *Cleveland Press* "Church Editor" Frank Stewart wrote in a 1939 issue of the trade journal *Editor & Publisher* that he avoided such stories by creating a feature called "A Stranger Goes to Church," which was popular in the faith community. Stewart sought to replicate the experience of a worshipper visiting a new church. Stewart contrasted his column with typical religion reports of the time: "Very little space is devoted to the minister's sermon. Reading a cold sermon is like eating leftover food and I avoid long, dull quotations. But I do comment plenty on the style of his delivery, his voice, his pulpit mannerism and adherence to biblical background. The only big play the preacher gets is the use of his picture."[4] Stewart's reviews never strayed in focus, however, from Christian houses of worship and male clergy, evidence of a lingering status quo in the parameters of religion news.

The earliest books and trade magazine articles about religion journalism date from the late 1930s. A commonality of their content included framing religion as "Christian"—in particular, mainline Protestantism. Often, and unapologetically, the authors of these earliest professional guides to religion news were clergy, whose advice assumed a common Christian faith and a shared desire to cast faith in a positive light. No advice was given to covering non-Christian faiths or even the pejoratively labeled "fundamentalist" faith groups. So-called "fundamentalist" churches, including the fast-growing Pentecostal movement, were portrayed among public intellectuals and educators as oppositional to the secular media, to nonmainline Protestantism, and to socially progressive Christianity. Relations became strained between large Protestant institutions and newer, independent forms of Christianity. One prominent interdenominational organization, the Federated Council of Churches, became so incensed that in 1938 it rebuked the ethics, public interest, and quality of "religious" radio, especially radio's vitriolic anti-Semitic exhortations. The news media, in contrast, remained mainline Protestantism's powerful ally and perceived distributor of "truth."

Toward Editorial Independence: RNS, World War II, and the Search for "Objectivity"

Although professional notions of best practices for religion writing were emerging during the 1930s, no school of journalism yet taught "religious journalism"—the label used at the time for both denominational and secular religion writing. The only opportunity to learn the trade prior to 1949, outside of handbooks and denominational pamphlets, was through informal apprenticeships with working religion journalists. While no formal apprenticeships existed for aspiring religion reporters, RNS became in effect the training ground for dozens of mainstream religion reporters.

In 1943, RNS founder Minsky was joined by journalist Lillian Block, who became legendary in religion reporting circles during her forty-year career with RNS. Together, Minsky and Block took responsibility for training RNS correspondents in creating "objective," information-based news reports about religion. Because of RNS's large network of writers, Minsky's and Block's influence extended throughout the US secular press, far beyond the number of client dailies subscribing to RNS at the time. Strict adherence to fact- and institution-based reporting helped RNS avoid charges of bias or favoritism; the news service set the standard at the time for independent, wire-style coverage of religion.[5]

RNS covered World War II, but it did not send dispatches from the front lines—no known religion reporter covered World War II on the ground. Rather, RNS and others reported on the war's effect on religious groups and on the human spirit. The war also played an indirect role in changing the nature of newspaper "church pages." Because the government cut newsprint deliveries to conserve fuel and paper, newspapers were forced to consolidate content to fit smaller spaces. The elimination of "church announcements" was one space reduction measure recommended by *Editor & Publisher*. RNS's Minsky also took advantage of war-time frugality and lobbied newspapers to drop "church listings" as a strategy to free up space for substantive coverage. In a 1943 press release, RNS crowed that at Minsky's urging, the *New York Times* would drop its Saturday "church topics" feature and "will henceforth devote the space thus saved to religious news of local, national, and international importance."[6]

Clergy, scholars, and journalists noted these slow but steady improvements in religion news, too. Carl F. H. Henry, a founder of the National Association of Evangelicals and first editor of *Christianity Today*, wrote in 1943 about the "remarkable" change in the secular press toward religious news.[7] The number of religion specialists and editors climbed throughout World War II; by the mid-1940s, prominent newspapers such as the *Plain Dealer* in Cleveland and the *Chicago Sun-Times* had full-time reporters responsible for religion news and the content of weekly religion pages. Still, for most of the reported 500 newspapers with a religion reporter or editor at the time, the beat was part time.[8]

Postwar Religious Revival Ignites Formal Professionalization on the Religion Beat

The end of World War II in 1945 set the stage for the first real blossoming and growth of religion reporting into a respected newspaper beat. Revelations of Hitler's atrocities and the efficiency of the atom bomb in Japan led intellectuals, theologians, and the public to ponder existential questions about life, death, God, good, and evil. From 1945 to 1960, a baby boom, a church boom, a spiritual revival, Communism, Israel's birth, and public theologians all helped move secular religion news from beyond the ghetto of the "church page" and onto the front page. An overt evangelical, or as some called it, neo-fundamentalist, movement prompted intellectuals to position themselves in support or opposition to the movement—garnering news coverage. This religious revival also affected many aspects of the book and magazine publishing industry. By 1947, publishers reported that sales of books with religious significance were at an all-time high. The *New York Times* even published monthly lists of the top religion books from 1948 through at least 1950. Magazines frequently put religion on their front pages.

To get an idea of how prevalent religion was in magazines and elsewhere, consider a March 10, 1947, issue of *Life* magazine. A seven-page cover story was the culmination of an eight-month trip around the world undertaken by *Christian Century* Managing Editor Paul Hutchinson to assess the state of religion globally. The story framed Communism and its embrace of atheism as a rival faith to Christianity—an interpretation that would gain traction throughout the early 1950s. Although the religion feature was prominent, the magazine failed to expand its definition of "faith" much beyond Christianity.[9]

Another sign of the growing sophistication of religion news was the inclusion of faith as a component in political news reports. Journalists wed coverage of politics and religion in significant ways for the first time in the late 1940s. In a 1953 speech to the Religion Newswriters Association, RNS Managing Editor Louis Minsky identified Communism as the primary factor giving religion news "more prestige among newspaper editors at this moment than at any previous time in the history of the American press."

The growth of actual religion news nudged the staid sermon stories off of page one, except when the preacher was a religious celebrity such as Reinhold Niebuhr or Bishop Fulton Sheen. In addition to an increase in the number of secular daily newspaper reporters covering religion, RNS's importance and reputation grew throughout the 1940s. In April 1948, *Newsweek* praised the service. According to *Newsweek*, more than 600 newspapers, magazines, and radio stations paid up to $200 a month for a subscription to RNS. RNS subscribers, which then included the *New York Times, Time, Life,* and *Newsweek,* received between twenty-five and fifty stories a day.[10]

New Decade Signals Turning Point for Religion News

By 1949 at most secular newspapers, seasoned newspaper veterans began seeking the beat, raising the quality and independence of religion news reports. Perhaps predictably, mainline Protestant and Jewish institutions, which had always championed a free media, began losing enthusiasm for secular religion coverage. Complaints about religion news from religious leaders grew louder, appearing in journalism trade magazines and religious publications alike.

In one complaint about religion news reporting, the *Christian Century* criticized a 1949 news report about a four-year-old evangelist in Long Beach, California, who performed a wedding ceremony for members of his Old Time Faith Church. The Christian magazine—favored by mainline and other Protestants—ran a story in its January 19, 1949, issue headlined "Another incident of bad reporting" and said the newspaper "hullabaloo" over the story failed to answer essential legal questions involved. "We believe that much reporting of church news remains unsatisfactory, not because the papers don't want to report church news properly, but because the reporters they assign simply don't know enough to do their work well." The critique was novel, marking perhaps the first time a lack of specialized knowledge was cited as a deficiency for news reporters covering religion. This complaint from the leading liberal Christian magazine of the day also suggests that mainline Protestantism still perceived itself as oppositional to reports about evangelistic faith traditions—a viewpoint largely echoed in news reports during this era.

Five months after the *Christian Century* editorial, a group of newspaper reporters gathered to do something about perceptions of inadequate religion coverage. In May 1949, an informal gathering of twelve journalists covering the General Assembly of the Presbyterian Church in the U.S.A. in Buffalo, New York, founded the Religious Newswriters Association (RNA)—the first and only professional association for religion journalists working in the mainstream media. According to histories of the organization, Frank Stewart, religion editor of the now defunct *Cleveland Press*, and Henry McCorkel, news editor of *Presbyterian Life*, called the meeting. Stewart was elected the group's first president. Early participants banded together with the intention of raising the standards of religion reporting in newspapers, wire services, and news agencies. RNA also sought to elevate the religion beat's standing in newsrooms where it was considered a dreary necessity.

The creation of a professional association for religion beat reporters in the news media was long overdue. Professional associations for communicators at Protestant and Jewish denominational publications or the Roman Catholic Church had existed for decades and grown in political prestige. Members of the Associated Church Press were invited to meet the president at the White House at least seven times since the group's founding in 1916. The Roman Catholic Press Association was founded in 1910. Its fiftieth anniversary celebration in 1960 drew 750 attendees, including 150 members of Congress. The Evangelical Press Association, formed a few months prior to RNA's birth, already had more than 100 member publications attending its first conference in 1949.[11] The growth and power of these faith-based communicator associations magnified the differentiation between secular and faith-based journalists.

Later in 1949, *Chicago Sun-Times* religion writer James O. Supple wrote a two-page article in the *Christian Century* on "Church and Press: Enemies or Allies?" Supple bemoaned religion news' previously low status:

> Until recently the treatment of church news in the secular press bumped along at a deplorable low, paralleling the death notice, the betrothal announcement, and the garden party to raise funds for the Junior League's pet philanthropy. Church news consisted of an occasional sentence about mission collections or a report on the ladies' aid. The church made the front page only when death with due apology swooped down on a bishop of any denomination whatsoever (the press has always been morbidly fascinated by bishops) or on the pastor of the most fashionable local suburban congregation.[12]

Yet Supple also noted secular coverage of religion news was becoming more prominent. He attributed it to a social gospel orientation that emphasized action as an accompaniment to theological pronouncements. As faith's pervasiveness in society grew, content options expanded as well. The number of specialized reporters grew, representing higher professionalism. But non-news religion content options expanded, too.

By 1950, syndicated feature services distributed more than fifty religion-themed daily and weekly newspaper fillers, including cartoons, serialized books, and spiritual commentary. The *Chicago Daily News* ran parts of Fulton Oursler's best-selling book, *The Greatest Story Ever Told*, on page one for forty days in 1949. "People would have laughed you out of town if you had run that kind of stuff in the '20s," *Daily News* Executive Editor Basil "Stuffy" L. Walters told *Time* magazine that year. News syndicates also serialized books by *Power of Positive Thinking* Pastor Norman Vincent Peale and Bishop Sheen. The *St. Louis Post-Dispatch* ran religious columns prominently on its front page.[13]

The abundance of syndicated religion content says more about demand for such content at the time than it does about the quality of religion beat reporting. While large Protestant denominations rebuked the press from time to time, nomenclature of the era reflected continued professional coziness, at least on some level, between religion beat reporters and communicators charged with directing a faith group's public message. For example, no distinction was deemed necessary in naming the association of religion reporters "Religious" rather than "Religion." In fact, some RNA founders worked for religious media, such as Eric Modean of the New York-based Lutheran News Bureau. Religious denominational communicators formed their own association, now called the Religious Communicators Council, in 1929. But it wasn't until the late 1950s that the distinctions and tensions between religious public relations agents and mainstream journalists sharpened. Eventually, such distinctions would lead the Religious Newswriters to rename itself the *Religion* Newswriters Association and excise denominational press from its membership.

Despite improved professionalism of the beat, newspapers were not immune from asserting editorial influence and even promoting a faith leader. The best-known case is the reported order by newspaper magnate William Randolph Hearst to "puff Graham" when a young and largely unknown evangelist named Billy Graham was preaching at a 1949 revival set up in a tent erected in Los Angeles for the event. Although Graham had been preaching to evangelical circles since 1945, Hearst's telegram ignited a spectacle in which the original twenty-one-day revival extended to fifty-seven days, packing in more than 6,000 people every day.[14]

Some journalism educators at the time were convinced of the need for reporters who could decipher religious phenomena such as Graham. In September 1949, Syracuse University announced it would become the first school to offer courses in "religious journalism"—a term used synonymously for "secular" religion reporting and religion news produced by faith groups. Professor Roland Wolseley, who founded the Syracuse program, became the chief expert and cheerleader for such programs. Under Wolseley's leadership, Syracuse University became the national leader in research and training in religion journalism for more than two decades.

By the 1950s, newspapers expanded the coverage of Roman Catholicism, which had been previously overshadowed by reporting on Protestantism. More than three million pilgrims visited Rome in 1950—declared a "Holy Year" by Pope Pius XII. The pope also issued an encyclical exhorting the Christian faith as protection against Communism. That same year, the church celebrated sixteen canonizations and beatifications—more than in any other previous year in church history. The world also learned that the tomb of Catholic Church father Saint Peter was discovered under Saint Peter's Basilica in Rome.[15] Colorful religion news followed from each of these events. Yet it would take another two decades before Roman Catholicism would be the single most reported faith in the United States.

US newspapers in the early 1950s had never given so much newsprint to religion news stories and other religion-related copy, much of it from syndicated feature packages. Editor-in-Chief Grove Patterson of the *Toledo Blade*, while he refused requests to print the entire Bible chapter by chapter, called the trend an "astonishing" phenomenon that showed that the public sought reports of faith and values in their newspapers and identified the religion beat as deserving of dedicated space:

> No editor a few years ago would have believed that there was any circulation pull whatsoever in publishing religious articles . . . but people see their world as a changed world, which may be poised on the brink of disaster.[16]

Although some argued that the burgeoning television technology should include religious programming, neither the well-established religious radio nor secular television markets at the time included independent coverage of religion news. Broadcast media, it seems, preferred syndicated children's programming, worship services, or innocuous public service announcements to original reporting on religion.[17]

God on the Wire: Legitimization of the Beat

The vast majority of religion news coverage centered on local or metropolitan religion news. National news was covered by elite media outlets, including *Time*, *Newsweek*, and the *New York Times*. RNS also covered religion from a national perspective, but its reach was limited to subscribing newspapers. The beat might have largely remained the purview of local—some might even say parochial—religion news had it not been for the one man who, more than any other, legitimized the beat by giving it a high profile and visibility in media worldwide.

Oklahoma native George Cornell was a cub reporter when he arrived in New York City in 1947. Fresh out of the US Army and hoping for work at one of the several New York dailies, Cornell traipsed into the offices of one newspaper after another, searching for employment. In October of that year, Cornell was hired by the Associated Press (AP) after its New York City bureau chief asked Cornell to spell "accommodate." "I spelled it right. So I got the job," Cornell recalled in a 1991 interview with the author. By 1950, he was covering ships burning in the Hudson Bay and trials of alleged Communist spies.[18] The Associated Press, founded in 1846, already had beat specialists for topics such as medicine and science. But no single person ever covered religion.[19] Instead, AP treated religion as general news.[20]

Serendipity created an opportunity for Cornell to report on the 1950 founding assembly of the National Council of Churches—the earliest religion story Cornell recalls covering and one for which he volunteered. Although Cornell never envisioned being a religion reporter—few journalists at the time did—he saw it as an opportunity to distinguish himself from the dozens of other AP and New York–based journalists. The complexity and popularity of the topic drew him to religion news, and once drawn to the beat, he never left it. He continued to report on religion until his retirement forty years later. Cornell died in 1994.

Cornell credited his former New York AP Bureau Chief Samuel Blackman with the idea of making religion a beat. "We started out with one column a week. And then I got one day, then two days, and than all of the time," Cornell said. Speaking to the author in 1991, Blackman said AP's monitoring of about 100 newspapers showed that Cornell's religion stories, especially his occasional series, received prominent and frequent play. AP's creation of the beat was, ultimately, a shrewd business move that took advantage of the heightened interest in religion in public life.

Cornell wrote some thirty religion stories throughout 1950 before his byline became "AP Religion Reporter." AP archives show the new byline in a January 31, 1951, interview with the newly elected National Council of Churches president, Bishop Henry Knox Sherrill. Perhaps as a formal debut of the beat, the AP also distributed on that date a 5,500-word, three-part series by Cornell on important trends in American religion. AP's description of the series to wire editors said:

> Cornell has talked to religious leaders and surveyed church developments and organizations. He tells of the development of a stronger, more compact religious structure in the United States. And he tells how the churches are stepping more boldly into public affairs and asserting their interest in issues of collective concern.[21]

Highlighting the ecumenical movement, Cornell began the series noting, "American Churches today are pulling together. On a scale unprecedented in the nation's history, religious bodies have pooled their forces for common goals." Cornell delineated the very trends that had made religion salient to newspapers and magazines:

> With a Bible under one arm and a stack of pronouncements under the other, a new reinvigorated figure has stepped into the U.S. public arena.
>
> He represents American churches.
>
> Usually on the sidelines in the past, you'll find him today in the chambers of government, in the halls of labor and industry and sitting with the council of nations. In a strengthened voice, he states what he stands for. . . . Never before have churches moved on such a broad, allied front in seeking to inject the ethics of their faith into practical, working problems of society.[22]

Although the appointment of a religion beat reporter at the AP was highly significant, not everyone in the early 1950s believed religion reporting was credible. An essay in the *Christian Century* pronounced that, "Protestants can at best look for dutiful, apathetic, somewhat tone-deaf press coverage." Roman Catholics, according to the article, received better press than Protestants.[23] In 1951, the head of the Federal Communications Commission complained there were not enough religious television news reports or inspirational programs.[24] And twice that same year, reports issued from the Nieman Foundation for Journalism included articles about newspaper coverage of religion and religious institutions. In one Nieman report, former *Washington Post* "Church Editor" Martha Hall quipped that while respect for religion news had grown, such appreciation was not universal: "To many on the staff, the church beat is a joke."[25]

Another criticism of the media was its blatant promotion of elite religious celebrities. In 1952, the now elevated Catholic Bishop Sheen appeared on the cover of *Time* magazine and his orations were broadcast to a reported two million viewers via live television. Sheen had converted several notables, including author Clare Boothe Luce, wife of *Time* publisher Henry R. Luce. But some accused Luce of promoting both Sheen and Graham—and of supporting a religious piety that defined Christianity too narrowly. The media—especially Luce's *Time* and *Life* magazines—rarely covered the nation's growing religious diversity.

Despite some criticism, journalists covering the religion beat believed it was time to reward excellence in religion news. Professional standards for excellence in reporting were well established and rewarded with general news contests long before World War II. However, until 1951, no prize existed to honor religion news. But when James O. Supple, a founding member of the Religion Newswriters Association, died in a plane crash en route to cover the Korean War, RNA established an award in his memory. The award was first presented in 1952 "for excellence in the field of religious journalism with the object of interesting young writers in this field and of raising the caliber of writing done in it."

The expanded state of religion reporting was formally quantified for the first time in a 1952 unpublished study by Theodore B. Pratt, a graduate student in sociology at Syracuse University. Pratt's nationwide survey of mid- and large-sized daily newspapers identified 474 religion specialists—a gain of 18 percent in five years. Women had dominated the field since 1945, but the ratio of men to women was balancing out by 1952, Pratt reported. He predicted expansion on the beat.

In 1953, the AP's Cornell had certainly expanded his coverage—sixty-eight news stories carried his byline that year. It was also the first time that the wire service distributed Cornell's weekly Friday column "Religion Today," an AP fixture until the 1990s. Cornell's first column was a 710-word advance that moved over the wires for use beginning with Friday afternoon papers. The column "Religion Today" became the AP's first content marketed for use in the religion pages of client newspapers.[26] That year the National Religious Publicity Council honored the AP for its religion coverage. Soon after, United Press (a merger later created United Press International) followed the AP's lead and assigned Louis Cassels to cover religion—establishing the beat at the AP's primary rival.

The syndicated offerings at RNS also grew. By the mid-1950s, RNS published an inspirational editorial, a religion question-and-answer feature, a daily fifteen-minute radio news script, twenty to forty weekly photos, and a "Believe It or Not"-type cartoon illustrating little-known facts about religious groups and personalities. Although two-thirds of RNS copy was domestic, the rest featured faith around the world. A weekly trends feature called "Week in Religion" included stories on East German Communists campaigning against the Evangelical Church, Christianity in East Asian countries, the revival of tithing, and a congressional probe of revivals reported at meetings of secular groups such as the American Legion and Junior Chambers of Commerce.

Yet even when RNS covered international stories, the focus remained largely on Protestants, Catholics, and, to a much lesser extent, Jews. More often than not, newspapers during this era rarely covered African American Christians, who remained segregated even on newspaper religion pages. Newspapers in the South, especially, sometimes had "Negro churches" directories, but rarely were these churches' activities covered. Also absent from the news were African American Muslims and Muslim families who emigrated in the 1800s from Syria and Palestine. Likewise, Buddhism, Hinduism, and other world faiths were rarely mentioned. Moreover, though the press did cover Gandhi's activities in India before his assassination in 1948, such stories were framed as political, and not religious, news.

The cozy codependence between the religious press and secular journalists that framed mainstream media as an ally of faith from the 1930s through 1940s was challenged by the mid-1950s, as industry reports and new scholarship emphasized journalism's watchdog role. Although the title "religious journalist" still referred to both denominational and daily newspaper press, the word "secular" would increasingly be used to differentiate between journalists working for independent media and those on a church payroll. About half of the reported 650 journalists attending the 1954 World Council of Churches' first North American meeting were described as "secular." Scholars described the suburban Chicago event as setting all-time records for the amount of religion news coverage generated and of news emanating from a single source.

The portrayal of journalists as "profane"—lacking in religious sensitivities and beliefs—also grew in the 1950s. As one scholar noted in 1955:

> Most men in the practices of religion and most in the practices of journalism would acknowledge only a nodding acquaintance with each other and would not extend themselves far to make more intimate the relationship. The man in the street shares the same two-world opinion: that men of religion keep their eye on heaven and their hands on sacred things, that men of journalism focus attention only on the world and traffic in profane things.[27]

The issue of the "secular media" would become supercharged by the 1980s, but during the 1950s, that loaded phrase did not exist as the clichéd venomous put-down it is today. In many cases, those who staffed the religion beat until the mid-1970s either had a strong personal faith or were ordained clergy. In any case, most religion journalists were not closeted about their faith in the 1950s. But professional concerns such as how you fairly cover your own faith, or religions you do not follow, routinely emerged as important conversations during RNA gatherings. Such ethical standards are a hallmark of a profession, and throughout the 1950s, debates about how to be a good religion reporter—as distinct from general journalistic ethical norms—helped acknowledge religion journalists as true professionals.

Ethics and Responsibilities Encouraged Rigorous Religion Reporting

Millions of Americans watched Sen. Joseph McCarthy's inquisition of writers, actors, directors, and public figures during congressional hearings between 1953 and 1955. But the abuses of McCarthy's inquiries reenergized scholars and practitioners alike to embrace the recommendations of the landmark book *Social Responsibility of the Press*, originally published in 1947. *Time* and *Life* Publisher Henry Luce had recruited University of Chicago President Robert Hutchins to head a commission to evaluate the proper role of the media in a democracy. The thin but influential volume was the fruit of the group's work. Similarly, journalistic codes of ethics, which began with regional press associations in the 1920s, expanded to journalism trade associations between 1930 and 1960.

Similar to other professional beats and trade associations, religion reporters and writers had a distinct set of ethical norms. RNS Managing Editor Lillian Block enunciated these values in a 1959 speech at the University of Missouri School of Journalism. Block notes the importance of accuracy, among other values:

> A religious news story may have all the right names and titles, the facts it reports can be confirmed, and it may be written with absolute clarity—and yet be inaccurate and offensive to the religious constituency. It will be inaccurate and a distortion if essential details are omitted, if the specific development is not reported in the proper perspective of its background, if it plays up even though inadvertently the inconsequential, as far as religionists are concerned, and neglects the significant. This means that the writer of religious news, in addition to being an all-around good newspaperman, must have a wide knowledge of the field of religion.[28]

Block complained that an inordinate amount of religion news is labeled as "off the record" and urged religion journalists to stridently advocate for why religious groups should be forthcoming with information. She also said religion reporters should not give disproportionate time and space to, as she called them, the "lunatic fringe." With major issues such as racial discrimination, capital punishment, and birth control to cover, "to play up such lunacy for 'kicks' is a disservice to religion and to the press."[29]

Similarly, religion journalists were not obligated to give space based on the size of a religious group, Block told faculty and students attending her talk. Rather, news judgment should remain the basis for deciding which stories are covered.

By the mid-1950s, conflict as a frame for religion news was growing more common, but it wasn't always so. Block said newspaper editors once largely dismissed religious controversy as either insignificant or not worth any resulting public outcry.

"Within recent years, however, religious controversy, which after all is a sign of life and activity, has itself become news. Editors aren't as fearful of it as they used to be and perhaps the reason is that religious leaders themselves have brought such controversy out into the open and editors can no longer ignore it," Block said.[30]

One religious controversy on the cusp of the 1960s was coverage of a Roman Catholic senator running for president. Although John F. Kennedy persuaded the public that his politics were independent of his faith, the election elevated the importance of religious debate in the public square—and its resulting coverage. News reports of Roman Catholicism would grow in the 1960s and eventually supplant Protestantism as the most written about faith in US newspapers. But the professionalization of religion reporting that occurred between the 1930s and 1950s helped equip journalists to report on the turbulent 1960s, when pietistic outrage stoked religion news reports about civil rights, the Vietnam War, and waves of new immigrants who brought their Buddhist and Hindu faiths to US shores.

NOTES

1. Louis Minsky, "The Future of Religious News Coverage" (address delivered May 5, 1953, in Syracuse, NY, to the annual meeting of the Religious Newswriters Association—referred to elsewhere as Religion Newswriters Association. Name changed in 1971).
2. Ibid.
3. William B. Norton, *Church and Newspaper* (New York: The MacMillan Co., 1930).

4. Frank Stewart, "Church News Is Untapped Vein of Reader Interest," *Editor & Publisher*, September 2, 1939.

5. Elliott Wright, *RNS Reporting . . . 60 Years of Religious News Service* (Dallas, TX: United Methodist Reporter, 1993).

6. Ibid.

7. Carl. F. H. Henry, *Successful Church Publicity—A Guidebook for Christian Publicists* (Grand Rapids, MI: Zondervan Publishing House, 1943), 34.

8. Roland E. Wolseley, *Interpreting the Church Through Press and Radio* (Philadelphia: Muhlenberg Press, 1951), 66.

9. Paul Hutchison, "Religion around the World," *Life*, March 10, 1947, 107.

10. "News and the Churches," *Newsweek*, April 12, 1948, 76.

11. William B. Lipphard, *A Brief History of Associated Church Press* (Chicago: Associated Church Press, April 1966).

12. James O. Supple, "Church and Press: Enemies or Allies?" *Christian Century*, August 17, 1949, 960.

13. "Tales out of Sunday School," *Time*, October 10, 1949, 67.

14. Ben Bagdikian, *The Media Monopoly*, 6th ed. (Boston: Beacon Press, 2000), 39. ff.

15. "End of the Year," *Time*, January 1, 1951, 51.

16. "Greatest Stories," *Newsweek*, April 10, 1950, 58.

17. Charles M. Crowe, "Television Needs Religion," *Christian Century*, August 10, 1949, 938.

18. George Cornell, telephone interview with the author, February 3, 1991.

19. Debra L. Mason, "God and the News Ghetto: A Study of Religion News from 1944–1989" (PhD dissertation, Ohio University, 1995).

20. Cornell, telephone interview. Samuel Blackman, telephone interview with the author, February 17, 1991.

21. Associated Press, January 31, February 1, and February 2, 1951, series, in the "Religion-U.S." file for 1951, in Associated Press News Library, New York. None of these stories have headlines or numbers for more specific identification.

22. Ibid.

23. Maynard Kniskern, "Protestants and the Public," *Christian Century*, September 19, 1951, 1075.

24. "FCC Commissioner Coy Deplores Small Number of Religious TV programs," *New York Times*, June 23, 1951.

25. Martha Hall, "The Church Beat," *Nieman Reports*, no. 5 (1951): 21.

26. "Religion Today," May 29, 1953, from the "Religion-U.S." file for 1953, Associated Press News Library, New York.

27. Richard T. Baker, "Religion and Journalism," *Religious Education* 1, no. 6 (November/December 1955): 361.

28. Lillian Block, "Ethics and Responsibilities of the Religion Journalist" (text of address given at the University of Missouri School of Journalism in 1959).

29. Ibid.

30. Ibid.

REFERENCES

Bagdikian, Ben. 2000. *The Media Monopoly*, 6th ed. Boston: Beacon Press.
Buddenbaum, Judith, and Debra L. Mason. 2000. *Readings on Religion as News*. Ames, IA: Iowa State University Press.
Hall, Martha. 1951. The Church Beat, *Nieman Reports*, no. 5:21.
Wright, Elliott. 1993. *RNS Reporting . . . 60 Years of Religious News Service*. Dallas, TX: United Methodist Reporter.
Wolseley, Roland E. 1951. *Interpreting the Church Through Press and Radio*, Philadelphia: Muhlenberg Press.

CHAPTER 5

QUANTITY, QUALITY, AND RELIGION IN THE NEWS SINCE 9/11

STEWART M. HOOVER

THE events of September 11, 2001, and their aftermath challenge us to look again at religion journalism. The terrorist attacks on the United States by al Qaeda led to increased public interest in religion in general, and Islam in particular. It led to increased awareness on the part of journalists, editors, and publishers that religion should be nearer to the center of the news project. It led to a higher profile for public information and public understanding of religion in politics and in policy making. It led to a greater appreciation of religion in the foreign and domestic policy establishments. Each of these is important to the way news is produced and circulated.

There is little doubt that 9/11 sparked a boom in the coverage of religion in the news. Prior criticism had found consensus on one point: that whatever else one might say about religion journalism, all could agree there simply was not enough of it. This chapter will assess what really changed in this period, by way of asking the question of whether this increase in quantity has been accompanied by a change in the nature of religion news, and thus what the prospects are. An increase in quantity alone is not necessarily an improvement, particularly in a time of great upheaval in the news business and in the world of religion. This assessment is important because the significant changes of the twenty-first century can obscure ways that religion journalism was undergoing important shifts long before. The last half of the twentieth century set the scene for what has come since.

Journalism is a formal practice that operates within a number of constraints, including the professional conventions and standards followed by journalists; the routines, structures, and demands of the media industries; and the interests, expectations, and patterns of consumption of readers and audiences. As a result, journalism is limited in the things it can do and is in important ways inherently conservative. Religion is covered according to its own particular and unique conventions and boundaries of reception and interpretation that determine the ways its practitioners and wider publics can know and understand it. This all means that there will always be a tendency for journalism about religion to resist novelty and change and to aspire to describe the religion "object" in conventional and "known" terms.

Religion in the US media has seen a wide range of treatments, from the sensational and tabloid to the literate and broadsheet. What one might call the "normative view" of religion news (specifically "socially normative," or a model for practice derived from broader social goals and values) has much in common with the way other beats are seen. However, there are things about religion that are particular to it that still influence practice today.

Consistent with the architecture of the Anglo-American press tradition, coverage of religion aspires to be part of a larger project of social and political discourse that values both the widest representation and the widest dissemination of the intelligence of the day. It is thought that this intelligence will serve the larger purpose of truth and understanding through a process attributed to John Milton's classic treatise on press freedom, *Areopagitica*. In it, Milton argued that truth would emerge from a kind of discursive combat in the press. "Let her and Falsehood grapple; who ever knew Truth put to the wors, in a free and open encounter," he suggested.[1] The Miltonian ideal, then, as inscribed in press theory and practice, supports the notion of as free and open access to information as possible.

Milton's ideas were extended and elaborated by other figures of the Enlightenment, including Rousseau, who connected Milton's sphere of open exchange and debate to the empowerment of free individuals in a democracy.[2] In the Miltonian vision, the securing of truth and the sanction of falsity are functionally inseparable from the process whereby they are disseminated—their exposure in a free marketplace of ideas subjects them to public scrutiny. The important point here, and one that is inseparable from the problem of religion coverage, is that there is no need for any objective test or mechanism through which the truthfulness of a given bit of journalism is demonstrated. The system is thought to be self-regulating.

This "liberal-pluralist" notion of press freedom and its role in democracy has been linked to a broader conception of democratic action in the American state project.[3] This is seen most clearly in the confidence that the Founding Fathers placed in the press's ability to monitor and sanction public action. Toqueville, in his description of emergent American politics, provided evidence of this role of the press. More significantly, Toqueville also noted that religion could be seen to play an important part in these politics. Religion functioned as what sociologists call an "intermediate institution," a context of association and discourse through which and out of which interests could be formed and articulated.[4] Thus, from the earliest days of the republic, there has been reason to think that a free press and free religion were linked in the formation of public opinion and thus politics.[5]

This normative view of the press underlies high-minded perspectives on journalism, arrogating to the news media special responsibilities, but also special prerogatives. Within this view it is a foregone conclusion that those expressions of religion that seem most obviously consistent with democratic ideals are those that will be favored, and that all religions will on some level be evaluated in those terms. This means that religion makes the most sense to American media practice when it rises to a positive role in democratic society. The most valuable journalism about religion will be that which covers or encourages religious impulses that support, or at least do not hinder, democracy and democratically intended processes of understanding (see Richard Flory's contribution to this volume). Some traditional criticisms of secular journalism's treatment of religion have assumed that when secularists look at religion, they tend to trivialize its nonrational or spiritual functions because of a guiding humanist rationalism.[6] That may not be the issue so much as the normative view that religion must always be evaluated for its contribution to democratic participation. This conceives of religion as most important as news in relation to democratic practice in a way that is consistent with the normative hierarchy of all "news."

Within this large normative mandate for religion journalism in the Anglo-American tradition, a series of more mundane conventions of journalism in sourcing, narrative structure, and professional ethics also come into play in the way religion is covered. Religion, in fact, challenges journalism as a practical matter in the ways that it almost uniquely confounds such conventions.

Religion can always claim to be about something "beyond," something outside the tangible or material world. While religions abound in material, tangible practices and can be seen to have very worldly resources, expectations, and consequences, they can nonetheless lay claim to activity in other dimensions of experience, including spiritualities, which are hard to observe, describe, or confirm. Reporting is, on the other hand, all about the tangible and material. The whole point of sourcing and the practice of reporting involve documenting what the reporter can see and verify for himself or herself. Again, while all religions have observable and tangible elements, they can always reserve from view something that many would claim is the core of what they are.

Religion also defies conventional journalistic standards of evidence. It is hard to "source" in conventional terms. While its material and worldly practices are of course very conventional and in many cases readily accessible, the part of it that may be its real heart—the spiritual or supernatural—doesn't usually present itself. Again, while most religion scholars and religion reporters would argue that the part of it that is accessible is very often where the news is, there continues to be a sentiment among media people who are less sophisticated about religion that it is a challenge because the "real story" is outside the material realm. In such a view, this problem of sourcing also confronts the Miltonian ideal and more conventional perspectives on democratic discourse (Habermas, for example) about who and what should be admitted to the normative public sphere and under what conditions.[7]

Religions are also socially and structurally complex. There are many religions, with a wide range of truth claims, practices, and structures. It can be hard to find clear and consistent "sides" in many religions and religion stories. The notion that truth will prevail when competing voices are exposed to view is best realized when there are two clear sides to an issue. Religions often refuse to cooperate.

Religion also poses a challenge because journalists quite rightly fear being lured into the position of legitimating competing truth claims. In an era where media exposure is the primary context of expression and legitimation, religions have an interest in advocating for themselves in the media sphere. Journalists increasingly find themselves in the role of a gatekeeper to that sphere and thereby to broader influence and ascendancy in public discourse. Before the mid-twentieth century, when a kind of tacit accommodation between religious, political, and media establishments held sway, this was less of a problem.

Religion also challenges journalism in its implicit claims to authenticity. Simply put, the received view (expressed in such arguments as Tönnies's classic *Gemeinschaft und Gesellschaft*) holds that religion in its purest form is deeply embedded in human social relations and is by definition legitimate and authentic. Human societies the world over have, among their unique identities and resources of meaning and action, religious or religionlike impulses and values. Religions claim to be self-legitimating in an important way, and this confuses journalistic practice, which struggles with its role in certifying or legitimating aspirants to the public sphere, both resisting efforts at "spin" or manipulation and, as Richard Flory[8] has suggested, wishing to claim the authorizing function for itself.

This is important because religions, as they access the public sphere, often rely on their claim to this organic (Durkheim would say "mechanical") authenticity, and therefore they should be somehow "beyond criticism." As religious authorities enter political discourse, they understandably bring truth and values claims to the fore that are rooted in historic positions of their particular traditions. The most obvious example is the public voice the Roman Catholic Church expresses on important issues of the day. Conventional journalistic practice might regard papal pronouncements as one of many competing perspectives within a marketplace of ideas, while the Vatican thinks of them as, well, *papal*—and perhaps even divinely sanctioned. Religions then arrogate to themselves a special category of authority rooted in claims to authenticity. This can also be seen clearly in the way the clerical establishment in Iran expresses itself through its *fatwas*. The conflict between this self-understanding on the part of religious authority and the realities of journalistic coverage is only increasing as religion continues to be restructured.

Religions can, at the same time, direct attention away from their economic, social, and institutional sources and motivations. Religion journalists and religion scholars have long known and demonstrated that there is much more to religions than their transcendent and other-worldly claims. It is common in the West for religions to be organized with ecclesiastical and bureaucratic structures and to be extensively intertwined with state interests, as well as with social and economic systems and structures. These latter are the spheres where journalism is most comfortable. The challenge has always been to look beyond the claims to particular privilege that some religions make to their actions in the material sphere. The trends of the latter twentieth century, when the religious establishments that had previously defined the American religious sphere began to decline in influence, have led to a decline in the presumption of deference that once was more typical of journalistic treatment of these religions.

As the once-dominant institutions decline, the question of institutions and institutional authority is coming increasingly to the fore, at least in the US context. Recent trends in religion journalism have responded in two somewhat contradictory ways. On the one hand, much of the increased attention to religion has focused on personal stories of faith and practice, while what coverage has been devoted to institutions and structures has been primarily reactive to emerging internal struggles over authority in some groups and scandals in others.

With all of this, religion journalism continues to struggle against a widespread perception that it is inherently controversial. It remains a matter of faith in the news business that religion stories, particularly on the local level, result in more negative feedback than any other beat. This image of religion has not been helped by religion on the national and global stage becoming a site of increasing political and even violent struggle. The traditional calculus used to be the question of whether, given the potential complications and controversies, religion coverage was "worth the trouble." In the case of many local stories, and more important, in the case of some important national news outlets, the answer was "no."[9]

Revived Religion

The 1960s were a turning point for American religion and religion journalism. Until then, an easy accommodation had defined relations between religion and the press, when a still-regnant "Protestant Establishment"[10] held important sway over the nation's political and social life. A kind of deference marked the way the media of the time treated this situation. The media did not directly challenge religion, and the Protestant—and later the Catholic and Jewish—"establishments" both encouraged and benefited from this reticence. The religious landscape of the time was described by Will Herberg[11] as an America that could be defined in religious terms as a place where any of these faiths (and by extension only one from among these faiths) was a route to American identity.

Things began to change radically in the 1960s. Among the signal events were a series of court decisions, most notably the school prayer decision of 1962, which began to limit the tacit ascendancy of Protestantism as the dominant American religion. These decisions energized what had been since the 1920s a nascent fundamentalist movement. The campus unrest that was called by some a "social revolution" destabilized much of the postwar domestic calm that had been so prized during the 1950s. The Vietnam War and its widespread ramifications in social unrest and moral struggle remade important relations and interests within the dominant religious establishments. Probably most significantly, the civil rights movement also had important religious roots, motivations, and consequences. Like Vietnam, the civil rights movement fractured the religious "establishments" internally, reinscribing, for example, what had been long-standing accommodation between "northern" and "southern" branches of Protestantism. The increasing activism of the establishment Protestant groups on Vietnam, civil rights, and social reform more generally re-created in a new form the modernist controversies that had led to the original emergence of American fundamentalism at the turn of the twentieth century, and reinscribed the establishment groups as what we today think of as "liberal Protestantism."

The increasing social power and influence of the feminist movement, the introduction of the birth control pill as part of an overall "sexual revolution," and the briefly popular "death of God" movement further startled bourgeois sensibilities. It could seem like the whole world was being rocked to its foundation and, being very much at the center of these trends, the consequences to the world of religion were indeed profound.

Perhaps the most significant of these consequences was the emergence of a movement that brought together the remnants of the earlier fundamentalist movement with new resources in the culture and the conservative religious academy to become a force that came to be called "neo-evangelicalism," and later just "evangelicalism." This movement had social as well as theological roots and motivations, and was and is (in a way consistent with the fundamentalist movement itself) a phenomenon of modern communication media. Prominent leaders of fundamentalism were radio preachers. The rising star of the new evangelicalism was a radio, film, and then television figure, Billy Graham.[12] The media sphere became a context where important interests and resources surrounding the movement were articulated. The advent of television religion we now call "televangelism" was an important element but certainly not the only way in which evangelicalism was and continues to be a media phenomenon. Among other things, the emergent evangelical media sphere provided a context outside the control of national religious establishments where the issues and anxieties of concern to the conservative Christians at the core of this movement could be imagined, articulated, and focused.[13]

The rise of the evangelical movement became an important phenomenon for the public media. Politics and journalism took notice as a presidential candidate identified himself as a "born-again Christian" in the 1976 general election, a year that *Time* dubbed "the year of the evangelical." Evangelical spokespeople came to prominence in the media in a way that leaders of the establishment had not experienced since its heyday decades earlier. The rise of evangelicalism, and particularly its increasing politicization, served to undo one of the taken-for-granted conventions of religion journalism: that coverage of religion could be facilely assigned to the margins, to a religion section or a "church page," and could and should be covered, when it was covered, by a religion specialist. evangelicalism began to change that as religion increasingly found its way into conventional news, and in a way that had not been typical of the religions of the establishment era. Religion thus became differentiated and particularized in coverage in new ways, as the emergence of evangelicalism and Pentecostalism, as well as new forms and expressions, such as independent churches that would eventually be known as "megachurches," and extrainstitutional trends, such as the so-called New Age movement, began to achieve more notice. These trends both revealed a religious landscape more varied and complex than had been known before and revealed religion's role and expression across a range of social locations, from politics to the economy.

A second event, this time on the international scene, proved to be both significant and portentous: the Iranian revolution of 1979. Until that time, the US foreign policy and media establishments had thought of religion internationally through the influential social theory of "secularization." The conventional wisdom of the time expected religion to fade with increasing levels of education and social development. It was thought that Western societies were becoming increasingly "secularized," a process that was seemingly more advanced in Western Europe than it was in the United States.

A corollary to this notion held that the "less advanced" societies of the developing world would of course show higher levels of religiosity but that the overall trend would be the same. They would gradually secularize as development took hold. This idea was a matter of faith in foreign policy and development circles and in the media that covered international news. It was thus a shock to these sectors that there could be a revolution in Iran (the depth and breadth of which caught many flat-footed) and that this revolution could have religion at its base and that a religiously defined polity would result (one that has now lasted three decades). Iran was a major watershed for the American public as well, raising important questions about the direction of the so-called American century, not least because it was such a heavily mediated event. Media were at the core of the revolution itself, and its progress and the ensuing hostage crisis were exhibited in real time in American living rooms. ABC's nightly coverage of the crisis, for example, was the genesis of its long-standing evening news program, *Nightline*.

Iran put religion on the foreign news agenda in the same way the evangelical movement (and the earlier events of the 1960s) had put it on the domestic news agenda. Islam, though, largely remained a religion "over there," a situation that changed with the 1992 Gulf War and then 9/11.

The effects of evangelicalism and Iran were to begin to change the terms of religion coverage. Religion began looking more like other "beats" as domestic and international religion became increasingly entangled in politics, and as the deference once shown to the religions of the establishment began to fade. These faces of religion also began to reveal what should have been obvious all along: the real and material dimensions of religion. As the establishment religions, particularly Protestantism, continued to experience internal struggles rooted in the social changes of the times, they also began to reveal more and more internal politics, something that increased their accessibility to traditional journalistic scrutiny.

Deference further declined with the emergence of scandals as a staple of the religion beat. The televangelism scandals of the 1980s and 1990s were among the first and highest profile of these, but this period also saw the first of the sexual abuse scandals that would continue to roil the Catholic Church for decades to come. This period also saw the emergence of coverage of the Protestant establishment itself, particularly focused on its alleged political liberalism and "Marxism" and on its declining numbers and influence, which would have been unthinkable a generation earlier.[14]

The rise of evangelicalism and the increased profile of religion internationally underscored the sense that religion was not fading away and that the notion of secularization was being disproven. Outside the realms of electoral politics and internal struggles over doctrine and authority, however, the traditional conventions of religion news continued to hold sway. Struggling with the growing sense that religion was a story that could not be ignored, a certain category of religion story began to predominate: stories of personal faith.[15]

Beginning a historical narrative with the 1960s necessarily focuses attention on the eclipse of Will Herberg's tripartite religious establishment. This is an important perspective from which to view the events of the era, but it needs to be seen in relation to the larger and more fundamental social trends of which it is emblematic, and which have undermined the dominance of received approaches to religion coverage.

Sociologists have described the late twentieth century as a time of "restructuring" of American religion.[16] This restructuring was typified by the gradual decline in the institutions of religion, particularly of the Protestant establishment, since the 1960s. Mainline or liberal Protestant churches were no longer at the center of American culture and society. Continuing declines in membership and financing, their gradual withdrawal from the center of social and political discourse, and their struggles over doctrine and authority are also important components of this decline. Where their position was once one of tacit centrality, they have become less vital. Their institutional sources, prerogatives, and aspirations are now more visible and their internal and external struggles are more obvious. In different but no less significant ways, the Catholic and Jewish establishments also have lost authority and precedence and are increasingly subject to press scrutiny.

The decline of the establishment institutions is at the same time a challenge to journalism in that it removes them as assumptive "taken for granted" sources of religious information and authority. What emerged instead are a range of more "self-legitimating" authorities, some (Jerry Falwell and Pat Robertson, for example) who achieved prominence through their own media presence.

Linked to this decline in authority is the continuing emergence of individual autonomy as a determinant of the nature of contemporary religion.[17] This aspect of religious restructuring is remaking religion "from below," as adherents feel increasingly responsible for their own faith journeys and are less reliant on theological or clerical authority for guidance. This trend has led to a proliferation of "new religions" as well as to new and protean spiritual and religious practices. The so-called New Age spiritualities were an example, but today there is a dizzying array of ways that individuals choose to be religious or spiritual. This further decenters what once was the straightforward project of defining religion news. It was news about "the religions," and the question of their legitimacy could be taken for granted. Today, what is and is not a "religion" is much more complicated. This individualism in faith and spirituality can be seen within even conservative religious traditions, where adherents are becoming more suspicious of authority.

In the media age, religions must be in the media to exist in public discourse. Accordingly, it is nearly mandatory for contemporary religions to engage with the media sphere, and to do so entails surrendering authority over their symbols, values, and ideals. The rise of personal autonomy further introduces media and mediation into the equation, as the modern digital media provide enhanced and deepened opportunities for the religious quest.[18] New values, symbols, resources, and solidarities can and do form through online and social media forms. To an extent, some emerging spiritual and religious expressions exist primarily through their mediation.[19]

Digital media have, of course, provided new opportunities and forms for rather more traditional mediations as well. Online interactive sources such as Beliefnet, Religion Dispatches, Patheos, Killing the Buddha, and The Revealer do traditional things in new ways. They are information and opinion sources, but they are interactive, and as such they are not bound to traditional publication and broadcast cycles. They are nimble and flexible in the way older religion journalism could not be.

These and other forces of restructuring have had major consequences for religion journalism. The central one is what sociologists call the increasing "differentiation" of all religion and of religions. Where religion might once have been thought of as organically expressed in the fabric of culture and society, religions today are increasingly differentiated from that fabric, and from one another. While it was a complex and problematic example of integration (for a number of reasons), establishment religion of the mid-twentieth century was nonetheless tacitly integrated into structures of power and influence in ways that made these linkages invisible. For example, religiously defined associations and loyalties were deeply embedded in the network of political and economic relations that dominated the era, but they did not need to be expressed or shown to be powerful. That is how establishments work. As the institutions of religion have been subject to restructuring, they have at the same time become more visible through their mediation. They are now obvious in ways they never were before, and their implicit and tacit power is draining away as a result. And journalism both is complicit in this process and finds its received coverage conventions increasingly challenged by it.

Religion has been further differentiated in the post-9/11 era as public attention and discourse have increasingly focused on religion on the global scene and as the presence of Islam and other non-Western religions have made it more and more obvious that the religious landscape is a diverse one. As various "publics" came to think about religion and particularly religious migration, the emergence of what are commonly thought of as "immigrant religions" also subjected native adherents of these faiths (American Muslims, for example) to greater public and media scrutiny. The religious landscape began to look more and more diverse. Once-solid links in religion and culture also began to break down in this period, most notably as Latino Pentecostalism grew in importance.

Differentiation has additional implications in the area of authority. Almost by definition, an expanding marketplace of religious "supply" implies that a wide range of religious "truths" may exist, and that the ascendancy of any one truth is less important than it once was. Combined with the general tendency away from confidence in received clerical and theological authority that is typical of the age, a radical "horizontalization" of religions has become the overall tendency, once again challenging the practice of journalism as it might seek out and source religion stories. The traditional, centralized, and authoritative media find themselves in a media landscape defined by change, diversity, and a kind of differentiation of their own (for example, in the emergence of politically defined news channels on cable television). The digital revolution is in the process of developing its own structures of journalistic practice and authority. "Journalism" in the normative sense is no longer the sole source of news about religion, nor is it expected to be. Readers and news consumers today have less confidence in the press (along with other leading social institutions) and are less and less likely to think of what journalism does as a search for "truth"—Gallup data, for example, show a long-term decline in reader/viewer confidence in the press.[20]

This all suggests that the way journalism has traditionally thought about religion is a failure of its epistemology as much as anything else. Journalism professionals conceived of their project as gathering and circulating information, leaving the larger questions of truth, veracity, and reliability to the discursive marketplace. Many shrank from religion as a topic because it assumed that the whole point of religions is to prosecute claims to special and particular veracities, and journalists feared being drawn into this process. This view seriously misunderstands the nature of contemporary media practice and religious practice (and perhaps misunderstood them even before the digital age). In a way, audiences are treating all religion as practice. Doctrine is of less importance. New mediated forms of religion are emerging underneath and outside the boundaries of "big journalism." Readers and audiences don't expect journalism to legitimate and authenticate religious claims so much as they expect it to reflect the religious landscapes important to their lives and aspirations.

The underlying dynamic here is the overall crisis of the Enlightenment project, where unitary or central voices and sources are no longer valued. At the base of the received conventions of religion journalism, and indeed all journalism, is the implication of universal spheres of practice and of discourse—indeed, the implication of a (potentially) universal modernity.[21] These ideas are increasingly questioned, as emerging global "publics" have access to mediated sources of information, modes of dissemination, and spheres of discourse. Such publics are also increasingly positioned by global digital media as "prosumers," as both producers and consumers of information and ideas. The idea that there may in fact be multiple "publics," "discourses," and "modernities" makes particular sense when contemplating the expanding and differentiating religious landscape.

The question for emerging religion journalisms will continue to be whether they can accommodate themselves to this new situation.

The Post-9/11 Context

Absent the events of 9/11, there might have continued to be a tendency for religion journalism to proceed along the trajectory that had been set during the last years of the last century. The solution to religious restructuring and change had been to cover religion more, but as a matter of faith and individual practice and experience rather than as a matter of institutions, structures, doctrines, and histories. This approach solves a number of problems. It avoids conflict with the still powerful institutions and active and articulate movements. It focuses on the "particular" and "personal," which fits well with an era of media atomization and diversification, and with a generalized shift toward niches and cultural identity enclaves in the media in general. It is thus "worth the trouble" (in the received calculus) because it follows trends in media at the same time that it sidesteps conflict and controversy. Stories of institutions and structures remain important, of course, and continue, but the growth has seemed to be on the side of stories of individual faith.

Post-9/11 an entirely new field of religion has opened up alongside the continuing evolution of religion as a "domestic" story. At the center of this is the question of Islam and how to cover it, both domestically and internationally. Many of the same challenges exist as in the general case, but there are a few that are particular to the times and to covering this faith. First and foremost, for journalists (and reinscribing the general issue of religious authority), there is the question of ecclesiastical authority in Islam. While the establishment religions in the American context vary in their degree of hierarchy (with Catholicism the iconic example of hierarchies of authority), it is commonplace for Protestant and Jewish spokespeople to stand in for theological or clerical authority in the public sphere. For a variety of reasons, this is not the case with Islam, and this fact will continue to vex conventional journalism as it continues to judge this faith through the frame of its "known" religions.

Second, also flowing from the frame of known religions has been the tendency for journalists and public discourse in general to subject Islam and other "emergent" faiths to a test of moral equivalence. Is this faith more violent, or more charitable, or more modern, or more misogynist, or more enlightened than that one? Even opening this question puts the weaknesses and limitations of our received approaches to religion journalism into relief. The liberal-pluralist ideal specifically avoids such tasks, leaving it instead to the court of public opinion to decide. Instead of directly addressing widespread myths and shibboleths of religion—that is, applying the same sort of specialist lens journalism applies to beats like business and politics—journalism about religion continues to be cautious and risk averse, seeking to hide its own sense of equivalence under a veneer of "objectivity." But that has always been the danger. One can only hope for coverage that resists the temptation to overemphasize stories of personal faith as a way of avoiding these challenges. Exploration of the faith experience of American Muslims (or Sikhs or Scientologists for that matter) is an important story, but it is hardly all that journalists and publics need to think about.

The amount of religion that shows up in news will continue to increase, as contemporary forces continue to shape it. Domestic religion news will continue to be defined by the ongoing restructuring of religious institutions and reimagining of religious and spiritual practice. The mediation of religion will continue to play an important role in this restructuring. Fundamental "news values" mean that some stories, such as scandals, hypocrisy, internal political struggles, and struggles over doctrine, will continue to push religion forward in news. The global context of religion will also continue to be of vital interest and importance. The remaking of the news business may show some promise of sidestepping the lacunae that defined religion journalism before the period of revival of the late twentieth century. What remains to be seen is whether it actually does so.

NOTES

1. John Milton, *Areopagitica: A Speech for the Liberty of Unlicensed Printing*, ed. H. B. Cotterill (New York: Macmillan, 1905), 45.
2. Robert Schmul and Robert Picard, "The Marketplace of Ideas," in *The Press*, ed. Geneva Overholser and Kathleen Hall Jamieson (New York: Oxford University Press, 2005), 142.
3. Schmul and Picard, "The Marketplace of Ideas"; Fred Siebert, Theodore Peterson, and Wilbur Schramm, *Four Theories of the Press* (Urbana: University of Illinois Press, 1963).
4. Robert Bellah, "Civil Religion in America," *Daedalus* 96 (Winter 1967): 1–21.
5. Doug Underwood, *From Yahweh to Yahoo!: The Religious Roots of the Secular Press* (Urbana: University of Illinois Press, 2002); Underwood, this volume; Robert Putnam, "The Strange Disappearance of Civic America," *The American Prospect*, no. 24 (Winter 1996): 34–48.
6. Cf. S. Robert Lichter, Stanley Rothman, and Linda Lichter, *The Media Elite: America's New Power-Brokers* (Bethesda, MD: Adler and Adler, 1986).
7. Cf. Nancy Fraser, "Rethinking the Public Sphere: A Contribution to the Critique of Actually Existing Democracy," in *Habermas and the Public Sphere*, ed. Craig Calhoun (Cambridge: MIT Press, 1992), 109–42.
8. Richard Flory, "Promoting a Secular Standard: Secularization and Modern Journalism, 1870–1930," in *The Secular Revolution: Power, Interests, and Conflict in the Secularization of American Life*, ed. Christian Smith (Berkeley: University of California Press, 2003), 395–433.
9. Stewart M. Hoover, *Religion in the News: Faith and Journalism in American Public Discourse* (Newbury Park, CA: Sage, 1998).
10. E. Digby Balzel, *Protestant Establishment: Aristocracy & Caste in America*(New York: Random House, 1964).

11. William Herberg, *Protestant—Catholic—Jew: An Essay in American Religious Society* (Chicago: University of Chicago Press, 1983).

12. George Marsden, "Preachers of Paradox," in *Religion and America: Spiritual Life in a Secular Age*, ed. Mary Douglas and Steven Tipton (Boston: Beacon Press, 1983), 150–68.

13. Heather Hendershot, *Shaking the World for Jesus: Media and Conservative Evangelical Culture* (Chicago: University of Chicago Press, 2004).

14. For a detailed account, see Diane Winston, "Back to the Future: Religion, Politics, and the Media," *American Quarterly* 59, no. 3 (September 2007): 969–89.

15. Hoover, *Religion in the News*; Mark Silk, *Unsecular Media: Making News of Religion in America* (Urbana: University of Illinois Press, 1998).

16. Robert Wuthnow, *The Restructuring of American Religion: Society and Faith Since World War II* (Princeton: Princeton University Press, 1990); Donald Miller, *Reinventing American Protestantism: Christianity in the New Millennium* (Berkeley: University of California Press, 1999).

17. Philip Hammond, *Religion and Personal Autonomy: The Third Disestablishment in America* (Columbia: University of South Carolina Press, 1992); Wade Clark Roof, *Spiritual Marketplace: Baby Boomers and the Remaking of American Religion* (Princeton: Princeton University Press, 1999).

18. Christopher Helland, *Internet Communion and Virtual Faith: The New Face of Religion in the Wired West* (New York: Oxford University Press, 2010).

19. Heidi Campbell, *When Religion Meets New Media* (London: Routledge, 2010).

20. "Journalism," PollingReport.com, 2009, http://www.pollingreport.com/media.htm.

21. Fraser, "Rethinking the Public Sphere"; Talal Asad, *Formations of the Secular: Christianity, Islam, Modernity* (Palo Alto, CA: Stanford University Press, 2003).

REFERENCES

Campbell, Heidi. 2010. *When Religion Meets New Media*. London: Routledge.

Flory, Richard. 2003. Promoting a Secular Standard: Secularization and Modern Journalism, 1870–1930. In *The Secular Revolution: Power, Interests, and Conflict in the Secularization of American Life*, ed. Christian Smith, 395–433. Berkeley: University of California Press.

Helland, Christopher. Forthcoming. *Internet Communion and Virtual Faith: The New Face of Religion in the Wired West*. New York: Oxford University Press.

Herberg, William. 1983. *Protestant-Catholic—Jew: An Essay in American Religious Society*. Chicago: University of Chicago Press.

Hoover, Stewart M. 1998. *Religion in the News: Faith and Journalism in American Public Discourse*. Newbury Park, CA: Sage.

Siebert, Fred, Theodore Peterson, and Wilbur Schramm. 1963. *Four Theories of the Press*. Urbana: University of Illinois Press.

Underwood, Doug. 2002. *From Yahweh to Yahoo!: The Religious Roots of the Secular Press*. Urbana: University of Illinois Press.

SECTION II

THE MEDIA

CHAPTER 6

LATE-NIGHT COMEDY AS A SOURCE OF RELIGION NEWS

LYNN SCHOFIELD CLARK
AND JILL DIERBERG

THE "fake news": Journalists, pundits, and comedians have used this term to refer to television's contemporary political satire, including Jon Stewart's *The Daily Show* and Stephen Colbert's *The Colbert Report*, as well as important predecessors such as *Saturday Night Live*'s long-standing parody-of-news segment, "Weekend Update."[1] Such programs are about entertainment, surely. Yet recent studies have also demonstrated that for many, especially among the young adult and largely non-news reading population, these programs are an important source of information on political happenings.[2] Might such programs be a source of news about *religion* as well? Through an examination of *The Colbert Report*'s references to religion and the program's relationship to the changing face of journalism, this chapter argues that this question needs to be taken seriously in a book purporting to examine religion and the news. Given their popularity among a small yet influential audience of educated young adults and the fact that these programs are increasingly prominent in the public realm, this chapter argues that political satirical programs, by helping to shape the contours of how people think about religion today, will influence the religion news of tomorrow.

Viewers of political satire programs assign Stewart, Colbert, and other political satirists a certain amount of authority and credibility. A 2007 Pew Research Center study found that Jon Stewart was ranked as the fourth most admired journalist among the US population, tying Brian Williams, Tom Brokaw, Dan Rather, and Anderson Cooper.[3] Indeed, at an average of 1.8 million viewers per program, the audiences for *The Daily Show* are comparable to those of Fox News' *Hannity & Colmes* and CNN's most highly rated program, *Election Center*.[4] Thus, while these programs primarily aim for comedy, they also may perform a role in society that is in some ways journalistic in nature, as this chapter will discuss.[5]

The chapter begins by reviewing three reasons why scholars, religious leaders, reporters, and journalism educators need to consider popular political satire programming such as *The Colbert Report* and *The Daily Show* as sources of news about religion, and as portents for the future. Then, the chapter presents several examples of how religion has emerged in political satire and in the political humor of Stephen Colbert. As this chapter will demonstrate, like the *political* leaders who come in for the greatest criticism in programs of political satire, those leaders, representatives, and organizations related to *religion* that exhibit hubris or hypocrisy, and that make authoritative and manipulative truth claims, are the most likely to find themselves the focus of satirical jokes on Colbert's program. The chapter concludes by considering how *The Colbert Report* may be indicative of the ways in which religion will be approached in the news of the future, as religious and cultural pluralism becomes more normative in the United States, and as irreverence replaces deference in the emerging news media's stance toward religion and specifically toward those who would claim religious authority.

The Definition of News Is Changing

The 2004 inaugural report of *The State of the News Media* from the Project of Excellence in Journalism began with an observation about then-president George W. Bush's comment to ABC News correspondent Diane Sawyer. He told her that he preferred to get his news from people he trusted, who "give me the actual news" and "don't editorialize." The *State of the News Media* report then observed, "surveys suggest increasingly that the public agrees."[6] How did the journalism of major news outlets come to be labeled by the president of the United States as "editorializing," and how did the views of friends become preferable to reports from those who are professionally charged with seeing that the public's views are accurately informed?

Of course, many within the field of journalism still believe that journalists are society's gatekeepers, charged with helping the public to sort fact from fiction and truth from propaganda. These advocates worry that with the current decline in economic support for the news industry, that role is under threat. But others are more sanguine, noting that journalists had long ago moved from being the watchdogs to the lapdogs of power, and that the industry was in need of serious reform. Still others, like Bush, have accepted the view that all news is constructed, and thus they believe that they can choose which news to consume based on the sources that are most likely to support their own ways of viewing the world.

Wrapped up in the changes of the news industry (and indeed in Bush's and the public's declining support for the journalistic enterprise) are challenges to the professional practices of objectivity. According to journalism historian Michael Schudson, "the belief in objectivity is a faith in 'facts,' a distrust in 'values,' and a commitment to their segregation."[7] Critics have long argued that objectivity is an impossible standard, as journalists are always making value-based judgments about which stories to tell and how to tell them. The practice of objectivity can even obscure the truth, as David Mindich powerfully argued in his review of how the *New York Times*, in its attempt to provide "balance" in the late-nineteenth-century stories of lynching, may have actually normalized the practice.[8] Yet people in the news industry have continued to perpetuate the belief that their work mimetically reproduces "the truth." John Hartley has termed this the "fatal premise" of news. He saw it as fatal because once society began to question the belief in the ability of the news industry to reproduce reality, the news industry's legitimacy began to crumble.[9] And just as society came to question the unique ability of professional journalists to convey the truth through objectivity, digital technologies increasingly made it possible for others to enter the fray and tell their own stories with their own truth claims. Therefore, just as objectivity has come under fire within scholarship and in public reflection, the news industry has struggled to argue that there is a difference not only between fact and opinion but also between certain forms of journalism, with some that are better and others that are worse.

Today, political satirists have come to play an important role in helping citizens to ferret out the truth, Jones argues. Satirists do not *assert* the truth as mainstream news has done through notions of objectivity, nor do they *create* "believable fictions" as pundits, politicians, and other persons in positions of power have done. Rather, satirists use *redaction*—the process of taking apart and reassembling facts within a different frame to create a new meaning—to help citizens see patterns and come to their own conclusions about events and people.[10] As they engage in redaction, programs like *The Colbert Report* and *The Daily Show* therefore are performing a function formally assigned to journalism, encouraging people to become aware of how both punditry and mainstream news are constructed to create a particular narrative, and how the facts within a narrative might be alternately assembled to create a different, sometimes competing, meaning.

In his book *Entertaining Politics* and in subsequent reviews of political satire programs, Jeffrey Jones has argued that there are many reasons why *The Daily Show* and programs like it are important to consider in relation to the changing definitions of journalism.[11] Jones argues that political satirists take on the task of "adding it all up" for their viewers, which is important at a time when many reporters at the legacy news outlets seem to assume that the public has been paying as much attention to the minutia of their stories as they have.[12] Programs like *The Daily Show* and *The Colbert Report* are free to provide background information to the current event stories of the day. This kind of contextual information is rarely if ever provided in daily or nightly news. Yet without this information, it can be difficult for viewers—particularly younger ones—to understand the news.[13] And when guests are invited to *The Colbert Report* or *The Daily Show*, these guests are engaged in a conversation that can take them away from their talking points and can similarly provide greater context for their viewers.[14] Moreover, because these programs are produced outside of the institutional structure of journalism, they have no obligation to follow the news cycle. This means that programs like *The Daily Show* and *The Colbert Report* can ignore the tabloid topics, and may therefore actually cover more "hard news" than many other more traditional news outlets.[15] They also may be freer to explore controversial topics related to religion, and to question those who lay claim to authoritative positions on such topics, as will be seen below. And when it comes to newsworthy topics with a religious dimension, political satire has the added benefit of providing insights about religion to those who did not think they cared about religion and who therefore would not choose to read or view news about religion. Thus, political satire has an added value as a source of news about religion, particularly for those with little interest in it. As leaders, institutions, and practices of religion play a role in the bigger picture of society, they too become topics that can be contextualized and therefore better understood by those with limited background knowledge of religion.

Political Satire and Religious Commentary

The second reason for considering political satire programs as a source of religion news has to do with the long history of the relationship between news, political satire, and commentary about religion. People have long learned about the foibles of religious leaders and institutions in the context of humor and critique. As early as 1759, Voltaire was utilizing humor to point out the shortcomings of Christianity in *Candide*, a novella that, as the author had predicted, was banned on the accusation of blasphemy.[16] In the same era of the Enlightenment, Montaigne and Hume had similarly employed a satirical form of writing as a means of criticizing Christianity's powerful role within Eurocentrist beliefs, writing in indirect and ironic fashion to avoid the persecution that would come from direct criticism of religion.[17]

These early critiques of religion were not considered journalistic because, of course, today's concept of journalism did not emerge until the widespread and regular distribution of printed newspapers in the nineteenth century. But these early writings had a significant influence on the form that political satire would take within the pages of the early press and in the news commentary that would follow it. As Douglas Underwood has argued, the early journalist-literary figures of Mark Twain and Ambrose Bierce in the nineteenth century and H. L. Mencken and Sinclair Lewis in the early twentieth century were the "natural heirs to the Enlightenment rationalism that challenged Christian assumptions about the universe."[18] Mark Twain was particularly well known for his blasts against conventional Christianity, penning such witticisms as "The best cure for Christianity is reading the

Bible," and "Heaven goes by favor; if it went by merit, you would stay out and your dog would go in."[19] Bierce similarly coined unique and critical turns of phrase, such as his definition of religion in his 1911 book, *The Devil's Dictionary*: "Religion /n./A daughter of Hope and Fear, explaining to Ignorance the Nature of the Unknowable," and his association of worship with Western society's priorities: "ZEUS /n./The chief of Grecian gods, adored by the Romans as Jupiter and by the modern Americans as God, Gold, Mob and Dog."[20]

By the time of the *Scopes* trial in the mid-1920s, journalism had firmly aligned itself with modernism and science and against conventional Christian religion, and had professionalized its practices so as to distinguish reporting from political satire and social commentary. But whereas studies of journalists have found that they are often motivated by values that many have argued are rooted in Judeo-Christian ethics, journalist-literary figures and satirists from the 1920s to the present have tended to regard institutional religion with scorn when they regarded it at all.[21] Some of today's political satirists, such as Bill Maher in his comedic documentary *Religulous*, adopt this position of scorn, whereas others such as David Letterman and Dennis Miller have exhibited views that range from distaste to indifference, sometimes pretending to have less personal knowledge of religion than they might actually have.[22] In contrast, Jon Stewart enjoys foregrounding his Jewish identity, critiquing the universalizing claims of a "Christian nation" and mocking well-known stereotypes of Jews.[23] And Stephen Colbert has placed critiques of religious hubris at the forefront of his program. These comedians and the ways in which they incorporate religious humor into their political programs mark a distinctive period in comedy and in journalism, as they enable audiences to question US culture, religion, and society in a post-9/11 context. On his program, Colbert has pointed out that since that time, American markets have been banking on fear, and comedians like him have "made a killing" on creating humor based on those fears.[24] As religion has become linked with politics since that time, it has also increasingly come into focus in the contemporary writings of political satire.

How News Fits into Everyday Life

The third reason it is important to consider political satire as a source of religion news has to do with the changing ways in which people receive and share information today. Habits of reading the daily newspaper or watching the nightly news are being replaced as people use various media—mobile phones, laptops, radio—to be updated on news events. Of course, college students and young adults have always been less frequent consumers of news when compared to those who are in their forties or older.[25] The difference today is that social networking sites make it easier than ever for young people to share news items with their peers. Through links on social network sites such as Facebook or Twitter, young people are pointed toward stories that then stand out amidst an environment in which news is constantly available. And because people are more likely to pass along humor than any other kind of link, comedy and political satire have become important first glimpses into the news stories of the day for many of today's young adults.[26] Most news is constructed for passive consumption, but programs like *The Daily Show* and *The Colbert Report* are made for sharing—and are therefore a perfect fit for a socially networked style of sharing news.[27] Socially networked communication provides a way for people to say something about themselves in relation to the things they reveal to others. By passing along highlights from programs such as *The Colbert Report* or *The Daily Show*, young people can demonstrate to others that they are intelligent, aware of the current events of the day, and capable of critically reflecting on how those events relate to the structure of society. By passing along instances of humor that address religion, they can furthermore convey to others that even if they associate themselves with some form of religion, they can be critical of religion when it is marshaled in relationship with power.[28]

Stephen Colbert on Religion

Religion is not an infrequent topic on *The Colbert Report*. As a correspondent on *The Daily Show* from 2003 to 2005, Colbert frequently hosted the segment "This Week in God," a satirical look at how various newsmakers referenced religion. Religion has remained a topic of interest on *The Colbert Report*, sometimes serving as a source of parody and at other times a subject within segments featuring book authors.[29] Colbert himself has been interviewed numerous times about his own Catholic background and its relationship to his humor. In a 2005 article in the periodical *Time Out New York*, Colbert noted:

> I love my church, and I'm a Catholic who was raised by intellectuals, who were very devout. I was raised to believe that you could question the church and still be a Catholic. What is worthy of satire is the misuse of religion for destructive or political gains.[30]

He made similar statements when speaking with Terry Gross on her National Public Radio program *Fresh Air*.[31] Then, in 2010, when Colbert "broke character" during his testimony before a House subcommittee about the plight of migrant workers, he referenced Christian scripture. He had been asked why he was using his celebrity to advocate for migrant workers, and he replied:

> I like talking about people who don't have any power. It seems like the least powerful people in the United States are migrant workers who come and do our work, but don't have any rights. . . . And, you know, "whatsoever you do for the least of my brothers," and these seem like the least of our brothers right now. . . . Migrant workers suffer and have no rights.[32]

Making a direct connection between the Christian tradition of justice and the need for him to use his celebrity to bring attention to the lack of rights among migrant workers, Colbert's quoting of Matthew 25 was somewhat surprising but was consistent with his deep convictions about religion and his approach to satire as that which might reveal what Young and Tisinger call "the gap between what is and what ought to be."[33]

Colbert's humor focuses on leaders within religion and the news media who exhibit hubris as they claim the right to define for others what they should believe in relation to religious commitments. He has been especially astute in criticizing religious, political, and media personalities who are opposed to social programs. On March 2, 2010, for example, Glenn Beck announced on his radio broadcast, "Look for the words social justice or economic justice on your church website. If you find it, run as fast as you can. Social justice and economic justice . . . they are code words." On the March 18 episode of *The Colbert Report*, Colbert reported on and then wittily responded to Beck's comments, saying, "Yes! They are code words . . . (dramatic pause) . . . for helping people . . . code words used by communists and by Nazis. I know when I think Hitler and Stalin . . . (dramatic pause) . . . I think social justice." Colbert thereby highlights the irony in Beck's claim that social justice is somehow inherently associated with the evils of certain communist and Nazi leaders of the past.

Colbert similarly criticized the Christian Coalition's decision to force Rev. Joel Hunter to step down as candidate for president-elect of their organization after Hunter urged the evangelical movement to "broaden its agenda to include fighting poverty." In his segment "The Word," which juxtaposes ironic written statements on the screen during Colbert's monologue, Colbert noted:

> So the Christian Coalition [members] are afraid that they will be called liberals. I don't blame them. After all, there's nothing more Christian than refusing to do good works because you might be called a name, especially the name liberal! Because one thing we know for sure, Jesus was a conservative!

Colbert continued: "After all, [Jesus] hated welfare. Why do you think he was so upset when Judas took that government hand out [screen text: 'Thirty pieces of government cheese.']?" Later in his critique, Colbert went on:

> Now, if Jesus was so anti-poverty, how come he didn't end poverty? I mean he raised the dead, he made the blind see, and he made the lepers less lepery [screen says: "Apply Directly to the Forehead"]. No. Jesus instructed us that the poor will always be with us [screen says: "Like a Bad Penny—But without the Penny"].

The monologue encapsulates Colbert's simultaneous creation and parody of his conservative religio-political persona as he references the justifications some conservative Christians employ when they defend capitalism and simultaneously reason against a commitment to social justice. In bringing together these ideas, Colbert clarifies for viewers why Christian conservatives would be concerned about a potential leader who advocates an agenda of social justice, and why they would resist this particular linkage so strenuously.

Colbert continues:

> Now some of you are going to say, "Stephen, but Jesus said we should sell all our things and give the money to the poor." Exactly! Jesus contradicted himself a lot. It's hard to know what he meant sometimes [screen says: "Need Mel Gibson to Translate"]. Which is why it is so important that the Christian Coalition keep their focus on two things, reproductive rights and gay marriage [screen says: "Add Flag Burning for Holy Trinity"]. On those subjects, Jesus was very consistent. He never said a thing about either of them. So it's easy to know what he thought . . . [it's] whatever the Christian Coalition says he thought! You can trust that, 'cause no one thinks more right than them.[34]

In this passage, Colbert highlights an irony: leaders of the Christian Coalition claim to be the most orthodox followers of Jesus Christ, yet rather than focus on poverty, which is a frequent topic within the scriptural record, they focus on topics that have no direct reference within that record. Colbert thereby calls attention to the tenuous claims of authority upon which the coalition bases its arguments. In so doing, he enables viewers to examine the claims of authority that conservative religious leaders make about a host of related social issues.

Colbert's parody of conservative Christianity's focus on gay marriage is another such issue. On April 16, 2009, *The Colbert Report* aired both part of a public service announcement produced by the National Organization for Marriage (NOM) and then a parody of that ad. Although the NOM organization had been notoriously secretive about its ties to conservative religious organizations, Colbert made several comments that referenced the group's connections to religion, first using a religious reference to introduce NOM as "one group that is fighting to keep this ArmaGAY-don at bay," later praising the NOM ad as it was "like watching [the conservative Christian television program] *The 700 Club* and the Weather Channel at the same time," and still later ending his own parody with the following disclaimer: "Paid for by generous donations from an anonymous group that may or may not be the Church of Jesus Christ of Latter-day Saints."

The original public service announcement, called "The Gathering Storm," aired on mainstream television as a direct response to Iowa's and New York's decisions to lift the statewide bans on gay marriage. Referred to as an "Internet camp classic" by *New York Times* columnist Frank Rich, the commercial showed a diverse group of people standing apart from one another in the midst of ominous clouds, with lightning striking in the background.[35] Colbert aired the first part of this message, which begins with different people saying, "There's a storm gathering." "The clouds are dark, the winds are strong." "And I am afraid." The message then focuses on a white woman who says, "I'm a California doctor who must choose between my faith and my job." Moving from the excerpt to an in-character rant about the spread of gay marriage amendments from Massachusetts to Iowa to New York, Colbert then introduces his own commercial in response, called "The Colbert Coalition's Anti-Gay Marriage Ad."

Colbert's commercial starts out just as the NOM message does, with people speaking to the camera in front of storm clouds and lightning. "There is a storm gathering," the first person states. "A giant gay storm." "With rough winds blowing in from the east." "And even rougher winds blowing in from the west. Before long they will be blowing each other." "And I am afraid." Later in the commercial, an unhappy-looking white man standing next to his wife complains, "We're a perfectly normal, totally happy heterosexual couple, and I don't need gay couples flaunting how much fun they're having." He looks away and adds wistfully, "following their heart," parodying the closeted gay conservative Christians who speak out against gay marriage (most notably former Christian Coalition head Ted Haggard, who had been outed the year before).[36] The same unhappily married man later stumbles through his lines as he admires a well-built African American man getting soaking wet in the storm. The married man says to the camera, "I'm afraid about the church. . . . And how it's gonna get all—uh, wet." He then says to the man whose sculpted chest is now visible through his drenched shirt, "Do you work out? You've got a really good body." Finally, at the end of the commercial, Stephen Colbert appears as the clouds lift and a rainbow emerges, echoing the original message's sudden change of weather. Whereas the weather change in the original ad accompanied the announcement of the formation of the National Organization for Marriage, Colbert says in his ad, "But there is hope. Join the Colbert Coalition, A rainbow of proud people, coming together in a commercial." The use of the rainbow, a symbol of the gay rights movement, ironically comments on the fact that many disagree with the assumptions informing the original NOM commercial, as Colbert's parody highlights the misinformation, stereotypes, and fear of homoeroticism that underlie the opposition to gay marriage among conservative Christians as articulated in the NOM commercial.[37]

Each of these examples highlights the ways in which Colbert's humor turns on a historical understanding of Christianity and its relation to social justice that is at odds with conservative politics. The humor draws attention to the incongruities in the statements of those who claim to both support Christianity and oppose social programs while mocking the hubris of the authority claims of conservative Christian organizations.

Religious intolerance also becomes a source of humor in *The Colbert Report*. When the 2010 midterm elections saw Oklahoma banning state courts from considering Sharia law to reach their decisions, Colbert's persona characterized this as "great news." He continued:

> You can't be too careful, because there are 15,000 Muslims in Oklahoma: a full four-tenths of one percent of their population. Now sure, Oklahoma has a larger population of cows. But I say we keep an eye on them, too. Just in case any of them are practicing MOOslims.[38]

Islam is often the focus in *Colbert Report* segments that highlight religious intolerance. In a "Word" segment titled "It's a small-minded world," Colbert highlighted a story of an American Muslim that Disneyland had hired over the phone. When she arrived for work, she was told that wearing the hijab didn't "fit in" with the Disney "look." When she would not remove her hijab, she was escorted to a secluded stockroom. As Colbert explained:

> You see folks, when you work at Disney, you're not just an employee. You're a cast member. And you don't wear a uniform, you wear a costume. And Noor Abdullah was hired to play the role of Girl in Ticket Booth. Now, we all know that character has an elaborate back story. She's not a Muslim, and—that's it.

Colbert went on to discuss another Disney employee who had been asked to wear a hat over her hijab, and he compared the resultant look to that of a pimp. He then suggested that Disney could be helpful to other Muslims, too, noting, "Americans may fear an Islamic cultural center, but who wouldn't love a Mickey Mosque?" showing an image of a mosque with mouse ears.[39] Such humor is intended both to underscore Disney's intolerance for religious difference and, perhaps, to highlight Disney's history of adopting and transforming narratives from other cultures, imposing its own "brand" on those other cultures in the process.

Conclusion: The Rise of Irreverence

Like his predecessors in the political satire of a century ago, Stephen Colbert and other political satirists are not viewed as journalists in the "high modern" sense of those who report on the events of the day. But it is important to note that as commentators, they are not aiming to deceive or mislead, either. Colbert, Stewart, Maher, and others have used humor as a means of expressing criticism for the way things are in the hope that things could be different and better. Thus, although they do not set out to cover everything important in the day's events, they do play a role in helping people to recognize what is worth questioning or critiquing in the news of the times. And as they call attention to the hypocrisies of those who wield power, and in particular those who would marshal religious authority to do so, they play a role in society that parallels the classical definition of the watchdog role of the press, as Serra Tinic has pointed out.[40] Thus, in many ways, today's political satire and its critiques of conservative Christianity's claims to authority are not a revolutionary form of journalism so much as a revisiting of an older tradition of political commentary. In fact, in fifty or more years, it may be that the era of professionalizing journalism through notions of objectivity marked an unusual moment in journalism's history.[41] This, too, suggests that close attention should be paid to how today's political satirists approach subjects such as religion, particularly given the prominence and frequency of political satire and the authority of today's political satirists.

Conservative Christian leaders and organizations that seek to assert a particular narrative to influence public opinion are favorite targets of Stephen Colbert. Through redaction, or a reassembling of a conservative Christian narrative through the construction of a parodic counternarrative, Stephen Colbert and other political satirists allow conservative Christian leaders, groups, and viewpoints to indict themselves. By viewing how these leaders and groups would establish an authoritative yet manipulative and self-serving truth, viewers can call into question not only the religious leaders' version of a narrative, but the very authority the leader presumes in the first place.[42] In this way, *The Colbert Report* both repeatedly refutes the conservative Christian claim that its view of the world is somehow closer to "the truth" than other forms of religion and challenges its accompanying quests for political power. Colbert, and satirists such as Rob Corddry, Samantha Bee, and others who have followed in his footsteps, may therefore be creating an important metanarrative about conservative Christianity, suggesting that its leaders may simply be making these truth claims with more volume and insistence but not necessarily any more veracity or authority than anyone else.

In a democratic society in which many sources of news and commentary are available, there is a great need for people who can guide the population through the truth claims of those leaders who are in religious, as well as in political, organizations. Yet even as of the writing of this chapter, the situation in the United States is undergoing change. Today, there is increasing acceptance of same-sex marriage among the US population, and it is nearly a nonissue among a younger generation of voters.[43] Religious organizations with political ties were not credited with the Republican Party's success in the 2010 midterm elections. Such trends might indicate that conservative Christian partisan groups and their influence are on the decline. Yet recent evidence suggests that the emergent Tea Party, a group that received a great deal of coverage in the 2010 midterm election, seems to have a strong self-selection bias among conservative Christians. Tea Party members overwhelmingly identify themselves as Christian (81 percent), and nearly half (48 percent) are part of the religious Right or conservative Christian movement.[44] As political satirical humor follows the trends in power, this suggests that future redactional segments of *The Colbert Report* and other programs might by necessity become more nuanced in how they cover the relationship between conservative Christian religion and political power.

As political satirists such as Stephen Colbert and Jon Stewart rise to prominence, their particular approach to religion comes to carry a certain weight. And as they tend to highlight certain kinds of stories, and in a certain kind of tone, they signal a shift in how people might come to expect that journalists and other redactors might approach religious organizations and their claims of authority. Even in the recent past, the legacy news has approached the dominant US religion of Christianity with deference, highlighting stories of individual faith practices and private devotion. Yet rather than approaching religion from a position of deference, these satirists approach religion with irreverence. Religion comes to attention in these programs for its relationships to and abuses of power, and in the role that the dominant US religion of Christianity has played in relation to the perpetuation of misunderstandings and religious intolerance.

News organizations had certainly paid close attention to abuses of power among religious organizations in the past, but the standard tone of report had been (and still is) one of scandal and moral outrage. In the political satire of today, however, the tone is more frequently one of glee. The story of religion news in relation to political satire, therefore, is the story of an increasing critique of certain religious institutions in Western society. What comes into focus as a source of parody and satire is the hubris of certain religious leaders, institutions, or organizations. Religion becomes a focal point within these programs of political satire when its leaders or institutions lay claim to what in today's religiously plural world is considered an overreaching authority, or a power to define things, whether that includes the way others should live or how others should act. Claiming access to knowledge about the right way to do things is a problem in a pluralist society—and it is in this area that popular programs of political satire are particularly savvy not only in sharing information about but also in skewering religion. This is, of course, not the only role of religion in society, but with an assist from today's prominent political satirists, it is arguably the most public one.

In an increasingly individualistic culture, where how one practices or subscribes to religion is seen as a choice, perhaps any attempt to impose one's version of truth on others will continue to come under fire. Based on the news as it presently appears within programs of political satire, one might expect that the news of religion will continue to be reduced to its happenings and its controversies, and the stories of moderation and private devotion will become nonstories except among the sectarian press. And perhaps, after all, the removal of religious deference from the news agenda is not such a bad thing. It could be that satire, and perhaps especially satire regarding religion, is a return to a true calling of Western journalism as it holds accountable those laying claim to religious authority. After all, the disappearance of deference in favor of irreverence toward religions that lay claim to power may be a productive stance in a pluralistic society. And as Colbert's persona bumbles his way through the worst of the United States' religious hubris and insensitivities, perhaps the public is invited to reconsider and tend to its own proclivities for similar human failings.

NOTES

1. Norm MacDonald, who anchored SNL's "Weekend Update" from 1994 to 1997, opened each segment with, "I'm Norm MacDonald, and now for the fake news." http://en.wikipedia.org/wiki/Weekend_Update. About.com refers to Daily Show host Jon Stewart as a "Fake news icon." See http://manhattan.about.com/od/famousnewyorkers/p/jonstewart.htm. Leonard Doyle, "You Can't Be Serious: How a Comedian Became the Most Influential Voice in American Politics," *The Independent*, August 19, 2008, http://www.independent.co.uk/news/world/americas/you-cant-be-serious-how-a-comedian-became-the-most-influential-voice-in-american-politics-901828.html.

2. "Cable and Internet Loom Large in Fragmented Political Universe: Perceptions of Partisan Bias Seen as Growing," Pew Research Center for People and the Press, June 8, 2004, http://people-press.org/report/200/cable-and-internet-loom-large-in-fragmented-political-news-universe; "Today's Journalists Less Prominent," Pew Research Center for the People and the Press, March 8, 2007, http://people-press.org/reports/display.

php3?ReportID=309. See also Julia Fox, Glory Koloen, and Volken Sahin, "No Joke: A Comparison of Substance in The Daily Show with Jon Stewart and Broadcast Network Television Coverage of the 2004 Presidential Campaign," *Journal of Broadcasting & Electronic Media* 51, no. 2 (June 2007): 213–27.

3. "Today's Journalists Less Prominent," Pew Research Center, March 8, 2007, http://www.people-press.org/2007/03/08/todays-journalists-less-prominent/.

4. Ibid.

5. "Journalism, Satire, or Just Laughs? The Daily Show with Jon Stewart Examined" (a report on the Pew Research Center's Project for Excellence in Journalism, May 8, 2008), http://Journalism.org/node/10953#fn1.

6. The Excellence in Journalism Project, "The State of the News Media," 2004, http://www.stateofthemedia.org/2004.

7. Michael Schudson, *Discovering the News: A Social History of American Newspapers* (New York: Basic Books, 1978).

8. David Mindich, *Just the Facts: How Objectivity Came to Define American Journalism* (New York: New York University Press, 1998).

9. John Hartley, "Communicative Democracy in a Redactional Society: The Future of Journalism Studies," *Journalism* 1, no. 1 (2000): 39–47. Cited in Jeffrey P. Jones, "Believable Fictions: Reactional Culture and the Will to Truthiness," in *The Changing Faces of Journalism: Tabloidization, Technology and Truthiness*, ed. Barbie Zelizer (London and New York: Routledge, 2009), 127–43.

10. Jones, "Believable Fictions."

11. Jeffrey Jones, *Entertaining Politics: New Political Television and Civic Culture* (Lanham, MD: Rowman and Littlefield Publishers, 2004).

12. Jones, *Entertaining Politics.*

13. Geoffrey Baym, "Using the 'Fake News' in Journalism Education" (paper presented at the annual meeting of the Association for Education in Journalism and Mass Communication, Denver, CO, August 2010).

14. Jones, *Entertaining Politics.*

15. Baym, "Using the 'Fake News' in Journalism Education."

16. Ian Davidson, *Voltaire in Exile* (New York: Grove Press, 2005).

17. Krystle Hernandez, "Literary Analysis: Comparing Montaigne's Essays and Hume's Dialogues Concerning Natural Religion," *Helium.com*, http://www.helium.com/items/1305741-literary-analysis-comparing-montaignes-essays-and-humes-dialogues-concerning-natural-religion.

18. Douglas Underwood, "Transcending the News: Religious Ambivalence Among the Famous Journalist-Literary Figures and Literature as the Uncertain Path to Immortality," *Journal of Media and Religion* 6, no. 4 (2007): 241–71.

19. R. Kent Rasmussen, *The Quotable Mark Twain: His Essential Aphorisms, Witticisms, & Concise Opinions* (New York: McGraw-Hill, 1998).

20. See Rasmussen, ibid. Also online: http://www.csmngt.com/religion_quotes.htm.

21. Douglas Underwood, *From Yahweh to Yahoo!: The Religious Roots of the Secular Press* (Urbana: University of Illinois Press, 2008). See also Mark Silk, *Unsecular Media: Making News of Religion in America* (Urbana: University of Illinois Press, 1995).

22. Katy Perry on *The Late Show with David Letterman, YouTube*, August 24, 2010, http://www.youtube.com/watch?v=UjhcJA6O1PA.

23. When Rick Sanchez was fired from CNN for calling Jon Stewart a bigot, denying the oppressed history of Jews, and then suggesting that the networks were run by Jews, Stewart's rejoinder was this: "All he has to do is apologize to us, and we'll hire him back."

"Jon Stewart Breaks Rick Sanchez Silence, Responds," *Huffington Post*, October 3, 2010, http://www.huffingtonpost.com/2010/10/03/jon-stewart-rick-sanchez_n_748348.html.

24. Stephanie Brehm, *Jon Stewart and Stephen Colbert: Exposing Religious Incongruity* (unpublished master's thesis, Florida State University, 2009).

25. David Mindich, *Tuned Out: Why Americans Under 40 Don't Follow the News* (New York: Oxford University Press, 2005). See also Todd Gitlin, *Media Unlimited: How the Torrent of Images and Sounds Overwhelms Our Lives* (New York: Metropolitan Books, 2001).

26. Deborah Fallows, "How Women and Men Use the Internet" (a report of the Pew Internet and American Life Project, December 28, 2005), http://www.pewinternet.org/Reports/2005/How-Women-and-Men-Use-the-Internet/07-Functions-of-the-Internet/02-Communications.aspx.

27. Baym, "Using the 'Fake News' in Journalism Education."

28. See Jill Dierberg, *Evangelicalism and the Colbert Report* (unpublished dissertation, University of Denver, forthcoming).

29. For a content analysis of the use of religious humor in the "This Week in God" segment of *The Daily Show*, see Stephanie N. Brehm, *Jon Stewart and Stephen Colbert: Exposing Religious Incongruity* (unpublished master's thesis, Florida State University, 2009). See also Lynn Schofield Clark and Jill Dierberg, "Religion and Authority in a Remix Culture: How a Late Night TV Host Became an Authority on Religion," in *Reader in Religion, Media, and Culture*, ed. Gordon Lynch and Jolyon Mitchell (London: Routledge, 2012).

30. Article from *Time Out New York* excerpted on the blog *The Largest Minority*, December 5, 2006, http://www.jwharrison.com/blog/2006/12/05/the-colbert-report-the-christian-right/.

31. Stephen Colbert interview with Terri Gross, *Fresh Air*, National Public Radio, November 19, 2008.

32. Dan Zak, "Stephen Colbert, in GOP Pundit Character, Testifies on Immigration in D.C.," *Washington Post*, September 25, 2010, http://www.washingtonpost.com/wp-dyn/content/article/2010/09/24/AR2010092402734.html. This article does not include Colbert's reference to Matthew 25 in the New Testament, but it is available in his testimony. See, e.g., "Stephen Colbert Cites Matthew 25," in the blog *The Deacon's Bench*, September 25, 2010, http://blog.beliefnet.com/deaconsbench/2010/09/stephen-colbert-cites-matthew-25.html.

33. Dannagal G. Young, "Dispelling Late-Night Myths: News Consumption among Late Night Comedy Viewers and the Predictors of Exposure to Various Late-Night Shows," *Harvard International Journal of Press/Politics* 11, no. 3 (2006): 113–34.

34. *The Colbert Report*, December 5, 2006.

35. Frank Rich, "The Bigot's Last Hurrah," *New York Times*, April 19, 2009.

36. Dan Harris, "Evangelical Leader Denies Accusation of Paying Former Gay Prostitute for Sex," *ABC News*, November 3, 2006.

37. In September 2010, a campaign titled "NOM Exposed" was launched by the Human Rights Campaign (HRC) and Courage Campaign, according to Wikipedia's entry on NOM. The campaign has exposed funding connections between NOM and the Church of Jesus Christ of Latter-day Saints, the conservative Catholic body Opus Dei, the Knights of Columbus, and Focus on the Family. Online: http://en.wikipedia.org/wiki/National_organization_for_marriage#cite_note-Rich-22.

38. *The Colbert Report*, November 3, 2010.

39. *The Colbert Report*, October 5, 2010.

40. Serra Tinic, "Using the 'Fake News' in Journalism Education (paper presented at the annual meeting of the Association for Education in Journalism and Mass Communication, Denver, CO, August 2010).

41. Jones, *Entertaining Politics.*

42. This is an insight building upon Jones's analysis of how filmmaker Errol Morris uses the same strategy in his documentary filmmaking. Jones, *Entertaining Politics.*

43. CNN Opinion Research Poll, released Wednesday, August 11, 2010.

44. J. J. Sutherland, "New Poll: Tea Party Overwhelmingly Christian and Socially Conservative," *The Two-Way: NPR's Blog*, October 5, 2010, http://www.npr.org/blogs/thetwo-way/2010/10/05/130353765/new-poll-tea-party-overwhelmingly-christian-and-socially-conservative.

REFERENCES

Doyle, Leonard. 2008. You Can't Be Serious: How a Comedian became the Most Influential Voice in American Politics. *The Independent*, August 19. http://www.independent.co.uk/news/world/americas/you-cant-be-serious-how-a-comedian-became-the-most-influential-voice-in-american-politics-901828.html.

Excellence in Journalism Project. 2004. The State of the News Media. http://www.stateofthemedia.org/2004.

Fox, Julia, Glory Koloen, and Volken Sahin. 2007. No Joke: A Comparison of Substance in *The Daily Show with Jon Stewart* and Broadcast Network Television Coverage of the 2004 Presidential Campaign. *Journal of Broadcasting & Electronic Media* 51 (2 [June]): 213–27.

Gitlin, Todd. 2001. *Media Unlimited: How the Torrent of Images and Sounds Overwhelms Our Lives.* New York: Metropolitan Books.

Hartley, John. 2000. Communicative Democracy in a Redactional Society: The Future of Journalism Studies. *Journalism* 1 (1): 39–47.

Jenkins, Henry. 2006. *Convergence Culture: Where Old and New Media Collide.* New York: New York University Press.

Jones, Jeffrey. 2004. *Entertaining Politics: New Political Television and Civic Culture.* Lanham, MD: Rowman and Littlefield Publishers.

Lynch, Gordon and Jolyon Mitchell, eds. 2012. *Reader in Religion, Media, and Culture.* London: Routledge.

Mindich, David. 1998. *Just the Facts: How Objectivity Came to Define American Journalism.* New York: New York University Press.

———. 2005. *Tuned Out: Why Americans Under 40 Don't Follow the News.* New York: Oxford University Press.

Pew Research Center for People & the Press. 2004. Cable and Internet Loom Large in Fragmented Political Universe: Perceptions of Partisan Bias Seen as Growing, June 8. http://people-press.org/report/200/cable-and-internet-loom-large-in-fragmented-political-news-universe.

———. 2007. Today's Journalists Less Prominent, March 8. http://people-press.org/reports/display.php3?ReportID=309.

Schudson, Michael. 1978. *Discovering the News: A Social History of American Newspapers.* New York: Basic Books.

Silk, Mark. 1995. *Unsecular Media: Making News of Religion in America.* Urbana: University of Illinois Press.

Underwood, Douglas. 2008. *From Yahweh to Yahoo!: The Religious Roots of the Secular Press.* Urbana: University of Illinois Press.

Young, Dannagal G. and Russell M. Tisinger. 2006. Dispelling Late-Night Myths: News Consumption among Late Night Comedy Viewers and the Predictors of Exposure to Various Late-Night Shows. *Harvard International Journal of Press/Politics* 11 (3): 113–34.
Zelizer, Barbie, ed. 2009. *The Changing Faces of Journalism: Tabloidization, Technology and Truthiness*. London and New York: Routledge.

CHAPTER 7

RELIGION IN PRINT MEDIA

DOUG UNDERWOOD

ALTHOUGH modern, secular readers don't necessarily pay much attention to it, the most important thing to happen to Robinson Crusoe on his deserted island was a religious epiphany, whereby he recognized the disobedience of his past life, acknowledged Providence's role in casting him ashore as a shipwrecked sinner, and dedicated himself to a "reborn" relationship with God. In his creation of what many now call the first novel in English literature, Daniel Defoe drew upon the skills that he had demonstrated as the editor of *The Review*, one of the early examples of the modern newspaper in England. But he also built his *Adventures of Robinson Crusoe* upon the foundation of his Puritan beliefs, which were being challenged by the developments in literature and journalism, trade and shipping, and business and political life in the late seventeenth and early eighteenth centuries.

Defoe's place as a pioneer in the literary forms that today we call "journalism" and the "novel" is well established with scholars. But his position as a transitional figure who blended deep religious faith with the increasingly secular values of commercial publishing is less recognized. Defoe saw God's hand everywhere, including in the events that today we call the "news." For example, Defoe's concerns that there might be a recurrence in England of the 1665 plague of his youth—which he discussed in 1722 in a lengthy, journalistic tome, *Due Preparations for the Plague*—was turned into a best seller when Defoe also cast the material as a fictional narrative, *A Journal of the Plague Year*. In it, a fictional protagonist recounts the scenes of drama and suffering that he encounters in the plague. Although Defoe's early "novel" is today most noted for the way that it blends journalistic fact gathering with literary narrative techniques, a key feature of *A Journal of the Plague Year*, which would not have been lost on his contemporaries, was its persistent discussion of religious questions and Defoe's ruminations about the message that God was sending with the plague's devastation (particularly to those who were struck down after mocking God and refusing to change their moral behavior).[1]

In the Massachusetts colony, the Puritans carried on this teleological view of the "news." Natural events (ranging from disease to disasters to military defeats to the workings of Satan within people) were presented as the providential framework for interpreting God's unfolding plan for humans. Marvin Olasky, the conservative scholar and editor-in-chief of the Christian magazine *World*, has pointed out how the Puritans thought that journalism was important because "events were their report card signed by God, and they wanted to know where they stood, for better or for worse." Like other Puritan journalists, Increase Mather delivered "news sermons" and published his writings to the Massachusetts community, where storms, earthquakes, and fires gained significance because they were "ordered by the Providence of God." As Mather wrote, "When a fire is kindled among a people, it is the Lord that hath kindled it."[2]

This was the background for the famous clash in 1721 between James Franklin, Benjamin's older brother and the editor of the *New England Courant*, and Cotton and Increase Mather. James Franklin was jailed by the British authorities for the printed abuse that he heaped upon the Puritan leadership's plans to inoculate citizens against smallpox (ironically, he was neither on the side of science nor history here). Benjamin, who was working as an apprentice in his brother's print shop in Boston, took two important lessons from the controversy. Although a Deist, a believer in "rational religion," and a critic of Puritan authoritarianism like his brother, Benjamin decided that he never wanted people to point at him with horror for his "indiscreet" religious opinions (as he confessed in his *Autobiography*). He also decided that he wanted to print a newspaper (which he did after he ran away to Philadelphia and established his own publishing career with the founding of *The Pennsylvania Gazette*) that would provide balanced opinion as a mechanism for maintaining respectability and good public standing.

J. Herbert Altschull has called Benjamin Franklin's strategy the "price of truth." He argues that Franklin's advocacy of the use of even-handed opinion and civil discourse was as much a device for marketplace success as it was based in principle.[3] One of the ironic elements of Franklin's public image was that he came to be seen as the embodiment of the Puritan virtues of thrift and shrewd enterprise, even though he wanted nothing to do with Puritan theology. The merging of Franklin's religious notions with his entrepreneurial interests was commonplace for the early editors of his day. Defoe, along with Joseph Addison's and Richard Steele's *Tatler* and *Spectator* newspapers, were great influences on Franklin's development as a writer and journalist, as he also attests to in his *Autobiography*. For example, he may have noted the careful and clever manner in which Addison would needle religious enthusiasts and advance his rationalist views about religion, all the while maintaining his own good standing by publishing reverent poetry that was turned into Christian hymns, or the tactics of Steele, who, although a legendary drinker and glutton, wrote a book, *The Christian Hero*, about living the pious Christian life. (Franklin also may have noted how Defoe was jailed and put into the pillory for satirically attacking government restrictions upon dissenters from the Anglican church.) In fact, Max Weber held up Franklin as the journalistic personification of what has become known as the "Weber Thesis." Weber argued that Calvinistic values (which Franklin endorsed in a cultural sense, despite his theological misgivings) have become infused in American business attitudes so that commercial success can be seen as a sign of spiritual success (i.e., that one is among the elect and has been "predestined" for salvation by God, as John Calvin taught).

The political dominance of Puritans in Massachusetts didn't last long, nor did the era when editors opined openly about the religious aspects of their thinking. But the tension between traditional Christian and Judaic viewpoints about God's role in human affairs and the challenge to those viewpoints by Deists and Enlightenment-influenced thinkers (who nonetheless still retained strong vestiges of Judeo-Christian moral thinking in their rationalist and scientific worldview) have continued to provide the philosophical, moral, and intellectual foundation for the news business. This has been the case, even as secularism has made continuous inroads into the ranks of the press and left many people to believe (including many journalists themselves) that they operate free of religious impulses.

Religion and Print in Western History

Print culture and the Western religious tradition have been inextricably linked since the time of Jesus and before that in Hebraic, Babylonian, Egyptian, and Greco-Roman history. Religious developments often have occurred in tandem with the changes in communication technology brought about by such advancements as the coming of print writing and manuscript culture, the invention of the printing press, the industrialization of newspapers that came with the steam-powered printing press, and the inroads into the once dominant role of print brought about by movies, television, and linked computer networks.

As Harold Innis, Marshall McLuhan, Walter Ong, Elizabeth Eisenstein, and others have posited, the dominant form of communication goes a long way in explaining the nature of a civilization and how its members think and operate. In this scenario, the notion of the "word" and written language has infused and reshaped religious values and belief since the coming of writing in symbols and script. The ancient Egyptians attributed to written communication a divine power, and their system of communication—using hieroglyphic pictorial symbols first on stone and then papyrus—reflected a hierarchical culture where literacy was limited largely to the priesthood and the technical professions, who not coincidentally used this system to engineer the building of the pyramids with slave labor.

The Babylonians refined writing on stone by developing a mobile and more flexible form of communication (cuneiform writing on clay tablets) that supported their system of loosely confederated city states and a highly developed trading culture. The Phoenicians developed the phonetic alphabet where sounds were translated into symbols as a way to interpret and understand different languages that they encountered in their trading activities around the Mediterranean Sea. Amid the more powerful empires that surrounded them, the Hebrews utilized written texts to preserve their tribal chronicles and religious stories and to maintain cultural identity and resist assimilation during times of warfare and exile. The Athenians in classical times debated the benefits of adopting written textual communication. This was a feature of the dialogue between the literate student Plato and his teacher, the illiterate Socrates, who feared what would be lost if writing undermined the Greek educational tradition that relied on rhetorical training and memorization of ancient poetry as a way to transmit cultural values and notions of the ideal Greek citizen. The Romans, in turn, borrowed from the Greeks their use of written language as a way to support expansion and empire building and to make permanent records of rhetorical debate and intellectual discourse upon which they based much of their thinking in the realm of politics, science, and engineering.

Jesus, Paul, and the Role of Text in Christianity

All of these developments had a profound impact on the emergence of Christianity, which came into being within the cauldron of a Mediterranean and Middle Eastern world being transformed by the advancement of print culture. Jesus contested in the learned debates within the rabbinical temple discourse. Although we don't know the full level of his literacy, scholars speculate that he knew Aramaic, probably Hebrew, and perhaps Greek (even though a reference to his writing on sand is the only biblical mention of his skills in writing or reading). Despite this, Jesus's was largely an oral ministry among illiterate people, and most of his followers (with the possible exceptions of his brother, James, and Levi, the tax collector) almost certainly couldn't read or write. Even so, in the practice of ancient times, a number of chapters of the Bible were written in the names of Jesus's followers (ancient writers often attributed important sayings or documents to legendary figures), which signaled the power that writing had come to exercise in the years after Jesus's crucifixion by the Roman authorities. The earliest writings in the New Testament are generally attributed to the apostle Paul, and his epistles are foundational to understanding the role that print culture played in memorializing Jesus's life and establishing the authority of the early church. Paul's use of letter writing to communicate with the far-flung communities of Christian followers in the Mediterranean region can be seen as an early form of the "news" (and certainly the "good news"). His epistles (designed to be read aloud to the congregations) helped to reinforce solidarity and loyalty in times of persecution and group in-fighting. Paul's rhetorical skills as a Jew trained to be a Roman official were critical in establishing as church doctrine the interpretation of the meaning of Jesus's life by his early followers. Paul's level of literacy also is debated by scholars. Some believe he wrote by himself the letters attributed to him in the New Testament. Others believe they were dictated to a scribe or teams of assistants, and many attribute a number of the Pauline chapters to people writing in his name. However, Paul's rhetorical sophistication was critical in developing the theological principles of the early church. His views became fixed in doctrine when his letters were among the texts assembled by Jerome in the late fourth and early fifth centuries to become the official church version of the Bible at the Council of Trent in the mid-1500s.

A growing scholarship has focused on the interplay between oral and print traditions during this era to better understand how Jesus evolved from his role as an itinerant preacher seeking to reform Judaism into the cosmic figure of worship and salvation that he represents within Christian teachings. In this schemata, the period when the stories of Jesus's life circulated in largely oral form (roughly 50 years) is seen as critical to the establishment of the concept of the divinity of Jesus. The period when these accounts were written down, as well as which ones were selected as canonical texts, established the permanent record of Jesus's life and teachings. As the printed text gained authority, the Bible as it was constructed came to reflect aspects of Judaic, Persian, Greek, and Roman thought. In particular, Platonic viewpoints—such as the notion of the "word" as a primal and divine force in the universe as expressed in the Gospel of John (where Jesus is seen as the manifestation on earth of the "word," or "logos" in Greek terminology, as it has come into the world)—became a symbol of the spiritual power that written communication took on in early Christian thought.

The use of textual tools was blended into the history and politics of Christianity from the start, and by the sixth-century church scriptoriums where monks copied sacred texts produced most of the written manuscripts available in Western Europe. The employment of Latin and Greek in church documents, the illiteracy of the peasantry and common people in dealing with Latin-speaking priests, and the lack of written material in colloquial languages or a transportation system to disseminate them has led to McLuhan's theories about text- and manuscript-based culture as supportive of hierarchies and nondemocratic elites. The time it takes to become initiated into print literacy, the deference given to teachers and authorities, and the power of written documents as supportive of established authority were all features, McLuhan argued, of a rigid system that constrained human psychology, human scientific exploration, and the human spirit under the dominance of print-based dogmas and ideologies.

Religion, Journalism, and Capitalism

The invention of the printing press in the mid-1400s put an end to the church's monopoly of print culture and famously led to Martin Luther's protest against Catholic practices, the Protestant Reformation, and what many commentators see as the beginnings of the modern age. Historians have long viewed the invention of the printing press as key to the release of empirical and inductive forces in the population, making possible a whole host of advancements toward "modernity." Among these were an explosion of cheap printed materials in colloquial languages, the growth of literacy among the population, the circulation of scientific documents chronicling new experimental discoveries, the production of reliable maps for exploration, and the use of writing in trade and commercial activities. The first volumes to come off Johann Gutenberg's printing press were Bibles, and they were quickly sold by his major financier, Johann Fust, as a way to recoup his investment. The spur to capitalism brought about by the printing press was an irony not lost on Luther, who was critical of the church for putting elaborate property assets and money (in the form of the sale of indulgences) ahead of the welfare of the German peasantry. Luther was troubled by printers and booksellers who profited from his writings, but he decided not to support the traditional church policy of regulating usury and the economy (which he felt should be determined in the conscience of the individual businessperson). From that time forward, historians have seen Protestantism and communication advancements linked in the development of the capitalist marketplace in Western culture. This was particularly the case with Calvin, whose alliance with the merchant class of Geneva became an important practical element in his preaching that worldly business success could be seen as a sign that one was among those predestined for salvation.

The development of journalism as an extension of capitalism became a critical aspect in the emergence of the "news" values that would provide the impetus to the spread of ideas about commerce and democracy. Historians have identified the first "newspapers" as appearing in England, Holland, Switzerland, Germany, and other places in Western Europe beginning around 1600. Most were the products of print shops where editor-printers produced publications under a masthead that contained information that was perceived as marketable to audiences willing to pay for it. What became known as "newsbooks" appeared at about the same time in England as vagabond writers and merchants traded upon the public's appetite for information about current affairs by marketing their printed wares at fairs and markets. Religion commonly was featured in these broadsheets and pamphlets, and political and religious controversy often constituted the "news" of the day. Writers and printers typically were subject to censorship under the vying forces of the English Civil War era and afterward, including during the periods when the monarchy, Parliament, and Puritan authorities vied to gain the upper hand in controlling the English government. However, press rights slowly expanded throughout the century, and a key element of the "Glorious Revolution" of 1688 was an agreement increasing press freedoms and limiting the English government's licensing and censorship powers.

By the eighteenth century, newspapers and periodicals had become an established feature of public life, although they looked only vaguely like the newspapers of today. Many were edited and/or owned by figures who have become famous in literary history—Defoe, Addison, Steele, Jonathan Swift, Anthony Smollett, Henry Fielding, Samuel Johnson, James Boswell, and Oliver Goldsmith, among others.

Jurgen Habermas has argued that these newspapers were critical components of the emerging "public sphere" that he views as key to the emergence of democratic institutions. However, these publications had as many things in common with what we now call "literature" and "fiction writing" as they do contemporary journalism, and many see it as no coincidence that the earliest fictional "novels" were written by important periodical writers and editors of the day. Most of their publications were supported—as Defoe's and Swift's were—by political factions; the writings typically were anonymous or written under pseudonyms, and a variety of literary devices (including satire and caricature, brief narratives, and editorially inspired letters to the editor) were used to evade punishment by authorities enforcing on-again, off-again censorship and libel restrictions and to give signals to readers who knew how to "read between the lines." Religious controversy was a staple of these publications, even as Enlightenment rationalism and secular notions were making inroads into the hold of religion upon the culture. Defoe and Swift, for example, feuded in print over their religious opinions (Defoe and his *Review* were allies of the trading classes and the dissenters from Anglicanism; Swift, an Anglican clergyman, was a supporter of the state church, the landed gentry and aristocracy, and the Tory party as editor of the Tory *Examiner*), and they disagreed vehemently over efforts to limit the rights and opportunities of those who refused to take communion in or pledge their loyalty to the state church.

Religion, Secularism, and the Influence of the Enlightenment

The Enlightenment values that so influenced Addison, Steele, Franklin, and others played a profound role in shaping the value system of American journalists to come—but in ways that don't make the journalistic tradition as irreverent as it sometimes seems. The seventeenth-century poet John Milton can be seen as a key figure in this development, and the embrace by the press of his "self-righting" principle ("Let [Truth] and Falsehood grapple; whoever knew Truth put to the worse in a free and open encounter?") as articulated in his pamphlet *Areopagitica* is seen by historians as a foundational statement about modern press freedoms. Today, many secularly oriented journalists and scholars don't pay particularly close attention to the fact that Milton capitalized "T" in his notion of "truth." As a Puritan influenced by classical and Enlightenment thought, Milton largely had in mind right-thinking and believing Protestants as those who could be trusted to express themselves freely (this later became demonstrated when Milton, as an official in the Puritan interregnum government of Oliver Cromwell, helped to persecute English Catholics for their writings). However, Milton's dictum has evolved over time and can be seen as the basis of its modern, secular equivalent—the notion of Oliver Wendell Holmes's "marketplace of ideas" as the basis for supporting unfettered press and speech freedom.

At the same time, "prophetic" voices sometimes discovered that this emerging "marketplace" of opinions could still constrain radical ideas that challenged establishment thinking. Franklin's friend and Revolutionary War ally, Thomas Paine, was tolerated despite his advocacy of world revolution against the aristocracy until he penned *The Age of Reason*, which attacked the "irrationality" and mythological basis of biblical stories. Although Franklin privately agreed with much of what Paine wrote about religion, he counseled him against "intemperate" expressions. Paine's other friend, President Thomas Jefferson (a Deist, too, who sat in the White House in the evenings and excised passages from scripture that he felt violated rationalist moral thought; the volume, known today as the "Jefferson Bible," was never published in his lifetime), would only meet with Paine outside of public view. Paine's outspoken French counterpart, the Deist Voltaire, didn't have the benefits of even incipient press freedoms that came about in France only after the French Revolution. He put himself in great danger with the French monarchy for his ringing endorsement of press freedom ("I disapprove of what you say but I will defend to the death your right to say it"). Interestingly, Voltaire, too, was a confounding figure when it came to the mixing of journalistic and religious thought. Even though he hated clerical authority and celebrated skepticism and contrarianism, historian Carl Becker has argued that Voltaire only believed that he was antireligious in outlook, and that Christian idealism deeply imbued his philosophy and journalistic values.[4] Paine, who had rebelled against his Quaker upbringing, also was a deeply spiritual person who became a follower of the French Illuminists and believed passionately in God as the animating principle in all people (at the end of his life he also hoped to be buried in a Quaker cemetery but was denied his request because of his Deist beliefs).

Jefferson and his ally, James Madison, greatly loathed the party press newspapers of the postcolonial era in America but put great faith in the press at the same time. As the major author of the language of the First Amendment, with its guarantees of speech, press, and religious freedom, Madison was heavily influenced by his experiences growing up in the colony of Virginia, where he witnessed Baptists and other religious minorities being persecuted by the allies of the Anglican church, which was briefly adopted as Virginia's state church. Alexis de Tocqueville complained during his visit to the United States in the early 1830s that American newspapers were too provincial, too shallow in their political views, and bound too closely to local public opinion—and he worried that newspapers encouraged Americans to put too much faith in majority viewpoints. But his observations occurred on the cusp of the industrialization of newspapers that—with the coming of the steam-powered printing press to the United States in the 1830s—would transform the way news and information was packaged and marketed. At the very apex of the influence of the party press—President Andrew Jackson's electoral victory in 1828 was engineered by his allies in the press, a number of whom served as advisers in his "kitchen cabinet"—the forces of change that came with Benjamin Day's creation in 1833 of the *New York Sun*, the first "Penny Press" newspaper in the United States, were on the horizon.

Darwin, the Industrialized Newspaper, and the Waning of Religion Coverage

Although an important feature of the early Penny Press, religion coverage within the industrialized newspapers and periodicals declined throughout the nineteenth century. The pioneering Penny Press editor James Gordon Bennett started out extensively covering religion, including the continuing wave of "great awakenings" and other evangelical and revival movements of the period. But Bennett's greatest priority—despite his claim that, as a former Roman Catholic seminarian, he was a religious enthusiast who loved the "delicious and charming mysteries" of faith—was to make money, and he never ceased to nettle the religious, along with the business and political, establishment. Bennett's determination to build circulation by maintaining political independence and by relying on marketing tactics to attract an audience became a feature of the Penny Press business model. However, this led to the so-called Moral War by church and establishment forces in New York City in the early 1840s against Bennett's *New York Herald* for its sensationalistic approach to news coverage. In the face of the growth of the large, urban, industrialized newspapers, the supporters of the religious press—who had come to see the commercial press as irredeemably "worldly"—soon retreated to coverage of denominational news and the promotion of evangelical mission activities.

Technological, scientific, and cultural changes during the Industrial Age also played into the trends that de-emphasized news about religion. The ascendancy of science and the empirical tradition were absorbed into journalistic methodology with the "objective" approach to reporting and presenting news. Journalistic pretensions to a neutral form of news coverage were catalyzed by the invention of the telegraph in the 1830s, which encouraged news writing in brief and economically efficient forms, and the establishment of the wire services, which utilized a spare and distilled method of writing that would be acceptable to publications of a range of editorial viewpoints. In this environment, religion became more marginalized within press discourse, particularly as Darwinian theory arose to offer a competing cosmological account of the origins of life found in the Bible. Although Darwin's ideas originally were resisted in some quarters of the press, by the time of his death in 1882, the journalism community had largely come to side with the scientific establishment in the disputes that pitted biblical literalists against the supporters of evolutionary theory. At the same time, in its growing search for controversy, the press often pitted biblical conservatives against secular and "liberal" Christian proponents in the news columns. The press's growing secularization and skepticism about traditional Christian explanations can be seen, for example, in the polemics of such scathing critics of conventional Christianity as the journalists-turned-fictionists Mark Twain and Ambrose Bierce, as well as in the coming of the great literary "naturalists"—Stephen Crane, Theodore Dreiser, Jack London, Frank Norris—who apprenticed at urban newspapers and absorbed into their journalism and their literary themes many of the principles of evolutionary determinism of Darwin's followers. Many journalists of this period came to embrace the pragmatic, opportunistic, and sensation-seeking values of a news business that was coming to identify with science and commercialism more than that "old time religion." This chasm came into dramatic public view with the 1925 *Scopes* "monkey trial," where most American newspapers editorially sided with the defenders of a Tennessee science teacher who was prosecuted for violating a state law barring the teaching of evolution in the schools.

Interestingly, the most important reform movement of the nineteenth and early twentieth centuries—the so-called "muckrakers" who battled and exposed the industrial trusts and municipal graft—gained its sustenance from religion. Many of the well-known muckrakers and radical reform editors were followers of Jesus as a figure of moral reform and social justice values, even though they rejected conventional Christian theology as a subversion of Jesus's message. In his *Autobiography*, Lincoln Steffens placed the muckrakers in the direct lineage of the Hebrew prophets, and Upton Sinclair added: "The world needs a Jesus more than it needs anything else." In this respect, the muckrakers followed in the tradition of the Chartist and British reform newspapers of the nineteenth century, led by the crusading journalists G. W. M. Reynolds, Ernest Jones, and W. T. Stead, in which Christian moral principles—known as the "social gospel"—led to a blending of radicalism and sensationalism as a way to draw working-class readers.

Marketing, Media Criticism, and the "Liberal" Contemporary Journalist

By the 1920s, the "social gospel" campaigns that were led by religious activists soon faded from the public eye, and Christian agitators increasingly became associated with culturally and politically conservative movements. Religious conservatives came to identify the mainstream press as an enemy of traditional religious beliefs, and surveys throughout the twentieth century often have shown reporters and editors to be political liberals (at least in the cultural and social sense, if not always in economic terms). Studies also have shown that journalists today—and particularly top-level editors and publishers, journalists in smaller communities, and journalists in certain regions of the country (such as the South)—are not as secularly oriented as journalists in urban markets and on the East and West coasts.[5] But as Eric Alterman has said, if religion was the only issue, then conservatives would have a strong case in labeling journalists as liberals and secularists.[6] In the twenty-first century "red state, blue state" world of polarized politics and the culture wars, there are those who have compared the decline of the mainstream media to the decline of the mainline Christian churches. The gravitation to the extremes in political, cultural, and religious life can be seen in the comments of the Christian scholar Olasky: "If a person . . . is unwilling to accept the testimony of others, and thus assumes internally-generated psychological change rather than God's grace, he will see Christian fact as imagination, and Christian objectivity as subjectivity. In the long run, journalistic differences between Christians and non-Christians are inevitable."[7]

The debate about the "liberal" media has tended to obscure another important issue—the emergence of marketing and commercialism as a competing ideology with traditional religious values. Beginning with the muckraker Will Irwin, a long line of critics have complained about the corrupting influence of commercialism within the industrialized newspaper industry and its deleterious impact upon "public discourse." Although the leftist "moralistic" critique has been a persistent one in the twentieth and twenty-first centuries (and particularly so as media conglomerates have risen up and chain newspapers spread), it was the coming of the market-driven journalism movement—done in the name of using market research to address stagnant and declining circulation numbers of major daily newspapers—that focused at least some of the discussion on how religious news was being covered. A burst of expanded religion coverage in the 1980s and 1990s was motivated, at least in part, by the recognition by marketing-minded editors that the American population continued to be quite religious compared to other Western, developed countries, and that readers' interest in spirituality and other forms of worship went beyond the traditional audience for Christian church news.[8]

The polarization and hostilities surrounding the press in the national political discourse also encouraged a response from editors who believed that newspapers and other media were exacerbating the toxic elements of public life by focusing too much on controversy and sensationalism. The "civic" or "public" journalism movement was hardly new on the American scene in its campaign for a more "communitarian" approach to coverage of public issues. The sociologists Robert Park and John Dewey pushed for a similar, community-oriented approach to newspapering in their call at the turn of the twentieth century for a richer and more intelligent form of journalism that utilized the techniques of social science to provide context and perspective to the day's events. Dewey's and Park's notion that Christian values were reinforced by focusing on community rather than commercialism as the core principle of communication can also be seen within the public journalism movement, though few editors would identify it that way.

Meanwhile, communication scholars interested in the religious elements inherent in the modern communication process—ranging from James Carey (with his distinction between the spiritual and community-building "ritualistic" function of communications versus the utilitarian "transmission" function) to John Durham Peters (who has studied the "dream" of communication by idealists, mystics, and others searching for a transcendent meaning in media developments) to Jack Lule (who has analyzed the narratives and news formulas used by journalists as examples of Jungian archetypes)—reflected the growing interest in the academic world in discerning how the spiritual needs of society were being met within the fast-changing structures of the media industries.[9]

Postmodernism, Digitization, and Religion Coverage in the Internet Age

With all of these changes, the typical newspaper newsroom and its journalists still tend to reflect the Enlightenment worldview of skeptical secularism and belief in "objective" news, even as the twenty-first century has brought about increasing postmodern challenges to this viewpoint, growing pluralism in the population (religious and otherwise), and rapid changes in information technologies that are revolutionizing the field of communications. Print media on paper has found itself under assault from all corners—from digitization and the personal computer revolution (leading to the "convergence" of print, video, and mobile graphics in the electronic interactive world of the Internet), demographics (as fewer young people, along with everyone else, read traditional newspapers on the printed page), and economics (as Wall Street's and stockholders' analysis of a bleak future for traditional media companies has led to their plummeting stock prices). Few might call it a "spiritual" crisis as the newspaper industry has shed jobs and widespread angst has settled over traditional news workers. But the palpable anguish has given an apocalyptic flavor—to borrow terminology from the religious realm—to the discourse about preserving journalism's role in public life. Meanwhile, some of the Western press's most fundamental values are being challenged by the growing diversity and pluralism within American and Western European culture, and the once monolithic hold of the Judeo-Christian worldview is being diluted by globalism, immigration, and the expanded communication possibilities available on the Internet. One can no longer simply presume that Western media models will be the driving force of the future, according to Shelton Gunaratne, author of *The Dao of the Press* (who claims, for example, that Eastern thought is more compatible with the discoveries of science).[10]

The revolution that personalized, interactive, digital media has brought to the journalism landscape can make it difficult to discern the future for religion's role within it. The Internet has spawned extravagant claims for its potential shaping function in the future of religion—including among both traditional religious groups that have used it for proselytizing and outreach and "techno-mystics" who claim that online, electronic interaction can be a transformative process in itself and is changing the very nature of religion. The ability to put print into a converged environment where it competes with the power of visuals and other highly stimulating forms of electronic communication is clearly breaking down the old gateways that allowed for one-way control of the printed news product. But as their historical linkage would imply, it is unlikely that journalism in print will disappear any more than traditional religion will disappear—even as the permutations that have taken place throughout history persist in their ever-changing transformation of the religion and media landscape.

NOTES

1. Many of the references for quotations from historical figures and other material in this article can be found in Doug Underwood, *From Yahweh to Yahoo!: The Religious Roots of the Secular Press* (Urbana: University of Illinois, 2002); Doug Underwood, *Journalism and the Novel: Truth and Fiction, 1700–2000* (Cambridge, UK: Cambridge University Press, 2008); Doug Underwood, "The Problem with Paul: Seeds of the Culture Wars and the Dilemma for Journalists," *Journal of Media and Religion* 5, no. 2 (2006): 71–90; Doug Underwood, "Transcending the News: Religious Ambivalence Among the Famous Journalist-Literary Figures and Literature as the Uncertain Path to Immortality," *Journal of Media and Religion* 6, no. 4 (2007): 241–71.

2. Marvin Olasky, *Telling the Truth: How to Revitalize Christian Journalism* (Wheaton, IL: Crossway, 1996), 103–6.

3. J. Herbert Altschull, *From Milton to McLuhan: The Ideas Behind American Journalism* (New York: Longman, 1990), 105–8.

4. Carl L. Becker, *The Heavenly City of the Eighteenth-Century Philosophers* (1932; repr., New Haven, CT: Yale University Press, 1966), 30–31.

5. One of the best-known studies of American journalists, by the conservative media scholars S. Robert Lichter, Stanley Rothman, and Linda S. Lichter, found that top journalists seldom attended church—but the study has been criticized for focusing only on East Coast journalists. Other studies of a broader sampling of journalists from other regions of the country have found them to be more religiously oriented than the Lichters and Rothman. Underwood, *From Yahweh to Yahoo!*, 130–47, 296–300; S. Robert Lichter, Stanley Rothman, and Linda S. Lichter, *The Media Elite: America's New Powerbrokers* (Bethesda, MD: Adler and Adler, 1986).

6. Eric Alterman, *What Liberal Media?: The Truth About Bias and the News* (New York: Basic, 2003), 104.

7. Marvin Olasky, *Prodigal Press: The Anti-Christian Bias of the American News Media* (Wheaton, IL: Crossway, 1988), 71.

8. Alicia C. Shepherd, "The Media Get Religion," *American Journalism Review*, December (1995): 19–20; Underwood, *From Yahweh to Yahoo!*, 42–43.

9. James W. Carey, *Communication as Culture: Essays on Media and Society* (Boston: Unwin Hyman, 1989); John Durham Peters, *Speaking into the Air: A History of the Idea of Communication* (Chicago: University of Chicago Press, 1999); Jack Lule, *Daily News, Eternal Stories: The Mythological Role of Journalism* (New York: Guilford, 2001).

10. Shelton A. Gunaratne, *The Dao of the Press: A Humanocentric Theory* (Cresskill, NJ: Hampton Press, 2005).

REFERENCES

Alterman, Eric. 2003. *What Liberal Media?: The Truth About Bias and the News.* New York: Basic, 2003.

Altschull, J. Herbert. 1990. *From Milton to McLuhan: The Ideas Behind American Journalism.* New York: Longman.

Underwood, Doug. 2002. *From Yahweh to Yahoo!: The Religious Roots of the Secular Press* Urbana: University of Illinois.

CHAPTER 8

RELIGION NEWS ON THE RADIO

PETER MANSEAU

For a fleeting hour one winter Sunday in 1921, a pious, infirm Massachusetts woman joined a religious community without leaving home. Her son had recently become a radio enthusiast, and though she had never imagined she would have much use for his wireless receiving set, he sat her down that evening and cupped two aluminum headphones over her ears. Four hundred miles away, in Pittsburgh's Calvary Episcopal Church, a congregation had just gathered for Vespers in the presence of four microphones, arrayed to capture the sounds of the pastor, the chimes, the organ, and the choir. Then, miraculously, she heard them.

"Last night for the first time in twenty years, I heard a full church service," the woman wrote the next day. "I could scarcely believe my ears when the organ music and the choir sounded distinctly. Then afterwards, the voice of the pastor thrilled me as few things have in the long suffering years. I kept the phones on all through the service and at the end felt at peace with the world." With a scriptural flourish, she added that this was no ordinary feeling of calm, but "the peace that passeth all understanding."[1]

Perhaps the previous century's most important writer to be forgotten because of the medium he chose, Norman Corwin once described radio with a phrase that today could be applied to any of the technologies that make possible the digitally connected world: "the miracle, worn ordinary now."[2] When he wrote those words in 1939, it had been just nine years since a majority of Americans began to welcome voices from beyond into their homes, and less than twenty years since the earliest regional "radio-phonic" transmissions, and already it seemed perfectly natural for men, women, and children to sit for hours in their living rooms without saying a word, staring at the hearth of a talking wooden box.[3]

Before then, hearing voices had been very much an in-body experience. For a number of people to hear the same words spoken at the same time, they needed to be in the same place, near the one doing the speaking. Oral narrative was embodied both in the sense of coming from a body and in the sense of being heard in the company of bodies. With the advent of radio, the word and the flesh were divided. Communication, which in both its religious and its rhetorical sense had always implied communion, a bringing together of the many into the one, could suddenly be a solitary affair. Even if radio at times made its listeners feel "at peace with the world"—as it did for that unlikely early adopter listening to the first-ever broadcasted church service on January 2, 1921—it had also undeniably and irrevocably changed the terms of engagement with that world.

The nature of the change brought by radio was not as straightforward as it might at first seem, for it did not produce the immediate rejection of long-held life ways that sometimes follows adoption of a new technology. Consider the context the Massachusetts woman provides for her initial encounter with radio: *for the first time in twenty years*, she heard a full church service, some of which excited her *as few things have in the long suffering years*. For her, radio was significant not only because it allowed her to experience something new but also because it allowed her to reexperience something old. Radio meant a recovery of a feeling lost but apparently longed for. The world-shrinking invention her son had installed in their home could have been brought from the future. Yet, in its ability to approximate the sensations of a bygone community within the confines of her isolation, radio for her was primarily a nostalgia machine.

In this, at least, she was not alone. Among the most popular programs in radio's first decades was Charles Fuller's *Old Fashioned Revival Hour*. A Baptist preacher, Fuller became interested in radio in 1925, and within fifteen years claimed his Sunday religious variety show had "the largest primetime distribution of any radio program in the country."[4] Much of the draw came from the use of "old time" hymns, which appealed not only to churchgoers but also to those with perhaps more memories of Sunday services than histories of active participation. Letters sent to Fuller echoed the Massachusetts woman's yearning for an abandoned community, for the Proustian sounds of worship in the company of other bodies:

> We do enjoy the broadcasts and can hardly wait from one Sunday to the next. Our radio battery was down this last Sunday night, so we drove six miles over to another old couple's house to hear your sermon and that wonderful singing, and listened altogether to the songs we used to hear when we were children.[5]

Notes of thanks for the reconnection Fuller provided to the remembered religious past came from those disconnected by age, illness, and geography:

> I cook on a ranch out in the country and never get to go to church. I have not been to a church in nine years. God has blessed my little radio and through it the message has saved me. I am so hungry to hear more I can't wait from one Sunday to the next.[6]

Providing a glimpse into the spiritual lives of Americans during the interwar period, letters such as these also highlight a great irony hidden in the success of religious broadcasting: among parts of the rural population in the United States, wireless receiver set ownership rose as community membership fell; radio became "church" for those who had left actual churches behind.

Despite the variety of religious expression on early radio, however, information about religion—news—was virtually nonexistent. Unlike newspapers and the then-ascendant weekly magazines, which had regular religion sections before 1930, radio networks and wire services established focused religion coverage only a half century later, beginning with UPI in the 1980s, then NPR in the 1990s.

A survey of trends in American radio from its beginnings to the present suggests that the void in news coverage of religion was not an oversight, but rather a product of the ambivalence about the place and purpose of religious content in broadcast media. This ambivalence had something to do with the fact that radio technology itself seemed to have qualities that seemed "religious" in the broadest sense. Both in the numinous quality of its invisible presence and in the legislated requirements of its content, radio was received not merely as a novel medium but as a potentially unifying moral force. While there have always been proudly sectarian figures on the airwaves, their voices usually served to bolster the cause of those who claimed the "miracle" of radio should be used for nonsectarian ends. The commercial requirements and technical limitations of radio often served to support this notion. Lacking the visual frames of headlines or images, aware that anyone might tune in at any time, many early radio producers saw the necessity of appealing to audiences instant by instant, and thus were careful not to drive listeners away with divisive or contentious content. As a result, radio more than any other medium has approached the subject of religion as if the particularities of religions could be transcended.

Beginning as early as the experience of that Massachusetts woman listening to a broadcasted church service in 1921 and continuing until today, radio's approach to religion has not been without spiritual consequences. On the radio, it did not matter what sort of vestments a pastor was wearing, nor which denomination was named outside the church's door. In both expressions of religion and its coverage, radio transformed the categories of community—neighborhood, church, nation, faith—by shifting freely between the frequencies of the particular to the universal.

As Tona J. Hangen recounts in *Redeeming the Dial*, religion was among the earliest uses of commercial radio. Before the rise of the national networks, radio stations were locally owned, with 10 percent of the licenses held by religious organizations. It was a surprisingly natural fit. While there were a few religious professionals who feared broadcasted spiritual messages would be debased if heard in the wrong places, many more focused on radio's evangelical possibilities from the start.[7]

To some, the new technology seemed a divinely inspired tool for the propagation of the faith. James Gillis, then-editor of the *Catholic World*, wrote in the 1930s of radio's "Pentecostal" capacity, acknowledging that through the new medium evangelists could finally make good on the charge given to the apostles to speak to all peoples of the earth. "If St. Paul could return to take up his unfinished work of the conversion of the Gentile world, he would praise God—God and man—for the radio," Gillis wrote. "If, in Heaven, he is aware that his successors in the apostolate can reach millions where he could be heard by only hundreds, perhaps he renews with emphasis that he was 'born of due time.'"[8]

For others, radio became the perfect religious metaphor. Its invisible ubiquity was seen as very much like the universal availability of grace. Radio waves were an all-encompassing reality, and yet they were accessible only if one had the proper equipment for receiving them. As the Chicago radio minister Paul Rader preached: "There are some of you folks who have no radio in your heart. You could have heard glorious harmonies from heaven. In your bosom God's pipe organ could be playing." But if you have no receiver set, Rader warned, you would miss out on the benefits freely received by your friends and neighbors and would have no one blame but yourself.[9]

The early adoption of radio by religious professionals was not without conflict, however. Competition for the vast but rapidly crowding airwaves created a battleground on which to fight the long-contested role of religion in the public life of the nation. This was primarily an intramural Christian dispute, with liberal church groups squared off against conservative voices as they vied for radio time.

Into this breach stepped the rising national radio networks. The first, the National Broadcasting Company (NBC), determined at its 1926 founding that it would not sell access to radio broadcast to religious groups, but would instead provide airtime each week for religious purposes, which were regarded as a public good, similar to providing equal time to political candidates. However, unlike the equal opportunity rule, which became law as part of the 1934 Communications Act, the place of competing religious perspectives on the radio was not legislated directly. Rather, it was influenced by church-affiliated organizations that worked diligently on behalf of their own denomination's particular positions.

The most powerful of these organizations, the National Religious Radio Committee, moved NBC in the direction of defining the public good offered by religion in terms set by its ecclesiastical alter ego, the Federal Council of Churches of Christ in America. Through the National Religious Radio Committee, the Federal Council suggested five guidelines to NBC, providing a template for the norms of religious broadcasting for years to come:

> 1. The National Broadcasting Company will serve only the central [*sic*] of national agencies of great religious faiths, as for example the Roman Catholics, the Protestants and the Hebrews, as distinguished from individual churches or small group movements where the national membership is comparatively small.
>
> 2. The religious message broadcast should be non-sectarian and non-denominational in appeal.
>
> 3. The religious broadcast message should be of the widest appeal—presenting the broad claims of religion, which not only aid in building up the personal and social life of the individual but also aid in popularizing religion and the Church.
>
> 4. The religious message broadcast should interpret religion at its highest and best so that as an educational factor it will bring the individual listener to realize his responsibility to the organizational Church.
>
> 5. The national religious messages should only be broadcast by the recognized outstanding leaders of the several faiths.[10]

While the networks that followed (CBS, ABC, Mutual) developed their own policies regarding religion, NBC's five commandments set the tone. Each of the four major broadcast companies sought to be first of all a *national* company, and so the repetition of that word in the guidelines was not incidental, nor was its use in the phrases "national agencies of great religious faiths" and "national religious messages."

As Tom Lewis has noted, radio in many ways brought the beginning of national culture, which at the onset of the 1920s did not exist to the extent it did by its close. Writes Lewis:

> By the end of the decade . . . it was clear to all that radio was changing the interior life of the country in ways that few could have envisioned. The invisible sinews of electromagnetic waves were binding the country together as never before. . . . Increasingly, people ceased to refer to themselves just as Pennsylvanians, Coloradans, Californians, Oregonians, or Texans; radio brought the nation into their homes and gave them a national identity. A single event, a boxing match, an inauguration, a football game, a concert, a comedy sketch, a political speech, or a sermon, gave Americans the chance to share in a common experience.[11]

Thus, the religion appropriate to the national airwaves was to be *national* religion. To be a national religion, it must be also *nonsectarian* religion. In this context, nonsectarian meant a variety of liberal Protestantism in keeping with that first broadcasted church service of 1921: soaring music and soothing words adding up to "the peace that passeth all understanding."

While not formally bound by the guidelines limiting religious broadcasts, the news and dramatic divisions of the networks—often with less separation between them than we might suppose today—came to approach the subject of religion in much the same spirit that governed religious broadcasters.

Radio drama troupes, for example, regularly broadcast holiday plays offering vague spiritual messages without getting too specific about the reason for the season. Among the most well known, the popular weekend program "Grand Central Station" broadcast the same holiday play every year through much of the 1940s. "Miracle for Christmas" told of a doctor arriving at a hospital for his scheduled ambulance duty only to be told that his co-workers had heard he'd died earlier that day. As he rides around in an ambulance on Christmas Eve, the doctor is revealed to be none other than God himself, though not an especially biblical God, not a God identifiably Christian, and certainly not Jesus Christ, just a fellow riding through New York City whose voice occasionally is made to echo like rolling thunder as he helps a drunk to his feet or heals a crippled baby.

Such "religious" offerings—marked by a general avoidance of theological interest or any appearance of sectarian bias—reinforced the Federal Council's notion that the only radio ready, nonsectarian faith was that which claimed to represent religion at its "highest and best."

The implication, of course, was that religious broadcasts that did not fall in step with the National Religious Radio Committee's guidelines represented religion that was somehow lower and less. Inevitably, dissenting opinions arose, some noting that any Christian minister adhering to such guidelines was likely not fulfilling his biblical mandate to be a voice crying out in the wilderness, prophetically taking the culture to task rather than engaging in the kind of conflict-averse boosterism the NBC guidelines seemed to require.

Even Father Gillis, the *Catholic World* editor, while praising the unprecedented reach of radio, also lamented the limits the medium imposed: "Quite naturally, radio corporations and sponsors do not want disturbers on their programs," he wrote. "They favor conciliators, pacifiers, minimizers of differences between sect and sect, not delvers into fundamental dogma, but sippers and samplers, tasters, purveyors of sweetness and light." He went further, attacking directly the language of the guidelines and the mindset of the committee members behind them:

> In the judgment of those who own and control the great radio systems, the ideal speaker is the indifferentist who says, or more likely lets his hearers infer that he believes, one religion to be as good as another—"You are a good fellow, and I am a good fellow and all the world is a good fellow." They indulge in some smooth pronouncement as that radio must "interpret religion at its highest and best. . . ." They deprecate conflict of religious opinion over what one of them has called "petty inconsequentialities."

"If we are meticulously careful to hurt no one's feelings," Gillis concluded, "if we shy away from controversial topics, there is danger of our lapsing into innocuous banality."[12]

In response to fears that liberal Christians sought to ban conservatives from the airwaves, conservatives side-stepped the public allocation of airtime system in favor of purchasing time on their own. As paying customers rather than beneficiaries of network largesse, religious broadcasters were free—for a time—not "to shy away from controversial topics," and to venture as far from "innocuous banality" as their massive radio audiences would bear. Among the most successful in this strategy were Fuller and Rader, mentioned above, and the firebrand Roman Catholic priest Father Charles Coughlin.

Coughlin, who began his radio career as a labor advocate and ended it as one of the most notorious anti-Semites in US history, had a weekly audience of ten million at the peak of his popularity. Yet his influence led directly to revised network guidelines, which came to include not only airtime provided gratis to religious organizations but also purchased time as well. Overriding existing individual network policies, the National Association of Broadcasters (NAB) adopted a religion standard for the industry as a whole in 1939:

> Radio, which reaches men of all creeds and races simultaneously, may not be used to convey attacks upon another's race or religion. Rather it should be the purpose of the religious broadcast to promote the spiritual harmony and understanding of mankind and to administer broadly to the varied religious needs of the community.[13]

While the need for an industry-wide religion policy arose as a means to make plain what did *not* belong on the radio, the new code was primarily a positive statement of what did belong. Significantly, this statement was not concerned with religion per se, but rather with the meaning and responsibilities of radio itself.

And what that meaning amounted to was this: Radio was not just a neutral conveyer of sounds. It was a technology with a perceived moral component, as the first phrase of the code's second sentence—"it should be the purpose"—makes clear. Moreover, by reaching "men of all creed and races simultaneously," radio was understood to be transforming the nature, and the distance between, the diverse communities that had for so long shaped individual and national identity.

That a technology of communication should raise questions of morality and the meaning of community is not unique. Indeed, the questions raised by radio are very much like those asked of new media today: is it bringing people together, or driving them apart? Yet what is most striking is that, where radio is concerned, the answers tended to be as affirmative of technology's moral role as were the NAB guidelines, which could not seem less applicable to the perceived chaos and amorality of the Internet.

In assuming its moral role, however, radio revealed a paradox within itself: broadcast technology had a religious purpose, but many religious broadcasters, precisely because they were particularly and often parochially religious, seemed not to be in a position to serve the purpose claimed by those with most control over the airwaves. As the first two decades of radio came to an end, a question lingered: what would religion on the radio sound like if it was at once truly nonsectarian and yet was not full of "innocuous banality"?

Unexpectedly, other elements of radio began to provide an answer. In 1939, the same year the National Association of Broadcasters adopted its industry-wide code of standards on religion, it also began a campaign to make listeners across the country "radio conscious"—that is, more aware of just what sort of device they had en masse invited into their homes. Norman Corwin, a twenty-nine-year-old former newspaper reporter now writing and producing for CBS, took up the challenge with a short dramatic piece called "Seems Radio Is Here to Stay." It was the third broadcast from Corwin's pen, and his words spoke directly to the kind of congregation-of-one that a generation before might have been listening for an organ drone from a far-off church.

> Do we come on you unaware,
> Your set untended?
> Do you put down your paper to lift up an ear,
> Suspend what you were just about to say,
> Or stay the finger tip that could snap shut
> The traps of night between us?
>
> Were you expecting us?
> Your dial deputized to let us in
> At thirty minutes after ten along the seaboard on the east,
> Nine-thirty inland by a thousand miles,
> A mountain's half-past eight,
> And dinner dishes still uncleared on shores that face Japan?

In either case, good evening or good afternoon, good morning or
good night,
Whichever best becomes the sector of the sky
Arched over your antenna.

Corwin was the first radio writer who wrote for the medium with full awareness of what the medium meant and what it could do. Radio was, he knew, nothing less than a technology that had the power to make intimacy of distance. It spoke with a voice that was allowed to enter even the most hidden spaces, the most private moments. Corwin also intuited, like the radio preachers who had claimed radio as a spiritual metaphor, that there was something almost mystical at work whenever a sonic signal reached a human ear. Unlike those preachers, however, Corwin had the greater insight that the mystical nature of radio had nothing to do with the content of religious messages. The ability to broadcast—to seem to be everywhere at once, a power Corwin's scripts effortlessly conveyed—and to hear that broadcast was itself a religious experience, providing what can only be called a God's eye view of the world, "seen" through the miracle of radio.

We wish a thousand words with you
Concerning magics that would make a
Merlin turn pistachio with envy:
The miracle, worn ordinary now, of just
such business as this . . .

This sense of radio's miraculousness was not a foolish notion he cynically projected upon the public, but an apparently widely held belief. Just a few years before Corwin noted that the miracle of radio had been "worn ordinary," his near-contemporary E. B. White captured the feeling the technology had inspired when its wonder still was new.

"I live in a strictly rural community, and people here speak of 'The Radio' in the large sense, with an over-meaning," White wrote in 1933. "When they say 'The Radio' they don't mean a cabinet, an electrical phenomenon, or a man in a studio, they refer to a pervading and somewhat godlike presence which has come into their lives and homes."[14]

It was to those lives and homes Corwin wrote; it was their "radio consciousness" he hoped to raise by lingering on the seemingly divine amalgam of elements that made that "godlike presence" possible:

We speak now of the innards of this radio,
The dials, filaments, and microphones,
The crystals, coils, and rheostats and rectifying tubes
And towers that inject the sky
With certain ectoplasms;
And there where you are listening,

O listener,
The gadgetry inside your set
Selecting, sifting strands of ether, letting pass
That only which it pleases you to hear.
Let's see the gods do better!
Dare they vie
With engineers of radio?

Corwin was not a religious man. A Boston-born Jew of Hungarian and Russian descent, he spent Friday evenings in his youth not in a synagogue, but cleaning house and reciting poetry with his family. Son of an immigrant milieu, Corwin has described his own beliefs as essentially American. As he said in 2010 (at the age of 100), "My religion is Jeffersonian and based upon personal freedom. I am opposed to most organized religions, because they all have wicked origins and emphasize cruelty and godlessness and compete with each other, but I think that ethics are terribly important, and search for them in the Bible and elsewhere."[15]

With a voice unabashedly lyrical—at times self-consciously biblical—Corwin did not often make religion his subject, but he did not shy away from either history or prophecy. His radio scripts were thick with literary and religious allusions, as well as with predictions that have come to bear. In one of the closing notes of "Seems Radio Is Here to Stay," Corwin reminded his listeners that radio was only the latest miracle, not the last:

There may this very moment be,
As close to us as one discoverer away,
Whole firmaments of stuffs awaiting comprehension.

Along with a production earlier that year ("They Fly Through the Air with the Greatest of Ease," a chilling sound portrait of an Italian bomber crew destroying Guernica), "Seems Radio Is Here to Stay" made Corwin famous. Just barely out of his twenties, he became the first radio writer to have his name on a network program: *Norman Corwin's Words Without Music*. His rise to national prominence came at a crucial point in the development of American radio. With the United States' entry into World War II, the network system shifted from its focus on entertainment to news, and Corwin was enlisted to take on subjects of global concern. As a result, the place of religion on American radio also changed.

In Corwin's hands, the war became the guiding narrative that the implicit morality and mysticism of radio had been waiting for. He produced dozens of programs related to the war effort between December 7, 1941, and May 8, 1945, many of which had been commissioned by the Office of War Information. His role as an occasional propagandist did not blinker his creativity, however. In fact, it seems that playing a part in a communal national enterprise only heightened his individual artistic aspirations.

The larger the assignment (first to strengthen Americans' wartime resolve, then to explain what they had been fighting for), the larger Corwin's ambitions became. And the larger his ambitions, the loftier his language, until he settled quite naturally into the rhythms of prayer. This was the case at several points in his masterpiece, *On a Note of Triumph*, broadcast on V-E Day, 1945. Celebrating the Allied victory in Europe, Corwin used the opportunity not for chest thumping but for inquiry and introspection. He surveyed what had been gained and what had been lost in the war, and in the closing moments of the fifty-eight-minute broadcast, entwined the ancient tradition of divine petition with the technologies and politics destined to grant or deny the prayers of the future:

> Lord God of test-tube and blueprint
> Who jointed molecules of dust and shook them till their name was Adam,
> Who taught worms and stars how they could live together,
> Appear now among the parliaments of conquerors and give instruction to their schemes:
> Measure out new liberties so none shall suffer for his father's color or the credo of his choice:
> Post proofs that brotherhood is not so wild a dream as those who profit by postponing it pretend:
> Sit at the treaty table and convoy the hopes of the little peoples through expected straits,
> And press into the final seal a sign that peace will come for longer than posterities can see ahead,
> That man unto his fellow man shall be a friend forever.

It bears repeating here that, at the time he composed these lines, Corwin was not an obscure poet working in a garret on his pseudo-biblical verses. Already a major force in American culture, Corwin found with "On a Note of Triumph" a larger simultaneous audience than any writer in history had before then. The broadcast ran twice on all four networks and was heard by sixty million people in the United States alone. In German translation, it was made mandatory listening for every German POW held by the US Armed Forces.

"On a Note of Triumph" was first of all an American paean to military victory, but it was also deeply religious. Though representing none of the major faith traditions, as those early radio religion standards had stressed as necessary, it nonetheless would have been seen as in keeping with other guidelines for religious broadcast. Called upon to explain the cost and purpose of the war to his country, Corwin had crafted an intentionally nonsectarian promotion of spiritual harmony. Rather than nonsectarian as a variety of liberal American Protestantism, however, it represented the nonsectarianism of a Jeffersonian secular Jew put in the unlikely position of being given the largest pulpit on the biggest holiday in an overwhelmingly Christian country.

Though written for starkly different purposes, Corwin's "Triumph" had much in common with earlier religious broadcasts. His language looked both forward and back, making use of religious categories but tying them together with the terms of modern age: "Lord God of test-tube and blueprint, Who jointed molecules of dust and shook them till their name was Adam. . . ." In this he was attempting to express what was "highest and best" in religion, yet he did so in a way the framers of the industry's religion guidelines could not have imagined.

Corwin began his career as a newsman, and it is mostly as a pioneer of narrative nonfiction storytelling that he should be remembered, but he made a mark on both the expression and coverage of American religion as well. Thirty years after its broadcast, the closing stanzas of "On a Note of Triumph" were included in *Gates of Prayer*, Reform Judaism's 1975 prayer book. More than this institutional affirmation, however, evidence of Corwin's religious influence can be heard in the echoes of his work sounding through the varieties of American religion that blend the scientific and the scriptural, the future and the past, as well as in contemporary radio depictions of faith.

Since Corwin's day, the poles of religion on the radio have shifted from liberal Christian versus conservative Christian voices, to religion's advocates versus its opponents. Those who would approach religion with the same spirit Corwin did rightly look for a middle path in between. Sharon Ball, a former National Public Radio editor who was instrumental in the beginning of NPR's focused religion coverage in 1993, recalls that, "At the time, it seemed new and necessary to treat religion as something other than a sideshow, or a site of controversy; to go beyond what those who were for it and those who were against were saying, to find out what was really going on."[16]

While NPR's coverage rarely becomes an outright expression of religious ideas, as Corwin's flights of lyricism did, there have been public radio broadcasts when one can sense an intention to describe religion as if from above, not merely "going beyond" partisan positions, but observing from a great enough height that the particulars of religious sentiment are obscured.

First broadcast by Minnesota Public Radio in 1999, *Speaking of Faith*—like Norman Corwin's *Words Without Music*—is the brainchild of a single charismatic creator/producer, in this case the former print journalist and Yale Master of Divinity Krista Tippett. After a decade abroad, Tippett returned to the United States and "saw a black hole where intelligent coverage of religion should be." To fill this void, she started *Speaking of Faith*, which for a decade delivered interviews with religious scholars and faith leaders through more than 200 public radio stations.

In recent years, however, Tippet decided that the act of—and the program title—"speaking of faith" was too narrow. In her view, not only particular religion but also religion in general had come to seem too limited a subject to attract the show's intended audience. Rather than merely concerned with faith, the program she intended was "a spacious conversation . . . about the big questions at the center of human life, from the boldest new science of the human brain to the most ancient traditions of the human spirit."

In 2010, *Speaking of Faith* made the bold move to transcend the category of religion altogether, ultimately changing its name to *On Being*. The reason for the change, the show's website explains, was that Tippett "envisioned a program that would draw out the intellectual and spiritual content of religion that should nourish our common life, but that is often obscured precisely when religion enters the news."[17]

One obstacle to covering religion, in other words, is religion itself. Framed with a new brand, *On Being* is both a product of and a response to "a cultural shift that seeks conversation, shared life, and problem-solving within and across religious traditions and across categories of belief and non-belief."

While *On Being's* mention of a "cultural shift" suggests this is something new, on radio it seems quite familiar. It is at once an attempt to represent that which is "highest and best" in religious ideas and to blend, as Corwin did, the scientific with the sacred. *On Being* also suggests that, even as religion is no longer considered a universal, unifying force, some still believe that radio can be.

Looking for a contemporary analog to the woman borrowing her son's wireless receiver set in 1921, one might find a family not listening together to the radio, but creating their own podcast. It is now possible for anyone with a microphone and a high-speed Internet connection to broadcast his or her own religious service. Not only does it not matter what sort of vestments the pastor might be wearing or which denomination's name is on the door, but also now no church, no pastor, and none of the long-established trappings of religious authority are necessary to create an aural experience indistinguishable from the kind of sanctioned service first broadcast from Pittsburgh eighty years ago. The same obviously is true of coverage of religion: today one need not be Norman Corwin to record biblically inflected interpretations of current events and send them off into the ether. One result of this democratized dissemination of information is that while *On Being* may in some ways carry on the long-standing radio tradition of attempting to transcend the particulars of religion, the universalizing trend of religion on the radio has largely passed. With thousands of religiously themed podcasts available to listeners worldwide at any moment of the day, recorded and transmitted representations of religion reflect an ever greater social fragmentation that can be seen also in the increasingly partisan nature of the professional press and the voices of talk radio.

Yet the relationship between particular and universal depictions of religion on the airwaves has always been one of creative tension. Perhaps without the Father Coughlins of radio making use of religious rhetoric to divide the nation, there would be no Norman Corwins arising to act as counterbalance with attempts to tell stories of religion that might transcend the divisions religion has helped create.

NOTES

1. Quoted in Spencer Miller, "Radio and Religion," *Annals of the American Academy of Political and Social Science* 177, *Radio: The Fifth Estate*, January (1935), 135–36.
2. Norman Corwin, *Untitled and Other Radio Dramas* (New York: Norman Corwin Papers, Special Collections Research Center, Syracuse University Library, 1942), 213.
3. For more on radio adoption in the United States, see Steve Craig's "The More They Listen, the More They Buy: Radio and the Modernizing of Rural America, 1930–1939" Agricultural History, Vol. 80, No. 1 (Winter, 2006), 1–16.
4. Steve Craig, *Out of the Dark: A History of Radio and Rural America* (Tuscaloosa: University of Alabama Press, 2009), 107.
5. Ibid., 108.
6. Ibid.
7. Tona J. Hangen, *Redeeming the Dial: Radio, Religion, & Popular Culture in America* (Chapel Hill: University of North Carolina Press, 2002), 21.
8. James M. Gillis, "The Radio and Religion," *Public Opinion Quarterly* 2, no. 1, *Special Supplement: Public Opinion in a Democracy*, January (1938): 74.
9. Hangen, *Redeeming the Dial*, 46.
10. Hangen, *Redeeming the Dial*, 25–26.
11. Tom Lewis, "A Godlike Presence: The Impact of Radio on the 1920s and 1930s," *Organization of American Historians Magazine of History*, Spring (1992).
12. Gillis, "The Radio and Religion," 76.
13. Hangen, *Redeeming the Dial*, 34.
14. E. B. White, quoted in Tom Lewis, "A Godlike Presence: The Impact of Radio on the 1920s and 1930s," *OAH Magazine of History*, 1992.
15. Norman Corwin, e-mail to the author, November 21, 2010.
16. Sharon Ball, interview with the author, November 29, 2010.
17. http://being.publicradio.org/about/.

REFERENCES

Corwin, Norman. 1942. *Untitled and Other Radio Dramas*. New York: Norman Corwin Papers, Special Collections Research Center, Syracuse University Library.

Craig, Steve. 2009. *Out of the Dark: A History of Radio and Rural America*. Tuscaloosa: The University of Alabama Press.

Gillis, James M. 1938. The Radio and Religion. *Public Opinion Quarterly* 2 (1): *Special Supplement: Public Opinion in a Democracy*.

Hangen, Tona J. 2002. *Redeeming the Dial: Radio, Religion, & Popular Culture in America*. Chapel Hill: University of North Carolina Press.

Lewis, Tom. 1992. A Godlike Presence: The Impact of Radio on the 1920s and 1930s. *Organization of American Historians Magazine of History*, Spring.

Miller, Spencer. 1935. Radio and Religion. *Annals of the American Academy of Political and Social Science* 177: *Radio: The Fifth Estate*, January.

CHAPTER 9

COMMERCIAL TELEVISION NEWS, CRISIS, AND COLLECTIVE MEMORY

MICHELE ROSENTHAL

INTRODUCTION

As a primary source for collective memory, television news not only provides images and narratives that shape American perspectives on religion and culture at the moment when an event occurs but also defines critical moments, like 9/11, for generations to come.[1] News about religion on the small screen has been noted for its scarcity and bias (i.e., more coverage of the Roman Catholic Church and less of other varieties of Christianity), but there is simultaneously a broad consensus among media scholars as to the ritual importance of television news in the "construction and maintenance of an ordered, meaningful cultural world."[2] In other words, television news is deemed worthy of study as a central site for the creation and apprehension of "significant symbolic forms."[3] So while television network news may not provide substantive critical accounts of religion as it is practiced and understood by many Americans in everyday life, it nonetheless functions as an important source for understanding the world beyond the screen.[4]

If journalists and audiences once viewed television news as an objective or even neutral source for information, changes in the media landscape in the twenty-first century have ushered in a new sense of reflexivity and cynicism. In lieu of the familiar network anchor who offered a seemingly "neutral" fixed point from which to view the world "out there," viewers now choose ideologically transparent programming that appeals to their own demographic and worldview. Current events are commercialized and packaged for multiple markets (national and global) and multiple screens (computer, telephone, tablet). In that sense, contemporary television news bears little resemblance to its network ancestors. No longer an ephemeral text by definition, television news can be recycled and replayed on YouTube and throughout the blogosphere. Despite these technological and sociological changes, there are still moments when live television news has an important cultural and ritual function.[5] This chapter examines three moments when television news broadcasts operated in such a fashion, with particular emphasis upon the religious dimension: (1) the Waco siege in February–March 1993; (2) Pope John Paul II's funeral on April 8, 2005; and (3) the Fort Hood shooting on November 5, 2009.[6]

The Waco siege case study begins the discussion by examining nonmainstream religion and the ways in which it is visually and orally framed in the television news. Pope John Paul II's funeral provides an excellent example of a transnational media event even in an age of segmented television audiences. The Fort Hood shooting demonstrates the ways in which civil religion remains dependent on the small screen. In each case, the film footage and the transcripts are explored, paying close attention to what appears and what is absent in these accounts of religion. The result suggests how the "narrative" can be "read" as part of a broader discourse about religion and media in America. The chapter concludes with reflections on TV news and religion within the current context of technological and cultural convergence in which TV news is increasingly (re)played in segments as streaming video and on YouTube.

Waco: A Religious Disaster Marathon[7]

On April 19, 1993, the Mount Carmel Center near Waco, Texas, that was home to the Branch Davidians burned to the ground along with at least seventy-four members of the community.[8] Television cameras captured the tragedy on live broadcasts as American audiences bore witness from their living rooms.[9] Stationed about three miles away from the center (by request from the US government troops) and subject to thirty-mile-an-hour winds, the television crews filmed jumpy images of the rural landscape, with green grass in the foreground and flames rising out of wooden frame buildings in the center on the horizon. Viewers watched as the fire burned out of control, leaping from building to building, with large clouds of black smoke rising above. CNN commentators asked about the arrival of the fire department and its ability to fight such intense flames with limited manpower, equipment, and access to water since the center was not hooked up to the municipal water system. As the fire grew larger and larger and the buildings disappeared in its wake, news commentators queried "experts" about the ability of the inhabitants to survive in concrete bunkers or with gas masks. But the answers given made clear that the possibility of survival was very small given the intensity of the flames. While the fire blazed, CNN reporters telephoned Brad Branch, an imprisoned Branch Davidian, to ask if he knew about a plan by the community to set a fire. He responded in the negative, providing a strong indictment of the government:

> This is a systematic character assassination by the FBI to eliminate the crime scene. Now they are finishing the job right now. Destroying the crime scene. America: this is the biggest lie that has ever been put before the American public ever. Mr. Clinton wants to scapegoat the Attorney General—I don't buy it.[10]

As Branch spoke, images of the fire dominated the screen. The commentator responded with another question about whether there was a plan to set a fire—and then a firm "thank you" that made clear that these controversial comments would not be discussed further. No investigative or critical analysis followed during the subsequent coverage. Instead, commentary focused on conversations with "experts" regarding fire control and the possibility of human survival under the extreme physical circumstances. Later that day, when the flames had been put out and the question of survivors was no longer relevant, the question of responsibility arose more directly. The White House issued a statement that placed responsibility for the fire on the Branch Davidians.

Throughout the conflagration, the images remained constant. The green grass in the foreground and the fenced-off area (with tanks at the border) and the blazing buildings served as the backdrop for voice-overs, usually between the news commentator and an "expert" or between the two commentators.[11] Due to the wind conditions and the uncertainty involved (was there an arms or explosives stock pile?), the cameras remained fixed in their visual perspective producing the images that would be engrained in the collective memory of the audience viewing the final hours of the Waco siege on live television.

And while these images were visually static, they were symbolically dense. They evoked historical connotations as diverse as the viewers watching: the biblical story of Elijah on Mount Carmel when he challenged the prophets of Baal to see which deity could light a sacrifice by fire[12]; book burnings; witch burnings; cross burnings; church burnings; the Holocaust; and other fiery cataclysms. Given that religious history is replete with images of fire and violence against a backdrop of intolerance and prejudice, the potential repertoire for interpreting the image of the burning church in a nondescript rural (read, heartland) setting was vast. The fire could be interpreted as a suicidal death wish or a just punishment for religious apostasy, an operative mistake, a misunderstanding, a lack of religious tolerance, or even government interference and oppression of a minority group. In the aftermath of the tragedy, explanatory narratives offered by the government, anticult advocacy groups, religious studies scholars, right-wing militias, and the media competed for primacy.

Accusations against the FBI, BATF, Janet Reno, President Clinton, and "the media" surfaced from unexpected sources. Religious studies scholars accused the media and the government agencies of dehumanizing the Branch Davidians by their use of terminology such as "cult," "cult leader," and "compound" (instead of "religious community," "sect," "pastor," "spiritual leader," "Mount Carmel Center").

The Branch Davidians, they argued, had been fundamentally misunderstood by the agencies making decisions regarding the siege. Images from the Jonestown mass suicide on November 18, 1978, may have fed the government agencies' sense of urgency to enter the compound. In the aftermath of Jonestown, there had been criticism that authorities had been too slow to interfere until Congressman Leo Ryan was assassinated. Eagerness to preempt a "Jonestown" scenario may have motivated government agencies to intervene more quickly than necessary during the Waco crisis. Scholars also pointed a finger at the media for directly and indirectly assigning the Branch Davidians to the religious fringe, thus legitimating a severe government reaction.[13] By framing the Branch Davidians as a cult rather than a small religious community or religious minority, the media evoked a repertoire of preexisting motifs and themes (child abuse and teen marriage, for example) that demonized the community and ultimately informed the government's decision to act sooner rather than later.[14]

But apart from the question of responsibility or blame for the deadly fire, the Branch Davidians posed a dilemma for mainstream media and religion because of their religious choices, including loyalty to a charismatic leader. Although historians of American religion for almost a decade prior had been revising conceptions of a mainline Protestant America in favor of a more inclusive and pluralistic narrative that accounted for the true diversity in the landscape, these perspectives were notably absent in the journalistic and government accounts of the community.[15] While religious pluralism was tolerated in the historical abstract, the Branch Davidian religiosity and lifestyle violated the transparent consensus (the liberal mainline Protestant paradigm) and by that standard the community could not even be considered Christian by some commentators, despite their clear lineage from Seventh Day Adventism.[16] Government agencies that worked during the siege (BATF and FBI) employed similarly prejudiced understandings when formulating their plans of action. The mainstream media cooperated by adopting this language and approach in an almost uncritical manner.[17]

In a parallel yet different mode of critique, white militia groups likewise pointed a finger at the government's seemingly disproportionate use of force against its own citizens (symbolized by images of tanks stationed around the border of the compound). In the initial coverage of the siege and tragedy, this perspective was not emphasized in the news coverage. Subsequently, the image of Mount Carmel going up in flames was interpreted by some as a symbol of government interference with two basic American "rights"—the right to bear arms and the right to practice religion without hindrance. As sociologist Joel Martin notes: "After Waco, a small minority of Americans developed a different view, one that accuses the federal government of heinous intentional crimes against its citizens. These Americans see Waco as a profound instance of galloping federal domination crushing freedom, a wake-up call for true patriots."[18] There is an irony involved in this interpretation: the icon of the burning church and oppressed religious minority was co-opted by white supremacist militias despite the multiracial nature of the Branch Davidian community. While this tradition may make some of its liberal counterparts uncomfortable, including the journalists who report about it, it is nonetheless an integral part of the broader American narrative about religion, religious freedom, and, ultimately, religious pluralism, providing a competing narrative and tradition to that of the Protestant liberal mainline.[19]

The competing narratives about Waco—the responsibility of the government and the moral problematic of allowing polygamy and underage marriage—reemerged on two future occasions in the media. After the Oklahoma City bombing, the militia critiques of the government's approach in Waco resurfaced as Timothy McVeigh's stated justification for his act of terror. The framing that received so little credence in the media coverage following the Waco siege was front and center during the investigation and media coverage of the Alfred P. Murrah Federal Building bombing.

In April 2008, another image of Waco was recalled when the Texas Child Protective Services removed all children younger than age seventeen from the Fundamentalist Church of the Latter Day Saints (FLDS) property. The media interviewed former Branch Davidians and asked them about underage marriage. A clear parallel was drawn between the Branch Davidians (charismatic leader, plural marriages, teen brides) and the closed community of the FLDS that Warren Jeffs headed. This parallel theme was pursued from another angle in the blogosphere. For example, the conservative blog "Sword-At-The-Ready" (April 24, 2008), titled: "FLDS Tragedy: First they came for the Branch Davidians," is illustrated with a photograph of the FLDS women being separated from their children alongside a photograph of a police tank and armed soldiers. Beneath the photomontage is a reworking of Pastor Martin Niemoller's famous anti-Nazi statement:

> First they came for the Branch Davidians at Waco
> and I did not speak out
> because I was not an alleged wacko Christian cultist with guns.
>
> Then they came for the FLDS church in San Angelo
> and I did not speak out
> because I was not an alleged child-abusing polygamist.
>
> Eventually they came for me, and my church
> and there was no one left
> with any courage or outrage
> to speak out for me.[20]

While broadcast television had employed the comparison with the Branch Davidians to legitimate government intervention, this blog turns the comparison toward another end: to critique government interference in matters of faith.

In both cases, the media coverage generated competing senses of moral panic: on the one hand, the conception of plural marriage with young girls living in a closed religious community with a charismatic leader promoted worries about safety and liberty, and on the other hand, the encroachment of big government appeared to threaten the protected sphere of "freedom of religion." Fifteen years after the event, the images broadcast on television from Waco remained vivid enough to be evoked in the FLDS case as a touchstone for debate about freedom of religion, the rights of children, and the role of the government in the lives of its citizens. While the original television news broadcast provided an alternate framing of this event, marginalizing the Branch Davidians by assuming a mainline Protestant norm and by employing language such as "cult," the competing interpretative frames that emerged almost immediately after the event have had a long afterlife. Reflecting upon the role of the media during disaster events (such as terror attacks), communication scholars Tamar Liebes and Menahem Blondheim have suggested that disaster marathons, like the Waco siege, do not necessarily promote national unity, and may be characterized as "co-productions" of broadcasters and antiestablishment agencies (i.e., the "perpetrators of disruption").[21] Viewed from this perspective, the television coverage of the Waco siege was indirectly coproduced by Branch Davidian leader David Koresh and ironically served to highlight and even promote his antigovernment, antiestablishment agenda. By portraying the Branch Davidians and their leader through a normative mainline Protestant frame (i.e., questioning their "Christianity" and marginalizing them as a cult), the television news broadcast unknowingly played into the hands of right-wing militias and other like-minded antigovernment groups.

The Waco siege was particularly significant to American viewers, but in an increasingly globalized context, television allows for viewers worldwide to participate in celebrations (i.e., the Olympics) and to witness disasters (i.e., earthquakes and tsunamis) as they take place. The second case study focuses on such a global media event—Pope John Paul II's funeral—and illustrates how the small screen continues to have a ritual function, albeit limited to particular (and arguably more sporadic) moments.

The Funeral Mass of Pope John Paul II: The Campaign for Sainthood

The television coverage of the funeral mass of Pope John Paul II on April 8, 2005, was a coproduction of the networks and the Vatican's press office. While nominally a sad occasion, the pope had passed away on April 2, 2005, at the mature age of eighty-four, after serving over twenty-six years as pope.[22] In an Easter week homily the week before, Father Raniero Cantalamessa had noted: "No one knows whether things will really go that way or some other way, but faith gives us the assurance that, whatever may happen, it will not be the total and final end."[23] Pope John Paul II not only adhered to such a vision of death but also had made explicit plans regarding the execution of his funeral and place of burial.[24]

In the days leading up to the funeral, television viewers witnessed long lines of pilgrims arriving in Rome to pay their last respects. During this time, the networks began the buildup for the media event to follow: the funeral itself. Broadcasters in this period emphasized Pope John Paul II's global popularity, noting the funeral was expected to attract over a billion viewers. Implicitly, the televised discussions and references that focused on vast numbers of potential viewers worked to the advantage of the coproducers, the networks, and the Roman Catholic Church, but for different reasons. The former were interested in promoting the rite, and their upcoming television special. Large numbers of viewers generally translates into larger advertisement revenues, a boon in an increasingly competitive television market. For the Vatican, the broadcasters' discussions of audiences operated as a proof text for the strength and relevance of the contemporary Roman Catholic Church. In this liminal moment, prior to the burial of the pope and the election of a new pope, when the future contours of the church were momentarily unclear, the television broadcasts of the crowds affected with such grief portrayed the contemporary relevance and strength of this ancient institution to both members and other viewers at home. Already at this stage, supporters of the pope were beginning to build a campaign for sainthood; establishing Pope John Paul II's worldwide, intergenerational popularity was an important first step on the long road to beatification and canonization. The television broadcasts were an integral part of this process.[25]

In their book *Media Events: The Live Broadcasting of History*, Daniel Dayan and Elihu Katz provided a framework for analyzing three kinds of media events: contest, conquest, and coronation.[26] These are not ordinary television broadcasts: they are by definition (the time in the schedule, type of advertising, camera angles, and commentary) events that are meant to make the viewer feel that he or she is experiencing something out of the ordinary. Notably, since *Media Events* was published in 1992, television has been transformed. With the advent of cable channels that program for every imaginable kind of audience, television viewing rarely unites viewers on a national level like the evening news did during the heyday of network television.[27] Increasingly, television audiences are found in segmented niches and, under these circumstances, media events have an increasingly important ritual function integrating disparate viewers from a variety of contexts that would not have shared the experience otherwise.[28] TV coverage of the pope's death and funeral integrated audiences from around the world, allowing both church members and other interested viewers to participate in the event in a manner different from those that were present in Saint Peter's Square. Lacking the physical sensations of being present at the event (experiencing the smells, noises, and frisson of immediacy), viewers watching from home were compensated with close-up images of the rituals that generated a sense of intimacy and privilege—a sense of being there together. For those less familiar with the rites they were witnessing, commentators provided explanation, allowing for an informed kind of participation. Through the television broadcast, viewers around the world witnessed and participated in a ceremony celebrating the life of one of the most popular popes ever.

Respecting the solemnity of the funeral (like actual participants in the ritual who don't usually speak ill of the dead), television commentators generally refrained from making critical observations either about the Roman Catholic Church or about the pope's leadership. Instead, commentary focused on John Paul II's legacies both to the Roman Catholic Church and to the broader world. Major themes that recurred across the networks included the following: Pope John Paul II's contributions to political change in Poland and Eastern Europe, his policy of promoting tolerance and ecumenism (particularly with Anglican, Orthodox, and Protestant churches), his support for interfaith dialogue (he was the first pope to visit a synagogue and a mosque), his strong relationship with Catholic youth, his media savvy, and his travels around the globe to further his projects and to promote the Roman Catholic Church worldwide.[29]

Perhaps some of the most interesting commentary from the prefuneral coverage concerned the pope's approach to media. John Paul II seemed distinctly different from his predecessors, who had generally viewed secular media with suspicion. In that spirit, on the evening prior to the funeral, ABC's *Nightline* broadcast a show titled "The Media and the Messenger," which began with host Chris Bury proclaiming that the funeral "may be the biggest television event ever." Guests, including Archbishop John Foley, chimed in that John Paul "was convinced that the media were the new means of making contact with people."[30] Bury continued:

> Though he was born seven years before the very first television broadcast, the pope became the most media-savvy religious figure of his time, mastering TV, radio and the Internet as instruments of faith . . . the television audience will number in the billions. Rituals that are centuries old will be beamed and streamed to every corner of the planet. In other words, the pope remains as much a media star in death as he was in life.[31]

The *Nightline* show highlighted this theme with commentators and guests citing the pope's media skills, as well as the ways in which the funeral would be used as a symbolic touchstone by the church: to celebrate the pontificate, to reinforce values that the pope promoted, to promote solidarity among Roman Catholics, and to evoke ecumenical sympathy for the religious leader among non-Catholics. Commentator Cokie Roberts noted that Pope John Paul II learned to use the press conference for dialogue with the world outside the Vatican and unlike his predecessors was therefore willing to answer reporters' questions:

> All the pomp and circumstance of a royal wedding. All the hype of a Super Bowl. All the uproar of a rock concert. He was the most media-savvy pope in history. Theology and technology, two powerful forces, turned out to be even more powerful in union with John Paul's papacy. Rather than railing against the press, as many public figures do, the pope used the media to deliver his message. The year he became pope, 1978, was the same year instant global television first became available, making way for John Paul, Superstar.[32]

These comments and the historical survey of the pope and his media savvy functioned as the prelude to ABC's live coverage of the funeral—which began a few hours later.

As the funeral rite began, the television hosts became participant-observers, quietly explaining behaviors and customs that might seem strange to viewers at home. As the crowds in Saint Peter's Square applauded, the commentators explained for overseas viewers that the practice was quite common in Italian funerals and was meant to express appreciation. The din of the hand clapping could be heard in the background while commentators continued with their explanations of the order of things to come: the colors of the priestly vestments, the uniform long black skirts and *mantias* worn by women in the crowd, the liturgy (translated simultaneously into English when possible), and the provenance and meaning of the rituals.

Meanwhile, the camera panned across the crowds before sharing a historic moment: leaders from the Eastern Orthodox Church offered prayers from the Eastern funeral liturgy, reflecting the efforts of John Paul II to reconcile and bridge the gap with the East. These kinds of details, including the presence of Jewish and Muslim leaders, suggest that the funeral's content had been highly scripted to produce as universal (read, global) an effect as possible. The television coverage was almost anthropological in nature: thick description for the noninitiated. Solemn in tone, the commentators guided viewers through the unfamiliar rituals, providing a visual perspective that those present would be unable to see firsthand (including close-ups of the coffin and the Bibles placed on top of it), except via the large screens that had been set up in the square and nearby.

Reflecting upon the mood in the street, Terry Moran of ABC News reported that people came for different kinds of reasons, including Polish patriotism: "There's a lot of that. But there is also something else in these crowds, and something that undoubtedly John Paul would have enjoyed. Solidarity, for a lack of a better word, really a Christian fellowship in this crowd that you can hear in the songs and prayers that are breaking out in the streets."[33] Comments like these signified to the viewer that television was in a different mode—a ritual mode—and momentarily viewers could join Moran in discarding their critical apparatus and simply feel the "solidarity" on the street. Anchor Charles Gibson asked Bill Blakemore, who covered the two previous papal funerals, if this one was similar. Blakemore's answer not only reinforced the power and hierarchy of the church but also indirectly promoted the cause of the pope's sainthood:

> Charlie, this crowd is just the same as it looked back in 1978. The Saint Peter's Square completely filled. And it reminds me of the fact that what we're seeing here today is the ancient heartbeat of the church reasserting itself. No matter how spectacular a pontificate is, and this one was certainly spectacular, the third longest papacy ever, and an amazing figure of a pope who helped advance the cause of nonviolence in the world, no matter how spectacular, that pope will be buried with the same basic ceremony that all the others were.[34]

Newscasters reinforced the idea of the funeral as a world gathering; the Fox News team noted: "It was the largest gathering of world leaders ever, testament to his ability to bring people together in life and death: seventeen reigning kings, queens, and princes, more than seventy presidents and prime ministers among numerous others." In death, too, the ecumenical, peace-seeking pope was portrayed as sparking rapprochements that he had been unable to achieve during his life. CNN's Wolf Blitzer told viewers that the Israeli president, Moshe Katzav, actually shook hands with the Syrian president, Bashar al-Assad, and exchanged words in Farsi with the Iranian president, Mohammad Khatami.[35]

While the coverage of the Waco siege left the audience divided and conflicted in its interpretation of the events, John Paul II's funeral was scripted with the intention of uniting even disparate and warring factions. The camera focused upon mourners holding signs calling for his beatification, and the media coverage seemed to endorse this sentiment and even predict its occurrence.[36] "Coronation" events with such global appeal are rare in the contemporary media market, but Pope John Paul II's funeral indicates that there are still moments when television acts to provide and promote consensus, including feelings of solidarity among viewers. Reflecting upon the Vatican's approach to the mediation of the funeral on television, Jonathan Mann, CNN correspondent, in conversation with Christiane Amanpour, noted: "even in conversations I've had with the clergy here in Rome over the past few days, they are delighted. They value the message that the media is spreading not only because they are eager to see the pope honored but the message of the church is being spread to places where the church is, quite frankly, not welcome."[37]

The funeral was a natural extension of Pope John Paul II's "friendly" relationship with the media, and the American news media's positive coverage reflected a broader change of attitude toward Catholicism in the contemporary context. Gone were the off-the-cuff critical comments about the papacy and the fears about the Roman Catholic Church's role in the United States that had provided fodder for the popular press in early nineteenth- to late-twentieth-century America.[38] While the commentary surrounding the funeral rituals assumed that audiences would not be familiar with Catholic protocol, the overall tone was ecumenical and respectful. The media coverage of the funeral promoted a positive, consensual image of Pope John Paul II as an important first step in the beatification process. As a quintessential media event, the funeral momentarily united a fractious audience, creating a ritual moment that transcended the screen. For both the networks and the Vatican, the televised funeral was a successful, solidarity-promoting event that emphasized both the importance of the contemporary Roman Catholic Church and the ritual importance of television. While the funeral was not viewed or portrayed through the prism of anti-Catholicism, the comments suggested that the broadcasters assumed that non-Catholics might constitute the principal audience at home.

At the funeral, the Catholic Church employed television broadcasts to enhance and reinforce the authority of institutional religion. The next and last example focuses on civil religion and its dependence upon the small screen.

Fort Hood Eulogy: Civil Religion on the Screen

In his classic 1967 essay, sociologist Robert Bellah argued for a distinctive American civil religion, based on biblical archetypes but separate from particularistic religious traditions.[39] Holidays and rituals that fall under this rubric include Memorial Day, Independence Day, inaugural addresses, presidential holidays, and state funerals. On these occasions, the broadcast audience becomes synonymous with the nation, and leaders have the opportunity to express "deep-seated values and commitments that are not made explicit in the course of everyday life."[40] Given that most citizens are not physically present when a president takes office or delivers a eulogy, television broadcasts of the events are the usual manner in which individuals participate in national rituals. Television coverage of the rituals is an indelible part of contemporary civil religion, and it is also a site for exhibiting conflict. Here, the argument is expressed in terms of liberals and conservatives and their differing understanding of America's divine calling.[41]

On November 5, 2009, a report of a shooting at the United States Army base in Fort Hood, Texas, flashed across the media. Television news teams struggled to eke out information from bystanders, spouses of soldiers inside the base, or anyone else with a connection to Fort Hood. Initial reports suggested that there was more than one shooter and at least one shooter had been killed. Only later were journalists able to relay accurate information about the events. At approximately 1:30 p.m., an army psychiatrist entered the Soldier Readiness Center, shouted "Allah Akbar," and started firing at soldiers. He killed thirteen and wounded thirty more before being shot by a civilian police officer, who then disarmed and handcuffed him. The shooter was identified as Major Nidal Malik Hasan.

At first, television reports simply tried to reassure viewers that it was a single incident and not the beginning of a coordinated attack like 9/11 or bombings in Mumbai, the London Underground, and Spain. The news commentators' initial speculation on the shooter focused on posttraumatic stress disorder (PTSD). Stressing this angle, television coverage focused on the traumas suffered by soldiers who were sent overseas for a second or third round of combat duty. Notably, none of the commentators on CBS, NBC, ABC, and CNN explicitly mentioned the possibility of religious terrorism during the early broadcasts. Even when the news crews had received the name of the shooter, indicating his Middle Eastern origin, most commentators continued to focus on his profession as army psychiatrist—and the possibility that stress propelled him to a shooting rampage. Hesitant to focus on his ethnic origins or his religious affiliations, the television news circled around Nidal's possible motivations, perhaps as part of an effort to avoid the negative stereotypes of Muslims that had become prevalent in post-9/11 American media. One exception to this general approach was Fox News, which notably also received the highest rating on the day of the shooting.[42]

Fox commentators quickly criticized President Obama and the White House for their cautious response to the event, noting from the beginning the possibility that the shooter was a terrorist and that his religious orientations may have provided his motivation. The difference in coverage between Fox News and CNN, NBC, ABC, and CBS was notable.

The events of the Fort Hood shooting challenged the delicate equilibrium that President Obama's administration had been striving toward. His speech in Cairo, only a few months earlier on June 4, 2009, had been a cornerstone in an effort to reformulate American foreign policy toward Islam and Muslim countries. Speculating on the importance of the occasion, Fox News commentator Bill Sammon commented:

> I think it's really going to be key to see the tone and tenor of the Commander in Chief when he addresses this crowd because it's actually a very important moment in his presidency.
>
> Think about this. This is the first time that he's going to be responding in a major way to, really the first major act of terrorism against the United States on our soil. And there's some similarities and some analogies to when President Clinton addressed the nation after Oklahoma City, to when George W. Bush went to address the nation from Ground Zero—both of those times, just like this, were early on in the presidencies, and really, in those earlier two examples, to some extent, they were, uh, forums in which the presidents sort of found their voices, especially if you think about Ground Zero, where President Bush had trouble sort of presenting a real strong, uh, public face for the first couple of days, and then he went to Ground Zero and said, "I can hear you, and pretty soon the people here are going to hear from all of us."

While Sammon viewed the Fort Hood shooting as part of a longer narrative about terrorism beginning with 9/11, Obama's eulogy explicitly sought to counter this framing with a revised version of liberal civil religion, in contrast to the evangelically informed rhetoric of his predecessor.[43]

Network television stations covered the memorial service at Fort Hood on November 10, 2009, and President Obama's eulogy was considered by some to be one of his finest rhetorical moments. Rather than focusing on the shooter or his motivations, or on the war against terrorism, he noted the diversity of American soldiers, celebrated their contributions to the war effort, and noted that their efforts would be remembered and appreciated by future generations. Drawing upon a tradition of civil religion that embraces unity and diversity, he declared powerfully:

> We are a nation that guarantees the freedom to worship as one chooses. And instead of claiming God on our side, we remember Lincoln's words, and always pray to be on the side of God.

The filmed funeral thus was legitimated as a moment of national healing, rather than a means of divisiveness. Yet by invoking Lincoln's words, Obama criticized both the actions of the shooter and those who might justify retaliatory actions by claiming that "God is on our side."

Despite recent technological innovations such as Twitter, Facebook, and the blogosphere that provide audiences with almost immediate means to respond to current events, television continues to endow official ceremonies with an imprimatur of solemnity and to allow audiences to participate in civil life despite geographical distance. After the live broadcast, the television text of the ceremony is often reaired: as a story in the evening news, uploaded on YouTube, and embedded in web pages and blogs for readers to potentially share again and again.[44] If broadcasters frame the live event in a consensual manner, venues such as YouTube provide a forum for viewers with competing interpretations to express their opinions. In the case of the Fort Hood shooting and eulogy, conservative blogs and websites continually contested the official White House version both before and after the broadcast. While the Waco disaster occurred prior to the age of web 2.0 and audience talkbacks, it is similarly invoked retrospectively in the blogosphere, with uploaded television texts available to viewers on YouTube,[45] where interpretations of the events (including documentary films promoting one theory or another) compete for primacy. As a ceremonial media event, Pope John Paul II's funeral generated far less controversy than either of the two disasters reviewed above, but nonetheless, the funeral can be (re)viewed on YouTube and also partially on the Vatican's official website, as well as comments on various blogs and forums about the Roman Catholic Church.[46] Cultural and technological convergence has not diminished the strength of television, but in some cases it has actually amplified texts that would have been ephemeral in the past. These television texts that are recycled and reinterpreted in light of new current events bear witness to the richness and diversity of audience interpretations, which vary from religion to religion and cross the ideological spectrum from liberal to conservative. Still, even in this varied field, the three case studies interpreted above suggest that the implicit frame of comparison for religion in American news remains vaguely Protestant.

NOTES

1. Barbie Zelizer, *Covering the Body: The Kennedy Assassination, the Media, and the Shaping of Collective Memory* (Chicago: University of Chicago, 1992).

2. Judith Buddenbaum, in *Channels of Belief*, ed. John P. Ferré (Ames: Iowa State University Press, 1990); James W. Carey, *Communication as Culture: Essays on Media and Society* (Boston: Unwin Hyman, 1989), 20–21; Stewart Hoover, *Religion in the News: Faith and Journalism in American Public Discourse* (London: Sage, 1998).

3. Carey, *Communication as Culture*, 30.

4. Elizabeth Bird, "Myth, Chronicle and Story," in *Social Meanings of the News: A Text Reader*, ed. Dan Berkowitz (Thousand Oaks, CA: Sage, 1997), 333–50.

5. Daniel Dayan and Elihu Katz, *Media Events: The Live Broadcasting of History* (Boston: Harvard University Press, 1992); Simon Cottle, "Mediatizing Rituals: Beyond Manufacturing Consent," *Media, Culture and Society* 28 (2006): 411–32, doi: 10.1177/0163443706062910; and the response to Cottle by Nick Couldry and Eric Rothenbuhler, "Simon Cottle on Mediatized

Rituals: A Response," *Media, Culture and Society* 29, no. 4: 691–95, doi: 10.1177/0163443707078430.

6. Herbert J. Gans, *Deciding What's News: A Study of CBS Evening News, NBC Nightly News, Newsweek, and Time* (Evanston, IL: Northwestern University Press, 2004); Mark Silk, *Unsecular News: Making News of Religion in America* (Urbana: University of Illinois Press, 1995); Sean McCloud, *Making the American Religious Fringe: Exotics, Subversives, and Journalists, 1955–1993* (Chapel Hill: University of North Carolina Press, 2004). Gans does not address religious preferences of journalists directly in his work, but notes how middle-class values are universalized in the news. McCloud suggests similarly that fringe religion is what defines the mainstream in newsmagazines from the 1950s to the early 1990s.

7. Menahem Blondheim and Tamar Liebes, "Live Television's Disaster Marathon of September 11 and its Subversive Potential," *Prometheus* 20, no. 3 (2002): 271–76; doi 10.1080/08109020210141434; Elihu Katz and Tamar Liebes, "'No More Peace!' How Disaster, Terror, and War have Upstaged Media Events," *International Journal of Communication* 1 (2007): 157–66.

8. The exact number varies report to report from seventy-four to eighty members.

9. Paul Frosh and Amit Pinchevski, eds., *Media Witnessing: Testimony in the Age of Mass Communication* (New York: Palgrave Macmillan, 2009).

10. Waco CNN Live Coverage—Parts 1–3 [Video]. (1993). *YouTube.* Retrieved from http://www.youtube.com/watch?v=5O5TILBOBgk&;feature=related; http://www.youtube.com/watch?v=jUdANLoYtSQ&;feature=related; http://www.youtube.com/watch?v=jRTfEjhdvSo&;feature=related.

11. See, for example, http://abcnews.go.com/video/playerIndex?id=9574125.

12. 1 Kings 18.

13. Scholars have written extensively about Waco and the media. See, for example, James T. Richardson, "Manufacturing Consent About Koresh: A Structural Analysis of the Role of the Media in the Waco Tragedy," in *Armageddon in Waco*, ed. Stuart A. Wright (University of Chicago Press, 1995), 153–76; Anson Shupe and Jeffrey K. Hadden, "Cops, News Copy and Public Opinion," in *Armageddon in Waco*, ed. Stuart A. Wright (University of Chicago Press, 1995), 177–202; John D. Tabor and Eugene V. Gallagher, *Why Waco? Cults and the Battle for Religious Freedom in America* (Berkeley: University of California Press, 1995); James R. Lewis, ed., *From the Ashes: Making Sense of Waco* (Lanham, MD: Rowman and Littlefield, 1994), particularly James A. Beckford, "The Media and New Religious Movements," 143–49, Constance A. Jones and George Baker, "Television and Metaphysics at Waco," 150–56, I. Lamar Maffett, "Waco and the War of the Worlds: Media Fantasy and Modern Reality," 157–64; McCloud, *Making the American Religious Fringe*. As Joel Martin summarizes: "The shocking thing is that most of them agree about what happened: the 'cult' label distorted how journalists and government officials did their jobs" ("Interpreting Waco," *Religion and American Culture* 8, no. 1 [Winter 1998]: 9).

14. See McCloud, *Making the American Religious Fringe*, on the print media's framing of Koresh, 183–91.

15. See R. Laurence Moore, *Religious Outsiders and the Making of Americans* (New York: Oxford University Press, 1987); Catherine L. Albanese, *America: Religions and Religion*, 3rd ed. (Belmont, CA: Wadsworth, 1999). Also see McCloud, *Making the American Religious Fringe*, 187–91, on print coverage of Waco.

16. McCloud, *Making the American Religious Fringe*, quoting James Wall of *The Christian Century*, 187.

17. Martin, "Interpreting Waco," 1–30.

18. Martin, "Interpreting Waco," 12–13.

19. R. Laurence Moore, *Religious Outsiders and the Making of Americans*; Paul Boyer, *When Time Shall Be No More: Prophecy Belief in American Culture* (Cambridge, MA: Harvard University Press, 1992).

20. "FLDS Tragedy: First They Came For The Branch Davidians. . . .," April 24, 2008, http://swordattheready.wordpress.com/2008/04/24/flds-tragedy-first-they-came-for-the-branch-davidians/.

21. Katz and Liebes, "'No More Peace!'" 157.

22. See, for example, the rules that Pope John Paul II formulated regarding photographing the Pope in death: http://www.vatican.va/holy_father/john_paul_ii/apost_constitutions/documents/hf_jp-ii_apc_22021996_universi-dominici-gregis_en.html.

23. http://www.vatican.va/liturgical_year/holy-week/2005/documents/holy-week_homily-cantalamessa_20050325_en.html.

24. See the changes he implemented in the funeral procedures and electoral process of a new pope in the document he wrote in 1996: http://www.vatican.va/holy_father/john_paul_ii/apost_constitutions/documents/hf_jp-ii_apc_22021996_universi-dominici-gregis_en.html.

25. See, for example, the US Conference of Catholic Bishops website on John Paul's beatification: http://www.usccb.org/popejohnpaulii/.

26. Dayan and Katz, *Media Events*.

27. See Menahem Blondheim and Tamar Liebes, "Television News and the Nation: The End?" *Annals of the American Academy of Political and Social Science* 625, no. 1 (2009), 182–95, doi: 10.1177/0002716209338574.

28. Dayan and Katz, *Media Events*, 23.

29. He visited a synagogue in Rome, the Wailing Wall in Jerusalem, and a mosque in Damascus.

30. ABC News Transcripts, *Nightline*, April 7, 2005. Retrieved from LexisNexis Academic.

31. Ibid.

32. Ibid.

33. Ibid.

34. Ibid.

35. Wolf Blitzer, "Pope John Paul II Buried," *CNN News*, CNN, April 7, 2005. Retrieved from LexisNexis Academic.

36. See about the beatification: http://abcnews.go.com/International/pope-benedict-beatifies-pope-john-paul-ii-vatican/story?id=13500062; http://articles.cnn.com/2011-01-14/world/vatican.john.paul.beatification_1_sainthood-process-beatification-ceremony-theological-experts?_s=PM:WORLD; http://www.bbc.co.uk/news/world-europe-13251415.

37. Anderson Cooper, *Anderson Cooper 360*, CNN, April 7, 2005.

38. Philip Jenkins, *The New Anti-Catholicism: The Last Acceptable Prejudice* (New York: Oxford University Press, 2003) 23, http://books.google.com/?id=p5SWol7ciokC&pg=PA23&lpg=PA23&vq=%22the+most+luxuriant,+tenacious+tradition+of+paranoiac+agitation+in+American+history%22. Also note that the blogosphere does suggest alternate interpretations of Pope John Paul II's funeral (i.e., funeral of anti-Christ, etc.). See, for example, http://www.cephasministry.com/index2.html#anchor124274, which is a self-defined fundamentalist Christian website against "cults and false doctrines," which comes up fifth in a Google search for Pope John Paul II's funeral.

39. Robert N. Bellah, "Civil Religion in America," *Dædalus, Journal of the American Academy of Arts and Sciences* 96, no. 1 (Winter 1967): 1–21, http://www.robertbellah.com/articles_5.htm

40. Ibid.

41. On two competing versions of civil religion see Robert Wuthnow, "Divided We Fall: America's Two Civil Religions," *Christian Century*, April 20, 1988, 395–99, http://www.religion-online.org/showarticle.asp?title=235.

42. "Fox News Channel Draws Large Audience for Coverage of Fort Hood Shootings," Media Decoder, *New York Times*, November 6, 2009.

43. Wuthnow, "Divided We Fall."

44. See, for example, the videos of the eulogy uploaded on different websites: http://www.cbsnews.com/video/watch/?id=5604162n; http://www.c-spanvideo.org/program/289929-1; blogs: http://hotair.com/archives/2009/11/10/video-obamas-eulogy-at-fort-hood/; http://www.lifeafterpowerpoint.com/?p=1213; http://www.mofopolitics.com/2009/11/10/video-president-obama-ft-hood-eulogy-111009/; and YouTube analyses: http://www.youtube.com/watch?v=rRKpzHsN1-w&;feature=watch_response_rev; http://www.youtube.com/watch?v=J9pmtfoN2NU.

45. See, for example, the different versions of the pope's funeral that were uploaded on YouTube: http://www.youtube.com/results?search_query=pope+john+paul+funeral&aq=2&;oq=pope+john+paul; and of Waco on YouTube: http://www.youtube.com/results?search_query=waco+texas+branch+davidians&;aq=f.

46. See, for example, references to the mediated funeral: http://forums.catholic.com/showthread.php?t=81007; http://saliu.com/pope-dream.html.

REFERENCES

Bird, Elizabeth. 1997. Myth, Chronicle and Story. In *Social Meanings of the News: A Text Reader*, ed. Dan Berkowitz, 333–350. Thousand Oaks, CA: Sage.

Dayan, Daniel, and Elihu Katz. 1992. *Media Events: The Live Broadcasting of History*. Boston: Harvard University Press.

Frosh, Paul, and Amit Pinchevski, eds. 2009. *Media Witnessing: Testimony in the Age of Mass Communication*. New York: Palgrave Macmillan.

Hoover, Stewart. 1998. *Religion in the News: Faith and Journalism in American Public Discourse*. London: Sage.

McCloud, Sean. 2004. *Making the American Religious Fringe: Exotics, Subversives and Journalists, 1995–1993*. Chapel Hill: University of North Carolina Press.

Silk, Mark. 1995. *Unsecular News: Making News of Religion in America*. Urbana: University of Illinois Press.

CHAPTER 10

RELIGION NEWS ONLINE

DEBRA L. MASON

BLOGGER Rocco Palmo is an apt case study of how the Internet changes the reporting of religion as news. Although Palmo is barely thirty, his *Whispers in the Loggia* is among the most influential religion news blogs in the world.

Scores of journalists in recent decades have tried, but largely failed, to break stories about ecclesiastical appointments and other moves within the Vatican hierarchy. Yet Palmo does so with some success, relying on tips from Vatican insiders, US clergy, lay men and women, and other journalists. While Palmo is certainly a secular media darling, he's also respected within the Roman Catholic Church. In 2010, the Aquinas Institute of Theology in St. Louis bestowed Palmo, then twenty-seven, with an honorary doctorate.

Palmo blogs primarily about issues and appointments within the Roman Catholic Church, employing the standard tools of professional journalism: original reporting and verification. While he is often the first to break a story, Palmo's pledge to verify a news item by three sources before it is published has also earned him a reputation for accuracy. His formula seems to work: more than twenty-one million visitors have viewed *Whispers in the Loggia* since it was established in 2004.

Religion News Online and the Search for Sustainability

Yet Palmo's blog also is emblematic of the problem that has plagued almost all online news outlets in the early twenty-first century: financial viability. Palmo makes meager money from *Whispers in the Loggia*—insufficient even to allow him to afford to move out of his parents' basement. The donation link is prominent on *Whispers in the Loggia*'s home page, but Palmo mostly ekes out his living with freelance assignments.

This disconnect between the perceived importance of an online news site and its profitability has afflicted even the largest online religion news and content site, Beliefnet. In 2002, just two years after being founded with an enviable $26 million in venture capital funding, Beliefnet filed for bankruptcy. When it emerged from bankruptcy several months later, Beliefnet had revamped its mission from a site focused on reporting news as the end goal into a site nurturing feel-good spirituality.

Stark economic forecasts confound every online religion news site referenced in this chapter. Moreover, its discussion of niche online religion sites, mainstream media online religion pages, and independent religion news blogs like Palmo's will show that a sustainable formula for funding online religion news remains elusive.

While delineating this chapter's premise, "news" is interpreted broadly to include the large religion-only site Beliefnet and independent religion blogs such as *Whispers in the Loggia*, along with mainstream news outlets that include *USA Today* and Religion News Service. Although it's clear that social networking sites such as Twitter, Facebook, and YouTube, along with aggregators such as Yahoo! News, act as powerful curators of religion news, the impact of social media on news creation remains in flux. For that reason, social media as a source of religion news is largely omitted from this chapter. Also absent is an analysis of how religion is practiced, transformed, and communicated among the faithful online. Research into how religion is practiced online is well established, with a growing body of work by cultural studies and media scholars across the globe.

One of the earliest examples of religion news online also grew to become the largest independent religion website. Yet as the following case study shows, Beliefnet's early mission to focus on original religion news shifted as its founders sought profits.

Diminishing Returns: News Takes Backseat at Online Niche Pioneer

Steve Waldman, former *U.S. News and World Report* national editor, became the best-known pioneer of and evangelist for online religion news after conceiving of Beliefnet in 1998. Beliefnet was the first major online site intended to bring diverse religion news to national prominence—independent of a traditional news media outlet. The site, cofounded by Waldman and magazine publisher Robert Nylen, launched December 28, 1999, after potential funders passed on Waldman's first pitch to underwrite a print religion magazine to be called *Belief*. Venture capitalists urged an online site instead, showing their enthusiasm with initial investments of $26 million pledged during Beliefnet's first eight months of operation. Nylen, who died in late 2008, served as Beliefnet's first board president and remained on the board until 2007, when News Corp. bought Beliefnet. The site, however, primarily developed under the leadership of Waldman, who was touted as a visionary entrepreneur and shrewd businessman. As Beliefnet's first editor-in-chief, Waldman hired away one of the country's top religion reporters—Deborah Caldwell of the *Dallas Morning News*—to serve as news editor for Beliefnet.

As Beliefnet built its audience, the site looked to other sources of revenue, such as providing websites for churches and other religious groups. Beliefnet created massive e-mail lists, sending out a religious joke of the day or a daily inspiration drawn from every major world religion to subscribers. Beliefnet was a pioneer in creating online communities, too, with forums for support, prayer, and commentary.

At Beliefnet's launch in 1999, "News" was the fourth highest item on the navigation bar and included subcategories such as "Politics," "Science," "Millennium," and "Holidays." The only sections on the navigation bar above "News" were a reference link, "Spirituality," and "Morality." Below the "News" section was "Culture"—defined as books, movies, music and television, humor, and travel. "Family and Parenting," "Teen," and "Milestones" completed the left-side navigational bar of Beliefnet in early 2000. In the early Beliefnet, even pages not labeled as "news" carried significant reporting and news feature content.

Beliefnet also was a pioneer in all of the multimedia components that help distinguish online news content from print, television, or radio. In April 2000, the site featured its first interactive chart asking, "What is an Evangelical?" as part of a column by Fuller Seminary President Richard Mouw on reclaiming the use of "evangelical" from the religious Right. The topic was timely; the religious Right was mobilizing voters in support of George W. Bush's GOP presidential bid in the US primaries. Beliefnet often featured high-profile religious commentators to raise the site's prominence and traffic, some of whom were paid a token fee for their contributions. The site ran news from Associated Press and Religion News Service as well, often supplementing these wire stories with surveys on related topics to engage Beliefnet's audience.

But only six months after its launch, Beliefnet had already been redesigned and had added the statement, "We all believe in something" under its logo. News moved lower in its priorities, too. On the right menu bar, "News" moved from the fourth to fifth position, trumped by the new category of "Community." Community, in various iterations, would become increasingly important—not just to Beliefnet but to many other news sites as well.

Beliefnet, launched in the midst of the Internet boom, reflected the availability of early, easy cash. The company's headquarters in New York City were expensive. To handle its advertising, Beliefnet contracted with famed marketing firm Saatchi & Saatchi for an estimated $15 million in billings. "The pervasive and in turn mainstreaming of spirituality has created a renaissance for matters of the soul in the U.S. and around the world," Beliefnet CEO Tony Uphoff said at the time.[1] The addition of e-commerce to sell books, recordings, and merchandise meant the site's staff grew to more than eighty. A report on Beliefnet by the Project for Excellence in Journalism (PEJ) describes the site's early news focus and quotes a former Beliefnet editor, Paul O'Donnell, who explained that editors hoped Beliefnet would become a forum for the nation's intellectuals to debate the political, cultural, and theological issues shaping culture war debates.

> The times played into Beliefnet's mission during those times. It seemed like almost every story from then had to [do] with religion and culture, from the debate over stem cell research to the battle between the West and Islam after 9/11.[2]

The site's initial editorial approach was guided by core journalistic values, in that it attempted theological and sectarian neutrality, and focused largely on the same sorts of news issues popular in traditional mainstream media.

Despite its early promise, by 2002, Beliefnet had exhausted its venture capital funds and was forced to declare Chapter 11 bankruptcy. The tech bubble burst, leaving Beliefnet cash poor and unable to raise more venture capital dollars. At that time, Waldman was named CEO and was tasked with steering Beliefnet out of bankruptcy. His strategy included freeing the site of labor-intensive nonmedia content, such as the sale of books and merchandise. Waldman laid off all but five of Beliefnet's employees, who had each agreed to work for minimum wage plus a share of company stock. According to one report, the company even sold all its furniture and its employees cleaned company bathrooms. Despite this, Beliefnet remained the only significant online religion news site, with one million unique viewers per month.[3]

Yet as Beliefnet worked to find a profitable business strategy, its content moved farther from an online newsmagazine about religion and more toward a site whose primary mission was to inspire and nurture spirituality. The placement of "Belief-O-Matic," a popular quiz that assigned the user a religion based on the answers to multiple choice questions, was featured more prominently as the years went by. Redesigns were ongoing, and by the start of 2005, the site looked lighter and brighter, reflecting the content as well. "News" as a stand-alone category was renamed "News Features" and promoted content such as "What to Say to Children" and "Interactive Multi-Faith Prayer Circle." A new "Headlines" section midway down on the navigation bar listed mostly wire stories. The "Headlines" category made it easy for Beliefnet to offer RSS feeds beginning in 2005, an important mechanism to distribute religion news—or any other content—directly to readers' computer desktops.

Another redesign in January 2006 put "News" rather than "News Features" as a category back on the home page navigation menu—but positioned it ninth in a list of eleven categories on the navigational bar beneath "Belief-O-Matic," "Spirituality," "Inspiration," "Health and Healing," "Entertainment," "Faiths," "Relationships," and "Astrology." Only the "Discussions" and "Family Life" categories ranked lower. Beyond the navigational menu, Beliefnet's home page included links to popular items, such as "Prayer Finder," "Meditations," "Quizzes," "Sacred Texts,"

"Houses of Worship," "Soulmatch," "Columnists," "Prayer Circles," "Calendar," and "Memorials." The site also became truly multimedia, with the inclusion of audio.

By its seventh year of operation, Beliefnet's business strategy had grown in sophistication, with advertisements and content more closely aligned. Online advertisements for diets and dating took advantage of audience research indicating that Beliefnet's largely female audience valued these topics. Expanded health and wellness content filled Beliefnet's pages. Ironically, as Beliefnet's audiences expanded—albeit at the expense of fewer and less prominent news reports—respect for the site grew, as it won a number of awards for both its content and design. Beliefnet started to benefit from some buzz in news reports, including favorable articles in the *New York Times*, *Time*, and Pew's Project for Excellence in Journalism. Revenues grew, too, at a pace of 50 percent per year between 2003 and 2007. In 2006, Beliefnet reported revenues of $12.6 million, with Disney, Eli Lilly Company, and Pfizer among its advertisers.[4] The new influx of cash allowed Beliefnet to rebuild its staff.

Beliefnet was among the first national sites to build major communities of newsletter subscribers on literally dozens of topics. But during its first seven years, technology had advanced significantly, making the "Religious Joke of the Day" and "Buddhist Meditation for the Day" seem anemic as a community builder when compared to Myspace, Facebook, and the many religion-specific social networks such as www.shmooze.com, www.muslimspace.com, and www.Xianz.com.[5] The personal data that users of social networking sites surrender was recognized as a digital goldmine for marketers. Although Beliefnet was late to include true social networking as part of its business strategy, the potential for revenue proved persuasive.

On October 21, 2007, Beliefnet's home page invited audiences to "Check out our new community." Social networking was promoted as a core feature of Beliefnet and the company put significant resources into developing the network, hoping to benefit from the revenue derived from expanded user data. On November 1, 2007, Beliefnet unveiled a redesigned home page that featured community conversations displayed prominently in a lengthy center column called "Get Involved." Other user-generated content was featured in the "Photo of the Day" and "Video of the Day." This era also began Beliefnet's reliance primarily on "expert" bloggers for news. Although Beliefnet's expansion into social networking was not exceptional, the site was unusual, given its multifaith identity.

With reported unique visitors at three million each month, the site was ripe for acquisition. In 2007, Rupert Murdoch's News Corp. bought the site for an undisclosed price. Beliefnet retooled itself as primarily a site for lifestyle-related spirituality stories and features about popular culture. Beliefnet's themed blogs opined about the religion angles on a diverse array of topics, including politics, popular culture, and the environment.

In November 2009, observers were surprised to learn that after a decade, Waldman was resigning from Beliefnet to lead a project on the future of the media for the Federal Communications Commission. A few months later, News Corp. announced that it was selling Beliefnet, presumably because it failed to generate the desired profits. In late June 2010, after once again laying off a sizable number of its staff, Beliefnet executives announced that BN Media LLC had purchased Beliefnet for an undisclosed sum. BN Media is the investment group behind Cross Bridge Media, a religious online video operator, with several prominent evangelical Christians on its board of directors.

Since the sale to BN Media, some non-Christian content has been sanitized and Christian-themed content displayed more prominently than content of other faiths. "News," as listed on Beliefnet's home page in early 2012, was primarily blog content—void of audio, video, or photos. Among recent news headlines were "So, you're getting married! What kind of wedding do you want?" and "Does the Bible ban tattoos?" Site visitors took note; less than a year after BN Media acquired Beliefnet, audiences—whether measured via page views or time on the site or number of pages viewed—dropped by 25 percent, according to the web analytics site Alexa.[6]

What's proprietary, and thus, unknown to the public, is whether or not changes at Beliefnet in 2010 and 2011 resulted in increased revenues. The question is not immaterial. Ultimately, for religion news to remain online, someone has to pay for it. Until it's clearer what audiences want and how readership affects profitability, economics and online religion content will remain scrutinized in complex ways that are nearly impossible to measure in print and broadcast media.

Search for the Holy Grail: What Audiences Seek Online

Studies show that more than two-thirds of US adults get at least some of their news online—a proportion that is growing. As Kristen Purcell, assistant director for the Pew Internet Project, told Catholic News Service in early 2011, the Internet has blurred the line between news and information, with audiences expecting that information is free and available in multiple places. Online news, particularly, is "portable, participatory, and personal," with consumers increasingly accessing news via mobile phones or mobile applications for phones or tablets.[7]

But what are the interests, in terms of religion news and information, of this growing online audience? According to 2010 data, about half of US adults say there is currently enough coverage of religion and spirituality. In the same survey, 41 percent reported wanting more religion news online. By comparison, 87 percent of those surveyed said sports and athletes get adequate coverage. Out of eleven such categories of news, the only topic with more people seeking expanded coverage was that of scientific news and discoveries.[8]

A 2007 Pew Research Center for the People and the Press report found that when surveying about actual online use, 35 percent of Internet users reported searching for information about religion, which includes but is not limited to news about religion.[9] Precise numbers are hard to gather from media outlets, which view such data as proprietary, yet indicators of the popularity of online religion content can be found. When Cathy Lynn Grossman started her *Faith & Reason* blog at USAToday.com in 2008, it outstripped the paper's most popular blog in the number of comments after only two months. The *Washington Post–Newsweek* collaboration panel blog called *On Faith* claims hundreds of thousands of visitors each month, making it one of the paper's most popular blogs. *Grand Rapids (Michigan) Press* religion columnist Charles Honey's columns are among the most popular content at Mlive.com, a site for all of the Michigan-centric Booth Newspaper chain's most popular online news content. In every case, this popular online religion content was delivered to audiences in the form of blogs or columns.[10]

Online Unable to Reinvigorate Newspaper Religion Sections

But mainstream news' migration online initially went beyond the growing number of metropolitan daily religion news specialists being recast primarily as bloggers. Early on, increased focus by newspapers on their online adjuncts seemed a promising medium for continuing or recreating the 120-year-old tradition of religion sections. These were popular in most metropolitan print newspapers until about 2000, when they began going extinct. Newspapers such as the *Houston Chronicle*, *Arkansas Democrat-Gazette*, and *Salt Lake Tribune* strategized ways to boost their online religion sections, creating faith directories, religious glossaries, databases of religious holidays, diverse blog rolls, and multimedia components such as slideshows or audio stories. But with news staffs at bare-bone levels, few journalists have the time or expertise to develop an online, local replica of printed news sections for faith and values. Today, while online religion news sections exist at some metropolitan-sized newspapers, they are often devoid of locally generated professional religion news and instead filled with user-generated content, such as blog comments, amateur photographs, and forum discussions.

Religion news is further marginalized online because it is so difficult to find on traditional news sites. No direct link to "Religion" or "Faith" news exists on most mainstream news sites' home pages; for most, religion or faith is only included within the submenus of "News," "Local," or "Lifestyle" home page links. One review of home pages for every US daily newspaper showed fewer than 14 percent had any home page link or sublink to faith and values news.[11]

Blogs Fill Gaps Left by Print and Broadcast Media

With mainstream media abandoning coverage of religion, independent blogs such as Rocco Palmo's *Whispers in the Loggia* have grown as a venue for religion news and discourse in the public sphere. In a 2010 report on religion blogs of all kinds, the Social Science Research Council noted:

> Because of their ease of publication and use, blogs have changed the shape of public discourse in society as a whole, and around religious questions in particular. They adjust the bar for entry, making dissemination to a great many readers possible for those who previously couldn't. Blogs also alter the content of that discourse, often privileging the immediate over the reflective and opinion or original research. Nevertheless, blogging is a powerful and flexible medium, one uniquely suited to providing the space for vibrant, diverse, and productive discussions about religion.[12]

Although scant, studies comparing topics covered in legacy news sites versus blogs begin to suggest differences in the themes and topics of such content. Pew data analyzing news events in 2010 showed that religion received more attention in online news blogs than in mainstream print and broadcast media, where religion news typically makes up just 1 to 2 percent of all news. Religion was one of the most-discussed topics on blogs in one-fourth of the forty-eight weeks studied by the Project for Excellence in Journalism and Pew Forum. Stories about the plan to build a Muslim community center and mosque near Ground Zero, for example, were among the top stories in the blogosphere for three weeks in 2010.[13]

The ease with which blogs can be created is also one of their weaknesses. By mid-2011, the blog tracking site BlogPulse.com estimated about 162 million blogs. On May 15, 2011, it reported more than 64,000 blogs created in the previous twenty-four hours. Although ranking sites such as Readit.com, Digg.com, and Technorati.com help curate blogs and posts, religion subjects rarely rank high enough to be prominent on these sites. A fall 2011 Nielsen report ranked the popularity of religion and spirituality sites at fifty-third among seventy-one broad categories of sites, including retail venues and adult entertainment.[14]

Quality among even the most popular religion blogs varies widely, and efforts to use metrics to validate a blog's importance produce wildly divergent lists of the most important religion blogs. What can be said of all such blogs is that they generally include an overt tone, such as the progressive bent in Religion Dispatches—popular among religious studies scholars—or the conservative Christian perspective of former "Crunchy Con" Beliefnet blogger Rod Dreher, who blogged at Beliefnet before he was hired by the John Templeton Foundation in 2009 to edit "Big Questions Online," as well as other publications. Dreher now blogs for the American Conservative.

Even before many of the most popular current blogs got their start, a number of specialized blogs emerged to critique media coverage of religion. A study released jointly by the Project for Excellence in Journalism and Pew Forum in February 2011 described the religion blog scene:

> Get Religion and The Revealer have developed loyal followings for their discussions of how religion is represented in news stories. These blogs, their authors say, have pushed reporters in old and new media alike to be more careful and nuanced in their coverage of religion, suggesting that—contrary to some conventional wisdom—blogs are capable of elevating the level of public discourse and expanding its breadth.[15]

Technology and New Business Plans Key to Future

Recasting religion beat specialists as bloggers and the emergence of popular independent religion blogs is more than a hunch by publishers, editors, or entrepreneurs. It's based in part on better understanding of audience metrics, more accurate analysis of what such metrics mean, and new technologies that are better able to use market data to generate revenue. With these developments, niche sites of all topics are seen as winners in the quest for profitability. Media economists argue that specialized news, honed into online niche news, is the future of news.

"A new generation of innovators is already building 21st century newspapers: nichepapers," Havas Media Lab Director Umair Haque writes in the *Harvard Business Review*'s online site. "Nichepapers are different because they have built a profound mastery of a tightly defined domain—finance, politics, even entertainment—and offer audiences deep, unwavering knowledge of it."[16]

Large media enterprises have adapted the notion of niche papers by creating specialized subpages housed within larger sites. Thus, in the past two years some of the largest online news sites have added niche pages, sometimes called "verticals." This trend is particularly evident at the *Huffington Post*, CNN.com, and USAToday.com, all of which have added online religion sections since late 2009. In every case, religion has been included among the first niche sections added at the media outlet, most often joining health, entertainment, sports, and business as specialized topics. At the *Huffington Post*, specialized journalists and religion experts have been hired to inform news choices. For example, in 2011, the *Huffington Post* hired Jaweed Kaleem away from the *Miami Herald*, where he was an award-winning religion journalist. Kaleem writes news features for the religion section of the *Huffington Post*. Similarly, CNN.com has increased its staff to include Dan Gilgoff, a specialist in religion and politics. At USAToday.com, religion content was expanded online by using wire service content and, as previously discussed, recasting its religion reporter as a blogger who posts frequently rather than writing longer features for the print version of *USA Today*.

These online verticals differ from the old-fashioned print religion sections in that they reflect a national and even global perspective on the news they distribute. The heavy reliance on blog content, editorially, can resemble advocacy. Notices of events, institutional religious activities, and non-deadline-style news are not hallmarks of these sites. As such, these strategies as a business model may not be effective at the local media market. Similarly, it is too early to determine how such niche components of larger sites are contributing to overall sustainability of the for-profit news sites that house them.

Some categories of online niche news sites—namely, investigative reporting and health news—have forsaken the search for profits altogether. Although nonprofit news entities have existed for decades, by 2010, news startups seeking nonprofit status to fund their sites via donations and foundations grew exponentially. The IRS has received so many applications that it crafted its own internal guidelines to help determine whether or not a news venture can be legitimately considered nonprofit.

Given this growing general interest in nonprofit media business models, it's not surprising that niche religion sites have also eyed the nonprofit model. Two nonprofit broadcast religion news and interview sites expanded their online presence with unique content: the PBS half-hour weekly program *Religion & Ethics Newsweekly* and the hour-long radio show *Krista Tippett on Being* (formerly called *Speaking of Faith*). *Religion & Ethics Newsweekly* content is viewed as much or more online than via local PBS television outlets, where the program often airs during the early morning hours. Yet neither program could exist without heavy subsidies from grant funders. Neither site has drawn significant donations from individuals, and both rely on administrative support from their public broadcasting partners—New York's WNET-13 in the case of *Religion & Ethics Newsweekly* and Minnesota Public Radio for *On Being*.

By May 2011, a new nonprofit religion news experiment was announced: the conversion of Religion News Service from for-profit ownership by Advance Communications to nonprofit ownership under a new nonprofit corporation created by Religion Newswriters Foundation. The project was funded by a three-year, nearly $3.5 million grant from Lilly Endowment Inc. The Washington, DC-based news service was founded in 1934 as a nonprofit but was acquired by the for-profit, privately held Advance Communications in 1994. The news service, which was distributed only to media subscribers for its first seventy-six years, sought to protect itself from declining subscriptions by traditional media outlets with plans for a robust, free website. The project included creating models for community-based religion news sites that could take advantage of preexisting social networks to fill the void in local models for quality religion news.

The nonprofit business model frees owners of online media from the need for profits; yet even nonprofit news organizations must break even. Thus, most nonprofit news sites continue to rely on a variety of revenue sources, including sponsorships, grants, individual donations, advertising, and merchandise sales. It remains to be seen if Religion News Service's return to nonprofit status and its network of local or regional sites will succeed.

Like hundreds of other media experiments across the globe, the Religion News Service quest to fund and sustain quality online religion news continues. Yet, hope remains that religion news will benefit from the plethora of new media experiments, refined business models, and technological advances creating solutions for the financial conundrums that plague all online news sites.

NOTES

1. Pamela Parker, "Spiritual Site Beliefnet.com Taps Saatchi & Saatchi for $15 Million," *Clickz.com*, February 29, 2000, http://www.clickz.com/312331.

2. "A Spiritual Network Grows on the Net: PEJ Backgrounder," *Journalism.org*, June 11, 2007, http://www.journalism.org/node/5982.

3. Joe Nocera, "Talking Business: Keeping Faith in a Venture Built on Faith," *New York Times*, May 5, 2007.

4. Ibid.

5. Katie Zezima, "Web Space: Where Religion and Social Networking Meet," *New York Times*, June 30, 2007.

6. http://www.alexa.com/siteinfo/Beliefnet.com# (accessed February 27, 2010).

7. "Trends to Watch: News and Information Consumption" (PowerPoint presentation by Kristen Purcell, Pew Internet Project, to *Catholic News Service*, March 24, 2011), www.pewinternet.org/~/. . ./KPurcell%20Catholic%20News%20Service.ppt (accessed April 6, 2011).

8. Ibid., 26.

9. "Pew Internet & American Life Project Poll, February 2007," Pew Internet & American Life Project, Pew Research Center, 2007.

10. Kimberly Winston, Untitled and unpublished report to Religion Newswriters, February 2009. Interviews conducted January 2009.

11. Mary C. Cupito, "The Missing Link: A Content Study of Religion as a Navigational Element on the Home Pages of U.S. Daily Newspapers" (paper presented at the annual convention of the Association for Education in Journalism and Mass Communication. San Francisco, CA, August 2006).

12. Social Science Research Council, "The New Landscape of the Religion Blogosphere" (undated PDF), p. 8. Released online March 2, 2010, http://www.ssrc.org/publications/view/F9D3E92C-2A2E-DF11-9D32-001CC477EC70/.

13. "Religion in the News: Islam Was No. 1 Topic in 2010," Project for Excellence in Journalism and Pew Forum joint release, February 24, 2011, 3.

14. Nielsen, "State of the Media: The Social Media Report," third quarter, 2011, http://www.nielsen.com/us/cn/insights/reports-downloads/2011/social-media-report-q3.html?status=success.

15. Social Science Research Council, "New Landscape," 29.

16. Umair Haque, "The Nichepaper Manifesto," *HarvardBusinessReview.com*, July 27, 2009, http://blogs.hbr.org/haque/2009/07/the_nichepaper_manifesto.html.

REFERENCES

Mason, Debra. 2010. Religious News in the Age of the Internet. In *Faith, Politics & Press in Our Perilous Times*, ed. Steve Burgard, 67–76. Dubuque, IA: Kendall Hunt Publishing.

Religion in the News: Islam Was No. 1 Topic in 2010. 2011. Project for Excellence in Journalism and Pew Forum joint release. February 24, 2011, p. 3.

Social Science Research Council. 2010. The New Landscape of the Religion Blogosphere. Undated PDF, p. 26. Released online March 2, 2010. http://www.ssrc.org/publications/view/F9D3E92C-2A2E-DF11-9D32-001CC477EC70/.

A Spiritual Network Grows On the Net: PEJ Backgrounder. 2007. *Journalism.org*, June 11. http://www.journalism.org/node/5982.

SECTION III

RELIGIONS

CHAPTER 11

AMERICAN CATHOLICISM AND THE MASS-MARKET NEWSWEEKLY

PETER MANSEAU

"Entwined . . . in Death as in Life"

Narratives of early American history often find their conclusion with the tale of the near-simultaneous demise of John Adams and Thomas Jefferson, on July 4, 1826. Daniel Webster, among other contemporary eulogists, spoke of the shared moment of death of the second and third presidents of the United States, arriving as it did fifty years to the day after the signing of the Declaration of Independence, as evidence that the young nation enjoyed the affection of the divine. According to David McCullough, the two men themselves had used their late correspondence to explore the influence each had on the other, as if they as much as any later historian saw their overlapping final days as an opportunity to take stock of an era at its end.[1]

Whatever one may say of the mythologizing attempt to make meaning of an accident, the connected deaths of Jefferson and Adams serve as a reminder of why such occurrences make for compelling storytelling, if not always reliable history: the coincidental endings of two distinct lives provide a lens through which to view both their joint significance and surprising interdependence.

To find a contemporary example of coincidental deaths that call out for interpretation as clearly as those which closed the book on the American Revolution, we would do well to consider not just human mortality, but the waning of cultural forces. Considered this way, it is noteworthy that, throughout the first decade of the twenty-first century, some heard death rattles of the dominant influence of two major players in twentieth-century American life: Roman Catholicism and the mass-market newsweekly.

Beginning with the clergy sexual abuse crisis in 2001, the Roman Catholic Church—not just as one faith tradition among others, not just as the single largest denomination in the United States, but as a molder and shaper of American culture and politics—suffered a blow to its credibility as never before. According to the John Jay Report on sexual abuse in the church, more than 10,000 victims in the United States made claims against more than 4,000 priests from the 1950s through the time of the 2004 study. By the decade's end, similar cases had sprung up in more than twenty countries, with more than a billion dollars spent on settlements and legal fees.

More costly still was the price the church paid in social capital. According to a May 2010 *New York Times* poll, 36 percent of the general population (as distinct from self-identified churchgoers) developed a more negative feeling toward the Roman Catholic Church as a result of its handling of the sexual abuse.[2] As the prominent dissident theologian Hans Kung noted midway through 2010, the church was at that time "going through its worst crisis of confidence since the Reformation."[3]

The situation was no less bleak for another major cultural force of the twentieth century: the mass-market newsweekly. The crisis it faced during this same period was one of not just confidence but also the bottom line. According to the Associated Press and Reuters, *Newsweek* lost $16 million in 2008 and $29 million in 2009, and, at the time of this writing, was on pace to lose more than $20 million in 2010. While once they were the dominant media of the "American century" (to use a phrase coined in *Time*), newsmagazines seemed already to have outlived their usefulness by that century's final days. Ten years into the new millennium, it was not just *Newsweek* that hit on hard times. *U.S. News and World Report* abandoned the newsstand for the web in 2008. Two years later, *Time* began offering subscriptions at 93 percent off the cover price, a desperate bid to bolster a subscriber base that hadn't grown in forty years.

The symbolic death of the newsweekly as a genre—or perhaps the moment when the next of kin must decide whether or not to allow life support to continue—came with the Washington Post Company's announcement that it would sell *Newsweek* lest it put the company as a whole at risk. It was, the *New York Times* said, the end of the era of the newsweekly.[4] As Slate.com's media watchdog Jack Shaffer wrote:

> The 30-year debate in the journalism reviews, among industry analysts, and over beers between reporters about the fate of the newsweekly category was settled today by Washington Post Co. Chairman Donald E. Graham, who announced that he wants to sell *Newsweek*. If the infinitely patient and hideously rich Graham can't see a profitable future for the money-losing magazine, that future doesn't exist.[5]

Like the church, the newsweeklies' financial loss was but a symptom of a larger problem: the loss of authority, and along with it, a near-complete diminishment of respect that until then had been taken for granted. A 2009 CBS/*New York Times* poll found that just 1 percent of the American public received its news mainly from magazines.[6] Compare that to the assessment made in the 1960s by Robert M. Hutchins, former chancellor of the University of Chicago, when asked about the cultural influence of *Time*, *Life*, and their progenitor, Henry Luce: "I might even say that Mr. Luce and his magazines have more effect on American character than the whole education system put together."[7]

It could be argued that in both cases—the church and the newsweekly—we have seen not a death but rather a moment of evolution, that the change forced upon each will ultimately lead to stronger institutions. Yet, given that no less a champion of the church than Pope Benedict XVI declared that "sins within" were the faith's greatest threat, and that no less a champion of the newsweekly than the editor of *Newsweek*, John Meachem, referred in the same month to the "existential crisis" of the format, it would seem the damage endured by each may indeed be transformative, but not positively so. If this was a moment of evolution, then newsweeklies and the church were perhaps the victims rather than the beneficiaries of natural selection.

While less dramatic than the dying breaths of Adams and Jefferson, the possible ends to be discussed here may yet prove more significant. An individual death ultimately dims only one set of eyes; institutional deaths are suggestive of the passing of ways in which entire cultures understand the world. Taken together, the rise and fall of the dominant influence of the Catholic Church and mass-market newsweekly demonstrate how two institutions separate in origin and purpose can come to seem, as McCullough noted of the last of the Founding Fathers, "entwined . . . in death as in life."[8] They may also mark the close of a larger era: the age of the iconic image.

Art, History, and the News

Throughout the twentieth century, no element of the media bestowed iconic status on an image with anything close to the force of the cover of a weekly newsmagazine. For a third of the nation's history (from the founding of the first newsweekly in the 1920s through the alleged end of the era of the newsweekly in 2010), the covers of the most influential magazines—*Time*, *Life*, and *Newsweek*—acted not only as windows into the soul of the nation but also as the stained glass of the newsstand. They retold the narratives of American concern in a medium more immediate than text, less ephemeral than radio, more concrete than television or any other flickering screen.

The bygone significance of newsweekly covers is captured well by one-time *Newsweek* editor Edward Kosner. Speaking of the highpoint of their influence in the 1960s and '70s, Kosner told the *New York Times*:

> [I]n those days . . . it was really important what was on the cover of *Newsweek* and what was on the cover of *Time* because it was what passed for the national press. They helped set the agenda; they helped make reputations. . . . On Monday mornings, on the advertising page of the *Times*, *Time* and *Newsweek* took out sort of quarter-page ads that showed the cover and everyone turned to that page on Monday mornings to see what each of them had done.[9]

The place of religion in these peculiar products of American media is noteworthy in general—*Folio* magazine has reported that putting the Bible on a magazine's cover can increase sales by 51 percent[10]—and the place of Catholic representation is particularly so. Throughout the twentieth century, the leaders, imagery, and concerns of the Roman Catholic Church appeared more often than those of any other religious group on the covers of newsweeklies. In *Time*'s archive of cover images, Catholic subjects—including depictions of prominent clergy and religious art, as well as newsmakers whose membership in the church was part of the magazine's coverage—rank among the top ten, behind categories like business, military, technology, and US presidents, but ahead of civil rights and space exploration. Even counting only those covers which show official representatives of the church, Catholics outnumber Jews, Muslims, Buddhists, Hindus, and Evangelicals combined.

Perhaps the main reason for the overrepresentation of Catholics is that, during their simultaneous rise and fall in public influence, the church and the newsweekly often seemed a message and a medium perfectly aligned in purpose and application. The roots of this alignment can be found in early Christian history: since the fourth century, when the faith adopted the cross as its symbol par excellence, the Catholic Church has survived and prospered in large part due to its success in filtering a world-conquering narrative through a single image. As the liturgical artist David Clayton suggests, the conversion of Constantine not only made Christianity the religion of the emperor but also created an opportunity for a new form of large-scale visual storytelling on the walls of the newly baptized buildings of the empire. Considering the mosaic "Justinian and His Retinue" in the Church of San Vitale in Ravenna, Italy, Clayton notes that compared to the art that had immediately preceded it, "the figures are much more stiff and formal. . . ."

> All are portrayed full-face, none in profile. The negative "space" around the figures is not devoted to the depiction of the illusion of depth. The figures almost give the appearance of cut-outs pasted onto a flat surface. [This] deliberate stylization and can be accounted for in terms of the Christian understanding of the human person and our place in Creation. For example, the flat negative space is a visual representation of heaven or the fullness of God, the eternal sphere where there is no time and no space.[11]

Christian iconography differed from the pagan and Jewish art that came before in part because it made one man—Jesus Christ—the prototype for the depiction of all others. A single face stood for every face; a single story came to be seen as the ultimate meaning of every other story. Even as Western Christian art matured and became increasingly ornate with each passing century, the beguiling simplicity of the iconic image retained its mystique, as well as its primary role in places of worship, which of course were also places of power. Icons were at once aspirational and prescriptive: they showed those who viewed them what men and women might be while simultaneously reminding those viewers that their lives would be judged against figures larger than life. Like the Emperor Justinian in the Church of San Vitale, to have one's own image rendered as an icon was to join the communion of saints. In the mass media of the day, iconic images were signifiers of unquestionable authority.

Sixteen centuries later, the newsweeklies found success through a similar form of visual narrative. The early covers of *Time* exclusively feature images much like those described by Clayton: single faces staring full-faced from the page, meeting the reader's gaze. Most of these images offered little in terms of context or decoration; the face was all, creating the dual impressions of immediate relevance and history in the making—the double promise of the bold red title three inches above the cover figure's eyes. It might even be said that while the "flat negative space" framing each cover figure was not "a visual representation of heaven or the fullness of God," it was a visual representation of "time" in the abstract, a secular translation of an icon's divine eternity.

Early covers of *Newsweek*, founded in response to *Time*'s success, broke with this tradition, but only briefly. Hoping to compete through difference, *Newsweek*'s first issue displayed seven images arranged as if in storyboard below the banner. The magazine's adoption of the *Time* approach in subsequent issues signaled that the newsweekly had found its dominant aesthetic. Though the early images looked, according to one contemporary wag, "like they had been engraved on pieces of bread,"[12] the act of reducing all the world's events to a single face immediately captured an audience, setting the newsweeklies apart in a media marketplace nearly as crowded as today's.

Yet of course, just as Christianity signified by the cross might be charged with reducing the Gospels to the crucifixion, so too did the newsweeklies' single-image design reduce the world to an ongoing narrative of "great men" (and occasional "great women" as well) shaping the world in which the rest of humanity lived. The Catholic Church, likewise invested in a narrative of "great men," not only benefited from this approach but also contributed to it. Inevitably, the frequent use of Catholic imagery by the newsweeklies affirmed some aspects of Catholic culture at the expense of others, creating a variety of Catholic expression codified not by Rome but by New York. This influence was not one-directional, however. For even as the newsweeklies began to shape the image of Catholic culture in America, the aesthetics of that culture helped inform the distinctive visual storytelling of the new medium.

Much like Gutenberg's printing revolution and Luther's Reformation in the sixteenth century, Catholicism and the mass-market press made in the twentieth century a near-perfect marriage of technology and theology. For this reason, the changing meaning and status of the Roman Catholic Church in the United States can be seen, as if in a slideshow, through a survey of the covers of the three most influential newsmagazines from their ascendency to their current decline.

Newsweeklies and Religious Authority

The mass-market American newsweekly was not a Catholic creation, but rather the creation of a man who found himself in bed with the church in more ways than one. For Henry Luce, there was of course the actual Catholic with whom he shared his home—his second wife, Clare Boothe Luce—but there was also, through her influence and through his own political sensibilities, the common cause to which he and the midcentury church were most piously devoted—the defeat of Communism wherever it arose in the world. Luce's primary weapon in this fight was *Time* magazine, which declared in its founding mission statement that on certain issues it would most definitely take sides: "The editors recognize that complete neutrality on public questions and important news is probably as undesirable as it is impossible, and therefore are ready to acknowledge certain prejudices which may in varying measure predetermine their opinions on the news."[13] Through *Time*, Luce made an ally of any institution that he deemed similarly biased, and in so doing, perhaps more than any other individual, he domesticated Catholicism for American consumption.

Time began as the brainchild of two recent Yale graduates: Luce and Briton Hadden, both just twenty-four years old. Boyhood rivals, they had pushed each other since prep school before finally making peace as collaborators rather than competitors. While Hadden was a son of privilege turned flamboyant figure of the Jazz Age, Luce was the son of missionaries. He was born in China to a former YWCA volunteer and a Presbyterian minister. The family's mission—spreading the Gospel—and its personal consequence—separation from America—instilled in young Luce an evangelical zeal less for the particulars of his faith than for that place he heard of constantly but would visit only once before the age of fifteen. The longing he felt for life in the United States made it his Zion, and the feeling did not fade when he was finally able to make the promised land his home. "No nation in history, except ancient Israel," he would later say, "was so obviously designed for some special phase of God's eternal purpose."[14]

Hadden died when *Time* was just five years old, and so it was the preoccupations of his partner that would come to control the future of the newsweekly. Whereas Hadden had been irreverent, sarcastic, and drawn to eccentricity, Luce was forever the missionaries' son, a man impressed by authority and its capacity to transform the world.

As one of his early biographers said, Luce "respected anybody who took a traditional religion seriously, whether Presbyterian, Roman Catholic, or Orthodox Jew, and deplored Unitarians, lapsed Catholics, and Reformed Jews." The magazine followed suit. Coverage of religion in *Time*—and to varying degrees in newsweeklies generally—tended toward the affirmation of the powers that be. Yet Luce also knew that he had a magazine to sell, and he recognized—perhaps through Hadden's lingering influence—that the occasional appearance of indifference to power created authority all its own.

Time's peculiar relationship to authority can be seen in its first conspicuously Catholic cover, which on June 16, 1924, featured a typical "great man" portrait of Pope Pius XI. It is an entirely straightforward cover but for the two-word caption printed beneath the pope's portrait: "No Popery!"

Luce in the beginning had been the business side of the collaboration with Hadden, and it is not hard to read this flourish as a business decision. The 1920s saw an explosion of anti-Catholic sentiment across the United States; according to Edward Cuddy, of all the many hatreds of the era, anti-Catholicism was arguably the strongest.[15] Not a few contemporary publications existed to exploit this fact. Luce, however, wanted to sell magazines to *everyone*.

How, then, to sell a publication to those who fear popery as well as those who fear the accusation of such? For Luce it was simple: put the pope himself on the cover directly above the word "popery" and let the interplay of text and image serve as a Rorschach for the prospective magazine buyer. Only after the article had been read would the reader wonder if there had been a bait-and-switch. The cover caption referred to words appearing in the related article, where "No Popery" was quoted as a cry often heard in England a full century before. Provocative on the cover, the caption was shown to be an archaism on the pages within. By the end of the article, the reader would find Pius XI described favorably as "a Pontiff who permits baseball to be played in the Vatican grounds and who enjoys watching the game from his window." Exploiting anti-Catholic shorthand for the threat Catholics offered to American ideals, this first appearance of the pope on the cover subtly suggested that *Time* readers had nothing to fear. No popery, indeed.

Putting the pope on the cover—as well as other prominent clergy—became a common trope for *Time*. Catholic clergymen provided the young magazine with the opportunity to maintain the "great man" approach to which it hewed through its first decade, even as it stretched the possibilities of the aesthetic. The choice to feature men of the cloth in their ecclesial finery, complete with vibrant trims and exotic hats, eventually allowed a quite natural use of color on an otherwise drab newsstand. The next Catholic cover of *Time* had the dual distinction of being the first depicting an American churchman (George Cardinal Mundelein, archbishop of Chicago) and the first to include color in the form of an eye-catching orange bar down the left side of the page.

With such covers, which included three others cardinals and two additional images of the pope in the magazine's first fifteen years, *Time* put faces to the Catholic hierarchy as never before. Other publications of the day often featured cartoons of the "Roman menace"—in the spirit of Thomas Nast's infamous tooth-hatted bishops crawling like crocodiles onto American shores—but Luce framed his Catholic cover subjects within a week-to-week serial of significant individuals of whom lesser mortals should take note. Moreover, when one of the cover cardinals—Eugenio Pacelli—eventually became pope himself, *Time* could claim status not merely as Catholic observer, but as Catholic kingmaker as well. No matter that much of the American reading public may fear "popery," Luce's belief in the positive power of religious authority extended well beyond the denomination of his youth.

But faith in authority could at times blind *Time* to other realities of belief. Nowhere was this better seen than in one of Luce's few misreadings of the American political landscape. Famously partisan in support of his beloved Republican Party, Luce broke ranks and supported Democrat Al Smith for president in 1928. Smith was the first Catholic nominated by a major party, as well as the four-term governor of New York. Luce backed Smith editorially and put him on the cover in the lead-up to the election. Rather than a liability, Luce saw Smith's Catholicism as an asset, an alternative to the "moral leaderlessness" he identified with the Republican candidate, Herbert Hoover.[16] "The gift [Roman Catholicism] has given," Luce would later say, was "the gift of moral authority." Discounting as a fringe position the virulent anti-Catholic rhetoric of the likes of Alabama Senator James Thomas Heflin, *Time* judged that "unless the U.S. is at heart intolerant, bigots of the Heflin type will have eliminated Roman Catholicism as a consideration in June and November."[17]

That crucial "unless," true to Luce's unshakable faith in the American proposition, assumed that the United States was *not* "at heart intolerant." In the 1928 election, however, this turned out to be a questionable conclusion. Luce believed, as if by creed, that the majority of Americans felt as he did, that all religious authority—even Catholic authority—was worthy of respect. Informed by that belief, he was caught off guard when Smith lost in a landslide. As Hadden's biographer suggested, "*Time* missed the big story of the election" by seeing only one way religion might influence the outcome.[18]

Perhaps chastened by this encounter with American anti-Catholicism, *Time* covers through the 1930s and '40s favored Catholic subjects with international frames of reference. In the magazine's second and third decades, the clergymen to appear on the cover were not unlike the magazine's editor: men of the missionary mold who did not shy away from politics. Each of the three American cardinals featured on covers during this time had cut their ecclesiastical teeth through postings in Asia.

In the postwar era, the surest way for a Catholic to find himself on the cover of *Time* was to share Luce's growing concern for the influence of the Soviet Union in Eastern Europe and around the world. The American Catholics appearing on covers in the 1950s—Cardinal Francis Spellman of New York, Cardinal Richard Cushing of Boston, the flamboyant television preacher Bishop Fulton J. Sheen—were all native-born prelates who saw their Catholicism as part of their patriotism and understood both as creeds that made Communism anathema. Likewise, *Time*'s coverage of the church in Europe favored those clergymen who served on the frontlines of the Cold War: Hungary's Cardinal József Mindszenty and Poland's Cardinal Wyszynski, each of whom had won victories over Soviet influence in Eastern Europe.

There were undoubtedly differences among the men chosen to represent the Roman Catholic Church on the cover of *Time*. (A champion of labor like Cardinal Mundelien would have been outraged that Cardinal Spellman's anti-Communism once led him to use seminarians as strikebreakers, for example.) Yet what they all had in common was a quality the early writers of the magazine liked to call "churchmanship."

Wherever it appears in *Time*, churchmanship seems to refer to an ability to use the resources of religion to effect practical change in the world. An echo of this can be heard in the commencement speech Luce gave at the Princeton Theological Seminary in 1962. With a joke about the differences between two churches celebrating the feast day Trinity Sunday, he suggested two ways of thinking about the power associated with religion. At an Episcopal church, he said, "the rector gave an extended explanation of the Holy Trinity. The children fidgeted almost beyond control, which was the only thing that kept their parents awake." Meanwhile, at a Catholic church, Luce continued, a pastor delivered a sermon of his own: "My friend, this is Trinity Sunday," the priest in Luce's story said. "I'm not going to tell you about the Trinity because you wouldn't understand it. But don't let that bother you—the Church understands it. Now, about the new parking lot which hasn't been paid for yet."[19]

Churchmanship, in Luce's estimation, was the ability to pay for the parking lot: temporal power as brokered by spiritual authority. Focus on churchmanship affirmed a vision of the Catholic Church as an overwhelmingly male, rigidly hierarchical organization that was primarily political rather than pastoral. As seen from the cover of *Time*, then, Roman Catholicism looks familiar to anyone whose sole view of the church is that which occurs behind the altar or in the inner sanctum of the Vatican. Only a handful of times over the course of hundreds of Catholic covers were *Time* readers shown anything of Catholicism as it is experienced in the pews—not to mention the hospitals, charities, and schools whose growth in the twentieth century was the surest sign that Catholics were enjoying a period of social ascendency.

As for those Catholics often credited with the success of such institutions, "churchmanship" was a quality categorically denied to them. While a handful of Catholic laywomen made *Time*'s cover through its first forty years, it was not until 1970 that a woman appeared to illustrate a story about the church.

Readers hoping to gain insight into what it actually might mean to live as an American Catholic who was not a member of the clergy were better served elsewhere. Through much of its history, *Time*'s blind spot to certain kinds of Catholic stories was compensated for, to some extent, by its sister publication, which came to being at the suggestion of Luce's second wife.

Claire Boothe Luce was not a passive influence in Luce's life, nor was she a passive Catholic. Perhaps one of the most influential Catholic converts in American history, she learned the faith at the knee of Bishop Fulton J. Sheen and counted among her friends the bestselling author and monk Thomas Merton. She persuaded Luce to transform their 7,000-acre South Carolina estate into a Trappist monastery (where they both were later buried) and likewise convinced her husband to break new ground with the first national magazine of photojournalism.

From its start in 1936, *Life* offered a very different take on the place of religion in America. While *Time*'s religious coverage moved within an orbit held by the gravity of political authority, *Life* offered glimpses of religion as lived. For example: The magazine's first Catholic cover showed a nun bent over an industrial-sized kitchen bowl, kneading a ball of dough so large it seems she might lose an arm. Over the caption "Franciscan retreat," the image forecasts that *Life*'s Catholic coverage will differ from *Time*'s in a number of ways. First and most obviously, it depicts a woman; second and perhaps less so, it depicts *work*. The lives of Catholics, the picture says, do not require the stillness or the clerical luxury depicted in many of *Time*'s cover images of prelates and popes. As if intentionally undoing the gender imbalance of the older publication, the next Catholic cover of *Life* (on September 2, 1940) showed the then-famous Dionne sisters (the first known quintuplets to survive infancy) as they prepared for their First Communion. Dressed in identical white dresses and holding gold-leafed prayer books, the five 6-years-olds equal the number of identifiably Catholic women to appear on the cover of *Time* throughout its full history.

Life's cover images of lived religion would continue with depictions of a Catholic baptism in the 1950s (part of the photo essay "Seven Sacraments" by Gordon Parks[20]) and a Catholic wedding in the 1960s (the marriage of Lyndon Johnson's Catholic-convert daughter Luci[21]). Added to this was *Life*'s frequent coverage of the Kennedy family, which John Kennedy himself would later acknowledge may have made the difference in 1960. This was no accident: Dating back to the 1930s, Luce personally played a role in the coverage of the Kennedy clan. After twice featuring his friend Joseph Kennedy on the cover of *Time*, Luce took a special interest when Kennedy's son John entered the world of publishing with his first book, *While England Slept*, for which Luce wrote an introduction. When the younger Kennedy became a Democratic senator and seemed likely to begin a bid for the presidency, Luce reined in his magazine's Republican bias. For arguably the first time, the news media promoted the narrative that a candidate's personality—and his image—trumped all other concerns.

Life offered similarly image-driven coverage of institutional Catholic events like the Second Vatican Council and the papal elections of John XXIII and Paul VI. With its focus on visual storytelling, *Life* was able to make human interest stories of events *Time* covered as "world affairs." Only *Life*, for example, made mention of what the bishops ordered for dinner when Vatican II's sessions overflowed to Roman restaurants. Despite the spread of sole, bass, and shrimp on display in one *Life* photograph, the caption noted that the picture was taken on a Wednesday, so the bishops chose steak.

Ultimately, *Life* would offer far fewer Catholic cover images than *Time*, but those it did feature suggested that Catholic lives were also family lives, American lives, and even sacramental lives—regardless of one's position within the church. It was a side of the Catholic experience left untold by the covers of *Time*, and if not for *Life*'s end in the 1970s, we might now be the beneficiaries of a fuller expression of the faith in the media.

Or perhaps not: differences of approach aside, *Time* and *Life* nonetheless told Catholic stories with similar relationship to authority. The notion that a religious organization as large as the Catholic Church might naturally include internal dissent was for the most part beyond the newsweeklies' narratives of Catholicism in America, at least through the first four decades of publication. Only with the shifting cultural sands of the 1960s and early '70s did *Time*'s Catholic covers diverge from this script. It did so not for any change of heart about the primacy of authority in its coverage of religion, but in answer to a marketplace challenge.

Thanks to their enormous popularity, Luce's publications had their share of imitators and would-be competitors. None came close to testing the dominance of *Time* until one would-be rival was bought by the Washington Post Company in 1961. *Newsweek* had been founded by an ex-*Time* staffer almost thirty years before, and perhaps as a filial rejection of a former employer's concerns, in the beginning *Newsweek* published very little about religion generally, and less about Catholics specifically. It featured the pope on its cover only at those unignorable moments such as the death of Pius XI in 1939 and the election of Pope John XXIII nine years later. (The 1939 election of Pius XII did not warrant a cover in *Newsweek*'s estimation.)

The advent of the 1960s, and the magazine's new status as subsidiary of the Post, led *Newsweek* to take a different approach. With the 1963 cover story "Catholicism in America" and 1967's "How Do Catholics View Their Church?" for the first time it seemed the coverage of the church in national newsweeklies might no longer be in the sway of the missionary's son. "Churchmanship" as the ultimate measure of the significance of a religious figure was replaced with a view from the pews. This was in keeping with the reputation *Newsweek* had begun to earn throughout the decade. As Richard Lentz has written, the younger magazine was "visibly ahead" of the older "in exploring social change and conflict. . . . Where *Time* delivered itself of received truth with one unwavering voice, *Newsweek* had a range of inflections, which better suited the cacophonous 1960s."[22]

When *Time* began to tell similar stories of religion and authority, it may have been as much due to the times as to the fact that Luce had died in 1967. Three years after *Newsweek* changed the unwritten rules of how the church might be covered, *Time* offered its first cover article—"The Catholic Exodus: Why Priests and Nuns are Quitting"—using a woman, in the figure of the former nun, to illustrate a story about the church. A year later, *Time* again entered the fray of religious controversy with a cover featuring "Rebel Priests" Phillip and Daniel Berrigan, the anti-Vietnam activists serving federal prison sentences for burning draft cards with napalm. Not to be outdone, *Newsweek* later that year brought out an issue with the words "Has the Church Lost Its Soul?" emblazoned on its cover. Taken together, the *Time* and *Newsweek* covers of the late 1960s and early 1970s suggest that, after nearly a half century, the newsweeklies' tendency to affirm the power of the church had given way to boldface questioning of its unity, legitimacy, and relationship to civil authority.

After the 1960s, the newsweeklies cut back on coverage of all religion, wanting to save space, and Catholic coverage was no exception. Treatment of the church fell through the 1970s and did not pick up again until the drama of the decade's end, when 1978 brought the year of three popes. The deaths of Paul VI and John Paul I provided opportunities for coverage much like *Time* had offered decades before, and then came the clergyman the newsweeklies seemed born to cover. A former actor and athlete, charismatic, indefatigable, and handsome, Pope John Paul II may have been an unknown quantity to many in the church, but he was an immediate hit on the newsstand. When *Time* touted him as a rising force against Communism—as it first did in 1983—it was as though the ghost of Henry Luce had returned to canonize the Polish pope as churchmanship personified.

Excluding US presidents, Pope John Paul II earned more *Time* covers than anyone—fourteen in eighteen years. *Newsweek* was similarly swayed. Describing John Paul II in 1979, covers of the two magazines differed only on matters of grammar: while *Newsweek* spoke of his "triumph," *Time* praised his "triumphal return." In return, he provided both with endless opportunities to feature the kinds of instantly iconic images upon which newsweeklies had been built.

As wholeheartedly as *Time* and *Newsweek* endorsed the "triumph" of John Paul II, the newsweeklies' born-again fondness for religious authority has not endured until today. Since the explosion of the clergy sex abuse scandals in the media, a curious trend has emerged on the covers of newsmagazines. In three *Time* covers—April 1, 2002, November 27, 2006, and June 7, 2010—the familiar figure of the pope appears, but altered. Unlike the scores of previous covers featuring the bishop of Rome, the pope now stands with his back to the reader. Where once the face on the magazine cover was all, here were three images in which the pope was literally de-faced. They may have once been influenced by Christendom's reverence for a single image that could stand for all others, but newsweeklies now seem equally at home with iconoclasm.

Conclusion

Despite the newsweeklies' eagerness to exploit the church's fall from grace, they have been slow to recognize that the mass-market media has suffered potentially fatal wounds from the same slings and arrows endured by the church. To put it too simply: each has had its influence and authority challenged by a radical change in the control of information. The mechanisms that have made news and opinion available from thousands of sources are the same that have revealed as systemic clerical scandals that once might have been dismissed as isolated events.

Whether or not they will truly prove "entwined . . . in life and death," as David McCullough wrote of Adams and Jefferson, is a question for future historians. Yet even today one point of connection is clear: the fates of both the Catholic Church and the mass-market newsweekly may depend on how well each institution adapts to a world in which the unquestionable power of the iconic image has been replaced by an endless mosaic of information uncontained.

NOTES

1. David McCullough, *John Adams* (New York: Simon and Shuster, 2001), 628–48.

2. "Americans, Catholics React to Reports of Child Abuse by Priests," CBS/*New York Times*, May 4, 2010.

3. Nick Squires, "Pope Says Catholic Church Needs to Do 'Penance,'" *Telegraph*, April 15, 2010.

4. Stephanie Clifford, "Newsweek on the Block as Era of the Newsweekly Fades," *New York Times*, May 5, 2010.

5. Jack Shaffer, "*Newsweek* Has Fallen Down and Can't Get Up," *Slate.com*, May 5, 2010, HREF="http://www.slate.com/articles/news_and_politics/press_box/2010/05/newsweek_has_fallen_down_and_cant_get_up.html" target="l">http://www.slate.com/articles/news_and_politics/press_box/2010/05/newsweek_has_fallen_down_and_cant_get_up.html.

6. CBS News/*New York Times* poll, January 11–15, 2009.

7. John Kobler, *Luce: His Time, Life and Fortune* (New York: Doubleday, 1968), 2.

8. McCullough, *John Adams*, 248.

9. Clifford, "Newsweek on the Block," 2010.

10. Report cited in *Mother Jones*, December 2005.

11. David Clayton, "How the Iconic Tradition Relates to the Catholic Worldview," *New Liturgical Movement*, February 2010.

12. Kobler, *Luce*, 53.

13. Kobler, *Luce*, 45.

14. Matthew Fox, *Religion USA* (Dubuque, IA: Listening Press, 1971), 53.

15. Edward Cuddy, "The Irish Question and the Revival of Anti-Catholicism in the 1920's," *Catholic Historical Review* 67, no. 2 (1981): 236–55.

16. Isaiah Wilner, *The Man Time Forgot* (New York: Harpercollins, 2006), 206.

17. *Time*, April 30, 1928.

18. Wilner, *The Man Time Forgot*, 210.

19. John K. Jessup, ed. *The Ideas of Henry Luce* (New York: Antheneum, 1969), 325.

20. *Life*, December 17, 1956.

21. *Life*, August 19, 1966.

22. Richard Lentz, *Symbols, the News Magazines, and Martin Luther King* (Baton Rouge: Louisiana State University Press, 1990), 14.

REFERENCES

Jessup, John K., ed. 1969. *The Ideas of Henry Luce*. New York: Antheneum.

Kobler, John. 1968. *Luce: His Time, Life and Fortune*. New York: Doubleday.

CHAPTER 12

MAINLINE PROTESTANTS AND NEWS NARRATIVES OF DECLENSION

J. TERRY TODD

"'God is killing mainline Protestantism in America,' says Methodist theologian Stanley Hauerwas of Duke Divinity School, 'and we goddam well deserve it.'" That provocative quote ran in a 1993 *Newsweek* article headlined "Dead End for the Mainline?" Kenneth Woodward, who reported the story, went on to take stock of the sorry state of mainline Protestant churches and denominations in the United States. "Their flocks are aging, their budgets shrinking. Morale is low. Many local congregations are rejecting control by denominational leaders and cutting back funds to support their national programs. From every angle, mainline Protestantism is gripped by crisis of identity and loyalty, membership and money, leadership and organization, culture and belief." The churches that had once claimed so much power and authority in the United States, helping "define America and its values," had now fallen on hard times, retreating into a "mood of embattled introspection."[1]

The 1993 *Newsweek* article is a notable example of a major narrative in religion news coverage stretching back over four decades, the story of mainline Protestant denominations and their catastrophic loss of power, prestige, and membership. It is true that over the last forty years there have been dramatic losses in the membership of churches in denominations considered to form the core of mainline Protestantism—the United Methodist Church, the Evangelical Lutheran Church in America, the Presbyterian Church (USA), the Episcopal Church, the American Baptist Churches in the USA, and the United Church of Christ (UCC).[2] After 1965, when membership in mainline Protestant churches reached a postwar peak, there was a precipitous slide that continued into the 1990s. In that period, for example, the major Presbyterian body in the United States lost 28 percent of its membership and the United Methodist Church recorded a 17 percent drop. Given these realities, it's not difficult to see how news stories about mainline Protestantism, in the years since the late 1960s, have focused on what the mainline churches have lost.

What is particularly notable about religion news coverage from the late 1960s to the present is how the demographic realities of mainline Protestantism are woven into a highly politicized narrative of decline. For over forty years, news writers have reported on how mainline churches have fought over racial justice, war, peace, nuclear disarmament, feminism, abortion, economic justice, and, perhaps especially, sexuality. Stories about mainline Protestantism tended to place these controversies in the foreground of reporting, an unremarkable observation in itself, since conflict drives the mainstream media's attention to most stories. Yet this bias has given a political edge to reports about the demographic realities within mainline Protestant churches. Many news stories represented mainline leaders as determined to take political stands antithetical to most Americans, even as mainline institutions sank deeper into trouble. The mainline churches were often represented as spiritually and intellectually bankrupt, especially when compared to the mainline's principled if controversial opponent, an evangelical faction within American Protestantism that had successfully challenged the mainline's earlier hold on cultural power and influence. Of course, such reportage did not appear in a vacuum. These conflict-driven stories tracked many of the overall social and political divisions in the period, even as they left largely unexamined other aspects of life within the mainline Protestant churches.

The terms "mainline Protestant" and "mainline Protestantism" came into widespread usage only in the last half of the twentieth century, referring to the predominantly white Protestant denominations, headquartered in the Northeast, that have enjoyed a degree of cultural, economic, and political hegemony in the United States from early on in the nation's history. The University of Pennsylvania sociologist E. Digby Baltzell's 1964 book *The Protestant Establishment: Aristocracy and Caste in America* describes a world of genteel suburbs with exclusive country clubs, day schools, and Protestant churches spread along the Main Line of Philadelphia's commuter rail system. The term "mainline Protestantism" is nowhere found in Baltzell's book, yet this influential work set up the idea of a Protestant world of power and privilege crumbling under the weight of rapid social, political, and economic change. Baltzell's book puts forward a declension narrative, and a version of it was soon launched into popular media accounts of mainline Protestant church life.

The news media helped to popularize the term "mainline Protestant" in reportage that linked the situation of the mainline churches to the larger political crises of the nation. The earliest usage of the term "mainline Protestant" in the *New York Times* dates from 1968. In a story headlined "Clergy Meeting Strong Resistance to Involvement in Secular Causes," the *Times* reported the findings of a Gallup poll showing that many Catholics, Jews, and Protestants did not want their clergy taking sides in political matters. One of several Christian ministers quoted in the article used the term "mainline Protestant" to note how social class affected the churches' response to the pressing issues of the moment. "'Especially in the mainline Protestant denominations, upper-middle-class people feel most threatened concerning race, open housing, any form of dissent by young people,'" declared the Reverend Everett C. Parker, communications director of the United Church of Christ (UCC). The article quotes unnamed UCC and other Protestant sources as saying that while some parishioners had withheld contributions in protest of clergy political involvement, others had increased their giving to make up for the loss. The story represents the nation's mainline Protestant churches as divided by the very same issues tearing at the nation's fabric.[3]

These conflicts had been in the making for years, especially in the wake of Protestant church leaders' involvement with the civil rights movement earlier in the decade. As the 1960s progressed, there was an increasing convergence between the movement for civil rights and the campaign against the war in Vietnam, perhaps best symbolized by Rev. Martin Luther King Jr.'s 1967 appearance before a meeting of Clergy and Laity Concerned About Vietnam (CALCAV). When King announced his opposition to the Vietnam War, he did so in a highly publicized speech at New York's Riverside Church, citadel of what would become known as "mainline Protestantism." That same year, the Good News Movement formed in the Methodist Church as part of a conservative reaction brewing within mainline churches, a harbinger of the fierce intradenominational struggles soon to come. Good News and similar "renewal" groups in other denominations wanted to halt what they understood to be the churches' liberal theological drift.

As fears about the nation's crises continued to reverberate through public discourse into the early 1970s, news stories about the mainline's decline began to appear with regularity. In 1972, *Time* magazine ran an article about dropping enrollments and financial challenges facing Yale Divinity School, Union Theological Seminary, and the Divinity School at the University of Chicago, elite institutions associated with mainline Protestantism. The article offered explanations that would appear time and again in news reports about mainline decline—the disappearance of serious public theologians like Reinhold Niebuhr and Paul Tillich, lax intellectual standards, the substitution of politics for piety, and clergy radicalism. There was even a hint that the feminization of the clergy might also be a factor in the mainline crisis. "Liberal seminaries are suffering because of the failure of the congregations they are closest to in motivating men for the ministry," remarked the president of the evangelical Fuller Theological Seminary, just at the moment when the first generation of women had taken up positions in mainline pulpits.[4]

Media reports of the decline of mainline Protestantism coincided with the media's growing awareness of the cultural power of other Protestants, especially evangelicals. Before the 1960s, the Protestant churches, denominations, and clergy that were later dubbed "mainline" had cornered the market on the label "Protestant," particularly when it came to media visibility. Clergy and laity from many of the other multiple forms of Protestant faith—Pentecostalism, the Holiness movements, fundamentalism, African American and Latino Protestantism—all stood somewhere closer to the cultural margins. While white evangelical Protestants had received media attention in the past, evangelicals were often covered for their sensational stage antics, not for their contributions to public discourse. When journalists needed a representative of American Protestants, they usually turned to an upstanding white Methodist, Presbyterian, Congregationalist, or Episcopalian.

This closeness between certain Protestant leaders and mainstream media power brokers is nowhere more evident than in the career of Henry Luce, founder of the *Time-Life* empire. Notoriously reticent about his own faith according to his biographer, Alan Brinkley, Luce was nonetheless thoroughly enmeshed within an elite Protestant world. Luce was born in China to parents serving as Presbyterian missionaries and later funded a Presbyterian chapel in Taiwan built in their memory. He was a faithful member of New York's tony Madison Avenue Presbyterian Church and a close friend of its pastor, David H. C. Read. During the Eisenhower administration, Luce helped raise funds for a national Presbyterian Church in Washington, DC, a project intended to stake a claim for the importance of Presbyterianism in the life of the nation.

More to the point, Luce made sure that *Time* promoted Protestant theologians as key figures in the postwar revival of American intellectual life. Whatever men like Reinhold Niebuhr, Harry Emerson Fosdick, and Paul Tillich said in their books, from their pulpits, or in their classrooms was news, according to Luce. It's true that Luce also showed great interest in Billy Graham, the most visible leader of postwar Protestant evangelicalism, in large part because of Graham's strident anti-Communism. But *Time*, like most other mainstream news outlets, presented Graham as a *doer* who could move tens of thousands of people in his stadium rallies. In contrast, notable Protestant figures were newsworthy because they were *thinkers*. Niebuhr appeared on the cover of *Time* in March 1948 and two years later was named "the number one theologian of United States Protestantism." Luce lavished even greater attention on his friend Paul Tillich. Tillich made it onto the cover of *Time* in March of 1959, along with the pretentious headline "A Theology for Protestants." Luce embraced Tillich's message of cultural engagement in the face of doubt and despair and gave the theologian top billing at the Waldorf-Astoria banquet celebrating *Time*'s fortieth anniversary in May 1963.[5]

Although no other news outlet matched the attention *Time* gave to Niebuhr and Tillich under Luce's editorship, newspaper writers and editors considered these figures to be spokesmen for American public values, addressing the entire society, not just the churches. A testament to Niebuhr's importance was the decision of both the *New York Times* and the *Los Angeles Times* to run his obituary on their front pages when he died in 1971. As Tillich and Niebuhr shuffled off the historical stage, mainline Protestants lost not only cherished figures with cultural gravitas and intellectual stature but also recognized (and recognizable) media personalities whose publications and pronouncements made news.

In 1974, the *New York Times* published its very first note about the growing demographic crisis in the mainline, titled "Mainline Protestantism on Decline." A dry recitation of statistics from the 1974 Yearbook of American and Canadian Churches, the article left no doubt that while membership in mainline churches plummeted, conservative churches had made gains. In 1976, *Time* magazine carried pollster George Gallup's assessment that this was the "year of the evangelical," and *Newsweek* delivered a cover story on evangelical Protestantism, with the headline "Born Again!"[6] In media reports for years to come, mainline decline was depicted in the mirror of an insurgent evangelicalism. The not-so-subtle message was that as mainline Protestants deepened their political involvement, their theology had become confused and muddled, and thus had opened a path for a principled evangelical opposition.

Throughout the period under review, narratives of the mainline's decline regularly relied on history lessons that closely bound the nation's destiny to the strength of its Protestant churches. "In the beginning was mainline Protestantism," Richard Ostling and his co-writers at *Time* declared in their 1989 story "Those Mainline Blues," a first line that echoed the Bible's opening words. "At Plymouth Rock and Jamestown, and for 3 ½ centuries thereafter, the denominations known today by that label defined the spiritual and moral ethos of the U.S." These are the churches that imparted "notions of republican government and individual freedom." Then came the bombshell: "The central fact about mainline Protestantism is that it's in deep trouble." Who or what was to blame? "A preoccupation with political and social issues at the expense of good old-fashioned faith has alienated many members."[7] In formulations like these, the loss of membership within mainline denominations was caused by a vanguard of clergy activists whose faith had been exchanged for radical politics, with consequences not just for the churches but also for the nation itself.

Narratives that combined fears about national security with challenges to Protestant clergy activism had their roots in the red-baiting days of the postwar era, but they reappeared with renewed force in the waning days of the Cold War. In 1983, a number of media reports linked mainline Protestant denominations and agencies with anti-American Marxist groups in the developing world. The accusations were launched in two of the most popular media forums in the United States, *Reader's Digest* and the CBS newsmagazine *60 Minutes*. The January 1983 edition of *Reader's Digest* carried an article with the provocative title "Do You Know Where Your Church Offerings Go?" The piece claimed that two ecumenical organizations closely linked to the mainline denominations in the United States—the Geneva-based World Council of Churches (WCC) and the New York–based National Council of Churches (NCC)—had channeled money to communist groups in Vietnam. It was an explosive charge given the tinderbox of resentments that lingered in the wake of the Vietnam War.[8]

A program that aired on *60 Minutes* in the same month carried similar accusations about money from American churches funneled to liberation fronts in Central America and in Africa. The segment, reported by Morley Safer, opened with a shot of a collection plate at the United Methodist Church in Logansport, Indiana. The program then cut immediately to scenes of Fidel Castro and Red Square in Moscow. In a voice-over, Safer tells viewers that the NCC had taken money from the heartland of the United States to use "on causes that seem closer to the Soviet-Cuban view of the world than Logansport's." The two stories remain astonishing examples of journalistic red baiting in the closing days of the Cold War.

Both the *Reader's Digest* and *60 Minutes* stories relied heavily on accusations launched by the Washington-based Institute for Religion and Democracy (IRD). Founded in 1981 as an outgrowth of the neo-conservative Coalition for a Democratic Majority and funded by the Olin, Scaife, and Bradley foundations, the IRD was formed to combat the supposed leftist influence in mainline Protestantism and the NCC and WCC. Conservatives in the mainline denominations had distrusted these ecumenical organizations for decades, accusing them of promoting a radical agenda on domestic and international policy matters. The IRD was formed to work alongside "renewal" movements within the mainline churches. Groups such as the United Methodist Good News Movement and the Presbyterian Laymen's Committee insisted that the leftist bias and radical initiatives of mainline leaders had led to a massive exodus from the mainline churches. These groups were determined to save the churches through a process of "renewal," by which they meant a return to so-called "traditional" or "orthodox" biblical teachings that radicals had supposedly abandoned. Critics of the renewal movements saw something different: a well-funded attempt to silence the social witness of the mainline denominations by seizing control of its forms of governance.

Writing in *Newsweek*, Kenneth Woodward and David Gates dismissed both the *Reader's Digest* and *60 Minutes* stories as "an overwrought attack" on the NCC and the WCC. Yet, they criticized those organizations as opaque and bloated bureaucracies, tone-deaf to their local constituents. The syndicated columnist Colman McCarthy defended the NCC in a strong rebuttal that appeared in the *Los Angeles Times* under the headline "Council of Churches Suffers Unjust Stonings." Criticizing both *Reader's Digest* and *60 Minutes* for uncritically airing the IRD's accusations, McCarthy went on to set the record straight with a cooler-headed investigation of whose money went where.[9]

Conservative activists had found a compelling story that explained why mainline denominations were hemorrhaging money and members: a radical chic vanguard had taken money from people in the pews and funneled it into activities that most American churchgoers found abhorrent. It appears that the conservative strategy involved the news media in disseminating an image of mainline denominations and church agencies as cauldrons of radical activism. As Diane Winston has noted, one of the most important effects of both the story and the strategy was that it put mainline Protestant leaders on the defensive, as old charges of leftist bias in the mainline churches haunted just about every programmatic initiative of the WCC, the NCC, and the mainline denominations for years afterward.[10]

The fall of the Soviet Union in 1989 helped push concerns about Marxist guerillas into the background, leading conservative activists struggling to identify the next line of attack on the leadership and direction of mainline denominations. In a 2004 *New York Times* interview, IRD President Dianne Knippers reflected on a decisive moment in the early 1990s when there had been some talk of folding the

IRD. Instead, its leaders decided to shift course, focusing the organization's efforts to counter what it saw as the menacing influence of feminism and homosexuality in mainline churches and seminaries.[11]

Even though women's full and equal ordination to the ministry in the mainline Protestant churches was one of the most important and far-reaching developments of the twentieth century, it took a bold event to get the media's attention. On July 29, 1974, at Philadelphia's Church of the Advocate, four retired Episcopal bishops consecrated eleven women as priests, defying their denomination's rules against the ordination of women to the priesthood. On the following day, both the *New York Times* and the *Los Angeles Times* ran the story on their front pages, with reportage highlighting the dramatic objections staged by conservatives at the ordination rites. The newsweeklies also covered the Philadelphia event, but it was the dailies, especially the *New York Times* and the *Los Angeles Times*, that extended coverage throughout the summer, reporting on the threats of clerical trials, excommunication, and schism that followed the ordinations. Just two years later, in 1976, the Episcopal Church's governing body formally voted to open the priesthood to women. Coming as it did in the context of a bureaucratic church conference, that vote was hardly as dramatic and confrontational as the Philadelphia ordinations, yet it did make the news.

A small number of Protestant churches had ordained women since the nineteenth century, but most mainline denominations did not grant full ordination rights until the 1950s and 1960s, in response to both a clergy shortage and growing demands from women. In media accounts, those developments were noted almost in passing. For various reasons, the move for the full inclusion of women in ministry came most slowly in the Episcopal Church, yet when the breakthrough arrived at the moment of the 1974 Philadelphia ordinations, the event pushed women and their demands into the headlines.

Women's leadership in the churches made news once again in 1989, with the consecration of Barbara Clementine Harris as the Episcopal Church's first woman bishop and one of its few African American bishops. Although women had achieved top leadership positions in some mainline churches before that date—Marjorie Matthews had been elected the first woman bishop in the United Methodist Church in 1980—women in the episcopacy proved especially controversial in the Episcopal Church, in part because of that church's connection to the Anglican Communion and its more conservative church bodies. News of Harris's election had already caused a heated reaction in some Anglican circles in England, Australia, and other places around the globe, accompanied by the usual pleas for delay and threats of schism if the deed were done. Harris's consecration as the first woman Anglican bishop made the front pages not only in the Boston dailies but also in the *New York Times*, with reports focusing on the pageantry of the event and the controversy it unleashed.[12]

In 1992, just three years after Harris's consecration and soon after the IRD decided to turn its attention to the effects of feminism within the mainline churches, a lengthy and wide-ranging article appeared in *Time* magazine surveying the women's movement in modern Christianity and its theological challenges to the churches. What lay behind the demand for women's ordination, Richard Ostling and his colleagues asked? In their approach to the question, *Time*'s writers suggested that the women's movement might be undermining classical Christian teaching and practice. Conservative churches that maintain the traditional faith flourish, we are told, while "the women's rights crusade increasingly is enmeshed with divisive projects of social, moral and theological reconstruction." The article included reports on the impact of women's organizations within the Catholic Church, as well as in mainline Protestant denominations, warning, "the new Christian feminism must not only claim power and authority for women but also demonstrate that gender equality enhances the church's spiritual and moral strength."[13] *Time*'s reportage was exceptional in its degree of editorializing about women's leadership in mainline denominations.

Of all the issue-related battles that have raged within and across mainline Protestant denominations since 1970, none has been as protracted or as bitter as the struggle over homosexuality. News stories generally have represented debates about homosexuality as another instance in the persistent crisis of mainline churches in the United States. A few of those stories hinted that the pro-gay stances of some clergy led to alienation from people in the pew. Most of the debate focused on two matters in particular, the ordination of lesbians and gay men and the blessing of same-sex unions. Skirmishes over these two issues have led to charges of heresy, ecclesiastical trials, and, in the case of the Episcopal Church, actual schism as hundreds of local churches and at least two dioceses have broken with the church to affiliate with like-minded bodies elsewhere within the Anglican Communion. These battles have been so acrimonious that Laurie Goodstein and David Kirkpatrick, reporting in a 2004 *New York Times* article, called the mainline's divisions over homosexuality "the biggest battle over the future of American Protestantism since churches split over slavery at the time of the Civil War."[14]

Although the clashes seemed to explode onto the pages of the news media only in the 1990s, dissension over sexual matters had long been brewing in mainline denominations. A search of the *Time* magazine archives reveals that the first use of the term "mainline Protestant" in that newsweekly occurred in a 1972 reader's response to an earlier article about clergy views of sex outside of marriage. The respondent writes from a Lutheran seminary, where debates about sexuality already were raging. Incensed by the article's description of the "new morality" in Christian sexual ethics, he criticized "the accelerating paganization occurring among some of the 'mainline' Protestant churches," linking sexual liberalism to a move away from Christian orthodoxy, a charge that would reappear time and again in debates about sexuality, especially homosexuality.[15]

In the mainline Protestant churches, as elsewhere in the United States during the period after 1970, concerns about normative sexual behavior and the meanings of marriage often focused on homosexuality. Mainline denominations occasionally debated sexual ethics more broadly, setting up study commissions and issuing reports that sometimes captured the interest of news media, such as the controversial 1991 Presbyterian report that discussed homosexuality within the larger framework of human sexual ethics. But nothing seemed to galvanize conservative reaction within the denominations like the subject of homosexuality itself. Why was homosexuality so threatening? In 1977, *New York Times* religion reporter Kenneth Briggs wrote, "The sanctify of family life, built on a model of heterosexuality, has come down through Christian history as an integral part of the faith that is deeply ingrained in most Christians. Under this view, the homosexual poses a threat to the accepted moral order and provides an illegitimate example for others to follow."[16]

Not every mainline Protestant considered homosexuality such a threat, of course. Since the early 1960s, a small number of ministers had formed alliances with the nascent movement for lesbian and gay civil rights, understanding their ministry as a logical extension of their work in the black freedom movement. The Council on Religion and the Homosexual (CRH) was founded in San Francisco in 1964 as the first organization to bring together gay and lesbian leaders with Protestant clergy. On January 1, 1965, a CRH fundraising ball was raided by San Francisco vice officers, giving the ministers in attendance a glimpse of the indignities regularly visited upon the city's lesbian and gay population. Outraged, the clergy called a news conference to denounce the raid as an example of an ongoing pattern of police harassment. The San Francisco dailies prominently covered the event, making it the first widely publicized action of mainline support of gay and lesbian civil rights.[17]

Six years later, Edward Fiske of the *New York Times* reported on the *Times*' religion page that some gay Christian leaders had grown impatient with what they considered to be the liberal paternalism of the Protestant denominations. "Homosexuals in the American churches have gone militant," Fiske wrote, "and are looking beyond tolerance and integration toward running their own religious affairs."[18] The formation of independent churches for gay and lesbian Christians found additional coverage in a 1970 *Los Angeles Times* story about the founding of "the nation's first religious denomination for homosexuals," the Metropolitan Community Churches (MCC). A 1971 *Time* magazine article is notable for its prescient sense of the struggle ahead in Protestant denominations. "The Gay Church" reported that while some mainline churches seemed open to the presence of gay men and lesbians in the ministry, many others did not. It cited the case of Rev. Gene Leggett, a United Methodist minister from Texas whose conference suspended him after Leggett acknowledged he was gay.[19]

A number of mainline churches had ordained openly gay men and lesbians to the ministry since the 1970s, but it was only in the 1990s that the practice took on greater visibility—in part, because of the news media's growing interest. In 1996, conservatives within the Episcopal Church charged Bishop Walter Righter of the Diocese of Newark with violating canon law for ordaining an openly gay man to the priesthood. After Righter's acquittal in a well-publicized trial, things moved very swiftly in the Episcopal Church, so much so that by 2003 the Diocese of New Hampshire had elected an openly gay bishop, Rev. V. Gene Robinson. Much like Barbara Harris's consecration as the first woman Anglican bishop in 1989, Robinson's election received media attention throughout the world. Many Anglican churches, particularly in the developing world, regarded the election of a gay bishop as nothing short of heretical. News coverage continued to trace the far-reaching effects of the Episcopal Church's action, with representative headlines from the *Los Angeles Times* giving some indication of the story's local and global importance: "Gay Bishop Spurs Spirited Debate; Episcopalians are split at Southland meetings on the church's decision to elevate a gay priest and allow blessing of same-sex unions" (September 28, 2003) and "Anglicans Say Split May Occur if Gay Man Ordained as Bishop; Archbishops rebuff conservatives' wishes to eject the U.S. church from the world body" (October 17, 2003). The international perspective continues to frame almost all news coverage of the Episcopal Church's debates over homosexuality.

In no other denomination has the battle over homosexuality been as protracted as in the United Methodist Church (UMC), the largest of the mainline denominations. In a story about the prosecution of an openly lesbian minister in a church court in 2004, Laurie Goodstein of the *New York Times* called the UMC a "church at war with itself."[20] Homosexuality first emerged as an issue in 1972, when the denomination's General Conference voted down a gay-friendly proposal and adopted instead a resolution that declared "homosexuality is incompatible with Christian teaching." Debates within the UMC quickly turned to a blanket proscription against the ordination of gay people to the ministry. And while that issue continued to fester into the 2010s, resulting in highly publicized trials of UMC gay clergy, another front in the struggle opened in the 1990s, the blessing of same-sex unions.

Debates about same-sex unions in mainline denominations tracked legal and legislative developments on same-sex marriage at both the state and federal levels. In 1996, President Bill Clinton signed the Defense of Marriage Act (DOMA), which for the first time defined marriage, in the eyes of the federal government, as a union between a man and a woman. In that same year, a bitterly divided UMC General Convention adopted a church law forbidding Methodist ministers from sanctioning same-sex unions. In the years immediately following, a number of dissenting clergy violated the rule, setting the stage for several highly visible church trials in which one UMC minister was defrocked for his role in blessing a same-sex union. In January 1999, sixty-eight UMC ministers jointly presided at the union of two longtime lay church leaders, Ellie Charlton and Jean Barnett, in Sacramento, California. Billed as a massive demonstration of support for equality within the church, this event also made it into the news. Writing in the *New York Times*, Gustav Niebuhr reported reaction to the ritual as illustrating "the tension within many mainline Protestant churches over how to respond to gay and lesbian members."[21] The UMC's battle over homosexuality ramped up at the denomination's 2004 General Conference, where a representative of the conservative Good News Movement proposed that the church formally divide because of the denomination's intractable disagreements about homosexuality. Though ultimately defeated, the proposal attracted much attention in the print media, where stories reported the calls for schism as one effect of the denomination's continuing debates.

News stories about pitched battles within mainline denominations regarding homosexuality appeared at the same moment as reports about the decline of mainline

Protestantism. For instance, *Time*'s 1989 article about the sorry state of mainline Protestantism, "Those Mainline Blues," appeared in the very same year as the magazine's "Battle Over Gay Clergy." "The penchant of mainline leaders for embracing progressive causes has sparked bitter internal disputes, especially over homosexuality and women's rights," Richard Ostling and his colleagues at *Time* noted in the first article. The second story paints a picture of a gay-led assault on the churches: "Not so long ago, Christians who were homosexual devoted much of their energy to cloaking that fact. Today not only have many of them come out of the closet, but they are also staging rallies, disrupting worship services and aggressively demanding church endorsement of their life-styles." When read back to back, the linkages those stories draw between crisis, decline, radical feminism, and homosexuality are not difficult to notice, although of course it is impossible to tell how many readers drew such a connection at the time.

What is certain is that conservative opponents of marriage equality and the ordination of gay or lesbian ministers placed the church's pro-gay movement within the frame of mainline declension. These views were circulated in media stories about the denominational battles over homosexuality, in the form of quotations offered by conservative activists. For example, Mark Tooley, director of the United Methodist Church project for the Institute for Religion and Democracy, claimed in a *New York Times* story that the UMC's liberal and pro-gay Western jurisdiction continued to lose members rapidly, while UMC churches in more conservative regions such as the South were growing. Tooley positioned the homosexuality debates within the UMC as a fight between an old, decaying liberal base in the Northeast and the West and a vital, insurgent "traditional" base in the South and Midwest. While Tooley acknowledged that homosexuality would continue to be a point of contention within the churches, "Those of us on the traditional side are at least hopeful that in a demographic sense, the church is going in our direction."[22]

Over the last four decades news reports have woven observations about the sobering membership losses of mainline Protestantism into complex declension narratives involving conflict and crisis, mostly at the denominational level. Academic studies have confirmed the loss of membership in the mainline churches, but they do not support the claim, made in conservative partisan attacks and reflected in some news stories, of dissatisfied members voting with their feet to leave mainline denominations because of theological confusion or dissatisfaction with clergy activism. "The trouble was mostly a demographic problem," Robert Wuthnow and John Evans have observed. "Being better educated and more upscale economically, mainline members married later, had fewer children, and waited longer to have them."[23] Also contributing to the demographic crisis was the fact that mainline churches were not able to hold on to their younger members, although on the whole those people did not flock to evangelical churches. They simply became part of the growing number of Americans who are unaffiliated with any religious group.

Narratives about the decline of mainline Protestantism tracked many of the larger political and social developments of the last half century, including the eclipse of the civil rights movement, the rise and splintering of the New Left, the emergence of identity politics, the birth of the LGBT movement and the fight for marriage equality, and the resurgence of conservative electoral politics in the United States. News reporters rightly understood that these trends influenced denominational battles over myriad issues. Such reportage gave a highly politicized spin to developments within the mainline, lending the impression that mainline Protestant churches were embroiled, like the rest of America, in never-ending conflict. It is impossible to tell to what degree news accounts fed fears of declension and debates about revitalization among mainline Protestants, and to what degree Protestant fear and dissension shaped those news stories. Most likely, there was a feedback loop at work, helping to sustain the storyline of declension for over four decades.

Among the effects of conflict-driven reportage is a tendency to minimize or ignore altogether the theological rationales for some of the controversial political stances taken by mainline Protestant leaders. Another effect is to miss the subtler, less visible realities of life in the mainline. For example, very little of the news coverage of mainline churches in the last forty years has focused on congregational church life.

News coverage of mainline Protestants in the period reviewed too often missed perspectives that might have challenged simplistic narratives involving declension, crisis, and clergy political involvement. Take, for instance, the case of South African Anglican Archbishop Desmond Tutu. It was Tutu's role in the struggle against South African apartheid and his attempts to peacefully bring about change that made him an international religious celebrity in the years after 1980. Over a span of three decades, television news and print media alike seemed riveted by Tutu's twinkle-in-the-eye charisma, as well as his brave willingness to carry a torch for social justice. In a manner that recalls how Henry Luce touted elite Protestant "great men" as spokesmen for public values, *Time* magazine represented Tutu as a fearless example of faithfulness in a globalizing world. For instance, a *Time* story on Tutu's retirement from public life in the fall of 2010 declared him "our global guardian."[24] The magazine's stories about Tutu were accompanied by a panoply of website content, including still photographs and video montages and a virtual space where *Time* readers could pose questions to Tutu.

It is tempting to speculate just how differently the story of mainline Protestantism might have been reported if stories like this had explored Tutu's deep connections to mainline Protestant churches in the United States. Tutu was a popular and respected church leader who visited the United States frequently, preaching in mainline pulpits, greeting churchgoers, and meeting with clergy and lay leaders to coordinate plans for global social justice initiatives. He promoted women's leadership in ministry and supported the ordination of gay men and lesbians, not only in the South African Anglican Church but also in churches elsewhere. Tutu did not register as a "mainline Protestant," and so his complex connections to mainline Protestant churches in the United States passed largely unexamined. Media representation of Tutu is yet another instance of how our available terms, such as the relatively new coinage "mainline Protestant," have limited our understanding of the complexities of religious life, trapping us in storylines that won't seem to go away.

NOTES

1. Kenneth L. Woodward, "Dead End for the Mainline?" *Newsweek*, August 9, 1993, www.newsweek.com/1993/08/08/dead-end-for-the-mainline.html.

2. This listing of mainline denominations follows the one developed by the Public Role of Mainline Protestantism Project of Princeton University's Center for the Study of Religion. Some lists also include one or both of the much smaller Reformed Church in America and the Christian Church—Disciples of Christ. See Robert Wuthnow and John H. Evans, eds., *The Quiet Hand of God: Faith-Based Activism and the Public Role of Mainline Protestantism* (Berkeley: University of California Press, 2002), 4.

3. Paul Hofman, "Clergy Meeting Strong Resistance to Involvement in Secular Causes," *New York Times*, April 12, 1968.

4. "The State of Union," *Time*, October 9, 1972, www.time.com/time/magazine/article/0,9171,906547-1,00.html.

5. Paul Tillich, "The Ambiguity of Perfection," *Time*, May 17, 1963, http://www.time.com/time/magazine/article/0,9171,830363,00.html.

6. "Counting Souls," *Time*, October 4, 1976, www.time.com/time/magazine/article/0,9171,918414,00.html; "The Evangelicals," *Newsweek*, October 25, 1976.

7. Richard Ostling and others, "Those Mainline Blues," *Time*, May 22, 1989, www.time.com/time/magazine/article/0,9171,957726,00.html.

8. Rael Jean Isaac, "Do You Know Where Your Church Offerings Go?" *Reader's Digest*, January 1983: 120–25.

9. Kenneth L. Woodward and David Gates, "Ideology Under the Arms," *Newsweek*, February 7, 1983, 61–62; Colman McCarthy, "Council of Churches Suffers Unjust Stonings," *Los Angeles Times*, February 23, 1983. See also Richard Ostling and others, "Warring Over Where Donations Go," *Time*, March 28, 1983, www.time.com/time/magazine/article/0,9171,923427,00.html.

10. Diane Winston, "Back to the Future: Religion, Politics, and the Media," *American Quarterly* 59 (September 2007): 978–79.

11. Laurie Goodstein and David D. Kirkpatrick, "Conservative Group Amplifies Voice of Protestant Orthodoxy," *New York Times*, May 22, 2004.

12. James L. Franklin, "Woman Consecrated as Episcopal Bishop; 8,500 See Rev. Barbara Harris Make History in Boston Rite," *Boston Globe*, February 12, 1989; Peter Steinfels, "Woman Is Consecrated as Episcopal Bishop," *New York Times*, February 12, 1989.

13. Richard Ostling and others, "The New Reformation," *Time*, November 23, 1992, www.time.com/time/magazine/article/0,9171,977073-9,00.html#ixzz1CeIjq9F5.

14. Goodstein and Kirkpatrick, "Conservative Group Amplifies Voice of Protestant Orthodoxy."

15. Thomas Elliott Blanch, "Rats Aboard," *Time*, January 3, 1972, http://www.time.com/time/magazine/article/0,9171,879009-2,00.html.

16. Kenneth Briggs, "Homosexuals Among the Clergy," *New York Times*, January 24, 1977.

17. Donovan Bess, "Incidents at a Homosexual Benefit: Angry Ministers Rip Police," *San Francisco Chronicle*, January 3, 1965; "Uproar over Dance," *San Francisco Examiner*, January 3, 1965. See also an online exhibition about the Council on Religion and the Homosexual, including media responses to its work. LGBT-Religious Archives Network, www.lgbtran.org/Exhibits/CRH/Exhibit.aspx?P=I.

18. Edward Fiske, "Color Some of the Churches Lavender," *New York Times*, March 28, 1971.

19. "The Gay Church," *Time*, August 23, 1971, www.time.com/time/magazine/article/0,9171,877276,00.html.

20. Laurie Goodstein, "Methodists Put Pastor on Trial for Declaring Herself a Lesbian," *New York Times*, March 18, 2004.

21. Gustav Niebuhr, "68 Clerics Face Judgment Over a Same-Sex Union," *New York Times*, June 11, 1999.

22. Goodstein, "Methodists Put Pastor on Trial."

23. Wuthnow and Evans, *The Quiet Hand of God*, 7.

24. Alex Perry, "The Laughing Bishop," *Time*, October 11, 2010, www.time.com/time/magazine/article/0,9171,2022647,00.html.

REFERENCES

Baltzell, Edward Digby. 1987. *The Protestant Establishment: Aristocracy and Caste in America*. New Haven, CT: Yale University Press.

Brinkley, Alan. 2010. *The Publisher: Henry Luce and the American Century*. New York: Knopf.

Tipton, Steven A. 2007. *Public Pulpits: Methodists and Mainline Churches in the Moral Argument of Public Life*. Chicago: University of Chicago Press.

White, Heather Rachelle. 2008. Proclaiming Liberation: The Historical Roots of LGBT Religious Organizing. *Nova Religio* 11 (4 [March]): 102–19.

Winston, Diane. 2007. Back to the Future: Religion, Politics, and the Media. *American Quarterly* 59 (3 [September]): 969–89.

Wuthnow, Robert, and John H. Evans, eds. 2002. *The Quiet Hand of God: Faith Based Activism and the Public Role of Mainline Protestantism*. Berkeley: University of California Press.

CHAPTER 13

ORTHODOX JUDAISM AND THE NEWS

NORA L. RUBEL

JEWS BEHAVING BADLY AND *CHILUL HASHEM*

Zionists once dreamed of a state where Jewish criminals, arrested by Jewish cops, would be tried by Jewish judges. In other words, normalization occurs when all Jewish behavior becomes unremarkable. Jews in America feel differently. Just as wealthy and acculturated German Jews attempted to civilize poor and superstitious Eastern European Jews in early twentieth-century America, so too do twenty-first-century Jews look out for one another to protect the group's standing in American eyes. American Jews, in other words, do not need Jewish criminals to signify their acclimation to American society. In fact, American Jews are obligated to refrain from unethical or illegal acts lest they be found guilty of what is known as *chilul haShem*, the desecration of God's name. Jews are accountable to the laws of the land in which they reside, but if they break this law, they not only are responsible for breaking civil law but also have committed chilul haShem, which adds the extra burden of having besmirched the reputation of the Jewish people. For example, if a Jew commits a crime of theft, the anxious logic of chilul haShem worries that non-Jews will think, "All Jews are thieves." The converse is also true; if a Jew performs a particularly charitable or respectable act, this behavior is known as *kiddush haShem*—a glorifying of God's name. This kiddush haShem reflects well on the Jewish community.

Accordingly, many American Jews are horrified to see the bad behavior of fellow "members of the tribe" splashed across headlines. And since the turn of the millennium, this has been a frequent occurrence. The first decade of the twenty-first century saw Americans reeling from one of the worst Ponzi schemes in history, put in place by the Jewish financier Bernie Madoff. Three years earlier, Washington lobbyist—and Modern Orthodox Jew—Jack Abramoff pled guilty to five counts of felony corruption for his involvement in defrauding American Indian tribes. The high-profile crimes committed by Madoff and Abramoff were decried as unforgiveable acts of greed by the public, and thus condemned as acts of chilul haShem by members of the Jewish community.

Equally embarrassing were the allegations plaguing Agriprocessors, a kosher meat company owned by the Rubashkin family, who are Hasidim—the most visibly identifiable of Jews. Hasidic Jews are a subset of what are generally referred to as ultra-Orthodox (or *haredi*) Jews. For almost a decade, a litany of the Rubashkins' wrongdoings has appeared in the media. Accusations included inhumane slaughter practices that first came to light in 2004, a largely undocumented workforce reported on in 2006, and later charges of child labor violations, unreasonably low wages, poor safety training, extortion, and physical and sexual abuse. The saga ultimately resulted in a 2008 federal raid of the plant and a subsequent trial of the former CEO, Sholom Rubashkin, both of which became the subject of intense regional and national scrutiny.

This chapter will examine how the mainstream secular press—both regional and national—reported on the Agriprocessors scandal. It pays particular attention to the way that Rubashkin's Jewishness—and specifically his Orthodoxy—factored into this coverage. Disparate images of Rubashkin emerged, depending on the source. The local Iowa papers focused on what was depicted as his foreignness and odd behavior. The national press viewed Agriprocessors and Rubashkin as symbols of a greater problem of corruption, and the subsequent schadenfreude over the hypocrisy of both a religious business and a religious businessman was hard to miss. In many ways, large city papers like the *New York Times* and the *Los Angeles Times* shared the progressive outlook of several Jewish papers. The Jewish press in general was split, running the gamut from vilifying the plant for the shame of chilul haShem to the outright martyrdom of Rubashkin as an innocent scapegoat.

High-profile trials always raise questions. In this case, many were about religion. What kind of religion is our society comfortable with and what seems unreasonable? In cases involving Jewish defendants, does the type of Jewishness matter? How much attention does the press pay to this element of the defendant's identity? Since the site of the Agriprocessors case is a kosher slaughterhouse, does this become a Jewish crime? Examining the media coverage of religious Jews on trial can begin to answer some of these questions.

The 2006 trial of Jack Abramoff offered an example of conflicting media coverage. When Abramoff wore a black fedora to court, the mainstream press described his appearance as reminiscent of a 1940s gangster movie. Robin Givhan of the *Washington Post* wrote:

> Abramoff emerged from U.S. District Court in Washington on Tuesday dressed like a crime boss. He could not have appeared more guilty, more menacing and more unsympathetic than if he had walked out wielding a baseball bat and muttering something about so-and-so sleeping with the fishes.[1]

But the Jewish press seized on something quite different. Many reprinted a piece by *Boston Globe* columnist Jeff Jacoby, which pointed out another reading of Abramoff's attire:

> For his appearance in the U.S. District Court in Washington last Tuesday, Abramoff made a point of wearing a black fedora, an element of attire that is de rigueur for men in certain Orthodox Jewish circles.[2]

Jacoby then dissected the black fedora. Was the hat Abramoff's way of playing at piety? Or was it a sign of true adherence to this religious community? The *Forward*—a Jewish weekly—asked, "What's with the hat?"[3] After examining the media's response to the controversial headgear, it added,

> Whatever fashion statement he was trying to make, Abramoff purchased the hat from Bencraft Hatters, a Brooklyn-based haberdasher that caters largely to Orthodox Jews. The hat in question, a Como II fedora made by Borsalino, retails on the Bencraft Web site for $200.[4]

The unasked question of the Jewish press was: how would the wider culture (i.e., the *goyim*) read that? Certainly any overt claim of Jewishness by Abramoff was *not* good for the Jews. What elements of religious identity can be reconciled with the greater culture and what is too Jewish? Despite internal Jewish anxiety, non-Jews were likely unaware of the sectarian meaning behind a fedora acquired in a certain shop in Brooklyn. The gentiles were more apt to read the hat as a reference to the *Godfather*.

Unlike Abramoff's scandalous Borsalino, which was read one way by mainstream media and yet another by the Jewish press, Sholom Rubashkin's hat can be read only way: Jewish. A member of the Lubavitcher Hasidic movement (also known as Chabad), Sholom Rubashkin is what is commonly referred to as an ultra-Orthodox (or haredi) Jew. Haredi men are easily identifiable by the black hats, black coats, and long beards that they wear. Similarly, haredi women follow a common dress code: sleeves that cover elbows, high necklines, and long skirts (pants are considered immodest). Married women cover their hair, wearing wigs or headscarves.

The majority of religiously affiliated American Jews identify with moderate and liberal Jewish movements such as Reform, Reconstructionist, and Conservative Judaism, all of which can be characterized by a willingness to adapt to changes brought on by modernity.[5] Orthodox Jews distinguish themselves from their more liberal coreligionists by their close adherence to Talmudic law. Historians have made a distinction between segregationist and integrationist Orthodox Jews, categorizing the haredim (of which the *hasidim* are a subset) as the former.[6] Followers of Modern Orthodoxy, a designation that is constantly changing, fall into the integrationist category. Since the haredim view the secular world as full of corrupting influences, they choose to live in insular communities.[7] While most of these communities are in larger cities, the Rubashkins and their fellow haredim in Postville created a Lubavitch enclave in Iowan farmland. And that is when the trouble started.

Nonkosher Exposure

Agriprocessors first came to national attention with the publication of journalist Stephen Bloom's 2000 book *Postville: A Clash of Cultures in Heartland America*. Bloom's critique of the Iowa plant centered in what he perceived as the arrogance of the new Jewish inhabitants toward their Iowan farmer neighbors. Bloom observed a blatant disregard for social and ethical norms. He also made note of some criminal acts by residents of the Postville Hasidic community, as well as the employment of illegal immigrants from Eastern Europe.[8]

In 2004, a brutally graphic exposé by People for the Ethical Treatment of Animals (PETA) raised questions about Agriprocessors' kosher slaughter practices. When reporting on the PETA exposé, the *New York Times* quoted celebrated Colorado State veterinarian Temple Grandin. "She called [the tapes at Agriprocessors] 'an atrocious abomination, nothing like I've seen in 30 kosher plants I've visited here and in England, France, Ireland and Canada.'"[9] In another article, the paper cited "a representative of Israel's chief rabbinate [who] said AgriProcessors' meat would no longer be accepted in Israel if the scenes he saw on tape were standard practice."[10]

The haredim dismissed PETA's allegations as troublesome muckraking at best and as overt anti-Semitism at worst. A Jewish paper in California quoted a spokesman for the Orthodox organization Agudath Israel of America who described the Nazi campaign against the Jews as including inflammatory photographs of kosher slaughter practices. "'Shechitah often comes under attack by elements that are unsavory, and in general, PETA is not an organization that commands our great respect.'" Also quoted was Nathan Lewin, an attorney for Agriprocessors: "'We'll put them [PETA] on the wall with Hitler.'"[11] PETA denied any sort of anti-Jewish bias. In addition to the USDA's subsequent investigation of the plant for its slaughter practices, the Environmental Protection Agency simultaneously took legal action against Agriprocessors for environmental violations.

Two years later, a series of investigative reports by Nathaniel Popper in the *Forward* described complaints about the unethical treatment of workers, as well as the hiring of illegal immigrants primarily from Guatemala. In May 2008, a federal raid of the plant led to arrests of over 300 undocumented workers, the second largest such raid in US history. The following months brought increased assessment of the whole Rubashkin family enterprise, a kosher monopoly that supplied over half of the nation's kosher meat. In the end, Agriprocessors declared bankruptcy and its CEO Sholom Rubashkin was convicted of eighty-six counts of bank fraud and sentenced to twenty-seven years in prison.

Suddenly America required a lesson in certain aspects of Jewish dietary laws, as well as the processes of kosher slaughter. The actual definition of *kosher* has nothing to do with food. The slang use of the term ("Something's not kosher here") is actually correct. A rabbi does not bless kosher meat, nor is it "cleaner" than other meat. After the raid, Rabbi Menachem Genack, the president of the Orthodox Union Kosher division, appeared on National Public Radio and explained:

> Kosher means fit, proper in accordance with Jewish law, *Halakha* and in this particular context, the way it's usually used is in reference to food products that they meet the kosher standards formulated. Initially actually in the Bible, in Leviticus, and there's rabbinic legislation which expands on it through the centuries.[12]

The allegations against Agriprocessors, however, led some to question whether unethical behavior would render otherwise kosher slaughtered meat *treyf* (nonkosher). But Agriprocessors was not just responsible for kosher meat; it was in charge of the production of *glatt* kosher meat. In its early coverage of the plant, the *New York Times* explained: "The plant is the country's largest producer of meat certified as glatt kosher, the highest standard for cleanliness under kosher law."[13] The juxtaposition of this espoused high standard with the details of violations at Agriprocessors led to a sketchy picture of the company in the media.

Iowa: A Stranger in a Strange Land

Regional Iowa papers reported on every step of the process, from the earliest charges of pollution and animal cruelty to the sentencing and its aftermath. There was not much regional discussion of Rubashkin's Jewishness until the trial began, presumably because the details of the allegations had little to do with religion. Once trial was under way, however, Rubashkin himself was the center of scrutiny and his Orthodoxy became a matter of curiosity. The regional papers offered a crash course in observant Judaism and attempted to explain some of Rubashkin's unfamiliar religious practices. The *Des Moines Register* described Rubashkin's daily routine:

> Rubashkin prays three times a day, always before eating. He must wash his hands before either act, using water from anywhere but a bathroom tap. Attached to the black straps Rubashkin wraps on his body for prayer are little black boxes containing pieces of parchment inscribed with verses of the Torah.[14]

During the trial, the *Waterloo Courier* article reported testimony from Rubashkin's wife, which explained her husband's clothing and beard.

> Asked about her husband's appearance, Leah Rubashkin said he wears the yarmulke cap to remind him that God is always above him. She said he dons his long black coat daily—an item some Jewish men only wear on the Sabbath—because of his dedication. She said the religion forbids him from shaving off his beard.[15]

Both papers also detailed the issues that Rubashkin's Jewishness caused in the jail. These began as soon as he entered custody. Rubashkin's religious observance required specific attire, food, and ritual articles for prayer. In all three instances, he met with difficulty.

> The Black Hawk County Jail staff removed Rubashkin's yarmulke and tzistzis—his skull cap and cloth white strings that hang from the hips of a man's pants.... His faith as a Hasidic Jew prohibits him from moving more than about 18 inches without the religious garb. So staff carried Rubashkin to move him around the jail before eventually providing his religious attire, according to statements made in court.[16]

In addition to the difficulties presented by the lack of a yarmulke and tzitzit, Rubashkin refused to eat.

> Defense attorney F. Montgomery Brown said Rubashkin, a Hasidic Jew, had not eaten for nearly 24 hours because the Black Hawk County Jail failed to provide kosher food that met his strict dietary requirements. "I can't represent a client that's not going to eat," he said. The county sheriff agreed to meet with a rabbi who will detail Rubashkin's religious needs. The jail provided kosher food, just not at the level Rubashkin requested, the county attorney said.[17]

This "kosher" but not "kosher enough" problem led to the media having to further explain that *kashrut* also involves the vessels for cooking and utensils.

Once the immediate needs of clothing and food were resolved, Rubashkin came up against another hurdle—his *tefillin*, those black straps and black boxes mentioned earlier, and his *tallit*, the prayer shawl. The *Des Moines Register* reported, "It was the leather straps and a prayer shawl—all viewed as potential weapons—that caused the Black Hawk County sheriff last week to deem Rubashkin's religious needs too dangerous for the local jail, county officials and Rubashkin's rabbi said."[18] These issues of religious accommodation are not unusual in prison, but it was clear that this jail had not yet encountered the needs of a prisoner like Rubashkin. "A constant tension exists between a prison's need to maintain discipline and safety and a prisoner's right to practice religion because there is no clear legal line defining when a religious accommodation becomes unreasonable, officials said."[19] As reported in the *Des Moines Register*, Rubashkin's needs began to seem unreasonable, particularly when juxtaposed with the working conditions of the illegal workers at Agriprocessors.

In addition to describing Rubashkin's distinctive behavior, the regional papers seemed fascinated with his supporters. Grant Schulte, who had been covering the trial for the *Register*, reported, "Behind him, in a wood-paneled federal courtroom, throngs of Orthodox Jews with beards and skullcaps gather to watch his trial."[20] Schulte continues: "The supporters range in age from teenagers to men with white beards hanging over their chests. They squeeze into rows of wooden courtroom benches, muttering prayers and listening to testimony. Some sway back and forth—'shuckling' in Yiddish—while reading psalms."[21] These men seem as odd and foreign as Rubashkin, with their muttering and Yiddish swaying. Photographs accompanied much of this coverage, demonstrating the physical distinctiveness of Rubashkin and his defenders.

Schulte, also reporting for the *Waterloo Courier*, captured a different scene of supporters: "More than 40 young men, most in their 20s, huddled around a big-screen television in a spillover room to watch. Some recited psalms in Hebrew. A black fedora, filled with crinkled dollar bills, passed from hand to hand."[22] Filling the fedora raised money to support Rubashkin, but given common stereotypes about Jews and money, the image is striking. Between the photographs and the written imagery, the American-born Rubashkin comes off as a caricature of a foreign Eastern European Jew.

This outsider image was not lost on Rubashkin's supporters. Schulte reported their perspective:

> Some supporters expressed anger at what they view as an unfair crackdown on Rubashkin and the plant he managed for years. Orthodox Jewish supporters point to the industry practice of hiring immigrant workers and ask why Agriprocessors was targeted. "This is a witch hunt," said David Moskovitz, an Orthodox Jew from Chicago. "And you can quote me."[23]

Rubashkin's supporters consistently argued that he shouldn't serve time due to the difficulty that a religious person would face in prison. They also argued that his ten children, particularly his autistic son, would suffer. Supporters also cited the charitable nature of the Rubashkin family. As with Jack Abramoff's black hat, Jews read the Agriprocessors/Rubashkin goings on with both a different perspective and a different investment than non-Jewish readers of the mainstream press.

Outside of Iowa: The Hypocritical Hasid

Even though Nathaniel Popper broke the Agriprocessors story in the Jewish *Forward*, it was quickly picked up by mainstream press, which had widely reported on the PETA exposé. Parallels were quickly made to *The Jungle*, Upton Sinclair's 1906 classic novel about the horrors of the American meatpacking industry. A century later, the spotlight was on a subset of this industry, the kosher meat business. Thus, while the Iowa papers focused on day-to-day events, the national news paid more attention to the ethical implications of the raid. Initially, the emphasis reflected sympathy for exploited workers. Unlike the Iowa press, papers such as the *New York Times* assumed some reader familiarity with Judaism and took greater note of Jewish issues, such as the cultural rift between different Jewish movements and ethical issues of kashrut. An editorial in the *Times* described "evidence of rampant illegal hiring at the plant," which has been called "a kosher 'Jungle.'"[24] The year 2008 was an election year, and the plight of illegal immigrants was at the forefront of presidential debates. The editorial criticized the purpose of the raid, claiming that the wrong people were vilified: "By treating illegal low-wage workers as a de facto criminal class, the government is trying to inflate the menace they pose to a level that justifies its rabid efforts to capture and punish them. That is a fraudulent exercise, and a national disgrace."[25]

Several days later, Shmuel Herzfeld, an Orthodox rabbi of a popular Washington, DC synagogue, published an op-ed titled "Dark Meat" in the *New York Times.* Herzfeld not only expressed outrage about the Orthodox community's reluctance to denounce Agriprocessors' alleged behavior but also provided Jewish precedent for declaring something *treyf* due to poor treatment of employees. Herzfeld wrote, "We need to express shame and embarrassment about the reports coming out of Iowa, and we need to actively work to change these matters."[26] A subsequent letter to the editor applauded Herzfeld, asserting, "I must rely on rabbinical supervision to determine if foods are fit to be put in my mouth. I don't need anyone to tell me that the plant's actions cannot be stomached."[27]

Not everyone heralded Herzfeld as a hero, however. More critical letters to the editor followed. Rabbis Shlomo Hochberg and Basil Herring, leaders of the Rabbinical Council of America, protested that Herzfeld greatly overstated the Orthodox community's indifference to the matter, writing:

> The council issued a lengthy public statement on June 3, expressing our concern about the allegations and calling for a full investigation of the facts. Unlike Rabbi Herzfeld, we believe that no rabbinic body—expert or otherwise—can do a better investigation than the federal and state authorities now engaged in such a review of the legal, non-kashrut aspects of Agriprocessors' operations.[28]

Menachem Genack, of the Orthodox Union, while concerned about the ethical issues raised by the raid, agreed. "We also believe, however, that the definition, assessment and enforcement of these standards are best placed in the hands of the governmental agencies that have the expertise, resources and regulatory authority to deal with them appropriately."[29]

Others criticized Herzfeld for suggesting that "kosher" should mean anything other than the proper slaughtering of a *halakhicly* sanctioned animal. Michael J. Broyde, a rabbi and law professor, wrote:

> In my view, the job of rabbis is not to certify that food is healthy, or the workers are fairly paid, or that they can legally work in the place that employs them, or that the treatment of the animals is ethical or even that the laws of the United States are followed. The job of the rabbis is to certify that the food is kosher—nothing more and nothing less.[30]

In response to the hullabaloo following Herzfeld's editorial, NPR's talk show *Tell Me More* featured both Genack and Herzfeld. Host Michel Martin posed the question: "Are people of faith call[ed] to higher standards in choosing what to buy and eat?"[31] Genack hesitated in his support for additional levels of certification, claiming again that government agencies are better suited for that sort of thing.

Herzfeld, in contrast, asserted that the Jewish community had to do more.

> I literally have received countless, countless of requests by congregants and by people in our community who have said that they're embarrassed and that they're ashamed. And they've come to me, and many of them have been crying. And they said this is dragging our name down. And it's one thing if you're in an insular Jewish community to say, OK, well we don't believe that, we can fight through this. But the world at large doesn't see it that way. If these allegations are true, this is absolutely something we need to be ashamed and embarrassed about.[32]

Others in the Jewish press criticized Herzfeld more harshly. Rabbi Avi Shafran, director of public affairs for Agudath Israel of America, responded to Herzfeld in the *Jewish Exponent*, calling his piece a "high-minded but innately ugly op-ed piece" and arguing that "the rabbi marches proudly in step with the editorial page's drumbeat, nobly slapping his fist against the collective Jewish breast in penance for the unproven sins of others."[33] Shafran echoed some of his coreligionists who have suggested that liberal Jews have mistaken liberalism for Judaism.

In response to the ongoing inter-Jewish quarrel over the scandal, the *Times* explained the players:

> The Agriprocessors raid in May fueled a fundamental debate between the Orthodox and Conservative movements of Judaism. The Orthodox, who include the majority of Jews who keep kosher, adhere to a strict interpretation of Jewish law, while the Conservative movement has a more liberal interpretation emphasizing social justice. Among Conservative Jews, a minority observe kosher laws strictly.[34]

The article also reprinted comments from Menachem Lubinsky, a spokesman for Agriprocessors, who claimed that the plant had been wrongly pursued for unproven labor violations. "Mr. Lubinsky told the *Jewish Week* newspaper that Agriprocessors was facing a 'Dreyfus trial in the media,' referring to the case of a Jewish military officer in France who was unfairly tried for treason in the late 19th century."[35] The invocation of Dreyfus's name would come up throughout this process.

Once the Rubashkin trial was under way, national attention shifted from the issues of exploited workers and the kosher industry to the person of Sholom Rubashkin. In the past, high-profile Jewish defendants such as the Rosenbergs and Leo Frank may have been coded as Jewish, but the current climate takes little notice of Judaism as a defining characteristic. The haredim *are* different, however. They look different and act different. In contemporary America, the Orthodox community stands out, and the haredim are a minority within that minority. Since haredim in America are largely disinterested in approval from the outside world, they have made little attempt to court popular opinion.

The *Village Voice*'s Elizabeth Dwoskin described the fallout from the raid and subsequent trial in her in-depth feature "The Fall of the House of Rubashkin." Dwoskin interviewed several women from the Lubavitcher stronghold of Crown Heights. Her interviewees expressed a siege mentality. Channeling statements made by Agriprocessors spokespeople, the women appear to think that this is the way the meat industry works, and that Rubashkin's plant was unfairly singled out. "'I'm just wondering if this is some old garden-variety anti-Semitism that they would be treating them [Agriprocessors] so differently,' says Chani Seligson."[36]

The haredi press highlighted protests over the "different" treatment Rubashkin received, but even secular sites like the *Huffington Post* made note of this concern:

> "He looks different, and he's being treated differently," argues Rabbi Menachem M. Katz, of the Aleph Institute, a nonprofit organization that serves Jewish inmates. . . . "[H]e's an ultra-Orthodox Hasidic Jew dealing with the justice system in a place that doesn't have Jews, in a jury pool that doesn't have Jews, in a state with very, very few Jewish residents."[37]

Dwoskin also notes a haredi finger pointing toward other Jews. Writing about Rochel (no last name given), Sholom Rubashkin's sister, Dwoskin cites a growing rage:

> Normally an amicable woman who helps out in her mother's restaurant, today she is irate. She says that liberals—including the "Jewish press"—will destroy the Jewish people and, also, the world. ". . . These are people who will fight for the rights of animals but not for the rights of an unborn child," she says.[38]

What "Jewish press" does Rochel indict? As the trial moved on, the response of the Jewish media largely fell into two distinct and vocal camps: critics gunning for Rubashkin's conviction and supporters claiming he was an innocent victim of a smear campaign. Those who fell in between found their voices drowned out by the cacophony that surrounded them. Presumably Rochel meant the *Forward*, but she could just as easily be speaking of the *New York Times*—long considered by some to be a "Jewish" paper by virtue of its Jewish ownership.

Ironically, the haredim and anti-Semitic white supremacists share an antipathy for the liberal Jewish press. In addition, haredim on the whole tend to ignore the mainstream press; Lubavitchers specifically have felt burned by secular news outlets since the early 1990s coverage of the Crown Heights riots.[39] They get their news from Internet blogs and papers deemed "safe." In Dwoskin's *Village Voice* feature, one woman shared an e-mail she received that

> asserts that the government crackdown on Agriprocessors is part of a plot by conservative Jews to take over the kosher-meat industry. "There's a lot of money in that," Ginsburg whispers. The e-mail also claimed that the government is unfairly victimizing Agriprocessors.[40]

Confirming Dwoskin's reporting, Rabbi Asher Zeilingold wrote in the Orthodox blog *Vos Iz Neias* (Yiddish for "What is News?"):

> I am deeply saddened to have to tell you that I believe without question or doubt that the Conservative Movement beleaguered Sholom Rubashkin with charges that were totally unproven only because they wanted to promote their Hekscher Tzedek. . . . They [the Conservative Movement] transgressed the most fundamental

> law of ethical and moral conduct by preaching to their constituency charges that were nothing more than the self-serving fabrication of the labor unions and the malicious design of Nathaniel Popper, who wrote his contemptible diatribe in the Forward newspaper, forming the basis of the Conservative jihad against Agriprocessors and Sholom Rubashkin.[41]

Much of the outrage about the conditions at Agriprocessors did begin inside the progressive Jewish community. Protests arose most notably from the Conservative movement, which had raised the idea of the ethical stamp of approval known as *hekhsher tzedek*. This stamp would be put on products already determined to be kosher by recognized authorities (such as the Orthodox Union), but also would signify that those goods were produced in an ethical and socially responsible manner. This proposal drew ridicule from some segments of the Orthodox community who saw it as hypocritical coming from a movement where a large number of practitioners eschew the dietary laws of kashrut.

Nonetheless, statements such as these point to an increasing paranoia on the part of the Rubashkins and their supporters. Not only is anti-Semitism a possible reason behind this "witch hunt," but the liberal Jews are in on it as well. Pinchos Lipschutz, publisher of a haredi newspaper, *Yated Ne'eman*, was quoted also placing blame on non-Orthodox Jews: "'Some liberal secular Jews look at the Orthodox like they are dirty. I think this was the secular Jews against the religious.'"[42]

Liberal Jewish media outlets publicized scandals related to the family, but not necessarily connected to Agriprocessors. One *Forward* headline read "Rubashkin Kin Guilty in Sex Case" and described the case of Yaakov Weiss, a son-in-law of Rubashkin who was found guilty of molesting a young boy at a mikvah in Albany.[43] The haredim, despite being a Jewish minority, carry with them the mantle of being considered "real" Jews due to their traditional appearance and practices. Accordingly, those who are by implication less "real" sometimes resent them.[44] Thus, schadenfreude is a frequent response to haredim caught behaving badly.

J'Accuse?

Beyond such "pleasurable anger" came outrage about the chilul haShem committed by Rubashkin. After the trial, Rubashkin's oldest daughter, Roza Weiss, was quoted in the *Des Moines Register* saying: "My only comment is, we're Jewish and we're proud of it."[45] Weiss's comment was reprinted widely in liberal Jewish media and commented upon with dismay. The *Forward* responded: "It should be deeply embarrassing to the Jewish world that a man who wraps himself in the garb, language and rhythm of an observant life should be guilty of such base behavior."[46] What was Weiss's point in asserting her family's Jewishness at that moment? Was she claiming it as a defense? Or that Jewishness was the cause of the conviction?

Like many minority groups in the United States, Jews follow the news through a lens of self-preservation. The understandable desire to point out that Jews are *not like that* is sometimes tinged with the worry that non-Jews are indeed motivated by not only a desire to bring (Jewish) criminals to justice but also latent anti-Semitism. In a world where Jewish criminals are less likely to be arrested by Jewish policemen, the question of motive might always be asked. But while many American Jews expressed horror at the continuous stream of allegations against Agriprocessors, the haredim increasingly began to close ranks around Rubashkin.

Rubashkin's twenty-seven-year sentence for bank fraud, two years more than the prosecution requested and admittedly high for a nonviolent crime, drew fury from the haredim.

"'Once again, a Jew has been scapegoated,'" declared Pinchos Lipschutz of *Yated Ne'eman* to a largely black-hatted crowd the night before Rubashkin's sentencing.[47] Lipschutz's words echoed a widespread haredi belief that Rubashkin was just one more Jew, in a long line of Jews, to suffer condemnation because of anti-Semitism.

Ultimately, the crime for which Rubashkin was found guilty had nothing to do with kashrut, but between his outfit and his occupation, his Jewish identity was hard to set aside. Unlike other infamous Jewish defendants (e.g., Frank, the Rosenbergs, or Madoff), Rubashkin was not an acculturated Jew. In some ways, the foreignness as depicted in the Iowa press—while reflecting a general ignorance about Jews—may have been helpful in creating a sympathetic portrait of a bumbling newcomer who just did not understand the type of business he was in (a portrait the right-wing Jewish press continues to perpetuate).

The true bias appears to be in the mainstream press's distraction from the specific crimes and emphasis on broader, ethical issues. Both the local papers' coverage of Rubashkin's foreignness and the national papers' coverage of ethical issues obscured the real crime and the real victims. While Rubashkin was cleared of the child labor charges—due to the admitted false documentation by the workers themselves—the acquittal doesn't change the fact that there were minors working at Agriprocessors. The conviction on fraud charges alone doesn't change the fact that the management turned a blind eye to the hundreds of undocumented workers, many of whom have been deported (some without their American-born children). Exploitation of foreign workers and minors is not new, or even unique, in American history. But by highlighting the foreignness and holy hypocrisy of the bearded man in the black hat, the victims left behind in Postville seem to be forgotten.

NOTES

1. Robin Givhan, "Jack Abramoff, Wearing a Guilty Look," *Washington Post*, January 6, 2006.
2. Jeff Jacoby, "Bringing Faith into Contempt," *Boston Globe*, January 8, 2006.
3. "A Lobbyist's Hat Raises Eyebrows," *Forward*, January 13, 2006.

4. Ibid.

5. For more information on American Jewish movements, please see Jonathan D. Sarna, *American Judaism: A History* (New Haven, CT: Yale University Press, 2004); Jack Wertheimer, *A People Divided: Judaism in Contemporary America* (Waltham, MA: Brandeis University Press, 1997).

6. Jacob Neusner, *Judaism: An Introduction* (London: Penguin, 2002).

7. Samuel Heilman, *Sliding to the Right: The Contest for the Future of American Jewish Orthodoxy* (Berkeley: University of California Press, 2006), 4.

8. Stephen G. Bloom, *Postville: A Clash of Cultures in Heartland America* (New York: Harcourt, 2000).

9. Donald G. McNeil, Jr., "Videos Cited in Calling Kosher Slaughterhouse Inhumane," *New York Times*, December 1, 2004.

10. Donald G. McNeil, Jr., "Kosher Authority Seeks Change in Steer Killings," *New York Times*, December 3, 2004.

11. Peter Ephross, "Kosher Slaughter Controversy Erupts," *Jewish Journal of Greater Los Angeles*, 2004, http://www.jewishjournal.com/world/article/kosher_slaughter_controversy_erupts_20041203/.

12. "Kosher Slaughterhouse Raises Ethical Dilemma," *Tell Me More*, National Public Radio, August 8, 2008.

13. McNeil, "Videos Cited in Calling Kosher Slaughterhouse Inhumane"; "Kosher Slaughterhouse Raises Ethical Dilemma."

14. Jens Manuel Krogstad, "Rubashkin Dispute Highlights Faith Issue," *Des Moines Register*, May 9, 2010.

15. Jeff Reinitz, "Rubashkin's Wife Takes Stand near End of Testimony," *Waterloo Courier*, June 1, 2010.

16. Krogstad, "Rubashkin Dispute Highlights Faith Issue."

17. Jens Manuel Krogstad, "Rubashkin Starts Jail Hunger Strike," *Des Moines Register*, May 5, 2010.

18. Krogstad, "Rubashkin Dispute Highlights Faith Issue."

19. Ibid.

20. Grant Schulte, "Rubashkin Draws a Loyal Following," *Des Moines Register*, November 8, 2009.

21. Ibid.

22. Grant Schulte, "Update: Rubashkin Supporters Show up as Trial Begins," *Waterloo-Cedar Falls Courier*, 2009, http://wcfcourier.com/news/local/article_bfd8d1ce-b80b-11de-8a07-001cc4c002e0.html.

23. Schulte, "Rubashkin Draws a Loyal Following."

24. "'The Jungle,' Again," *New York Times*, August 1, 2008.

25. Ibid.

26. Shmuel Herzfeld, "Dark Meat," *New York Times*, August 6, 2008.

27. "Letters: What Happened at the Meatpacking Plant?" *New York Times*, August 13 2008.

28. Ibid.

29. Ibid.

30. Ibid.

31. "Kosher Slaughterhouse Raises Ethical Dilemma."

32. Ibid.

33. Avi Shafran, "In Agriprocessors Case, Does Journalism Play Judge, Jury?" *Jewish Exponent*, August 28, 2008.

34. Julia Preston, "Rabbis Debate Kosher Ethics at Meat Plant," *New York Times*, August 23, 2008.

35. Ibid.

36. Elizabeth Dwoskin, "The Fall of the House of Rubashkin: As the Nation's Largest Kosher Empire Implodes, Brooklyn's Ultra-Orthodox Jews Begin to Break Ranks," *Village Voice*, December 3, 2008.

37. Nicole Neroulias, "Jews Worry as Slaughterhouse Chief Faces Jail Time," *Huffington Post*, April 19, 2010, http://www.huffingtonpost.com/2010/04/19/jews-worry-as-slaughterho_n_543288.html.

38. Dwoskin, "The Fall of the House of Rubashkin."

39. Ibid.

40. Ibid.

41. Asher Zeilingold, "The Conservative Movement Needs to Take Responsibility and Admit the Truth," *Vos Iz Neias*, 2010, http://www.vosizneias.com.

42. Edwin Black, "Is a Life Sentence for Iowa Kosher Butcher Disproportionate Justice?" *The Cutting Edge*, 2010, http://www.thecuttingedgenews.com/index.php?article=12123%3Cbr%20/%3E.

43. Debra Nussbaum Cohen, "Rubashkin Kin Guilty in Sex Case," *Forward*, January 22, 2010.

44. For more on this conflict, see Samuel G. Freedman, *Jew vs. Jew: The Struggle for the Soul of American Jewry* (New York: Simon & Schuster, 2000).

45. Grant Schulte, "Sholom Rubashkin Guilty on 86 Charges in Fraud Trial Involving Postville Meat Plant," *Des Moines Register*, November 13, 2009.

46. "Rubashkin's Crimes," *Forward*, November 27, 2009.

47. Michael Orbach, "Saving Sholom Rubashkin," *Jewish Star*, June 23, 2010, http://www.thejewishstar.com/stories/SavingSholomRubashkin,1816?content_source=&category_id=&search_filter=rubashkin&event_mode=&event_ts_from=&list_type=&order_by=&order_sort=&content_class=&sub_type=&;town_id=.

REFERENCES

Bloom, Stephen G. 2000. *Postville: A Clash of Cultures in Heartland America*. New York: Harcourt, 2000.

Dwoskin, Elizabeth. 2008. The Fall of the House of Rubashkin: As the Nation's Largest Kosher Empire Implodes, Brooklyn's Ultra-Orthodox Jews Begin to Break Ranks. *Village Voice*, December 3, 2008.

Forward. Rubashkin's Crimes. November 27, 2009.

Freedman, Samuel G. 2000. *Jew vs. Jew: The Struggle for the Soul of American Jewry*. New York: Simon & Schuster.

Heilman, Samuel. 2006. *Sliding to the Right: The Contest for the Future of American Jewish Orthodoxy*. Berkeley: University of California Press.

Preston, Julia. 2008. Rabbis Debate Kosher Ethics at Meat Plant. *New York Times*, August 23, 2008.

Rubel, Nora L. 2010. *Doubting the Devout: The Ultra-Orthodox in the Jewish American Imagination, Religion and American Culture*. New York: Columbia University Press.

Sarna, Jonathan D. 2004. *American Judaism: A History*. New Haven, CT: Yale University Press.
Shafran, Avi. 2008. In Agriprocessors Case, Does Journalism Play Judge, Jury? *Jewish Exponent*, August 28, 2008.
Shalit, Wendy. 2005. The Observant Reader. *New York Times*, January 30, 2005.
Wertheimer, Jack. 1997. *A People Divided: Judaism in Contemporary America*. Waltham, MA: Brandeis University Press.

CHAPTER 14

MEDIA REPRESENTATIONS OF "SUNBELT" EVANGELICALISM

DARREN DOCHUK

"Born Again"

With a flash of fresh insight that historians now consider strikingly prescient, *Newsweek* declared 1976 the "year of the evangelical." Amid bicentennial celebrations and Jimmy Carter's campaign for the fall election, evangelicals seemed to be everywhere, thinking, talking, and acting as a new cultural force—*the* new cultural force—in modern America. "There is a hidden religious power base in American culture which our secular biases prevent many of us from noticing," Michael Novak opined in *Newsweek*'s pages. "Jimmy Carter has found it."[1]

What Carter had found required a careful elucidation of new trends in American religious sensibility, regional alignment, economy, and political mobilization, which *Newsweek* provided in rich detail. Evangelicals, the magazine explained, "are Protestants who take a conservative view of Christian doctrine, emphasize morality rather than social ethics, look to the Bible as the sole authority in faith and practice and tend to regard themselves as the only true heirs of the New Testament church." Found throughout the country, they nevertheless gather in largest numbers along the southern rim of the country, *Newsweek* noted, creating a regional imbalance with important cultural and political implications. Unlike evangelicalism in the "Middle West," where Christian citizens "embrace Jesus" with little "effusiveness," "in the South, religion is traditionally a more demonstrative affair, and revivalism . . . a form of people's theater." What did this mean? It meant a new era of evangelical "political muscle-flexing," and in the immediate, flexing for Carter. "In Texas, where Southern Baptists have literally inherited the earth and faith is as partisan as football," *Newsweek* teased when making this point, "furor over the Carter candidacy has stripped away the last veneer of Southern Baptist [and evangelical] claims to political nonpartisanship." To add a serious bent to its playfulness, the magazine next quoted James L. Sullivan, president of the Southern Baptist Convention, whose forthrightness made it clear that evangelicals meant business in their engagement with the political world: "If we do not seize this opportunity . . . I think God's condemnation will be upon us."[2]

Newsweek was not the only media outlet to ruminate on evangelicalism's remarkable and seemingly sudden climb into mainstream status. Throughout the 1970s, other major periodicals, most notably *Time* and the *New York Times*, profiled evangelicalism's ascent. They did so to understand the internal workings of this faith community, but also to grasp the social, economic, and political forces thrusting this movement forward. Evangelicalism's rise, the press emphasized, was the product of a "power shift" in American society away from the urban centers of the "Rustbelt" Northeast and Midwest to the sprawling metroplexes of the emerging "Sunbelt" South. Whether referencing the Jesus People and mega-churches of Southern California or Tom Landry and the Dallas Cowboys, Billy Graham and Richard Nixon or Oral Roberts and Jimmy Carter, the nation's media establishment seemed enthralled with evangelicalism as a window onto the Sunbelt's soul and, in essence, the emerging America of the 1970s.

Through a survey of articles published in the three periodicals highlighted above, this chapter briefly tracks evangelicalism's rise in the 1970s and demonstrates how media portrayals of it became catchall critiques of society. In this volatile moment, evangelicalism was converted into a lightening rod as much as a measuring stick for scrutiny of America's encounter with regional change and all of the pronounced cultural divides it seemed to create—between North and South, certainly, but also between industrial and postindustrial economies, urban and suburban communities, conventional and innovative cultural styles, white and nonwhite citizens, and liberal and conservative political interests. As this chapter will show, pundits reached no consensus in their appraisal of America's 1970s turn, but they did agree on one essential truth: as Sunbelt evangelicalism went, so would go the nation.

With a Bible in One Hand and a Computer in the Other

In the same way *Newsweek* attributed America's "born again" phenomenon of 1976 to new Sunbelt trends, the *New York Times* and *Time* connected evangelicalism's rise to an emerging New South that stretched from Southern California to South Carolina. "Evangelicals flourish in many parts of the country," *Time* conceded in an editorial that appeared just weeks before *Newsweek*'s "Year of the Evangelical" issue, "but nowhere are they more identified with the prevailing religious culture than in the South."[3] What made the evangelical South so powerful was that it was emboldened by America's economic revolution, which was transforming the nation from a modern industrial state into a postindustrial, high-tech society. In an editorial published in conjunction with *Time*'s look at the New South, one astute commentator suggested that evangelicalism's ascent came because it was eager to meld traditional values with the requisites of cutting-edge economy. "The New South is carrying a computer in one hand and the Bible in the other," he declared.[4]

Two journalists had already underscored this feature when introducing the "Sunbelt" concept at the decade's beginning. It was Kevin Phillips who resurrected a 1940s military term—"sunshine belt," used to describe favorable testing conditions south of the thirty-seventh parallel—and applied it to the new realities of American politics. In his best seller *The Emerging Republican Majority*, the pundit described a new alloy of conservatism that united voters across the southern rim of the country behind a pro-growth, pro-family, pro-defense, pro-business, antistatist agenda.[5] Whereas Phillips heralded this developing trend as a boon to the GOP, Kirkpatrick Sale decried it. In his book *Power Shift*, Sale spoke critically of the way a new class of boosters had pried "the balance of power in America away from the Northeast and toward the Southern Rim."[6] Here, along the "broad band . . . that stretches from Southern California . . . into the Deep South," a "power base" had taken shape, built upon unsurpassed in-migration and "the giant new postwar industries of defense, aerospace, technology, electronics, agribusiness, and oil-and-gas extraction."[7] Sale saw that this "Southern Rim" had achieved supremacy by the 1970s and would dictate American politics for the "foreseeable future."[8] From his perspective, the rise of the Sunbelt portended the nation's decline.

Despite their differences of opinion, Phillips and Sale crafted the concept of a region that cohered around a distinctive economic and religious culture. Postindustrial in its new dependence on the service, technology, defense, and leisure sectors, Phillips's Sunbelt (Sale's Southern Rim) was also poststructural in its urban layouts, with communities sprawling out from the city's edge. In this expansive landscape, residents internalized free market assurances and sought to limit the reach of the federal state. They also championed an assertive evangelicalism that sanctified suburban emphases on local autonomy and community protection. Many of Phillips and Sale's contemporaries helped them unpack the priorities of this evangelical subculture. In 1976, Carey McWilliams, editor of *The Nation*, explained that the "God-fearing, up-and-coming types" who lived in the "missile crescent," stretching from "Florida . . . to Southern California," constituted a "movement" ideally suited to their "jerry-built suburban" communities built on "cheap land" with the aid of "tax inducements, lower wage scales, less union activity . . . [and] defense spending." The "God factor" now overtaking the country, he summarized, was a producer and product of the Sunbelt economic juggernaut, and it promised to have a commanding presence for years to come.[9]

As Sale's and McWilliams's writings suggest, much of the print media's take on the economic power of the Sunbelt and its evangelical constituents clanged with criticism, some of it explicit and biting, most of it implicit and searing. Folded into journalistic accounts of Sunbelt religion and economy were critiques of the corporate turn driving 1970s America into a new economic order. The *New York Times* encouraged this reasoning by publishing a series of articles in 1976 that stressed regional change in a national context of financial strain. Wayne King opened the discussion by announcing, "The factors behind the emergence of the Sunbelt as a powerful and cohesive region are multiple rapidly changing industrial, economic and population patterns, new living styles, a balmy climate."[10] King's piece made it clear that, even as the country paused to commemorate its past, impatient citizens clustered along its southern rim were far ahead in imagining an illustrious future where old, Rustbelt styles of labor politics were about to be jettisoned for good. To be sure, critics of this corporate turn admitted that the antiquated ways of the industrial North were partly to blame for the predicament. When referencing union struggles in Houston, for instance, the *New York Times* admitted, "labor's problems seem to be mostly of its own making: unions, once powerful, have not adapted themselves to the changing labor force."[11] Still, as far as *Time*, *Newsweek*, and the *New York Times* saw it, the Sunbelt insurgency came courtesy of a business strategy to freeze out unions and undermine principles of industrial unionism—in short, to keep the new America "untarnished" by Rustbelt ways.

Evangelicalism, critics pointed out, helped shape this system by sanctifying a gospel of bootstrap entrepreneurialism, anathema to the industrial economy of the North. Indeed, any talk about shifting realities in America's political economy frequently came paired with commentary on evangelicalism's role in this process. "The movement is now richer and more powerful than it has been in half a century," *Time* emphasized, before pointing out Sunbelt evangelicalism's reliance on business tycoons, ranging from Dallas billionaire Nelson Bunker Hunt to Holiday Inn's founder and "praying millionaire," Wallace Johnson.[12] Ready to fund evangelical ministries like the Sunbelt-based Campus Crusade for Christ as eagerly as they fought labor unions, the Hunts and Johnsons of the Sunbelt evangelical world were, in a majority of journalists' opinions, the face of America's new economy.

Many pundits took the critique of the new evangelicalism one step further by lambasting its commercialization. Fueled by Hunt and Johnson's booster class, Sunbelt evangelicalism fell easy victim to charges that it now blended "show biz and salvation" with willing ease.[13] Oft-cited facts about evangelicalism's growing media enterprises helped journalists shore up this conclusion. Reporting on the Christian Booksellers Association convention in 1978, *Time*, for instance, noted that the meeting's "sometimes strange mix of piety and commerce . . . is the central show of a big business," with 263 retailers selling their wares of "mawkish, illuminated paintings of Jesus, T-shirts that proclaim HE IS RISEN, PRAISE THE LORD paper napkins and LAST JUDGMENT AT HAND bumper stickers" and books and music written by a host of "Born-Again" celebrities.[14] *Newsweek* provided its own coverage of evangelical consumption by profiling Christian nightclubs. At nightspots like the Daisy in Beverly Hills, *Newsweek* explained, religion is offered with hip music and cherry Cokes, making it "more alive and fun than going to church." Elsewhere, in Dallas and Atlanta, clubs with names like King's Village and Joyful Noise offered "supper-style buffets and name gospel singers." There, *Newsweek* quipped, evangelical club members could, for a dollar, purchase "non-alcoholic drinks with names like Promised Land and Samson's Delight."[15]

To be sure, *Time*, *Newsweek*, and the *New York Times* typically left room for counterarguments, noting that the new corporate evangelicalism was a natural challenge to "dead churches" and "the more staid religious establishment" of the Protestant mainstream.[16] By supplying cradle-to-grave ministries that employed all the latest strategies in corporate outreach and expansion, evangelicalism, they conceded, was reaching a vast pool of people that older methods and institutions could not.[17] Still, the overriding sense that emerged from these periodicals was that the "Fervor and Froth" of the Sunbelt enterprising evangelicalism came at the cost of authenticity.[18] Though able to reach the masses with unmatched efficiency and effect, evangelicalism, it seemed to many commentators, was about to be consumed by the secular forces of commerce it had once stood so fearfully against.

The "Unbuckled" Sunbelt

Even as they critiqued Sunbelt evangelicalism's affinity for free market economics, journalists found it difficult to resist fascination with the "unbuckled" look of Sunbelt evangelicalism. What caught their eye most was the youthful confidence and exuberance it exuded.[19] Beginning in 1970 and continuing throughout the decade, *Time*, *Newsweek*, and the *New York Times* kept their gaze on evangelicalism's young baby boomers. In 1971, for instance, *New York Times* reporter Douglas Kneeland penetrated the ranks of California's "Jesus People" to understand how they were supplanting the counterculture spirit of the 1960s with a counter-counterculture spirit of the 1970s. "Just as the radicals gained adherents because of the wide disenchantment among the young," he explained, this "Christian movement is attracting many who are disillusioned with . . . the quality of American life, including . . . the so-called counterculture."[20] Kneeland was struck with the sense of community that permeated the Jesus People, as well as the simple gospel it endorsed, which allowed for creative forms of worship. America's next generation of leaders, he mused, participated in rituals of devotion that blended the contemporary with the ancient. They published a newspaper called *The Fish*, met in seminar groups where "cheerful smiles and friendly hugs" were common greetings and debates about current events were common occurrences, and gathered in cavernous auditoriums to sing emotional choruses about Christian sacrifice and Christ's return.[21]

For detractors, such displays seemed dangerous. By replacing a "drug high" with a "spiritual high," one critic offered, the Jesus People simply traded one questionable dependency for another, and by teaching a gospel of personal redemption it was shunning social involvement. "The Jesus Movement is not going to lift a finger to change the status quo," a worried observer noted. "They're waiting for the Second Coming and Christ is going to take care of all that."[22] A few evangelicals chimed in with their own caution, stating that the Jesus People "might become a fad."[23] But others like Reverend Billy Graham countered such criticisms. He joked that "even if the craving for Christ was a youthful fad, it was better than organized brick-throwing parties," encouraged by the Left.[24] In his eyes, the "unbuckling" of evangelicalism that the Jesus People epitomized was a good thing, for it encouraged Protestantism to regain its energy amid rising secularism, and America to regain its moral compass in the face of cynicism and despair.

Graham's celebration of California's Jesus People received even greater attention in 1972 as their movement went national. In March of 1972, Edward B. Fiske offered *New York Times* readers a glimpse into the future when he suggested "the 1970s will be a decade of evangelical revival,"[25] a claim he based on the way the young people's awakening continued to spread. Though noticeably objective, Fiske's article did not avoid liberally tinged worries that this phenomenon was promoting excesses. "It has already developed to the point where it has produced its own institutions, mainly communes, and some groups have all the earmarks of developing into regular cults." Fiske was most concerned, though, with predicting how the Jesus movement would affect societal trends, and here he pointed to "Explo '72," a Christian rock festival planned for Dallas in June. The "Jesus People" are only "the tip of the iceberg," Fiske insisted, for this small cohort's fervor was driving a mass happening for America's middle-class youth.[26] Fiske was there to cover this happening in Dallas later that year, and his reporting for the *New York Times* joined a chorus of commentaries that appeared in *Time* and *Newsweek*.[27] "It's a religious Woodstock," he explained, in one of his first articles about Campus Crusade's weeklong festival, and "it has drawn more than 75,000 . . . high school and college students—to sing, pray, study their Bibles and learn new techniques for winning souls for Christ." Though many of Explo's participants arrived barefooted and dressed casually in T-shirts and shorts, they were hardly radical, Fiske emphasized. "Most delegates are white and still sympathetic to middle-class values. All are neat and well-mannered."[28] If otherwise in appearance, the "unbuckled" Sunbelt, in his estimation, was more single-minded than laid back.

It was also more masculine. Journalists who critiqued the Sunbelt's youthful evangelicalism underlined its "muscular" qualities. In an article titled "Religion: God's Muscle," a 1973 *Time* issue traced the evangelical youth movement's impact on sport. *Time* teased:

> When God created man he set him up to score big in life. He put Adam on first base and gave him a choice: he could run with God and never get thrown out—or he could try it on his own. Adam chose to go it alone and was nailed. In fact, the attempted steal failed so miserably that the team still hasn't recovered. God never meant for it to be so difficult. He sent a pinch runner, Jesus Christ. . . .[29]

This was an "inelegant . . . sweat-soaked version of the Gospel," *Time* admitted, but one that resonated with the Fellowship of Christian Athletes (FCA) and Athletes in Action (AIA), two Sunbelt-centered ministries in which muscular metaphors permeated daily discourse. In this and subsequent articles that appeared in its pages, *Time* noted that hundreds of "prominent athletes" were "practicing locker-room piety alongside the swingers of sport."[30] This tongue-and-cheek tone was not uncommon in the print media's dealings with 1970s evangelicalism and athletics, but behind the humor stood a truth journalists took seriously: the Sunbelt knew no boundaries when it came to exporting its values, whether they were harnessed to lessons from the gridiron or lessons from the pulpit and pew.

One of the ways in which journalists traced the emergence of Sunbelt evangelicalism's masculinity was by way of spiritual biographies.[31] In Dallas Cowboy Coach Tom Landry, writers found the perfect case study. A stately gentleman known for patrolling the sidelines in a suit, Landry was all business in his coaching, as well as his faith. As president of the FCA, he offered emotional testimonials of faith at Billy Graham revivals, but he was also cerebral to the core, *Newsweek* emphasized, and liked to apply an "orderly, computerized approach" to his weekly game plans.[32] "Landry once sold insurance," *Time* joked in 1978, "so he is quite at home in Dallas, one of the country's major insurance centers. As any good actuary should, he relentlessly computes the possibilities and probabilities that govern the chaotic life span of a football game."[33] Landry's team embodied his outlook, as well as the "unbuckled" Sunbelt style. Led by their celebrated coach whose cool professionalism never got in the way of his emotive Christianity or passion to win, the Cowboys also consisted of dazzling athletes, glamorous cheerleaders, and an oil-tycoon owner (Clint Murchison) whose personalities captured the "born-again spirit of nouveau riche Dallas society."[34] As the representative of Sunbelt fortune, the Cowboys emblemized the America to come, just as the team it faced in several Super Bowls during the 1970s—the Pittsburgh Steelers—stood for Rustbelt grit amid a dying way of life.

"The New Ellis Island"

Journalists embedded evangelicalism in another narrative during the 1970s, one that portrayed the Sunbelt as "The New Ellis Island." In an article that used this phrase as its subtitle, *Time* analyzed immigration patterns to Los Angeles. There, sojourners from Latin America and Asia had turned Southern California into a haven of multiculturalism.[35] "Stretched and shaped by the automobile into a half urban, half suburban archipelago," *Time* explained, Los Angeles was "the first great Sunbelt city" and hence the first to be transformed by the new immigration, but it was not the last.[36] As the 1970s unfolded it became evident that other Sunbelt cities, which shared Los Angeles' burgeoning economy and layout, were favored destinations of the world's migrants. Developing alongside this dramatic growth, journalists surmised, was a new pattern of race relations, one in which "color-blindness" and multicultural cooperation was encouraged on the surface, but conflict brewed below. As an indelible feature of the Sunbelt, evangelicalism was considered a force that stirred up these tensions as much as it helped ameliorate them.

Pundits were openly surprised by the way evangelicalism performed the second of these functions. Almost counterintuitively, they remarked, evangelicalism's rising fortunes in the American South were tied to an impressive degree of multiculturalism. When describing the "God factor" in American politics, Carey McWilliams, for example, emphasized that the Christian citizens who inhabited the missile crescent's "jerry-built" suburbs were "by no means exclusively white." "Thousands of Blacks, Chicanos, Orientals, Indians and White ethnics," he stressed, called this region's suburbs home.[37] And the suburban churches these citizens frequented, other journalists pointed out, were growing at unprecedented rates. Throughout the 1970s, religion reporters kept readers updated on church growth trends that reflected a steep rise by evangelical bodies and a decline by liberal ones. It was their theological strictness combined with broadening social inclusiveness, experts suggested, that made evangelical churches attractive.[38] Reporting just before decade's end, Kenneth Briggs of the *New York Times* succinctly summarized ten years of development: "Knots of religious enthusiasts formed outside the ecclesiastical mainstream; many of the great historic Protestant churches took a statistical nosedive, and 'born again' Christianity emerged as the success story in growth and vitality."[39] Evangelicalism, Briggs and his cohort concluded, could no longer be dismissed as parochial.

Journalists, meanwhile, located additional evidence of evangelicalism's expanding global vision in its vibrant ecumenism. Their accounts came wrapped in a language of surprise tinted with skepticism. In one of many reports on American evangelicalism's attempts to build an international alliance, *Time* tracked Billy Graham and his contemporaries as they coordinated ecumenical meetings in Switzerland and Mexico, with hopes of forming an international governing body. "Individualists all," *Time* quipped, "evangelicals are loath to construct a bureaucracy, and many of them think that church movements should adopt a low profile at a time when the secular world seems hypnotized by power."[40] Nevertheless, evangelicals were now penetrating Eastern Europe and forging impressive alliances with "Third World churches."[41] Graham's Jesus was no longer a "Westerner," pundits jibed, nor was he Baptist or Presbyterian.[42] Even as evangelicals pursued connections abroad, they fashioned a cooperative spirit at home, and the product was striking as far as journalists were concerned. Proof of this came at the 1978 Congress of the Laity, organized by Texas millionaire Howard E. Butt, Jr.[43] According to Briggs in another *New York Times* essay, the meeting was "the latest in a series of moves by evangelicals to reach across the chasm that has divided conservatives from liberals, and it relates to what some churchmen call 'the second stage' of the evangelical awakening."[44] Evangelicalism, Briggs and his cohort concluded, could no longer be dismissed as sectarian.

When commenting on evangelicalism's new inclusiveness, journalists often singled out a third factor in this global force: Neo-Pentecostalism, otherwise known as the Charismatic Movement. In much the same way the Jesus People mystified journalists for the way they translated New Testament notions of community to the modern day, Neo-Pentecostals mystified pundits for the way they channeled the "gifts of the spirit" into everyday life. This emphasis on the outpouring of supernatural powers—evidenced by speaking in tongues, prophesying, and healing—were staples of the Charismatic Movement and made it a reforming impulse within the broader evangelical scene. The *New York Times*, *Time*, and *Newsweek* accounted for the intensity with which Neo-Pentecostalism contributed to the venture. "Pentecostalism Surges in Brazil," a *New York Times* headline from 1972, was typical for the way it announced the Charismatic Movement's exportation to the global South.[45] This same year, another article outlined other reasons for Neo-Pentecostalism international prominence. Besides offering new theological emphases on spiritual experience, upon which Protestants and Catholics could unite, Neo-Pentecostalism also compelled devotees to embrace biblical prophecy. End-times theology was popular among all evangelicals, but Neo-Pentecostals latched onto it as a map of God's active work around the globe, among peoples of all nationalities, but especially among Jews in the Middle East, where Christ was expected to return.[46] Suddenly, reporters opined, Protestants, Catholics, and Jews seemed swept up together in anticipation of Christ's Second Coming.

Neo-Pentecostalism's globalizing impulses played out on American soil as well. Throughout the 1970s, journalists watched closely as the Charismatic Movement expanded its institutional base. In 1972, Edward Fiske profiled Oral Roberts and his new university in Tulsa, Oklahoma. Roberts "is a former tent evangelist and faith healer who never finished college," Fiske began, yet here he was overseeing a modern educational empire, whose focal point was a "shiny 200-foot space needle known as the Prayer Tower." What was most surprising, Fiske's *New York Times* article pointed out, was that Roberts had "demonstrated that it is possible to run a modern university under traditional disciplinary methods and values."[47] Technologically sophisticated, theologically conservative, and commercially savvy, Oral Roberts University was proving that the new Pentecostalism was perfectly suited for its Sunbelt setting. By the late 1970s, pundits saw this marriage on a wider plain among Neo-Pentecostal preachers whose appeal across cultural boundaries outshone even Roberts's. In San Diego, reporters noted as an example, Morris Cerullo was setting the pace by building a $100 million "futuristic 'world outreach center'" that included "a 6,000-seat worship center, elaborate television studios, a school for training ministers, housing for the elderly, a 200-bed convalescent hospital, a kindergarten-through-12th grade private school and Mr. Cerullo's staff headquarters."[48] Cerullo, more than Roberts, truly stood for Neo-Pentecostalism's dispensation of multicultural success.

This success, though, came clouded in controversy. As much as journalists conceded Sunbelt evangelicalism's ability to unite people from all walks of life, they also cautioned that its internationalism opened the door for scandal and exclusion on different grounds. In the first place, critics pointed out, pastors like Cerullo were building international empires on shaky foundations by shady means. In one of his signature articles on the "Electronic Church," Briggs provided a penetrating account of the televangelism Neo-Pentecostals were using to reach their audience. "Religious commitment has traditionally meant joining a church," he began. "But the advent of television has added an option and perhaps changed the spiritual habits of millions of Americans. Those who look for hymns, sermons and Biblical advice can turn to an array of preachers with a flick of the switch."[49] This flick of the switch was too easy, he suggested, because it drained the gospel of substance.

Charges that televangelism was vapid were not uncommon, nor were more searing criticisms that its Sunbelt booster spirit lacked propriety. Years before televangelism's scandals of the 1980s, the press was already hinting at the ways Southern television preachers like Jim Bakker were employing questionable tactics to take their ministries global. In 1978, Betsy Carter offered *Newsweek* readers one of the first looks inside Bakker's North Carolina Praise the Lord (PTL) television network. It was Bakker's funding that caught Carter's attention. "While the talk and music of PTL are spiritual," she wrote, "there is also a strong secular pitch for fund-raising."[50] Where were the dollars going, she asked? To PTL's "Heritage Village," a 25-acre complex that "houses a $5 million TV studio, several red-brick Colonial style buildings, [and] a swimming pool, that doubles as a baptismal font and meditation gardens filled with magnolias and azaleas."[51] Bakker's cash flow, Carter added, was also going to PTL's work in South Korea and Japan, which she let Bakker describe as a close to her piece. "'Our goal is to reach every human being on earth and teach them there is only peace through Christ. . . . I believe that Christian television will be the tool that ushers in the triumphant return of Jesus Christ.'"[52]

If Carter's treatment of Bakker hinted at charges of hypocrisy that would become commonplace in *Time*, *Newsweek*, and the *New York Times* during the PTL scandal in the 1980s, it also employed a tone that pundits would use when leveling more damning criticism of Sunbelt evangelicalism in the 1970s. The "New Ellis Island" was not so inclusive when viewed closely, some contended. In the first place, evangelicalism's rank and file did not necessarily accept the diversity evidenced in evangelicalism's ecumenical overtures, not without questioning it at least.[53] Secondly, the "color-blind" conservatism to which Sunbelt citizens looked for answers to society's racial strife was not without racial prejudices. The very notion of color-blindness struck critics as naïve at best, and manipulative at worst. By moving past the rhetoric of race, an emerging Sunbelt GOP was able to escape the demons of a Jim Crow past, pundits observed, but this did not mean that Jim Crow did not persist in subtler (and more odious) forms in the shimmering white suburbs of Atlanta, Dallas, and Los Angeles. Sunbelt evangelicalism, in other words, was contributing to a dangerous illusion of racial innocence.

It was also participating in the political enforcement of other prejudices based on gender and sexuality. Indeed, if Sunbelt evangelicalism seemed remarkably determined to put race on the political backburner, it also seemed equally resolute to ensure that traditional, heterosexual "family values" dictated daily life in the suburbs.

Between 1978 and 1980, as political fights over the Equal Rights Amendment, abortion, and gay rights intensified, evangelicals across the southern rim of the country carried the mantle as protectors of a conservative social order, and reporters covered their every move. One illustrative article from *Newsweek* in 1978 suggested the scale of the new crusade when covering the campaign against gay rights in South Florida. With extensive detail, and an impressive impartiality that would become rare as the war over gay rights heated up, *Newsweek* profiled Anita Bryant, who now donned the role as "the Carry Nation of the sexual counter-revolution."[54] "All over Miami, sexual fundamentalists and gay activists are mobilizing for a somewhat bizarre but deadly serious battle over gay rights," *Newsweek* offered, before explaining how the fight was triggered by a referendum on a county ordinance banning discrimination in employment and housing based on a person's sexual preference. While Florida's gay activists saw the ordinance as a way to secure their public freedoms, Bryant and her grassroots warriors vowed to defeat it through a "decency crusade."[55]

Bryant's promises were being felt nationwide, *Newsweek* emphasized, but especially across the South, all the way to California. For Sunbelt evangelicals, gay rights sparked several anxieties, not the least of which was the possibility of gay teachers using "the schools to influence children in favor of homosexuality and perhaps even to molest them."[56] With such a severe threat facing them, Bryant and her coalition of fundamentalists employed severe language, calling homosexuals "human garbage," contending that Miami's "antidiscrimination law could protect the right to have 'intercourse with beasts,'" and speculating that the "drought in California might be God's punishment . . . for passing liberal antidiscrimination laws."[57] Such rhetoric covered over several complex issues that could be debated rationally from both sides of the battle, *Newsweek* emphasized, but the reality at hand was that Sunbelt inclusivity had clear limits, and these limits were about to be imposed on the rest of the nation. Regardless of whether it wins or not, *Newsweek* concluded, "Anita Bryant's crusade will be felt for years to come."[58]

"The Americanization of Dixie"

Bryant won, of course, paving the way for a broader quest by Sunbelt conservatives to capture national power with Ronald Reagan in 1980. Throughout the lead-up to the 1980 election, and well into the Reagan years, the Sunbelt and its distinctive evangelical subculture would continue to be critiqued by *Newsweek*, *Time*, and the *New York Times*. As they did in 1976, during the "year of the evangelical," these periodicals would use developments within the New South's evangelicalism as a window into the soul of the country. With increasing regularity, however, their assessments would lean to the negative side.

In this sense, they would follow the lead of John Egerton, who, with Kirkpatrick Sale and Carey McWilliams, was among the first outspoken liberal critics of the

Sunbelt evangelical dispensation. In the mid-1970s, this proud southerner and accomplished journalist wrote with resignation that Sunbelt spirituality was a sign of the "southernization of America" and the "Americanization of Dixie." "The modern, acquisitive, urban, industrial, post-segregationist, on-the-make South," he wrote, is "coming back to the Mother Country, coming back with a bounce in its step, like a salesman on the route, eager to please, eager on making it. There ain't no revolution."[59] For Egerton, as for many of his colleagues by the mid-1980s, if there was a Sunbelt "revolution," it was nothing to celebrate.

Indeed, what journalists increasingly agreed upon by the mid-1980s was that the nation glimpsed an increasingly ominous future in the Sunbelt, one that was not nearly as bright as this region's gilded veneer suggested. During this time, pundits took special aim at the New South's evangelicalism as it became more heavily politicized. Whereas in the 1970s their appraisal of this entity displayed as much curiosity as disdain, in the 1980s they would grow sharper and more impatient.[60] In an expansive, front-page article, whose title incorporated this language, John Herbers outlined point by point how the trends journalists once found intriguing about 1970s evangelicalism—its economic power, cultural style, global outlook, and media capabilities—were now being marshaled to create "a surging new force in politics."[61] Evangelicalism, Herbers suggested to his *New York Times* audience, was now the glue in a conservative bloc that combined the priorities of family, basic morality, free market economics, and opposition to government into one potent political force. For the next decade, journalists would watch closely as this "ubiquitous" "Sunbelt churchianity" continued to tilt the region and country toward the right.[62]

And they would also watch closely as this force, combined with darker trends of economic decline and environmental disaster, further exposed the Sunbelt's troubled core.[63] Their observations would come packaged in a discourse of dramatic contrast between the utopian dreams of Sunbelt boosters and dystopian realities of this region's inhabitants—between the "sense of excitement" that the Sunbelt elicited and the good deal of "terror" it stirred up, between the "excellent and beautiful" it possessed and the "bad and ugly" that often overshadowed all else.[64] As an essential part of this equation, the new evangelicalism would continue to be portrayed as a movement plagued with its own Sunbelt excesses, unable ever to escape the existential contradictions of the region it helped create.

NOTES

1. "Born Again!" *Newsweek*, October 25, 1976, 68.
2. Ibid., 69, 70.
3. "A Born-Again Faith," *Time*, September 27, 1976.
4. "A Computer and a Bible," *Time*, September 27, 1976.
5. Kevin Phillips, *The Emerging Republican Majority* (New Rochelle, NY: Arlington House, 1969).

6. Kirkpatrick Sale, *Power Shift: The Rise of the Southern Rim and Its Challenges to the Eastern Establishment* (New York: Random House, 1975), 6.

7. Ibid., 5–7.

8. Ibid., 7.

9. Quoted in Darren Dochuk, *From Bible Belt to Sunbelt: Plain-folk Religion, Grassroots Politics, and the Rise of Evangelical Conservatism* (New York: Norton, 2011), 370.

10. Wayne King, "Federal Funds Pour into Sunbelt States," *New York Times*, February 9, 1976.

11. "Labor Union Problems in the Sunbelt," *New York Times*, March 5, 1983.

12. "That Old Time Religion," *Time*, December 26, 1977.

13. Ibid.

14. "Fervor and Froth," *Time*, July 26, 1976.

15. "Nightclubs for Christ," *Newsweek*, June 13, 1977, 98.

16. "That Old Time Religion," *Time*, December 26, 1977.

17. Ibid.

18. "Fervor and Froth," *Time*, July 26, 1976.

19. "The Unbuckled Sunbelt Look," *Time*, February 21, 1977.

20. Douglas E. Kneeland, "The Jesus Movement Spreading on Campus," *New York Times*, December 26, 1971.

21. Ibid.

22. Ibid.

23. "Youth Is Stressed by Evangelicals," *New York Times*, April 25, 1971.

24. Ibid.

25. Edward B. Fiske, "The Strong Current of Spiritual Revival," *New York Times*, March 5, 1972.

26. Ibid.

27. Edward B. Fiske, "A 'Religious Woodstock' Draws 75,000," *New York Times*, June 16, 1972; "The Jesus Woodstock," *Time*, June 26, 1972; "The Christian Woodstock," *Newsweek*, June 26, 1972, 52.

28. "'Holler For Jesus,'" *New York Times*, June 18, 1972.

29. "God's Muscle," *Time*, May 21, 1973.

30. Ibid.

31. Ibid.

32. Pete Axthelm, "The Steelers—I Think," *Newsweek*, January 19, 1976.

33. "It's Denver and Dallas," *Time*, January 16, 1978.

34. Ibid.; "Bootlegs and Saddles," *Time*, November 7, 1983; quote from "A Locker Room With Soul," *Newsweek*, August 6, 1979.

35. "Los Angeles: The New Ellis Island," *Time*, June 13, 1983.

36. Ibid.

37. Quoted in Dochuk, *From Bible Belt to Sunbelt*, 370.

38. Kenneth A. Briggs, "Report Finds Evangelical Churches Continue to Grow as Others Decline," *New York Times*, April 29, 1977.

39. Kenneth A. Briggs, "The Evangelical Boom Keeps Going," *New York Times*, December 30, 1979.

40. "Evangelicals Unite," *Time*, February 3, 1975.

41. Ibid.; "Graham Goes East," *Newsweek*, August 29, 1977.

42. "Evangelicals Unite."

43. Kenneth A. Briggs, "Evangelical Shift to Pluralism," *New York Times*, February 24, 1978.

44. Ibid.

45. "Pentecostalism Surges in Brazil," *New York Times*, December 10, 1972.

46. Edward B. Fiske, "There Are Those Who Think It Is Imminent," *New York Times*, October 8, 1972; Kenneth L. Woodward and Rachel Mark, "Evangelism for Jews," *Newsweek*, August 13, 1979.

47. Edward B. Fiske, "Oral Roberts College Has Grown in 7 Years," *New York Times*, June 13, 1972.

48. Kenneth A. Briggs, "Of Evangelicalism and Architecture and a Wave of Heady Spending," *New York Times*, June 3, 1978.

49. Kenneth A. Briggs, "The Electronic Church Is Turning More People On," *New York Times*, February 10, 1980.

50. Betsy Carter, "The Lord's Network," *Newsweek*, March 20, 1978.

51. Ibid.

52. Ibid.

53. Briggs, "Evangelical Shift to Pluralism."

54. Tom Mathews, with Tony Fuller and Holly Camp, "Battle Over Gay Rights," *Newsweek*, June 6, 1977.

55. Ibid.

56. Ibid.

57. Ibid.

58. Ibid.

59. John Egerton, *The Americanization of Dixie: The Southernization of America* (New York: Harper's Magazine Press, 1974), xx, 24–25, 192–96.

60. "Best and Worst of Times," *Time*, May 30, 1983.

61. John Herber, "Ultraconservative Evangelicals a Surging New Force in Politics," *New York Times*, August 17, 1980.

62. "Power, Glory—and Politics," *Time*, February 17, 1986.

63. "Hot Times for the Old Orb," *Time*, October 31, 1983.

64. "California: A State of Excitement," *Time*, November 7, 1969.

REFERENCES

Dochuk, Darren. 2001. *From Bible Belt to Sunbelt: Plain-folk Religion, Grassroots Politics, and the Rise of Evangelical Conservatism*. New York: Norton.

Egerton, John. 1974. *The Americanization of Dixie: The Southernization of America*. New York: Harper's Magazine Press.

Phillips, Kevin. 1969. *The Emerging Republican Majority*, New Rochelle, NY: Arlington House.

Sale, Kirkpatrick. 1975. *Power Shift: The Rise of the Southern Rim and Its Challenges to the Eastern Establishment*. New York: Random House.

CHAPTER 15

THE LEGENDS OF THE "ASSASSINS" IN NEWS COVERAGE OF MUSLIMS

KARIM H. KARIM

Introduction

The portrayal of Muslims in the news did not become salient only after the terrorist attacks of September 11, 2001. This has been a long-standing issue that has acquired increasing attention over the last few decades as the coverage of the adherents of Islam has steadily grown in American news coverage. The image of the "*Islamic* terrorist" has come to dominate among various depictions of Muslims. It tends to take at face value the claims of some who perpetrate political violence in the name of Islam at the expense of more than a billion followers who see the religion as a source of harmony. This chapter asserts that the image of the endemically violent Muslim has currency in American news media because it rests on many centuries of the cultural portrayal of Islam as a source of conflict. The endless stream of depictions beginning with some of the earliest encounters of Europeans with the "Saracens" have produced a strongly embedded set of core stereotypes that make plausible depictions that would seem outrageous when applied to other groups.

Both journalists and their audiences are familiar with the cultural narratives about Muslims, which provide for ways to construct and interpret accounts about them. News reporting does not exist in a vacuum, but has an integral relationship with the contents of other media to which it contributes information and from which it draws material. The news portrayals of Muslims are echoed by producers of television drama, literary fiction, and computer games, and journalists regularly make cultural references to non-news media content. This chapter shows how the intertextual weaving of the legends of the medieval "Assassins" into contemporary American news and entertainment media draws upon and reinforces the ingrained image of the violent Muslim.

The Cultural Shaping of News

Robert Ivie[1] found a remarkable consistency in American characterizations of the successive military enemies (the British, Native Americans, Mexicans, Germans, Japanese, Koreans, Vietnamese, etc.) the United States faced over two centuries. The "self" was almost always portrayed as peaceful and defensive and the "other" as aggressive and violent. This tendency is not limited to Americans but seems to be shared by all societies. The self is good; the enemy is evil. Whereas criticism of the self is not completely absent, the overall premise is that one's own society's cultural and moral ideals are of a high, if not the highest, order. Ivie's work helps in understanding how some basic stereotypes (topoi) are reproduced over a long period of time to fulfill a consistent cultural and ideological purpose. His method can be applied to study the images that one group of people have about another: "The topoi, metaphorically speaking, are a 'reservoir' of ideas or core images from which specific rhetoric statements can be generated."[2]

Such images also shape the cultural frameworks of a society's media. Despite claims of objectivity, journalists are inescapably immersed in the assumptions of their respective cultures. They draw on the collective memories and received knowledge of the societies in which they live and work. The media utilize various narrative modes in attempting to get their interpretations of reality across to their publics. Journalists make the implicit assumption that audiences share the same general ways of understanding information. Such consonance is vital in making their accounts seem reasonable, rational, and logical. For this to happen, writer and reader have to adhere to generally similar cognitive structures that frame the images about specific groups of people. The topoi of the "other" forms the cognitive basis for understanding them. These stereotypes shape our thinking about how we expect members of an ethnic group, adherents of a religion, etc., to behave in particular situations. These expectations construct a specific rationality and logic that is at the basis of news reports. Even the most high-minded journalists who are committed to imparting news with integrity have the functional imperative to make their material interesting to readers and audiences. Notwithstanding a dedication to facts and the "truth," copy has to be written in a way that does not appear overly factual and dry. Many reporters are given to colorful language that may often be emotionally charged—frequently drawing from the stereotypes of groups under discussion.

It is common also for news stories to be constructed as dramatic conflicts between various social actors.[3] Protagonists and antagonists may be set up implicitly in narratives that portray "good" and "bad" sides of a confrontation. Heroes and villains emerge from the way that they deal with each other, symbolically portraying good and bad, right and wrong, and winners and losers in society.[4] News about war and terrorism is often narrated in a dramatic manner. The impetus for journalists to act like propagandists grows as the cultural and ideological stakes are high when established structures of society are seen as being under threat. Elisabeth Anker[5] discusses how media coverage of 9/11 constructed an interplay of villains, victims, and heroes to reinforce American identity.

The news media do not operate in isolation from other media but participate in a cultural environment that broadly shares common understandings of the events taking place in the world. Material from news becomes fodder for late-night talk shows and drama series, and journalists often make cultural references to non-news media content. Such intertextuality[6] between various media enables audiences to develop common reference points about specific groups such as Muslims. Semati states that Hollywood films in which Arabs have appeared as enemies "provided the interpretive framework to render intelligible"[7] the conflicts against Saddam Hussein's regime in Iraq. These perceptions are supported by the topoi about Muslims that underpin the narratives in newspapers, television dramas, movies, novels, and computer games. Journalists themselves develop their narratives about the events involving Muslims within the cultural frameworks that exist in society, as well as in other media, the contents of which they also consume. Their reporting therefore appears reasonable, rational, and logical to their audiences who similarly derive information from a range of sources that corroborate one another because they are shaped in similar cultural manners. The contents of the entertainment media act as cognitive reinforcements for the news media, and vice versa.

Core Stereotypes of Muslims

Muslims have emerged as a primary enemy in American news coverage following the terrorist attacks of September 11, 2001.[8] Whereas the daily coverage is about current events, their narration has roots in age-old ideas about Islam. Certain basic notions about the characteristics of Muslims, having survived hundreds of years, feed the discourses of contemporary media—just as the primary stereotypes that Muslims have about Europe inform their current constructions of America.[9] However, Muslim societies have not institutionalized their imaginaries about Western societies to the extent that the latter have done of Islam, especially over the last two centuries. In the seminal *Orientalism*,[10] Edward Said analyzed the works of Europeans to demonstrate the links between knowledge and power in the relationship between Western and Muslim societies. He described Orientalism as "the corporate institution for dealing with the Orient—dealing with it by making statements about it, authorizing views of it, describing it, by teaching it, settling it, ruling over it: in short, Orientalism as a Western style for dominating, restructuring, and having authority over the Orient."[11]

Each generation of Orientalist writers was influenced by previous ones, absorbing the biases and prejudices that went back centuries. "Transmitted from one generation to another, it was part of the culture, as much a language about a part of reality as geometry or physics. Orientalism was able to survive revolutions, world wars, and the literal dismemberment of empires."[12] This is true not only in academia but also in the domain that has a more ubiquitous presence in the contemporary world—the mass media, which "raid the orientalist cupboard for alimentation, picking up old prejudices and scatological bits of information."[13] The dominance of the American and European transnational news agencies and the communications structures, whose foundations were built under colonialism, reinforce the largely one-sided views of the world.[14] "Islam" becomes a timeless entity in much of the reporting, which is replete with stereotypical generalizations and clichés. Phrases such as "the Islamic mind-set," "the crescent of crisis," and "the Shi'ite penchant for martyrdom" have posed as standard explanations for events that most journalists do not explore in a meaningful way.

The topoi in the Western depictions of Muslims that have been most consistent over the ages are those of violence, lust, greed, and barbarism.[15] Although the specific depictions generated from the core stereotypes may vary from time to time, they remain the most resilient images about Muslims in American media. Variations of the four primary stereotypes of Muslims as being endemically violent, indulging in sexual excess, having fabulous but undeserved wealth (they have not *earned* it), and being barbaric and regressive have not only been reproduced in newspapers and television but also generally appear as the representations of the Muslim other in popular culture, art, music, literature, school textbooks, computerized formats, and public discourse. Some Muslims may indeed exhibit such characteristics, but it would be grossly inaccurate to suggest that they are shared by significant proportions of Islam's adherents. Yet the stereotypes, particularly that of violence, have a strong influence on news coverage about Muslims. Indeed, they form the discursive grammar for reporting about Muslims, which would not be intelligible without both journalists and their audiences sharing in the cultural memory of the topoi.

Emerging centuries ago as the basic frames in the European Christian polemic against the "Saracens," the generic notions about Islam often discursively interlink with one another in contemporary American narratives about Muslims. The image of Muslims converting by "the sword of Islam" those whom they conquered is a popular image in the United States. For example, this phrase served as the title of the June 15, 1992, cover story of *Time* magazine. Out of the scores of Muslim caliphs and sultans, the few despots who persecuted non-Muslims, as well as Muslims, are often presented as being typical. Violence has come to be linked with the very nature of Islam as a religion and of its followers. This image intermingles with that of Arabs as lovers of luxury with the implication that their wealth is an indication of avarice and is usually obtained through illicit means. Linked to the desire for worldly pleasures are the notions of sloth and greed, as well as of lust for sexual and political power. Technological and cultural differences between Muslim and Western societies are often viewed as evidence of barbarism and intellectual backwardness. Personifications of these topoi are to be found in figures such as the cruel, barbaric, and lascivious but fabulously wealthy sheikh, who is a common figure in American representations of Muslims.[16]

Inherent in these imaginaries is the idea of exoticism: "the exotic East" evokes simultaneous but contradictory feelings of attraction and revulsion, of fascination and terror; it invites prurient indulgence, but it is to be kept at a distance. Shakespeare's *Othello* seems to imply that a violent end awaits European women who choose to consort with such men as the "Black Moor": lust and greed come together here in the form of sexual jealousy, which ultimately explodes in violent rage. The immense popularity in Europe and North America of the "Arabian Nights" (out of all the literature produced in Arabic), the depictions of exotic Muslims in alternatively violent or languorous poses by artists such as Eugène Delacroix and Jean-Léon Gérôme, the early Hollywood production of *The Sheik* (1921) followed by the numerous films of this genre, and the portrayal of "oil sheiks" by editorial cartoonists all illustrate, despite their internal contradictions, the seeming inseparability of the images of "sensuality, promise, terror, sublimity, idyllic pleasure, intense energy"[17] in Western ideas about the Muslim other.

Reeva Simon has traced portrayals of Middle Eastern characters in British and American crime fiction, indicating how—whereas the images of Arabs or Turks as particular groups may change depending on the current political circumstances—the topos of the violent Muslim remains irrepressible.

> This perennial Western fear, that of a resurgent Islam, is part of the Western historical memory. The sword-wielding Muslim thundering across the Strait of Gibraltar or laying siege to Vienna, the Old Man of the Mountain's Assassins high on drugs launched to kill political leaders, white slavers, and Barbary pirates have been reincarnated as plane hijackers, embassy bombers, and nefarious creators of long gas lines. In the fiction of the "paranoid" and "vicious" categories, the conspiracy, the hero, and the villain are basic elements for thriller/spy novel success. One of the most popular conspiracies, the Islamic threat, has been a plot motif threaded throughout crime fiction since John Buchan's *Greenmantle* (1916).[18]

As one would expect, such tendencies intensified following 9/11.

The "Islamic terrorist" has become a major figure in the typology of characters who perform in American news and other media dramaturges about Muslim societies. It does not appear to require much ideological labor to create such a role given the repertoire of images arising from the topos of "the violent man of Islam." The widely reported activities of the relatively few Muslims who practice terrorism out of the 1.4 billion adherents of Islam also serve to strengthen this core image. The generative framework of the violent Muslim becomes the matrix upon which to base the portrayal of the careers of people as distinct in character and in time as the prophet Muhammad, Saladin, Rashid al-Din Sinan, Muammar Qadhafi, Yasser Arafat, Ayatollah Khomeini, Saddam Hussein, and Osama bin Laden.

The Assassins: A Tale of Sex, Drugs, and Violence

There is a particular trope in American media portrayals of Muslims that has centered on the medieval legends about the Assassins. They have served as a narrative theme that appears from time to time as a cultural backdrop in news coverage. In the months immediately following September 11, 2001, there was a strong concentration of media references to the Assassins legends. It appeared in a news backgrounder by Emily Yoffe[19] on MSN's online *Slate* magazine. The conservative news website WorldNetDaily circulated a long article making comparisons between "Bin Laden and the 'Old Man of the Mountain.'"[20] A *New York Times* article that apparently sought to provide a positive historical understanding about medieval Muslim science as a contrast to contemporary terrorism opened with the lead, "Nasir al-Din al-Tusi was still a young man when the Assassins made him an offer he couldn't refuse."[21] Nor was the script writer of the popular drama series *West Wing* on the NBC network immune to the Assassins bug: an episode titled "Isaac and Ishmael" that aired on October 10, 2001, referred to the legends.

These American references to the medieval group were part of an international media tendency. Links were made between the Assassins and Al Qaeda's attacks on 9/11 in a Canadian Broadcasting Corporation television program,[22] the Toronto-based the *Globe and Mail*,[23] the German national daily *Die Welt*,[24] the Moscow-based *Pravda*,[25] and a number of London-based papers: the *Financial Times*,[26] the *Daily Telegraph*,[27] and the *Times*.[28] It was as if a shared cultural memory was simultaneously awakened across North America and Europe.

The Assassins legends were first popularized in Europe by travelers like Marco Polo and then by Orientalist scholars. These stories, much embellished in the course of time, are about Nizari Ismailis, a branch of Shia Muslims, who had managed to acquire a number of forts in northern Iran and Syria during the late eleventh, twelfth, and thirteenth centuries. A significant amount of research has been carried out in the last few decades about this group.[29] Marshall Hodgson, a notable American scholar of Islam, wrote,

> The word "assassin," which the West used for terrorist murderers in general, was originally a nickname for the sect, and had nothing to do with killing. It received this connotation in our languages only by analogy to the famous murders of the "Assassins"—whose "chief object," however, was not murder, and especially not "to assassinate Crusaders."[30]

The Ismailis presented religious and philosophical positions that put them at odds with powerful forces. They founded the Fatimid Empire (tenth through twelfth centuries), building Cairo as their capital and making significant contributions to civilization. They were the patrons of sciences, the arts, and architecture and built libraries and centers of learning—like Al Azhar University in Cairo, which exists after a thousand years.

The claim of the Ismaili Imam as the lineal heir of the Prophet Muhammad's cousin, Ali, appears to have prompted unrelenting enmity from the Abbasid Caliphate and its successors. This produced a sustained stream of propaganda against them. "In time, the seminal anti-Ismaili 'black legend' came to be accepted by the Muslim majority as an accurate description of the motives, teachings and practices of the Ismailis."[31] This demonization was intensified in the descriptions about the Nizari Ismailis who broke away from the Fatimids in the late eleventh century. The Nizaris were mainly in Iran and Syria, which was hostile territory under Seljuk sultans who had designated them as heretics and whose forces frequently attacked and massacred Ismaili communities.[32] The Nizaris acquired several forts, which provided them with security. This also provided the opportunity to engage in scientific and philosophical pursuits: "we find the community cultivating the learned disciplines . . . [and] the library at Alamut, [which was] famous for its scientific collection. . . ."[33] A number of non-Ismaili and non-Muslim scholars also worked at Alamut, but upon its conquest by the Mongols, who massacred large numbers of Ismailis (especially its leaders and intelligentsia), they said that they had been there under constraint.[34]

Outnumbered by the vast forces of the Seljuk Empire, the Nizaris adopted the tactic of attacking selected military and administrative leaders responsible for the campaigns against them in particular localities. These killings were conducted in a public manner apparently to demoralize the Seljuk forces and dissuade them from destroying Nizari communities. However, the military and social context in which the Nizaris found themselves rarely features in the many descriptions of this group, who have mainly become known for their tactic of assassination. Quite apart from the accounts of their military methods, a number of fantastic legends were attached to the tales of the Assassins. These were built partly on the already existing black legend about the Ismailis and also on a series of new portrayals of them as a secretive, libertine, and murderous cult.

Over the last two centuries, scholars have sought to answer a number of questions about the legends attached to the Assassins such as "The Tale of the Three Schoolfellows," the "death leap," and the "training legend." These have each appeared in contemporary media in one form or another. Examining Muslim and Western textual sources, Farhad Daftary has carried out the most meticulous study of the genealogy of these stories.[35] He suggests that the emergence of the tales were prompted by the search for a rationale, especially among European travelers to the East, for the highly dangerous acts of the Nizaris who attacked the well-guarded leaders of their enemies in public. The Europeans usually did not understand the social, political, and cultural context and tended to put forward fantastic explanations for the Nizaris' daring.

The "death leap" legend had some followers of a Nizari leader jumping to their deaths from a high wall at his mere command—supposedly as an exhibition of the absolute devotion of the Assassins to their leadership and its murderous strategies. Daftary finds historical evidence for this story from European sources to be extremely weak[36]; however, it is frequently repeated in the retelling of the Assassins tale. In the even more fantastic "training legend," the "Old Man of the Mountain" drugs his recruits and, when they have passed out, takes them to a paradisiacal garden populated with enchanting damsels. Eternal residence in this garden was promised to them upon their death in the cause of the Nizari faith. Marco Polo's publication about his travels in the East was the source of this legend. No corroboration has been found in any historical accounts of the period,[37] but it is one of the most resilient myths about Muslims. Its imaginative inclusion of sex, drugs, and violence provides the very ingredients that make up populist news making. The story also appears plausible for the contemporary media because it is grafted so well upon the well-established Western topoi about Muslims, within which both journalists and their audiences tend to make sense of Islam.

One of the most long-standing discussions about the Assassins regards their appellation. The August 22, 1997, issue of the Atlanta-based periodical *Bioworld Today*, which describes itself as "the news source of record for the biotechnology industry, [that] is read by biotechnology professionals worldwide for its hard-hitting, objective news reporting," had the following lead for an article titled "Marijuana Compounds in Human Brain Hint at Drugs to Ease Cancer Chemotherapy,"

> A millennium or so ago, Christian warriors who sallied forth in the Crusades to liberate the Holy Land from its Islamic occupiers were often set upon and murdered by Moslem fighters who cultivated the cult of hashish. By smoking or chewing this [plant] . . . these sons of the prophet acquired a high that spurred them psychologically to kill a Crusader on sight. They called themselves "hashishins," after the Arabic word for the plant, which in Western language came out as "assassins."

Newspaper and magazine articles, whose content has often little to do with Muslims, endlessly repeat this baseless story.

The name's origin is thought to be from the Arabic term *Hashishiyya*—user of the narcotic drug hashish. Daftary notes that "early Saljuk chroniclers use the terms *hashishiyya*, *malahida* [heretics] and *batiniyya* ['esotericists'] interchangeably."[38] These were terms of abuse that appeared also in the anti-Nizari propaganda of other Muslim sources. However, none of these accounts presents explanations or details about the Nizaris' actual use of hashish. Daftary observes that the drug was the subject of discussion among some Muslim writers of the period who described its harmful effects "on the user's morality and religion."[39] He states, "It was in the abusive senses of 'low-class rabble' and 'irreligious social outcasts' that the term *hashishiyya* seems to have been used metaphorically in reference to the Nizari Ismailis."[40] Daftary, Hodgson,[41] and Lewis[42] assert that the self-discipline and asceticism displayed by the Nizaris would not have allowed for the systematic use of narcotic drugs. However, the influence of the writings of Marco Polo, as well as those of

Orientalists like Silvestre de Sacy and Joseph von Hammer-Purgstall, and the frequent repetition of the training legend in media contents have led to the entrenchment of the misnomer of the Nizaris as *hashishiyya* and as "*the* Assassins." The latter term has come to imply erroneously that they were the originators of the idea and practice of assassination. There were many instances of political murder around the world in earlier periods, including that by organized groups such as the first-century Jewish rebels known as the Sicarii ("dagger-men"), who carried out assassinations of Roman leaders.[43]

Discussion: "A Perfect Evil Enemy"

The references to the Assassins in the news are part of a broader tapestry of intertextual media reproductions of the tale. These present-day constructions continue a process that began in medieval times. The legends of the Assassins are integral to the global circulation of images about Islam. Apart from the news, these fabrications appear periodically in various media that serve to present a deceptive picture of the Assassins, who are recognized as a familiar historical group to audiences when they are mentioned in newspapers or broadcast news. Due to their longevity and ubiquity in Western discourses, the Assassins have been integrated into the cultural language of American narratives about Islam. Decontextualized from the religious, social, and military circumstances of their time, they have been defined as nefarious and highly dangerous terrorists reviled by other Muslims.

The description of the Assassins by Loren Miller, who ran an online forum on religions and secret societies for use in role-playing computer games, is indicative of the ways in which the group is viewed as a metaphor for the extreme form of malevolence. He stated that "the Assassins are a perfect 'evil' enemy for players. they [*sic*] could be the main enemy for a medieval campaign in the Levant, and would be a very dangerous one as they had the finest spy system in the world."[44] Despite the scholarly findings that have debunked the Assassins legends, it appears that this group of Muslims continues to serve as a trope for "the perfect 'evil' enemy" in media narratives.

A common narrative technique in demonizing an individual is to associate him or her with a person or group whose negative character is well established in dominant discourses. The Assassins have from time to time been linked in this way to a host of other Muslim figures whom the writer may want to disparage. This was done, for example, in the April 21, 1986, issue of *Time* magazine, in which the cover story, titled "Targeting Gaddafi," seemed to be making the case for an imminent bombing of Libya by American forces. A two-page article in that same issue by Richard Stengel with the headline "Gaddafi: Obsessed by a Ruthless, Messianic Vision" sought to link the Libyan leader's suspected support for terrorism with an "Islamic" fanaticism: "He has become the modern-day incarnation of the society of

Assassins, which flourished from the 11th to the 13th century in the Middle East, only his victims are random and spread over the entire map." This journalist links what he sees as Gaddafi's desire to overcome historical humiliation with figures from Muslim history. The relationship with the Assassins is very tenuous, but Stengel—implicitly drawing on the topos of the endemically violent and barbaric Muslim—makes the connection seem reasonable and logical to his readers.

References to the Assassins have appeared in numerous Hollywood movies over time. They include *Omar Khayyam* (1957), whose lead character overcomes hashish-addicted assassins; *Haram Scarum* (1965), where the hero (played by Elvis Presley) is kidnapped by Sinan—the "Old Man of the Mountain"; *The Prince of Persia* (2010), in which weapons of mass destruction are suspected to be hidden in a place called Alamut; and *The Seeds of Destruction: The Terror Beneath* (2011), in which an unscrupulous scientist has grown a latter-day Garden of Eden, operating under the name of "Alamut Corp. Industries." The Assassins legends seem to be an inexhaustible source for plots in which items from the news and fiction are liberally blended. Dennis MacEoin, an Orientalist who writes thrillers under the pen name Daniel Easterman, brings present-day successors of the Nizaris into the storyline of *The Last Assassin*[45] in which terrorists pose a global threat.

News reporting of contemporary acts of terrorism by Muslims has led to new editions of previous works on the Assassins. Bernard Lewis's *The Assassins: A Radical Sect in Islam*, which initially appeared in 1967, was republished in 2003 with a new preface by the author. The back cover states, "Particularly insightful in light of the rise of the terrorist attacks in the US and Israel, this account of the group that lent its name to politically motivated murder places recent events in historical perspective and sheds new light on the fanatic mind." It is interesting that Lewis's own preface[46] actually disavows any connection between the historical group and present-day terrorists. Freya Stark's *The Valleys of the Assassins and Other Persian Travels*, a travelogue that first came out in 1934, was reissued in 2001 with a new introduction by former *New York Times* journalist Jane Fletcher Geniesse. Stark's own writing does not dwell on the Assassins legends, but Geniesse reproduced the hackneyed tale in her introduction[47] and the back cover also referred to "hashish-eating terrorists." The medieval group's distorted image remains ever ready for exploitation by the unscrupulous.

Notwithstanding the general tendency of various media to reinscribe the false stories about the Nizaris, there is at least one recent media product that has partially resisted the trend. The enormously popular computer game *Assassin's Creed* presents a member of the group as the protagonist. Jade Raymond, the game's developer, said in an interview,

> We have . . . worked with cultural experts throughout production to make sure that we treat sensitive topics with respect. As the Saracens and Crusaders battle one another for control—the Assassins are working to find a way to end the hostilities. They see the war as pointless. There is no reason Crusaders and Saracens should not co-exist in peace. The Assassins are not allied with either side of the conflict, nor are they driven by a desire for profit or power. In *Assassins'*

> [*sic*] *Creed*, Crusaders (and the Saracens) are not the Assassins' true enemy. War is—as are those who exploit it.[48]

Given the vulnerability of Nizaris caught in the conflicts between various Muslim and Christian groups, this view may be closer to the historical truth than most media accounts of the Assassins.

Stories about the group in news media appear either as background material or passing references. The culturally entrenched image of the Assassins as nefarious murderers seeking to create mayhem and social discord is generally used as a narrative device to demonize others who are under discussion in news reports. It extends the topos of the essentially violent Muslim to provide for a picture of Islam at its darkest. This works ideologically to present "a perfect 'evil' enemy" when needed as a foil for the good self. Of course, journalists would deny that they indulge in such constructions. Nevertheless, some of them seem intent on perpetuating harm upon vulnerable religious communities by adopting unsubstantiated tales and presenting them as fact. The Assassins legends offer the reporter without integrity an easy way to grab the attention of readers with leads that foreground drug-induced murderers who have little to do with the story at hand. Conscientious journalists, on the other hand, would make the effort to become aware of the fuller story and context of the legends and, in the words of Jade Raymond, "treat sensitive topics with respect."

NOTES

1. Robert L. Ivie, "Images of Savagery in American Justifications for War," *Communications Monographs* 47 (November 1980).
2. Ibid., 280.
3. See Eric Rothenbuhler and Mihai Coman, eds., *Media Anthropology* (London: Sage, 2005).
4. George Gerbner, "Violence and Terror in and by Media," in *Media, Crisis and Democracy*, eds. Marc Raboy and Bernard Dagenais (London: Sage, 1992), 94–107.
5. Elisabeth Anker, "Villains, Victims and Heroes: Melodrama, Media and September 11," *Journal of Communication* 55, no. 1 (March 2005): 22–37.
6. B. Ott and C. Walter, "Intertextuality: Interpretive Practice and Textual Strategy," *Critical Studies in Mass Communication* 17 (2000): 429–46.
7. Mehdi Semati, "Islamophobia, Culture and Race in the Age of Empire," *Cultural Studies* 24, no. 2 (2010): 261.
8. Brigitte Nacos and Oscar Torres-Reyna. *Fueling Our Fears: Stereotyping, Media Coverage, and Public Opinion of Muslim Americans* (Lanham, MD: Rowman and Littlefield, 2007); Semati, "Islamophobia, Culture and Race"; Anker, "Villains, Victims and Heroes"; and Karim H. Karim, *Islamic Peril: Media and Global* Violence (Montreal: Black Rose, 2003).
9. Nabil Matar, ed. and transl., *In the Lands of the Christians: Arabic Travel Writing in the Seventeenth Century* (New York: Routledge, 2003); Kamal Abdel-Malek, ed., *America in an Arab Mirror: Images of America in Arabic Travel Literature* (New York: St. Martin's Press, 2000).

10. Edward Said, *Orientalism* (New York: Pantheon Books, 1978).

11. Ibid., 3.

12. Ibid., 222.

13. Akbar S. Ahmed, *Postmodernism and Islam: Predicament and Promise* (London: Routledge, 1992), 186.

14. Karim, *Islamic Peril*.

15. Ibid.

16. Ibid.

17. Said, *Orientalism*, 118.

18. Reeva S. Simon, *Spies and Holy Wars: The Middle East in Crime Fiction* (Austin: University of Texas, 2010), 53.

19. Emily Yoffe, "Bernard Lewis: The Islam Scholar U.S. Politicians Listen To," *Slate*, http://slate.msn.com/?id=2058632 (accessed November 13, 2001).

20. James Perloff, "Bin Laden and the 'Old Man of the Mountain,'" *WorldNetDaily*, November 2, 2001, http://www.worldnetdaily.com/news/article.asp?ARTICLE_ID=25181 (accessed November 20, 2001).

21. Dennis Overbye, "How Islam Won, and Lost, the Lead in Science," *New York Times*, October 30, 2001, E1.

22. Joe Schlesinger, "Foreign Assignment," *Canadian Broadcasting Corporation*, October 28, 2001.

23. Salim Mansur, "The Father of All Assassins," *Globe and Mail*, October 11, 2001, A6.

24. Berthold Seewald, "Die Assassinen: Vorbilder fur die Martyrer-Morder der Gegenwart," *Die Welt*, September 13, 2001, 14.

25. Anatoli Baranov, "American Tragedy: Who Needed It?" *Pravda*, September 12, 2001, 7.

26. Tom Scott, "Grim Lessons from a Legendary Muslim," *Financial Times Weekend*, October 6–7, 2001, 15.

27. Daniel Johnson, "War to the Death Between America and Islamic Terrorists," *Daily Telegraph*, September 12, 2001, 5.

28. Mary Ann Sieghart, "The Cult Figure We Could Do Without," *Times* (London), October 26, 2001, 20.

29. Marshall Hodgson, *The Order of Assassins* (The Hague: Mouton & Co., 1955); Farhad Daftary, *The Assassin Legends: Myths of the Isma'ilis* (London: I. B. Tauris, 1995); Bernard Lewis, *The Assassins: A Radical Sect in Islam* (New York: Basic Books, 2003); Peter Willey, *Eagle's Nest: Ismaili Castles in Iran and Syria* (London: I. B. Tauris, 2005).

30. Hodgson, *The Order of Assassins*, 1.

31. Daftary, *The Assassin Legends*, 88.

32. Hodgson, *The Order of Assassins*; Daftary, *The Assassin Legends*; Lewis, *The Assassins*.

33. Hodgson, *The Order of Assassins*, 239.

34. Ibid.

35. Daftary, *The Assassin Legends*.

36. Ibid., 113.

37. Ibid., 97.

38. Ibid., 89.

39. Ibid., 91.

40. Ibid., 92.

41. Hodgson, *The Order of Assassins*.

42. Lewis, *The Assassins*.

43. Nachman Ben-Yehuda, *The Masada Myth: Collective Memory and Mythmaking in Israel* (Madison: University of Wisconsin Press, 1995).

44. Loren Miller, "GRASS/Assassins," http://hops.wharton.upenn.edu/~loren/Links/grass/assassins.ss (accessed January 24, 2000).

45. Daniel Easterman, *The Last Assassin* (London: Grafton, 1984).

46. Lewis, *The Assassins*, xi.

47. Jane Fletcher Geniesse, Introduction to the Modern Library Edition of *The Valleys of the Assassins and Other Persian Travels*, by Freya Stark (New York: Modern Library, 2001), xiii–xiv.

48. Magy El-Nasr, Maha Al-Saati, Simon Niedenthal, and David Milam, "Assassins Creed: A Multi-Cultural Read" (unpublished paper, circa 2008).

REFERENCES

Abdel-Malek, Kamal, ed. 2000. *America in an Arab Mirror: Images of America in Arabic Travel Literature*. New York: St. Martin's Press.

Ahmed, Akbar S. 1992. *Postmodernism and Islam: Predicament and Promise*. London: Routledge.

Anker, Elisabeth. 2005. Villains, Victims and Heroes: Melodrama, Media and September 11. *Journal of Communication* 55 (1 [March]): 22–37.

Baranov, Anatoli. 2001. American Tragedy: Who Needed It? *Pravda*, September 12, 2001, 7.

Ben-Yehuda, Nachman. 1995. *The Masada Myth: Collective Memory and Mythmaking in Israel*. Madison: University of Wisconsin Press.

Bioworld Today. 1997. Marijuana Compounds in Human Brain Hint at Drugs to Ease Cancer Chemotherapy, August 22, 1997, 7–11.

Bioworld Today. 2010. About Us. http://216.54.230.15/servlet/com.accumedia.web.Dispatcher?next=aboutUs (accessed August 7, 2010).

Daftary, Farhad. 1994. *The Assassin Legends: Myths of the Isma'ilis*. London: I. B. Tauris.

El-Nasr, Magy, Maha Al-Saati, Simon Niedenthal, and David Milam. Assassins Creed: A Multi-Cultural Read (unpublished paper, circa 2008).

Easterman, Daniel. 1984. *The Last Assassin*. London: Grafton.

Gerbner, George. 1992. Violence and Terror in and by Media. In *Media, Crisis and Democracy*, ed. Marc Raboy and Bernard Dagenais, 94–107. London: Sage.

Geniesse, Jane Fletcher. 2001. Introd. to the Modern Library Edition of *The Valleys of the Assassins and Other Persian Travels*, by Freya Stark, ix–xvi. New York: Modern Library.

Hodgson, Marshall. 1955. *The Order of Assassins*. The Hague: Mouton & Co.

Ivie, Robert L. 1980. Images of Savagery in American Justifications for War. *Communications Monographs* 47 (November).

Johnson, Daniel. 2001. War to the Death Between America and Islamic Terrorists. *Daily Telegraph*, September 12, 2001, 5.

Karim, Karim H. 2003. *Islamic Peril: Media and Global Violence*. Montreal: Black Rose.

Lewis, Bernard. 2003. *The Assassins: A Radical Sect in Islam*. New York: Basic Books.

Mansur, Salim. 2001. The Father of All Assassins. *Globe and Mail*, October 11, A6.

Matar, Nabil, ed. and transl. 2003. *In the Lands of the Christians: Arabic Travel Writing in the Seventeenth Century*. New York: Routledge.

Miller, Loren. 2000. GRASS/Assassins. http://hops.wharton.upenn.edu/~loren/Links/grass/assassins.ss (accessed January 24, 2000).

Nacos, Brigitte, and Oscar Torres-Reyna. 2007. *Fueling Our Fears: Stereotyping, Media Coverage, and Public Opinion of Muslim Americans*. Lanham, MD: Rowman and Littlefield.

Ott, B., and C. Walter. 2000. Intertextuality: Interpretive Practice and Textual Strategy. *Critical Studies in Mass Communication* 17: 429–46.

Overbye, Dennis. 2001. How Islam Won, and Lost, the Lead in Science. *New York Times*, October 30, E1.

Perloff, James. 2001. Bin Laden and the "Old Man of the Mountain." *WorldNetDaily*, November 2. http://www.worldnetdaily.com/news/article.asp?ARTICLE_ID=25181 (accessed November 20, 2001).

Rothenbuhler, Eric, and Mihai Coman, eds. 2005. *Media Anthropology*. London: Sage.

Said, Edward. 1978. *Orientalism*. New York: Pantheon Books.

Schlesinger, Joe. 2001. Foreign Assignment. *Canadian Broadcasting Corporation*, October 28.

Scott, Tom. 2001. Grim Lessons from a Legendary Muslim. *Financial Times Weekend*, October 6–7, 2001, 15.

Seewald, Berthold. 2001. Die Assassinen: Vorbilder fur die Martyrer-Morder der Gegenwart. *Die Welt*, September 13, 2001, 14.

Semati, Mehdi. 2010. Islamophobia, Culture and Race in the Age of Empire. *Cultural Studies* 24 (2): 256–75.

Sieghart, Mary Ann. 2001. The Cult Figure We Could Do Without. *Times* (London), October 26, 2001, 20.

Simon, Reeva S. 2010. *Spies and Holy Wars: The Middle East in Crime Fiction*. Austin: University of Texas.

Stark, Freya. 2001. *The Valleys of the Assassins and Other Persian Travels*. New York: Modern Library.

Stengel, Richard. 1986. Gaddafi: Obsessed by a Ruthless, Messianic Vision. *Time*, April 21, 1986, 8–10.

Yoffe, Emily. 2001. Bernard Lewis: The Islam Scholar U.S. Politicians Listen To. *Slate*, November 13. http://slate.msn.com/?id=2058632

Willey, Peter. 2005. *Eagle's Nest: Ismaili Castles in Iran and Syria*. London: I. B. Tauris.

CHAPTER 16

NEWS COVERAGE OF THE CHURCH OF JESUS CHRIST OF LATTER-DAY SAINTS

JANA RIESS

In *The Angel and the Beehive*, sociologist Armand Mauss finds that Mormon Americans have, in recent decades, struggled with two competing archetypes of what it means to be a Latter-day Saint. On the one hand, Mormons have been driven to assimilate—becoming financially successful, politically powerful, and culturally integrated into the American mainstream. Mauss uses the beehive, long an emblem of Mormon industry, to symbolize this trend. On the other hand is the angel, a sign of Mormons' theological distinctiveness and self-understanding as a peculiar people.[1] Throughout the last few decades of Mormon history, those two archetypes have pushed and pulled against one another not only within the fold, as Mormons try to understand who they wish to be in the twenty-first century, but also in media representations of Mormonism, as Americans grapple with whether to accept or reject this homegrown faith.

In media coverage of Mormonism, we see both archetypes, sometimes even in the same news story. This chapter examines representative print media coverage of Mormonism since 1970, exploring the interplay between these two tropes. In keeping with the "beehive" archetype, some media representations suggest that Mormons are "just like us"—or even slightly better—as seen in stories about strong families, successful church programs, and financial prosperity. This approach was capped by the highly positive media coverage of Mormonism in Salt Lake City in 2002. A competing trope is that Mormonism is inherently "other," with enough lingering concerns from its past (polygamy, theocracy, and extrabiblical beliefs) to cause disquiet.

Because this chapter cannot cover all forms of media in all of Mormon history, it will focus attention on five major metropolitan newspapers outside of the Mormon-dominated Wasatch Front: the *New York Times, Washington Post, Los Angeles Times, Denver Post*, and *Chicago Tribune*. Where appropriate, mentions will also be made of smaller regional papers, as well as the two dominant newspapers in the Salt Lake area, the *Salt Lake Tribune* and *Deseret News*. In addition, the chapter canvasses articles about Mormonism that appeared in the nation's two major newsweekly magazines, *Newsweek* and *Time*. Although for comparative purposes some attention will be paid to print media coverage of Mormonism in the nineteenth and early twentieth centuries, the bulk of this chapter concentrates on reportage from 1970 to 2010, tracking trends and changes over time.

Then and Now: Sweeping Changes in Media Coverage of Mormonism

Although this chapter focuses on media coverage in the late twentieth and early twenty-first centuries, it's important first to recognize major shifts that have occurred in reporting about Mormonism since the religion's founding. These have happened quietly, and it's only in comparing coverage from the distant past with news analysis of Mormonism today that these changes even become noticeable. Three deserve particular mention.

The first is that, despite Mormons' perception of themselves as being under a national microscope, in reality, overall media coverage of Mormonism has decreased over time. In the nineteenth century, Mormonism routinely made front-page headlines, and most non-Mormon Americans could identify current leaders of the Church of Jesus Christ of Latter-day Saints (hereafter "LDS church") like Joseph Smith and Brigham Young. Everyone, it seemed, had an opinion about Mormonism, and overwhelmingly negative nineteenth-century news reports avidly fanned the flames of public fury. Today, Brigham Young University scholar Eric Eliason observes, most non-Mormon Americans would be hard-pressed to name the LDS prophet.[2]

Secondly, although news reports in the nineteenth century routinely dismissed Mormonism as a pernicious cult, today's news articles rarely pass judgment on its religious tenets. In part, this is due to the secularization of the mainstream print media itself. Most journalists today do not view it as part of their job to warn others of possibly dangerous religious heresies in their midst or to offer theological evaluations of beliefs. Mormonism has benefited from this media secularization, with the church anxious to define its own theology (e.g., its self-branding of "Christian, but different") and news outlets seemingly willing to take many of Mormonism's self-characterizations at face value. Theological outcries about Mormonism still exist, but they are largely found on blogs and websites, not in mainstream media.

Finally, although the media have always been fascinated by Mormonism's material success and political leverage, news coverage today views this in a less damning light than in the past. In the nineteenth century, legitimate outcries about theocracy arose repeatedly as news organs complained about Brigham Young being the prophet of the LDS church, the governor of Utah Territory, a key shareholder in all of the area's major utilities, and one of the wealthiest men in the West. Today, although complaints about LDS interference in politics still occur (as we will see in the discussion of same-sex marriage below), the tenor is far less shrill: in recent memory, no credible media outlet has built a case for the LDS church to be secretly trying to overthrow the government.

Mormons in the News, 1970–2000: An Overview

The 1970s

In January 1970, beloved LDS prophet and president David O. McKay passed away. While in the early twentieth century the death of a prophet might have been a mere footnote in the national media, *Time* magazine and other outlets covered it at some length, with *Time* gushing that McKay had "done more in his nineteen-year tenure to change the image and direction of the Mormon Church than any president since Brigham Young himself." Chief among his cited accomplishments were nearly tripling membership (from one million to almost three) and pouring energy into the globalization of the church, breaking down what *Time* called "Mormon exclusivism" to engage with the "wider, friendlier world."[3]

This eulogizing of McKay set a tone for a mostly positive media presence throughout the 1970s. Under new president Joseph Fielding Smith, the church reinstituted Family Home Evening, designating Monday nights as a time when all Mormon families should come together for religious instruction and intentional bonding. The idea was widely admired in the media through the decade, with a 1975 *National Geographic* profile lauding Mormonism's "family comes first" ideology as a viable answer to the generation gap then splitting the nation. The *New York Times* likewise held up Mormon family traditions as a bulwark in troubled times, claiming that "for at least one sizable group in American Society, the family is still the thing."[4]

Media coverage of the Mormon family in the 1970s stretched beyond the major metropolitan dailies and the primary newspapers of Mormon-dominated areas to embrace smaller regional outlets such as the *Cleveland Sun Press, Salem Oregon Statesman, Columbia Missourian, Baton Rouge State Times, Indianapolis News*, and many others. This new regional diversity in coverage was made possible in part by the Mormon diaspora, which had accelerated rapidly in the years after World War

II as Mormon wards were created in places far from the Utah-Idaho Mormon belt. With the advent of Mormons living among non-Mormons, some of the exoticism of depicting the Mormon "other" decreased in the media. Having Mormons in places like Southfield, Michigan, and Houston, Texas, meant that reporters could and did interview local LDS families, lending local flavor and authenticity to their coverage. And of course, from 1976 to 1979, all of America could tune in to witness one Mormon superfamily on television, as the variety show *Donny & Marie* showcased not only wholesome skits and songs but also an idealized version of Mormon family life.

In keeping with the media's admiring tone, the 1970s also saw an uptick in the number of stories written about Mormon welfare and food storage programs. In a decade marked by stock market declines, skyrocketing oil prices, and stagflation (high inflation matched by high unemployment), the Mormon commitment to emergency preparedness and helping one another sounded increasingly attractive to the general public. Politically, faith in government was at record lows, so the rationale behind some of Mormonism's stockpiling—prepare for the future so that you'll never have to depend on government welfare—also struck a chord among Americans. "Few Mormons Need Public Aid" proclaimed a headline in the Huntington, West Virginia, *Advertiser*, while Kansas's *Garden City Telegram* praised the fact that the Mormon welfare plan "doesn't encourage idleness."

Amidst all this puffery, one persistent sticking point in media coverage in the 1970s was the church's refusal to grant the priesthood to African American males. In 1971, *Newsweek* affirmed the centrality of this topic, saying that no "other single subject seems to dominate" public conversations about Mormonism. Criticism of the priesthood ban was leveled by various media quarters, from the *New York Times* and *Los Angeles Times* to religious publications like *Christian Century* and *Christianity Today.*

On June 9, 1978, LDS President Spencer W. Kimball made the surprise announcement that he had received a revelation from God that "all worthy males" would henceforth be eligible for priesthood ordination. (Alongside that policy change was another, just as important but rarely reported upon: all worthy church members of African descent—both male and female—could receive temple ordinances such as anointing, eternal marriage, and the endowment. This change recognized the increasingly global nature of Mormonism and allowed converts access to the new LDS temple in racially mixed São Paulo, Brazil.) In Utah, Kimball's priesthood announcement was broadcast immediately, with some Mormons who heard the news over the radio in their cars reportedly becoming so overwrought they had to pull over to weep with joy and relief. The next morning, many newspapers featured the story on the front page, and in the ensuing days major metropolitan dailies also invited commentary from scholars such as Edwin Gaustad and Mario DePillis, as well as columnists such as Molly Ivins.

In retrospect, some of these stories appear premature and optimistic; the *Washington Post*, for example, featured the next-day headline "Mormon Church Dissolves Black Bias," apparently not anticipating that although the policy had been changed, none of the racist folklore that had propped it up for so long had been officially repudiated; many LDS church members persisted in believing and teaching that blacks had been "less valiant" in the premortal life, resulting in a curse of black skin. In the coming years, this theological failure would be a minor but persistent focus of media coverage, as journalists followed black LDS converts through some of their adjustments to Mormon faith and culture while chronicling the racism some continued to encounter within the LDS ranks.

The 1980s

If the 1970s were generally a time of appreciative media coverage for Mormonism, the 1980s would prove quite different. In December of 1979, Virginia feminist Sonia Johnson was excommunicated from the LDS church for, among other things, hindering missionary activity, campaigning for the Equal Rights Amendment (ERA), and lodging public complaints about Mormon patriarchy. The publicity surrounding Johnson did not abate after her excommunication, however, with the media opinion makers generally siding with Johnson and against the LDS hierarchy. In a *Chicago Tribune* editorial, Charles Madigan compared the charges against her to ones that had been trumped up during the Spanish Inquisition: "knowingly preaching false doctrine, [and] undermining the Church's missionary efforts and its authority."[5] A *Washington Post* editorial charged that in going after Johnson, the LDS church "attempted to silence a voice—not just a Mormon voice, but a voice. If the Church succeeds, not just Mormon women will suffer, but women in general."[6]

This was not how the LDS hierarchy had hoped to mark 1980, its sesquicentennial year. Even amidst the publicity for the 150th celebration, Mormon leaders were dogged by media questions about Johnson and the church's continued denouncement of the ERA. In April of 1980, the *Miami Herald* ran an exposé demonstrating that the LDS church had used its own funds to defeat the ERA in Florida, channeling at least $60,000 into last-minute efforts before the pivotal November 1978 election.

The unease that many Americans had begun to express about Mormons' political agenda and financial prowess worsened in 1981, when the LDS First Presidency issued a statement opposing the placement of an MX missile system in Utah and Nevada. Many major metropolitan papers carried the story as front-page news. The *New York Times* called the church's stance "an oddly selective summons to national morality in the service of an obviously parochial interest."[7] In contrast, the *Washington Post* observed that although the church's statement had been catalyzed by the threat of an MX missile in Utah, it had actually expressed opposition to MX missiles being placed anywhere at all, a position the *Post* hailed as "unexpectedly progressive." That was a rare voice of support in a broad sea of media criticism, as most outlets complained that the church was practicing a convenient and provincial morality. What outsiders found perhaps most alarming about the church's statement against the MX missile was that it proved successful: the military proposal, already controversial, was dead in the water after the LDS church announced its opposition.

The political clout manifested by the LDS church's opposition to the MX missile and its defeat of the ERA in key states raised the sinister specter of "Mormonism, Inc.," as a long-form series in the *Nation* called it. Through the years, the media had always expressed an interest in the financial holdings of the LDS church, but in the 1980s this concern took on greater urgency. The new media interest appeared fueled in part by Mormonism's well-financed entries into the political arena, but also by the decade's booming economy and a renewed American emphasis on wealth creation. In 1983, the *Denver Post* ran an eight-part series on the LDS church—an unprecedented number of column inches devoted to understanding Mormonism—which included an estimate that the church's business interests amounted to two billion dollars. Throughout the decade, other newspapers and periodicals attempted to revise that number, usually trending upward. This was a guessing game, since the LDS church had stopped releasing annual financial statements in 1959. Similar articles appeared throughout the 1980s, such as Robert Lindsey's "The Mormons: Growth, Prosperity and Controversy," which ran in the *New York Times Magazine* in 1986. Lindsey expressed simultaneous admiration for and concern about the wealth of the LDS church—anxieties that were expounded still further in his 1990 book *A Gathering of Saints: A True Story of Murder, Money, and Deceit.*

In addition to questions about money and politics, the LDS church in the 1980s faced significant challenges to its theological identity. A popular anti-Mormon film, *The God Makers*, enjoyed widespread distribution in the early 1980s; hundreds of thousands of people were influenced by its portrayal of Mormonism as a powerful cult that brainwashed members and had ties to Satanism. The LDS church's attempts to stake a claim to be Christian—and its 1982 rebranding of the Book of Mormon with the subtitle "Another Testament of Jesus Christ"—did little to mitigate the growing sentiment. Newspapers and newsweeklies largely stayed out of the theological fray, but there were exceptions, such as a *Los Angeles Times* review of the 1984 book *America's Saints: The Rise of Mormon Power*. Although the reviewer liked the book, he chided its authors for not exposing the dangers of Mormon theology. "Good Mormons routinely take oaths acknowledging God's right to slit their throats for revealing temple secrets," the reviewer claimed, also noting that even though polygamy had been officially disallowed, many Mormons believed they would become "polygamous Gods and Mrs. Gods" in the world to come.[8]

Other media troubles were also brewing. In the early 1980s, a young collector named Mark Hoffman approached the LDS church with a startling discovery: a document, written in the hand of founding prophet Joseph Smith, that clearly indicated Smith's intention to pass the mantle of prophecy not to Brigham Young or any other member of the Quorum of the Twelve Apostles, but to his eldest son, Joseph Smith III. The document received widespread press coverage, as did Hoffman's 1985 discovery of the "Salamander letter," a document by Joseph Smith's friend and financial backer Martin Harris that suggested that Smith had not been led to discover the Golden Plates by an angel, but by a white salamander that morphed into a spirit. Drenched in beliefs in magic and folklore, the document caused widespread consternation among many Latter-day Saints—apprehensions that were reported in the press. "It's an incredible crisis of faith for me," Mormon scholar Klaus Hansen told *Time* magazine. "It means our historical foundation becomes a nice story that has no connection to reality."[9] The *Los Angeles Times* quoted one scholar who suggested that after these damning revelations, the LDS church might stop emphasizing the allegedly divine origins of the Book of Mormon.

However, it all came crashing down within the year. The documents had been cleverly forged by Hoffman, who in the fall of 1985 set off three bombs in Salt Lake City to cover his tracks, killing two people. Now the LDS church had the ignominy of seeing its name in headlines alongside words like "murder," "fraud," and "conspiracy." As journalists fought to get to the heart of the complicated story, it became clear that the LDS church had quietly purchased more than forty documents from Hoffman over the years. "Some made their way into the public domain," said the *Los Angeles Times*. "Most did not."[10] Mormon leaders, it seemed, had acquired controversial documents at considerable expense so that Hoffman would not make them public, potentially embarrassing the church.

In 1987, when more of the facts of the story were known, the *Los Angeles Times* ran an exposé of 12,000 words that clarified the involvement of Gordon B. Hinckley, who had been a counselor (adviser) to two different prophets, Spencer W. Kimball (who served from 1973 to 1985) and Ezra Taft Benson (who served from 1985 to 1994). According to the *Times*, Hinckley repeatedly dipped into church coffers to purchase documents that might damage the church's reputation or history. Hoffman did not even have to make an appointment to see Hinckley, a privilege granted to very few. The *Times* also reported that Hoffman had obtained a bank loan of $185,000 through Elder Hugh Pinnock of the Quorum of the Twelve. In all, the Hoffman debacle was a public relations nightmare for the LDS church, and allegations of leaders' secret dealings dogged it through numerous news articles and journalistic true-crime books that emerged from the scandal.

The 1990s

Like the 1980s, the 1990s didn't begin well. In 1990, the church quietly instituted changes to its sacred temple endowment ceremony, a key ritual that teaches Mormons about God's history with humankind and occurs only in LDS temples. Several controversial elements were dropped, including the mocking of a Christian minister and some physical gestures that indicated the devotee would inflict violent self-harm before revealing temple rituals. *Time* reported on these changes, despite what it characterized as the "shroud of secrecy" surrounding them, and speculated that they had been made because of declining temple attendance. The *New York Times* ran the headline "Mormons Drop Rites Opposed by Women" and lauded "the evolution of Mormonism away from its stormy origins in 19th-century America to a multicultural world religion."[11] Although the media coverage of the temple changes was neutral or even positive, doubtless LDS leaders would have preferred to keep the story out of the news at all.

In 1993, the LDS church made headlines again with the disciplining of the "September Six," a half-dozen historians and intellectuals, most of whom had feminist leanings. All were excommunicated or disfellowshipped within weeks of one another. Although the *New York Times* had three years earlier praised Mormonism's apparent increased sensitivity to women's issues, it now saw Mormon women as "chafing at what they regard as sex discrimination."[12] While highlighting some of the doctrines that made Mormonism different (including a belief in a Mother in Heaven), the article also took pains to demonstrate that Mormons were becoming ever more like other Americans: their birth rates were declining, and the percentages of Mormon women in the workforce mirrored the national average. With that, the article suggested, more women would rise up to demand equality in the church.

Although the 1990s began with critical media coverage, a good deal changed when Hinckley became the prophet in 1995. He granted unprecedented access to journalists, breaking down some of the "prophet mystique" by appearing on *60 Minutes* and *Larry King Live*. Hinckley had been trained in communications himself, and one of his first jobs at church headquarters had been to spearhead the Mormon presence in radio in the 1930s. He understood the importance of good PR and cultivated better relationships with journalists. His achievements were widely reported in the press: an ambitious worldwide temple-building program, the creation of a Perpetual Education Fund to finance the educations of impoverished Latter-day Saints, and a grueling travel schedule that took him to sixty countries.

The church's significant growth during the Hinckley era was noted by the media. Each new temple announced or dedicated provided local news outlets an opportunity to explore the Mormon presence in their midst, and although these articles were not always free of controversy (in Boston, for example, a significant backlash occurred in the neighborhood proposed for the temple), they generally fostered understanding. The media also focused on Mormonism's rapid growth at a time when other religions seemed stagnant or dying. When Hinckley became the prophet in 1995, the church had nine million members, and when he died in 2008 it had grown to more than twelve million, more than half of whom lived outside the United States.

The Mormons Next Door: A Gold Medal Olympics

In 2002, the LDS church faced an unprecedented opportunity for media exposure as Salt Lake City played host to the Olympic Winter Games. In the months leading up to the Olympics, members of the media speculated about whether the event would be dominated by ill-placed Mormon attempts to convert the 1.5 million visitors and 9,000 journalists expected to attend. A September 2001 *Newsweek* cover story raised the specter of the "Mo-lympics," in which a PR-obsessed church would ruin the party for everyone else. "For some, it all boils down to a single question," *Newsweek* declared. "Will I be able to get a stiff drink in this town?"[13]

Although pre-Olympic coverage was cautious or even skeptical, reportage during and after the Olympics often presented Mormonism in a positive light. Historian Jan Shipps credits the 2002 Olympics for shattering two persistent public stereotypes of Mormons: that they belong to a backwater, provincial tradition and that their primary goal is to make converts.[14] According to the LDS Public Affairs Division, approximately 95 percent of the thousands of stories filed about the Olympics treated Mormonism in a manner characterized as "positive or fair." Utah came across not as a remote or isolated locale but as the site of a new IT boom. Mormons were portrayed as friendly but largely unobtrusive.

This was due in no small part to the LDS church's conscious and concerted efforts to correct misunderstandings and have church members serve as "gracious hosts" during the Olympics. Prior to the event, the church sent 3,600 journalists miniature briefcases with story ideas inside, suggesting features such as "a day in the life of a missionary" and "health code helps Mormons live longer." During the weeks prior to and during the Olympics, the church operated a News Resource Center to assist journalists with research about Utah and Mormonism.

So positive was the media coverage, in fact, that one scholar believes it presented Latter-day Saints as a "model minority": industrious, clean, virtuous, financially successful, and family oriented. Chiung Hwang Chen has chronicled the fawning tenor of some media coverage of Mormonism before and during the Olympics, noting the similarities in Mormons' portrayal to the model minority stereotypes of Asian Americans. Although such coverage is an improvement over inaccurate or intentionally negative reporting, Chen writes, it has its own problems by forcing members of a minority into well-contained boxes and erasing legitimate historical changes over time.[15]

The Persistence of Polygamy

Almost entirely absent from journalists' coverage of the Olympics were stories about polygamy and the persistence of underground plural marriages in Utah. In the years to come, however, that focus would change dramatically. In June 2002, fourteen-year-old Elizabeth Smart was kidnapped from her home in a prosperous area of Salt Lake City. Every major media outlet followed the story, with regular updates about the search and television news replaying a preabduction home video of a well-dressed blonde girl playing the harp. As the days turned into weeks and Elizabeth was not found, journalists began to scrutinize her family, debating whether a family member had murdered Elizabeth, or whether she had simply run away from home. Some perceptive media analysts began to wonder aloud why, after months with no news, the Elizabeth Smart kidnapping continued to *make* the news, especially when other children—children from poorer backgrounds, children without white skin—went missing with appalling regularity and far less fanfare.

After nine months, Elizabeth Smart was found in the company of polygamist Brian David Mitchell and his wife Wanda Barzee in a suburb of Salt Lake City. The nation was thrilled with her miraculous return and eager for news of what had happened to her during what the media referred to as her "captivity." Many speculated about Stockholm syndrome, in which an abductee bonds with captors, and suggested that it might explain why Elizabeth had not run away from her kidnappers when she had the chance, such as when Mitchell was jailed in California for a short period. *Newsweek* further conjectured that Elizabeth, with her squeaky-clean Mormon upbringing, would have been obedient to a fault—especially since Mitchell, an excommunicated Latter-day Saint, spoke her religious language. "Changing her name (she initially told police she was 'Augustine') and dressing her in white robes were acts that mirror sacred Mormon practices," *Newsweek* explained. "Members of the Church of Jesus Christ of Latter-day Saints wear long, white robes in the temple, and they are given new names (not used outside the temple) when they wed."[16]

Newsweek's coverage was suggestive of a dark connection between Smart's Mormon faith and polygamy, but did not cross any lines into factual inaccuracy. Other journalists were not so circumspect, labeling Mitchell and Barzee as "Mormon polygamists." The LDS church immediately set about correcting this, rather desperately attempting to separate the moniker "Mormon" from anything to do with plural marriage. "We remind journalists that the alleged perpetrators of this horrendous crime were not affiliated with the Mormon faith in any way, and had not been for years," the church said in a public statement. "There is no ambiguity about the teachings of The Church of Jesus Christ of Latter-day Saints relative to the practice of polygamy today. Simply, the practice of polygamy is grounds for excommunication."[17]

To some journalists and scholars, however, the Elizabeth Smart kidnapping placed in stark relief the tensions between historic and contemporary Mormonism, the angel and the beehive—tensions that were not going to disappear so easily. Mitchell represented an older form of the religion, one characterized not just by polygamy but by itinerancy, direct revelations from God, and a wild dissociation from mainstream culture. His actions also harkened back to the disturbing violence of the religion's earlier days. The Smart family represented what Mormonism had become—assimilated, wealthy, patriotic, peaceful, and dedicated to the flourishing of a tight-knit nuclear family. It was a dichotomy difficult to reconcile.

Over the next several years, the LDS church would have to repeatedly distance itself from plural marriage, as well-publicized arrests occurred among polygamists in Utah and elsewhere. Leaders of some polygamist communities, such as Tom Green and David Kingston, were convicted of incest, rape, and domestic violence. But the largest prosecution was against the FLDS (Fundamentalist Church of Jesus Christ of Latter-day Saints), led by Warren Jeffs. In 2003, the Attorneys General of Utah and Arizona jointly launched investigations into this group, an aggressive move for states that had long allowed polygamy to fly under the radar. Jeffs moved his compound to Texas to evade prosecution but was convicted in 2007 of statutory rape for marrying off young women under the age of eighteen against their will. In 2008, agents invaded the compound and removed 416 children—an eerie re-enactment of the infamous "Short Creek" raid the FLDS had endured in 1953[18]—while cameras captured footage of sobbing children being torn from their mothers.

A flurry of newspaper articles, radio pieces, and television news segments expressed outrage about the forcible separation, creating sympathy for the FLDS families and applying pressure to the legal system. "What Did the FLDS Kids Do to Deserve This?" screeched an editorial on CBS News. The *Christian Science Monitor* noted the unusual spectacle of polygamist wives taking their case to the media themselves, without male intermediaries; some even invited journalists into their homes to provide their side of the story or spoke to reporters outside the courthouse.

Mitt Romney

Along with polygamy, the other Mormon-related issue in the news in late 2007 and early 2008 was former Massachusetts governor Mitt Romney's bid for the US presidency. The son of late Michigan governor and 1968 presidential contender George Romney, Mitt Romney had grown up watching his father's faith publicly analyzed and criticized. Some conservative political commentators felt that Americans had progressed beyond old anti-Mormon stereotypes and were ready to seriously consider a Mormon candidate. However, this was not quite the case.

Romney's campaign got off to a strong start, aided by deep coffers and his reputation as a successful businessman who could turn the economy around. But in early December, a Vanderbilt University poll revealed that randomly selected voters had more prejudice against voting for a Mormon than a woman or an African American candidate. Interestingly, more than half of those surveyed revealed that they did not know a Mormon personally. Clearly, Romney had a problem, and against the advice of some of his aides, he decided to cancel a day of public appearances to address the charges head-on during a twenty-minute speech at the George H. W. Bush library in Texas.

Romney's speech was largely praised by pundits as being a relatively straightforward defense, not of Mormonism itself (Romney used the word "Mormon" only once) but of Americans' allegiance to ideals higher than denominationalism. Echoing John F. Kennedy's famous 1960 speech about religion, Romney called himself "an American running for president" and stressed the unity of all faiths. "The speech was peppered with declarations appealing to Christian conservatives about the importance of religious expression," concluded the *New York Times*.[19]

Despite the well-received speech, the entrance of evangelical Mike Huckabee into the race meant that Romney's Mormonism became more of a stumbling block than it had been before. After declaring that he was above taking potshots at distinctive Mormon beliefs, Huckabee accused Mormons of teaching that Jesus and Lucifer were brothers, a crude oversimplification of LDS theology. Yet Huckabee's message was clearly heard: Mormons are not like us. Romney's ratings began to fall in the polls.

By early February, the race was all over for Romney, and it was left to pundits to dissect where the campaign had gone wrong. *Newsweek*, surprisingly, accused Romney not of being too Mormon, but not Mormon enough. It lambasted him for appearing insincere about his religion, as well as his politics. When asked about polygamy, Romney had denounced it in the strongest terms possible, saying he "couldn't imagine anything more awful." *Newsweek* took him to task for protesting too much—after all, his great-grandparents were polygamists. Another *Newsweek* editorial went even further in criticizing Romney: the politician had failed completely and expensively, and it was his own fault. In the end, the one good, genuine act *Newsweek* columnist Howard Fineman found in the entire campaign was that Romney had left the trail on the eve of Super Tuesday to fly to Salt Lake City for the funeral of LDS prophet Gordon B. Hinckley. "It was a class act, one of the few in his otherwise misbegotten campaign," Fineman concluded.[20]

Mormons and Proposition 8

Although media coverage of Romney's Mormonism was pervasive, it was occasionally positive and generally fair. In late 2008 and early 2009, that changed as the church participated in a full-scale fight against same-sex marriage in California. In the summer of 2008, local LDS leaders in California were instructed to read aloud a statement from the First Presidency urging them to support Proposition 8, which would define marriage as exclusively between a man and a woman. Although the LDS church apparently did not provide money from its own coffers to pass the measure, it strongly encouraged individual California Mormons to do so, which resulted in the donation of an alleged twenty million dollars to the cause. Despite being only 2 percent of California's population, Mormons far outstripped any other single religious group in donations, with Yes on 8 estimating that Mormons had contributed over 40 percent of the total. This figure did not include the untold hours Mormons spent knocking on doors, circulating petitions, and working the phones. When all this became public knowledge in the weeks just before and after the election, the public backlash against the LDS church was immense.

On November 7, days after Proposition 8 passed with 52 percent of the vote, the *Los Angeles Times* reported that more than a thousand gay-rights activists had protested outside a Mormon temple. "It was the latest in an escalating campaign directed against the Church of Jesus Christ of Latter-day Saints for its role in marshaling millions of dollars in contributions from its members for the successful campaign to take away same-sex marriage rights."[21] However, the *Times* also noted that the criticism ran both ways: just as Mormons were accused of discriminating against gays and lesbians, so too did some of the backlash cross the line into antireligious discrimination, such as a widely televised video of two Mormon missionaries invading the home of a lesbian couple to destroy their marriage license. Mormons who found their names outed on websites or in full-page newspaper ads as donors to Proposition 8 wondered why their church was being so exclusively associated with the campaign when all of California's Catholic bishops, as well as many evangelical Christians, had also supported the measure. In fact, according to the *New York Times*, the LDS church had been the last major religious group to be invited to join the broad coalition of religious groups in favor of Proposition 8.

But the *Times* also pointed to a major reason that Mormons had been so singled out: in addition to the millions its members raised in a few short months, "80 percent to 90 percent" of the Yes on Proposition 8 volunteers were LDS. What's more, they were clearly mobilized by a centralized leadership, given precise canvassing assignments based on zip codes and talking points with detailed scripts to convey door to door. Some of those scripts included the false claim that same-sex marriage would lead to churches losing their tax-exempt status for refusing to marry gay couples.

Mormons had become the public face of the 52 percent of Californians who supported Proposition 8, and the backlash caught the church by surprise. In the coming months, Mormon leaders would continue to face criticism for the church's involvement—particularly when, in February 2009, the church revised its initial estimate of having spent approximately $2,000 in nonmonetary donations and volunteer labor to almost one hundred times that, or $189,903.58. News outlets pounced on the discrepancy, forcing the church to issue a statement clarifying the extent of its involvement.

It remains to be seen whether the LDS church plans to further its fight against same-sex marriage in other states. It won the battle in California, but in some senses this was a Pyrrhic victory, as the negative publicity generated by seemingly top-down Mormon involvement presented the very kind of cultlike image the church had spent the last forty years trying to avoid. As with the church's other major attempts to enter the political arena on what it perceived as moral issues—the ERA and the MX missile—its politicking generated unwanted and potentially lasting backlash.

In the fight over same-sex marriage as in so many other arenas, the push-pull dynamic of the angel and the beehive creates a constantly changing dialectic of Mormon involvement with the world, which is reflected in media coverage of the movement. Such media coverage also shapes Mormons' perception of themselves, whether they are basking in a post-Olympic glow or reeling from harsh criticisms about their political involvement. The future is uncertain: will Mormonism be regarded as a homegrown American faith to be cherished and celebrated, or an exotic, powerful other to be exposed as a danger to American freedom? If past trends are any indication, Mormonism will continue to receive its most positive media coverage when Latter-day Saints adhere to the beehive archetype of successful assimilation, and not when they call attention to the angel archetype through an emphasis on distinctive beliefs or political force.

NOTES

1. Armand Mauss, *The Angel and the Beehive: The Mormon Struggle with Assimilation* (Urbana: University of Illinois Press, 1994), esp. 196–201.

2. Eric A. Eliason, "Introduction," in *Mormons & Mormonism: An Introduction to an American World Religion*, ed. Eric A. Eliason (Urbana: University of Illinois Press, 2001), 5.

3. "Prophet, Seer and Innovator," *Time*, February 2, 1970.

4. Judy Klemesrud, "Strengthening Family Solidarity with a Home Evening Program," *New York Times*, June 4, 1973.

5. Charles Madigan, "A Woman's Anguish: Her Church or ERA," *Chicago Tribune*, December 16, 1979.

6. Richard Cohen, Op-Ed, *Washington Post*, January 3, 1980, quoted in Stephen W. Stathis, "Mormonism and the Periodical Press: A Change is Underway," *Dialogue: A Journal of Mormon Thought* 14, no. 2 (Summer 1981): 55.

7. "The Mormons and the MX," *New York Times*, May 9, 1981.

8. David Johnston, "Church of Choice and Ambition," *Los Angeles Times*, November 18, 1984.

9. Richard N. Ostling, "Challenging Mormonism's Roots," *Time*, May 20, 1985.

10. John Dart, "Letter Revealing Mormon Founder's Belief in Spirits, Occult Released," *Los Angeles Times*, May 11, 1985.

11. Peter Steinfels, "Mormons Drop Rites Opposed by Women," *New York Times*, May 3, 1990.

12. Dirk Johnson, "As Mormon Church Grows, so Does Dissent from Feminists and Scholars," *New York Times*, October 2, 1993.

13. Ana Figueroa, "Salt Lake's Big Jump," *Newsweek*, September 10, 2001.

14. Jan Shipps, "Spinning Gold: Mormonism and the Olympic Games," *Dialogue: A Journal of Mormon Thought* 36, no. 1 (2003): 134.

15. See Chiung Hwang Chen and Ethan Yorgason, "'Those Amazing Mormons': The Media's Construction of Latter-day Saints as a Model Minority," *Dialogue: A Journal of Mormon Thought* 32, no. 2 (1999): 107–28; also Chen, "'Molympics'? Journalistic Discourse of Mormons in Relation to the 2002 Winter Olympic Games," *Journal of Media and Religion* 2, no. 1 (February 2003): 29–47.

16. Elise Christenson, "How the Kidnappers Controlled Elizabeth," *Newsweek*, March 31, 2003.

17. "Erroneous Reporting of Elizabeth Smart Case," The Church of Jesus Christ of Latter-day Saints Newsroom: The Official Resource for News Media, Opinion Leaders and the Public, March 24, 2003, http://www.mormonnewsroom.org/article/erroneous-reporting-of-elizabeth-smart-case.

18. In July 1953, state authorities cracked down on polygamists in Short Creek (now called Colorado City), Arizona, in the largest-ever arrest of polygamists in American history. The story is recounted best in Martha Sonntag Bradley, *Kidnapped from That Land: The Government Raids on the Short Creek Polygamists* (Salt Lake City: University of Utah Press, 1993). The Short Creek polygamists later regrouped and became the Fundamentalist

Church of Jesus Christ of Latter-day Saints, which made headlines again in the 2000s with the arrest and trial of leader Warren Jeffs.

19. Michael Luo, "Romney, Eye on Evangelicals, Defends His Faith," *New York Times*, December 7, 2007.

20. Howard Fineman, "Burying Mitt," *Newsweek*, February 6, 2008.

21. Jessica Garrison and Joanna Lin, "Prop. 8 Protesters Target Mormon Temple in Westwood," *Los Angeles Times*, November 7, 2008.

REFERENCES

Chen, Chiung Hwang. 2003. "Molympics"? Journalistic Discourse of Mormons in Relation to the 2002 Winter Olympic Games. *Journal of Media and Religion* 2 (1 [February]): 29–47.

Chen, Chiung Hwang, and Ethan Yorgason. 1999. "Those Amazing Mormons": The Media's Construction of Latter-day Saints as a Model Minority. *Dialogue: A Journal of Mormon Thought* 32 (2): 107–28.

Eliason, Eric A., ed. 2001. *Mormons & Mormonism: An Introduction to an American World Religion*. Urbana: University of Illinois.

Mauss, Armand. 1994. *The Angel and the Beehive: The Mormon Struggle with Assimilation*. Urbana: University of Illinois Press.

Ostling, Richard N., and Joan K. Ostling. 2001/2007. *Mormon America: The Power and the Promise*. San Francisco: HarperOne.

Shipps, Jan. 2003. Spinning Gold: Mormonism and the Olympic Games. *Dialogue: A Journal of Mormon Thought* 36 (1): 133–49.

Stathis, Stephen W. 1981. Mormonism and the Periodical Press: A Change is Underway. *Dialogue: A Journal of Mormon Thought* 14 (2): 48–73.

CHAPTER 17

NEWS COVERAGE AND POPULAR PRESS REPORTS OF THE MAHARISHI MAHESH YOGI IN THE 1960S

JANE NAOMI IWAMURA

MASS media, especially the news industry, played a crucial role in the changing attitudes and consciousness of the 1960s. Surprisingly, the stories that stirred the most interest were not those that covered religiously motivated conflict in Asia or the example of a conventionally recognized religious leader. Rather, Americans' provocative and widespread initiation into an alternative worldview came through the media's intense focus on the Maharishi Mahesh Yogi and his Spiritual Regeneration Movement in the late 1960s. Mahesh's relationship with the Beatles and other high-profile Western celebrities made for good copy and hurled the guru, as well as Indian spirituality, into the headlines.

First, news reporting on Mahesh stimulated popular interest in Asian religious traditions. Although Westerners have historically held a fascination with the "spiritual East," and specifically India, the popular press during the 1960s transformed an esoteric interest into a popular phenomenon. This was achieved not only by the general media attention that Mahesh received but also through news reporting that included a heavy reliance on the visual image. Photographs that accompanied written accounts said as much about the story as the reporters' words. Second, celebrity journalistic accounts of the guru established the indirect route through which Asian religions and Asian-influenced movements would gain widespread recognition among Americans. Before the 1960s, coverage and references to Indian religions, especially Hinduism, were consigned to the international pages of newspapers and magazines. Mahatma Gandhi's nonviolent struggle against British colonial rule may be the only example in which Indian religions were prominently featured. While Gandhi's practices were shaped by his Hindu upbringing and his exploration of Hindu texts, American news reports stressed the universalistic dimensions of his thought. As the editorial that ran in *Life* magazine soon after Gandhi's assassination proclaimed: "Gandhi was not just a 'great man'; he was a universal saint, something the West has not produced for many generations" (February 9, 1948). Journalists also cast Jawaharlal Nehru—India's first prime minister, seemingly more secular in view—as someone who could overcome religiously informed internal divisions and move the "ancient civilization" into the modern world. Gandhi and Nehru, however, were the exceptions; the rest of India was portrayed as a poor and backwards people, mired in strange customs and religious conflict.

The treatment of India as a backwards nation and of India's most representative religious tradition as a living cultural artifact was also pronounced in *Life* magazine's extensive exploration of religion in India in its February 7, 1955, issue titled "Hinduism." This special report kicked off the periodical's ambitious series "The World's Great Religions." True to its format, *Life*'s coverage was supplemented by dramatic images of Indians engaged in exotic practices, from a Brahmin offering a simple prayer to Hindu ascetics on the shores of the Ganges. While the writers attempt to translate Indian thought for their Western audience, often emphasizing Hinduism's focus on the "one true reality" (in relation to practitioners' recognition of many deities) and the tradition's attempt to "adapt to the modern age," their efforts are undercut by the visual spectacle that the images provide. In these scenes (as well as their captions), "caste and certain primitive elements still cling to Hinduism like moss."

The Orientalist divide between a backwards India and the modern West was thus perpetually reinforced by American news reporters and cultural commentators. But it became much more difficult to maintain in the case of the Maharishi Mahesh. The yogi would travel beyond the Indian subcontinent, and by the mid-1960s he had established a global movement with followers in the United States and Europe. Mahesh and his Western adherents helped pave the way for Americans' eventual embrace of yoga, meditation, and Indian mysticism, with the help of the popular press that offered unprecedented exposure to the Asian religious figure and his growing, yet contested reputation and movement.

Mahesh is best known as the personal guru to the Beatles. Lead guitarist George Harrison, especially, found spiritual inspiration from the unconventional yogi, whose simple meditative technique refocuses the practitioner's mind on "pure being" and taps into a wellspring of "creative intelligence." By the time the Beatles first met the Maharishi Mahesh Yogi in London in 1966, Mahesh had already made seven trips around the globe, established 38 centers, and amassed more than 100,000 followers since his announcement about bringing peace to the world in 1957.[1] Despite these impressive achievements, he and his Spiritual Regeneration Movement did not capture widespread American interest until the late 1960s, when his name became associated with famous musicians and film personalities. By the end of 1967, the *New York Times Magazine* declared him "The Chief Guru of the Western World," and in 1968, *Life* magazine announced "The Year of the Guru." Transcendental Meditation, as an alternative to a drug-induced high, had become a full-fledged phenomenon in the United States, especially among the nation's youth.

In the late 1960s, the Maharishi's philosophy seemed to appeal to a generation that was increasingly disillusioned with traditional forms of religious belief and practice. As Americans faced a rapidly changing environment and increasing turmoil brought on by mounting racial tensions, urban uprisings, and the Vietnam War, the Maharishi offered a solution to problems that, to some, seemed insurmountable. With ease and confidence, he publicly asserted that "world peace would come if he could spread his teachings."[2] These teachings, the Science of Creative Intelligence, along with its practical component, Transcendental Meditation, focused on the inner world of the individual. The "bliss consciousness" and "illuminating expansion of the mind" the Maharishi promised made his spiritual alternative extremely compelling, if not magical.

Mahesh enjoyed spectacular attention by the American media from the autumn of 1967 to the spring of 1968 and constituted a photojournalist's dream. Encounters with the Maharishi took place through a colorful lens reflective of the psychedelic style of the time. This vibrancy made for eye-catching copy and reinforced long-embedded notions of a spiritual and exoticized India.

First Impressions

A small news item appeared in the Sunday edition of the *New York Times* on December 12, 1966: "Beatle Tells Preference for Religions of India." It reported that Harrison "believed much more in religions of India than in anything he ever learned from Christianity." This interest would lead Harrison and his bandmates to seek out the Maharishi in the winter of 1967.

The meeting took place in London, and the band then joined Mahesh on a five-day retreat in Bangor, Wales (a scheduled stop on the Maharishi's eighth tour around the world). The encounter was auspicious for both parties. The Beatles found a new spiritual guide, who offered consolation during a very difficult period of their lives. (During the retreat, the guru broke the news to the musicians that their long-time manager, Brian Epstein, had died.) As for Mahesh, the pop group represented unprecedented public exposure for his movement's mission to spiritually regenerate the world.

As the Beatles made plans to join the Maharishi in Rishikesh, India, the news media covered the spiritual alliance with increasing fervor. In the "Religion" pages of *Time* magazine's October 20, 1967, issue, the American public got their first glimpse of the guru who had so enthralled their musical idols. The photo offers a humble portrait of the Maharishi, in both gesture (with one hand rested gently on his forehead and another clasping a bouquet of flowers) and presentation (the photo's black-and-white medium). The unassuming representation befitted a spiritual luminary from the East in all his ascetic and mystical promise. However, any mystique the image evoked is offset by the article's caption: "How to succeed spiritually without really trying." The simple legend, paradoxically phrased, calls into question the Maharishi's authority by drawing attention to his potentially unscrupulous practice. The piece further dismisses Mahesh by generically identifying him as "The Guru."

Mahesh therefore was introduced to Americans as "hard news" copy (albeit in the religion sections of various venues). The Beatles' foray into a foreign and alternative religious system was deemed newsworthy, not only because of their pop star status, but also because of the seeming weight of their endeavor ("religion"). Journalists would turn this event into "soft news" fodder and follow up with more extensive offerings. The Maharishi would be featured in four full-length articles, visually supplemented with countless photos. Despite the representational abundance, the tone of most of these reports (e.g., the *New York Times Magazine*, *Saturday Evening Post*) would be similar, offering skeptical, if not critical, assessments of Mahesh and his movement. Only one, *Look*'s cover feature, would be deferential.

It is important to get a sense of how the extensive "soft news" coverage portrayed Mahesh, and especially how the visual image contributed to its overall tenor. By focusing on the photographic layout of two paradigmatic treatments—*Look*'s reverential portrayal and Lewis Lapham's critical exposé for the *Saturday Evening Post*—this chapter examines the journalistic trend toward reporting on Asian religions and Asian religious figures that has, since the 1960s, relied extensively on the visuals.

Look's Reverential Portrait

In January 1968, the Maharishi packed the Felt Forum in the newly built Madison Square Garden in New York City.[3] During his visit, he also met with United Nations Secretary-General U Thant to discuss ways of aiding "permanent peace."[4] Shortly after, on February 6, 1968, *Look* magazine featured the guru on its cover, with the headline "AND NOW—MEDITATION HITS THE CAMPUS; How Hindu monk Maharishi turns the students on without drugs." The magazine features two articles on the Maharishi phenomenon. The first piece, "A Visit with India's High-Powered New Prophet" by Paul Horn, is accompanied by an elaborate photo spread—eleven images of Mahesh and his ashram in Rishikesh, India. In the second feature, "The Non-Drug Turn-On Hits Campus," William Hedgepeth reports on student meditators at the University of California at Berkeley and at UCLA with seven photos throughout.

On the heels of the *New York Times Magazine*'s critical article on Mahesh (December 17, 1967), *Look*'s coverage resacralized the yogi's image. In "India's High-Powered New Prophet," Paul Horn, an American jazz musician, traces the development of Transcendental Meditation and explains its philosophy. The photos and their captions provide a separate text, in which Horn narrates his visit with Mahesh "on the Ganges." The primary photo of the yogi is minimalist, featuring a wind-swept, contemplative Maharishi. On the two-page opening spread, this image is supplemented by a host of other photos, most of which portray Mahesh as intimately connected with the Indian people.[5] Viewing the Maharishi ministering to the native population caters to a paternalistic vision shared by *Look*'s Western audience: a spiritual leader in tune with the needs of the "most oppressed." Hence, these photos lend a human dimension and spiritual legitimacy to Mahesh's mission.

Such legitimacy is also supplied by another image in the photo spread: a portrait of the Maharishi's own spiritual teacher, Brahmanda Saraswati or Guru Dev (as he was called by his disciples). The article describes Guru Dev as "a spiritual leader of the Hindus,"[6] who "revived the meditation technique Maharishi is now spreading."[7] The image is not simply of the portrait, but of Dr. R. C. Verma painting the likeness of Dev. According to Horn, Verma "supplies portraits of Dev to meditation centers in 50 countries."[8] This complex image is significant for two reasons. First, it places Mahesh within the spiritual lineage of a recognized religious tradition (Hinduism). Second, the fact that the paintings are made for meditation centers takes the focus away from the Maharishi's own image. This may seem contrary to the development of Mahesh's iconic status as a sagely Oriental Monk.[9] But given the "bad press" of previous articles, this referential nod toward Guru Dev, in fact, rehabilitates Mahesh's image.

This favorable view is also evident elsewhere. In yet another image, the Maharishi is shown with camera in hand, taking snapshots. This picture depicts the guru engaged with modern technology. Amid the photos of Mahesh in his "natural surroundings" in India, the camera appears as an anomaly, an amusement. And if there is any doubt to this read, the caption[10] confirms it: "Maharishi's message is that men are born to enjoy. He's a superb host, and loved to escort us on tours around India so we could take pictures. Sometimes, he borrowed cameras to take pictures himself." Mahesh's use of the camera is framed as a moment of unadulterated enjoyment. Image and text also lend the Maharishi's image a childlike simplicity: The guru is enthralled with a "new toy," in which he seems to delight.

The opening spread, for the most part, achieves the solemnity befitting a spiritual leader. The somber nature of its images demands the viewer-reader take seriously the Maharishi and his movement. The photo of Mahesh with camera is perhaps the exception. But even this somewhat amusing shot is clearly situated within the realm of the yogi's philosophy: *Men are born to enjoy*. Likewise, the three photos on the following page are meant to capture the essence of this philosophy. In each of these images, Mahesh's pleasant expression is the focus. The spiritual leader becomes the embodiment of his teachings. Surrounded by Indians in his native setting, the Maharishi's smile does not represent an indulgent decadence (as it will come to symbolize in later articles), but rather the nonattachment of a wise man.

In the second article of the same issue, "The Non-Drug Turn-On Hits Campus: Student Meditators Tune in to Maharishi," Mahesh's joyful face is superimposed on a group of meditators at Yale. His larger-than-life image looks down on a group of well-scrubbed youth with what can be read as a look of approval. The visual montage offers a study in contrasts. Each student is fairly clean-cut and seemingly happy. These images reflect the reporter's generally positive stance toward the Student International Meditation Society (SIMS) and favorably portray Mahesh's influence. The image of the student followers as respectful, drug-free individuals persuasively makes a case for Mahesh, as a general audience contrasts these with the stereotypical image of the disobedient, disheveled, and drugged-out youth of their time.

Look magazine's coverage of both the Maharishi in Rishikesh and the SIMS in California cast Mahesh in a favorable light, imbuing the chief mystic of the Spiritual Regeneration Movement with authority and grace. The persuasive force of the visuals is achieved not only by their arrangement within the separate articles but also by the manner in which they are collectively divided. Images of Mahesh are sequestered to Horn's visit to Rishikesh, which locates the spiritual figurehead squarely in India. Images of Western adherents occupy a separate textual and geographic domain. The single image connecting the two (the Maharishi and meditators at Yale) relies on two distinct images that are superimposed.

When one compares this visual separation of spheres (East and West) with the images in which Mahesh mingles effortlessly in a Western setting, the implication is subtle, yet clear. The Maharishi is awarded spiritual clout when he can be squarely located within certain bounds—geographic and racialized. Under *Look*'s surveilling eye, he conforms to this Orientalist contract. And any breach of this contract results in a negative assessment. Transcendental Meditation, as an Eastern spiritual alternative, is allowed legitimate consideration only when it can be properly managed.

"There Once Was a Guru from Rishikesh"

The cover image of the May 4, 1968, issue of the *Saturday Evening Post* provides the most direct visual link between the Maharishi and his Western celebrity following. Similar to *Look*, the *Post* cover offers a montage of images—this time a large profile of Mahesh juxtaposed with smaller images of actress Mia Farrow and the Beatles entourage. The magazine positions these celebrities as the main audience draw, even as the Maharishi visually dominates the frame. It also characterizes "the scene" as one in which Mahesh has considerable influence over youth and youth culture. His presence is cast as menacing, especially as the guru seems to gaze directly at a seemingly young and innocent Farrow.

The *Saturday Evening Post* ran a two-part report on the Maharishi and his Rishikesh settlement in successive issues. The series, in which correspondent Lewis H. Lapham offers an account of his visit to Mahesh's compound in India, was whimsically titled "There Once Was a Guru from Rishikesh." The images chronicle Lapham's trip and reflect the narrative development of his account. Unlike previous articles, the photos are scattered throughout the piece, but after scanning the photos, the story's progression is clear.

Part 1, which appeared May 4, 1968, begins with an image of Mahesh meditating on a sofa, microphone in front of him. The darkened auditorium in which the picture is set also serves as a textual backdrop against which the article's white print is highlighted, and the viewer-reader is visually drawn into the story. The Maharishi is photographed at a public event, but his meditative pose—eyes closed and hands folded—sets him apart from the mundane setting. Indeed, it is the microphone that appears as a curious and imposing probe. It beckons the yogi to speak. An instrument of amplification, it accentuates Mahesh's every sound, even his silence.

In the article, the image of the Maharishi's noninteraction with what is, at once, a Western technological device and an instrument of publicity establishes him as a serious spiritual figure—one who appears impervious to the microphone's corrupting presence. The sacred dimension of Mahesh's movement is further captured in the next photo, which depicts a group of student followers in California meditating peacefully in a grassy field. They are well dressed, well coiffed, and well behaved. Like the images in *Look*, these first two photos seem to make a distinction between the Indian leader (and the Eastern mystical realm he embodies) and his students (and their world in the West). Although the next photo includes both Mahesh and members of his Western audience, the initial setup allows the viewer-reader to interpret the interaction with requisite seriousness. The audience members, on which the camera is focused, seem intent on the Maharishi's every word.

These opening photos reflect Lapham's initial stance toward Mahesh and his Spiritual Regeneration Movement, developed through interviews with avid followers. Indeed, the images capture the Maharishi's movement through the eyes of American adherents, who view him as a spiritual icon and themselves as serious seekers. In the article, Lapham does not wholly adopt a convert's perspective but is heavily intrigued. The writer's ensuing visit to India serves as the critical event, and he seems to reserve final judgment until then.

Lapham eventually arrives at Rishikesh, where the fourth photo is taken. This visual moment foreshadows the perspective the reporter will eventually take. The image depicts a sentry stationed outside the Maharishi's compound, and its caption ironically reads: "A banner said WELCOME, but the way to the ashram was barred by a Hindu guard, a gate and a barbed wire fence."[11] For the author, these physical barriers symbolize an exclusionary attitude on Mahesh's part and seem to contradict his universally conceived message. Inevitably, it provokes suspicion in the mind of both author and viewer-reader.

The final two photos in Part 1 of "Guru from Rishikesh" visually distinguish those who are allowed to enter Mahesh's compound and those who remain outside its gates. The first of these photos shows the Beatles and their companions, along with Beach Boy Mike Love, engaging in conversation with the Maharishi. Within the circle, Mahesh sits cross-legged as before, but his celebrity guests appear nonchalant. Unlike the California students, the Beatles do not adopt a reverent attitude toward the guru. In fact, they appear rather bored; John Lennon looks idly at his fingernails, while George Harrison snaps a photo of another guest.

The flip attitude of the famous visitors stands in sharp contrast to the final image of Lapham's first installment. This picture depicts two Westerners meditating solemnly outside the walls of the Maharishi's settlement. According to the caption, these two individuals are among "a group of Americans living near the ashram, searching for a guru of their own." Compared with the Beatles, the unknown meditators represent serious spiritual seekers, unimpressed with Mahesh.[12] Together, the three photos taken on and around the premises of Rishikesh (guard, Beatles, Western meditators) help the viewer-reader distinguish the different types of adherents who journey to India. They also reflect Lapham's budding disillusionment with the Maharishi, whose fascination with Western fame and success seem to contradict his sagely status.

This interpretation is confirmed in the set of images that accompany Part 2 of "Their Once Was a Guru from Rishikesh" (May 18, 1968). The article opens with shots that emphasize the worldly nature of the guru's spiritual retreat. The first is of Mahesh, sitting cross-legged in the passenger seat of a helicopter. Once again, he appears overly enthusiastic about technologies and personalities from the West.

The other photo, on the facing page, shows Beatle Ringo Starr fiddling with an eight-millimeter movie camera. The famous guests appear to approach their spiritual instruction with all the seriousness of a holiday. In addition to Starr, Lennon and Paul McCartney are also caught filming their visit.[13] Farrow, in another image, is seen dining at the compound. According to the report, she "called her pilgrimage 'a romp,' but had left the ashram for a few weeks to go tiger hunting."[14] As the article progresses, the captions that frame the images take on an increasingly ironic tone.

The penultimate image shows two individuals meditating near the Ganges. Despite the irreverent activity that accompanies the celebrity visits, at least two adherents appear to seriously engage the Maharishi's technique. The caption acknowledges the pair as "Nancy Jackson and Beach Boy Mike Love." Jackson's dress and posture reflect her social status, which Lapham elaborates in the article: "A chic, blond woman in her 40's, Nancy . . . had a brisk way of talking that suggested she was accustomed to managing things and her conversation invariably contained references to the important people she knew."[15] Mike Love, in comparison with the maven's formal pose, sits cross-legged on the ground. At a glance, the image captures two very different individuals engaged in meditation, which lends the photo a peaceful and alluring tone. However, the caption once again calls into question the sincerity of the followers: "[Jackson] and [Love], two of the Maharishi's disciples from California, *meditate for the camera*" (my emphasis).[16] The textual commentary highlights the superficiality of the captured moment; the photograph's aura is shattered, and the meditators become little more than spiritual "posers."

Given the reporter's mounting skepticism, the final image of the article comes as little surprise: a photo of Mahesh on the phone in his office. Although the room appears modest, the few items captured within the frame are telling: a copy of the *Indian Express*, a notebook, and, of course, the phone. The way the Maharishi sits—upright in a cloth-covered chair, legs firmly planted on the ground as he leans forward to take the call—signifies the guru in a moment much more mundane. Indeed, a comparison of the first and final images of the two-part report captures the overall flow of the article, as it works to disrupt any "illusion" the viewer-reader may have about Mahesh and his Spiritual Regeneration Movement. Indicative of critical accounts, the *Saturday Evening Post* ultimately presents the Indian guru as an individual more interested in image than soul. The article does not necessarily place the entire onus for this situation on the Maharishi; his celebrity guests are partly to blame. The allure of the West provides a serious temptation (helicopters, cameras), which the presence of famous guests only seems to heighten. The Maharishi's ashram turns into "a scene"—one in which an American popular audience is critically distanced, yet phantasmically involved.

Through these first impressions of Mahesh and his followers, one immediately senses not only the two different attitudes—critical and reverent—that prevailed during the period but also the way in which they were constructed and communicated through the visual image. The battle between youth and adults—their divergent views on cultural authority—seemed to fuel the popular interest in Mahesh and his movement. Press reports generally conformed to an Orientalist narrative in which a lone monk figure of Asian origin transmits his spiritual wisdom to the West. This conventionalized narrative depends on two primary figures: the Oriental monk teacher (in this case guru) and his dedicated Anglo pupil. The character of the monk, mysterious and foreign, operates as the embodiment and transmitter of Eastern spirituality. His Western pupil functions as the figure with which the audience most identifies or, at the very least, serves as an entry point into the monk's mystical realm.

In representations of the Maharishi in the late 1960s, this narrative is maintained and developed. Mahesh is portrayed as a spiritual sage whose mission is to spread his teachings beyond his native homeland, specifically to the West. As the guru reportedly commented, he "admired the American mind and compared it to the flower of the tree, while the other peoples of the earth were bark and branches."[17] Whether Mahesh's comment is taken as genuine compliment or sycophantic gesture, it signals a particular type of recognition of the West (and specifically the United States) as a significant site of regeneration and reinforces Americans' own sense of self-importance.

Within the representative mix, the Beatles paradigmatically serve as the monk's Western pupils, who, disillusioned with their inherited spiritual heritage, are drawn to Mahesh's philosophy and practice. First, the Beatles primarily function as a synecdoche for Western youth. In press reports, the two are almost interchangeable, as the popular rock group is referred to as "the blessed leaders of the world's youth,"[18] and young people are seen as increasingly defining themselves in relation to their musical heroes. The Beatles seem to reflect both the exuberance and excess of their young audience. Given this metaphorical fluidity, American youth occupy a primary place in the Maharishi/monk narrative. It is members of this generation who are seen as most attracted to his wisdom.

The relationship between Oriental monk teacher and Western pupil is usually romanticized to legitimate the transfer of Eastern spiritual knowledge from one to the other and, more broadly, from the cryptic East to the white Western world. The more reverent accounts of the Maharishi phenomenon reinscribe this romantic account, akin to *Look*'s positive portrayal. Not only is Mahesh's image appropriately sacralized but also his American followers are represented as serious spiritual seekers. In addition, the clear distinction between East and West, maintained in the magazine's coverage, allows the transmission of mystical wisdom to serve as a dramatic event. Overall, positive reports adopt a tone that is fairly straightforward and respectful toward Mahesh and his philosophy. The audience is meant to identify (or at least sympathize) with the pupils—portrayed as earnest and reliable in their spiritual endeavors, as well as in their high regard for the yogi.

Compared to these reverent offerings, critical accounts are structured in a more complicated manner. Although the same elements of the conventional narrative are maintained, in media reports on the Maharishi, examples of verbal irony are plentiful. The writers for *Look*, *Life*, and other newsweeklies were usually viewed as reliable sources of information; at the very least, they were taken as commentators whose perspective offered insight into a phenomenon. Perhaps most significant is the set of shared assumptions between author and audience that provide instances of verbal irony and their force. Media reports critical of the Maharishi invoked deeply embedded notions of Christian asceticism to shape the public's opinion and encourage a skeptical view. For instance, a religious leader should be "in the world, not of it"—that is, not overly taken by celebrity, as Mahesh seems to be. Spiritual worth cannot be assigned a material value; in other words, the guru is not justified in charging the nominal fee for instruction. Spiritual insight requires dedicated commitment and practice; namely, there is no "Peace without Penance,"[19] as Transcendental Meditation is seen to achieve. In these underlying ways, Christianity provided the frame of reference for understanding the emergent Spiritual Regeneration Movement, as well as for the media commentator's critical rhetoric.

Back to the Orient

In the rhetorical ways just discussed, most press accounts dedicated to the Maharishi presented their subject with great ambivalence. One can easily discern the connection between 1960s American press reports of Mahesh and views upheld by Orientalists during the nineteenth century and the news reporting on India and

Indian religions that preceded the guru's appearance. As Edward Said astutely remarks about the latter:

> Language and race seemed inextricably tied, and the "good" Orient was invariably a classical period somewhere in a long-gone India, whereas the "bad" Orient lingered in present-day Asia, parts of North Africa, and Islam everywhere. "Aryans" were confined to Europe and the ancient Orient; . . . the Aryan myth dominated historical and cultural anthropology at the expense of the "lesser" peoples.[20]

Given Said's characterization, representations of Mahesh entail a significant difficulty because he seems to embody both "a long-gone India" and "present-day Asia." But any contradiction dissolves when one considers the conflicting opinions of the guru presented by the popular media. Reverent accounts primarily chose to see Mahesh merely as representative of an ancient Hindu tradition ("long-gone India"), whereas critical ones spoke only of the yogi's corrupted concerns ("present-day Asia").

Mahesh's mission was informed by similar views and expectations, and he could not escape this deeply ingrained Orientalist frame of reference. For instance, American reviewers could not adequately comprehend his attempts to employ modern means of communication and travel to disseminate his spiritual knowledge. Mahesh's mobility became an index of his agency and controllability; a monk who stays put in his Asian country of origin or whose mobility is limited is certainly preferred over one who seems on the go. But not only had the Maharishi made eight trips around the world (by 1968) but also these trips were part of a conscious plan to establish Transcendental Meditation centers and spread his teachings throughout the globe. On the one hand, this conscious plan demonstrated initiative on Mahesh's part that discomforted critical commentators. On the other, reverent reviewers, often followers of the movement, saw the guru's visits as a response to their call. They also saw themselves as providing Mahesh with the means to travel from one place to another. Hence, Mahesh, as historical figure, maintains the romantic composure of the icon as long as he is suitably dependent on the white host society and/or travels only according to their needs. In either case, his spiritual initiative and economic prowess was something that could not be adequately conceived by the American press. Initiative constituted a characteristic reserved solely for his pupils in the West.

Mahesh's Orientalized image did not exist independently but was supported by an equally Orientalized India. In his "Open Letter to the Beatles," Arthur J. Dommen, the *Los Angeles Times'* New Delhi bureau chief, invoked these notions to critically comment on the pop group's impending trip to India:

> But you will say, the mystical wisdom of India lies not in the illiterate, ill-nourished peasants, who are like the illiterate, ill-nourished peasants everywhere, but in the holy men, the gurus and the sadhus. Here indeed is an important difference. To observe these holy men in their faded pinkish orange robes trudging the roads of India, their bare feet stirring the dust and their matted hair their only protection from the beating sun or rain, does make one

> wonder whether they have not attained a higher plane of spirituality, where the afflictions of the body no longer exist.
>
> In so far as they do not collectively concern themselves with problems of bettering society, India's holy men have relinquished the temporal things of life, I agree.
>
> The influence of these holy men is said to be considerable, yet it seems insufficiently enlightening to prevent the suicide of an estimated 17,000 people every year, and it does not give salvation to the estimated 2 million beggars.
>
> I confess that the spirituality of the several thousand baked and near-naked sadhus who tried to storm the Parliament building last November in their frenzy to see a law enacted to ban the slaughter of cows, even if they had to lynch a few MPs in the process, still escapes me today.[21]

Here, Dommen references the stereotypical view of India as a third world country, typified by its teeming masses, superstitious tendencies, and chaotic mix of lifestyles. Like British writers such as Rudyard Kipling, he uses this characterization to posit the spiritual, moral, and political inferiority of the Indian peoples. Ironically, this same view was also upheld in more reverent portrayals. These accounts assumed that Indians' superstitious nature and their penchant to cater to religious folk like Mahesh meant excellent service at the Rishikesh ashram. India's nontechnological, agrarian setting provided a romantic backdrop. And the disorderly nature of Indian life translated into local color to be enjoyed and experienced by spiritual tourists from the West.

Although Americans at the time saw themselves as distinct from India's British colonizers of the past, they still adopted many of the same dispositions toward the former colony. Indeed, after declaring itself an independent state, India received financial and technical assistance from the United States.[22] In Americans' eyes, India could not survive on its own and would continue to be a "white man's burden,"[23] a view of Indian dependency that continued to underwrite Orientalist attitudes of pessimism and privilege.

On the Shoulders of (Celebrity) Giants

News coverage and popular press accounts, both reverent and critical, participated in a debate that had, in essence, very little to do with the Maharishi Mahesh Yogi and his Spiritual Regeneration Movement. The intense focus on famous converts, especially the Beatles, betrayed a riveting shift in the structure of cultural authority. Indeed, Mahesh's popularity emerged from a new countercultural outlook that seemed to resonate with the younger generation. This outlook eschewed traditional forms of American religion and embraced more mystical alternatives focused on individual fulfillment.

However, even more radically, this emerging sensibility brought forth a new authorial framework that featured pop celebrity as legitimating force and was inherently media driven in nature. *Look*, in its report registering the "Campus Mood, Spring, '68," spoke with student editors from twenty-three universities and reported: "The nearest thing to heroes for many students is the Beatles."[24] A similar observation was made in the December 4, 1967, issue of *Newsweek*, whose education column explored the demise of the campus hero. The magazine hints at several reasons that "college students no longer idolize political leaders, or try to imitate authors like Salinger or Tolkien."[25] These young people are either "too jaded" or "too busy." However, the piece paradoxically realizes: "The most popular non-ideological idols are the Beatles, particularly John Lennon. . . . 'They are saying that youth can be more successful than adults,' says Jon Ratner, a senior at Berkeley, 'and that the values of youth are important. All the new ideas of everything that's going on begin with the Beatles.'"[26]

The fact that college students so readily recognize and identify with entertainment figures reveals a new form of cultural authority. Such authority appeared not only unwieldy but also formidable, as other powerful influences, such as Mahesh, were spun off these figures. Cultural sanction seemed based on nothing more than the fluffiness of pop stardom, as Lapham's depiction of one adherent suggests:

> Characteristic of another type I found prevalent among meditators, [Kip] Cohen was young, engaging, very articulate and very hip. He had long blond hair and a mustache, and he was just past 26, which depressed him. He'd first seen the Maharishi on the Johnny Carson show, and he's heard that Donovan and the Beatles were into meditation.
>
> "With their endorsement," he said, "I knew the thing couldn't be too far amiss."[27]

Indeed, sensationalized image was often put forth as the foundation of Mahesh's "success" in the West. It afforded the guru and his movement widespread publicity, whether one felt he deserved it or not. As Hedgepeth observed: "Even if there were some who hadn't seen [Mahesh] on [the Berkeley] campus last year, there wasn't one who didn't realize that he was the same jet-age guru who had guided the Beatles off the psychedelic drug scene by way of a new, nonchemical turn-on."[28] All in all, the majority of American reviewers seemed most troubled not necessarily by *what* Mahesh had to say (which often perplexed commentators), but rather by *how* he achieved popular recognition, namely, through the authorial framework of celebrity. Critical accounts, ironically posed in a variety of ways, expressed their disdain or at least their ambivalence toward this new framework. In contrast, more reverent portrayals were readily at home within this framework or at least resigned to its presence.

Amid the larger battle for cultural authority and significance, the Maharishi's image served as a convenient screen on which to project these more immediate concerns. The ascendancy of television and other news media had transformed popular consciousness in ways that few predicted. The emphasis on more immediate experience (sight and sound) and the powerful circuits of pop celebrity[29] were just two of its many unintended effects. The fact that the Maharishi capitalized on both of these effects made him the perfect figure on which to project Americans' ambivalent feelings toward the new media environment. Such anxiety, especially over the emerging status of celebrity, was displaced onto Mahesh—a target made more acceptable through religious, racial, and colonial difference. The figure of the celebrity guru allowed an American audience to disavow pop culture's widening influence by drawing their suspicion onto the figure while simultaneously indulging their desire for celebrity spectacle.

Coverage of the Maharishi Mahesh Yogi during the late 1960s established significant patterns in regards to Asian religions and Asian religious alternatives and their coverage by the news media. While Asian religions still make "hard news" copy when linked to political events abroad, most attention is paid (and pages rendered) to "soft news" stories, especially ones that involve well-known entertainment stars and their embrace of Buddhism, Hinduism, or other Asian-influenced movements. Asian religions may not make headlines on their own, but with the right spokesperson and a few eye-catching images, reporters get their story.

NOTES

1. Barry Lefferts, "Chief Guru of the Western World," *New York Times Magazine*, December 17, 1967, 44–45, 48, 50, 52, 54, 57–58, statistic from 45.

2. "Yogi Speaks Here on Peace Teachings," *New York Times*, January 20, 1968.

3. See "Yogi Speaks Here on Peace Teachings"; "36,000 Hear Guru Urge Meditation," *New York Times*, January 22, 1968; "Preacher of Peace," *New York Times*, January 22, 1968.

4. See "Yogi Confers with Thant—to Aid 'Permanent Peace,'" *New York Times*, January 21, 1968.

5. This view was not commonly held by Western reporters, who painted Mahesh as more concerned with pleasing his Western audience than with the plight of the native population.

6. Paul Horn, "A Visit with India's High-Powered New Prophet," *Look*, February 6, 1968, 66.

7. Ibid., 65.

8. Ibid.

9. See Jane Naomi Iwamura, *Virtual Orientalism: Asian Religions and American Popular Culture* (New York: Oxford University Press, 2011) for a detailed analysis of how the icon and narrative of the Oriental Monk operates in mass media and has become a part of the American (religious) imagination. The narrative is explored briefly later on in this chapter.

10. Ibid., 64.

11. Lewis H. Lapham, "There Once Was a Guru from Rishikesh, Part 1," *Saturday Evening Post*, May 4, 1968, 26.

12. Lapham does eventually call into question O'Shea's spiritual journey in Part 2 of the series ("There Once Was a Guru from Rishikesh, Part 2," *Saturday Evening Post*, May 18, 1968, 30), but the visual image of the wandering seeker in Part 1 does not betray any such folly.

13. The caption does reveal: "John Lennon referred to the Beatles' photographs and records as diaries of their developing consciousness" (Lapham, "Part 2," 30).

14. Ibid., 31.

15. Ibid.

16. Ibid., 32.

17. Ibid., 33.

18. Ibid., 28.

19. "Soothsayer for Everyman," *Time*, October 20, 1967, 86.

20. Edward Said, *Orientalism* (New York: Vintage, 1979), 99. Here, Said generalizes upon the view of nineteenth-century "Darwinian anthropologists and phrenologists."

21. Arthur J. Dommen, "India Offers Plenty for Meditation," *Los Angeles Times*, September 10, 1967.

22. Ernest Dunbar, "India," *Look*, March 19, 1968, 31–37, quotation from 31.

23. Kipling's famous phrase.

24. Ernest Dunbar, "Campus Mood, Spring, '68," *Look*, April 2, 1968, 26.

25. "The Urug and the Grungey," *Newsweek*, December 4, 1967, 54.

26. Ibid.

27. Lapham, "Part 1," 25.

28. William Hedgepeth, "The Non-Drug Turn-on Hits Campus," *Look*, February 6, 1968, 68–69.

29. For an interesting examination of these circuits, as well as the function of celebrity in contemporary society, see P. David Marshall, *Celebrity and Power, Fame in Contemporary Culture* (Minneapolis: University of Minnesota Press, 1997).

REFERENCES

Carrette, Jeremy, and Richard King. 2005. *Selling Spirituality: The Silent Takeover of Religion*. New York: Routledge.

Ellwood, Robert S. 1994. *The Sixties Spiritual Awakening*. New Brunswick, NJ: Rutgers University Press.

Iwamura, Jane Naomi. 2011. *Virtual Orientalism: Asian Religions and American Popular Culture*. New York: Oxford University Press.

King, Richard. 1999. *Orientalism and Religion: Post-Colonial Theory, India and "The Mystic East."* New York: Routledge.

Lawrence, Bruce B. 2002. *New Faiths, Old Fears: Muslims and Other Asian Immigrants in American Religious Life*. New York: Columbia University Press.

Marshall, P. David. 1997. *Celebrity and Power, Fame in Contemporary Culture*. Minneapolis: University of Minnesota Press.

Prashad, Vijay. 2001. *The Karma of Brown Folk*. Minneapolis: University of Minnesota Press.

Wuthnow, Robert. 1990. *The Restructuring of American Religions*. Princeton: Princeton University Press.

CHAPTER 18

AMERICAN PRESS COVERAGE OF BUDDHISM FROM THE 1870S TO THE PRESENT

NICK STREET

AN article published in the *Chicago Daily Tribune* on September 19, 1886, inadvertently anticipated the cultural dissent of the Beats and the spiritual star power of the Dalai Lama in the twentieth century, as well as the rise of the religious "Nones" in the first decade of the new millennium. The anonymous reporter—writing before the advent of the byline as a standard feature of mainstream American journalism—also offered a distinctively nineteenth-century angle on "The Buddhist Mahatma Craze" then sweeping through the ranks of the urban elite in the United States:

> Chow-Ju-Tien, a veritable Buddhist priest, has arrived here, bringing in his carpet-bag all the paraphernalia of his ancient religion—the aura, the astral body, the Mahatma, tirthankars, and all. . . . In this age of religious transition many curious and dissatisfied people are reaching out for new forms of belief to take the place of the old. They are in a condition of discontent with the plain, old-fashioned practical doctrines of orthodox Christianity, which are too simple and easy of comprehension. They want something which is enveloped in an air of mystery, has a high-sounding vocabulary, and abounds in vague but delightful supernatural agencies. Buddhism seems to offer them all this.

If the *Tribune* article shows us that religious ferment is a constant feature of American religious life, it also highlights elements of American journalism that have dramatically changed since the 1880s. What we would now consider editorializing—particularly the decidedly pro-Christian tone that typified much reporting during the era of the partisan press—is mostly absent from current religion coverage in our mainstream news media. And, as we will see, an unalloyed element of racism, coupled with almost uniformly uncritical support for missionary and military enterprises in Asia, once informed most of the reporting on immigrant Buddhists and Buddhism in general.

A Zen saying goes: nobody knows the power of an old monk chanting sutras on a mountaintop; he turns the universe. Though the civil rights movement of the 1950s and a nascent antiwar movement had already provided the impetus for a shift in journalistic perspectives on race and American colonialism, a Buddhist monk in flames at a busy intersection in Saigon abruptly altered the way our news media have covered Buddhism in the United States and abroad since 1963.

This chapter will examine how the largest daily newspapers in our three most populous cities—the *New York Times*, the *Chicago Daily Tribune*, and the *Los Angeles Times*—reported on Buddhism before and after that pivotal event. Specifically, the sections that follow will look at how each paper covered immigrant, as well as convert, Buddhism at various key historical junctures (e.g., the *Tribune*'s reporting on the Parliament of the World's Religions in 1893, David Halberstam's war reporting for the *New York Times* in 1963, and the *Los Angeles Times*' coverage of the emergence of "medicalized" meditative practice and distinctively American forms of Buddhism since the 1980s).[1]

What becomes apparent from this broad historical perspective is, first, our news media's slowly evolving appreciation for religions as sets of activities and beliefs that help people form communities, shape identity, and give meaning to their lives. Also apparent in the coverage of Buddhism over the years is a steadily increasing journalistic awareness of the interplay between religious movements and the political, cultural, and physical environments they inhabit.

A consistent theme in the teaching passed on from the Buddha is that the more you think you know, the less you actually see. As the journalism of the 1950s and '60s began to cast off the last remnants of the partisan press, reporters began to see Buddhism—and most other religious traditions—a bit more clearly.

Putting Up with Nirvana

Though research into Buddhist literature—if not actual Buddhist practice—had begun to attract enthusiasts among the American intelligentsia before 1850, when Transcendentalists like Ralph Waldo Emerson and Henry David Thoreau were already prominent cultural figures, a widespread curiosity about Buddhism among educated elites didn't register in the national press until after the Civil War.

But in the couple of decades immediately following that conflict, many urbanites who had the means and the inclination to look beyond social convention for spiritual inspiration began to turn toward Theosophy, a philosophically oriented society of well-heeled mystics founded by Henry Steel Olcott (1832–1907) and Helena Petrovna Blavatsky (1831–91). Though the Theosophists sought to tease out elements of universal wisdom from all religious traditions, both Olcott and Blavatsky formally converted to Buddhism at a temple in what was then called Ceylon on May 25, 1880.[2] A few years before Blavatsky's conversion, the *New York Times* had already taken an interest in her as a sort of cultural curio—a notion that mirrored a description of Blavatsky's home that appeared in the paper on April 30, 1877:

> A select circle of Theosophists gathered in Mme Blavatsky's cozy apartments in West Forty-seventh-street last evening to listen to a short discourse on "China, and the Chinese Religion" by Wong Chin Foo, the native missionary. [A] huge tiger's head over the door, a miniature crocodile swinging from the ceiling, and elegant and curious bric-a-brac distributed about on the walls and mantel-pieces gave testimony to the untrammeled tastes of the hostess.

According to Blavatsky, her Chinese guest "has merely entered upon his present course for the purpose of disabusing the American mind of the gross errors and absurdities respecting the religion of China." Wong, himself the scion of a wealthy family, pointed toward American missionaries in China as the source of those "errors" and "absurdities." He might also have directed his criticism at the *New York Times*, which was scathing in its coverage of Buddhist converts long before and well after the apex of the Theosophy movement.

In a piece published on June 22, 1890, the *Times* said of intellectuals gathering at a Buddhist conference in Paris:

> [T]he same vastness of mind through which they have been enabled to accept the doctrines of Buddhism is the very reason why they never put them into practice . . . one of the most awful of these doctrines consists in standing for several years on one leg . . . another is being buried alive for a month or two. . . . Their great minds may put up with Nirvana, but not with the various ridiculous modes of getting there.

At this point in American history, media coverage of Buddhism—of most non-Christian religious practice, for that matter—was not so much a window into the unknown as a mirror reflecting the familiar and reassuring biases of America's Protestant majority.

Insolent People Without Attractive Characteristics

The *Chicago Daily Tribune* and the *Los Angeles Times* were equally contemptuous of convert Buddhism during this era. And, like the reporting in the *New York Times*, that tone of condescension was often tinged with disgust when the subject of reportage was Buddhism practiced by Asians.

Racism was an obvious reason for the distorted angle on religious practice that was both nonwhite and non-Christian. But the reportage of the late nineteenth century also spurred an increase in American missionary and military involvement in China, which had been weakened by the Opium Wars (1839–42, 1856–60) and hobbled by the punitive treaties imposed by Western powers.[3]

Playing to the sensibilities of readers supporting these colonialist activities, the *Tribune* published an article about "The Buddhist Priesthood" on June 27, 1879, in which the writer claimed that the ranks of young Chinese monks "are generally . . . purchased from their parents or from kidnappers. . . . [A]fter a required novitiate, [the monk] proves his constancy to the faith by standing unmoved while several pastilles burn down into his scalp, leaving the ineradicable scars which testify to the fact that he has put away forever the things of this world."

Similar—and similarly uncorroborated—accusations of barbarism among the colonized Chinese appear in a *New York Times* piece on June 20, 1891, about an uprising against a European outpost south of Shanghai. According to the *Times*, "The cause of the insurrection is stated to be that the Buddhist fanatics incited the mob to violence by continual preaching against the foreign missionaries, alleging that at the Catholic convent in Wuhu the Chinese children were tortured and maimed, and that their eyes were gouged out for the purpose of making medicine to bewitch the Chinese."

From the perspective of many white Californians, the barbarians weren't merely across the ocean; they were crossing it. The construction of the transcontinental railroad and the discovery of gold in northern California in 1848 had attracted tens of thousands of workers, including 25,000 Chinese immigrants, who by 1860 were the single largest foreign-born ethnic group in the state.[4] After the railroad was completed and the gold grew scarcer, white immigrants from other parts of the United States often found themselves competing for work with Chinese laborers in California's rapidly growing urban centers. That localized resentment, coupled with politicized racism at the national level, spawned the Chinese Exclusion Act of 1882, the first in a series of anti-immigrant legislative moves that severely curtailed the growth of immigrant Buddhist communities in the United States until the passage of the Immigration and Nationality Act of 1965.[5]

By the 1870s and 1880s, the *Los Angeles Times* had become instrumental in stoking this xenophobia. On March 23, 1888, the *Times* published a dispatch from Canton (modern Guangzhou) titled "Insolent People Without Attractive Characteristics":

> They repel one in every way, and I watch them as I would the gambols of apes or the antics of some half-civilized missing link tribe of heathens. . . . If in the heat of the anti-Chinese excitements in America some shrewd politician had only come to Canton, watched, studied and pried into the life of this crowded city, he could have gone home with an illustrated lecture that would have been the most forcible argument for the Restriction Act, or an Expulsion or an Extermination Act.

In the context of this widespread and deep hostility toward non-Christian Asians and condescension toward American converts to the tradition, the coverage of the Parliament of the World's Religions at Chicago's Columbian Exhibition in

September 1893 was, if not a turning point in American reporting on Buddhism, then at least a glimpse of brighter days to come.

A Day at the Fair

The religion parliament was one of several congresses held in conjunction with the Columbian Exhibition, a commemoration of the 400th anniversary of European arrival in the Americas that was billed as youthful Chicago's debut as a city with broad shoulders and worldly aspirations.[6] While the *New York Times* and the *Los Angeles Times* gave the parliament relatively scant coverage—New York had been passed over as the host city for the Columbian Exhibition—the *Tribune* reveled in its access to the parliament's luminaries and the chance to outshine its coastal competitors in reporting on an event of national importance. Compared to the acerbic tone of the newspaper's pre-1893 coverage of Buddhism, the pieces related to Buddhist delegates to the conference were fairly levelheaded, and even at times obsequious, as shown in this excerpt from "Disciples of the Sage of Asia at Christian Service," September 4, 1893:

> In ceremonial dress a party of Buddhist priests and monks attended divine service at the First Presbyterian Church yesterday morning. . . . For the first time in history have priestly followers of the gentle sage of India greeted with their presence a Christian form of worship in a Christian church in America. . . . Asked about the possibility of establishing Buddhism in the United States, Soyen Shaku of Kamakura, Japan said through his secretary: "Time only will tell what the result may be."

Shaku was one of six delegates representing the various schools of Japanese Buddhism at the parliament. His young student and translator, D. T. Suzuki, would eventually become one of the key figures in the counterculture movement of the 1950s and 1960s.[7] Anagarika Dharmapala, a Theravada Buddhist scholar and layman, was less circumspect than Shaku in his appraisal of Buddhism's encounter with the West. In "Buddhist Scholar's Rebuke" (September 19, 1893), the *Tribune* reported that in his speech before the parliament, Dharmapala excoriated "the missionaries of Christianity, who, he said, 'Go into the temples of the ancient faiths, where gentleness and love are taught, and revile and insult its teachers and the principles which they teach.'"

If the *Tribune* was willing to allow its readers to be challenged in their perceptions of nonwhite Buddhists, it was less eager to abandon the tendentious language that characterized its coverage of Westerners' interest in Buddhism. On September 27, the last day of the parliament, the paper ran "Convert to Buddha," a story about Charles T. Strauss, a prominent convert from Judaism:

> Mr. Strauss is related to some of the wealthiest and most exclusive Hebrew families in New York City, and his father before him was a strict observer of the

> Jewish ritual. They are astonished as well as indignant over Mr. Strauss' abjuration of the faith of his fathers, and they cannot understand his move toward the effete religious mysticism of the East.

The persistent journalistic suspicion toward Americans who were attracted to "effete religious mysticism" augured that the easing of antipathy toward Buddhism—among both immigrants and converts—would not last much past the closing days of the parliament. But Dharmapala returned to American to lecture in 1897 and from 1902 to 1904, and Soyen Shaku toured the country from 1905 to 1906, preparing the soil for Buddhist teachers who would arrive to plant spiritual seeds decades after them.[8] Ironically, the very place where American Buddhism is flourishing most dramatically in the early twenty-first century seemed the least hospitable terrain for the tradition at the beginning of the last century.

"Nothing but a Japanese Face"

If the United States has always been a society bubbling with religious ferment, Southern California has long seemed closer to the flame than other places. Currently the nation's most religiously eclectic region, Southern California's fervor in the early 1900s was mainly of the Christian variety, nurturing Pentecostalism, as well as several centers of higher education associated with mainline Protestantism, Roman Catholicism, and the evangelical movement.

During that period, the outlook of the *Los Angeles Times* usually matched the point of view of the conservative-minded developers and businesspeople who had begun to lay the foundations of a vast city atop the L.A. Basin's dusty chaparral. Also figuring into the editorial mix were the moral sensibilities of the latest generation of pilgrims to migrate westward in search of yet another New Eden. That sympathy for the zeal of the missionary—and wariness toward anything that might challenge the wider social order in which it flourished—is apparent in "Buddhists to Build Temple," an article that appeared in the *Times* on October 8, 1904:

> Only two days ago *The Times* announced . . . that the largest band of Christian missionaries ever sent out from the Pacific Coast would leave Los Angeles this week for China. Today comes an announcement of missionary work on entirely different lines—one that will cause the Christians who are attempting to evangelize pagan countries to sit up with a start. . . . A temple for the worshipers of Buddhism is soon to be erected on one of the fashionable streets of Los Angeles. . . . Los Angeles already has some people high in the seats of social activity and professional life who give allegiance to the idea of final absorption in the great Buddha, and it is expected that they will also help . . . in the campaign for the pagan propaganda in this city.

Though Soyen Shaku would visit Los Angeles in 1906 and dispatch another of his students, Nyogen Senzaki, to establish California's "floating zendo" in the 1920s, coverage of Buddhism in the *Times* continued to cast a suspicious gaze on immigrant Buddhists and to frame white practitioners as soft-headed dabblers. "Vows Taken as a Buddhist Nun: Former Chorus Girl Enters Upon New Life" (June 19, 1933), one of the few pre–World War II articles to provide any background on a convert's experience, trades on the sensational aspects of the story of Mrs. C. I. Chester, a divorcee who ended her career with the Ziegfeld Follies in 1913. Chester had become a student of Nyogen Senzaki and decided to take the vows of a nun because she had reached a time of life, as she said, "When a person grows old and fat and the world forgets about them." The *Times*' lead—Chester, "who was once a chorus girl, yesterday renounced the world of material delights"—appears to trade sneeringly on Chester's subsequent statement.

A decade later, that cynicism toward the tradition had mixed with inveterate racism and hardened into cruelty when the *Times* lent its vigorous support to the internment of tens of thousands of Japanese and Japanese Americans in relocation camps following the attack on Pearl Harbor. In a piece excoriating "Pro-Jap Sentimentalism" published on May 21, 1943, the *Times* reports:

> Representative J. Parnell Thomas, who, being from New Jersey, cannot be accused of sectional prejudice against Japanese, makes some revelations of Jap spy activity carried on in Los Angeles which are a full answer to the sentimentalists who want the Japs turned loose from relocation centers and allowed to wander at will throughout the United States. The pro-Japanese sentiments of most of those confined in relocation centers are testified to by Thomas, who adds that Shinto and Buddhist priests are allowed to disseminate pro-Jap propaganda in these surroundings. . . . [T]here is considerable pampering of traitors in the relocation centers.

Sourcing among the internees was rare, and while the *Times* regularly framed Buddhist clergy as agitators in the camps, none was interviewed in the articles captured by a ProQuest search into the *Times*' coverage of the internment period. In fact, the sources for stories about disquiet in the camps were almost always political figures or military personnel.

Following apparent incidents of sabotage at the Tule Lake War Relocation Center in northern California, the *Times* ran a representative piece on November 5, 1943 ("Army Takes Over Tule Jap Camp"): "[T]he regional field director for the War Relocation Authority, which has charge of the camp, disclosed that a 'Rev. Kai,' a Japanese Buddhist priest from Hawaii, told a crowd of his countrymen that 'You must give your all for Japan,' and after that several thousand took off their hats and bowed their heads." If an effort was made to interview Rev. Kai or any other internees at Tule Lake, it's not evident in the *Times*' reporting on the incident.

One of the priests netted in the relocation effort was Nyogen Senzaki, who was interned at Heart Mountain, Wyo., until after the end of the war. He produced this recollection of his internment in the style of Buddhist sutra fragment: "Thus have I heard—the army ordered all Japanese faces to be evacuated from the city of Los Angeles. This homeless monk has nothing but a Japanese face."[9]

Five years after the *Times'* lopsided coverage of events at Tule Lake and other relocation centers—and with grim images of internment camps elsewhere in the world fresh in readers' minds—the paper ran a front-page story on December 16, 1948, about a memorial service for Sadao S. Munemori, a second-generation Japanese American who was awarded the Congressional Medal of Honor. The medal "was bestowed posthumously," the *Times* reported, for Munemori's "gallantry near Seravessra, Italy, where, in April 1945, he single-handedly destroyed two German machine-gun nests and then flung himself atop a grenade to absorb its deadliness with his body and thus save the lives of his comrades."

The article said the services for Munemori, "which also were dedicated as a tribute to the sacrifices of all Japanese-American soldiers in the gallant 442nd Regimental Combat Team, were a mixture of ancient Buddhist rites and modern military ceremonies."

"Democracy looked its best yesterday," the lead declared. It had certainly looked much worse.

A House on Fire

In 1951, Cornelius Crane (of Crane bathroom fixtures) funded a Columbia University lecture series featuring D. T. Suzuki, the student-translator who had attended Soyen Shaku at the Parliament of the World's Religions a half century earlier. The lectures, which were open to auditors not enrolled in the university, attracted psychoanalysts, artists, and budding Buddhist practitioners who would eventually become expositors of their own distinctive interpretations of the Dharma.[10] Suzuki's writing on Buddhism and Zen had already begun to influence artists like John Cage, as well as a group of literary figures that included Jack Kerouac and Allen Ginsberg—the prince and the poet-muse of a loose coterie that would come to be known as the Beats.

All of these transmitters of Buddhist teaching benefited from the proliferation of paperback books after World War II; like the advent of the Internet a few generations later, paperback culture made previously esoteric or elite subject matter available to a larger, more demographically and geographically diverse audience. That late midcentury phenomenon was the subject of several stories in the *New York Times*, where coverage of Americans' dabbling in Dharma became more tempered as the trend lost some of its elitist associations.

"As the Fifties give way to the Sixties," begins a front-page article in the *Times* on January 17, 1960, "the paperback is 'the latest'—as much a part of the times as hi-fi and stereo records, compact cars and ranch houses, bongo drums . . . and electric can openers. Indeed, certain writers and their ideas—Jack Kerouac and his Beats, David Riesman and his lonely crowd, Jules Feiffer and his sick-sickery, D.T. Suzuki and Zen Buddhism—have gained their wide reputations and currency largely through the soft covers."

While the journalistic angle on non-Asian Buddhist practice softened and widened over the course of a couple of decades, coverage of Asian Buddhism changed abruptly and dramatically in the middle of 1963. The seminal event occurred on June 11, when Thich Quang Duc, an elder Vietnamese monk, assumed the lotus position at a crowded intersection in Saigon while several hundred monks and nuns blocked traffic. After a younger monk doused him gasoline, Quang Duc struck a match and burst into flames.

Malcolm Browne, a photographer and the only Western journalist at the scene, captured a sequence of images that later won him a Pulitzer Prize—and riveted the world's attention on the corrupt South Vietnamese regime, as well as the failure of military and political figures in the United States to control the violent inclinations of an American client state. Browne's pictures, along with subsequent on-the-ground reporting by the *New York Times'* David Halberstam—who also won a Pulitzer for his work in Vietnam—forever changed the way Americans saw Asian Buddhists, as well as the culture of East Asian immigrants to the United States.

On September 11, 1963, Halberstam published "The Buddhist Crisis in Vietnam: A Collusion of Religion, World Politics and Pride," a careful delineation of the conflict between the US-backed government of South Vietnam, which was dominated by the country's Catholic aristocracy, and an increasingly activist and politicized movement of Buddhists, whose cause became a matter for international diplomacy after Thich Quang Duc's death. What made Halberstam's article remarkable—and utterly distinctive from previous reporting on Asian Buddhism—was not only his thorough sourcing within both the government of Ngo Dinh Diem and the Buddhist movement but also his clear-eyed analysis of the forces at play in the unfolding drama.[11]

We learn from Halberstam that the country's minority Catholic government, bolstered and emboldened by the American aid it was receiving to support its war against communist insurgents from North Vietnam, had become increasingly unresponsive to the desires of the Buddhist majority. In March 1963, the government denied a request to fly the Buddhist flag in Hue, the seat of Vietnamese Buddhism, on the Buddha's birthday. Subsequent protests in that city drew thousands to the streets, and the government broke up the demonstration by firing into the crowd, killing nine. Over the next few months, the United States attempted to broker a settlement, which ultimately satisfied no one, and the Diem government's increasingly brutal acts of suppression transformed the younger Buddhist clergy into an organized resistance movement.

"[The protest] was a complicated force," Halberstam concluded. "It was in small part Buddhist against Catholic; it was in much larger part the protest of a large segment of the people who happened to be Buddhist against an authoritarian Government that happened to be Catholic-dominated. It was also, in small part, have-nots protesting against haves; it was in much larger part 20th-century Asians protesting against older Asians molded from a mandarin past."

Five months after Thich Quang Duc persuaded Americans to pay attention to a situation—a nation, a religious movement, a people, a war—they had preferred to ignore, Ngo Dinh Diem was assassinated during a military coup that toppled South Vietnam's minority government. The effects of the tectonic shift that Quang Duc brought about in our collective perception were felt for decades to come. The image of his immolation and subsequent images of Vietnamese suffering energized the antiwar movement, and aftershocks were still reverberating in 2007, when another brutal regime, this time in Burma, contended with its own community of dissident monks, who used the networked gaze of digital media and the memory of Quang Duc to full advantage.[12]

Before the Vietnam War flared into American public consciousness, the tropes employed in journalistic narratives about Buddhism, particularly those dealing with Asian Buddhists, had only slowly begun to change. By the war's end, the convergence of several factors—the wider availability of Buddhist writing through paperback culture, the end of national origins quotas in 1965, the humanizing power of the stories reported from Southeast Asia, and the flourishing of communities seeded by Nyogen Senzaki and other "import Buddhists"—had altered not only media coverage of Buddhism but also the character of the tradition in the American context.

From Horns to Halos

One of the *Chicago Tribune*'s earliest stories involving the Dalai Lama places the renowned pacifist and future Nobel Peace Prize winner in a veritable rogues' gallery of infamous dictators. According to "More Payoffs by CIA," an article published on February 19, 1977, for years His Holiness had secretly received funds from the Central Intelligence Agency along with the likes of Joseph Mobuto, Saddam Hussein, and South Vietnam's Ngo Dinh Diem.

Despite that shady association with Cold War intrigue, Tibet's most famous exile would become the embodiment of the American archetype of the Oriental monk: a scrim onto which many of us project our ambivalence about Western religious and political values, even as we continue to long for a savior to do the hard work of redemption on our behalf.[13] And while movie stars and PR-savvy convert-Buddhist disciples have worked to shape this cloying image, news media coverage of the Dalai Lama has generally employed a very light touch, making their work that much easier.

In "Dalai Lama's on a Pilgrimage to Make Friends" (September 3, 1979), the *Tribune* enlisted Buddhist author Terry Clifford to write a backgrounder in advance of the Tibetan leader's arrival in New York City for his first visit to the United States:

> [A]s almost everyone who meets him discovers, the Dalai Lama is a disarmingly generous, warm, and witty man, a person of great intelligence and presence, sublimely unattached to his power and prestige. . . . His impending visit has sent waves of anticipation through the New York Buddhism community. . . . While

there are fewer than 50 actual Tibetans in the city, there are a thousand or so New Yorkers seriously committed to Tibetan Buddhism and many more who have some interest in it.

The *Tribune*'s hagiographic angle on the Dalai Lama isn't unique; in fact, similarly effusive reporting has become common in both the secular media and the Buddhist press. While that development is arguably preferable to the partisan and often racist bias that tinged coverage of Asian and immigrant Buddhism prior to the Vietnam War, it has often led to a reflexive softness in tone and constriction of focus in reportage on Buddhist life and practice.

In that respect, the halo is only a marginal improvement on the horns. Still, the body of *Tribune* reporting in the decade after Vietnam also includes several pieces that manage to acknowledge the relative benignity of Buddhism and Buddhists even as they uncover the kind of grit and context that make for richer journalistic storytelling.

One such article from this period—"From Gunner Pilot to Monk, They Call Him Teacher" (October 22, 1982)—takes the reader to Bangkok, where, "At bars where the American expatriates hang out . . . they've all heard there is an American out there who became a Buddhist monk." Once a hard-drinking, pot-smoking soldier, Ahjun Pabakaro (who asked the reporter not to use his American name) recounted the grim details of his wartime service and the experiences with Vietnamese monks that led him toward monastic life. Following a conversion to Buddhism, he requested and was eventually granted conscientious objector status. After his discharge, he "went home for three months to try to explain his decision to his parents . . . then caught a plane for Thailand . . . where he has risen to the position of abbot of a jungle monastery."

Another well-sourced and thickly described *Tribune* piece from this period ("Clean Up Vandalized Temple," October 23, 1980) examined the multiple shifts in perspective that followed a street gang's desecration of a 1,200-family Japanese Buddhist temple on Chicago's multiethnic North Side:

> The Rev. Gyoko T. Saito, the head minister of the temple, said the incident sent a wave of anger and fear though the congregation. . . . "Many of the members raised the question of moving to a new location," he said. However, after a coalition of neighborhood groups . . . provided materials and volunteers to remove the paint, the Rev. Saito announced the temple would remain in Uptown Square. Arnie Owens, a 41-year-old community activist . . . said, "[I]t was a real shot in the arm for our block . . . those Buddhists are good neighbors, and the last thing in the world we need is to lose a good neighbor."

The depth of the background reporting and the curiosity with which the reporters approach their sources markedly distinguish this pair of stories and others like them from coverage of immigrant and convert Buddhists in earlier decades. These developments in mainstream journalism's angle on Buddhism came just in time; in Southern California, a crop of completely novel—and distinctively American—iterations of the tradition was just beginning to sprout.

Bonpu Soldiers and *Gedo* Punks

In a journal article framing their 2003 survey of attitudes toward Buddhism and Buddhists in the United States, sociologists Robert Wuthnow and Wendy Cadge say, with what sounds like a bit of social-scientific exasperation, "[W]e need to acknowledge that nobody knows precisely how many people there are in the United States who practice aspects of Buddhism and/or consider themselves Buddhists."[14] They cite "credible estimates of the numbers of Buddhists in the United States at the start of the 21st century" that range from 1.4 to 4 million—figures that are dramatically imprecise compared to tallies of, say, Mormons or Muslims in the United States.

Why the fuzziness of the math? Wuthnow and Cadge observe that "in many Buddhist groups the teachings and practices are, if anything, attractive to the people who participate in them because of their flexibility and nonexclusivity. . . . They do not require practitioners to identify as Buddhist, to give up other religious beliefs or traditions, or to go through a conversion experience, for example."[15]

It has long been thus. Guifeng Zongmi, a ninth-century master of Ch'an (the Chinese precursor to Japanese Zen), described a broad range of different aspirations that could attract a practitioner to Buddhist meditation. Someone might engage in *bonpu* or "ordinary Zen," for example, simply to sleep better, supplement an exercise regimen, or experience a lighter disposition. Another kind of motivation to practice—called *Gedo* or "outside way" Zen—is typically undertaken by someone who sees meditation as a natural complement to spiritual discipline in a non-Buddhist religious tradition.[16]

That openness to all comers has also allowed communities of practitioners to adapt received forms of Buddhism to suit their particular needs. And nowhere has the range of adaptations been more diverse than Southern California—which is, as the *Los Angeles Times* reported on November 14, 1998, home to about "40 percent of all Buddhists in the United States" and "the only place in the world where all of the more than 100 types of Buddhism are actively represented."

The *Times* has documented the profusion of Buddhist movements springing up in its own backyard with commendable thoroughness. And like the best *Tribune* pieces from the 1980s, the *Times*' coverage of Buddhism around the cusp of the new millennium has often benefited from reporting that tightly focuses on individuals whose stories reveal the bigger picture:

> She has led "street retreats" on skid row, injected feminism into a patriarchal liturgy and sponsored interfaith gatherings with a Jewish rabbi and a Catholic priest. It may not fit the cloistered, contemplative image of Zen Buddhism, but the new abbot of the Zen Center of Los Angeles is here to make changes. Last week's formal ascension of Wendy Egyoku Nakao, an American of Japanese and Portuguese descent, signifies a transition for one of the nation's most prominent Zen centers—from its Japanese roots to a more American combination of social action, interfaith work and egalitarian exchange.[17]

The *Times* has also managed to report on controversies associated with some of Southern California's Buddhist communities without losing sight of the complex evolutions unfolding in the same contexts. Several pieces on the Zen Center of Los Angeles and Nakao relate her actions not just to the history of Japanese Buddhism but also to the schismatic leadership crises that preceded her installation as abbot. And between May 1997 and April 2000, the *Times* published a series of investigative pieces on violations of campaign-finance law during Al Gore's 1996 fundraiser at Hsi Lai temple as well as several features that examined the blurring of traditional ethnic and sectarian boundaries at nearby Hsi Lai University ("Studying Buddhism's Many Denominations," March 15, 2000, for example).

Taking a cue from Wuthnow and Cadge—and from Guifeng Zongmi—reporting on the future development of Buddhism in Southern California and the rest of the United States will have to take into account the adaption of Buddhist practice not only for the next generation of immigrant and convert Buddhists but also for those who don't consider themselves Buddhists at all. Some non-Buddhist practitioners will likely emerge from the cohort of spiritual but not religious seekers that demographers have dubbed the "Nones." One such group covered by the *Times*: the Dharma Punx, founded by Noah Levine, a former crack addict who first learned meditation from a convert Buddhist teacher who also happened to be his father. "Except for his bald head, there isn't much monkish about Noah Levine," the *Times* reported on May 4, 2009. "His body is covered with tattoos, his speech is spiked with profanities, and his style . . . is a throwback to his days as a hard-core punk rocker. . . . Dharma Punx don't wear robes and they don't bow to statues of the Buddha."

Others will be the beneficiaries of "medicalized" Buddhist practice like Mindfulness-based Stress Reduction (MBSR) and similar meditative techniques that are currently being used to treat conditions ranging from attention-deficit disorder in adolescents to posttraumatic stress disorder among soldiers returning from Iraq and Afghanistan. In "Doctor's Orders: Cross Your Legs and Say Om," an article published on October 29, 2007, the *Times* closed with this prediction from Jon Kabat-Zinn, who developed MBSR at the University of Massachusetts Medical School in the 1980s: "We are headed toward development of a new kind of medicine that honors the profound dilemma of the person who presents to a doctor with suffering. Since Buddhism has a history of understanding suffering, and since nobody goes to a hospital without some kind of suffering, what better place than a hospital to be grounded in meditation?"

From Madame Blavatsky's bohemian apartment to Japanese American internment camps and from the Parliament of the World's Religions to Veteran's Administration hospitals, mainstream news media in the United States have depicted Buddhism as a folly, a scourge, a fad, and a source of salvation. Journalism itself has been pinned with those labels at various times. At their best, Buddhist practice and reporting are pursuing the same end: to see things as they really are.

NOTES

1. For an elaboration of "ethnic Buddhism," "import" or "elite Buddhism," and "export" or "evangelical Buddhism," see Charles Prebish, *Luminous Passage: The Practice and Study of Buddhism in America* (Berkeley: University of California Press, 1999), 60.

2. Thomas A. Tweed, *The American Encounter with Buddhism, 1844–1912: Victorian Culture and the Limits of Dissent* (Bloomington: Indiana University Press, 1992), 30–31.

3. See W. Travis Hanes and Frank Sanello, *The Opium Wars* (Naperville, IL: Sourcebooks, 2004) for an account of nineteenth-century Western imperialism in China.

4. Mark Kanazawa, "Immigration, Exclusion, and Taxation: Anti-Chinese Legislation in Gold Rush California," *The Journal of Economic History* 65, no. 3 (September 2005): 781.

5. Thomas A. Tweed and Stephen Prothero, *Asian Religions in America: A Documentary History* (New York: Oxford University Press, 1999), 163.

6. See Justin Nordstrom, "Utopians and the Parliament: The World's Parliament of Religions and the Columbian Exhibition of 1893," *Journal of Religious History* 33, no. 3 (September 2009): 348–51.

7. Rick Fields, *How the Swans Came to the Lake: A Narrative History of Buddhism in the United States* (Boulder, CO: Shambhala Publications, 1992), 126–27.

8. Tweed, *The American Encounter with Buddhism*, 32.

9. Tweed and Prothero, *Asian Religions in America*, 166.

10. Fields, *How the Swans Came to the Lake*, 196.

11. Portions of my analysis here were first published as "Ghosts of 9/11," *Trans-Missions*, September 13, 2010, http://www.trans-missions.org.

12. See Diane Winston, "Old Monks, New Media, and the Limits of Soulcraft: A Case Study of Burma's 2007 Saffron Revolution," in *Rethinking Religion and World Affairs*, ed. Timothy Samuel Shah, Alfred Stepan, and Monica Duffy Toft (New York: Oxford University Press, 2012).

13. For a fuller treatment of this archetype, see Jane Iwamura, *Virtual Orientalism: Asian Religions and American Popular Culture* (New York: Oxford University Press, 2011).

14. Robert Wuthnow and Wendy Cadge, "Buddhists and Buddhism in the United States: The Scope of Influence," *Journal for the Scientific Study of Religion* 43, no. 3 (2004): 365.

15. Ibid., 366.

16. Philip Kapleau, *The Three Pillars of Zen: Teaching, Practice and Enlightenment* (New York: Anchor Books, 1980), 48–50.

17. Teresa Watanabe, "Zen Abbot Gives a U.S. Look to an Asian Faith," *Los Angeles Times*, June 19, 1999, 1.

REFERENCES

Rahula, Walpola. 1974. *What the Buddha Taught*, rev. ed. New York: Grove Press.

CHAPTER 19

WICCA IN THE NEWS

SARAH M. PIKE

"Evil Worship Debated in Slayings" ran the headline in the *Commercial Appeal*, Memphis, Tennessee's daily newspaper, on June 6, 1993, after the arrest of three teenagers—one of them Wiccan—for the brutal murder of three young boys in West Memphis, Arkansas. The *Commercial Appeal*, the *Jonesboro Sun*, and other local papers kept the devil in the headlines over the weeks following the teenagers' arrest, subsequent trial, and, not surprisingly, eventual conviction. In 1994, with no motive other than "Satanism," Damien Echols, the oldest of the three teenagers, was sentenced to death, while the other two young men, Jason Baldwin and Jesse Misskelley, were sentenced to life in prison.[1]

Damien Echols was a working-class Wiccan teenager who dressed in black and listened to heavy metal music. As soon as his name was mentioned in the local paper, his guilt was assumed in West Memphis, a town of conservative evangelical Christians.[2] Journalist Mara Leveritt, who covered the trial for the *Arkansas Times*, blamed the media for perpetuating stereotypes and stoking fears about devil worship. According to Leveritt, during the investigation, a story in the *West Memphis Evening Times* hinted at "cult activity" and rumors of Satanism started to spread. From that point on, Leveritt and other critics have argued that the boys had already been found guilty in the court of public opinion and were unable to prove their innocence. As soon as the trial began, more headlines followed, such as "Satanic Dabblers Can Become Deadly Disciples." Reporters mentioned "evidence" such as the following without skepticism or explanation: the boys' age of eight being a sacred number in Wicca, the defendants' numerous black T-shirts, damage to the left side of one victim's face as a sign of the occult, the book *Never on a Broomstick* being found in Damien's house, a Metallica album cover, etc.[3] Reporters who covered the trial failed to consult experts on Wicca or Satanism; instead, they interviewed other high school students who recalled that Damien was "spooky" and always wore black clothes. One story also relied on a widely discredited "Satanism expert," Carl Raschke, who concluded: "Would people do this if not for Satan?"[4] Throughout the trial, most news coverage neglected to distinguish between "cult," "occult," "Wicca," and "Satanism."

The cult label triggered widespread fears because only two months earlier the public had witnessed the tragic deaths of a community of Branch Davidians in Waco, Texas. The Branch Davidians and their leader David Koresh were repeatedly depicted in news stories as dangerous child abusers. The "Satanic panic" of the 1980s was declining by the early 1990s, but suspicions lingered, leading to the demonization of teenage outcasts like Echols.[5] Reporters saw Echols's Wiccan identity as deviant and neglected to challenge the biases and stereotypes held by many of their readers. Damien's attorney argued to reporters during the trial that "Damien wasn't a suspect until he started talking about his Wiccan beliefs," but his point was lost in the rush to resolve the town's outrage and grief.[6] Investigative reporting years later by journalist Mara Leveritt and documentary filmmakers Joe Berlinger and Bruce Sinofsky revealed not only the effect of this stereotyping on the investigation and trial but also many other errors that contributed to a miscarriage of justice and likely resulted in placing an innocent man on death row.[7]

News coverage of the "West Memphis Three" trial exemplified two of the most egregious trends in reporting on new religious movements in general: stereotyping ("Satanism" and "cults") that has little basis in reality and using sources who are self-styled "experts" with an axe to grind. Since the "cult" scare of the 1970s that demonized new religious movements, scholars have been critical of reporters' lack of discrimination among sources. Short deadlines and ignorance about new religions often resulted in stories that quoted anticultists and Satanic rumormongers who sought to demonize cults and create Satanic conspiracies where none existed. News stories about the trial also revealed the common mistake of identifying Wicca with Satanism and ritual abuse. Wicca, the most common term for contemporary Witchcraft, is a new religious movement that emerged in Britain in the 1950s and began appearing in American news media in the mid-1960s, at the same time that other new religious movements were just taking root here.

Wicca is the largest movement under the broad umbrella of Neo-Paganism, which includes a variety of religions that re-create and reconstruct ancient pre-Christian traditions that honor nature as sacred and ritually observe the changing seasons. For the most part, coverage of the West Memphis Three case revealed many of the standard tropes appearing in newspaper stories about Witchcraft and Witches and paralleled many of the general trends in depicting new religious movements since the late 1960s.[8]

Wiccans like Echols have often found themselves caught in a net of misinformation. Wicca is unrelated to the religion of Satanism and to so-called "Satanic" crime, even though all three have been conflated in many news stories. From the 1960s through the beginning of the twenty-first century, Witches have been made into the "other" against which a religious norm is constructed, following the more general pattern of treating marginal religions in the news, or as religious studies scholar Sean McCloud puts it, "The American religious fringe functioned for journalists as a 'negative reference group' in a process of identity construction."[9] Stories about Witches, which almost never appear on newspapers' "religion" pages, often equate Wicca with Satanism and appear in conjunction with criminal activities or in trivialized representations of Witches in Hollywood or at Halloween.

Although media representations of Wicca have become more favorable and better informed since the 1960s, many of the ways that reporters discuss Witches remain the same. By 2010, news sources from local weeklies to the *New York Times* had countered negative stereotypes with stories introducing Witches as normal people, as the "Witch next door" or what author of the Pagan blog *The Wild Hunt* Jason Pitzl-Waters calls "meet the Witch" stories.[10] In response to Wiccans' complaints about negative media portrayals and the increasing accessibility of accurate information about their religion, reporters tamed Witches into nature-loving, cookie-baking neighbors. At the same time, as Wiccans became increasingly involved in religious freedom cases during the 1990s and 2000s and were persecuted for their beliefs by some conservative Protestant evangelicals, news coverage of Wicca grew more positive.

The Evil Witch Next Door

The harmless neighbor Witch is a recurring theme in articles at the beginning of the twenty-first century that challenges years of damaging reports about evil Witches who live next door and secretly worship Satan. Of course, equating Witches with evil has a long history in the West. David Frankfurter, in his study about discourses of evil, argues that the "myth of evil conspiracy," such as the belief in Satan-worshipping covens of Witches, provides a powerful way "of thinking about otherness," and for this reason has lasting and compelling power, even in the secularized West.[11] As contemporary Witches attempt to reclaim and revise old images into positive ones, they repeatedly come up against these intractable discourses. The image of the evil Witch has been deployed in a variety of contexts to demonize and marginalize certain people and practices. Most significantly, perhaps, Witches in the United States have been forced to contend with the widespread effects of Hollywood films.

Director Roman Polanski's 1968 film *Rosemary's Baby* put devil-worshipping Witches on the big screen and shaped attitudes toward Wiccans throughout the 1970s. In Polanski's film, a young couple moves into an apartment building and meets their eccentric but apparently harmless neighbors who turn out to be Satan worshippers. They drug the young wife so that she is impregnated by Satan and gives birth to the Antichrist. After *Rosemary's Baby*, Wiccan journalist Peg Aloi argues, "the idea that one might have Satan-worshipping Witches living right next door was clearly a very potent and titillating idea."[12] This image of devil worshippers lurking in one's neighborhood turned out to have lasting power through the 1980s and early 1990s, when the West Memphis Three trial took place.

Fears about dangerous neighbors were heightened by real-life events in 1969 when Charles Manson's young female followers brutally murdered actress Sharon Tate and six others in a spree of killings that were linked in news reports to "Satanism," "cults," and the "occult." Coverage of the Manson family marked a shift toward more suspicious treatment of what had previously been seen as weird but harmless interest in astrology, Witchcraft, etc., in the 1960s counterculture.[13] The demonic cult leader image began with Manson and persisted throughout the 1970s, as charismatic leaders of new religious movements were framed in most news coverage as deviant and threatening. Throughout the 1970s, new religions were typecast as "cults," resulting in the tendency of Witches and reporters to distinguish "white" magic from Manson's and *Rosemary's Baby*'s "black" magic.[14]

References to "the occult" in coverage of murders or Hollywood films are rarely specific but stir up fears of mysterious, secret, and even Satanic rituals. In the 1970s, the occult was associated with a mounting interest in astrology, Asian religions, and Witchcraft but often was mentioned in the news in connection to criminal activity. According to National Public Radio reporter Margot Adler in *Drawing Down the Moon*, her groundbreaking study of Neo-Paganism, "the occult" refers to "hidden or obscure forms of knowledge that are not generally accepted."[15] For this reason, it both intrigues and evokes images of dangerous, illicit practices occurring in hidden spaces. In many religions, there are occult teachings that are transmitted secretly from generation to generation, which has been the case in some traditions of initiatory Witchcraft. Evil connotations are only attached to the term when unfounded rumors spread of destructive or violent rituals, usually imagined to be the work of "Witches" or "Satanists." From the late 1960s on, the occult and Witchcraft were equated with myths about Satanism, especially in the context of violent crimes. As coverage of the West Memphis Three case demonstrates, even in the 1990s these terms were still confused in the minds of many journalists.

Covering Hollywood: From *Rosemary's Baby* to *Harry Potter*

Witches are not like the Satanic coven-mates in *Rosemary's Baby*, nor are they akin to the fictional characters in the hugely successful *Harry Potter* films and J. K. Rowling's best-selling novels on which the films are based. Controversy over the release of films depicting Witchcraft provides an opportunity for news stories that contrast real and screen Witches. In these stories, Witches and reporters convey new meanings about Wicca as a religion, always framing it in contrast to its misrepresentation in film.[16] By the early 1970s, then, at least three aspects of the Witch were in play in popular culture and encouraged by Hollywood films: the demonic and threatening witch of *Rosemary's Baby*, the sexy witch, and the quaint witch next door.[17]

In publicity for later films such as *The Witches of Eastwick* (1987) and *The Blair Witch Project* (1999), reporters responded to Wiccans' public relations efforts to normalize Wicca in contrast to these sensationalistic film portrayals.[18] As was noted by a reporter in the *New York Times* story "Updike Movie Dismays Followers of Witchcraft," *The Witches of Eastwick*, based on John Updike's novel of the same name, was "the latest misrepresentation of who witches really are."[19] In this story and others like it, Wiccans challenged and corrected portrayals of their religion in entertainment media. In fact, Wiccan organizations like Circle Sanctuary have made a concerted effort to reach out to reporters to tell their side of the story, resulting in fewer stereotypes about evil Witches in media coverage.

Hollywood witches are not just evil; they are sexy, too. This is not to imply that real Witches are unattractive, but rather that Hollywood depictions of Witches adhere to stereotypes. Films like *The Witches of Eastwick* and even the more sympathetic *The Craft* (1996) shaped Americans' attitudes toward their Wiccan neighbors and gave off-screen Witches a public relations challenge. Reporters often compounded the problem by focusing on certain aspects of Witches' lives and physical appearance while downplaying others. Teresa Watanabe's *Los Angeles Times* piece on the all-women Circle of Aradia preparing for a Samhain ritual noted that one witch named Dawn was "a glamorous blond in a black mini-skirt." A story on the same day in *USA Today* linked the images of Warner Brothers Television Network's series *Charmed* (1996–2001) to real Witches in Cathy Hainer's piece, "The New Face of Witches: After the Toil and Trouble, Media Have Fallen Under the Spell of Powerful, Sexy Women."[20] But the image is nothing new; what Hainer calls "the witch babe" has been around since at least the 1960s. As a pair of powerful stereotypes, representations of exoticized sexy teenage female Witches in *The Craft* contrast sharply with demonized teenage boys like the West Memphis Three.[21]

By the time the *Harry Potter* books and films had become so wildly successful, Witches had come to be depicted in more complicated ways. The Witches in *Harry Potter* tended to be seen favorably by Witches in the real world, if not by many conservative Christians who shunned the films. J. K. Rowling's books and their film adaptations presented all kinds of Witches, including heroic teenage boys like Harry, friendly neighbors like Mrs. Weasley, and attractive good Witches like Hermione, as well as evil Witches like Voldemort. In the *Harry Potter* books and films, Witches became ordinary and extraordinary human beings, who were as morally upright or powerfully corrupt as any other human beings, regardless of their magical powers. In this way, the Harry Potter phenomena revised stereotypes of Witches as evil and/or sexy and went a long way toward taming Witches. But Hollywood, of course, was not solely responsible for negative images.

"We Don't Eat Children": New Religions and the Satanic Panic

Halloween is when Americans are most aware of Witches as scary (kids' costumes) or sexy figures (teen and adult costumes). Halloween has also served for decades as one of the most common occasions on which Wiccans, who are often sought for interviews, take the opportunity to educate reporters and clear up misconceptions about Witchcraft as a religion. As Witches have become adept at public relations and as journalists want to appear tolerant of religious difference, many newspapers run stories on what real Witches do on Halloween. These Halloween stories do feature real Witches, but they often trivialize Wiccan celebrations, although they occasionally depict serious religious practices lurking beneath a thoroughly commercialized secular holiday. Many reporters and the Witches they interview use the occasion of Halloween to address stereotypes and provide alternate images of Witches. However, linking Witchcraft to Halloween perpetuates the very juxtaposition that Witches want to challenge. *St. Louis Post-Dispatch* reporter Kathryn Rogers tells her readers: "Those strange little people with big ugly noses and black pointed hats ringing your doorbell tonight are nothing like real witches" and "there is no devil in witchcraft."[22] The only real Witches most readers encounter, then, are those mentioned in the same stories that invoke the stereotypes they are concerned about.

While Witches sometimes appear in the news to confront Hollywood and Halloween stereotypes, another common occasion for media attention to Witches is in connection with crime and controversy. Many news stories involve custody battles and bizarre murders with pentagrams left at crime scenes.[23] Reporting on new religious movements during the 1970s usually equated Witches with "cults" and, in the 1980s, with "devil worship."[24] High-profile events like the 1993 siege and fire at the Branch Davidian compound in Waco, Texas, and the 1978 Jonestown, Guyana, murder-suicides of People's Temple members increased the tendency to label anything diverging from the norm a "cult." In their study of Witches in the news during the 1980s, Laurel Rowe and Gray Cavender focused on newspaper articles from 450 cities across the United States. They found that stories about "the occult" (which included Witchcraft) were more likely to be linked to crimes after Jonestown and appeared more frequently in local rather than national newspapers.[25] Anticult fears of the 1970s gradually gave way to rumors of Satanic conspiracy in the 1980s, with the same patterns of stereotyping and the same images of possessed youth held captive by evil (evil cult leaders in the 1970s, Satan in the 1980s).

During the 1980s, a rumor panic gripped the United States as media reports on Satanic rituals perpetuated unsubstantiated rumors about ritual murder and sexual abuse by supposed Satanic covens. Experts on "Satanic ritual abuse" traveled the country giving seminars for police officers and psychotherapists. According to sociologist Jeffrey Victor, the news media did not create these stories, but nevertheless validated them by uncritically reporting on unfounded allegations of Satanism. Victor argues that the news media spread rumors started by moral crusaders, especially conservative evangelical Christians.[26] One story in the *Los Angeles Times* characterized coverage of the Satanic panic as "hysteria, sensationalism and what one editor calls a 'lynch mob syndrome.'"[27] By the end of the 1980s, most of the rumors had been discredited, but crime, teenagers, and Satanism had become powerfully linked in the popular imagination.

At the same time that major news outlets criticized the Satanic rumor panic, many local newspapers continued to treat Witches and other Neo-Pagans as if they were Satanists. In response, Witches and Neo-Pagans worked hard to distinguish their religion from Satanism. Reporters at large city newspapers were more likely to treat Satanic rumors skeptically and chose to focus on stories that challenged stereotypes as being more compelling to their readers. In "Witches Spell It Out: Don't Stereotype Us," Karlyn Straganana, a Wiccan priestess, told *USA Today* reporter Maria Goodavage, "Witches cast only good spells."[28] The *San Diego Union-Tribune* ran several stories in the mid-1980s that also addressed stereotyping. In "They Turn to Magic, Not Satan," reporter George Flynn wrote about local Witches who became more secretive following two major media events in California: the Night Stalker murders (1985) and the McMartin Preschool Satanic ritual abuse accusations (1983), both of which featured "allegations of Satanism and the occult."[29] Witches were worried, Flynn noted, that their religion would be equated with Satanism. Like many stories during the 1980s, Flynn's also drew a sharp line of separation between Witches and Satanists.

Negative media coverage of Witches during the Satanic panic declined as reporters increasingly distinguished between good and evil uses of ritual magic and made the effort to contact local Witches, or were contacted by them. In news coverage of the Satanic panic during the late 1980s, Witches were usually given the chance to clear their names; in fact, 92 percent of newspaper stories in 1987–88 refuted the claim that Witches participated in black magic, and the majority of the stories connected Witchcraft to feminism, women's empowerment, and nature worship.[30] A positive outcome of these stories was increasingly accurate information about Witchcraft in the news.

But reporters and Witches sometimes turned Satanism into the "other" against which a real religion is measured, rather than recognizing it as a religious option, one that is distinct from instances of criminal "Satanism." With the Satanic panic of the 1980s and the simultaneous rise of conservative Protestant evangelicalism as a political and social force, Wiccans were besieged on all sides. While therapists and reporters sensationalized Satanic rumors, conservative evangelicals charged Witches with being in league with the devil. For this reason, many Witches felt forced to adopt a white magic versus black magic strategy by turning Satanists into their evil other.

From the 1980s on, Protestant evangelical parents publicly expressed concerns about demonic influences in public schools, while at the same time secular parents opposed Christian censorship of school materials. Some news stories focused on

Witches caught up in these culture wars. Wicca was covered in the context of controversies about the free exercise of religion, such as teenagers wearing pentagrams to school, or in response to efforts by conservative Christians to ban books and films that they claimed taught kids Witchcraft.[31] Coverage of these controversies in major newspapers inevitably took the side of religious freedom and portrayed conservative Christians, instead of Witches, negatively. In 1986, at the height of the Satanic panic, the *Omaha World-Herald* described Witchcraft as "an organized religion" in its coverage of a suit by Christians over films shown in Waverly, Nebraska, public schools that mentioned Witchcraft.[32] Christian attacks on films and books that they claimed promoted Witchcraft ironically resulted in further opportunities for Witches to clear up misconceptions and increased positive media coverage of Wicca.

"If Georgia Lawmaker Forces Witches Out of Military, Good Christian Bombs Will Reign Supreme"[33]

Most Americans first hear about real Witches in the news, usually in connection with crime, Hollywood films, Halloween, conflicts with neighbors, or religious freedom controversies in schools. The same holds true for new religious movements in general: they usually escape notice until something *bad* happens. For example, most Americans had never heard of the People's Temple before the mass suicide in Jonestown, Guyana, in 1978. And they did not know about the Branch Davidians before the Davidians' tragic standoff with the FBI in 1993. Sociologists Barend Van Driel and James T. Richardson have argued that new religious movements tend to be covered with a "stream of controversies approach," in contrast to "coverage of control groups that were allotted more balanced and diverse treatment frequently resembling a 'human interest' approach." Van Driel and Richardson concluded that the news media function as "institutions of social control that marginalize, delegitimize and discredit oppositional movements."[34] In other words, news stories imply that when new religious movements are mentioned in connection with crime or conflict, the religion is to blame, though this is rarely the case if a criminal is Buddhist or Christian.

Even articles that are relatively benign may result in controversy and further stereotypes, as was the case when a 1999 story describing Wiccan rituals at Fort Hood in Killeen, Texas, ran in the *Austin-American Statesman*.[35] A week later the same paper reported that after reading the story, US Congressman Bob Barr of Georgia called on top Army officials to put a stop to Wiccan rituals on Army bases. Subsequent coverage depicted Barr as an extremist and Wiccans as reasonable Americans exerting their constitutional right to freely practice their religion.

For instance, the *Atlanta Constitution* came down clearly on the side of religious freedom in "Whichcraft: Barr Would Like to Choose Which Religion You Follow." Editorial writer John Head criticized Barr's campaign to promote prayer in school at the same time that he wanted to ban military personnel from practicing Wicca. Barr and his supporters looked foolish and, even worse, un-American. At the core of the nation's religious balance, Head argued, are "public policies that try as much as possible to keep the government out of religion and personal practices that allow the other fella to believe or not to believe whatever he pleases, even if his religion is not your cup of tea. Or your boiling cauldron, for that matter."[36] Barr's position was so extreme that Wiccans were given favorable treatment in most news media. An article on the controversy that ran in the *Fort Worth Star-Telegram* included the most outrageous quotes from Barr and his supporters.[37] For instance, a minister in Killeen told one reporter, "I've heard they drink blood, eat babies. They have fires, they probably cook them."[38] As these examples suggest, this case marked a significant shift in coverage of Wicca as a serious religious choice deserving of constitutional protection as a contrast to the intolerance of some conservative Christian fanatics.

Stockbroker, Army Colonel, School Teacher: The Good Witch Next Door

Stories of conflicts with neighbors and controversies in schools and on military bases often made the news as "bad neighbor" stories. At the same time, depictions of the harmless Witch next door were common throughout the 1990s. Quite a few articles that intended to clear up misconceptions around Hollywood films, Halloween, and Satanic rumors ran with this phrase in their title as they presented a tamed version of Wicca for mass consumption.[39] Even smaller newspapers picked up on the Witch-next-door theme; in 2009, a Southern Maryland paper ran a story by Bob Renneisen: "Does a Witch Live Next Door? Wicca: An Oft Misunderstood—But Fast-Growing—Religion."[40]

And yet, the Witch-next-door image managed to keep alive 1960s stereotypes of both the cozy neighborly witch and the sexy playmate, as in a story in the *Las Vegas Weekly*: "Oh My Gods! Sex Rituals, Arcane Rites and Homemade Cookies."[41] Stereotypes have persisted, but because of Wiccans' public relations work, including their widespread presence on the Internet, journalists are much more likely to seek balance in their coverage.[42] After the Satanic panic of the 1980s died down, numerous stories appeared about conflicts between Christian and Wiccan "neighbors," often in small-town or rural communities.[43] In 1999, just a few weeks before the Fort Hood story broke, news outlets framed a conflict in Jonesboro, Arkansas, in terms of religious freedom versus Christian extremism. "New Occult

Shop Disturbs Citizens" proclaimed the *Jonesboro Sun* headline on April 28, 1999. In this case, Witches themselves created an outcry when several Christian ministers in the town told a landlord to cancel an occult bookstore's lease. Word spread across the Internet and soon a religious freedom march was planned as the national Neo-Pagan community geared up to fight: "Fort God vs. Born-Again Pagans" quipped Daniel Glick in *Newsweek*.[44] These 1999 stories suggest Wiccans were likely to gain more positive news coverage, as well as mainstream acceptance, in the new millennium.

According to Chas Clifton, editor of *The Pomegranate: The International Journal of Pagan Studies*, by the beginning of the twenty-first century, Wicca had become "the new Other." Clifton explains, "No longer is it 'How will this affect our Jewish friends?' or 'What will the Jehovah's Witnesses say?' Now—good or bad—people cite Wicca as the difficult religion that tests public policy."[45] The Jonesboro and Fort Hood cases made it clear that religious freedom could trump Satanic rumors and that Wiccans were a force to be reckoned with, stronger in numbers and more media savvy than they had been in the 1970s and 1980s.

"Praise the Goddess and Pass the Magical Candle—the Federal Department of Veterans Affairs Has Finally Recognized the Wicca Religion"[46]

Wiccans read, track stories, share news across vast Internet networks, and engage in constant critique of media coverage. If, in previous decades, news coverage could have negative effects for Wiccans even when the coverage was positive, the opposite was much more likely to be true during the early 2000s. Many factors have led to Wicca's change in status, two of which seem most significant: Neo-Pagan/Wiccan presence on the Internet and a backlash against politicized conservative evangelicalism.

Wiccans and other Neo-Pagans have made aggressive use of the Internet as a tool for educating the public and organizing around religious freedom issues. Jason Pitzl-Waters, author of *The Wild Hunt* blog and organizer of *The Pagan Newswire Collective*, observes that Neo-Pagans now play prominent roles in online journalism, including Beliefnet and the *Washington Post*'s online forum *On Faith*. Moreover, he argues, "It's important to note the role grassroots new media outlets have played in fueling and changing coverage of modern Paganism. Pagan blogs and podcasts . . . help drive the discourse, and influence the things that get covered."[47] Neo-Pagan news sites like *The Witches' Voice*; equal treatment of Wicca/Paganism by Patheos, an online "gateway" for information about the world's religions; and favorable coverage in the online daily Religion Dispatches are a few of many possible examples.[48] What was a coven-based and mostly hidden religion in the 1960s, with the exception of a few high-profile Witches like Sybil Leek and Raymond Buckland, is now a religion with hundreds of informative websites and media contacts ready to speak to reporters.

These trends were apparent in 2006, when Wiccans successfully sued the US Veterans Administration to have the pentacle, their sacred symbol, added to the list of religious emblems allowed on veterans' tombstones.[49] The case was widely covered by most major news outlets as a fight for religious freedom. The headline "Circle of Hope" in the Minneapolis *Star Tribune* was typical of this positive coverage and no doubt helped gain public support.[50] Selena Fox, high priestess of Circle Sanctuary, a Wiccan church, and a party to the suit, pointed out that favorable coverage of the "Pentacle Quest" was in part due to the "cognitive dissonance" in the term "Wiccan veteran." As Fox saw it, "Shed Wiccan patriot blood trumped religious bigotry. When you have Fox News, CNN, BBC, and other major news sources across the political and international spectrum all reporting on the situation and putting Wicca in the news along with religious freedom, it normalized Nature religion in some ways. . . . The Pentacle Quest was a turning point for Paganism."[51] Wiccan veterans challenged all the old stereotypes: evil Satanist, sexy young woman, cuddly witch next door, and long-haired "cult" member.

By the end of the first decade of the twenty-first century, most Wiccans believed that news coverage of their religion had significantly improved. As Margot Adler observed in 2010, "In general news coverage is much better: it's not just at Halloween, and often the coverage actually says that Paganism and Wicca are nature religions. . . . The coverage of Witches getting the Pentacle as a symbol that vets could use on headstones, and the fact that there are now headstones with Pentacles in Arlington and at other graveyards where veterans lie is a huge step forward."[52] Although some stereotypes endure, the extensive, nationwide publicity around this case makes it hard to imagine that reporters will continue to identify Wiccans with Satanism or evil.

Treatment of the West Memphis Three case and its growing numbers of celebrity supporters two decades later is a clear example of how media coverage and public understanding of Witchcraft has changed since the 1960s. In 2010, the West Memphis Three made news again when actor Johnny Depp took advantage of publicity for his new film *Alice in Wonderland* to speak out for the three young men who had by then served sixteen years in prison for crimes they probably did not commit. On February 23, 2010, the *New York Post* reported that Depp made an unusual public appearance on "48 Hours Mystery" to decry the miscarriage of justice in the case. Depp echoed other celebrities and supporters who over the years have repeatedly called the rumor that Satanism was to blame "totally baseless." Perhaps in 2010, Damien Echols and his teenage friends in West Memphis would have received more balanced coverage in the news, a fair trial, and, in the end, a different verdict.

NOTES

1. See the "Free the West Memphis Three" website: http://www.wm3.com.
2. Filmmakers Joe Berlinger and Bruce Sinofsky's award-winning 1996 documentary, *Paradise Lost: the Child Murders at Robin Hood Hills*, profiles the town's biases.
3. Rob Johnson's "Satanic Dabblers" piece ran in the Memphis *Commercial Appeal*, June 13, 1992. The *Jonesboro Sun* "cult" story is discussed in Mara Leveritt, *Devil's Knot: The True Story of the West Memphis Three* (New York: Atria Books, 2002), 231.
4. Rob Johnson, "Satanic Dabblers Can Become Deadly Disciples," the Memphis *Commercial Appeal*, June 13, 1993. A few reporters were more critical: see, for example, Leveritt, *Devil's Knot*, 269.
5. Jeffrey S. Victor, *Satanic Panic: The Creation of a Contemporary Legend* (Chicago and LaSalle, IL: Open Court Publishing, 1993).
6. Leveritt, *Devil's Knot*, 264.
7. See Berlinger and Sinofsky's *Paradise Lost* and Leveritt's *Devil's Knot*.
8. I capitalize "Witch" and "Witchcraft" throughout when referring to the religion of contemporary Witches.
9. Sean McCloud, *Making the American Religious Fringe: Exotics, Subversives, and Journalists, 1955–1993* (Chapel Hill and London: The University of North Carolina Press, 2004), 6.
10. E-mail to the author, May 28, 2010.
11. David Frankfurter, *Evil Incarnate: Rumors of Demonic Conspiracy and Ritual Abuse in History* (Princeton, NJ: Princeton University Press, 2006).
12. Peg Aloi, "Rooted in the Occult Revival: Neo-Paganism's Evolving Relationship with Popular Media," in *Handbook of Contemporary Paganism*, ed. James R. Lewis and Murphy Pizza (Leiden and Boston: Brill, 2009), 547.
13. Martin Waldron, "Witness Recalls Manson a 'Devil': He Says Murder Defendant Posed as Satan on Loose," *New York Times*, September 18, 1970.
14. Judy Klemesrud, "Witchcraft: Some People Find It a Serious Matter," *New York Times*, October 31, 1969.
15. Margot Adler, *Drawing Down the Moon: Witches, Druids, Goddess-Worshippers, and Other Pagans in America Today* (Boston: Beacon Press, 1986), 12.
16. "Wren's Nest," a collection of news stories on *The Witches Voice* listing over 400 stories related to Harry Potter and Wicca: http://www.witchvox.com.
17. McCloud discusses a slightly different variation of these stereotypes in *Making the Religious Fringe*.
18. Peg Aloi, "A Charming Spell: The Intentional and Unintentional Influence of Popular Media upon Teenage Witchcraft in America," in *The New Generation Witches: Teenage Witchcraft in Contemporary Culture*, ed. Hannah E. Johnston and Peg Aloi (Aldershot: Ashgate Publishing, 2007), 118.
19. August 31, 1986.
20. Both stories ran on October 29, 1998.
21. Aloi, "A Charming Spell," 113–27.
22. Kathryn Rogers, "Area Witches Worship Nature in Practice of Wiccan Faith," *St. Louis Post-Dispatch*, October 31, 1992.
23. "Rape Suspect Accuses Victim of Witchcraft," on *40/29 TV* (Springdale, AR), April 14, 2010; "Woman Accuses Husband of Child Abuse, Witchcraft," *Independentmail.com* (Anderson, SC), August 19, 2009, http://www.independentmail.com.

24. See, for example, my discussion of this dynamic in *Earthly Bodies, Magical Selves Contemporary Pagans and the Search for Community* (Berkeley and Los Angeles: University of California Press, 2001).

25. Laurel Rowe and Gray Cavender, "Cauldrons Bubble, Satan's Trouble, But Witches Are Okay: Media Constructions of Satanism and Witchcraft," in *The Satanism Scare*, ed. James T. Richardson, Joel Best, and David G. Bromley (New York: Aldine de Gruyter, 1991), 263–75.

26. Victor, *Satanic Panic*, 46.

27. Ibid., 117.

28. *USA Today*, June 2, 1992.

29. September 15, 1985.

30. Rowe and Cavender, "Cauldrons Bubble, Satan's Trouble," 265.

31. For example, David Shepardson, "School Relents on Anti-Witch Rule," *Detroit News*, March 3, 1999.

32. November 8, 1986.

33. *Salt Lake Tribune*, June 26, 1999, C1.

34. James Richardson and Barend Van Driel, "Journalists' Attitudes Towards New Religious Movements," *Review of Religious Research* 39, no. 2 (December 1997): 119.

35. May 11, 1999.

36. June 4, 1999.

37. August 7, 1999.

38. http://circlesanctuary.org/liberty.

39. See Kimberly Winston, "The Witch Next Door," *Beliefnet*, November 11, 2004.

40. The Calvert County (Maryland) *Recorder*, October 30, 2009, http://www.somd-news.com/stories/10302009/reccov151853_32184.shtml.

41. Lynette Curtis, Las Vegas *CityLife*, May 5, 2005.

42. See, for example, Sabrina Eaton, "Top Court to Hear Case on Inmates' Sacred Items," Cleveland *Plain Dealer*, March 21, 2005.

43. For instance, "Witch School Fails to Charm Town: Community on Edge After Wiccans Arrive," *Chicago Tribune*, December 19, 2005.

44. August 23, 1993.

45. E-mail to the author, May 27, 2010.

46. Lenore Skenazy, "Witching Hour in America," *New York Sun*, April 25, 2007.

47. E-mail to the author, May 28, 2010. See also http://www.wildhunt.org/blog/.

48. http://www.patheos.com and http://www.religiondispatches.org.

49. Sarah M. Pike, "The Pentacle Quest: Religious Freedom and the U.S. Department of Veterans Affairs," *Religious Studies News* 22, no. 2 (March 2007): 24.

50. March 3, 2007.

51. E-mail to the author, May 29, 2010.

52. E-mail to the author, May 28, 2010.

REFERENCES

Adler, Margot. 1986. *Drawing Down the Moon: Witches, Druids, Goddess-Worshippers, and Other Pagans in America Today*. Boston: Beacon Press.

Aloi, Peg. 2007. A Charming Spell: The Intentional and Unintentional Influence of Popular Media Upon Teenage Witchcraft in America. In *The New Generation Witches: Teenage*

Witchcraft in Contemporary Culture, ed. Hannah E. Johnston and Peg Aloi, 113–27. Aldershot: Ashgate Publishing.

———. 2009. Rooted in the Occult Revival: Neo-Paganism's Evolving Relationship with Popular Media. In *Handbook of Contemporary Paganism*, ed. James R. Lewis and Murphy Pizza, 539–74. Leiden and Boston: Brill.

Bromley, David. 1991. Satanism: the New Cult Scare. In *The Satanism Scare*, ed. James T. Richardson, Joel Best, and David G. Bromley, 49–72. New York: Aldine de Gruyter.

Cowan, Douglas E. 2005. *Cyberhenge: Modern Pagans on the Internet*. New York: Routledge.

Frankfurter, David. 2006. *Evil Incarnate: Rumors of Demonic Conspiracy and Ritual Abuse in History*. Princeton: Princeton University Press.

Leveritt, Mara. 2002. *Devil's Knot: The True Story of the West Memphis Three*. New York: Atria Books.

McCloud, Sean. 2004. *Making the American Religious Fringe: Exotics, Subversives, and Journalists, 1955–1993*. Chapel Hill and London: The University of North Carolina Press.

Patheos. http://www.patheos.com.

Pike, Sarah M. 2001. *Earthly Bodies, Magical Selves: Contemporary Pagans and the Search for Community*. Berkeley and Los Angeles: University of California Press.

Richardson, James T., and Barend van Driel. 1997. Journalists' Attitudes Towards New Religious Movements. *Review of Religious Research* 39 (2 [December]): 116–36.

Rowe, Laurel, and Gray Cavender. 1991. Cauldrons Bubble, Satan's Trouble, but Witches Are Okay: Media Constructions of Satanism and Witchcraft. In *The Satanism Scare*, ed. David Bromley, Joel Best, and James T. Richardson, 263–75 (New York: Aldine de Gruyter, 1991).

Victor, Jeffrey S. 1993. *Satanic Panic: The Creation of a Contemporary Legend*. Chicago and LaSalle, IL: Open Court Publishing.

The Wild Hunt. http://www.wildhunt.org.

The Witches' Voice. http://www.witchvox.com.

Wright, Stuart A. 1997. Media Coverage of Unconventional Religion: Any Good News for Minority Faiths? *Review of Religious Research* 39 (2): 101–15.

CHAPTER 20

MEDIA COVERAGE OF SCIENTOLOGY IN THE UNITED STATES

CAROLE M. CUSACK[1]

Introduction

Since the founding of the Church of Scientology (CoS) by L. Ron Hubbard in 1954, this controversial new religion has had a checkered relationship with the media. This chapter commences with a brief description of Scientology's teachings, organizational structure, and coverage in the media throughout its history. In early 2008, the changed nature of media coverage due to the Internet caused the viral propagation of two films (initially via YouTube). The first was actor and prominent Scientologist Tom Cruise discussing his beliefs, and the second was the first salvo by the anti-Scientology protest group Anonymous, which asserted that it would "expel the Church from the Internet." Project Chanology, initiated by Anonymous, used social news websites and whistleblower site WikiLeaks to escalate the exposure of Scientology's secrets. In 2009, media coverage of CoS was unprecedentedly constant and negative.

This chapter considers landmark media pieces in the United States, focusing on the work of crusading journalists Joe Childs and Thomas C. Tobin of the *St. Petersburg Times*: the three-part expose "The Truth Rundown" (June 2009); "Strength in Their Numbers" on Scientology defectors telling their stories (August 2009); and "Man Overboard," which told of Don Jason's escape from Scientology after doing forced labor on the ship *Freewinds*, on which he was illegally detained (November 2009). It is argued that the tactics used by the CoS in the past to quash negative publicity (mainly threatened or actual litigation against critics) are no longer effective in a world where breaking news is frequently generated by citizens blogging and posting mobile phone photographs and films online, and in which the Internet renders it virtually impossible to keep information out of the public sphere. CoS, which has always courted celebrity and strove to maintain a positive media image, now finds itself enmeshed in a mediatized world, where it is unable to control the exponentially multiplying negative images of itself.

Scientology: Founder, Teachings, and History

L. Ron Hubbard (1912–1986) founded the Church of Scientology in 1954 in the wake of the Dianetics movement. Hubbard, a science fiction author and former navy officer, had published *Dianetics: The Modern Science of Mental Health* in 1950. Dianetics (from the Greek for "through" and "mind") combined psychological and religious ideas into a "science of the mind."[2] Hubbard claimed the mind was divided; the analytical mind was "accurate, rational, and logical," but the reactive mind was "the repository of a variety of memory traces, or what Hubbard calls engrams."[3] Through auditing, a type of confessional or counseling process, these negative engrams can be banished, leaving the person "clear." *Dianetics* was a best seller and Dianetic auditing became a popular pastime. Hubbard attracted celebrity followers and the phrase *Dianetic processing* was used in a film due to a relation of Cecil B. De Mille being a Dianetic practitioner. The Church of Scientology formalized the Dianetics movement, with elaborated teachings. These included the Eight Dynamics of survival; the persistence of engrams from past lives; the existence of the Thetan, the spiritual part of the person; the "tone scale" measuring the state of the reactive mind, including "Apathy, Grief, Despair, Fear, Covert Hostility, Hate, Pain, Boredom, Mild Interest, Strong Interest, Cheerfulness, Enthusiasm and Exhilaration"; and the science fiction–influenced mythology of Xenu and the Galactic.[4]

In 1959, Hubbard moved to the United Kingdom and bought Saint Hill Manor, East Grinstead, Sussex, which became the headquarters of the Church of Scientology. CoS grew rapidly, with centers opening in New Zealand, Canada, South Africa, and Australia, among other countries. From its inception, Scientology (and Hubbard personally) had been criticized by journalists, government bodies, and medical organizations, among others. CoS teachings and practices, including auditing, the evils of psychiatry, and Hubbard's "Fair Game" principle, whereby those identified as major threats to CoS could "be harassed, threatened or punished using any and all means possible," attracted several investigations in the 1960s.[5] In the United States, the Food and Drug Administration (FDA) raided the CoS center in Washington, DC, in 1963 over false claims as to the health benefits of the e-meter (a device measuring electrical resistance used in auditing), and in 1967, the Internal Revenue

Service (IRS) ruled to strip Scientology of its tax-exempt status in a state of affairs that persisted until 1997.

The structures of Scientology became more complex with the introduction of the pseudo-naval Sea Organization (Sea Org) in the late 1960s, and its flagship, the *Apollo*. Members of Sea Org made a commitment to Scientology for all of their reincarnations. Advanced Organizations were also founded in a number of countries in the late 1960s to teach the newly released Operating Thetan (OT) Levels. The first major scandal involving CoS persecution of critics concerned freelance journalist Paulette Cooper, author of "The Tragi-Farce of Scientology," published by *Queen* (now *Harper's Bazaar*) in December 1969. This was expanded into a book, *The Scandal of Scientology* (1971). CoS restricted distribution of Cooper's book and launched "Operation Freakout," a program of harassment "intended to put Cooper either into prison or into a mental hospital."[6] In all, eighteen suits were brought against Cooper, and other critics had similar experiences. The 1979 convictions of nine senior CoS staff (including Mary Sue Hubbard) for offenses committed as part of "Operation Snow White," an exercise in domestic espionage including break-ins, thefts, and phone tapping, resulted from Federal Bureau of Investigation (FBI) raids in 1977.

The church also has a history of protecting its teachings, particularly the initiatory OT Levels, through complex legal actions under copyright and trademark laws. After the death of Hubbard in 1986, effective control of CoS passed to David Miscavige (b. 1960). The contemporary CoS has a complex institutional hierarchy, with the Church of Scientology International (CSI) and the Religious Technology Center (RTC) at the top. There is also Scientology Missions International (SMI), the Guardian's Office, Narconon (a drug rehabilitation program), Celebrity Center Churches, and the Sea Org. Critical press coverage of CoS increased after Hubbard's death, with the *San Diego Union* revealing the purchasing scams that put his science fiction novels onto the best-seller lists,[7] and the *Los Angeles Times'* six-part "The Scientology Story," both in 1990.[8] Yet Scientology's public reputation is zealously protected by the public relations and legal departments, and David Miscavige has demonstrated a continued commitment to controlling critics of CoS and to constructing a positive media profile for the church.

Media Coverage of Scientology Prior to 2009

Hubbard and CoS always maintained that there was an organized opposition to the religion, consisting of psychiatrists, certain government agencies, and the anticult movement. The Cult Awareness Network (CAN) was founded in 1978 after the deaths of members of the Jim Jones–led Peoples Temple in Jonestown, Guyana. CAN was a vocal opponent of Scientology; its representatives, including Executive Director Cynthia Kisser and Exit Counselor Rick Ross, had by the mid-1980s settled on CoS as CAN's particular target. Anson Shupe states that in "the 1980s and 1990s more than twenty-five lawsuits were filed against CAN by Scientology members" who had been denied entry to conferences or refused the right to join CAN.[9] Further, Sterling Management Systems, a group with links to Scientology, sued CAN for libel. There were countersuits initiated by CAN against Scientology. The case that brought CAN to bankruptcy involved the failed deprogramming of Jason Scott, an eighteen-year-old Pentecostal Christian. The lawyer acting on behalf of Scott, Kendrick Moxon, was a member of CoS. After criminal action against the deprogrammers failed, Moxon represented Scott in a civil action for damages in late 1995. The court awarded almost five million dollars in damages to Scott and CAN was liable for one million dollars. CAN went bankrupt in October 1996, partly as a result of pursuing an unsuccessful appeal against Scott, partly because of other lawsuits that it could not afford to settle, and partly because Jason Scott sold his compensation payment to a CoS member, Gary Beeny, for $25,000, making Scientology CAN's largest creditor. Bankrupt, CAN was sold to the Church of Scientology, which now operates as "NewCAN."[10]

CAN's opposition to Scientology was clearly important to the religion, in that it was the spur for David Miscavige to give his first media interview with ABC News, with journalists Ted Koppel and Forrest Sawyer, on February 14, 1992. This interview featured many ex-Scientologists and a range of accusations were made against CoS. Miscavige observed that Scientology did not "lend itself so well to the press," then countered the accusations by arguing that "every single detractor on there is part of a religious hate group called Cult Awareness Network . . . it's the same as the KKK would be with the blacks."[11] In 1998, his first and only newspaper interview was published, with Thomas C. Tobin, a journalist with the *St Petersburg Times*. This piece was a surprisingly courteous treatment in which the details of Miscavige's life and career within Scientology were confirmed for interested readers, and the strongest criticism of him was the suggestion that he was "a bully" and had possibly influenced the IRS decision to reinstate Scientology's tax-exempt status in 1996.[12]

With the development of the Internet, critics of Scientology found a new venue to share their concerns. In 1991, the Usenet group alt.religion.scientology was started by Scott Goehring.[13] In January 1995, lawyers for CoS attempted to have alt.religion.scientology removed from Usenet, because sensitive documents, including the OT teachings, had been posted. By the middle of 1995, a "flame war" was in progress, with Scientologists spamming alt.religion.scientology so as to make it unreadable, and raids by US federal marshals were taking place on the homes of those suspected of posting the copyrighted materials. In 1995, the Internet-based Church of the Dead Cow, a direct precursor of Anonymous, declared war on CoS, stating: "We fear plans for a 'Fourth Reich' to be established on our home soil under the vise-like grip of oppression known as Scientology!"[14] Between 1996 and Anonymous's 2006 debut as a "hacktivist" organization with its raid on Habbo, a social networking site, Internet access became the norm and media outlets such as newspapers and radio and television stations gradually created virtual presences. Outside of official media companies, citizens began blogging and posting short films and photographs of news flashpoints (the collapse of the Twin Towers on September 11, 2001, being the prime example). Copyright law, upon which CoS had relied for fifty years, was challenged over music downloads, the vast GoogleBooks digital library, and a multitude of other innovations.[15]

Anonymous, a loose group of computer enthusiasts and free speech activists, sought to take advantage of the radically deregulated nature of cyberspace and to position themselves aggressively as advocates of religious freedom and freedom of speech by painting Scientology as repressive and anti–freedom of religion and speech. On January 14, 2008, a video of Tom Cruise speaking to a CoS audience at a ceremony at which he received the International Association of Scientologists (IAS) Medal of Valor was uploaded to YouTube. Scientology promptly sued for breach of copyright and demanded the video be removed. In response, Anonymous formulated Project Chanology, an anti-Internet censorship protest aimed at CoS. This involved frequent demonstrations outside Scientology premises around the world (often wearing Guy Fawkes masks, referencing the anarchist vigilante protagonist of the film *V for Vendetta*, a move approved by Alan Moore, author of the original graphic novel), singing the 1987 Rick Astley hit "Never Gonna Give You Up," and posting their opening salvo on YouTube on January 21, 2008. This video stated:

> Hello, leaders of Scientology. We are Anonymous. Over the years we have been watching you. Your campaigns of misinformation, your suppression of dissent, your litigious nature, all of these things have caught our eye. With the leakage of your latest propaganda video into mainstream circulation the extent of your malign influence . . . has been made clear to us. Anonymous has therefore decided that your organization should be destroyed, for the good of your followers, for the good of mankind, and for our own enjoyment. We shall proceed to expel you from the Internet. . . . You have nowhere to hide, for we are everywhere. . . . Knowledge is free. We are Anonymous. We are Legion. We do not forgive. We do not forget. Expect us. . . .[16]

The continued existence of Anonymous, and its steadily increasing campaign against CoS, is evidence of the changed nature of both breaking news and activism.

The leaked Tom Cruise clip was a genuine embarrassment for CoS. The jargon that he employed was barely comprehensible ("the tech," "SP," and so on); the inexplicable laughter, the pulsating *Mission Impossible* soundtrack, and the claim that Scientology has the answer to the world's problems ("let's go!") have sparked myriad imitations, none as disturbing or as hilarious as the original.[17] Anonymous has also attacked the Sea Org (through Operation Sea Arrrgh, in which members used another important Internet meme, pirates, which also serves as a significant motif in the Church of the Flying Spaghetti Monster and is the object of devotion on September 19, International Speak Like a Pirate Day, to mock the uniform branch of the CoS), and they have gained respect through taking on board the advice of independent CoS critic Mark Bunker, who argued that they must work within the law or damage the anti-Scientology cause irrevocably.[18] The net effect of the Cruise and

Anonymous YouTube videos was to inform millions who had never given Scientology a thought that it might be worth thinking about and protesting against.

2009: The *St. Petersburg Times* Coverage of Scientology

Media coverage of Scientology in 2009 was unprecedentedly constant and negative. The first opportunity for journalistic comment was when Jett Travolta, the sixteen-year-old son of celebrity CoS members John Travolta and Kelly Preston, died in the Bahamas on January 2, 2010. Speculation about Jett's health had long dogged Travolta. Some observers conjectured that Jett was autistic and epileptic but that his parents concealed these conditions because Scientology is vehemently opposed to nonphysical illness and medication for psychological/psychiatric conditions.[19] When pressed, Travolta and Preston admitted Jett had suffered from Kawasaki disease and had seizures. Throughout their family tragedy, Travolta and Preston maintained their dignity in the face of media curiosity. Anonymous posted a YouTube video on January 3, 2009, narrated by a sympathetic female voice, which explained that although Anonymous "would not intrude upon your time of grief," they must explain how CoS treated disorders such as autism and epilepsy. Defectors informed Anonymous that they had to discontinue their medication, and instead psychological conditions were treated through a detoxification program called the "Purification Rundown," which involved auditing, large doses of vitamins, lengthy sessions in the sauna, and doses of oils.[20] Members of the medical profession have warned that the "Purif," as it is known, is potentially dangerous.

More damaging to Scientology was the increasing number of defectors who were willing to discuss their experiences. The classic account of Scientology by a former member was Jon Atack's *A Piece of Blue Sky* (1990), which is now available in its entirety on the Internet. In October 2008, former member John Duigan published *The Complex: An Insider Exposes the Covert World of Scientology* (with Nicola Tallant). CoS effectively stymied the distribution of this work, which had been published in Duigan's native Ireland, but another two damning memoirs were published by ex–Sea Org members late in 2009, Marc Headley's *Blown for Good: Behind the Iron Curtain of Scientology* and Nancy Many's *My Billion Year Contract: Memoir of a Former Scientologist.*[21] Both are still readily available for purchase. By 2009, there was a palpable sense that CoS was no longer able to stem the tide of negative publicity; specifically, the organization could no longer block distribution of books.

This changed climate was largely due to the media coverage that the religion received that year. *St. Petersburg Times* journalists Joe Childs and Thomas C. Tobin had a history of reporting on Scientology since the early 1990s, and on June 21,

2009, the first part of "The Truth Rundown" appeared. This article featured Scientology defectors Marty Rathbun, Mike Rinder, Tom De Vocht, and Amy Scobee, who testified that David Miscavige controlled CoS through violence and humiliation and that members were repeatedly subjected to security checks ("sec checks"), public confession of failures, hard labor with the Rehabilitation Project Force (RPF), and isolation as a "suppressive person."[22] The male defectors admitted to violent abuse of others to earn Miscavige's favor. Each article reviewed scandals in CoS's past, such as the acquisition of property in Clearwater, Florida, in 1975. The Sea Org headquarters, Flag Land Base, was later established there. Mayor Gabe Cazares labeled Scientology a "cult" and citizens rallied against Flag. CoS reacted with a smear campaign, alleging false sex offenses against Cazares and attempting to frame him for a fake car accident. Part 1 also covered the IRS scandals and Miscavige's rise to power during Hubbard's declining years.

The next day, Part 2 dealt in detail with the death of Lisa McPherson on December 5, 1995. On November 18, 1995, thirty-six-year-old McPherson had what appeared to be a psychotic episode during which she crashed her car. However, when she was apprehended and taken to the hospital, she refused treatment and was collected by CoS members who escorted her to the Fort Harrison Hotel, which was owned by Scientology. She was held in Room 174 for the next seventeen days, and by December 5 she had lost a great deal of weight and was gravely ill. David Minkoff, a Scientologist who was also a doctor, was consulted by telephone and recommended bringing her to Morton Plant Hospital, where he was. She was pronounced dead on arrival. It was later revealed that she had been put on an "Introspection Rundown," the goal of which is to "calm a psychotic person enough to be audited. She is to be kept in a silent environment with no one around to 're-stimulate' mental images that might upset her."[23] Minkoff, the doctor who treated McPherson, was disciplined by the state of Florida, and David Miscavige decided that the extremely large legal costs generated by the McPherson case would be borne by the Flag Land Base.

On June 23, Part 3, "Scientology: Ecclesiastical Justice," continued the revelations of life within CoS from the four high-profile defectors. The article's focus was life within the Sea Org and the mind games played by David Miscavige to control his lieutenants. Rinder and De Vocht recalled being made to jump fully clothed into a pool on a cold night early in 2005, a tradition based on "overboarding," which Hubbard enforced while in command of the *Apollo*. The grueling pace of work within CoS was exposed (with a focus on the reissue of Hubbard's writings and the push to get rank-and-file Scientologists to buy them), and the agony of being consigned to "the Hole" for offenses against the religion was discussed.[24] The CoS focus on confession and the relentless punishment of sins were particularly emphasized, and the autocratic and violent nature of Miscavige's leadership was seen to be a key factor in the decision of the defectors to leave CoS and attempt a life outside the religion. In August, CoS responded by calling Childs and Tobin "merchants of chaos" in the CoS publication *Freedom* magazine. Later pieces by Childs and Tobin included "Strength in Their Numbers," which appeared on August 2 and addressed the question of the increasingly large number of ex-Scientologists who were now willing to speak out against their former faith. Further cruelties were discussed, including the "tent punishment" and the "Cause Resurgence Rundown," in which Scientologists are made to run around a track until the point is reached in which "you have a realization that you're in control of your own body and mind."[25] Defectors Morehead and Rinder claimed that those being punished might run for twelve hours per day.

These insightful and well-written articles were supplemented in 2009 by a series of television interviews with high-profile defectors from CoS. KESQ TV's Nathan Baca did a series of interviews as part of a "Scientology versus Anonymous" series. Jeff Hawkins, a Scientologist of forty years' standing and the former marketing director of CoS, was the subject of Parts 6 and 7, broadcast on March 19, 2010. Hawkins spent many years at CoS's IntBase in Hemet, California, and he explained that celebrity members, like Tom Cruise, who visited IntBase were shown an attractive, staged tableau of what was happening at the site. Hawkins drew attention to human rights abuses such as hundred-hour working weeks, the guards at the gates to prevent people from leaving, wages set at forty cents per hour, the lack of holidays, and the brutal treatment meted out to those who do not comply. Substandard conditions, including ten-cents-per-hour pay and sleeping thirty to a room, affecting those assigned to the RPF also were discussed. Hawkins confirmed that members found it very difficult to leave the religion and were forced to "disconnect" from non-Scientologist family members and friends. He openly accused David Miscavige of violence and extremely controlling tendencies. Marc Headley's dramatic departure from Scientology was treated *en passant*, and Hawkins explained that he had done the same as Headley, leaving without his wife and entering a world in which he had nothing—no job, no savings, and no friends to support him.[26]

In an earlier interview from the same series aired on March 13, Nathan Baca interviewed Tommy Davis, the son of Hollywood actress Anne Archer (who starred in *Fatal Attraction*, 1987), who is head of the Celebrity Center in Los Angeles. The initial focus of the Davis interview was Anonymous, which he described as a "religious hate group" responsible for "hate crimes," "terrorism," and other largely unsubstantiated offenses. Davis asserted that CoS was a "huge advocate" of free speech and argued that Anonymous was not engaged in defending free speech but was rather harassing Scientologists because of their religious beliefs. Davis took pains to present the Anonymous protests as a law enforcement issue and the CoS response as one of concern for its members. The publication *Anonymous: Who They Are and What They Do* was discussed; Davis indicated that this was not put out by CoS. In the discussion of this publication, Davis attempted to connect Anonymous with the distribution of child pornography, random hacking, and illegal public demonstrations. Davis remained calm and was a credible representative of Scientology, but the overall impression given by this forty-five-minute interview was of a religion desperately trying to protect its image and discredit its critics, chief of which is Anonymous. The most provocative moment was when Baca began to read from the OT III materials referencing Xenu, and Davis admitted that he knew what Baca was talking about to prevent him from reading more. Davis's controlled delivery was meritorious, but Baca's mild questioning clearly unnerved and unsettled him.[27] A few months later, in October, when British journalist Martin Bashir again asked Davis about Xenu on camera, he was unable to maintain his equilibrium and walked out. It is worth remembering, however, that the Xenu materials are doctrinally sensitive within CoS and Baca and Bashir were both being extremely provocative in mentioning such esoteric teachings in a television interview.[28]

The year 2009 saw several high-profile defections from CoS, but Thomas C. Tobin's November article "Man Overboard" featuring 1996 defector Don Jason and his tale of escape from the Scientology ship *Freewinds* still made harrowing reading. Tobin (and his co-writer Childs) had a talent for presenting the defectors as real people, credible voices that readers could identify with and take seriously. Though Don Jason escaped from Clearwater, he missed his friends and Scientology and voluntarily returned to face his punishment. He was held a virtual prisoner on the ship *Freewinds*, where he did hard labor, and was later assigned to the Rehabilitation Project Force. At that point he asked to leave the ship and was refused. After six weeks on board and gradually worsening treatment, he escaped. This was great journalism; Don Jason's story had human interest, a taut thriller plotline, and a happy ending.[29]

One important factor at work in the defections of high-ranking Scientologists was that they were not necessarily known outside CoS. However, the defections of actor Jason Beghe and filmmaker Paul Haggis revealed cracks in Scientology's hold over its celebrity members. Hubbard was fascinated by Hollywood and had courted celebrities assiduously during his active leadership of CoS. Celebrity members were an important part of CoS's outreach to the public, as celebrities are powerful role models in the late modern West and serve to render Scientology potentially desirable to the wider public.[30] Jason Beghe, who had reached the level of OT V and was a trained auditor, left Scientology in late 2007. After the leaked Cruise video and Anonymous's YouTube debut, he decided to publicly criticize CoS and recorded a lengthy interview with Scientology critic Mark Bunker and Andreas Heldal-Lund, the founder of "Operation Clambake," a Norwegian nonprofit organization that publishes negative material about CoS. The full interview was made available on YouTube. Beghe has since attended public protests against Scientology and spoken of the abuses of the religion in a number of European countries. Paul Haggis (director of acclaimed films *Crash* and *Million Dollar Baby*), an active member of CoS for over thirty years, defected in October 2009 over the issue of Scientology support for Proposition 8, a California state ballot measure that banned gay marriage in the state. However, the most damaging criticism of CoS he made was about the process of "disconnection," in which Scientologists are forced to cut all contact with non-Scientologist family members.[31] This story was picked up by multiple media outlets and helped reinforce the impression among the public that CoS was a repressive and illiberal organization that violated human rights and interfered inappropriately in the familial and emotional lives of its members. Anecdotal evidence also suggests that, although not megastars like Tom Cruise or John Travolta, Beghe and Haggis were famous enough for their defections to significantly damage Scientology's outreach to celebrities, and for the celebrity-conscious public to register this fact.

In the wake of constant negative media coverage, Scientology's public reputation was in tatters: the celebrity blogger Queen concluded her final piece for 2009 with this comment: "Who knows what 2010 will bring for Scientology? Their downward spiral continues on a daily basis. Can they survive the continuing deluge of bad publicity, pending court cases, ex-members writing books, closing orgs, ex-members doing interviews, and members leaving weekly? I hope 2010 is Scientology's last year."[32] With blogs and YouTube now increasingly both the source of breaking news and the medium through which conversations are conducted and views formed, her comment has far greater power than is apparent.

The focus of this chapter is coverage of the Church of Scientology in the US media, but it is worth noting that 2009 was an unprecedentedly negative year for CoS in France, where in May six high-ranking Scientologists were charged with fraud and the illegal practice of pharmacy; in Britain; and in Australia, where independent Senator Nick Xenophon requested an independent parliamentary enquiry into CoS after being approached by two ex-Scientologists.

Conclusion: Scientology and the Media New World Order

Prior to the advent of the Internet, Scientology's relationship with the media was carefully controlled. Positive publicity was courted and exploited and negative publicity was neutralized by a combination of legal action and the harassment of journalists and academic researchers through the application of Hubbard's "Fair Game" policy.[33] Copyright and trademark law was used to keep CoS texts restricted, and the rhetoric of freedom of religion was employed to give the impression that Scientology's critics were in violation of the First Amendment. The ubiquity of the Internet has, however, profoundly altered religion, the dissemination of news, copyright law, and the whole of contemporary life, and this means that Hubbard's traditional methods of keeping critics at bay are no longer effective. Rothstein, analyzing the Xenu myth, has noted that scholars can no longer pretend that they are ignorant of the material, as "the texts are . . . made available on many different home pages."[34] If CoS forces a site to take down the OT materials, they will appear on another site or sites almost immediately. Likewise, while blocking the publication or distribution of a print book was relatively simple, once a book is digitized and available online, it will be constantly replicated and stopping its penetration into the reading public becomes impossible.

It is this "viral" nature of Internet dissemination that has most affected the news media. Traditional journalists have argued that the result is a decline of investigative reporting and a dearth of real news.[35] This may be the case if formal news agencies are the only sites consulted, but when citizen-generated news (YouTube footage, websites, blogs) is factored in, there is a great variety of content available. One question is whether news agencies deliberately report on trending topics, in which case the *annus horribilis* of media coverage experienced by Scientology in 2009 may be partially a result of web-savvy organizations like Anonymous causing a spike in trending through viral Internet memes. Anonymous views attempts to suppress, censor, or prosecute Internet dissemination as anathema and should be aggressively resisted. The CoS case against YouTube over the Tom Cruise video was a tipping point for Project Chanology, and the lesson learned by CoS in 2009 is that the "viral" nature of the Internet means that a single, insignificant leak can lead to headline news given the right news cycle combination of events.

Thus, the methods by which Scientology formerly kept control of its publications, its members, its public image, and its critics are obsolete. In the words of Anonymous, "Your orders are set out by L. Ron Hubbard, now long dead. You are bound to and by the tech. You cannot adapt. You cannot learn. The self-proclaimed *homo novis* is many decades out of date, trapped in the permafrost of your own dogma."[36] The Internet has also changed contemporary religion, being viewed by many as a "battleground for contending religious (and anti-religious) visions."[37] It is too early to predict whether the radically decentered nature of the medium will result in a revival of participatory democracy, but the Internet is increasingly the first port of call for people interested in breaking news, celebrity gossip, and information, *inter alia*, about science, art, politics, and religion. Typing "Scientology" into Google leads directly to negative media coverage; CoS knows that, and as yet has found no answer to it.

NOTES

1. I am grateful to my research assistant Alex Norman for his help in the preparation of this chapter. My thanks are also due to Don Barrett for his interest in my research and patience in assisting me to clarify my ideas prior to, and during, the writing process.

2. L. Ron Hubbard, *Dianetics: The Modern Science of Mental Health* (Los Angeles: Bridge Publications, 1986 [1950]), 7.

3. Hugh B. Urban, "Fair Game: Secrecy, Security, and the Church of Scientology in Cold War America," *Journal of the American Academy of Religion* 74, no. 2 (2006): 365.

4. Stoddard Martin, *Orthodox Heresy: The Rise of 'Magic' as Religion and its Relation to Literature* (New York: St Martin's Press, 1989), 214.

5. Urban, "Fair Game," 375–77.

6. Jon Atack, *A Piece of Blue Sky: Scientology, Dianetics, and L. Ron Hubbard Exposed* (New York: Carol Publishing Group, 1990), 223.

7. Mike McIntyre, "Hubbard Hot-Author Status Called Illusion," *San Diego Union*, April 15, 1990, http://www.ex-cult.org/Groups/Scientology/sandiego.txt (accessed May 29, 2010).

8. Joel Sappell and Robert W. Welkos, "The Scientology Story," *Los Angeles Times*, June 24–29, 1990, http://www.lermanet.com/scientologynews/latimes/latimes.htm (accessed May 29, 2010).

9. Anson Shupe, "The Nature of the New Religious Movements—Anticult 'Culture War' in Microcosm: The Church of Scientology versus the Cult Awareness Network," in *Scientology*, ed. James R. Lewis (Oxford: Oxford University Press, 2009), 277.

10. Ron Russell, "Scientology's Revenge," *New Times Los Angeles*, September 9–15, 1999, http://web.archive.org/web/20000120012331/www.newtimesla.com/issues/1999-09-09/feature_p.html (accessed May 29, 2010).

11. "Scientology Leader Gave ABC First-Ever Interview," *ABC News*, February 14, 1992, transcript at http://abcnews.go.com/Nightline/story?id=2664713&;page=1 (accessed May 29, 2010).

12. Thomas C. Tobin, "The Man Behind Scientology," *St. Petersburg Times*, October 25, 1998, http://www.sptimes.com/TampaBay/102598/scientologypart4.html (accessed May 29, 2010).

13. Wendy M. Grossman, "alt.scientology.war," *Wired* 3, no. 12 (December 1995), http://www.wired.com/wired/archive/3.12/alt.scientology.war_pr.html (accessed May 29, 2010).

14. http://www.cultdeadcow.com/news/scientology.txt (accessed May 29, 2010).

15. See, for example, Daniel J. Gervais, "Transmissions of Music on the Internet: An Analysis of the Copyright Laws of Canada, France, Germany, Japan, the United Kingdom and the United States," *Vanderbilt Journal of Transnational Law* 34 (November 2001): 1363–416.

16. Anonymous, "Message to Scientology," *YouTube*, January 21, 2008, http://www.youtube.com/watch?v=JCbKv9yiLiQ (accessed May 29, 2010).

17. "Tom Cruise Scientology Video," *YouTube*, http://www.youtube.com/watch?v=UFBZ_uAbxSo (accessed May 29, 2010).

18. Tom Whipple, "It's a Protest, Ron . . . But Not as We Know It," *The Times*, June 20, 2008, 1, 6–7.

19. Anon, "Travolta's Son 'Autistic,'" *Sunday Telegraph*, June 3, 2007, 43.

20. Anonymous, "Anonymous Explains Relationship Between Jett Travolta's Death and Scientology," *YouTube*, January 3, 2009, http://www.youtube.com/watch?v=LM1YobXaAEY (accessed May 29, 2010).

21. Marc Headley, *Blown for Good: Behind the Iron Curtain of Scientology* (available at BFG.com, 2009); Nancy Many, *My Billion Year Contract: Memoir of a Former Scientologist* (Northridge, CA: CNM Publishing, 2009).

22. Joe Childs and Thomas C. Tobin, "The Truth Rundown Part 1," *St. Petersburg Times*, June 21, 2009, www.tampabay.com/news/article1012148.ece (accessed May 29, 2010).

23. Joe Childs and Thomas C. Tobin, "Death in Slow Motion: Part 2," *St. Petersburg Times*, June 22, 2009, http://www.tampabay.com/news/article1012234.ece (accessed May 29, 2010).

24. Joe Childs and Thomas C. Tobin, "Scientology: Ecclesiastical Justice Part 3," *St. Petersburg Times*, June 22, 2009, http://www.tampabay.com/news/scientology/article1012575.ece (accessed May 29, 2010).

25. Joe Childs and Thomas C. Tobin, "Strength in Their Numbers: More Church of Scientology defectors come forward with accounts of abuse," *St. Petersburg Times*, August 2,

2009, http://www.tampabay.com/news/scientology/article1023717.ece (accessed May 29, 2010).

26. "KESQ: Jeff Hawkins on Scientology," *YouTube*, http://www.youtube.com/watch?v=YNf1qwoUb5E (accessed May 29, 2010).

27. "KESQ: Full Tommy David Interview," *YouTube*, http://www.youtube.com/watch?v=kLG3teVnszQ (accessed May 29, 2010).

28. Mikael Rothstein, "'His Name Was Xenu. He Used Renegades . . . ': Aspects of Scientology's Founding Myth," in Lewis, *Scientology*, 365–87.

29. Thomas C. Tobin, "Man Overboard: To Leave Scientology, Don Jason Had to Jump off a Ship," *St. Petersburg Times*, November 3, 2009, http://www.tampabay.com/news/scientology/article1048124.ece (accessed May 29, 2010).

30. Carole M. Cusack, "Celebrity, the Popular Media, and Scientology: Making Familiar the Unfamiliar," in Lewis, *Scientology*, 389–409.

31. Xan Brooks, "Film-maker Paul Haggis Quits Scientology over Gay Rights Stance," *The Guardian*, October 26, 2009, http://www.guardian.co.uk/world/2009/oct/26/paul-haggis-scientology-prop-8 (accessed May 29, 2010).

32. Queen, "Scientology 2009 . . . Year of Epic Fail," *GlossLip.Com*, December 31, 2009, http://technorati.com/entertainment/glosslip/article/scientology-2009-year-of-epic-fail/page-14/ (accessed May 29 2010).

33. Urban, "Fair Game," 358.

34. Rothstein, " 'His Name Was Xenu," 368.

35. Chris Paterson, "News Agency Dominance in International News on the Internet," in *Converging Media, Diverging Politics: A Political Economy of News Media in the United States and Canada*, ed. David Skinner, James R. Compton, and Michael Gasher (Lanham, MD and Oxford: Lexington Books, 2005), 145–64.

36. Anonymous, "Message to Scientology: We Still Run This," *YouTube*, January 2, 2009, http://www.youtube.com/watch?v=uB8ZrM3Adxk (accessed May 29, 2010).

37. Douglas E. Cowan, "Religion on the Internet," in *The SAGE Handbook of the Sociology of Religion*, ed. James A. Beckford and N. J. Demerath III (Los Angeles: SAGE Publications, 2007), 359.

REFERENCES

Atack, Jon. 1990. *A Piece of Blue Sky: Scientology, Dianetics, and L. Ron Hubbard Exposed.* New York: Carol Publishing Group.

Headley, Marc. 2009. *Blown for Good: Behind the Iron Curtain of Scientology*. Burbank, CA: BFG Books.

Lewis, James R., ed. 2009. *Scientology*. Oxford: Oxford University Press.

Melton, J. Gordon. 2000. *The Church of Scientology*. Salt Lake City: Signature Books.

Miller, Russell. 1988. *Bare-Faced Messiah: The True Story of L. Ron Hubbard*. Boston: Sphere Books.

Wallis, Roy. 1977. *The Road to Total Freedom: A Sociological Analysis of Scientology*. New York: Columbia University Press.

Whitehead, Harriet. 1987. *Renunciation and Reformation: A Study of Conversion in an American Sect*. Ithaca, NY: Cornell University Press.

SECTION IV

ISSUES AND BEATS

CHAPTER 21

RELIGION AND POLITICS IN PRINT

MARK SILK

COVERAGE of religion in American politics is shaped by the Constitution's mandate in Article VI, Section 3, that "no religious test shall ever be required as a qualification to any office or public trust under the United States." Because of it, the press tends to shy away from focusing on the religious commitments of candidates for public office. These are things that in the American system should not matter. But sometimes they do, and since the beginning of the republic the mandate has from time to time been honored in the breach. In such cases, the rhetorical struggle is generally to portray the opponent as intolerant—hostile to the values that Americans (are supposed to) hold dear.

That was the case in the elections of 1796 and 1800, when Thomas Jefferson and John Adams faced off for the presidency. In those days the press was highly partisan, with most newspapers tied to either Adams's Federalists or Jefferson's Democratic-Republicans. In addition, there were numerous pamphleteers who took advantage of the First Amendment to indulge freely in hyperbolic attacks on politicians they didn't like, and preachers who gave political sermons that they were happy to publish for general consumption.

By 1796, the antireligious activity of the revolutionaries in France had become widely known in the new American republic, and Jefferson, Francophile and free-thinking advocate of separation of church and state, paid the price. "We are not Frenchman," wrote a "correspondent from Connecticut" in the New York *Minerva, & Mercantile Evening Advertiser* on September 3, "and until the Atheistical Philosophy of a certain great Virginian shall become the fashion (which God of his mercy forbid) we shall never be." Jefferson lost. Four years later, the Federalists played the same tune, but this time to less effect; the French threat had receded. For his part,

Jefferson had his enthusiastic defenders—Baptists and Methodists, Unitarians and Jews—who appreciated his support for their interests, as enshrined in the Virginia Statute for Religious Freedom, drafted by him in 1789. According to the pamphleteer "Timoleon," his tolerance for different sects flowed from an understanding that coercion "never has been, and never will be of service to christianity." From this perspective, it was the Federalists who were intolerant of religion. In the end, the ad hominem attacks on Jefferson as an atheist who would lead the country into orgies of immorality did not succeed. It would be a long time before an American presidential candidate would again be subjected to such faith-based vituperation.[1]

THE CATHOLIC BEAT

If it was secularism, French style, that pushed religion into the forefront of electoral politics at the end of the eighteenth century, it was Roman Catholicism that brought it back in the 1840s and kept it there for more than a century. Anti-Catholicism was deeply engrained in American society, but the flood of Irish and (to a lesser extent) German Catholic immigrants into the cities of the North transformed theological hatred into social prejudice. The new Penny Press drew up sides, with some newspapers appealing to the recent immigrants and others to the old-time Protestants or "Native Americans," as they called themselves. Was the problem intolerance of Catholicism, as the one side charged, or was it the Catholics, whose church disapproved of separation of church and state, who were the truly intolerant? In 1844, bloody riots broke out between the two sides in the Kensington section of Philadelphia, to the distress of the *Philadelphia Times*, which wrote on May 9:

> The late riots between the Native Americans and the Irish Roman Catholics—for the feud is now a *religious* one entirely, conceal the fact as we may—have filled our city with excitement, and every thoughtful mind with deep reflection. What are we coming to? Are the people forgetting at once the elements of Republicanism, viz: tolerance of opinion, freedom of thought and action, and obedience to the laws . . . ? As a Protestant and a Native born citizen we protest against this unnatural admixture of religion and politics.

It did seem that the people had forgotten that there was something unnatural in that admixture, at least in their country.

The diverse membership of the nativist American Party, which swept to power in many states in the election of 1854, had little in common except antipathy to the political powers that be and hostility to the new Catholic immigrants. Organized in semisecret lodges, pledged to say nothing when asked about their organization, they came to be known as the Know-Nothing Party; in Massachusetts, the epicenter of Know-Nothingism, they caught the press, as well as the political establishment, completely unawares. In due course they acquired their own papers—the *Boston Bee* and the *Baltimore Clipper*, for example—and they published an almanac that circulated widely. But the rest of the press roundly condemned them for their anti-Catholicism, which was expressed in legislative deeds, as well as words on the stump. In 1855, the Bay State's Know-Nothing-dominated government passed an array of anti-Catholic laws; most notorious was a new Nunnery Committee that had special powers to inspect parochial education and investigate Catholic religious institutions suspected of holding women against their will and concealing firearms. Significantly, it was the Know-Nothings' religious bigotry that the press focused on, passing over largely in silence their populist efforts to rein in the political power of the wealthy.[2]

In the late nineteenth century, the country became one-quarter Catholic; overt anti-Catholicism was not only a violation of civil propriety but also politically perilous in a national campaign. A case in point occurred on October 28, 1884, when Republican presidential candidate James G. Blaine appeared at a rally of almost exclusively Protestant clergy in New York City. The idea was to contrast Blaine as a man of impeccable family values to Democratic candidate Grover Cleveland, who had become embroiled in scandalous charges that he had fathered a child out of wedlock and was a wife beater to boot. The master of ceremonies was an elderly Presbyterian minister named Samuel D. Burchard, who declared, "We are Republicans, and don't propose to leave our party and identify ourselves with the party whose antecedents have been rum, Romanism, and rebellion." It took a few days for the remark to become a full-fledged scandal of its own—reported and denounced across the country—and then to cost Blaine the election. It was, he later said, "an ass in the shape of a preacher" that had kept him from the presidency.[3]

An anti-Catholic slur was one thing; electing a Catholic to the presidency was another. The two acts of that drama took place thirty-two years apart, in 1928 and 1960, and both Governor Al Smith of New York and Senator John F. Kennedy of Massachusetts had to persuade the country that a man of their faith could be trusted to embrace separation of church and state and declare their independence from ecclesiastical authority. Once they did, the press, both pro and con, rejected religious opposition to their candidacies as un-American.

Smith took the pledge by way of a response to an "open letter" from a New York lawyer that appeared in the April 1927 issue of *Atlantic* magazine. Responding to the charge that there was an "irrepressible conflict" between the US Constitution and the claims of his church, Smith, in the following issue, said he recognized no power in his church to interfere with the Constitution. Even newspapers like the *New York Herald Tribune*, which would not end up supporting him, greeted the statement with approval. That paper's lead story on April 19 reported that "religious and political leaders throughout the country joined yesterday in acclaiming Governor Smith's reply," while an editorial the same day underscored the approval, calling Smith's avowal "a refreshing statement of sound Americanism that will give the bigots of every church pause," and saying it "may well prove to be a landmark in the history of American tolerance." In the heart of the Bible Belt, similar sentiments were expressed the same day by the Dallas *News*.

Just as the Know-Nothings sought to keep their purposes under wraps, Smith's religious opposition was christened "the whispering campaign"—a quiet but deadly effort to torpedo the New York governor's campaign on religious grounds. For its part, the opposition press blamed Smith for exaggerating the amount of whispering. When he blamed the Republican National Committee for stirring up religious opposition to his candidacy in a speech in Oklahoma City, the *Herald Tribune* and the *Los Angeles Times* accused him of exploiting the religious issue for his own benefit. As the *Herald Tribune* editorialized, "To attempt, as Governor Smith is doing, to manufacture political capital out of such a situation is hostile to the cause of true tolerance." A study of press coverage of the campaign concludes that newspapers supporting Herbert Hoover "attempted to ignore Smith's religion as much as possible while the Smith supporters kept the issue before the public and depicted Smith as the heroic victim of bigotry."[4]

In 1960, the press took an even dimmer view of anti-Catholic prejudice than it had thirty-two years earlier. Like Smith, Kennedy won widespread approval for disavowing church influence, famously telling the Houston ministerial association, "I believe in an America where the separation of church and state is absolute—where no Catholic prelate would tell the president (should he be a Catholic) how to act, and no Protestant minister would tell his parishioners for whom to vote." Now, however, the *Herald Tribune*—as Republican as ever and supporting Richard Nixon—declined to charge the Massachusetts senator with exploiting the issue. The newspaper even went so far as to actively combat what had come to be called "the underground campaign." Thus, in a lead Sunday editorial on September 18, it praised Protestant clergy who pledged not to oppose Kennedy on religious grounds, and in an October 16 article it warned of a "massive new religious attack" on Kennedy's candidacy. Overall, the press played a significant role in lessening the impact of religious bigotry and thereby making it possible for the United States to elect its first Catholic president. As was usually the case, it stood up for the principle of "no religious test."

The Rise and Nonfall of the Religious Right

The 1960 election brought the curtain down on anti-Catholicism as a perennial issue in American political culture. When religion next arose as a significant story in national politics, it would concern the "born again" identity of the Democratic candidate for the presidency in 1976, Jimmy Carter. Carter turned out to be a harbinger of the return of evangelical Protestantism to the American public square, a phenomenon that turned into the most important ongoing religion story in American political history. To be sure, religion had played a noteworthy role in earlier sociopolitical movements—from antislavery and women's rights to temperance and, in the middle of the twentieth century, civil rights. But as an explicitly religious enterprise linked to a major political party, the religious Right has been unique. It began in the 1970s as conservative religious figures and groups emerged on the front lines of various social battles against the Equal Rights Amendment, gay rights ordinances, and the teaching of evolution. As a force engaged in the mobilization of voters on behalf of political candidates, it properly dates from the 1980 campaign cycle, which resulted in the election of Ronald Reagan to the presidency and the replacement of a clutch of liberal Democratic senators from the heartland with conservative Republicans.

The creation of the religious Right was accompanied by a number of culture-war tropes, one of which was to charge the "liberal media" with embracing a double standard with respect to religion in politics: it was fine when the cause was liberal, but if conservative, it represented an unwholesome violation of the separation of church and state. In fact, the charge was more clever cultural politics than empirically based demonstration. From the outset, Jerry Falwell and other leaders of what was initially termed the "New Christian Right" delighted in asserting that they were doing nothing other than what religious liberals had done in supporting the civil rights and anti–Vietnam War movements. "Nobody ever criticized Martin Luther King when he was using the churches for political activity," an October 13, 1980, story in *Time* quoted Falwell as saying. "No one has ever criticized the National Council of Churches and its leaders for 50 years of active political involvement."

Yet *New York Times* religion writer Kenneth Briggs beat that story to the punch on October 3 with an article quoting constitutional experts supporting the right of religious activists of all stripes to engage in politics. "The tradition of the intermixture of religion and politics is too ingrained in our national life to be eliminated," said Lawrence Tribe, the liberal Harvard Law School professor par excellence. "It is extremely important to the principle of freedom of speech that this process not stop just because some are distressed by the content of the speech or the speaker." His point was echoed by a *Times* editorial two days later: "Liberals further confuse the matter when they applaud the political passions of, say, Martin Luther King, but denounce Jerry Falwell's as illegal. The 'wall' that Jefferson envisioned between church and state will not stand if conceived as a barrier to political speech by religious sects."

By the 1984 campaign cycle, the "liberal media" had lost none of its readiness to acknowledge the legitimacy of faith-based politicking. When, at the end of the summer, the Reagan campaign sent out word that it had emphasized religion enough, a September 2 editorial in the *Washington Post* declared: "We see no reason for anyone to fall silent on the subject now just because Reagan strategists are having a case of nerves." Signaling how much the worm had turned in a quarter century, in its September 17, 1984, issue, *Newsweek* asserted that the "absolutism of John Kennedy in his address to the Houston ministers" had "raised the wall of church-state separation to unrealistic heights." If the Christian Right was on the march, the black church had likewise backed the Reverend Jesse Jackson in his run for the Democratic presidential nomination; for their part, Catholic bishops had been active in the campaign, especially in the matter of abortion. Religion and politics drew on the same "ethical imperatives," and "no arbitrary dividing line can ever completely separate religious beliefs from political passions." By the late 1980s, such views had become virtually the party line among the media elite. As the 1988 campaign geared up, the *Washington Post*'s David Broder gave his blessing to "the two reverends" who were running for the presidential nomination of their respective parties: Jackson again and Pat Robertson. "It's a healthy phenomenon, in the eyes of this secular reporter-critic, and not the menace some see," Broder wrote on December 23, 1987. "The clerics often speak uncomfortable truths to the mighty."

None of this is to say that journalists were enthusiastic about the religious Right as such. By the late 1980s, after the collapse of Falwell's Moral Majority and the Bakker-Swaggart televangelist scandals, political reporters and pundits began what would become periodic flurries of stories suggesting that the movement was finished as a political force. When Newt Gingrich's Republican Revolution ran aground in late 1995 and Bill Clinton coasted to an easy re-election, analysts speculated on why the movement had failed and was all but spent. During the late 1990s, the press was filled with reports that conservative evangelicals were abandoning political activity. In early 2000, because neither George W. Bush nor John McCain was closely identified with the Christian Right, pundits concluded that social conservatism was becoming a lonely voice in American politics. In this, they had help from academic experts, who kept telling them that the steep decline of the national Christian Coalition, infighting within the movement, and the negative impact of politically charged comments by Jerry Falwell and Pat Robertson were evidence of Christian Right crackup. It is hard to believe that there was not at least some wishful thinking in all this.

Part of the difficulty in getting a proper fix on the religious Right was that the stories tended to be viewed from a national perspective and written by journalists specializing in politics rather than religion. Their Rolodexes had the names of the marquee players—the Falwells and Robertsons and James Dobsons—who were always good for a quote but unlikely to disclose anything of importance. What was lacking was on-the-ground investigation by reporters who knew their way around evangelical churches and had sources to tell them what was going on inside by way of political mobilization. That this shortcoming was not characteristic of national political reporting was evident in Georgia in 2002, when Governor Roy Barnes and incumbent U.S. Senator Max Cleland went down to ignominious defeat and the state government flipped to Republican control for the first time since the Reconstruction. Despite the fact that former Christian Coalition executive director Ralph Reed had become chairman of the state Republican Party the year before, pre-election news coverage ignored Christian Right mobilization. Instead, Georgia newspapers focused on internal GOP disgruntlement with Reed's leadership.

Even after the election, Reed was portrayed not as a maestro of movement politics but as someone who had successfully morphed into a practical, mainstream politician. "Democrats snickered and even some Republicans scowled when the

Georgia GOP, still trying to broaden its mainstream appeal, elected Ralph Reed as its new party chair last year," wrote the AP's Russ Bynum from Atlanta on November 10, 2002. "But a quieter, more low-key Reed helped Republicans take a historic sweep of Georgia elections." Bill Torpy of the *Atlanta Journal-Constitution* noted Reed's success in mobilizing volunteers and paid staff to knock on doors, get out mailings, and make phone calls. The GOP ground campaign was likewise highlighted by David Halbfinger of the *New York Times*, Ken Ellingwood of the *Los Angeles Times*, and Manuel Roig-Franzia and David Broder of the *Washington Post*. But none of the above so much as mentioned the possibility that the Christian Right had been involved.

The evidence that it had was in part obscured by the absence of exit poll data after the election, but the story was there for those with eyes to see and shoe leather to tread—or at least some local sources. The story that should have been told can be found in the following series of e-mails the present author received from a woman in suburban Atlanta describing political activity in her middle-sized Southern Baptist Church.

> The old saw is "You can't take politics out of politics." But it has happened—politics have been taken out of politics and put into our churches. In north DeKalb County where I live, as well as in Gwinnett and other areas, the churches have become political power brokers under the rule of Ralph Reed and the "Christian" coalition. . . .
>
> The "in crowd" at my church is all Republican and regularly encourage others in the church to attend the Christian Coalition meetings and rallies. They also ask for volunteers to help them in the election campaigns of Republican candidates. The Deacons and Pastor invite Republican candidates to come speak at our church, but never invite Democrats. . . .
>
> In all meals or meetings in the Church Fellowship Hall, whenever talk turns to politics and current affairs, the Church leaders always point out that the Republican Party is the one that represents "Christian values" and "Christian people" should always support them. During the Clinton presidency, there were 8 years of demonizing him and all things Democratic. If I ever spoke up in defense of a Democratic politician, I was talked down and sometimes actually yelled at by red-faced Deacons saying that the Democrats are the work of the devil. Whenever I tried to point out church is not the appropriate place for secular politics, I've also been pooh-poohed. . . .
>
> [M]any politically unsophisticated Christians allow themselves to be told how to vote by "wolves in sheep's clothing." . . . It is now commonly accepted in the Christian community that the Republican Party is the Christian political party. . . . Because I am a Democrat, I have actually been pulled aside by fellow church members and told I'd better not let people in my church know that!
>
> Sunday morning before an election day, the so-called Christian Coalition's Voter Guide is distributed in the vestibule of my church (and hundreds of other churches across the state). The preacher always makes an announcement about it and exhorts everyone to be sure to pick one up as they leave the sanctuary. There is always a stack of these "voter guides" (which amount to Republican tickets) left in the vestibule, easily available to voters when they come to vote on Tuesday. . . .

> The Republican political activities continue year-round, no matter whether an election year or not. For an example . . . a so-called "Families & Freedom Rally" was held at Mt. Vernon Baptist [January 25, 2003]. This was a fundraiser for "little people" at a cost of $20 per head. The program consisted of all Republican elected officials. . . . The Mt. Vernon Baptist Church is used for many of the "Christian Coalition" meetings; it is a huge church (about 3,000 members I believe) and has plenty of room to accommodate these sorts of Republican political rallies. Although the U.S. Constitution calls for separation of church and state, the Georgia Republican Party actually uses church properties (as evidenced by this recent event) and calls on so-called Christians to join them and be used as operatives for the Republican Party. My own church actually sent a church van to carry people to this event, as they do for most of these things. . . .
>
> To protect their religious tax-exempt status, the politicized churches do not speak openly with academic people, and especially not with journalists!! The political leaders in church are usually hesitant to speak freely even with fellow church members until they feel you share their beliefs. Open church comments are normally guarded, e.g., "Be sure to pick up the voter's guides in the vestibule as you leave" or "See John Doe for information about the Christian Coalition meeting next week."

In due course, the Georgia press did catch up with the important figures—most significantly Sadie Fields, who as director of the Christian Coalition of Georgia was the critical link between the state Republican Party and the churches the lady from suburban Atlanta was talking about. Under the Republican administrations of the decade, Fields got all the coverage she needed from local media, and then some.

The Bush Presidency and the God Gap

In the 2004 campaign cycle, it became clear to the press that the religious Right was very much alive and kicking, and that its core constituency—conservative white evangelicals—were now the base of the Republican Party. In the wake of the 9/11 attacks, George W. Bush had emerged as the Christian leader the movement had been looking for from the beginning. By contrast, the Democratic Party, which in Bill Clinton had its second evangelical president in a row, now appeared intolerant of religion. The emblem for the contrast was what came to be called the "God gap"—the tendency for more religiously observant Americans to vote Republican regardless of religious preference. This gap, which began widening in the 1990s, reached twenty points in the evenly divided 2000 election and stayed there in 2002 and 2004. The contention, endlessly reiterated by reporters and commentators, was that, in a religious country, the Democrats had become the party of irreligion—and would have to do something about it if they ever expected to recapture Congress and the presidency. Massachusetts Senator John Kerry, their 2004 standard bearer, was the first Catholic since Kennedy to head a major party ticket, but the question now was not whether he was too Catholic but whether he was Catholic enough. A typical New Englander, Kerry was a strong supporter of church-state separation, part of a political culture in which religion did not have a place on the campaign trail—and pro-choice. Around the country, hard-line bishops did not hesitate to make clear that pro-choice Catholic politicians should not present themselves for Communion in *their* dioceses. "What next?" asked the *Boston Globe*'s Ellen Goodman in an April 15 column. "Will we have a political reporter to cover John Forbes Kerry at each Sunday Mass from now to November? Will there be a Holy Communion beat? A wafer watch?" In fact, a wafer watch was what there was, with reporters trailing Kerry to see what happened when he turned up for mass on Sunday. Writing in *The Christian Science Monitor* on October 26, Jane Lampman summed up, "Nearing the end of the most religion-infused election campaign since 1960, Sen. John Kerry is making a bid to close the perceived 'God gap' between the two political parties." It didn't work.

In fact, the God gap cut both ways. For even as the Democrats were losing the more religious voters, the Republicans were losing the less religious—and the less religious were on the rise in twenty-first-century America. Politically, the situation harked back to the era of Jefferson and Adams, with the country divided into religious and secular camps. By the 2006 midterm elections, there was a sense in the news media that the GOP had pushed the spiritual envelope too far, that its success with religious voters was turning into intolerant zealotry. As a case in point, TV news shows seized on "Jesus Camp," a documentary about three children from Missouri who attend a summer camp run by a Pentecostal pastor named Becky Fischer. In its most striking scene, the campers are shown praying at the feet of a cardboard George W. Bush, chanting for righteous judges to end abortion. "I mean, obviously, a lot of people would look at that scene and they would be concerned, saying, 'My gosh, they're sending little kids up there after brainwashing them,'" remarked Joe Scarborough on MSNBC's *Scarborough Country* on September 27. The film, ABC's Diane Sawyer announced on *Good Morning America* the same day, "is electrifying the culture wars." After the Democrats swept back to power, it appeared that between Republican fanaticism and a vigorous Democratic effort to reach out to religious voters, the partisan religious divide of the Bush years was coming to a close. "It's finally time to retire that tiresome, inaccurate phrase 'the God Gap,' so beloved by pollsters and commentators after the 2004 election," wrote Amy Sullivan, an editor of the *Washington Monthly*, in the *New Republic*'s online edition November 8. "Yesterday the God Gap all but disappeared." On November 11, Alan Cooperman reported in the *Washington Post*: "As the results of the midterm elections sank in this week, religious leaders across the ideological spectrum found something they could agree on: The 'God gap' in American politics has narrowed substantially." This new conventional wisdom was, however, wrong. Exit poll data released a few months later showed that while the proclivity of the more religious to vote Republican had shrunk somewhat, the less religious flocked to the Democrats in considerably greater numbers. The God gap was greater than ever.[5] This did not prevent

Sullivan, now with *Time* magazine, from writing a book titled *The Party Faithful: How and Why Democrats Are Closing the God Gap*. Nor did it prevent E. J. Dionne, another leading journalistic student of religion and politics, from writing *Souled Out: Reclaiming Faith and Politics After the Religion Right*.

The 2008 Campaign and the New Media

Never in American political history has religion played such a varied and active role as in the 2008 presidential campaign. Covering the stories was made more complex by a radical shift in the nature of the news media. Traditional print journalism had, since the previous election, gone into serious decline, and increasingly stories were driven by online media—blogs and video available via high-speed Internet connection.

The Republican primary featured a struggle between the former Mormon bishop and stake president Mitt Romney and former Baptist preacher Mike Huckabee. That Romney would have difficulty with the evangelical base of his party was clearer to journalists than it was to the candidate himself—notably via a September 2005 *Washington Monthly* article by Amy Sullivan whose subhead said it all: "Everyone wants to believe the Massachusetts governor's Mormonism won't be a problem if he runs in 2008. Think again." To be sure, as with the anti-Catholic "whispering" and "underground" campaigns of 1928 and 1960, evangelical hostility remained for the most part *sub rosa*. At least one prominent evangelical pastor, Robert Jeffress of Dallas's famous First Baptist Church, did speak out—not against voting for a Mormon per se but against imagining that a vote for a Mormon would be equivalent to voting for a *Christian*. "It's a little hypocritical for the last eight years to be talking about how important it is for us to elect a Christian president and then turn around and endorse a non-Christian," Jeffress told the *Dallas Morning News* on October 18, 2007. "Christian conservatives are going to have to decide whether having a Christian president is really important or not."

What seemed to concern evangelicals most about Mormons was their claim to be Christians—a claim that evangelicals rejected out of hand. In November of 2007, Jonah Goldberg of *National Review*'s Corner blog quoted from some of the many responses he received to a post he made on evangelical anti-Mormonism. One of these, along the lines of which Goldberg said he received "piles," ran:

> Speaking for myself, there is no policy that I think a Mormon would pursue that I find objectionable. I will not vote for a Mormon because they claim to be Christian, when they are not Christians. Electing, or even nominating, a Mormon continues to send the message to Americans that Mormons are fine and dandy, Christians like everyone else. Thousands of Christians are converted to Mormonism each year, and it is done under false pretenses. From what I have read, Mormons are very good at appearing to be orthodox Christians with new recruits. It's only

> later that the blatantly non-orthodox views come out. So, I rule out voting for a Mormon not because of actual policies they might pursue, but because of the message their election would send to Americans.[6]

For his part, Huckabee did offer conservative evangelicals the prospect of having one of their own in the White House. While religious Right leaders kept away from him in hopes of a more electable candidate, the grassroots found him highly appealing, and he succeeded in racking up victories in Iowa and a number of southern states. That John McCain eventually prevailed was the result of Romney's inability to attract evangelical support and Huckabee's inability to attract anything but.[7]

In the Democratic primary, Hilary Clinton and Barack Obama vied to show that they could appeal to religious voters—laying on faith-based staff to demonstrate that they would succeed where Kerry had failed. In the spring, Obama's campaign was nearly shipwrecked when video clips surfaced showing his Chicago pastor, the Reverend Jeremiah Wright, talking about how 9/11 had been about chickens coming home to roost and, in full-throttle black preacher mode, prophesying: "God Damn America." That Obama managed to survive the video, endlessly looped on Fox News and called up on millions of computer screens, was a minor miracle. But this wasn't the only clerical video to disturb voters during the course of the campaign. Video of anti-Catholic prophecy and some odd preaching on the Holocaust forced McCain to disavow the endorsement of San Antonio pastor John Hagee, and then to do the same when anti-Muslim preaching by Columbus, Ohio, pastor Rod Parsley came to light. Later, a video showing Kenyan evangelical witch-hunter Thomas Muthee praying over Sarah Palin made the rounds, persuading the left-wing blogosphere that the Republican vice presidential candidate was part of a suspicious worldwide evangelical conspiracy.

But Palin's actual religious commitments were not so easy to pin down. After she received the Republican vice presidential nomination, reporters from several newspapers made the trek to Alaska to see what they could find out. Yet even as she sent verbal signals to the evangelical heartland that she belonged to them and made herself into a living endorsement of the pro-life cause, she remained studiously vague about where she stood religiously. She declined even to identify herself as having grown up in an Assembly of God congregation, to which she belonged until she ran for statewide office in 2003. In this, she stood in stark contrast to Obama, who on a number of occasions testified to his own journey from a nonbelieving Christian family through experiences of Islam and Catholicism in Indonesia to eventually accepting Jesus at Trinity United Church Christ. For all that, some 10 percent of the public—encouraged, perhaps, by his exotic name—remained persuaded that he was a Muslim, an adherent of the faith that outranked all others as an object of suspicion in post-9/11 America.

How responsible was the new media environment for the almost unhinged character of religion in the 2008 campaign? History shows that electoral politics can be disturbed by religion under any journalistic regime—and, indeed, whether the journalists are paying attention or not. No viral YouTube video had more of an effect in 2008 than Rev. Burchard's remark about Romanism, taken down by an

Associated Press stenographer and published by newspapers in the old-fashioned way in 1884. Yet there is no question that the nature of the game changed radically during the first decade of the twenty-first century. Coverage of religion in politics, like all other coverage, migrated into an online world that seemed more like Adams's and Jefferson's carnival of pamphleteers and sermonizers than the buttoned-down mainstream media of the 1980s and 1990s. More vituperative and partisan it certainly was, but not necessarily worse. Where most newspaper coverage of religion was undertaken by full-time religion reporters who knew their way around the subject, the political side of religion generally fell to political reporters as an occasional feature of their main business. Their grasp of the motives and language and institutional context of the actors was limited at best. In the history of the religious Right, the best daily coverage was provided by the *New York Times*' David D. Kirkpatrick, who beginning in 2004 had the job of covering conservatives as a political beat for several years. But Kirkpatrick was the exception that proved the rule.

Compared to that less-than-impressive performance, the new media environment did not look so bad. By the end of the Bush presidency, a wide variety of blogs, online magazines, multipurpose websites, and news aggregators were providing a wide variety of perspectives, from a wide variety of points of view, on the religion that washed through the nation's politics. In the new era, the pastor of a small mainline Protestant congregation in the Midwest could make a name for himself as one of the country's leading progressive religious bloggers and a professor in a small New England ivory tower could find himself being offered credentials to presidential press conferences and fielding annoyed phone calls from White House officials. Together, freelance writers, academics, religious professionals, and members of the beleaguered legitimate press came to constitute a community that offered up the kind of context, informed insight, and even original reporting that many critics of conventional media treatment of religion and politics had for years been calling for. As one of them tweeted on May 21, 2010, "Realizing how much GOOD writing there is on religion these days." But was it too good to last?

NOTES

1. Quotations cited in Robert M. S. McDonald, "Was There a Religious Revolution of 1800?" in *The Revolution of 1800: Democracy, Race, and the New Republic*, eds. James Horn, Jan Ellen Lewis, and Peter S. Onuf (Charlottesville: University of Virginia Press, 2002), 173–98.

2. See John R. Mulkern, *The Know-Nothing Party in Massachusetts: The Rise and Fall of a Peoples' Movement* (Boston: Northeastern University Press, 1990), 175–85.

3. Mark Wahlgren Summers, *Rum, Romanism, and Rebellion* (Chapel Hill: University of North Carolina Press, 2000), 303.

4. Donald Frederick Brod, "Church, State, and Press: Twentieth-Century Episodes in the United States" (unpublished PhD dissertation, University of Minnesota, 1968, ch. 5).

5. Mark Silk and John C. Green, "The GOP's Religion Problem," *Religion in the News* 9, no. 3 (Winter 2007): 1.

6. http://www.nationalreview.com/corner/153273/beware-mormon-captivity-contd/jonah-goldberg.

7. See John C. Green and Mark Silk, "No Saints Need Apply," *Religion in the News* 11, no. 3 (Winter 2009): 4–7, 26.

REFERENCES

Schneider, Nathan, and Ruth Braunstein. 2010. *The New Landscape of the Religion Blogosphere*. Social Science Research Council. http://blogs.ssrc.org/tif/religion-blogosphere/.

Silk, Mark. 1995. *Unsecular Media: Making News of Religion in America*. Urbana: University of Illinois Press.

CHAPTER 22

MEDIA PORTRAYALS OF THE MORAL MAJORITY

JOHN P. BARTKOWSKI AND ASHRAF ALAM

Introduction

The New Christian Right or "religious Right" was an influential and widely covered movement during the latter decades of the twentieth century. This chapter examines media representations of the Moral Majority, the movement's touchstone organization, with an emphasis on the variegated narratives that swirled around its rise, apex, and fall.[1] The Moral Majority is situated within the religious Right, which itself is characterized by public activism and political engagement in defense of "traditional family values" (e.g., opposition to abortion, divorce, and gay rights), voter registration and education, and political endorsements and campaigning animated by Christian theological orthodoxy.[2] Nevertheless, conservative Christians are a loose coalition that does not always agree on key theological, cultural, and political issues.[3]

This chapter utilizes a social constructionist approach to media representations.[4] Social constructionism identifies how portrayals of social groups are created, legitimated, and contested. Using the Lexis/Nexis search engine, a media data archive of 1,000 articles on the Moral Majority was generated.[5] The analysis of this archive focused on media claims (descriptions, characterizations) and narrative frames (stories, metaphors, motifs) pertaining to the life course of the Moral Majority, with attention to both primary articulations (e.g., self-characterizations by movement insiders) and secondary representations (e.g., media interpretations, critics' portrayals).

Genesis: Representing the Rise of the Moral Majority

How did the press depict the rise of the Moral Majority in its early years? Articles published from 1979 through the middle of 1980 reveal the widespread use of metaphors of awakening and militancy.[6] One early article in the *Washington Post*, tellingly titled "Ready on the Right: Christian Soldiers Are on the March," illustrated these intertwined themes.[7] This article portrayed the rise of the Moral Majority as part of a larger mobilization of previously apolitical "right-leaning Christians" by "leading fundamentalist preachers." Just as religious revivals and born-again experiences promote spiritual awakening, the New Christian Right was portrayed as fomenting a political awakening among religious conservatives who had previously shunned the "worldliness" of politics.

Although journalists did not invent the militaristic metaphor of "Christian soldiers" (popularized through religious hymns), this depiction made for good news copy. Given the nature of this political awakening, there was clearly a story here. And, at least initially, this was one metaphor that both journalists and religious conservatives could embrace as a depiction of the New Christian Right. Moral Majority founder Jerry Falwell employed the "marching" metaphor himself in offering sound bites, while at the same time taking pains to underscore the interdenominational and inclusive character of these allied forces. As Falwell put it, "Religious organizations are marching together who never worked with each other. . . . Evangelicals, fundamentalists, conservatives, Catholics and Mormons are all working together now."[8]

Like other early treatments of the Moral Majority, this particular article called attention to the national reach of the New Christian Right, coupling coverage of the California-based Christian Voice with that of the Washington-based Moral Majority. Estimates of influence varied widely within the first wave of press coverage, with early projections that the Moral Majority and other New Christian Right organizations could affect the political sensibilities of anywhere between fifteen and seventy-five million Americans.[9]

Like several other early articles on the subject, "Ready on the Right" sought to provide balance by giving due space to the concerns, criticisms, and countermobilization plans of groups opposed to the New Christian Right. Critics described the religious Right as "show[ing] considerable arrogance," propagating "bad theology," and serving as "shelters for racism, reaction, and intolerance."[10] Although such criticisms were typically relegated to the end of articles, journalists' sympathies for critics' concerns were sometimes evident. Kotkin's[11] own description of the ascendancy of the religious Right as an "interlock between religious fervor and practical politics" seemed to indicate his own wariness of a movement in which faith and politics were so closely allied.

Interestingly, the *Washington Post* did not speak with one voice on the Moral Majority or the New Christian Right. Writing for the paper in March of 1980,

Garrett Epps[12] provided an extensive analysis of conservative Christian groups, including the Moral Majority, in Virginia. The motif of internal diversity and factionalism in this article ran directly counter to monolithic, militant characterizations of "Christian soldiers" who "march" in lockstep to the dictates of their leaders. Articles of this sort sought to quell the hype surrounding the New Christian Right by lending texture and complexity to the movement.[13] Epps described Christian Right leaders as "boldly . . . step[ping] over the line separating church and state" but was quick to add that "there is no guarantee that the ordinary Christian conservative will follow."[14] Showing an unusual amount of awareness about significant religious and theological differences among conservative Christians in early treatments of the topic, Epps wrote an extensive article using *Washington Post* and Gallup poll data to underscore the heterogeneity within the Christian Right, including distinctive levels of political engagement among religious conservatives, as well as rifts between evangelicals ("who rely solely on the Bible") and "'charismatics' or 'pentecostals'" ("who practice the 'Baptism of the Holy Spirit,' or 'speaking in tongues'").[15] He also conducted interviews with conservative Christians in Norfolk and found that while "there is widespread agreement on certain 'family' or 'moral' issues" such as the Equal Rights Amendment (ERA), abortion, and homosexuality, "beyond this, the unity disappears. There is little general agreement on religious issues, much less political ones."[16]

In seeking to explain this state of affairs, Epps described conservative Christianity as an "American religious tradition which holds that anybody with a Bible can form his own opinions without clearing them with ecclesiastical authorities of any kind," while also suggesting that some Bible-believing Christians reject political involvement altogether because they are confident that their worldview will ultimately be vindicated in the end regardless of their own political (in)activity.[17] Interweaving threads of optimism and fatalism, one local Norfolk citizen with conservative Christian sensibilities told Epps, "To be involved in politics is wrong, because you can't change destiny. . . . And why be afraid of destiny? The final winning is with Christianity."[18] Thus, in contrast to monolithic and militant representations of the New Christian Right as an "awakening giant," Epps concluded that "upon close examination, the evangelical movement of Norfolk resembles less the 'sleeping giant' of which its leaders like to boast than the biblical Tower of Babel."[19] The Tower of Babel motif of diversity and disunity, then, stood in direct contradiction to the Christian solider metaphor of monolithic militancy and a "lieutenant-to-troop" line of command.

As prescient as the Tower of Babel metaphor might have been given later academic research, the Christian soldier motif quickly became the dominant narrative during the early years of the Moral Majority.[20] Abetted by leading fundamentalists who wore the label of militancy as a badge of honor, early media coverage seized on the characterization of "Christian soldiers" as "true believers" waging "crusades" against their opponents, including gays, secular humanists, feminists, liberals, and other proponents of "godlessness."[21] Among these commentators, some warned that such "crusades" could lead to "political tyranny."[22] The *New York Times* op-ed

"Junking Democracy" was highly instructive in just this way.[23] Penned after Moral Majority "fundamentalists . . . seized control of Alaska's Republican Party" in 1980, this op-ed lamented that a "small, well-organized special-interest group" coupled with flagging voter participation "threatens the whole democratic process."[24]

Others echoed these concerns about the Moral Majority's undermining of democracy, while enlisting more of a comparative logic. One *New York Times* op-ed drew connections between the New Christian Right and other totalitarian movements that have sought to promulgate ideologies of narrowness and intolerance:

> The last few years have seen a surge of fundamentalism, a demand to return to old-time beliefs, in many different societies. . . . It illuminates how much the militant believers have in common. There are certain profound similarities in the theses advanced by the Red Guards who rampaged through China a few years ago in the name of Mao, the Ayatollah Khomeini's wild-eyed Islamic disciples, the orthodox militants of Israel, and the Americans who call themselves the Moral Majority.[25]

In short, while various accounts of the Moral Majority's rise to prominence emerged through early media coverage of the organization, the dominant media frames were those of awakening (transition from apathy to mobilization) and militancy (marching "Christian soldiers"). As the movement began to capture national media attention, New Christian Right leaders did not reject these characterizations but rather seemed to embrace them. Indeed, such depictions served as positive public relations by emphasizing the movement's cohesion and shared vision, its unyielding commitment to moral principles, and its wide appeal to a large sector of American society—the very essence of a "moral majority." But to what degree did such depictions of this organization persist as the movement took off and pursued its goals and strategies?

Promised Land? Media Frames of the Moral Majority's Goals and Tactics

During the organization's heyday of the early 1980s, media depictions generally took one of two forms, "standing-for" narratives or "standing-against" narratives. "Standing-for" narratives discussed the movement in terms of its vision for American society, essentially its desire to spread a gospel of "born-again politics" that was "a pro-family, pro-life, pro-morality platform."[26] More specifically, the media—seemingly aided by the public relations wing of the Moral Majority—focused on the organization's initiatives to promote school prayer, parents rights (e.g., corporal punishment), and school choice.[27]

Far more common were "standing-against" narratives in which the media and, to a degree, the organization itself portrayed the Moral Majority as opposed to the "liberal, humanist, and secular tendencies" in American society.[28] Press accounts seized on the Moral Majority's opposition to abortion, the Equal Rights Amendment, gay rights, the teaching of evolution and sex education in schools, drug use, and "immorality" on television and print media (e.g., pornography).[29] In this sense, the Moral Majority effectively used the media as a vehicle for underscoring its adversarial posture toward what it sometimes termed the "immoral minority."[30]

However, the emphasis that the news media and Falwell's organization itself placed on the Moral Majority's opposition to social trends in an American society soon became a double-edged sword. An organization that aims to project itself as the arbiter of moral virtue can seem lacking in a constructive, inclusive vision if it plays the condemnation card too heavily. Not surprisingly, *Newsweek* characterized the Moral Majority as "considerably more 'anti' than 'pro.'"[31] There is a potential downside associated with being reduced to a reactionary protest movement with no positive vision for American society. Consequently, the Moral Majority sought to recast its "Christian soldier" image. A *Washington Post* headline declared, "Falwell Denies 'Moral Majority' Seeks to Dictate Nation's Moral Philosophy."[32] In this article, Falwell countered charges of intolerance and exclusion, while highlighting the softer, more pluralistic aspects of his organization.[33] In a *Meet the Press* interview, he added: "We're not trying to jam our moral philosophy down the throats of others. We're simply trying to keep others from jamming their amoral philosophies down our throats."[34]

Charges of intolerance were not the only drawback associated with the militancy metaphor of fundamentalist "Christian soldiers." In the early 1980s, metaphors of militancy associated with the Moral Majority ran the risk of becoming equated with the violent tendencies exhibited by some Islamic fundamentalists and by movements that critics portrayed as reactionary predecessors. Norman Lear's comparison of the Moral Majority and the Ku Klux Klan was one such example.[35] Falwell tried to dispel such linkages in the press by drawing distinctions between influence and control: "We're not religious fanatics who have in mind a Khomeini-type religious crusade to take over the government. We support the separation of church and state.... We want influence, not control."[36] In fact, Falwell went so far as to disavow any aspirations for a nation governed through religion: "The one thing we are very much opposed to is the formation ... of a Christian Republic. We have been very much misunderstood along that area."[37]

How, then, did the media depict the tactics the Moral Majority used to pursue its objectives? Here, proactive and oppositional narratives were dual lenses through which organizational tactics were depicted and contested. And, like coverage of the Moral Majority's goals, considerably more attention was given to oppositional tactics. Proactive tactics used by the Moral Majority included voter drives, door-to-door canvassing, fundraising efforts, and how-to workshops in political engagement. To be sure, the press covered such efforts,[38] but they rarely made riveting news copy.

For example, a *New York Times* reporter described how the Moral Majority was "[building] up a substantial treasury through television appeals and sophisticated direct-mail techniques, ... by providing literature and holding lengthy 'workshops' on fund raising, public relations, and organizing."[39] Enlisting somewhat more colorful language, *Newsweek* covered the movement's effort to "run massive voter-registration and education drives designed to turn traditionally apolitical elements of the evangelical community into a potent force at the polls."[40] Other reporters sought to emphasize the human interest element of the Moral Majority, thereby breathing life and personality into media accounts of otherwise dry and mundane activities such as door-to-door canvassing. Adams,[41] reporting on a Moral Majority member who knocked on her door during a canvassing effort, shared the following account: "The lady's name was Dorothy, and she was delighted to come in for a cup of tea; mostly, she said, she'd had the door slammed in her face and people laughing when she handed them her brochures."

By contrast, oppositional narratives produced more inherently provocative storylines, while also extending the "Christian soldier" metaphor of an angry, resurgent fundamentalism. Consequently, oppositional tactics, which included (1) policy changes effected through boycotts, protests, and letter writing and (2) opposition to candidates who espoused "liberal" agendas, received the lion's share of media attention. Of course, sensational "standing-against" narratives did a great deal to bring attention to the combative and, quite often, successful campaigns waged by the Moral Majority. So this press coverage was not unwelcome by them.

Much was made of conflicts between the Moral Majority on the one hand and activists and politicians on the other who supported abortion rights, gay rights, the ERA, and other "liberal" causes. These conflicts were portrayed variously as "fights," "takeovers," "attacks," and "crusades."[42] The language in the print media reflected the culture wars being waged in American society. A *New York Times* editorial characterized the Moral Majority's book-banning campaign in just such a fashion: "Having tasted blood in November by defeating a number of 'targeted' liberal senators, the Moral Majority is apparently getting ready to tackle the shelves of the nation's libraries. An increasing number of people identifying themselves as members of the organization . . . [have] complain[ed] about books they consider unfit for public consumption."[43] A number of media outlets also covered the Moral Majority's plans to boycott advertised products in an effort to remove television programming containing "excessive and gratuitous sex and violence and profanity" from the airwaves.[44]

Perhaps the most sensational of all the oppositional tactics used by the Moral Majority was its efforts to challenge gay rights. Here again, press coverage emphasized the idea of cultural warfare and often served to trumpet the religious angle that the Moral Majority adopted in waging such battles. The *New York Times* article "Coalition in San Francisco to Fight Homosexuality" described the efforts of a group of conservative Christian groups including the Moral Majority in this light:

> Calling San Francisco the "Sodom and Gomorrah" of the nation, a coalition of fundamentalist groups has announced that it intends to spend $3 million on a media campaign attacking homosexuals. The coalition said that it would buy advertisements in an attempt to build anti-homosexual feeling in the community and attempt to persuade homosexuals to give up their lifestyle.[45]

While the Moral Majority engaged in these tactical maneuvers to change public policy and social sentiment, newspaper coverage also surfaced on their efforts to defeat political rivals.[46] Nationwide expansion of the Moral Majority that encouraged politicians to "examine their records" and comport to "conservative values" was described in the *New York Times*. In its report, the *New York Times* further highlighted that the organization had "spent $3 million to oppose liberal Senate candidates . . . and would become active in every state by means of self-sustaining chapters. [Falwell] warned officeholders with liberal records that they 'would do well to examine their records and get in step with conservative values or be prepared to be unemployed.'"[47]

After the Moral Majority defeated candidates, these ex-politicians sometimes used the media to criticize the organization. One particular case was that of Representative John H. Buchanan (R-Alabama).[48] Buchanan, a former Baptist minister, had served in the House of Representatives for sixteen years before being defeated in his 1980 renomination bid by an "ultraconservative" who had previously been allied with the John Birch Society. Buchanan charged that the Moral Majority "sent out letters saying [he] was un-Christian" and mobilized 2,500 volunteers to go door to door telling voters not to support him. As Buchanan explains it, he had

> engaged in a lively Biblical discussion with [members from the organization prior to the election] . . ., telling them that "the voice I hear is the burden [of] fifteen million people on earth who will die this year" because of hunger and other deprivation. "God has laid that burden on me," he told the visitors, citing scriptures of Jesus' challenge to his followers to care for the poor. "They seemed to respond warmly at the time," Buchanan recalled, "then they went back home and beat my brains out."[49]

In this particular story, the Tower of Babel motif of factionalism and division among conservative Christians was revived. For his part, Buchanan underscored the dangers of a monolithic political point of view among conservative Christians, issuing his own call for "other Christians, particularly evangelicals, to speak up" against the Moral Majority. He charged: "God expects us as Christian people to be concerned, to be informed, to be active, to be involved. . . . But to contend that there is only one 'Christian' position on complex political issues is a violation of both the Christian and the democratic traditions."[50]

Defeated candidates were not alone in offering such criticism. Barry Goldwater, often called the father of modern political conservatism, was quoted as saying that "every good Christian ought to kick Falwell right in the ass."[51] Americans might have gladly lent their feet to such an effort. A 1982 Gallup survey revealed that the Moral Majority had gained in visibility, with over half of Americans recognizing the name, as reported in the *New York Times*.[52] However, a glance beneath the *Times* headline "Moral Majority Gains in Poll on Recognition" revealed that greater visibility was a mixed blessing. Americans opposed the Moral Majority by a two-to-one margin, and conservative affect toward the group was evenly divided between supporters and critics, each registering at just over one-fifth of those surveyed.[53]

These public relations problems led the Moral Majority to reframe the ways the press depicted its tactics. The organization did not dispute the media's portrayal of its aggressive oppositional tactics at the ballot box, because such "successes" demonstrated its viability. However, the Moral Majority disputed its characterization as a political entity, redefining itself simply as an interest group advancing a morally conservative Christian platform. As such, its leaders were "adamant that their public education efforts are not aimed to endorse candidates, but to make clear their stands on moral issues so that voters can decide."[54] Although treated with some suspicion by journalists, the Moral Majority used the commercial side of the news media to take out "full-page newspaper advertisements insisting . . . that the group's concerns are moral rather than political. The advertisements also state[d] that the conservative group is 'not a religious organization attempting to control the Government.'"[55] For his part, the Moral Majority's founder echoed these claims, with the *Washington Post* reporting that "Falwell denies [that] he or his Moral Majority movement are interested in political parties. The only interest they have, says Falwell, is in backing Bible-based policies."[56] Yet, although the organization took pains to avoid the appearance of "trying to throw its political weight around," it remained politically influential through the mid-1980s.[57] At that time, the momentum enjoyed by many New Christian Right organizations receded in the wake of scandals that embroiled several of Falwell's fellow televangelists, notably Jimmy Swaggart and Jim Bakker. Just a short time before their downfalls, these "celebrity preachers" had "pooled their organizations" with Falwell's Moral Majority to form the ill-fated American Coalition for Traditional Values, whose goal, in the words of *Newsweek*, was to "'take dominion' over fallen America."[58]

Exodus: Making Sense of the Fall of the Moral Majority

How did press accounts portray the dimming cultural spotlight on the Moral Majority at the close of the 1980s? Some journalists framed their accounts as an epitaph by adapting earlier motifs. The Moral Majority, in the eyes of some, was little more than a "spent crusade" by the close of the 1980s.[59] Others balanced the epitaph metaphor with prospects for movement resurrection and resurgence through more grassroots approaches that would focus less on personalities and more on principles.[60]

As Falwell retired from such high-profile political activism and sexual scandals rocked the credibility of televangelists at large, he sought to reframe the Moral Majority's denouement as a story of rebirth rather than decline. In doing so, he continued to embrace military motifs, albeit softened with populist shades that the Reagan revolution had made common political currency. As Falwell reflected on the fruits of his political activism, he argued against the epitaph metaphor and rejected characterizations that placed him in charge of the movement: "I see the religious right [as] much, much stronger than it was five years ago, even with the difficulties we've had. It has diversified into the scores of medium-size organizations and literally hundreds of small local organizations. The new right has no general, and it never will again; just lots of privates and corporals, with a few lieutenants."[61]

On this point of grassroots activism, proponents and critics of the New Christian Right could agree. Doug Gould, communications vice president for Planned Parenthood Federation of America, echoed this portrayal of a grassroots transition within the religious Right.[62] This transition did not stop journalists from speculating about possible successors to Falwell and the Moral Majority, including Operation Rescue's Randall Terry and Focus on the Family's James Dobson.

Conclusion

This chapter has explored formative media representations of the Moral Majority and, among other findings, revealed that a dominant narrative of militancy ("attacks" waged by "Christian soldiers") was coupled with a subordinate narrative of diversity and factionalism on the Christian Right ("Tower of Babel"). Interestingly, the Moral Majority and New Christian Right initially embraced the militancy frame because it suggested a united movement committed to "saving" America from moral decay. However, as the movement gained recognition and successfully defeated candidates and policies it opposed, the militancy moniker became a liability and likely contributed to its unpopularity. Ultimately, the Moral Majority sought to brandish a more populist and less political image. Ironically, the decade closed with Jerry Falwell, the icon of the New Christian Right, disbanding the Moral Majority and emphasizing the leaderless character of his grassroots movement.

Interestingly, media frames that initially seized on the religious elements of the Moral Majority ultimately gave way to a focus on the political dimensions of the organization. Media interests were served by this emphasis on political factors in the Moral Majority because a more compelling storyline could be created about a group that demonstrated real-world political efficacy sufficient to tip elections in its favor. A media focus on religious beliefs—and heterogeneous ones at that—is a more complicated and less provocative motif, one that does not lend itself to such clear and compelling news copy. The media's emphasis on the political dimensions of the organization also served the interests of the Moral Majority. This focus on the political influence of the Moral Majority permitted the organization to stress its defense of "traditional morality" and "family values" while enabling it to evade charges of religious extremism, a particularly shrewd movement strategy given the rise of violent forms of fundamentalism in other parts of the world.

NOTES

1. In examining media framings of the organization's mission and tactics, we restrict ourselves to early press accounts. These "formative frames" set the tone and trajectory for later press coverage and constitute the first 500 items in our database (a full half of our archive) consisting of articles published through November 1982.

2. See Lynn M. Hemple and John P. Bartkowski, "Scripture, Sin, and Salvation: Theological Conservatism Reconsidered," *Social Forces* 86 (2008): 1647–1674.

3. E.g., John P. Bartkowski, *Remaking the Godly Marriage: Gender Negotiation in Evangelical Families* (New Brunswick, NJ: Rutgers University Press, 2001); John P. Bartkowski, *The Promise Keepers: Servants, Soldiers, and Godly Men* (New Brunswick, NJ: Rutgers University Press, 2004); Christian Smith, *Christian America? What Evangelicals Really Want* (Berkeley: University of California Press, 2000).

4. E.g., John P. Bartkowski, "Claims-Making and Typifications of Voodoo as a Deviant Religion: Hex, Lies, and Videotape," *Journal for the Scientific Study of Religion* 37 (1998): 559–579; Joel Best, ed., *Images of Issues: Typifying Contemporary Social Problems* (Hawthorne, NY: Aldine de Gruyter, 1995).

5. Our Lexis/Nexis archive composed of 1,000 articles, including editorials, was generated on May 13, 2010. We entered the search string "Moral Majority Right" with January 1, 1978, through January 1, 1990, date parameters. The vast majority of our archive was published in newspapers ($n = 917$), with over 300 hits each from the *New York Times* ($n = 329$) and the *Washington Post* ($n = 315$). Seventy-nine items in our archive were published in magazine format, with most of those ($n = 41$) generated by *Newsweek* and several others from the *Economist* ($n = 13$).

6. E.g., Haynes Johnson, "The Terrible Swift Sword of the True Believer," *Washington Post*, September 7, 1980; Joel Kotkin, "Ready on the Right: Christian Soldiers Are on the March," *Washington Post*, August 25, 1979; Allen J. Mayer and others, "A Tide of Born-Again Politics," *Newsweek*, September 15, 1980; Tom Nicholson, "The Reverend Jerry Who?" *Newsweek*, December 22, 1980.

7. Kotkin, "Ready on the Right."

8. As quoted in Ibid.

9. E.g., Dudley Clendinen, "Rev. Falwell Inspires Evangelical Vote," *New York Times*, August 20, 1980; Kotkin, "Ready on the Right."

10. Kotkin, "Ready on the Right."

11. Ibid.

12. Garrett Epps, "Born-Again Politics Is Still Waiting to Be," *Washington Post*, March 30, 1980.

13. See also, e.g., Kenneth A. Briggs, "Leader of Jews and Evangelical Christians Work Together for Better Relations," *New York Times*, December 14, 1980; Megan Rosenfeld, "The New Moral America and the War of the Religicos: Born Again Political Forces Not Singing the Same Hymn," *Washington Post*, August 24, 1980.

14. Epps, "Born-Again politics Is Still Waiting to Be."

15. Ibid.

16. Ibid.

17. Ibid.

18. Ibid.

19. Ibid.

20. E.g., Smith, *Christian America?*

21. See, e.g., Edward N. Costikyan, "Junking Democracy," *New York Times*, June 20, 1980; Johnson, "The Terrible Swift Sword of the True Believer"; Kathy Sawyer and Robert G. Kaiser, "The Republicans in Detroit; Evangelicals Flock to GOP Standard Feeling They Have Friend in Reagan," *Washington Post*, July 16, 1980.

22. Costikyan, "Junking Democracy." See also Johnson, "The Terrible Swift Sword of the True Believer."

23. Costikyan, "Junking Democracy."

24. Ibid.

25. Flora Lewis, "The Fundamental Urge," *New York Times*, November 28, 1980.

26. Mayer and others, "A Tide of Born-Again Politics."

27. David S. Broder, "The Social Agenda Could Spoil the Party," *Washington Post*, November 23, 1980; Marjorie Hunter, "Tuition Tax Credits Backed at Hearing," *New York Times*, June 5, 1981; Marjorie Hyer, "Drive to Put Prayer in Schools Gets Strong Backing," *Washington Post*, June 6, 1980; Kotkin, "Ready on the Right"; Stewart McBride, "Evolution in Court: 'Both Sides Win,'" *Christian Science Monitor*, March 9, 1981; Joyce Purnick, "Moral Majority Establishes Beachhead in New York," *New York Times*, February 5, 1981; Wallace Turner, "Group of Evangelical Protestants Takes over the G.O.P. in Alaska," *New York Times*, June 9, 1980.

28. Kotkin, "Ready on the Right."

29. Briggs, "Leader of Jews and Evangelical Christians Work Together for Better Relations"; Broder, "The Social Agenda Could Spoil the Party"; Denis Collins, "TV Evangelist Snags Reagan, but Not Everyone Down Home," *Washington Post*, October 4, 1980; Blaine Harden, "'Shocked' Va. Preacher Trying to Ban 'Hard-Core Porn' from Town's Library," *Washington Post*, December 1980; Mayer and others, "A Tide of Born-Again Politics"; McBride, "Evolution in Court"; Bill Roeder, "Monitoring TV for Sex and Violence," *Newsweek*, January 26, 1981; Rosenfeld, "The New Moral America and the War of the Religicos"; Margot Slade and Eva Hoffman, "Ideas and Trends in Summary; Evangelicals Get Inspiration and Warnings, Too," *New York Times*, February 1, 1981; Stuart Taylor, Jr., "Leading Lawyers Defend the Courts," *New York Times*, January 25, 1982; Turner, "Group of Evangelical Protestants Takes over the G.O.P. in Alaska"; Bernard Weinraub, "Liberal Group Report Surge Since Reagan Election," *New York Times*, December 9, 1980.

30. See Warren Brown, "Falwell Denies 'Moral Majority' Seeks to Dictate Nation's Moral Philosophy," *Washington Post*, October 13, 1980.

31. Mayer and others, "A Tide of Born-Again Politics."

32. Brown, "Falwell Denies 'Moral Majority' Seeks to Dictate Nation's Moral Philosophy."

33. Ibid.

34. As quoted in Ibid.

35. See Richard Cohen, "The New Hype," *Washington Post*, January 24, 1982.

36. As quoted in Mayer and others, "A Tide of Born-Again Politics."

37. Brown, "Falwell Denies 'Moral Majority' Seeks to Dictate Nation's Moral Philosophy."

38. E.g., Jane Adams, "Hers," *New York Times*, October 2, 1980; Richard M. Harley, "Evangelicals May Not Fall into Ranks Behind 'New Right,'" *Christian Science Monitor*, October 29, 1980; Kotkin, "Ready on the Right"; Mayer and others, "A Tide of Born-Again Politics"; Purnick, "Moral Majority Establishes Beachhead in New York"; Sawyer and Kaiser, "The Republicans in Detroit."

39. Purnick, "Moral Majority Establishes Beachhead in New York."

40. Mayer and others, "A Tide of Born-Again Politics."

41. Adams, "Hers."

42. Briggs, "Leader of Jews and Evangelical Christians Work Together for Better Relations"; Costikyan, "Junking Democracy"; Mayer and others, "A Tide of Born-Again Politics"; Paul Moore Jr., "True Conservation," *New York Times*, November 16, 1980; "Nays on Gays," *Newsweek*, May 8, 1978; Rosenfeld, "The New Moral America and the War of the Religicos"; Turner, "Group of Evangelical Protestants Takes over the G.O.P. in Alaska"; United Press International, "Moral Majority Official Attacks Council Head," *New York Times*, January 22, 1982.

43. Eric Nagourney, "Enter the Book-Burners," *New York Times*, December 19, 1980.

44. Roeder, "Monitoring TV for Sex and Violence"; Rosenfeld, "The New Moral America and the War of the Religicos."

45. "Coalition in San Francisco to Fight Homosexuality," *New York Times*, February 11, 1981.

46. E.g., Robert M. Press, "The Bible and the Ballot: How Strong Is the Religious Right?" *Christian Science Monitor*, May 26, 1982.

47. Joseph F. Sullivan, "Falwell Warms Jersey Liberals at Capitol Rally," *New York Times*, November 11, 1980.

48. Hyer, "Drive to Put prayer in Schools Gets Strong Backing."

49. Ibid.

50. Ibid.

51. Tom Morganthau and John J. Lindsay, "Barry Goldwater Tastes New Life," *Newsweek*, July 27, 1981.

52. "Moral Majority Gains in Poll on Recognition," *New York Times*, January 24, 1982.

53. Ibid.

54. Harley, "Evangelicals May Not Fall into Ranks Behind 'New Right.'"

55. Adam Clymer, "Moral Majority Starts Ad Campaign to Counter Critics," *New York Times*, March 26, 1981.

56. Collins, "TV Evangelist Snags Reagan, but Not Everyone Down Home."

57. Jack Eisen, "Metro Notes," *Washington Post*, January 26, 1982.

58. Kenneth L. Woodward, "Playing Politics at Church," *Newsweek*, July 9, 1984.

59. Gustav Niebuhr, "Spent Crusade: Why Moral Majority, a Force for Decade, Ran out of Steam," *Wall Street Journal*, September 25, 1989.

60. E.g., Mathew Scully, "Right Wing and a Prayer—Still Alive and Kicking," *Washington Times*, November 8, 1989; Larry Witham, "LaHaye Continues Ministry on Local Level," *Washington Times*, October 20, 1989.

61. Scully, "Right Wing and a Prayer."

62. Ibid.

REFERENCES

Adams, Jane. 1980. Hers. *New York Times*, October 2.

Bartkowski, John P. 1998. Claims-Making and Typifications of Voodoo as a Deviant Religion: Hex, Lies, and Videotape. *Journal for the Scientific Study of Religion* 37:559–79.

Bartkowski, John P. 2001. *Remaking the Godly Marriage: Gender Negotiation in Evangelical Families*. New Brunswick, NJ: Rutgers University Press.

Bartkowski, John P. 2004. *The Promise Keepers: Servants, Soldiers, and Godly Men*. New Brunswick, NJ: Rutgers University Press.
Best, Joel, ed. 1995. *Images of Issues: Typifying Contemporary Social Problems*. Hawthorne, NY: Aldine de Gruyter.
Briggs, Kenneth A. 1980. Leader of Jews and Evangelical Christians Work Together for Better Relations. *New York Times*, December 14.
Broder, David S. 1980. The Social Agenda Could Spoil the Party. *Washington Post*, November 23.
Brown, Warren. 1980. Falwell Denies 'Moral Majority' Seeks to Dictate Nation's Moral Philosophy. *Washington Post*, October 13.
Clendinen, Dudley. 1980. Rev. Falwell Inspires Evangelical Vote. *New York Times*, August 20.
Cohen, Richard. 1982. The New Hype. *Washington Post*, January 24.
Collins, Denis. 1980. TV Evangelist Snags Reagan, but Not Everyone Down Home. *Washington Post*, October 4.
Costikyan, Edward N. 1980. Junking Democracy. *New York Times*, June 20.
Clymer, Adam. 1981. Moral Majority Starts Ad Campaign to Counter Critics. *New York Times*, March 26.
Economist. 1980. Born Again Political. October 4.
Eisen, Jack. 1982. Metro Notes. *Washington Post*, January 26.
Epps, Garrett. 1980. Born-Again Politics Is Still Waiting to Be. *Washington Post*, March 30.
Harden, Blaine. 1980. "Shocked" Va. Preacher Trying to Ban "Hard-Core Porn" from Town's Library. *Washington Post*, December 1980.
Harley, Richard M. 1980. Evangelicals May Not Fall into Ranks Behind "New Right." *Christian Science Monitor*, October 29.
Hempel, Lynn M., and John P. Bartkowski. 2008. Scripture, Sin, and Salvation: Theological Conservatism Reconsidered. *Social Forces* 86:1647–74.
Hunter, Marjorie. 1981. Tuition Tax Credits Backed at Hearing. *New York Times*, June 5.
Hyer, Marjorie. 1980. Drive to Put Prayer in Schools Gets Strong Backing. *Washington Post*, June 6.
Johnson, Haynes. 1980. The Terrible Swift Sword of the True Believer. *Washington Post*, September 7.
Kotkin, Joel. 1979. Ready on the Right: Christian Soldiers Are on the March. *Washington Post*, August 25.
Lewis, Flora. 1980. The Fundamental Urge. *New York Times*, November 28.
Mayer, Allan J. and others. 1980. A Tide of Born-Again Politics. *Newsweek*, September 15.
McBride, Stewart. 1981. Evolution in Court: "Both Sides Win." *Christian Science Monitor*, March 9.
Moore, Paul, Jr. 1980. True Conservation. *New York Times*, November 16.
Nagourney, Eric. 1980. Enter the Book-Burners. *New York Times*, December 19.
New York Times. 1981. Television "Censors" Criticized. April 10.
New York Times. 1981. Coalition in San Francisco to Fight Homosexuality. February 11.
New York Times. 1982. Moral Majority Gains in Poll on Recognition. January 24.
Newsweek. 1982. Scenes and Echoes. January 4.
Niebuhr, Gustav. 1989. Spent Crusade: Why Moral Majority, a Force for Decade, Ran out of Steam. *Wall Street Journal*, September 25.
Nicholson, Tom. 1980. The Reverend Jerry Who? *Newsweek*, December 22.
Press, Robert M. 1982. The Bible and the Ballot: How Strong is the Religious Right? *Christian Science Monitor*, May 26.

Purnick, Joyce. 1981. Moral Majority Establishes Beachhead in New York. *New York Times*, February 5.
Roeder, Bill. 1981. Monitoring TV for Sex and Violence. *Newsweek*, January 26.
Rosenfeld, Megan. 1980. The New Moral America and the War of the Religicos: Born Again Political Forces Not Singing the Same Hymn. *Washington Post*, August 24.
———. 1981. The Battle for Prime-Time Decency; the National Federation for Decency's Battle with Prime-Time Television. *Washington Post*, February 3.
Sawyer, Kathy, and Robert G. Kaiser. 1980. The Republicans in Detroit; Evangelicals Flock to GOP Standard Feeling They Have Friend in Reagan. *Washington Post*, July 16.
Scully, Matthew. 1989. Right Wing and a Prayer—Still Alive and Kicking. *Washington Times*, November 8.
Slade, Margot, and Eva Hoffman. 1981. Ideas and Trends in Summary; Evangelicals Get Inspiration and Warnings, Too. *New York Times*, February 1.
Smith, Christian. 2000. *Christian America? What Evangelicals Really Want*. Berkeley: University of California Press.
Sullivan, Joseph F. 1980. Falwell Warms Jersey Liberals at Capitol Rally. *New York Times*, November 11.
Taylor, Stuart, Jr. 1982. Leading Lawyers Defend the Courts. *New York Times*, January 25.
Turner, Wallace. 1980. Group of Evangelical Protestants Takes over the G.O.P. in Alaska. *New York Times*, June 9.
United Press International. 1982. Moral Majority Official Attacks Council Head. *New York Times*, January 22.
Weinraub, Bernard. 1980. Liberal Group Report Surge Since Reagan Election. *New York Times*, December 9.
Witham, Larry. 1989. LaHaye Continues Ministry on Local Level. *Washington Times*, October 20.
Woodward, Kenneth L. 1984. Playing Politics at Church. *Newsweek*, July 9.

CHAPTER 23

EVOLUTION, CREATIONISM, AND OBJECTIVITY IN THE PRESS

LAURI LEBO

H. L. MENCKEN'S derision for William Jennings Bryan was hardly a subtle subtext in his dispatches from Dayton, Tennessee. During the infamous 1925 trial of *Tennessee v. Scopes*, which Mencken dubbed the "monkey trial," the *Evening Sun* columnist spared no brutal adjective in his tirades against the populist orator known as the Great Communicator.

In one of his daily front-page pieces, Mencken wrote of the prosecution's chief counsel, "This old buzzard, having failed to raise the mob against its rulers, now prepares to raise it against its teachers. . . . It is a tragedy indeed, to begin life as a hero and to end it as a buffoon."[1]

It's hard to imagine such words appearing in today's newspapers, dictated by the demands of "objectivity" and fair-and-balanced journalism. But Mencken's dispatches were written at a time when the word *objectivity* was only beginning to appear in conversations about the American media. Mencken's often hyperbolic coverage took the form of columns, in which strong and entertaining opinion was not only encouraged but also eagerly sought by devoted readers. His words became the voice of the *Evening Sun*. While Mencken's articles are the best remembered, he was not the only skeptical reporter impatient with religious attacks on science. Two years after the trial, an analysis of news articles indicated that most journalists who covered *Scopes* "were temperamentally inclined to the pro-evolution side of the case" and "as a whole . . . on the side of science."[2]

Fifty-six years later, the media would turn out for another battle over evolution, this time in Little Rock, Arkansas. But by then, journalism's approach to covering such issues had changed. The lively and often snide reporting of the *Scopes* trial had been replaced with a neutral voice in which the arguments of both sides were carefully balanced. Accordingly, half a century after Mencken called Bryan a buffoon for his antievolution crusade, an Associated Press article printed in the *New York Times* summed up the trial of *McLean v. Arkansas* with cautiously crafted wording:

> Evolutionists believe that the earth is billions of years old and that scientific data show man evolved over long ages from creatures of lower order, which in turn developed from the first organism that came into existence in a lifeless world.
>
> The creationist view holds that data show the earth to be much younger, perhaps 10,000 to 500 million years old, and that man came into existence suddenly and fully formed.[3]

The clash between religion and science is nothing new. It has existed at least since Galileo was arrested at the behest of the Roman Catholic Church for arguing the Earth revolved around the sun. But it wasn't until 1859 when Charles Darwin provided a materialist explanation for man's origins that science directly challenged church teachings. At its most basic, evolution refers to the incremental and inheritable changes within a population over time, and yet it is the elegant driving force behind life's awesome diversity. But in the court of public opinion, it has become a lightning rod in the culture wars, with few signs of waning. Americans are just as divided today over it as they were in 1925.[4]

Newspapers have long struggled with culture war issues and the task of sifting through facts and emotions without appearing to take a side. Seeking to project neutrality, newspapers, beginning in the 1920s, gradually developed a style in which the writer carefully balanced two opposing sides.[5] This chapter will analyze the impact of this desire for objectivity on coverage of the battle between religion and science. Because evolution speaks directly to these two often diametrically opposed domains, it is the focus for this analysis of newspaper reporting on the courtroom trials of *Tennessee v. Scopes*, *McLean v. Arkansas*, and *Kitzmiller v. Dover*. The chapter will review the institution of "objectivity" as a practice of modern American journalism and its limitations in producing fair and accurate newspaper coverage of these antievolution battles. It also will examine the press's tendency, in its bid for objectivity, to treat science and faith as two sides of the same coin. The general tone of local and national trial coverage will be compared to determine whether the pressures of objectivity are different when reporting in one's own small town or for a city newsroom hundreds of miles away. For purposes of this comparison, the chapter will look at *Scopes* coverage by the national media, with an emphasis on the *Baltimore Evening Sun* and Science Service, and by the local press, focusing on the *Chattanooga Daily Times*. For the *McLean* trial, it will analyze the *New York Times* and Associated Press for national coverage and the *Arkansas Democrat* and the *Arkansas Gazette* for local coverage. For *Kitzmiller*'s national coverage, it will examine *USA Today*, the *Washington Post*, and the *New York Times*. It will also look at the *York Daily Record* and the *York Dispatch* for local coverage.

While the modern notion of newspaper objectivity, in which equal treatment is provided to both sides, may be an effective tool in covering political horse races, it does a poor job at conveying scientific realities and an injustice to readers trying to understand the issues. Worse, it balances truth with fallacy and creates the impression that there is a controversy in the scientific community when none exists.

"Agent of Beelzebub Once Removed"

In the storytelling shorthand of daily newspapers, *Tennessee v. Scopes* is the original source from which this particular modern culture war flows.

To understand the nature of the *Scopes* newspaper coverage, one first has to understand the cultural forces of its day. Despite some initial resistance, Darwin's theory of natural selection had gained general public acceptance in America by the 1920s.

Following World War I, prominent national business leaders believed that science and technology, as well as an educated workforce, were key to the nation's successful future. Many newspapermen rallied around this idea of an enlightened readership and dedicated themselves to improving scientific literacy. In 1921, with the cooperation of national science organizations, publisher E. W. Scripps created Science Service, dedicated to improving public scientific literacy.[6] The not-for-profit became a syndicated service like Associated Press, selling articles devoted to scientific issues to newspapers and magazines. In 1924, Managing Editor Watson Davis developed a popular radio series, *Adventures in Science*, bringing research news into the homes of a burgeoning radio listening public.

However, as this scientific movement was developing, a parallel antiscience movement had been quietly growing in the evangelical community. Historians say the movement started soon after the turn of the century with a series of pamphlets called *The Fundamentals*, which called for a return to biblical orthodoxy.[7] Supporters argued for a literal reading of Genesis and blamed evolution for fostering moral relevance and social engineering. William Jennings Bryan, an ardent progressive and three-time failed presidential candidate, championed the cause against "social Darwinism," arguing it allowed the rich to oppress the poor and was responsible for societal ills such as child labor and worker exploitation. In response, Tennessee lawmakers passed the 1925 Butler Act, which stated no teacher in a publicly funded school may "teach any theory that denies the story of the Divine Creation of man as taught in the Bible, and to teach instead that man has descended from a lower order of animals."

Seizing on opportunity, the newly formed American Civil Liberties Union ran advertisements in Tennessee newspapers, offering to represent anyone accused of teaching evolution. A Dayton businessman spotted the ads and convinced community leaders that a court case would be great publicity for the town. John Scopes, a football coach and substitute teacher, was enlisted.

It was evolution's first court challenge. On May 7, 1925, the *Washington Post* announced the impending circus with a front-page brief: "J.T. Scopes, of the science department of the Rhea County High School, was arrested Tuesday by a deputy sheriff, charged with violating the Tennessee law prohibiting the teaching of evolution in the State public schools."[8]

That July, more than 100 reporters from across the country descended on the small rural town, straining the local infrastructure. The new medium of radio jumped on the opportunity to provide live coverage of what many predicted would be the "trial of the century." WGN of Chicago earned the distinction of becoming the first radio station to broadcast from a courtroom. To cope with the national media's need to disseminate information from the isolated Cumberland Mountains of southeastern Tennessee, the American Telephone & Telegraph Company laid ten and a half miles of temporary wire. Western Union's twenty-two on-site telegraphers transmitted more than 1.5 million words throughout the trial, "and at least another half million went out over a private wire leased by four of the press associations."[9]

Mencken spent little time on the science of evolution, choosing instead to rail against the superstitions of religious fundamentalists, whom he said portrayed scientists as "sworn and sinister agents of Beelzebub" and Scopes, therefore, as an "agent of Beelzebub once removed."[10] But his depictions of Dayton as a backwater were not isolated portrayals. Headlines across the country labeled Dayton "Monkeyville." A *Baltimore Evening Sun* headline read "Man with a Tail Reported Located in Tennessee."[11]

Other reporters took a more serious tone. Philip Kinsley of the *Chicago Tribune* wrote that Scopes was "nervous but undaunted" and "passionately sincere in his conviction that the evolution law is a form of mental slavery."[12]

Watson Davis, covering *Scopes* for Science Service, provided some of the trial's most powerful and picturesque reporting about the science of the case:

> After the sun has moved in its daily journey across that flat earth believed in by some Tennesseans and has disappeared behind the mountains, the stars in all their glory shine in the sky each night. . . . There, milky ways as vast as the one in which our earth is a mere grain of sand are among the most impressive evidences of evolution that may be presented in the case of the state of Tennessee vs. John T. Scopes. Yet most of the facts that the scientists are ready to present do not come from the ends of space. Barnyards, fields, forests, rocks, animals and man himself will furnish exhibits for the defense.[13]

While the national media were enjoying themselves with at times amused and at other times elegant prose, the state newspapers generally provided sober coverage. The *Chattanooga Daily Times* had opposed the Butler Act, but its trial coverage carefully aired both sides. While the *Daily Times* ran Davis's pro-evolution articles from Science Service, they also employed a Baptist preacher whose stories took a decidedly pro-prosecution tone. One of the Reverend T. W. Callaway's articles accused Scopes's father of being a socialist and not a Christian.[14] Another chastised one of Davis's articles with the headline "Baptists Resent Davis' Statement" after Davis referred to Tennessee Baptists as pagans.[15]

While Mencken praised the *Daily Times*' editorial stance, he believed that once the trial began, the paper became too cautious. He had no patience with its attempt to appease its religious readership. He wrote:

> The newspapers of the State, with few exceptions, are very feeble. One of the best of them, the *Chattanooga News*, set up an eloquent whooping for Bryan the moment he got to Dayton. Before that it had been against the anti-evolution law. But with the actual battle joined, it began to wobble, and presently it was printing articles arguing that Fundamentalism, after all, made men happy—that a Tennessean gained something valuable by being an ignoramus—in other words, that a hog in a barnyard was to be envied by an Aristotle.[16]

At end of the trial, the jury deliberated briefly before returning with a verdict of guilty. In a gesture that would be almost impossible to imagine by contemporary newspaper ethics, the *Evening Sun* chipped in to cover Scopes's bail. The newspaper noted simply: "Bail for Scopes was fixed at $500, pending appeal of the case to the Supreme Court of Tennessee, at Knoxville. Dudley Field Malone announced that the *Baltimore Evening Sun* had offered to go on the bond, and the offer had been accepted."[17]

While Scopes's conviction was later overturned on a legal technicality—in Tennessee, the jury was supposed to set the amount of the fine, not the judge—the teaching of evolutionary theory would languish in the following decades, both in Tennessee and across the country. Those who opposed evolution didn't disappear for eight decades only to reappear in 2004 with the intelligent design trial of *Kitzmiller v. Dover*. Rather, several states, including Arkansas, joined Tennessee and passed laws that prohibited the teaching of any science that contradicted the Bible. It would take the Space Race to turn things around.

"Two Sides to Every Question"

In 1957, the Soviet Union shocked Americans with the launch of Sputnik, the first Earth-orbiting satellite. The realization that the United States was losing the Space Race sparked a renewed interest in science among the public, the media, and the government. The ACLU believed the time was ripe to challenge antievolution statutes. In 1965, the Arkansas ACLU chapter convinced Susan Epperson, a twenty-four-year-old Little Rock biology teacher, to be the face of the first test case since *Scopes*. Epperson sued the Arkansas public school system to challenge her state's antievolution law, which had been on the books since 1928. Arkansas's Chancery Court sided with Epperson and ruled that the law violated the Fourteenth Amendment. When the Arkansas Supreme Court overturned the lower court decision, the ACLU appealed. Three years later, the US Supreme Court sided with Epperson, determining the sole reason for the antievolution law was religious belief: the theory conflicted with Genesis's account of creation. The news media, preoccupied by the escalating Vietnam War and assassinations of Martin Luther King, Jr. and Bobby Kennedy, provided little national coverage. If anything, reporters expressed mild surprise that the issue still existed. In a short news item, *Newsweek* summed up the Supreme Court decision: ". . . finally last week, 43 years after Scopes' conviction, the Supreme Court struck down one of the monkey laws."[18]

In response, creationists changed their tactics. Instead of outlawing evolution, they started calling for equal-time clauses, a strategy rooted in the Fairness Doctrine, the Federal Communications Commission regulation that required that television and radio provide "a reasonable opportunity for the presentation of contrasting viewpoints on controversial issues of public importance."[19]

By the end of 1970s, creationists had refined their strategy, demanding that evolution be balanced with the teaching of creation science. Supporters claimed the concept was based on solid empirical evidence that proved a 6,000-year-old Earth with an entire fossil record laid down during the Great Flood. Thirteen years after *Epperson v. Arkansas*, in March 1981, Arkansas became the first state to adopt the "Balanced Treatment of Creation-Science and Evolution-Science Act." At the behest of the academic and science communities, as well as members of the religious community, the constitutionality of the law was immediately challenged. Rev. William McLean, a United Methodist minister, was the lead plaintiff. A trial was set for December before US District Judge William Overton. The media dubbed the scheduled trial as *Scopes* II.

After giving the Epperson case barely a yawn, newspapers were excited by the coming showdown and provided extensive coverage on whether or not creation science should be taught in science class. Seventy-five news organizations from across the country and overseas attended the first days of the two-week-long trial. But while the national media editorialized against the law, there was almost no mention in news stories that the scientific community unanimously accepted evolution. The narrative voice of the amused observer so prevalent in the *Scopes* trial had been replaced by a carefully crafted tone of bland and balanced objectivity. As evidenced in the following examples, rather than address the scientific issues, much of the coverage followed the "horse race" model, pitting secularism against religious fundamentalism and treating them as equally valid.

Typical of coverage was a lengthy Associated Press article setting up the debate: "The curtain rises in December on another act in the long battle between creationists and evolutionists over what children should learn about the beginning of mankind. The trial of an American Civil Liberties Union suit attacking a creationist-backed Arkansas law is to start December 7."

The article devoted equal space to defining the two sides: "Creation Science (CS): Sudden creation of the universe, energy and life from nothing. Evolution Science (ES): Emergence of the universe and life from disordered, non-living material by natural processes. . . ."

The article concludes, "if either view is taught in a class, the act says, balanced treatment must be given the other view."[20]

Another piece by the defunct United Press International (UPI) sought a neutral overview:

> One of the main issues of the trial was whether a creator could ever be discussed in the classroom in non-religious terms. Norman Geisler of Dallas Theological Seminary said telling students a supernatural being may have brought the earth into existence is not the same as telling them how to worship. But Langdon Gilkey, a theologian from University of Chicago, said, "A creator is certainly a god. The idea of a creator has its source in religious tradition."[21]

Just as the Arkansas statute required equal time for creation science, so too, it seemed, did reporters. The problem was a misunderstanding of the original meaning of objectivity.

The term *objectivity*, as it relates to newspapers, was coined by media critic and Pulitzer Prize winning columnist Walter Lippmann in the 1920s. The word arose from a discussion of ways to address prejudice in reporting that often led to distortions of fact.[22]

Lippmann called for an objectivity of method, a way to set aside one's prejudices and sift through the evidence to find the truth. But by the 1980s, the term had been reinterpreted in response to accusations of biased reporting. Seeking to meet the demand for objectivity, reporters were pressured to write articles that concealed the fact that they might regard one side of a debate more credible than the other.

The two Little Rock papers exemplify this kind of balanced approach. While they took opposing editorial positions, their coverage, for the most part, followed a "he said, she said" format, devoting equal space to both sides. In a few cases, however, the *Arkansas Gazette*, which editorialized against the law, allowed some breathlessness to creep into its front-page coverage. Clearly excited at having a nationally watched test case in its back yard, it ran numerous photos of a man dressed as a gorilla mugging for cameras outside the courthouse. It ran clever headlines, such as "Creation Took Week in Bible, Trial Is Expected to Last Two."[23] The *Gazette* also spent a good bit of its coverage laying out the constitutional issues at stake in the trial. On the first day of the trial, its edition devoted an extensive amount of space to dissecting what the law actually requires, which included the teaching of "catastrophism," the belief that the Earth was shaped by sudden cataclysmic events, including the occurrence of a worldwide flood.[24]

Meanwhile, the *Democrat* seemed steadfastly against explaining anything. After the first day of trial, it reported, "Expert witnesses also testified Tuesday, saying that creation science is not a science. The state attorney general's office, which is defending the law, objected to their testimony, saying that the definition of science was not an issue in the case."[25]

No details or explanation of creation science or of evolution were provided.

Despite the fact that the trial featured the testimony of renowned paleontologist Stephen Jay Gould, there was surprisingly little information about scientific issues. Nor was there much discussion about whether evolution and religion can coexist—even though much of the plaintiffs' case was devoted to making that point.

Gene Lyons, a columnist for the *Arkansas Gazette*, remembers that the trial was treated by the press as a "regional curiosity." The national media typically sent general assignment reporters rather than science journalists, aiming, he supposed, to foster a more "balanced" approach to the trial.[26]

But if this was the rule, Lyons was the exception. He wrote a brilliant, if scathing, piece for *Harper's* that appeared three months after Judge Overton's decision. In it, he addressed the national media's coverage:

> The statute's very concept of "balanced treatment" derives from, and therefore appeals to, the idea of journalistic fairness taught in the nation's "Schools of Communication." Are there not, after all, "two sides to every question"? Unfortunately that concept, which is shallow enough when dealing with persons holding a post-Enlightenment world view, ill equips a reporter to get at the truth when confronted with persons who do not. Creationists, you see, do not believe that there is or can be a distinction between the sacred and the secular. All ideas to them are religious ideas. Hence they do not hold themselves to the arbitration of facts, evidence, and logic; they reject the metaphysics of science even while claiming its cultural authority.[27]

On January 5, 1982, Overton ruled that the teaching of creation science in public school science class violated the First Amendment's Establishment Clause because it was religion with "no scientific merit or educational value."

Ever balanced, a UPI article said, "ACLU attorney Jack Novik said Overton's ruling had dealt a 'fatal blow' to creation science. But Arkansas Atty. Gen. Steve Clark, who defended the law, said an appeal was 'very probable.'"[28]

In the end, the state declined to appeal Judge Overton's decision, but five years later, the US Supreme Court would strike down another balanced treatment act, the Louisiana case of *Edwards v. Aguillard*. Relying on evidence first presented at the *McLean* trial, the court reached the same conclusion as Judge Overton. Once again, antievolutionists needed to evolve their strategy.

Of Pandas and Bacterial Flagella

ACLU attorney Novik's prediction was correct: *McLean* dealt a fatal blow to creation science. But the trial didn't kill the antievolution movement. Instead, creationists developed a new concept, this one called intelligent design. Similar to creation science, they said intelligent design was based on solid empirical evidence. Reasoning that life was too complex to have evolved through natural selection, they said it must have been intelligently designed, a design that scientists can detect in nature.

After spending years searching for a constitutional test case of intelligent design, in 2004 a Christian legal organization settled on a zealous group of school board members in Dover, Pennsylvania, who wanted to help, as their attorney with the Thomas More Law Center told them, lead "a revolution in evolution."

At the same time, a group of progressive bloggers, including scientists and science writers, were finding their voice. Unlike the conventional media, they felt unconstrained by demands to provide balance or objectivity. Their scientific analyses emerged just in time to become a valuable resource for members of the traditional media who were struggling to understand the issues.

As Ed Brayton, of the science blog *Dispatches from the Culture Wars*, explained, "The nature of online media, both professional and amateur, was so rapidly changing at the time, the number of things one could find on the Internet, and blogs were a huge part of that. . . . [T]he Dover trial came along at a time just when people were starting to take advantage of it."[29]

The science blogs paid close attention in the lead-up to the trial of *Kitzmiller v. Dover*, the first constitutional test case of the concept of intelligent design.[30] Many of the posts revealed the history of intelligent design. On the first day of the trial, Nick Matzke wrote for *Panda's Thumb*, "Due to the *Kitzmiller* case, it is now becoming widely known that the modern 'intelligent design' movement originated as nothing more than a new label for 1980's creationism."[31]

At the same time, many national newspapers focused on dissecting intelligent design and explaining the process of evolution. Unlike articles previewing the start of the *McLean* case, this *Washington Post* article provided a thorough and lovely description of the process of evolution:

> By some accident of nature whose workings neither man could explain, an organism may exhibit a variation in shape, color or body function new to the species. Although most of these new traits are damaging—probably lethal—a small fraction actually help. They may make it easier to hide from predators (like a moth's coloration), exploit a food source (an anteater's long tongue), or make seeds more durable (the coconut's buoyant husk).
>
> If the trait does help an organism survive, that individual will be more likely to reproduce. Its offspring will then inherit the change. They, in turn, will have an advantage over organisms that are identical except for that one beneficial change. Over time, the descendants that inherited what might be termed the "happy accident" will outnumber the descendants of its less fit, but initially far more numerous, brethren. . . .[32]

Cornelia Dean, then science editor of the *New York Times*, neatly addressed the inherent deception in the intelligent design argument, noting, "In theory, this position—'teach the controversy'—is one any scientist should support. But mainstream scientists say alternatives to evolution have repeatedly failed the tests of science, and the criticisms have been answered again and again. For scientists, there is no controversy."[33]

Still, a few strange aspects about the coverage emerged. Rather than sending Dean, the *New York Times* sent its religion reporter Laurie Goodstein to the Harrisburg courtroom. Goodstein's balanced approach to coverage stressed the religion angle and didn't delve into evolution as deeply as a science reporter would have. Still, she offered a complete narrative of daily events and her definition of evolution was concise but forthright:

> Evolution finds that life evolved over billions of years through the processes of mutation and natural selection, without the need for supernatural interventions. It is the foundation of biological science, with no credible challenges within the scientific community. Without it, the plaintiffs say, students could never make sense of topics as varied as AIDS and extinction.[34]

For the most part, when the issues were presented in the clear format of courtroom debate, Goodstein and other nonscience reporters could articulate the science. But when reporters were forced to sift through the information on their own, coverage rapidly fell back on the false dichotomy of "he said, she said."

Evidence of this occurred when President George W. Bush, a month before the trial, said that intelligent design should be discussed alongside evolution in science class. Political reporters, used to covering two-party contests, cast it as a debate between religious conservatives and secular scientists. *New York Times* political correspondent Elisabeth Bumiller interviewed three people who defended Bush and three who opposed him, balancing quotes from scientists with the pro–intelligent design Discovery Institute. She also called intelligent design a theory:

> Intelligent design, advanced by a group of academics and intellectuals and some biblical creationists, disputes the idea that natural selection—the force Charles Darwin suggested drove evolution—fully explains the complexity of life. Instead, intelligent design proponents say that life is so intricate that only a powerful guiding force, or intelligent designer, could have created it. Intelligent design does not identify the designer, but critics say the theory is a thinly disguised argument for God and the divine creation of the universe.[35]

Another example is the coverage by *USA Today*, which noted in one article, "To most scientists, evolution is defined as changes in genes that lead to the development of species. They see it as a fundamental insight in biology. Creationism is the belief that species have divine origin. Another alternative to evolution is called 'intelligent design.' Proponents believe some cellular structures are too complex to have evolved over time."[36]

As these attest, the Seattle-based Discovery Institute was able to exploit reporters' relative ignorance and quest for balance, arguing that intelligent design has been denied a fair hearing. Unlike Dean and even Goodstein, Bumiller and the *USA Today* reporters presented the opposing arguments with equal emphasis, creating the false notion that there was a legitimate debate within the science community and dismissing the overwhelming body of scientific evidence for evolution.

Just as with Mencken in the *Scopes* trial and Lyon in the *McLean* trial, columnists had a terrific time writing about Dover. The *York Daily Record*'s Mike Argento, in homage to Mencken, dubbed *Kitzmiller* "the Dover panda trial," a reference to *Of Pandas and People*, the intelligent design textbook at the center of the debate.

In one dispatch, Argento wrote:

> As an example of their theory, the intelligent design people like to show a photo of Mount Rushmore and ask people to look at it. They ask, could Mount Rushmore have been carved by natural processes? Or was it designed?

> That's the wrong question. The question for these guys should be, can you tell the difference between an inanimate object and a biological organism? So, the Big Bang is supported by physical and experimental evidence that other scientists have confirmed.
>
> And intelligent design is supported by the notion that people can't tell the difference between their lawnmowers and their dogs.[37]

By the end of the six-week trial, few journalists sitting in the courtroom believed that intelligent design was anything but revamped creationism. Judge John E. Jones III reached the same conclusion about intelligent design that Judge Overton had come to about creation science twenty-three years earlier—it was nothing more than religion masquerading as science. In his decision, he wrote, "It is our view that a reasonable objective observer would, after reviewing both the voluminous record in this case, and our narrative, reach the inescapable conclusion that intelligent design is an interesting theological argument. But it is not science."

After Judge Jones settled legal fees for the trial, Christina Kauffman of the *York Dispatch* wrote:

> Legal fees for thousands of hours of attorney services and a six-week trial: $1 million.
>
> Damages paid to 11 parents whose rights were violated in the Dover Area School District: $1 each.
>
> A sense of closure: Priceless.[38]

Objectivity: The Journalist's Scientific Method

At the conclusion of the *Scopes* trial, Mencken famously wrote:

> . . . [E]ven a superstitious man has certain inalienable rights. He has a right to harbor and indulge his imbecilities as long as he pleases, provided only he does not try to inflict them upon other men by force. . . . But certainly he has no right to be protected against the free criticism of those who do not hold them. He has no right to demand that they be treated as sacred. He has no right to preach them without challenge.

The trials of *Scopes*, *McLean*, and *Kitzmiller* reveal the difficulty in covering scientific issues in a fair context.

The coverage of *McLean*, for the most part, followed the dictates of "fair and balanced" journalism. While some newspaper analysis was devoted to the legal and constitutional issues, little space was devoted to exploring the scientific issues that were the reasons for the trial.

Readers who espoused creationism would have come away from such articles with little understanding of how evolution works. While coverage of *Scopes* was often sensationalistic and, at times, filled with cultural stereotypes, there was also reliable coverage about the scientific issues.

Like *Scopes*, *Kitzmiller* captured and sustained national interest, certainly more so than did *McLean*. New media may have played a part in the increased attention. Just as the emergence of radio helped spark national interest in the *Scopes* trial, excitement over *Kitzmiller* was fueled by the Internet. In some cases, blog writers provided sophisticated commentary and helped educate readers about evolution, as well as intelligent design's creationist history. In both *Scopes* and *Kitzmiller*, many mainstream newspapers provided scientific explanations of evolutionary theory, as well as detailed its opponents' failure to present a credible case.

Despite the very good reporting that came from *Kitzmiller*, there also were weaknesses, particularly among general assignment and political reporters who may have felt pressured by standards for objectivity. Those weaknesses were especially apparent in stories by reporters who never came to the courtroom.

The case studies of the trials show that general assignment reporters are most vulnerable to being exploited by parties seeking to portray an issue as controversial and who manufacture controversy through journalists' adhering to a false notion of balance.

The problem, as best evidenced in the *McLean* trial, is that there is a vast misunderstanding of the word *objectivity* among journalists. But Lippmann, in calling for an objective method, was not arguing that reporters should strive to be sponges, soaking up information and then wringing themselves dry again, with nothing retained from their research. Rather, he was calling on the profession to acquire more of "the scientific spirit," that saw objectivity as the "unity of method rather than aim; the unity of disciplined experiment."[39]

Essentially, he was saying that objectivity is the reporters' version of the scientific method. But this notion of objectivity has all too often been replaced by a false equivalency that is devoid of context.

As Mencken so fervently believed, it is the responsibility of the press to challenge false assertions rather than just repeating the two sides of a disagreement.

Journalists have a responsibility to foster an informed citizenry. In the scientific community, there is no debate over evolution. To present the information in any other way coddles lies and does a disservice to readers trying to sort through the information to get to the truth.

NOTES

1. H. L. Mencken, "Mencken Declares Strictly Fair Trial Is Beyond Ken of Tennessee Fundamentalists," *Baltimore Evening Sun*, July 16, 1925.
2. Marcel Chotkowski LaFollette, *Reframing Scopes: Journalists, Scientists, and Lost Photographs from the Trial of the Century* (Lawrence: University Press of Kansas, 2008), 52.

3. Associated Press, "Bill on Creationism Passes in Arkansas," *New York Times*, March 18, 1981, http://www.nytimes.com/1981/03/18/us/bill-on-creationism-passes-in-arkansas.html.

4. David Quamman, "Was Darwin Wrong?" *National Geographic*, November 2004. In a 2001 Gallup poll study, 45 percent of respondents "agreed that 'God created human beings pretty much in their present form at one time within the last 10,000 years or so."

5. David T. Z. Mindich, *Just the Facts: How Objectivity Came to Define American Journalism* (New York: NYU Press, 1997), 9.

6. LaFollette, *Reframing Scopes*, 11.

7. Edward J. Larson, *Trial and Error: The American Controversy Over Creation and Evolution*, 3rd ed. (New York: Oxford University Press, 2003), 42.

8. LaFollette, *Reframing Scopes*, 11.

9. Ibid., 50.

10. H. L. Mencken, "Mencken Likens Trial to Religious Orgy," *Baltimore Evening Sun*, July 11, 1925.

11. "Man with a Tail Reported Located in Tennessee." *Baltimore Evening Sun*, July 6, 1925.

12. LaFollette, *Reframing Scopes*, 27.

13. Watson Davis, "Scientists Begin Reaching Dayton," *Chattanooga Times*, July 14, 1925

14. Rev. T. W. Callaway, "Father of Scopes Renounced Church," *Chattanooga Times*, July 9, 1925.

15. "Baptists Resent Davis' Statement," *Chattanooga Times*, July 13, 1925.

16. H. L. Mencken, "Tennessee in the Frying-Pan," *Baltimore Evening Sun*, July 20, 1925.

17. United Press International, "Scopes Declared Guilty of Violating Tennessee Law Against Evolution," *Baltimore Evening Sun*, July 21, 1925.

18. Larson, *Trial and Error*, 120.

19. Ibid.

20. United Press International, "Creation Science Trial Called Valuable Seminar," *Sarasota Herald-Tribune*, December, 21, 1981, http://news.google.com/newspapers?id=cpocAAAAIBAJ&sjid=GWgEAAAAIBAJ&pg=5867,3488586&dq=creation+science+arkansas&hl=en.

21. Bill Kovach and Tom Rosenstiel, *The Elements of Journalism: What Newspeople Should Know and the Public Should Expect* (New York: Three Rivers Press, 2007), 73.

22. Associated Press, "Creationist-Evolution War Ongoing," Oxnard (CA) *Press Courier*, October 11, 1981, http://news.google.com/newspapers?id=gx1KAAAAIBAJ&sjid=DSINAAAAIBAJ&pg=6676,2575377&dq=mclean+v+arkansas+washington+post&hl=en.

23. George Wells, "Creation Took Week in Bible, Trial Is Expected to Last Two," *Arkansas Gazette*, December 6, 1981.

24. Ibid.

25. Larry Ault, "Battle over Origin Theories Begins Today in Court," *Arkansas Democrat*, December 9, 1981.

26. E-mail interview with Gene Lyons, November 23, 2010.

27. Gene Lyons, "Repealing the Enlightenment," *Harper's Magazine*, April 1982.

28. Associated Press, "Backers of Creation Science Probably Will Appeal Ruling," *Milwaukee Sentinel*, January 6, 1982.

29. Phone interview with Ed Brayton, November 15, 2010.

30. As a newspaper reporter for the *York Daily Record*, the author was a primary reporter covering the trial for the local press. In the interest of fairness, this chapter has no analysis of the author's articles.

31. Nick Matzke, "Why Didn't They Tell Us?" *Panda's Thumb*, September 21, 2005, http://pandasthumb.org/archives/2005/09/why-didnt-they.html#more.

32. Rick Weiss and David Brown, "New Analyses Bolster Central Tenets of Evolution Theory," *Washington Post*, September 26, 2005, http://www.washingtonpost.com/wp-dyn/content/article/2005/09/25/AR2005092501177_pf.html.

33. Cornelia Dean, "Opting Out in the Debate on Evolution," *New York Times*, June 21, 2005, http://www.nytimes.com/2005/06/21/science/21evo.html.

34. Laurie Goodstein, "A Web of Faith, Law and Science in Evolution Suit," *New York Times*, September 26, 2005, http://www.nytimes.com/2005/09/26/education/26evolution.html?scp=1&sq=dover,%20laurie%20goodstein&st=cse.

35. Elisabeth Bumiller, "Bush Remarks Roil Debate on Teaching of Evolution," *New York Times*, August 3, 2005, http://www.nytimes.com/2005/08/03/politics/03bush.html?_r=1&scp=1&sq=elisabeth%20bumiller,%20intelligent%20design&st=cse.

36. Dan Vergano and Greg Toppo, "'Call to Arms' on Evolution," *USA Today*, March 23, 2005, http://www.usatoday.com/news/education/2005-03-23-evolution_x.htm.

37. Mike Argento, "ID—Out with a Bang," *York Daily Record*, October 30, 2005.

38. Christina Kauffman, "Dover Gets a Million Dollar Bill," *York Dispatch*, February 22, 2006, http://www.yorkdispatch.com/searchresults/ci_3535139.

39. Kovach and Rosenstiel, *The Elements of Journalism*, 73.

REFERENCES

Kovach, Bill, and Tom Rosenstiel. 2007. *The Elements of Journalism: What Newspeople Should Know and the Public Should Expect*. New York: Three Rivers Press.

LaFollette, Marcel Chotkowski. 2008. *Reframing Scopes: Journalists, Scientists, and Lost Photographs from the Trial of the Century*. Lawrence: University Press of Kansas.

Larson, Edward J. 2003. *Trial and Error: The American Controversy Over Creation and Evolution*, 3rd ed. New York: Oxford University Press, 2003.

Lebo, Lauri. 2008. *The Devil in Dover: An Insider's Story of Dogma v. Darwin in Small-Town America*. New York: New Press.

Lyons, Gene. 1982. Repealing the Enlightenment. *Harper's Magazine*, April.

Mindich, David T. Z. 1997. *Just the Facts: How Objectivity Came to Define American Journalism*. New York: NYU Press.

Rosenhouse, Jason, and Glenn Branch. Media Coverage of "Intelligent Design." *BioScience* 56 (3): 247–52.

CHAPTER 24

ALTERNATIVE MEDICINE IN THE PRESS

STEVEN BARRIE-ANTHONY

Introduction

In the last few decades, stories about "complementary and alternative medicine" have increasingly become a staple of domestic and international newspaper health coverage. These are often pegged to the dramatic upsurge in the use of alternative health practices or to scientific research on the efficacy of particular treatments. Coverage reporting the rise of alternative health practices does not generally overplay the trend. Research suggests that in the United States roughly 40 percent of adults utilize some form of complementary and alternative medicine and that visits to such practitioners actually exceed visits to conventional primary care physicians.[1] Clearly there is a significant shift happening that merits ink.

But whether journalists are getting at the nature of that shift and its relationship to broader cultural trends and changes is a reasonable question. Print coverage tends to focus most readily on aspects of complementary and alternative medicine (CAM) that can be observed physically and measured scientifically. The philosophical and spiritual systems underlying many CAM modalities, their effects on practitioner and patient, and their relationship to the overall spiritual and religious scene receive less substantive attention. A small amount of research has been conducted on media coverage of CAM, mostly in the United States, Canada, and the United Kingdom (summarized below). Some studies suggest that reporters are far more likely to cite conventional scientific and biomedical rather than CAM sources, and that US newspaper reporters in particular seem dedicated to upholding journalistic "objectivity" in their coverage. The more ephemeral, experiential, spiritual bases of many CAM systems often fit uneasily—or do not fit at all—into a reportorial matrix favoring the objectively observable and measurable.

This approach to reportage, at first glance, seems commonsensical. A pill or procedure either improves ill health or it doesn't, and the scientific method is well credentialed to gauge such black-or-white efficacy. Why should a reporter, assigned to examine the effects of acupuncture on infertility, ask questions about spirituality? Would he or she, in covering the debut of a new Pfizer blood-thinning drug, query scientists or patients about its effects on faith? The National Center for Complementary and Alternative Medicine, a branch of the National Institutes of Health, says nothing of spirituality in defining CAM as "a group of diverse medical and health care systems, practices, and products that are not generally considered part of conventional medicine."[2]

On the other hand, perhaps it is journalistically relevant that many CAM therapies either are directly rooted in religious structures or are more unselfconsciously steeped in spiritual principles. Furthermore, there is religious/spiritual continuity among the therapies. As Michael S. Goldstein and others argue, CAM is more than simply treatments excluded from biomedicine; it also has philosophical and spiritual coherence as a category. For Goldstein, this includes a belief in holism; a focus on the integration of mind, body, and spirit; and a sense of flowing energy that suffuses the body.[3] Granted, particular treatments such as acupuncture are occasionally practiced divorced from religious or spiritual context. More commonly, however, Western practitioners de-emphasize partisan religious content in favor of ecumenical spiritual principles in tune with CAM as a category.[4]

This all might be beside the point for journalists if patients were largely unaffected by the spiritual orientations of practitioners and drawn to CAM as a purely physical alternative when biomedical treatment fails. But on the contrary, mounting research on CAM utilization in the West suggests that (1) the failure of biomedicine is not the most significant predictor of CAM use and (2) spiritual and philosophical content is important to patients. A landmark study conducted in the United States by John A. Astin is persuasive on these points. Contrary to his expectations, Astin did not find "dissatisfaction with conventional medicine" to be predictive of CAM use. Instead, the study indicated that "for many individuals, the use of alternative health care is part of a broader value orientation and set of cultural beliefs, one that embraces a holistic, spiritual orientation to life."[5]

Astin viewed his findings as potentially "reflective of shifting cultural paradigms regarding beliefs about the nature of life, spirituality, and the world in general."[6] The swelling interest in alternative medicine, he suggested, "may represent a type of cultural (Kuhnian) paradigm shift regarding health beliefs and practices"—a paradigm shift in which spiritual and philosophical variables play either *a* key role or *the* key role.[7] If this and numerous subsequent congruent studies are taken seriously, it would seem that attempts to understand the ascent and nature of CAM require inquiry into spirituality as much as into science. And yet, newspaper journalists often prefer biomedical sources and a sense of scientific objectivity in their reporting, which edges out consideration of spirituality. Coverage will occasionally reference the foreign, mysterious religious roots of alternative medicines—often positively—but rarely do reporters situate CAM within the shifting tides of contemporary spirituality and religion.

The present analysis examines journalistic coverage of CAM in light of this disconnect between the religious/spiritual nature of CAM, on the one hand, and the paucity of journalistic attention to such on the other. This entails taking a wide view. American newspaper coverage of CAM since the mid-1960s has taken place in an ideologically polarized environment—for instance, as manifest in the culture wars. Certain scholars have interpreted individual conflicts as symptomatic of overarching tension between opposing frameworks of meaning, between what might be called opposing bases of social solidarity. The present analysis continues in that vein, drawing particularly on categories of solidarity developed by Charles Taylor. Simply put, mainstream US newspaper journalism tends to be more in line with one style of solidarity, and the particular spiritual quality of CAM with another. This often results in implicit competition between observer and observed, which helps account for the de-spiritualization of CAM within the journalistic frame.

Situating US newspaper journalism and CAM within competing bases of solidarity allows for their contextualization as parts of larger movements with coherent historical roots. The trajectories of journalism and modern science are intertwined. Journalists self-consciously molded the "objectivity" ideal, the guiding principle of contemporary newspaper journalism, on the empiricism and rationalism of the scientific method. But despite its affinity with science, there is continuity here with what Robert Bellah calls "civil religion," and the close alliance of church, family, and the state that peaked in 1950s America. The solemn evocation by journalists of their role as the Fourth Estate expresses this civil religious heritage, this authority conferred by divine appointment.

Complementary and alternative medicine, on the other hand, emerges from a different stream. Within the contemporary American religious landscape, the underlying spiritual coherence of CAM aligns with the worldview characteristics of the rapidly expanding category that scholars call "new spirituality," such as the individually defined identity of "spiritual but not religious." As in many CAM systems, the focus within new spirituality is on the authority of individual experience, which often serves as a felt connection to a deep, shared reality whose name (God, nature, energy, oneness) is accepted as variable. Institutional authority loses its jurisdiction here. Recent studies indicate significant overlap between new spirituality and CAM demographics.[8] In terms of historical narrative, it seems reasonable to agree with scholars who interpret the mass adoption of CAM[9] and new spirituality[10] as a diffusion into culture of metaphysical and mystical spirituality.

All of this suggests that the newspaper journalist writing about CAM is involved in profound tensions and shifts. Sticking to the usual scientific and biomedical sources lends the story an air of objective truth, and the reporter feels a reassuring connection to the quasi-religious journalistic tradition; but the story may fall short of its representational aim. Broadening the sourcing and questioning to include spiritual variables on equal footing with scientific ones may better access the phenomenon in question, but it simultaneously lends credence to a framework of meaning that competes with the journalist's professional identity.

A Wide View

Taylor lays out three models of social solidarity, each defined in relation to Emil Durkheim's argument that a healthy society coheres at its base through a religious collectivity.[11] Taylor poses these as ideal types (i.e., there is inevitably some mixing of types within a given society), but he suggests that there is nonetheless chronological momentum, with the dominance of one type transforming into the dominance of the next. Of the three "Durkheimian dispensations," the first is "paleo-Durkheimian," which refers to baroque Catholic societies in which the Catholic Church claimed an overall monopoly on shaping and expressing the social sacred. In these societies a generally shared religiousness and religious authority was woven into the fabric of everyday life.

The second type, "neo-Durkheimian," refers to a society that no longer coheres through a universal church—in the American case, the one church fractured into many denominations. But there remains in the overarching vehicle and spirit of the state a feeling of collective belonging and mission, and therefore coherence in the Durkheimian sense. This is essentially what Bellah refers to as civil religion.[12] In the United States, neo-Durkheimian solidarity peaked in the 1950s, before its widespread contestation in the cultural revolutions a decade later. During this period, "American patriotism, religion, and a sense of family values seemed to be in perfect lock step."[13]

Finally, Taylor discusses a third type, "post-Durkheimian," which surged in the 1960s in the form of numerous interlocking critiques of neo-Durkheimian solidarity. Resistance to the war in Vietnam, adoption among American youth of Eastern religious forms, criticism of conventional sexual mores and gender roles, and a quilt of related movements rapidly undercut the experience of combined purpose that had united church, family, and state just a decade before. The previously shared religious or civil religious framework is here diminished in favor of the authority of individual experience and the inwardly guided search for personal authenticity, wholeness, and integrity. Within this mode of solidarity, the "spiritual" edges out the "religious."

This use of Taylor's latter two categories of solidarity is in line with their recent application by Wade Clark Roof, in which Roof emphasizes "less the shift from one to the other than the tensions existing between the two competing factions who endorse one model or the other, and the ways in which these conflicts are playing out at present."[14] Taylor seems to generally agree that the United States is currently torn between the neo- and post-Durkheimian dispensations and that the resultant tension pervades the culture and destabilizes or "fragilizes" worldview constellations at both ends of the spectrum.[15] Understood as such, the culture wars can be seen as individual flare-ups of an overarching negotiation between these types of solidarity. And insofar as newspaper journalism is rooted in neo-Durkheimian and CAM in post-Durkheimian solidarity, their interaction can be interpreted as a site of this overarching negotiation.

Newspaper Journalism as Neo-Durkheimian

The history of newspapers in the United States is inextricably bound up with the civil religious fabric of the polity. The nation's founders, Jefferson and Madison particularly, spoke reverentially about the free press as fundamental to democracy. Jefferson went as far as to assert, "Were it left to me to decide whether we should have a government without newspapers, or newspapers without a government, I should not hesitate a moment to prefer the latter."[16] The press has never been a monolith, and self-interested publishers and yellow journalism have run astray of Jefferson's vision. But prominent newspapermen and -women have repeatedly sounded a return to the animating charge of the whole enterprise—to defend and promote the hallowed values of the Republic. Writing in 1904 of his founding of the Columbia School of Journalism, newspaper publisher Joseph Pulitzer could have been channeling Jefferson: "In all my planning the chief end I had in view was the welfare of the Republic. . . . Our Republic and its press will rise or fall together."[17]

Scholars have generally focused on expressions of civil religion in the words and documents of the founding fathers, presidential inaugural addresses, ritual displays of patriotism, and so forth. These were on broad display during the 1950s, contributing to the peak of neo-Durkheimian solidarity that Taylor describes above. But the first half of the twentieth century is also replete with civil religious expressions within journalism, functioning to guide an occasionally errant nation back to its (civil religious) roots. The press has, in other words, often operated as the conscience of neo-Durkheimian solidarity, redirecting society to that basis whenever it begins to drift.

In his analysis of civil religion and journalism, Leo Sandon, Jr. nominates the longtime *New York Times* reporter and editor James Reston (1909–95) as a prophet of American civil religion, a "spokesman for the national covenant."[18] Reston is an excellent example of this tradition; his statement of moral philosophy resounds with civil religious feeling:

> The government of our country, I still believe, is the real hope of any moral basis for political action in the world. . . . [T]hat is *the* role of America and has been throughout our history. When we get a Watergate and a Cambodian bombing, that to me is like my country being unfaithful. It is almost as if my wife were unfaithful. This is letting down the noble tradition of America. So I criticize it. It isn't a criticism from a strictly religious point of view. It is an ethical point of view.

> It is historically an effort to remind us that the democratic political system was really "political affirmation" of certain religious concepts . . . the basic ethics of all religions for that matter, but it's not a sectarian thing.[19]

In order for reporters such as Reston to speak "truth to power," to serve as the conscience of neo-Durkheimian solidarity, newspaper journalism has adopted models of truth and authority that are continuous with neo-Durkheimian solidarity. The particulars of such models have shifted over time, and those currently dominant took shape during the process of journalistic professionalization beginning in the late 1880s. During this period, as Richard W. Flory argues, journalism "explicitly patterned itself after the established scientific professions" such as biomedicine.[20] The empiricism and rationalism of modern science became the adopted basis for journalistic truth, and journalistic authority therefore became allied with modern scientific authority.

The modeling of professional journalism after the sciences was in part a simply pragmatic decision. Science conferred great clout. But there was also congruence between the scientific worldview and the mode of solidarity from which journalism emerged and which it was tasked with protecting. Neo-Durkheimian solidarity refers to a diverse society unified by an overarching and implicitly religious vision. This implies that univocal truth is possible, as fundamentally rooted in that vision and mediated by those with the greatest claim to that vision. Positivistic science expresses a consonant objectivism and authority structure, in which truth is discernable via rational observation and dissection. Furthermore, during the neo-Durkheimian high tide, science was widely interpreted harmoniously with civil religion, as advancing the national destiny. So it made sense for journalists to secure special access to scientific authority to keep journalistic truth recognizably true and therefore an efficacious counterbalance to power.

By the 1920s, "objectivity" and "impartiality" had become the creedal watchwords of the journalistic profession. Much as the chemist approaches his laboratory or the surgeon her operating theater, their personal contexts ostensibly irrelevant to the scientific process, so the newspaper journalist attempted to set aside personal bias in favor of "just the facts," of the objectively true. In the following decades, however, as objectivity continued to gain traction as the modus operandi of the American press, countervailing winds were blowing. And in the 1960s, the post-Durkheimian mode of solidarity emerged to powerfully challenge the neo-Durkheimian form. Numerous counterrational movements—in philosophy, art, literature, religion—questioned the very possibility of univocal truth, many advocating instead a radically personal and experiential basis for authenticity. The shared fabric of neo-Durkheimian solidarity was imperiled.

Journalists were not immune to post-Durkheimian momentum. Practitioners of the "new journalism," such as Hunter S. Thompson, Tom Wolfe, and Joan Didion, embraced the subjective lens. Thompson maintained that "objective journalism is a contradiction in terms."[21] But the new journalism appeared mostly in magazines and books, forms less steeped than newspapers in neo-Durkheimian solidarity, less chromosomally invested in its upkeep. More common than defection to outright subjectivism was the sense that, as former *New York Times* foreign editor Sydney Gruson put it, "pure objectivity might not exist, but you have to strive for it anyway."[22] This ambivalent objectivity remains in large part the operative framework in American newsrooms today.

Complementary and Alternative Medicine as Post-Durkheimian

The neo-Durkheimian mode of solidarity assumes a shared ground of belonging upon which individual choice operates. The post-Durkheimian mode, on the other hand, removes that shared ground; there is here "no necessary embedding of our link to the sacred in any particular broader framework, whether 'church' or state."[23] This dynamic tends to undermine historically dominant Western religious, civil religious, scientific, and journalistic claims to univocal truth and top-down authority. Truth is no longer conferred by outside authorities, but emergent from within.

In the 1960s and 1970s, countercultural youth and others within the post-Durkheimian frame moved away from institutional religion and toward a culture of seeking, of spiritual quest.[24] This shift was influenced, after the Immigration and Naturalization Act of 1965 particularly, by the emergence in the United States of numerous Eastern gurus espousing various mystical religious systems and by the intermarriage of those systems with already long-present metaphysical movements and ideas. Many of these mystical and metaphysical forms advocated a personal, experiential approach to spiritual growth that meshed well with the expressive individualism of the post-Durkheimian model. A small but significant percentage of Americans converted to Buddhism, Hinduism, or other Eastern forms or to new religious movements expressing variants thereof. More commonly, seekers adopted aspects of multiple Eastern and Western traditions to form their own pastiche spiritual identities.

This overall genre of spirituality was not confined to the 1960s counterculture. A large body of research on new spirituality indicates "a widespread autonomy of individuals across faith traditions, an openness to mixing and matching of beliefs and practices from a variety of sources independently of religious authority, plus the rise of a self-proclaimed identity as 'spiritual but not religious.'"[25] Studies suggest that roughly 20 percent of the population currently identifies as "spiritual but not religious" and nearly 40 percent as "more spiritual than religious."[26] Clearly, new spirituality and related post-Durkheimian movements are contributing to a major reconfiguration of American religion.

Simultaneously, the widespread adoption of CAM in the United States (and the West more generally) has contributed to a dramatic reconfiguration of medicine and healing. This new medical geography can be seen as substantially divided between neo- and post-Durkheimian modes of solidarity.[27] The biomedical model of truth and authority, which largely reduces the patient to a body subject to physical laws, is here counterbalanced by the surging popularity of numerous CAM systems that view the patient as a fluid constellation of physical, psychological, and spiritual forces. Much as there are philosophical and historical links between newspaper journalism and biomedicine upon the shared foundation of neo-Durkheimian solidarity, so there are links between new spirituality and CAM upon post-Durkheimian ground. Taylor comments on this connection directly:

> A link is created here between spiritual and physical health. . . . Mainstream medicine objectifies the body. . . . But contemporary links between health and spirituality usually take off from alternative kinds of medicine. Far from seeing the body as just an object of natural science, they see it as the site of spiritual currents and flows. Recovering health requires that one put oneself right with these, and this can only be done by opening oneself to them, the very opposite stance from objectification.[28]

Of course, many CAM systems are rooted in ancient Eastern religious systems that long predate contemporary new spirituality. Traditional Chinese medicine emerged substantially from Taoism, Buddhism, and Confucianism; Ayurveda from Hinduism; Tibetan medicine from Buddhism. These medicines often retain their explicit religious foundations when practiced in their countries of origin or in ethnic communities in the West. However, this chapter addresses the widespread adoption of CAM in the United States, where many patients are not intimately familiar with the religious and cultural origins of the treatments in question. In this case, practitioners and patients often replace culturally and religiously specific vocabularies with generalized metaphysical language in tune with CAM as a category. Undoubtedly, spiritual and cultural depth is lost in translation.[29] But for many Western patients, a sense of the spiritual nonetheless remains integral to their experience of treatment.

Other CAM modalities have roots within American metaphysics. Historians have usually ignored the role of metaphysical spirituality in American religious history in favor of churched denominational and evangelical Christianity. However, as Catherine L. Albanese documents, metaphysical spirituality has always been an important part of the American religious picture, and it has often been concerned with healing.[30] Robert Fuller argues that "a good many of our alternative healing systems are far more than purveyors of unorthodox medical treatments. They are also purveyors of a rich spiritual heritage—the American metaphysical tradition."[31]

A growing body of research on CAM includes spirituality as a variable, much of it confirming the importance of spirituality in CAM treatments for both practitioners and patients. Studies along these lines often corroborate and expand upon Astin's conclusion that alternative health care involves "a broader value orientation and set of cultural beliefs, one that embraces a holistic, spiritual orientation to life."[32] Patients may initially seek out CAM for purely physical reasons, but many experience broader effects of treatment, such as what researchers refer to as "whole person effects" including "changes in personal and social identity."[33] Furthermore, some studies indicate that patients who seek CAM for purely physical conditions tend to later revise their treatment aims to include nonphysical effects, sometimes as a higher priority than physical ones.[34]

Several recent studies of spirituality in CAM make it sound distinctly post-Durkheimian. One representative 2009 study compared the religious perspectives of biomedical doctors and CAM practitioners. CAM practitioners were three times more likely than the biomedical doctors to have no particular religious affiliation, but were more likely to self-describe as "very spiritual" and to "agree they try to carry religious beliefs into life's dealings." The authors surmise that "interest in CAM is related to shifts away from religious orthodoxy and tradition toward more individualized notions of spirituality."[35] Other studies likewise characterize CAM patients as more spiritual than religious[36] and as expressing individualized spiritual worldviews that sound much like new spirituality in their mystical and metaphysical valence.[37]

In all, it seems fair to say that for many CAM patients and practitioners, spirituality is a vitally important ingredient within the experience of treatment—and that such spirituality overlaps substantially with new spirituality. Furthermore, the intertwining CAM and new spirituality movements in the United States can be seen as largely post-Durkheimian.

Representation Across Paradigms

One of the earliest newspaper accounts of acupuncture arrived when James Reston—the *New York Times* reporter and exemplar of civil religion mentioned earlier—was struck with appendicitis during a 1971 reporting trip to Beijing. Chinese biomedical doctors performed his appendectomy, but the crux of Reston's front-page *Times* article came when an acupuncturist treated his postoperative discomfort by inserting "three long thin needles into the outer part of my right elbow and below my knees and manipulated them in order to stimulate the intestine and relieve the pressure and distention of the stomach."[38] Reston felt better, and he spent his convalescence interviewing hospital staff about this modality and its "dramatic cures" reported in the Chinese press.

To gauge the veracity of this "needle and herb medicine," Reston turned mostly to the biomedical doctors surrounding him, whose locus of medical truth was the objectified body. One doctor had been a skeptic at one time, but he had seen the needles work, and "facts are facts." Another recounted having studied the use of acupuncture to treat postoperative constipation by "putting barium in a patient's stomach and observing on a fluoroscope how needle manipulation in the limbs produced movement and relief in the intestines." Reston spends little time on his own interior experience of treatment, beyond the straightforward shift in his physical symptoms, nor on discussing with his acupuncturist the treatment system in any depth. These potential sources of truth appear radically epiphenomenal to the rational and objective truth that the journalist and scientists are here seeking together.

Newspaper coverage in the 1970s and 1980s of meditation as a healing modality tended to adopt a similar frame. Such stories were commonly pegged to the research of cardiologist Herbert Benson, who had studied the physical changes during meditation of practitioners of Transcendental Meditation and Tibetan Buddhist monks with an eye toward secularized medical application. On a research trip to India in 1981, Benson measured the temperature of Tibetan monks engaging in "heat meditation" and recorded a skin temperature elevation of as much as eleven degrees. The *Washington Post* covered Benson's findings under the headline "A Team of Western Researchers Verifies Effectiveness of Tibetan 'Heat Meditation'"—language that lays out a top-down authority structure in which Western scientific objectivity is the arbiter of truth. The reporter went into great detail regarding scientific methods and results, whereas interviews about the experience of meditation or its effects beyond the body are absent.[39]

As Americans' interest in CAM grew, the biomedical establishment took greater notice, and newspaper coverage ratcheted up accordingly. In 1991, the National Institutes of Health established the Office of Alternative Medicine (later renamed the National Center for Complementary and Alternative Medicine). The *New York Times* headlined this development "U.S. Opens Door Just a Crack to Alternative Forms of Medicine," straightforwardly conflating the collective United States with the biomedical authority of the National Institutes of Health.[40] The new office aimed to hold CAM up to "rigorous science," and nobody in this lengthy front-page article questions that basis for truth or mentions CAM aims or effects that are off the scientific radar. While the *Times* story quotes both proponents and critics of CAM, the assumed basis for truth is clearly the rationalism and objectivism of the biomedical—and journalistic—model. All of the eleven sources quoted or paraphrased are biomedical doctors. The single CAM practitioner quoted is a "family doctor . . . who practices homeopathy," and her argument is that homeopathy deserves the chance to prove its scientific veracity within the biomedical establishment.

The only mention of spirituality comes at the end: ". . . Many researchers worry that the underlying message of the new office might be part of a larger social trend toward rejecting science and bringing mysticism and New Age culture into the mainstream." Here in bold relief is the tension between scientific objectivism and top-down authority, and the Trojan horse of individualized, experiential new spirituality and healing. The last word of the article goes to a virologist who tries "to be open minded, but I fear this could be part of a general anti-intellectualism. . . . The reality is that the establishment often ignores certain alternative practices for a good reason."

In 1993, the *New England Journal of Medicine* published a study illustrating the tectonic reconfiguration of medicine taking place. Its authors reported that one in three of the adult Americans surveyed had used "unconventional therapy" in the year prior, whether self-applied or through visiting a practitioner. Extrapolating to the full population, the authors suggested that in 1990, Americans had made roughly 425 million visits to CAM providers—more than the number of visits to primary care physicians—and had spent approximately $13.7 billion on such care, roughly on par with the annual out-of-pocket expenses for all hospitalizations in the United States.[41] This and subsequent studies confirming the mass adoption of CAM have inspired a stream of coverage reporting the trend, frequently against the backdrop of biomedical acceptance or rejection of CAM.

New biomedical research evaluating specific CAM treatments serves as a regular peg for stories. The editors of scientific journals will often provide prepublication research findings to journalists, and the resultant newspaper dispatches are typically brief and to the biomedical point; for example, "Acupuncture alleviates pain and improves movement for elderly people suffering from arthritis in their knees, according to a major federally sponsored study released yesterday."[42] Coverage may lead with the popularity of a treatment, followed by a summary of relevant biomedical research. Feature-style reporting on CAM often builds stories around anecdotes of successful treatment, with a coda summarizing the opinion of biomedical authorities.

The small amount of research conducted on US and Canadian print media coverage of CAM suggests that it is often positive (although perhaps less so in newspapers than magazines).[43] But research emphasizes that coverage relies far more heavily on biomedical rather than CAM sources[44] and that it is particularly invested in maintaining journalistic objectivity.[45] This leads newspaper journalists to focus on the aspects of healing over which biomedicine and objectivity exercise most naturally their claim to authority, in other words on the physical body and to a lesser degree on the mind.

This framing of CAM limits the journalistic ability to persuasively explain its widespread adoption. As mentioned, CAM patients may initially seek treatment for purely physical conditions, but its effects are often much broader. As one homeopathy patient explained, "What she treats is not just the physical symptoms, but the emotional, the spiritual, the mental as well as the physical."[46] And an acupuncture patient recalled: "So I did get a glimpse of how the ultimate will be when I get there."[47]

The result is representation across paradigms of truth and authority, or modes of solidarity. Newspaper journalism, on the one hand, assumes a shared ground on which to operate, a fundamental civil religious consensus that provides coherence within a diverse society. This is the essence of neo-Durkheimian solidarity. The role of the Fourth Estate as a pillar of this arrangement allows journalism to stand within the consensus and speak truth upon this basis, and its adoption of scientific objectivity reemphasizes its authority in a modern scientific age. CAM and new spirituality, on the other hand, individualize truth and authority. They turn inward, not often to rootless solipsism but rather to deep rootedness in spheres of reality that go by many names—*qi*, truth, energy, God, Goddess, light—or a combination of names, or that are nameless altogether. This internal, experiential ground for truth and authority is the essence of post-Durkheimian solidarity.

Covering complementary and alternative medicine thus puts the journalist in a difficult position. Representing CAM according to the dominant journalistic paradigm entails its description and evaluation according to an objectivist standard of truth in which measurable effects on the body are most important. Such representation is often misrepresentation. However, adopting a representational formula in tune with CAM radically undermines the journalistic claim to truth and authority. How is the journalist to report experiential, spiritual truth as being as valid as empirically demonstrable truth and still maintain authority rooted in a shared reality? And more broadly: if journalism cedes its unitary basis for truth to multiplicity, upon what ground will it speak truth to power and redirect the nation when it goes astray? Reporters on the alternative medicine beat are working across a fault line.

Conclusion

The last half century has witnessed the ascent of CAM into the American mainstream. Newspaper journalists seeking to understand and represent this reconfiguration have generally done so through the lens of objectivity, which entails the application of biomedical measures of efficacy. This vision of CAM largely reduces its analysis to effects upon the physical body, or occasionally upon the mind. However, this hypothesis is hard pressed to explain the full breadth of the trend, and it is undercut by convincing research on CAM emphasizing the importance for its practitioners and patients of spiritual and other nonphysical effects and its overlap with new spirituality.

The models of social solidarity advanced by Taylor help to explain this disconnect between observer and observed. American newspaper journalism can be seen as largely rooted in neo-Durkheimian solidarity, which assumes a shared ground of civil religious belonging that peaked with the 1950s-style alliance of family, church, and state. CAM as it has been widely adopted in the United States, on the other hand, can be understood as rooted within post-Durkheimian solidarity, which eschews the interposition of an externally applied collective basis for truth and top-down authority in favor of experiential approaches to health and well-being. When journalism and CAM converge, tension between their underlying modes of solidarity commonly results in de-spiritualized representations of CAM. Journalistic coverage of CAM thus provides a window into the ongoing negotiation between overarching models of solidarity that constitutes a key project in American culture at large.

NOTES

1. David M. Eisenberg and others, "Trends in Alternative Medicine Use in the United States, 1990–1997: Results of a Follow-up National Survey," *Journal of the American Medical Association* 280, no. 18 (1998): 1569. More recently, adult CAM utilization in the United States has been estimated at 38 percent.

2. The National Center for Complementary and Alternative Medicine, "What Is Complementary and Alternative Medicine?" http://nccam.nih.gov/health/whatiscam/.

3. Michael S. Goldstein, *Alternative Health Care: Medicine, Miracle, or Mirage* (Philadelphia: Temple University Press, 1999), 40–73.

4. Ibid., 90–91.

5. John A. Astin, "Why Patients Use Alternative Medicine: Results of a National Study," *Journal of the American Medical Association* 279, no. 19 (May 1998): 1553.

6. Ibid., 1552.

7. Ibid., 1553.

8. Regarding clinicians, see Farr A. Curlin and others, "Religion, Clinicians, and the Integration of Complementary and Alternative Medicines," *Journal of Alternative and Complementary Medicine* 15, no. 9 (2009): 991. Regarding patients, see Merrijoy Kelner and Beverly Wellman, "Health Care and Consumer Choice: Medical and Alternative Therapies," *Social Science and Medicine* 45, no. 2 (1997): 205.

9. Robert C. Fuller, *Alternative Medicine and American Religious Life* (New York: Oxford University Press, 1989).

10. Catherine L. Albanese, "Introduction," in *American Spiritualities: A Reader*, ed. Catherine L. Albanese (Bloomington: Indiana University Press, 2001), 1–15.

11. Charles Taylor, *A Secular Age* (Cambridge: Harvard University Press).

12. Bellah equates civil religion with neo-Durkheimianism in Robert Bellah, "New-Time Religion," *Christian Century*, May 22–26, 2002, 20–26.

13. Taylor, *A Secular Age*, 505–6.

14. Wade Clark Roof, "Religion and Social Solidarity: The Case of the United States," unpublished.

15. Taylor, *A Secular Age*, 506, 510.

16. John J. Patrick, ed., *Founding the Republic: A Documentary History* (Westport, CT: Greenwood Press, 1995), 136.

17. James Boylan, *Pulitzer's School: Columbia University's School of Journalism, 1903–2003* (New York: Columbia University Press, 2003), 19.

18. Leo Sandon, Jr., "James Reston: Prophet of American Civil Religion," *The Christian Century*, January 1977.

19. Ibid.

20. Richard W. Flory, "Promoting a Secular Standard," in *The Secular Revolution*, ed. Christian Smith (Berkeley: University of California Press, 2003), 429.

21. David T. Z. Mindich, *Just the Facts* (New York: New York University Press, 1998), 113.

22. Michael Schudson, *Discovering the News* (New York: Basic Books, 1978), 161.

23. Taylor, *A Secular Age*, 487.

24. Cf. Wade Clark Roof, *Spiritual Marketplace* (Princeton and Oxford: Princeton University Press, 1999); and Taylor, *A Secular Age*, 506–8.

25. Roof, "Religion and Social Solidarity."

26. Heinz Streib, "More Spiritual than Religious: Changes in the Religious Field Require New Approaches," in *Lived Religion: Conceptual, Empirical and Practical-Theological Approaches*, ed. Heinz Streib, Astrid Dinter, and Kerstin Söderblom (Leiden: Brill, 2008), 57–60.

27. As in the journalistic and religious realms discussed above, there is within the medical and healing realm some mixing and intermarriage between particular expressions of the solidarity types; but tension between the types significantly colors the realm as a whole.

28. Taylor, *A Secular Age*, 507.

29. Cf. Linda L. Barnes, "Spirituality and Religion in Health Care," in *Cross-Cultural Medicine*, ed. JudyAnn Bigby (Philadelphia: American College of Physicians, 2003), 248.

30. Catherine L. Albanese, *A Republic of Mind & Spirit: A Cultural History of American Metaphysical Religion* (New Haven, CT: Yale University Press, 2007).

31. Robert Fuller, "Subtle Energies and the American Metaphysical Tradition," in *Religion and Healing in America*, ed. Linda L. Barnes and Susan S. Sered (New York: Oxford University Press, 2005), 384. See also Fuller, *Alternative Medicine and American Religious Life*.

32. Astin, "Why Patients Use Alternative Medicine," 1553.

33. Charlotte Paterson and Nicky Britten, "Acupuncture for People with Chronic Illness: Combining Qualitative and Quantitative Outcome Assessment," *Journal of Alternative and Complementary Medicine* 9, no. 5 (November 2003): 671.

34. Tina Cartwright and Rebecca Torr, "Making Sense of Illness: The Experiences of Users of Complementary and Alternative Medicine," *Journal of Health Psychology* 10, no. 4 (2005): 565. See also Alison Gould and Hugh MacPherson, "Patient Perspectives on Outcomes After Treatment with Acupuncture," *Journal of Alternative and Complementary Medicine* 7, no. 3 (2001): 265–66. Gould and MacPherson suggest that this may be limited to acupuncture.

35. Curlin and others, "Religion, Clinicians, and the Integration of Complementary and Alternative Medicines," 987–92.

36. Kelner and Wellman, "Health Care and Consumer Choice," 205.

37. Goldstein, *Alternative Health Care*. See also Jan Van den Bulck and Kathleen Custers, "Belief in Complementary and Alternative Medicine Is Related to Age and Paranormal Beliefs in Adults," *European Journal of Public Health* 20, no. 2 (2010): 229.

38. James Reston, "Now, About My Operation in Peking," *New York Times*, July 26, 1971.

39. Philip J. Hilts, "A Team of Western Researchers Verifies Effectiveness of Tibetan 'Heat Meditation,'" *Washington Post*, January 31, 1982.

40. Natalie Angier, "U.S. Opens Door Just a Crack to Alternative Forms of Medicine," *New York Times*, January 10, 1993.

41. Eisenberg and others, "Unconventional Medicine in the United States," 246.

42. Rob Stein, "Study Says Acupuncture Eases Arthritis Pain," *Washington Post*, December 21, 2004.

43. Cf. Laura Weeks, Marja Verhoef, and Catherine Scott, "Presenting the Alternative: Cancer and Complementary and Alternative Medicine in the Canadian Print Media," *Support Care Cancer* 15 (2007): 937.

44. Brian Vastag and others, "Complementing the Alternative: Newspaper Sourcing of Complementary and Alternative Medicine" (presentation, Association for Education in Journalism & Mass Communication, November 2, 1998). Cf. also Tania Bubela, Timothy Caulfield, and Heather Boon, "Trends in Evidence Based Medicine for Herbal Remedies and Media Coverage," *Health Law Review* 15 (2006): 4.

45. Stephanie Dube and others, "International Coverage of Alternative Medicine: A Comparison of Stories Appearing in American, Asian, British and Israeli Newspapers," *Southwestern Mass Communication Journal* 14, no. 2 (1999): 33.

46. Cartwright and Torr, "Making Sense of Illness," 567.

47. Paterson and Britten, "Acupuncture for People with Chronic Illness," 676.

REFERENCES

Astin, John A. 1998. Why Patients Use Alternative Medicine: Results of a National Study. *Journal of the American Medical Association* 279 (19 [May]): 1548–53.

Taylor, Charles. 2007. *A Secular Age*. Cambridge and London: Harvard University Press.

CHAPTER 25

NEWS COVERAGE OF RELIGION, SEXUALITY, AND AIDS

DIANE WINSTON

On Thursday, November 7, 1991, Earvin "Magic" Johnson stunned fans with the news that he was retiring from basketball. Just days before, during a routine blood test, the Los Angeles Lakers superstar discovered he'd contracted the AIDS virus. The newly wed but legendary ladies man seemed as surprised as everyone else that a disease once thought to plague only homosexuals, Haitians, and hemophiliacs had struck him.

"It can happen to anybody, even me," Johnson said in words that the *New York Times* selected as the quote of the day.[1]

That day, the *Times* featured a slew of stories on Johnson's revelation. There was the requisite page one piece, but the paper also ran reaction pieces, analyses, and a health story that used Johnson to look at the spread of AIDS among heterosexuals. That Johnson, a heterosexual athlete, could have the disease both corroborated and upended many of the cultural and sexual tropes that had previously defined AIDS and its coverage. In the wake of the announcement, black churches vowed to raise the once-taboo topics of AIDS and safe sex, and heterosexuals realized that they, too, needed to take the disease, and precautions against sexual transmission, seriously.

This chapter will examine how the first decade of AIDS coverage at three large metropolitan newspapers was bound up with issues of religion and sexuality. It will probe the what, when, why, who, and how of coverage to ascertain patterns in framing, sourcing, and contextualization. It will argue that, by 1983, a medical/moral frame for the disease made religion an integral part of the story. Subsequent coverage reflected three dominant tropes: AIDS as a punishment for immorality, as a pastoral challenge for denominations, and as a spiritual trial for the afflicted. In conclusion, it will consider the impact of AIDS coverage in general and on reporting about sexuality specifically. The chapter uses three newspapers, the *New York Times* (*NYT*), the *Los Angeles Times* (*LAT*), and the *Dallas Morning News* (*DMN*), for its analysis.[2]

In 1981, ten years before Johnson's announcement, the *NYT* printed its first story on AIDS, a brief about an unusual cancer occurring among homosexual men. Over the subsequent decade, the *NYT*, reflecting the quandary of newsrooms nationwide, grappled with reporting on the mysterious outbreak. AIDS exposed social and cultural fault lines that made coverage more than just a medical story. Its initial outbreak in the homosexual community made it a story about sexuality and religion, too. In 1981, the majority of American Christians, including Roman Catholics, evangelicals, Mormons, and some mainline Protestants, believed that the Bible not only forbade homosexuality but also strongly condemned it.

Some of those Christians, seeing the success of coreligionists engaged in the civil rights movement, had already organized political campaigns in support of their religious beliefs. If the Supreme Court decisions to ban school prayer (1962) and Bible reading (1963) were not bad enough, these believers felt the so-called "sexual revolution," especially the 1973 Supreme Court decision legalizing abortion, would undermine the traditional family, the backbone of American religion and society. Moreover, the immoral behavior of feminists, pro-choice advocates, and homosexuals would bring God's wrath on the nation.

By the early 1980s, reporters incorporated these believers' frames into stories on religiously contentious social issues. According to popular televangelists, God was angry at America for its sexual offenses. While readers in some regions were familiar with such beliefs, other readers were oblivious. For these news consumers, journalists mainstreamed the televangelists' perspective; large newspapers in particular cited the Reverends Jerry Falwell and Pat Robertson since both had national audiences. (Falwell led the Moral Majority and Robertson headed the Christian Broadcasting Network.) When the ministers said feminists (or "abortionists" or homosexuals) flouted biblical teachings, most reporters neither put the teachings in perspective nor noted what other scriptural texts were disregarded (a list that countenanced slavery and stoning disobedient children).

AIDS appeared against this backdrop, and the tangled narrative of medical and social pathology, overlaid with biblical morality, make coverage of its first decade an intriguing case study of reporting on religion and sexuality. Sex sells because it's replete with magic, mystery, and secrecy. Religion is, too. When mixed together, the combustible energy explodes into headlines of orgiastic cults, adulterous ministers, and abused acolytes. Some nineteenth-century editors, knowing the appeal of a religiously inflected sex scandal, were lax about facts in the rush to publication.

Respectable twentieth-century newspapers had higher scruples, at least when it came to same-sex encounters. According to author Edward Alwood, "Until World War II, homosexuals were unmentionable in American newspapers and magazines."[3] The only exceptions were tabloids and the African American press, which mockingly covered drag balls. The 1948 publication of Alfred Kinsey's *Sexual Behavior in the Human Male*, reporting that male-on-male sexual encounters were more common than previously imagined, could have signaled a change. But another fifteen years passed before most newspapers took note of an increasingly visible gay community and another thirty years elapsed before coverage was routine. That shift was due, in part, to the outbreak of AIDS, a story that the mainstream media initially missed.

In the 1980s, national and regional papers played a primary role in setting the news agenda. Despite audience gains for television news, prestige newspapers, especially the *NYT*, functioned as agenda setters. Print and broadcast outlets nationwide checked them to guide their own coverage, government officials used them for leaks and trial balloons, and policymakers sought to effect change by influencing reportage. The *NYT* and the *LAT* covered cities with large gay populations and significant numbers of AIDS cases. The *DMN* also covered a city with a considerable gay population, but Dallas's location on the buckle of the Bible Belt put its AIDS coverage in a different context. The chapter's first section looks at reporting on the gay community before AIDS, as well as early coverage of the epidemic. Subsequent sections explore three tropes: AIDS as God's punishment, pastoral responses to AIDS, and the epidemic's heterosexual martyrs and homosexual saints. All three overlapped from 1983 on, but by the late 1980s the second and third were ascendant. In conclusion, the chapter examines the impact of AIDS coverage.

"Growth of Overt Homosexuality in City Provokes Wide Concern," *NYT*, December 17, 1963

According to Alwood and other chroniclers of AIDS coverage,[4] gays and lesbians began forming advocacy and support groups in the 1950s. But their outreach efforts had little success. Most mainstream newspapers ignored their bids for accurate coverage. Instead reporters focused on "perverts" whose sexual deviance made them suspect as neighbors, employees, and citizens. In 1963, when the *NYT* finally ran a front-page story ostensibly (or so gay sources thought) on the growing presence of homosexuals in the city, the tone was hostile. An increasingly large and open homosexual population "has become the subject of growing concern of psychiatrists, religious leaders and the police."[5] Not only did homosexuality pose a public safety risk but also its practitioners were deviants who needed psychological help and religious counseling.[6]

As the decade passed, homosexual groups, following the example of civil rights activists, led protests against discriminatory employment practices, police entrapment, and raids on gay bars and clubs. The press paid scant attention. The notorious Stonewall raid, the June 1969 clash between police and gays in New York's Greenwich Village, was barely noted by the mainstream news media. The *NYT's* piece was on page thirty-three and the *Daily News'* story ran on page thirty, inauspicious coverage for a pivotal event in the gay liberation movement.

Coverage picked up in the 1970s as gays and lesbians, similar to members of other liberation movements, marched and lobbied. Mainstream news outlets noted when gays challenged psychiatrists whose denunciations of their alleged deviancy was a media staple. In 1973, when the American Psychiatric Association withdrew its classification of homosexuality as a "mental illness," the decision was widely reported.[7] Gay activists won other battles, too. A growing number of cities added "sexual orientation" to antidiscrimination laws, and an increasing number of public figures—including authors, athletes, and politicians—came out, openly acknowledging their sexual identity.

By the end of the decade, many reporters—encouraged to write about this "new" constituency—profiled a community with its own bars, clubs, music, and fashion, as well as a distinctively uninhibited sexual scene. Journalists also covered an emerging religious backlash against gay rights, coalescing in the 1977 campaign to rescind a Dade County, Florida, antidiscrimination ordinance. Entertainer Anita Bryant, crusading to "Save Our Children," rallied Christians to repeal the statute, which they did by an overwhelming majority. Both types of coverage set gay sexuality over and against monogamous heterosexual families. In stories such as the Florida repeal, opponents of homosexuality explicitly argued the ordinance was immoral and antifamily. In articles about gays' open sexuality, narratives implicitly set "us" against "them," inviting readers to pruriently observe and judge gay behavior.

A mysterious cancer that afflicted gay men did not initially strike mainstream journalists as newsworthy. In 1981, when physician Lawrence Mass wrote about it for the *New York Native*, a small gay newspaper, the disease did not have a name. Several weeks later, the Centers for Disease Control and Prevention (CDC) in Atlanta reported an outbreak of a rare cancer among a handful of gay men in Los Angeles. Soon after, several news outlets, starting with the *LAT*, briefly reported the findings. Another month passed before the *NYT* mentioned the unknown cancer that by then had killed forty-one homosexuals.[8] Despite the rapid spread of the disease, few news outlets provided ongoing or thorough coverage. Communications scholar Larry Gross has speculated that a mix of homophobia, disinterest, and squeamishness kept the press at bay.[9] If a reporter came forward to cover the story, his editor would assume he was homosexual, a liability in many newsrooms. Editors also assumed that readers would not care about a disease that did not directly affect them.

According to Alwood, reporters at the *NYT* had an especially difficult time if they wanted to write about homosexuals or AIDS. Iphigene Sulzberger, the daughter of the newspaper's owner, the wife of its second publisher, and the mother of the then-current publisher, was removed from daily decision making, but her wishes were generally followed. Sulzberger did not want homosexuality to receive prominent coverage. In a 1966 letter to her son, the publisher, she described it as a "perversion," adding, "it should not be played on the front of a section."[10] Moreover, Abe Rosenthal—the metropolitan editor who oversaw the 1963 story on homosexuals' growing visibility and the executive editor when the AIDS crisis began—was considered homophobic by many *NYT* staffers.[11] Thus, despite covering the city with the largest gay community in the United States and the highest number of AIDS cases, the *NYT*'s reportage was, especially in the early years, spotty.

Dallas, despite its Southern locale and large evangelical population, provided a very different scenario. Exact statistics are hard to come by, but the metro area may have had the largest, if not the most visible, gay community in the South. The city also was home to the Cathedral of Hope, the country's largest gay church. Early on, editors at the *DMN* decided to provide aggressive and comprehensive coverage of AIDS. In the late 1980s, it was one of the few mainstream newspapers to assign a full-time reporter to the beat. Throughout the 1980s, the *DMN*'s coverage looked at AIDS from multiple local perspectives—including its impact on individuals, religious groups, and the public health system. It also ran national stories that put AIDS issues in a national context.

By the 1980s, the *LAT* had shed its parochial image. But while East Coast newsrooms were captive to Beltway politics or Wall Street, the *LAT* was known as a reporter's paper, where journalists were encouraged to follow their instincts. The *LAT* was the first mainstream newspaper to report on AIDS and the first to run a front-page story on its spread. The medical reporter wrote the early pieces, but others found angles to follow up. As at many papers, reporting on AIDS intensified as the decade progressed.

Notwithstanding the papers' different approaches, AIDS was not a big story in the early 1980s. Some outlets, including the San Francisco papers, the *Philadelphia Inquirer*, and *Newsday*, provided regular updates and features, but the reticence of the *NYT*, the industry's standard-bearer, provided cover for newsrooms that ignored the growing problem. According to James Kinsella, much of the early AIDS reporting fell to the wire services, the Associated Press (AP) and United Press International (UPI), and focused more on hard news than the crisis's human dimensions.

By 1982, nearly 800 AIDS cases were diagnosed. According to one study, children were increasingly infected, which meant that anyone could be at risk. Although a threat to the general population was quickly dismissed, the implications were clear. By 1983, newspapers were writing about not only the medical and scientific aspects of the disease but also its social and cultural ramifications, which according to religious conservatives were dire.

"Falwell Urges Government Officials to Launch Crackdown Against AIDS," *LAT*, July 13, 1985

The Reverend Jerry Falwell crystallized the conservative religious position when he declared in July 1983 that AIDS was God's punishment against those who "break the laws of nature and the laws of moral decency." A media-savvy fundamentalist, Falwell's pithy condemnations of abortion and feminism had garnered headlines; now reporters cited his, or as he would say God's, opinions on AIDS and gays. In a series of speeches and media appearances, Falwell stated that homosexuality was a sin and that AIDS was divine judgment against a nation that tolerated immorality. Visiting Washington, DC, he urged the federal government to close gay bath houses, monitor gays donating blood, and provide safety guidelines for professionals—including police, doctors, and morticians—who worked with people with AIDS.[12]

The theme of divine judgment had surfaced before Falwell became the go-to source connecting AIDS with God's wrath. In May 1983, an *NYT* piece quoted the Reverend William Sloane Coffin, previously university chaplain at Yale and now the minister of New York's Riverside Church, who ministered to people with AIDS. "'Some felt that this was in some way God's punishment,' he said. 'I reassured them that they have no right in the world to feel in any way that this is God's will. Being gay is not a sin.'"[13] Yet, given societal attitudes toward homosexuals—a 1983 poll found 70 percent of respondents were unsympathetic to gays[14]—AIDS sufferers' internalized shame and guilt was unsurprising. When Falwell gave voice to these sentiments, news outlets used the opportunity to quote a nationally known religious leader. Even opponents repeated Falwell's stance; it was the de facto conservative position.

Throughout the mid-1980s, reporters also cited the argument in articles that treated gays sympathetically. The patient, his family, or a pastor would opine that AIDS was a supernatural judgment and then another religious figure would disagree. Even if this harsh conclusion was absent, Falwell's other concerns—the homosexual threat to families, the need to proactively protect citizens from gays with AIDS, and the immoral nature of homosexuality—were raised by patients' families or religious spokesmen. According to a 1985 *NYT* article, after one of the ministers of the historically "liberal" Riverside Church preached a sermon saying heterosexual marriage was biblically based and deviations were "therefore sin," the congregation was more deeply divided than it had been on any issue since the Vietnam War.[15] Several months later, the paper reported on churches "that have had to struggle with fears over drinking from a common communion cup, even though clerics have said in sermons that there is no evidence that the disease can be transmitted that way."[16] The article noted that ministers nationwide regretted they had not done more to combat negative religious stereotypes about gays and AIDS. These clergy, typically mainline Protestants, had been slower to develop a religious response to AIDS than conservatives whose beliefs led to quick condemnations. The AIDS epidemic pushed many mainliners to reexamine their theological positions on sexuality; several years passed before they could articulate them to the media.

In July 1985, actor Rock Hudson gave AIDS its first celebrity face. Hudson's homosexual orientation had been rumored for years, but speculation became rampant when he began to appear gaunt and listless. His announcement that he had AIDS triggered a media frenzy. According to Kinsella, "media coverage tripled," papers that had relied on the wires started writing their own AIDS stories, and "reporting in print media increased by 270 percent between Hudson's diagnosis and the end of 1985."[17] Hudson's admission spurred a slight change in public opinion, confirmed by an *LAT* poll. While 73 percent of respondents said homosexuality was wrong (the same percentage as in 1973), 41 percent said they "were sympathetic to gays," a rise of 11 percent in two years. Still 28 percent agreed that "AIDS is God's punishment for homosexuals" and 23 percent concurred: "AIDS victims 'are getting what they deserve.'"[18] A subsequent *LAT* article, "AIDS: Rigid Church View Is Fading," reflected both negative and positive findings. Beginning with an anecdote about an evangelical church that refused to baptize an AIDS patient because members feared he would pollute the water, the article documented instances of religiously based prejudice. Yet, midway through, the reporter noted, "religious voices are increasingly departing from the theme that AIDS is God's wrath on homosexuals."[19]

Both New York and Los Angeles papers were particularly attuned to Roman Catholic reaction to AIDS since both cities had large Catholic populations. Coverage illuminated the church's desire to act compassionately while also decrying homosexuality. Reporting on a new Vatican document that did not mention the disease but condemned the "pro-homosexual movement," the *NYT* quoted an unnamed Vatican source who noted, "In 1986 AIDS cannot be ignored in any consideration of the moral and ethical issues raised by homosexuality."[20] The pope's words and actions also were scrutinized. The decision whether or not John Paul II would visit an AIDS hospice during his 1987 visit to San Francisco was widely reported (he didn't), as were his attempts to confront the growing health crisis.

Likewise, any time either Cardinal John O'Connor of New York or Archbishop Roger Mahony of Los Angeles addressed the problem, their respective papers took notice. While the *NYT* covered O'Connor's efforts to help people with AIDS, it also reported his strong denunciation of homosexuality and condom use. In 1989, Act Up, an AIDS advocacy group, organized a "Stop the Church" demonstration at St. Patrick's Cathedral to draw attention to O'Connor's opposition to safe sex and abortion. More than 4,500 protesters tried to obstruct services. Even the *Times'* trademark staid reportage could not mask the antic disruption: "Some of the protesters chained themselves to pews inside the cathedral, while others shouted or lay in the aisles."[21] The following day, O'Connor told a reporter that mass would be interrupted only "over my dead body."[22]

A similar protest occurred several weeks later in Los Angeles. But this time, only ten of the fifty activists present participated. During Archbishop Mahony's sermon at midnight Christmas mass, demonstrators walked silently to the altar then left. The archbishop, who hewed the same line as O'Connor but with less edge, elicited less hostility. New York reporters quoted O'Connor's tough talk; journalists in Los Angeles described Mahony's bridge building. At a 1986 prayer vigil, Mahony "broke new ground by addressing Catholic homosexuals for the first time as 'gay Catholics' instead of 'homosexuals.'" Many in attendance were visibly touched: "Morris Kight, a veteran gay activist, leaped to his feet, murmuring: 'This is awesome, simply awesome.' In the pew behind him, a man wearing a tan leather jacket rose, weeping silently and applauding."[23]

Yet a letter that Mahony sent to 2,500 nuns and priests older than the age of sixty-five sparked incredulous headlines. The archbishop requested volunteers for an experimental AIDS vaccine. Since the HIV virus was in the serum, there was a chance that volunteers could be infected, thus spurring a national debate over the ethics of recruiting human subjects for medical trials. Between mid-March and mid-April, the *DMN* ran three stories on Mahony's letter. Dallas's own bishop, Thomas Tschoepe, told the paper that the request did not represent a softening in church policy toward homosexuals but rather an attempt to alleviate suffering.[24] The bishop made clear and the paper made known that compassionate religious responses to AIDS did not mitigate the divine judgment on homosexuality.

"Clerics Offering Support on AIDS," *NYT*, February 24, 1985

As the decade progressed, reporters wrote less about religious condemnations of gays even if, as Bishop Tschoepe insisted, there was no change in the conservative position. But as AIDS coverage shifted from medical reports on the spread of the illness to feature stories on its human toll, journalists wrote more about coping with AIDS and caring for its victims. Inasmuch as people with AIDS asked, "Why me?" and the unaffected wondered, "What should I do?" religion entered many subsequent stories. Even in the earliest days of the crisis, newspapers quoted religious leaders such as Bishop Paul Moore of the Episcopal Diocese of New York affirming the humanity of people with AIDS and seeking ways to serve them. But such stories were more about individuals than institutions, reflecting the time it took for churches and denominations to work through the issues. In 1985, two chaplains at the Texas Medical Center's Institute of Religion in Houston called on *Christian Century* readers to meet the spiritual test: "to abandon a group of people who have almost no one to cry out in their behalf for justice and mercy, would constitute a failure in Christian discipleship."[25]

By the mid-1980s, reporters increasingly explored how religious folks met the pastoral and prophetic challenges posed by the epidemic. Stories usually included a nod to the Falwellian perspective, but religious censure—implicitly contrasted with religious caregiving—appeared misguided, if not wrongheaded. Summing up the sentiment, the lead of a 1985 *NYT* story reported that religious leaders "called on the public 'not to stand in judgment' of AIDS victims, 'but to grow in compassion' for them."[26] Other stories tracked how different faith groups were responding to the illness: the *NYT* reported on a new Passover *haggadah* for people with AIDS, the *DMN* covered Southern Baptist efforts to establish a special ministry, and the *LAT* profiled a gay black pastor starting an outreach program for black AIDS patients.[27] Even articles that were not about religious outreach frequently cited the work of religiously motivated volunteers.

Stories stressing the humanity of AIDS patients and their caregivers coincided with the growing number of people who had contracted the disease through blood transfusions or heterosexual contact. But the religious issue of homosexuality did not go away. In the mid- to late 1980s, stories about clergy with AIDS constituted big news. The *DMN* reported that the disease had struck rabbis, ministers, and priests; there were more than a dozen cases among the nation's 57,000 Roman Catholic clerics and an additional 9 had already died.[28] The news was bad enough for Jews and Protestants, who believed sexual relations should be confined to heterosexual marriage. But it was especially embarrassing for the Catholic Church, which demanded priestly celibacy. It also was the perfect "gotcha" story for newspapers that relished exposing religious hypocrisy.

Still, it was one thing to report on nameless priests who, dying of AIDS, were "transferred into relative obscurity." It was another to disclose that a prominent Methodist bishop, a family man and longtime church bulwark, had died of the disease. Soon after retired United Methodist Church Bishop Finis Crutchfield passed away on May 20, 1987, rumors circulated that he had succumbed to AIDS. The family initially denied the story, but on May 24, the Reverend Charles Crutchfield acknowledged that his father died of AIDS but was not homosexual. The subsequent *DMN* story quoted Crutchfield's supposition that he might never know how his father was infected.[29] A follow-up piece reported that the bishop's death "humanized" AIDS for the church and might nudge it toward accepting homosexuality.[30] Several months later, the *Texas Monthly* broke the story of Crutchfield's closeted gay life, belying his son's speculation that the bishop caught the disease by ministering to AIDS patients.[31]

The *DMN* found members of other faith groups with their own "come to Jesus" AIDS experiences. Two Episcopal priests, the Reverends Chris Steele and Ted Karpf, made AIDS central to their ministries after life-changing encounters. Steele, appointed chairwoman of the Texas Joint Committee on AIDS, was a hospital chaplain when she met a heterosexual businessman who contracted the virus through a blood transfusion. Soon after, she started counseling AIDS patients facing imminent death. "It's the finest thing one can do," Steele told the paper. "To give people hope when they go through the shadow of death was tremendously rewarding for me."[32] Karpf likewise developed an AIDS ministry by chance. A dying young man appeared at his church after other congregations refused to help him. Karpf couldn't turn him away. "I was scandalized that anyone could tell another human being, 'No, we are not going to take care of you.' But it happened."[33]

Religious attitudes were in flux. A 1987 Gallup poll found that Roman Catholic and nonevangelical Christians were among "the strongest supporters of the rights of AIDS victims" and that 50 percent of the public (up 8 percent in four months) disagreed that AIDS was "a divine punishment for moral decline."[34] But the news media singled out one church group as aloof from the crisis. Despite the rising number of African Americans with AIDS, black congregations offered little comfort and even less outreach to the afflicted, according to press reports. In a 1987 *NYT* story, city health officials said there were more cases of AIDS among black and Hispanic men than whites, and that intravenous drug users, 90 percent of whom were black or Hispanic, accounted for over half of AIDS deaths.[35] Two years later, the paper reported that black clergy, "breaking what they say is the silence of many blacks about AIDS," had launched "a local campaign to mobilize nearly 600 congregations by next fall."[36] Public officials, noting that "a disproportionate number" of blacks and Hispanics had contracted the disease, said community activism, especially by churches, is "long overdue." Black churches had been slow to respond, reporters noted, because most believed that homosexuality was a sin.

The combination of a public health crisis and religious conflict kept black churches in the news. A 1991 *DMN* piece reported that even though black gay and bisexual men were two to three times more likely to contract AIDS than whites, AIDS remained a taboo subject in many black congregations. The story profiled the Reverend Willie C. Champion, one of the few ministers who had seen the light. Champion previously preached that God "was using AIDS to punish gays and lesbians." But after a conversion experience, he convinced church members to help people with the disease.[37]

Several months later, after Magic Johnson's announcement, many papers ran stories about the black church response. "Black Ministers Break Silence, Discuss AIDS," read the *LAT*'s headline. The *NYT's* story, "Reluctantly, Black Churches Confront AIDS," was as much about the theological issues that stymied outreach as new church activities. The focus on black churches took the spotlight off white ones with similarly homophobic beliefs. Yet, no black minister threatened Falwell's perch as the conservative quote maker on AIDS and morality.

"'It Was So Unnecessary': S.F. Nun Succumbs After Contracting AIDS from a Blood Transfusion," *LAT*, February 14, 1985

Magic Johnson was not a homosexual, a Haitian, or a drug user, nor had he contracted the virus through a blood transfusion. He was a successful athlete whose irresponsible behavior had disastrous consequences. But even before Johnson proved AIDS could affect anyone, the news media profiled individuals whose tragic plight might stir public sensibilities. Most of these stories fell into two categories: heterosexual martyrs and gay saints. The former were typically women who, infected by tainted blood or bisexual male partners, went public—hoping they could educate others about AIDS. Saints were gay men whose personal sufferings were rendered as public performances of love and religious affirmation.

Sister Romana Marie Ryan was an early AIDS martyr. A "magically gifted" kindergarten teacher, she injured her knee on a class trip and was infected by a blood transfusion during surgery. According to her rector, the "66-year old celibate nun" was "the last person anyone would think would get this kind of disease." Yet even as she faced death, Ryan prayed for the person whose blood she had received and hoped that her passing would spur the search for a cure.[38]

AIDS martyrs usually lived in the paper's catchment area or were types familiar to local readers. The *DMN* profile of Atlanta native Belinda Mason depicted a "white, middle-class, non-drug-using heterosexual housewife from the mountains of Kentucky" who received a transfusion of infected blood. Learning she had AIDS, Mason "dedicated her life to helping others understand the pain, fear and tragedy." Physically devastated with only months to live, Mason remained steadfast in her commitment to changing public opinion—starting with her own Southern Baptist denomination. "It has been dreadful—the way people have acted and the things that people have done in the name of God. . . . It almost makes me ashamed to be a Baptist because I think we can do better than that."[39]

In terms of ink spilt, the martyr most covered during the decade was Ryan White, an Indiana teenager. Beginning in 1985, White—a hemophiliac who had contracted AIDS from a blood transfusion—waged an extended legal and political battle to attend public school. After he won, classmates taunted him and his family was physically attacked. The Whites moved to another town, and Ryan found acceptance in the last years of his life.

AIDS saints likewise modeled grace and courage. Unlike sufferers who said AIDS was a divine punishment, these men felt God's love and yearned to spread it. A 1985 *LAT* profile of the Reverend Steve Pieters explained that the thirty-three-year old gay activist "believes that his sexuality is a gift from God." Pieters, who had AIDS, added, "I believe God is with me, struggling with this disease."[40] Another cleric with AIDS, a Roman Catholic priest in San Diego, told the paper that he could not now go public because of family issues. "But when I die, I think it's important that people know about me and know that I died of AIDS—sexually transmitted AIDS."[41]

Not all saints were clerics or even religiously committed. In a series of stories about people who tested positive for the HIV virus, the *DMN* included twenty-three-year-old Charles, a gay intravenous drug user. Since learning his status, Charles stopped taking drugs and started helping people with AIDS. Although he did not belong to a religious group, Charles saw himself on a spiritual mission, telling the paper that "he was 'standing in the way of the hand of God' until he dedicated himself to helping people with AIDS."[42]

"A Mixed Picture of AIDS at 30," *LAT*, June 5, 2011

At the outset of the AIDS crisis, mainstream news outlets marginalized AIDS coverage. The straight white men who staffed most newsrooms believed their perspectives represented the population at large. Most reporters were uninterested in the gay community unless they saw a sensationalist story or a political fight. As the dimensions of the AIDS epidemic became clear, these two themes—gay libertinism and religious condemnation—created a frame for seeing AIDS as a moral, as well as medical, problem. Some AIDS patients corroborated the theme of disease as punishment for their sins, and conservative clergy avowed it. Even stories that were not about religious responses to AIDS often evoked the moral/medical axis.

As the gay community responded to the crisis and heterosexual caregivers became involved, real life caught up to religious platitudes and many Christians reconsidered their moral positions. When believers interrogated their faith, journalists repeated their questions: Was God a God of love or judgment? Were biblical injunctions against homosexuality cultural artifacts or eternal truths? At the same time, AIDS spread into the straight community, infecting unsuspecting heterosexual partners, as well as infants and children, and weakening the force of religious tropes that blamed the disease on immorality. Religious people told reporters that AIDS called them to serve. Did working through their theological response to AIDS enable some mainline Christians to accept gay, lesbian, bisexual, and transgender (GLBT) people as equal members of the congregation, deserving of ordination and entitled to the sanction of religious and civil marriage? Likewise, did reporting on mainline Protestants' beliefs about gays and activities around AIDS predispose news consumers to rethink their own opinions? Or, on other hand, did hearing Falwellian assertions about gay immorality harden some hearts and convert others?

Academics wrestle with the question of whether journalism reflects public opinion, shapes it, or does a little of both. Insofar as religion influences attitudes about sexuality—which it does directly to the faithful and indirectly through cultural osmosis to many others—coverage of religious responses to homosexuality provides a glimpse into living history. It also offers a way to chart broader and deeper currents of cultural change. Assessments of AIDS need to consider the altered landscape of American discourse. In 1981, for example, few Americans would have taken seriously the possibility of gay marriage—including many gays, who would have scoffed at the notion that mirroring what they saw as an inherently (hetero)sexist, monogamous lifestyle could be a milestone on their own path to liberation. What caused the change? AIDS for one, evolving religious opinion for another, and—arguably—the news media's role in bringing both to the public's attention.

NOTES

1. Richard Stevenson, "Magic Johnson Ends His Career, Saying He Has AIDS Infection," *New York Times*, November 8, 1991, http://partners.nytimes.com/library/national/science/aids/110891sci-aids.html.
2. The *DMN*'s digital archives do not cover 1977 to 1985.
3. Edward Alwood, *Straight News* (New York: Columbia University Press, 1996), 19.

4. Larry Gross, *Up from Invisibility* (New York: Columbia University Press, 2001); James Kinsella, *Covering the Plague: AIDS and the American Media* (New Brunswick, NJ: Rutgers University Press, 1989).

5. Robert Doty, "Growth of Overt Homosexuality in City Provokes Wide Concern," *New York Times*, December 17, 1963.

6. Robert Trumbull, "Homosexuals Proud of Deviancy Medical Academy Study Finds," *New York Times*, May 19, 1964.

7. Richard D. Lyons, "Psychiatrists, in a Shift, Declare Homosexuality No Mental Illness," *New York Times*, December 16, 1973.

8. Lawrence Mass, MD, "Disease Rumors Largely Unfounded," *New York Native*, May 18–31, 1981; Harry Nelson, "Outbreaks of Pneumonia Among Gay Males Studied," *Los Angeles Times*, June 5, 1981; Lawrence K. Altman, "Rare Cancer Seen in 41 Homosexuals," *New York Times*, July 3, 1981.

9. Gross, *Up from Invisibility*, 95–101.

10. Alwood, *Straight News*, 45.

11. Ibid., 163–67.

12. Eleanor Randolph, "Falwell Urges Government Officials to Launch Crackdown Against AIDS," *Los Angeles Times*, July 13, 1985.

13. Glenn Collins, "Facing the Emotional Anguish of AIDS," *New York Times*, May 30, 1983.

14. John Balzar, "American Views of Gays: Disapproval, Sympathy," *Los Angeles Times*, December 20, 1985.

15. "Sex Issue Divides Riverside Church," *New York Times*, May 26, 1985.

16. Joseph Berger, "AIDS Patients Pose Difficult New Test for Clerics," *New York Times*, January 10, 1986.

17. Kinsella, *Covering the Plague*, 144.

18. Balzar, "American Views of Gays," *Los Angeles Times*, December 20, 1985.

19. Russell J. Chandler, "AIDS: Rigid Church View Is Fading," *Los Angeles Times*, June 12, 1986.

20. Roberto Suro, "Vatican Reproaches Homosexuals with A Pointed Allusion to AIDS," *New York Times*, October 31, 1986, A17.

21. Jason DeParle, "111 Held in St. Patrick's AIDS Protest," *New York Times*, December 12, 1989.

22. Todd Purdum, "Cardinal Says He Won't Yield to Protesters," *New York Times*, December 12, 1989.

23. Stephen Braun and William Nottingham, "L.A. Hospice for Victims of AIDS Planned by Archdiocese," *Los Angeles Times*, February 3, 1986.

24. Helen Parmley, "AIDS Vaccine Won't Alter Teaching on Gays, Bishop Says," *Dallas Morning News*, March 14, 1990.

25. Earl E. Shelp and Ronald H. Sunderland, "AIDS and the Church," *Christian Century*, September 11–18, 1985, 797–800.

26. Ari L. Goldman, "Clerics Offering Support on AIDS," *New York Times*, February 24, 1985, 33.

27. Ari L. Goldman, "Modern Concerns Enrich Passover Rituals," *New York Times*, April 18, 1989, B1; Helen Parmley, "Ministry on AIDS Suggested," *Dallas Morning News*, November 5, 1986; Lynn Simross, "Reaching out to Minority AIDS Victims," *Los Angeles Times*, August 15, 1985.

28. Frank Bajak, "Spread of AIDS Forces Homosexuality out of the Clergy's Closet," *Dallas Morning News*, March 22, 1987.

29. Helen Parmley, "Retired Bishop Dies of AIDS," *Dallas Morning News*, May 24, 1987.

30. Tracy Everbach, "Death Seen as 'Humanizing' AIDS," *Dallas Morning News*, May 25, 1986.

31. Emily Yoffe, "The Double Life of Finis Crutchfield," *Texas Monthly* 15, no. 10 (October 1987): 102–6, 188, 190, 192–200.

32. Bill Deener, "Keeping the Covenant Rector Says North Dallas Church Has Commitment to Welcome AIDS Victims," *Dallas Morning News*, August 15, 1987.

33. Sherry Jacobson, "Pastor Active in AIDS Work Quits," *Dallas Morning News*, September 12, 1988.

34. "Gallup Poll Shows Rise in Compassion For People With AIDS," *New York Times*, November 23, 1987.

35. Ari L. Goldman, "AIDS Patients in Dire Need of Finding Solace," *New York Times*, December 12, 1987.

36. Bruce Lambert, "Black Clergy Set to Preach About AIDS," *New York Times*, June 10, 1989.

37. Toni Y. Joseph, "Invisible Men Fear, Denial, and Isolation Touch Gay Men of All Colors, but Black Gays Say Their Suffering Is Doubled," *Dallas Morning News*, June 23, 1991.

38. Dan Morain, "'It Was So Unnecessary': S.F. Nun Succumbs After Contracting AIDS From a Blood Transfusion," *Los Angeles Times*, February 14, 1985.

39. Angela Curriden, "The Face of AIDS Belinda Mason Calls Herself the Conscience of the National Commission on AIDS. Now She Is Dying," *Dallas Morning News*, July 30, 1991.

40. Patricia Ward Biederman, "AIDS-Stricken Pastor Clings to Faith," *Los Angeles Times*, October 10, 1985.

41. Miles Corwin, "Priest with AIDS—'It's Important That People Know,'" *Los Angeles Times*, February 16, 1987.

42. Sherry Jacobson, "The Life Sentence if HIV+," *Dallas Morning News*, May 29, 1988.

REFERENCES

Alwood, Edward. 1996. *Straight News*. New York: Columbia University Press.

Gross, Larry. 2001. *Up from Invisibility*. New York: Columbia University Press.

Kinsella, James. 1989. *Covering the Plague: AIDS and the American Media*. New Brunswick, NJ: Rutgers University Press.

CHAPTER 26

RACE AND RACISM IN NEWS COVERAGE OF RELIGION

MARCIA ALESAN DAWKINS

"MALCOLM X Scores U.S. and Kennedy; Likens Slaying to 'Chickens Coming Home to Roost' Newspapers Chided" read the *New York Times* headline of December 2, 1963.[1] In the 1960s, the American public was embroiled in the civil rights movement that would grant people of color equal rights. At the same time, the nation's newspaper-reading public was preoccupied by an outrage involving Nation of Islam Minister Malcolm X. Malcolm had said that the assassination of President John F. Kennedy was an instance of "the chickens coming home to roost." He went on to characterize Kennedy as a "prison warden," "segregationist," and "crook."[2] Fast forward forty-five years to April 2008, during the candidacy of America's first black president and an infamous YouTube clip titled "God Damn America." The video depicted a sermon in which Rev. Jeremiah Wright expressed anger toward injustices and moral crimes committed by the United States government against people of color. "God damn America for treating our citizens as less than human," Wright declared. "God damn America for as long as she acts like she is God and she is supreme." He continued by stating that the September 11 attacks were a direct consequence of the nation's wrongdoing at home and overseas. "You cannot do terrorism on other people and expect it never to come back on you," he said. The headline for the *Washington Post's* story read "The Audacity of Rev. Wright; A Tale of a Candidate, a Pastor and Some Repugnant Remarks."[3]

Malcolm's and Wright's remarks demonstrate how narratives about race and religion are intertwined in headlines and ideals that suggest "a chosen people" and "a chosen nation." Specifically, America is framed as a chosen nation, and white Christians have been framed as appropriating the status of "chosen people," which once belonged to Jews. However, the presence of black Christians and Muslims in

America complicates and at times opposes this narrative. The press picks up these concurrent themes and turns them into headlines. White Christians' "chosen" status is often treated as a humbling one, as the *Washington Post* reflected when it ran the story "Among Evangelicals, A Kinship with Jews."[4] Black Christians and Muslims (of all racial and ethnic backgrounds) are not assumed to have "chosen" status, so when it is declared the press equates it with claims of racial superiority and ethnocentrism. Journalist Pamela G. Wilson calls this "racialism," explaining that religion reporting depicts black Americans' worldviews to be shaped more by race than by religion.[5] Reporting in the *Washington Post* and the *New York Times* reflects a racialized, and somewhat politicized, view of religion. Headlines about black Muslims read "Cult of Hate: Black Muslims Told They're Chosen People,"[6] "Black Muslims' Hate Campaign Criticized,"[7] and "Farrakhan's Angry World Tour Brings Harsh Criticism at Home."[8] Even today, though the Nation of Islam is not the same movement with the same constituency as it was when Malcolm was alive, it and other Muslim coalitions are often compared to Nazis.[9] Black Christianity also rings of racism in the press, with headlines that read "Pastor Says Race Remains a Big Issue"[10] and articles that quote Wright about attempted reconciliation with the president as "them Jews aren't going to let him talk to me."[11]

These headlines reflect journalistic tropes, as well as the presuppositions of racial groups that believe themselves to be selected uniquely by God to prosper, proselytize, and lead. These headlines also generate important questions about how the press frames race and religion as racism. Some of these questions are philosophical: How is religious practice reported along racial and ethnic lines? Is religion used to justify racism and/or racial privilege? Can religion be framed as a force that inherently resists racism? Or, is it the case that the more devout the religious practitioner, the more extreme the racial pride and/or racism that will be covered? Other questions are more practical: why does so much coverage of race and religion reflect "the tragic fact that when [we] stand at 11:00 on Sunday morning . . . [we] stand in the most segregated hour of . . . America?"[12]

Not much has changed since Rev. Dr. Martin Luther King, Jr. posed that question to Protestants in the 1960s. Today, according to a 2008 US Religious Landscape Survey released by the Pew Forum on Religion & Public Life:

> [O]f the country's estimated 1.6 million adult Buddhists . . . only one-third are Asian—despite the religion's roots in Asia—while a slim majority (53 percent) are white. Among Catholics, 29 percent are Hispanic—the largest proportion in any faith—while Muslims are the most ethnically diverse group, spread among whites, blacks and Asians. Jehovah's Witnesses, meanwhile, are about half white, a quarter black and almost a quarter Hispanic.[13]

Despite current growth trends in racial diversity across religious lines, a recent meta-analytic review since the 1964 Civil Rights Act found that religion, and Protestant Christianity in particular, is practiced mainly within racial groups and, as a result, "a strong religious in-group identity" is often accompanied by "derogation of racial out-groups."[14] In other words, there is an "us" versus "them" paradigm inherent in much of America's religious practice that does not seem to be changing. Only about 5 percent of the nation's Protestant churches are racially integrated and half of these are in the process of becoming all-black or all-white. This trend is reflected in news coverage of race and religion, which generally focuses on the race angle at the expense of the religion angle. In other words, stories about black Christians focus more on race than on religion, and stories about white Christians focus more on religion than on race. Similarly, stories about black Muslims focus more on race, while stories about nonblack Muslims focus more on religion. Thus, reporting of African American religion tends toward racialism at the expense of religion and encourages racism.

Few scandals in recent memory reflect the nature of this racial and religious polarization more concretely than the 1963 controversy over Malcolm X's comments about President Kennedy's assassination and the 2008 controversy over Jeremiah Wright's sermon "Confusing God and Government," dubbed by YouTube "God Damn America." This chapter will compare and contrast these controversies as bookend events for how the mainstream press, represented by the coverage of the *New York Times* and the *Washington Post*, frames race and religion as racism. In this chapter, coverage of race is limited to, but not conflated with, the black-white divide and coverage of religion is limited to Protestantism and the Nation of Islam. Arguing that American religious and racial histories are intertwined, the chapter begins by exploring the coverage of Malcolm's and Wright's comments as examples of how racialized religion is reported. Specifically, the chapter addresses how reporting of African American religion tends to racialize religion and encourage racism by and against African Americans. With that frame in place, the chapter continues by discussing the similarities in coverage between the scandals on the basis of race. Namely, commentary is taken out of context and used to represent the totality of Malcolm's and Wright's messages, as well as the totality of "angry" and racist African American sentiment. The chapter then discusses differences in coverage between the two racist scandals on the basis of religion, focusing on how Protestant/Christian and Nation of Islam/Muslim identities lead to variations in coverage. Despite charges of racism, black Christians fare better in the press than black Muslims because they are seen as members of a preferred religious group. The chapter concludes with a discussion of how reporting on similar controversies differently in the future could aid in resolving a troubled narrative concerned with absolving national sins by overcoming racism.

Race and Religion: A Story in Black and White

David Wills, a historian of African American religion, argues that the most common way of reporting "the story of the United States' religious past is to center it on the theme of pluralism and toleration, the existence of religious variety in America and the degree to which it has or has not been tolerated and even affirmed."[15] Ironically, Willis also argues that the most common way of reporting the story of the United States' racial past is to center it on the theme of an "intractable" racial divide that "seems always to endure."[16] Part of the reason for this intractability is that the concept of race has "varied enormously over time"—having been interpreted scientifically, politically, economically, rhetorically, and religiously.[17] In other words, race also has a creation story and this story affects how issues of race and religion are framed and reported. Sociologists Michael Omi and Howard Winant call this story "racial formation," describing the ways in which "social, economic and political forces determine the content and importance of racial categories, and by which they are in turn shaped by racial meanings."[18] These stories of "racial formation" and separation and "religious pluralism and toleration" represent two sides of the same coin for news coverage. They also shed light on a critical question raised in the remainder of this chapter: why are leaders who endorse religious ideologies of egalitarianism, like Malcolm and Wright, often represented as endorsing racial and ethnic prejudice by the news media?

The best way to answer this question, and explore the controversy over Malcolm's and Wright's remarks, is to understand that adjectives matter—in the sense that there has been something called "African American" or "black" religion.[19] In their particulars these religious traditions stand as refutations of white racism, "a system of meaning and value that could only have arisen out of the peculiar conjunction of modern ideas and values with the political, economic, and technological realities of colonialism and slavery."[20] In one sense, black religion challenges basic assumptions of religious discourse and practice that might be immune, because of racism's deafening qualities, to the available means of persuasion that circumscribe it.[21] In another sense, black religion has provided some of the first public space for African Americans to engage in deliberations around their own material existences and life circumstances. News media generally cover black religion from this deliberative perspective as a primary site for the exercise of citizenship and democratic participation, especially in terms of civil rights and politics.[22] For instance, both the *New York Times* and the *Washington Post* characterized the Nation of Islam as an extremist group who believed that Christianity was the white man's religion and that Islam was closer to African roots and identity. Coverage explained how the movement mixed religious tenets of Islam with black pride and black nationalism, a formula for which Malcolm X became infamous. Jeremiah Wright also comes out of a black nationalist tradition, as he explained to Bill Moyers in a PBS television interview on the *Bill Moyers Journal* on April 25, 2008.[23] However, it is also important to note that Wright's denomination, United Church of Christ, is predominantly white with origins in Puritan New England. Under Wright's guidance Trinity United adopted the slogan "Unashamedly Black and Unapologetically Christian." Keeping in mind that Trinity is part of the United Church of Christ and not part of the African Methodist Episcopal Church, a historically African American denomination, it is important to acknowledge the interracial dialogue that was taking place within that denomination, with Wright at the forefront. Consequently, Wright is a complicated figure. This could account for why his brand of black religion fares somewhat better in the press than the Nation of Islam's, particularly in the *Washington Post*, where coverage addresses black liberation theology in the context of African American political history.

These details are relevant to a discussion of race in the news coverage of religion for several reasons. First, both the *New York Times* and the *Washington Post* concentrate most on the intersection of race (black and white) and religion (Protestantism and Nation of Islam) framed as racism. However, their foci and descriptions of racism vary in relation to whether the parties involved are Christian or Muslim ministers, particularly in a post-9/11 context. When religion and race are at the center of stories in both newspapers during the civil rights era, the primary focus is on Christianity, with lesser focus on race and religion in Judaism and Islam. Since the civil rights era, both newspapers' reporting on religion and race has skewed increasingly conservative and Christian, though issues of equal rights, racial violence, interracial associations, sexual behavior, racial superiority, and racial reconciliation are covered. Since September 11, 2001, both newspapers' reporting on religion and race has increased focus on Islam, while also maintaining a sharp focus on conservative Christian themes and Islamophobia.[24] One interesting aspect of this coverage is that Islamophobia is framed as a relatively recent sentiment sparked by the 9/11 attacks. In addition, the majority of Muslims in the United States are represented as Arab Americans in the press, when the reality is that the majority of US Muslims are African American.[25] So, racialized coverage of religion has now extended from African Americans to include Arab Americans. This is due in part to the fact that Islam has been framed as a foreign religion practiced by foreigners (and though African Americans are racial "others," they are not considered foreigners). Finally, both papers depict anger from black Christians and/or Muslims as misplaced, unfounded, unwelcome, and threatening. This type of anger, seldom heard in mainstream religious discussions, makes some white newspaper-reading audiences uncomfortable and fearful because it not only seems radical and contagious but also emphasizes the legacy of a racial divide. This type of anger also disrupts the preferred religious narrative of pluralism and tolerance, and instead presents Americans with a call to action that would make justice and equality a reality for all. This focus on anger is indicative of what sociologists Lawrence Bobo and Ryan Smith refer to as a "laissez-faire racism" reflected in news reporting—the idea that principled conservative ideals are actually bound up with subtle (and often unspoken) antiblack stereotypes that actually justify or legitimate political inaction.[26]

Laissez-Faire Racism in the Coverage of Malcolm X and Jeremiah Wright

Malcolm X, a minister and national spokesperson for the Nation of Islam, is best known for his tireless efforts in the US civil rights movement. Malcolm used newspaper columns, radio, and television to communicate the Nation of Islam's message across the country and world. Dubbed a "fiery renegade of the Negro radical movement" by the media, Malcolm's ability to attract crowds and controversy made him a news magnet.[27] For instance, in 1959 he was featured in a week-long television special with Mike Wallace. The show, called *The Hate That Hate Produced*, explored fundamentals of the Nation of Islam and Malcolm's emergence as one of its most important leaders. During the early 1960s, racial tensions ran increasingly high and Malcolm was called to comment on a host of incidents, including the Kennedy assassination. In an address delivered on December 1, 1963, at the Manhattan Center, Malcolm talked about how Allah would continue to wreak vengeance on white America until it let its black population go free. When he was asked about the assassination during the question-and-answer period, Malcolm described it as a case of "chickens coming home to roost" and compared it to the assassinations of African freedom fighters that died in coups the Kennedy administration condoned. Malcolm said he "was an old farm boy" and that "chickens coming home to roost never did make me sad; they've always made me glad."[28] When asked to elaborate on these comments in a subsequent interview with Louie Lomax, Malcolm said:

> I meant that the death of Kennedy was the result of a long line of violent acts, the culmination of hate and suspicion and doubt in this country. You see . . . this country has allowed white people to kill and brutalize those they don't like. The assassination of Kennedy is a result of that way of life and thinking. The chickens came home to roost; that's all there is to it. America—at the death of the President—just reaped what it had been sowing.[29]

As a result of these comments and the news frenzy they provoked, Malcolm was silenced, suspended, and later demoted by Nation of Islam officials. Elijah Muhammad was quoted in the *New York Times* saying that Malcolm X did not speak for him or for the Nation of Islam. Yet the paper later reported that "Malcolm has contended that the present civil rights struggle is destined to fail and to provoke bloodshed. This is the traditional view shared by all Muslims."[30]

History seemed to repeat itself when, in March 2008, the media honed in on excerpts from Rev. Jeremiah Wright's sermons that had been telecast in their entirety years before. ABC News and Fox News Channel aired clips of Wright's sermons on March 13, 2008. The excerpted and edited segments appeared on the Internet and other broadcast and cable news outlets in what the press called a "constant loop." Among the clips was the sermon "Confusing God and Government," delivered on April 13, 2003, but now given the new, more sensational title "God Damn America" on YouTube. Viral Video Chart, which catalogs popular videos posted on Google, YouTube, and My Space, identified it as the most viewed video online that week.[31] In the sermon, Wright expressed anger toward hypocrisies, injustices, and moral crimes committed by the US government against Native Americans, African Americans, Africans, and nations of the Middle East. Wright's thesis was three pronged: Governments lie and God does not lie. Governments change and God does not change. Governments fail and God does not fail.[32] According to Wright, the sermon was prepared specifically to address the needs of his black congregation and, at the same time, to provide a warning that God's wrath will be visited on the United States if its hypocrisies, injustices, and moral crimes continue to be ignored. According to ABC News,

> Wright's sermons, offered for sale by the church, found repeated denunciations of the US based on what he described as his reading of the Gospels and the treatment of black Americans. "The government gives them the drugs, builds bigger prisons, passes a three-strike law and then wants us to sing 'God Bless America.' No, no, no, God damn America, that's in the Bible for killing innocent people," he said in a 2003 sermon. "God damn America for treating our citizens as less than human. God damn America for as long as she acts like she is God and she is supreme."[33]

Many black scholars, theologians, reporters, and laypeople resented the way in which Wright's theology was taken to stand in for African American Christian communities at large. An editorial in the *Washington Post* criticizes the coverage of religious rhetoric on the basis of race on several points:

> The media continues to misunderstand religion, whether Islam or black Christianity. Religious rhetoric and sermons are frequently taken out of context and sensationalized for five-second sound bites. Nuance is completely absent. In the Wright case, for example, no sincere attempt has been made to distill the history, theology or circumstances behind any of his comments. We can disagree with what he said, but let us do so with knowledge, not ignorance.[34]

Several themes surface in this editorial. First are the difficulties surrounding racial difference, when those differences disrupt the dominant American religious narrative of unity, universalism, community, and family. Embedded within this discomfort with difference is the need to critique Wright's and Malcolm's black nationalism. As Obama explained in his public response to Wright's remarks, speaking out for racial equality and progress means recognizing what has not changed but also, just as importantly, what has.[35] Gordon Jackson took a different approach in a BlackPressUSA.com article titled "The Wright Stuff: Preacher Preach On" on March 22, 2008. According to Jackson, Wright's perspective "does not assume superiority, nor does it assume separatism. It assumes Africans speaking for themselves as subjects of history, not as objects of history." Mainstream coverage disagreed with this assessment and fired back through opinion pieces expressing that

> if the members of Trinity United believe the reaction to . . . Wright's unmistakably racist remarks has been unfair, they need to reconsider . . . and come up with a fairer approach that can be applied equally to anyone of any race who uses racist language. Otherwise members of this Christian congregation are engaging in un-Christian, race-based hypocrisy of the kind strongly condemned by Jesus. See, for example, Matthew 23:13–36.[36]

Second, mainstream press coverage of Malcolm's and Wright's remarks highlights the "taken for granted" nature of white cultural, political, and economic power.[37] As a result, Malcolm and Wright come off as racial "others" whose religions are "angry" and "radical" in news coverage. Moreover, they appear to undermine the cultural unity that Americans should strive for, a "unity" that has been dominated historically by and continues to privilege white Americans. At the same time the rich religious diversity of African American communities is elided when the press uses Wright and Malcolm to represent black churches and mosques and then to imply that religious institutions would hold similar opinions. An April 27, 2008, an *On Faith* post by Eboo Patel explains why this is an unfair characterization.

> So, how well do the twelve words we know about Jeremiah Wright define the man, the nearly four-decades of ministry, the church he built, the denomination it belongs to, the black community, and whatever else we think he might represent? Are those words the right grain of sand? The Bill Moyers interview with Wright last Friday night went a long way towards illuminating other dimensions of the man. My father—no fan of lefty politics of any stripe—called me after watching the segment with some surprise in his voice. Perhaps he was expecting Wright to cite Stokely Carmichael as his most important intellectual influence instead of Martin Marty, who is probably the most distinguished scholar of religion in America and the very model of thoughtful moderation.

Wright himself echoed these sentiments in an interview with Hamil R. Harris of the *Washington Post* on March 11, 2010, when he said that "they don't hear the whole sermon, and they think that is the story of the church. They need to know the story of the church. It is a profound story." This is one of the reasons Wright addressed the National Press Club on April 28, 2008. Wright asked, "How long do you let someone say something about your faith tradition before you speak up and say something?"[38] Wright went on to answer questions about his sermons, his church, his patriotism, his thoughts on Nation of Islam Minister Louis Farrakhan, and his relationship with then-candidate Obama. In an interview with Michel Norris of National Public Radio titled "Religious Scholars Discuss Liberation Theology," on March 21, 2008, Rev. William B. McClain elaborated on the problem with coverage of black religion in general and Wright in particular: "part of the problem with the snippets that we're hearing of Dr. Wright's sermon is that we don't hear the whole thing. . . . What you don't get is the end of the sermon."

Finally, mainstream press coverage ultimately flattens out differences within racial and religious lives and at the same time raises anxiety levels among many racial groups about all involved. When the mainstream press represents Malcolm and Wright as stand-ins for the whole of black Christianity or Islam, they fail to report that African American religion is made up of a variety of figures, as well as many perspectives.[39] Further, the image of a radical Malcolm X or an angry Jeremiah Wright overshadows the many conservative black congregations that have always been a part of African American religious communities. This kind of shallow representation in the news media forecloses opportunities to redefine, much less accurately report on, what it means to be black or white and Christian or Muslim. Moreover, by overplaying the black-white divide, the press subsequently underreports other demographics, particularly Native American, Pan-Asian, Pan-Hispanic, and new immigrant congregations. In other words, black ministers and preachers appear to be stuck in historical moments that paint their congregants as victims and white Christians as racist oppressors and turn a deaf ear to the experiences of everyone else.[40] For this reason, it is also important to address how news coverage of these laissez-faire racist incidents varies on the basis of religion.

Different Religion, Different Coverage

Historically, stories on white Protestants have dominated religion coverage in the *New York Times* and the *Washington Post*.[41] This white "Protestant bias" has meant that new religions (whether new to the United States or newly minted) such as the Nation of Islam were generally framed as cults. Cults were assumed to brainwash individuals, who would then pose a threat to society. By the late 1980s, the amount of coverage of conservative Protestantism increased sharply and focused largely on local stories. After the terrorist attacks on September 11, 2001, however, more in-depth coverage of Islam began. On one hand, both papers did take time to focus on the various strains within Islam and to provide context and meaning for the events covered. On the other hand, both papers published reports that focused on opinions of government officials and people on the street that equated the word *Muslim* with the word *terrorist* and the words *Nation of Islam* with *radical black movement*.[42] On the whole, today's coverage of the Nation of Islam remains episodic, controversial, and focused on one key figure, the Honorable Minister Louis Farrakhan. Reporting on the current state of the Nation of Islam, the *New York Times* maintains that "the Nation promotes both racism and anti-Semitism and incites hatred of others more than it empowers its own members."[43] This view is in line with the historical news coverage of the Nation of Islam and Malcolm X, which failed to frame Malcolm as the leader of a religious movement but instead portrayed him as an angry black radical. Strikingly, however, something about Malcolm's coverage has changed, particularly in the *Post*: "The Malcolm revered today is the same Malcolm X who stunned a grieving nation when he described President Kennedy's violent death as a case of 'the chickens coming home to roost.' That is now forgotten or forgiven or simply ignored."[44]

Despite today's more favorable memorialization of Malcolm, based largely on the critical acclaim of Spike Lee's 1992 biopic *X*, as well as the popularity of Malcolm's autobiography, news coverage continues to focus superficially on discrete statements made by Nation of Islam ministers. These discrete statements are pigeonholed as racist rather than reported on as statements with underlying religious motivations or connections.[45] Coverage also portrays the Nation of Islam as under attack from within.[46] A notable exception appeared in the *Post* on December 17, 2009, when it was reported that "The Department of Homeland Security improperly gathered intelligence on the Nation of Islam for eight months in 2007."[47] More well-rounded coverage on the Nation of Islam as a bona fide religious movement is scarce.

In contrast, most news reports about Wright's remarks either challenged or disavowed what he said, but none questioned his status as a religious leader and a member of a mainstream religious institution.[48] Yet it is important to note that, except in cases of racist scandal, "newspapers quote, mention and interview conservative religious leaders nearly three times more often than their moderate and progressive counterparts."[49] For instance, most articles in the *Times* reported on Wright from a conservative postracial frame that increasingly distances itself from nostalgia for the civil rights era. This reframing both may be shaped by and may be reflective of the needs and expectations of youthful audiences, who require conversations that are updated for the twenty-first century. *Times* columnist Matt Bai affirms as much when he writes that "for a lot of younger African-Americans, the resistance of the civil rights generation . . . signified the failure of their parents to come to terms . . . with the success of their own struggle—to embrace the idea that black politics might now be disappearing into American politics."[50] In other words, today's post-9/11 and conservative religious coverage precludes affirmations of an oppressed racialized experience like Malcolm's or Wright's. This is because the press has labeled the contemporary moment as a "post-racial" era in which race—read, racism—is dead. Consequently, Wright's framing as someone who cannot let go of the past—read, racism—is what makes him appear dangerous and out of control.[51] What is more, unlike other Christian ministers embroiled in scandal, Wright refused to apologize. This foreclosed any narrative of redemption that the press may have made available to him. It also suggests a continuing discomfort among news organizations in tackling deep questions of how religion may influence many Americans' racial identities and interracial communication practices.[52]

Given the ways in which race and religion have intersected historically, Malcolm's and Wright's cases show why it remains increasingly important for the news media to address the constraints and possibilities of focusing on both race and religion instead of on race at the expense of religion or on different religions. One way of accomplishing this might be to eschew laissez-faire racism by determining whether seemingly nonracial religious stories in fact have racial dimensions. In a diversifying world it behooves reporters to consider how race may operate around issues deemed worthy of news coverage. Journalists should seek out data that disaggregate information by racial groups, seek out diverse sources and news outlets that offer varying perspectives, and consider the ways in which policies, programs, and issues may impact different communities or groups differently. Similarly, news professionals should also determine whether seemingly nonreligious racial stories have religious dimensions by attending to the historical relationships between races and religions. Determinations like this would also help to increase newspaper-reading audiences' general knowledge of religion. This is especially important in light of the *Times'* recent report that "Americans are by all measures a deeply religious people, but they are also deeply ignorant about religion."[53] When this kind of reporting becomes standard practice, then experiences like Malcolm's and Wright's—that are equally spiritual, theological, political, racial, and cultural—can be covered with more accuracy, relevance, and dimension.

NOTES

1. "Malcolm X Scored U.S. and Kennedy: Likens Slaying to 'Chickens Coming Home to Roost' Newspapers Chided," *New York Times*, December 2, 1963.

2. Bruce Perry, *Malcolm: The Life of a Man Who Changed Black America* (Barrytown, NY: Station Hill, 1991), 239–40.

3. "The Audacity of Rev. Wright; A Tale of a Candidate, a Pastor and Some Repugnant Remarks," *Washington Post*, April 29, 2008.

4. Alan Cooperman, "Among Evangelicals, a Kinship with Jews," *Washington Post*, January 8, 2006.

5. Pamela G. Wilson, *Finding Soul Brothers: Dismantling Black Christian Racialism* (Bloomington, IN: AuthorHouse, 2007).

6. Wallace H. Terry, "Cult of Hate: Black Muslims Told They're Chosen People," *Washington Post*, December 15, 1960.

7. Wallace H. Terry, "Black Muslims' Hate Campaign Criticized," *Washington Post*, December 16, 1960.

8. Steven A. Holmes, "Farrakhan's Angry World Tour Brings Harsh Criticism at Home," *New York Times*, February 22, 1996.

9. Brad Hirshfield, "Who's Your Nazi?" *On Faith*, August, 26, 2010, http://newsweek.washingtonpost.com/onfaith/brad_hirschfield/2010/08/whos_your_nazi.html; Richard Cohen, "Obama's Farrakhan Test," *Washington Post*, January 15, 2008.

10. Gregory B. Hladky, "Pastor Says Race Remains a Big Issue," *New York Times*, November 6, 2008.

11. Kate Phillips, "Wright Defends Church and Blasts Media," *New York Times*, April 28, 2008.

12. Martin Luther King, Jr., "Paul's Letter to American Christians," November 4, 1956, http://www.mlkonline.net/christians.html.

13. Brittani Hamm and Adelle M. Banks, "Study Shows Racial Diversity Across U.S. Faiths," The Pew Forum Religion News Service, http://pewforum.org/Religion-News/Study-Shows-Racial-Diversity-Across-US-Faiths.aspx.

14. Deborah L. Hall, David C. Matz, and Wendy Wood, "Why Don't We Practice What We Preach? A Meta-Analytic Review of Religious Racism," *Personality and Social Psychology Review* 14 (2010): 126–39.

15. David W. Willis, "The Central Themes of American Religious History: Pluralism, Puritanism and the Encounter of Black and White," in *African American Religious Thought: An Anthology*, ed. Cornel West and Eddie S. Glaude, Jr. (Louisville, KY: Westminster John Knox Press, 2003), 209.

16. Ibid., 216.

17. Michael Omi and Howard Winant, *Racial Formation in the United States: From the 1960s to the 1980s* (New York: Routledge, 1989), 57.

18. Ibid., 62.

19. In a piece for the *Huffington Post* on February 24, 2010, called "Is the Black Church Dead?" Eddie Glaude advances the claim that the black church is dead, awaiting a resurrection. Glaude notes that a change in historical context has occurred and that there is now a need to change religious tide. This would mean moving away from nostalgia for the civil rights era and moving toward the needs of the current moment. As yet, outside of opinion pieces in the *New York Times* and the *Huffington Post*, this approach has not been taken up by mainstream media outlets. It has, however, been addressed through new media outlets like Facebook and Bloggingheads.tv. In an April 30, 2010, interview with National Public Radio entitled "Is the Black Church Dead: Part Two," Anthea Butler argues that we have imagined the black church to be a powerful source of civic engagement and that we should reimagine it as the "black show." The "black show" is about traditional African American oratorical performance and about how what was known as the black church gets reconfigured in a "post"-racial era. For Butler, the black church is not so much a relic of an ideological past; it is a relic of a media past. While the black church may have been a safe space for intraracial communication, the "black show" is not as insulated.

20. George D. Kelsey, *Racism and the Christian Understanding of Man* (New York: Scribner, 1965), 19.

21. Stephen C. Finely and Torin Alexander, *African American Religious Cultures Volume 1: A-R* (Santa Barbara, CA: Greenwood Publishing Group, 2009).

22. W. E. B. DuBois, *The Souls of Black Folk: Essays and Sketches* (Chicago: A. C. McClurg & Company, 1903).

23. Jeremiah Wright Jr., email to author, November 22, 2009. Wright professes a philosophy that links African American political and social activism with Christianity. Wright served as senior pastor of Trinity United Church of Christ in Chicago, Illinois, from 1972 to 2008. In a personal interview with the author via e-mail, Wright expressed that his "greatest life accomplishment has been helping young people accomplish goals they never dreamed possible by showing them the unlimited potential and possibility God had placed within them when God created them." In conjunction he has also argued with vitriol against events, actions, and attitudes that impact African Americans negatively.

24. Robert Wright, "Islamophobia and Homophobia," *New York Times*, October 26, 2010.

25. "Muslim Americans: Middle Class and Mostly Mainstream," Pew Research Center, May, 22, 2007, http://pewresearch.org/pubs/483/muslim-americans.

26. Lawrence D. Bobo and Ryan A. Smith, "From Jim Crow Racism to Laissez-Faire Racism: The Transformation of Racial Attitudes," in *Beyond Pluralism: The Conceptions of Groups and Group Identities in America*, ed. Wendy Freedman Kakin, Ned C. Landsman, and Andrea Tyree (Champaign: University of Illinois Press, 1998), 182–220.

27. "Extreme Remarks Led to Ouster," *Herald-Journal*, February 22, 1965.

28. Bruce Perry, *Malcolm: The Life of a Man Who Changed Black America* (Barrytown, NY: Station Hill, 1991), 241.

29. Louis Lomax, "A Summing Up: Louis Lomax Interviews Malcolm X," 1963. http://teachingamericanhistory.org/library/index.asp?document=539.

30. M. S. Handler, "Malcolm X's Role Dividing Muslims," *New York Times*, February 26, 1964.

31. Jose Antonio Vargas, "Internet Congregation Responds in Many Voices," *WashingtonPost.com*, March 19, 2008, http://www.washingtonpost.com/wp-dyn/content/article/2008/03/18/AR2008031803229.html.

32. Jeremiah Wright, Jr., "Confusing God and Government" (sermon preached at Trinity United Church of Christ, April 13, 2003).

33. Brian Ross and Rehab El-Buri, "Obama's Pastor: God Damn America, U.S. to Blame for 9/11," *ABCNews.com*, March 13, 2008, http://abcnews.go.com/Blotter/DemocraticDebate/story?id=4443788&;page=2.

34. "Wright Case Misunderstood," *Washington Post*, May 3, 2008, B.9.

35. Barack Hussein Obama, "Remarks of Senator Barack Obama: A More Perfect Union," March 18 2008, http://my.barackobama.com/page/content/hisownwords. (accessed June 9, 2010).

36. Donald M. Malone, "The Rev. Wright's Remarks," *Washington Post*, March 20, 2008.

37. Ashley W. Doane, Jr., "Dominant Group Ethnic Identity in the United States," *Sociological Quarterly* 38 (2005): 375–97.

38. "Jeremiah Wright at National Press Club: Watch Video," *Huffington Post*, April 28, 2008, http://www.huffingtonpost.com/2008/04/28/jeremiah-wright-at-nation_n_98949.html.

39. Jonathan L. Walton, "A Cultural Analysis of the Black Electronic Church Phenomenon" (PhD dissertation, Princeton Theological Seminary, 2006).

40. Eddie S. Glaude, Jr., *In a Shade of Blue: Pragmatism and the Politics of Black America* (Chicago: University of Chicago Press, 2007).

41. Stephen L. Vaughn, *Encyclopedia of American Journalism* (Boca Raton, FL: CRC Press, 2008), 446–47.

42. Ibid., 446.

43. "Nation of Islam," *New York Times*, October 25, 2010.

44. Colbert J. King, "Meir Kahane as Malcolm X," *Washington Post*, November 25, 1990.

45. "Blacks Superior, Students Told," *Washington Post*, February 16, 1996.

46. Peter Noel, "Nations of Islam at War," *Washington Post*, May 25, 1999.

47. Spencer S. Hus and Carrie Johnson, "Documents Show DHS Improperly Spied on Nation of Islam in 2007," *Washington Post*, December 17, 2009.

48. Herb Boyd, "Rev. Jeremiah Wright speaks at CEMOTAP," *New York Amsterdam News*, May 5–11, 2009.

49. Diane Winston, "Press Coverage of Religion Tilts Right," *Huffington Post*, June 7, 2007.

50. Matt Bai, "Is Obama the End of Black Politics?" *New York Times*, August 6, 2008.

51. Colbert I. King, "The Next Willie Horton," *Washington Post*, May 3, 2008.

52. Winston, "Press Coverage of Religion Tilts Right."

53. Laurie Goldstein, "Basic Religion Tests Stumps Many Americans," *New York Times*, September 28, 2010.

REFERENCES

Bobo, Lawrence D., and Ryan A. Smith. 1998. From Jim Crow Racism to Laissez-Faire Racism: The Transformation of Racial Attitudes. In *Beyond Pluralism: The Conceptions of Groups and Group Identities in America*, eds. Wendy Freedman Kakin, Ned C. Landsman, and Andrea Tyree, 182–220. Champaign: University of Illinois Press. http://www.brothermalcolm.net.

Doane Jr., Ashley W. 2005. Dominant Group Ethnic Identity in the United States. *Sociological Quarterly* 38:375–97.
DuBois, W. E. B. 1903. *The Souls of Black Folk: Essays and Sketches*. Chicago: A. C. McClurg & Company.
Glaude, Jr., Eddie S. 2007. *In a Shade of Blue: Pragmatism and the Politics of Black America*. Chicago: University of Chicago Press.
Hall, Deborah L., David C. Matz, and Wendy Wood. 2010. Why Don't We Practice What We Preach? A Meta-Analytic Review of Religious Racism. *Personality and Social Psychology Review* 14:126–39.
Kelsey, George D. 1965. *Racism and the Christian Understanding of Man*. New York: Scribner.
Lomax, Louis. 1963. A Summing Up: Louis Lomax Interviews Malcolm X, 1963. http://teachingamericanhistory.org/library/index.asp?document=539.
Omi, Michael, and Howard Winant. 1989. *Racial Formation in the United States: From the 1960s to the 1980s*. New York: Routledge.
Perry, Bruce. 1991. *Malcolm: The Life of a Man Who Changed Black America*. Barrytown, NY: Station Hill.
Pew Research Center. 2007. Muslim Americans: Middle Class and Mostly Mainstream. http://pewresearch.org/pubs/483/muslim-americans.
Willis, David W. 2003. The Central Themes of American Religious History: Pluralism, Puritanism and the Encounter of Black and White. In *African American Religious Thought: An Anthology*, ed. Cornel West and Eddie S. Glaude Jr. Louisville, KY: Westminster John Knox Press, 2009.
Wilson, Pamela G. 2007. *Finding Soul Brothers: Dismantling Black Christian Racialism*. Bloomington, IN: AuthorHouse.

CHAPTER 27

FOOTBALL AND CHRISTIANITY IN THE NEWS

ANNIE BLAZER

In 1976, *Sports Illustrated* published a series of articles by Frank Deford criticizing the practices of Christian athletes. According to Deford, "Sportians" were not interested in addressing the moral issues of sport like cheating, racism, or exploitation for profit. Instead, "as long as it can work the territory, Sportianity seems prepared to accept athletics as is, more devoted to exploiting sport than to serving it."[1] Deford noticed the prevalence of Christian professional athletes using their sports media coverage to preach an evangelical gospel message. Renowned athletic personalities like Dallas Cowboys coach Tom Landry took an especially big hit as Deford accused Sportians of selling religion "much as they would a new sneaker or a graphite-shafted driver."[2] Football was central to Deford's critique as, much like today, Christian athletes seemed to appear most often in football coverage.[3]

Since the rise of sports ministry organizations in the 1950s and 1960s, Christian sports stars have become adept at using news coverage to promote an evangelical agenda. Celebrity evangelism of this sort is a prominent strategy within the Christian athletic community. For example, a magazine devoted entirely to narratives and successes of Christian athletes, *Sports Spectrum*, has been in print since the 1990s, and a quick search of Christianbook.com returns 473 sports-related books, many the stories of Christian athletic celebrities.[4] Additionally, sports ministry organizations have a definitive presence at big-time sporting events, often hosting events like prayer breakfasts before major tournaments. Deford's critique that evangelicals are more likely to exploit sport than to improve it remains relevant as Christian athletic practices continue to be scrutinized for their moral value in Christian and popular presses.[5]

The now-cliché postgame thanks to God by football players and coaches brings up an important question: how did Christian witnessing become a part of our sports media landscape? And how is football in particular part of this story? This chapter endeavors to answer these questions. While the relationship between media, sport, and Christianity has a long history, the 1950s are particularly important for understanding this relationship in contemporary sports culture. The 1950s saw the rise of national evangelical Christian organizations like Billy Graham's Youth for Christ and Bill Bright's Campus Crusade for Christ. These groups were interested in using popular culture to convey an evangelical message, and one of the most powerful popular culture avenues at the time was televised football. Though Deford heavily critiqued Christian athletes in the 1970s, Christian athletic witnessing did not decline. As this chapter will show, stories of evangelical coaches and athletes fit easily into media narratives of football that have been circulating since the sport was first covered in the popular press in the late nineteenth century. Football, as an unquestioned domain of masculine authority, is particularly appealing for evangelicals who want to present their lifestyle as powerful. Given the masculine narratives that frame sports coverage and evangelicals' ability to use popular culture strategies, Christian athletes will likely remain a part of our sports landscape as these tools remain an effective means of communicating religious belief and garnering press coverage.[6]

The Central Narratives of Football

Newspaper coverage of sports expanded significantly in the late nineteenth century. According to historian of American football Michael Oriard, football became a press staple, appealing because of the format of the sport itself. Football demonstrated American cultural values coming into prominence in the late nineteenth century—specifically corporate efficiency and individual genius. Reflecting this, two narratives consistently emerged in press coverage of the sport—the narrative of the coach as a leader of an efficient corporation and the narrative of the All-American as a hard-working, creative individual demonstrating success through merit.

Walter Camp, the leading football expert in the country at the turn of the century and a major force in promoting the narrative possibilities of football, focused on rationalization and hierarchy in his descriptions of the game. "Camp's own narrative for football's development had a distinct plot: the rationalization and tactical development of the game's action, driven by the object of winning, developed in young men the character and experiences essential for success in America."[7] These experiences were at heart the experience of belonging to a highly efficient workforce headed by a mastermind with grand vision, the coach. The professional coach emerged as a key figure in football at the turn of the century, and media narratives of the coach as visionary (still prominent today) emerged at this time.

A second narrative figure also appeared in late-nineteenth-century football coverage, the All-American. All-Americans, the best eleven players of a season, were selected personally by Walter Camp. According to Oriard, the All-American served to solidify the myth of individual success through hard work and determination. The quarterback was the position most favored for this narrative as the quarterback was seen as the director of the game on the field. The culture of celebrity intensified throughout the early decades of football coverage, and by the 1920s, news accounts conspicuously singled out individual heroes from the team at large.[8]

One reason that these narratives may have appealed to the popular press at the turn of the century was the cultural success of "muscular Christianity." A movement to masculinize religion, muscular Christianity emphasized strength and manliness as Christian obligations and promoted sport as a Christian enterprise.[9] According to historian Clifford Putney, as industry replaced agricultural labor as the defining force in men's lives, "another kind of male dominance, athletic prowess, became a central feature in the definition of manliness."[10] One Methodist minister summed up the ideology, noting that it was as much man's moral duty "to have a good digestion, and sweet breath, and strong arms, and stalwart legs, and an erect bearing as it is to read his Bible, or say his prayers, or love his neighbor as himself."[11] This sort of thinking firmly linked physical strength with moral character.

However, this idea did not catch on everywhere right away. Sport as a necessary feature of Christian manliness was less successful in the turn-of-the-century American South. Sport was banned on Sundays in some states until well into the twentieth century, and football in particular was seen as bestial and lacking in self-control. Many denominational schools in the South banned football until World War I. As historian of sport William Baker notes, "World War I did wonders for sport everywhere in the United States. . . . Newspapers gave extensive coverage to these activities, extolling sport as an indispensible ally in the struggle against the Hun."[12] By the 1920s, football was firmly embraced as part of Southern and Christian culture. This idea continued to undergird American perceptions of sport and, by the 1950s, evangelical Christians interested in presenting Christianity as manly (and therefore powerful) were drawn to professional athletes as particularly effective spokespeople given their prominence in the news.

Television, Advertising, and Sports Coverage in the 1950s and 1960s

Television proved integral to the rise of sports spectatorship on a grand scale. In the United States in 1947, there were around 14,000 television sets; in 1948, 172,000; and by 1950, four million. By 1954, there were thirty-two million sets, and before the end of the decade 90 percent of American homes had a television.[13] The rise of television ownership coincided with a rise in sports programming. According to sports historians Randy Roberts and James Olson, "Not only did sports programming please the affiliates, but it also provided a solid platform for launching the network's fall season. Good sports promoted good ratings."[14]

However, "good sports," in other words, sports that were accessible to more than just die-hard fans, required some technological innovations. In the 1960s, Roone Arledge, an employee of ABC, revolutionized televised sports through targeting the "casual viewer." For football in particular, Arledge saw it as his mission "to get the audience involved emotionally. If they didn't give a damn about the game, they might still enjoy the program."[15] Not surprisingly, the narratives that Arledge used to connect viewers emotionally to the game were the same narratives established by the popular press at the turn of the century. Just as in early football coverage, the coach and the quarterback were the most frequent protagonists.[16]

Sport spectatorship's growth through television and the increasingly common advertising strategy of celebrity endorsement made sports stars ideal candidates for commercials. As scholars of sport and advertising have noted:

> Arguably the entire structure of sport as a form of popular culture is ideally suited to advertising and promotional culture. It is global, yet local and particular. It is exciting for consumers because of its *uncertainty* of outcome, yet attractive to producers and advertisers because it is increasingly *certain* in terms of scheduling, rules and commercial breaks.[17]

This tension between certainty and uncertainty creates attentive consumers and grants sporting celebrities a unique endorsement position. This was a key factor in evangelicals' recruitment of professional athletes as Christian spokespeople. As scholars of postwar evangelicalism have noted, evangelicals were consumers of popular culture and were interested in implementing popular culture strategies in their outreach practices.[18] Evangelicals recognized Christian athletes as men with the power to communicate widely and recruited these individuals to demonstrate their faith publicly, often using the same narratives already established in football coverage.

Evangelical Endorsements

In 1954, Don McClanen wrote letters to a number of athletic celebrities that he knew to be Christian. He told them, "If athletes can endorse shaving cream, razor blades, and cigarettes, surely they can endorse the Lord, too. So my idea is to form an organization that would project you as Christian men before the youth and athletes of this nation."[19] McClanen's letter-writing campaign resulted in the formation of Fellowship of Christian Athletes (FCA), America's first sports ministry organization. Similarly, in the mid-1960s, Dave Hannah, founder of Campus Crusade's sports ministry branch Athletes in Action (AIA), employed advertising and celebrity endorsement language in describing his vision of an athletic ministry. According to AIA historian Joe Smalley:

> The idea for the project came to Hannah one day as he watched a Campus Crusade music group share an evangelistic message through its performance. Hannah thought out loud, "Why couldn't an athletic team be used in the same way? . . . Athletes are used to sell everything from candy bars to cars. Why not have them tell about something far greater—the message of Jesus Christ?"[20]

Two things are evident from McClanen and Hannah's statements. First, they saw the gospel as a consumable product that would benefit from advertising strategies. Second, McClanen explicitly saw a need to present Christianity as masculine by relying on male athletic spokespeople and projecting professional athletes as "Christian men before the youth and athletes of this nation." This demonstrates an enduring link between late-nineteenth-century muscular Christianity and emergent athletic evangelism in the 1950s and 1960s.

The idea of the gospel message as a consumable product had been popularized earlier in the twentieth century. On the campus of UCLA, Bill Bright began Campus Crusade for Christ in 1951. Bright's ministry defined itself through "aggressive evangelism" and prioritized the proclamation of belief and testimony as the first piece of information Christians should share about themselves. To assist Crusade members in this task, Bright created a mass-producible and mass-consumable version of the gospel, first in the form of a memorized verbal speech, and later in print materials. In 1965, he developed a booklet called *Have You Heard of the Four Spiritual Laws?* and, according to Campus Crusade's website, this is the most widely distributed religious booklet in history, with 2.5 billion printed to date.[21] Bright boiled down salvation through Jesus Christ to four concise statements, followed by a short example prayer that the reader could use to start his or her personal relationship with Christ.[22] The genius of the booklet was its high degree of portability and simplicity; salvation was treated as a step-by-step process that could and should be the same for everyone.

Religious studies scholar John Turner's work on Bill Bright emphasizes the impact of contemporary media on Bright's evangelical plan, noting that *Have You Heard of the Four Spiritual Laws?* may have been successful because "perhaps in the era of television, a brief advertisement for Jesus closed an evangelistic sale better than a wordy discourse."[23] It is important to remember that the era of television was also the era of big-time sports coverage on a grand scale. The narratives of sporting heroism circulating in press coverage may help explain why evangelicals would be drawn to athletes as ideal advertisers for the gospel as a product. Hannah and McClanen, the first to recruit Christian athletes as evangelical endorsers on a large scale, were interested in affirming the manliness of Christianity; they recruited athletes to publicly declare a Christian identity in order to grant their evangelical message power and strength.

Scholars of sport and gender have noted the special place of football in maintaining notions of male power and strength. Susan Cahn argues that the assumption of male sporting participation makes it culturally acceptable for men to behave in a dominant fashion.[24] Additionally, Mariah Burton Nelson notes in her book *The Stronger Women Get, the More Men Love Football*, football is routinely treated as evidence of male superiority in debates over co-ed sports. "In no sport are all men better than all women, I point out, and in many sports, women routinely defeat men. . . . So it intrigues me that in response to my discussion of women's athleticism, men change the subject to football. . . . Because 'women could never play football,' they imply, men are physically, naturally, biologically superior."[25]

This understanding of football as a realm of male dominance and male superiority is affirmed in the popular press. For example, ESPN reporter Sal Paolantonio's book *How Football Explains America* notes that one of the most powerful masculine narratives that football coverage provides is "the quarterback as individual protagonist—it had all the makings of compelling dramatic action . . . the violence of man against himself and the field."[26] Given the undeniable emphasis on masculinity in football coverage, it is easy to understand why evangelicals would be drawn to athletes as masculine spokespeople. It also may clarify why contemporary sports reporting tolerates athletes and coaches crediting Jesus in postgame interviews—religious language elevates the importance of football while using God to affirm football's most basic narratives.[27] But, as the following section demonstrates, this was not always the case.

Frank Deford and the 1970s Critique of Christian Athletes

In the 1970s, American evangelicals garnered increased national media attention. According to scholar of American evangelicalism Robert Wuthnow, political events at the time blurred public and private morality. He argues that morality prior to the 1970s was understood as a private choice that should not be dictated by the government. However, key political developments like the Watergate scandal and the Vietnam War served to blur this distinction. The Watergate scandal of 1972 demonstrated that private morality could have significant public effects, and reactions to the Vietnam War were construed as moral positions, with supporting or protesting understood as moral obligations. Wuthnow theorizes that these events led to greater evangelical political engagement by making morality a politically debatable and legally enforceable subject.[28] This was compounded by the election of America's first born-again president, Jimmy Carter, in 1976 and *Newsweek's* cover story labeling 1976 the "year of the evangelical." The popular press had discovered evangelicals and began to investigate them.

By the time *Sports Illustrated* writer Frank Deford published his critique of what he called "Sportianity," evangelical Christians had a presence in nearly every professional sport and had fully launched the campaign to have athletes endorse Christianity. According to Deford, Sportianity was a locker room religion on the rise in professional leagues that entailed a declaration of Christian beliefs yet did not require ethical improvement to sport. He wrote, "In the process of dozens of interviews with people in Sportianity, not one remotely suggested any direct effort was being considered to improve the morality of athletics."[29] Deford conjectured that this lack of attention to sporting morality was connected to sports ministry's dependence on athletic celebrity. According to Deford, the ministry benefited from media promotion of hero worship based on winning. Since sports ministry used the system for evangelism, sports ministers would be unlikely to seek significant changes in the organizing principles of competitive sport or the manner in which sport was covered. "[N]o one in the movement—much less any organization—speaks out against the cheating in sport, against dirty play; no one attacks the evils of recruiting, racism or any of the many other well-known excesses and abuses. . . . Sportianity seems prepared to accept athletics as is, more devoted to exploiting sport than serving it."[30]

Deford was not alone in identifying this relationship as problematic. In fact, his critique remains present in publications aimed at Christian audiences like *Christianity Today*, a high-circulation magazine targeting a Christian readership. In the cover story from February 2010, contributing writer and sports scholar Shirl Hoffman used Deford's terminology to critique contemporary Christian involvement in sports. "Rationalized and systematized, [Sportianity] is vigorously taught to college, high school, and even younger athletes. Its themes crop up in sermons preached from evangelical pulpits and in articles from the religious press. There are, in fact, few alternative ways of thinking about sports and faith in the evangelical community."[31] As Deford's critique remains relevant, it's worth exploring his claims in depth.

In Deford's articles, football received the harshest criticism. Deford presents football players as most susceptible to the evangelical message because they "live more intimately with violence and injury" than athletes in other sports.[32] He accuses sports ministers of confusing Jesus with football. "They worship both, it seems, and, after a time, Jesus and football become indistinguishable."[33] This conflation of football and Christianity relied on much the same narratives established in the popular press surrounding the characters of the All-American and the coach. Deford quotes sports ministers who state that the sports star has impressive selling power, while the coach has personal impact. Given his critique, it is clear that sports ministry programs envisioned athletic celebrities and coaches in much the same manner as they were established in popular press coverage.

In the second and third articles of his *Sports Illustrated* series, Deford tempered his critique somewhat and introduced "Sportians" who were interested in addressing moral issues in sport. In particular, he pointed to an article in the *Christian Athlete* (FCA's member publication) in 1972 entitled "Sports and War." This article included juxtaposed pictures of injured athletes and fallen soldiers in Vietnam, linebackers and the front line. "Sports and War" decried the growing emphasis on winning over team cooperation and cautioned against treating the world like a sporting competition.

> In the midst of the most complex time in our nation's history, we are witnessing a phenomenal growth of our athletic institutions. Sports has become the national conversation, complete with its own peculiar grammar and vocabulary. It has absorbed our passions in its fantasy world of winners and losers. Sports has proved compatible with our view of the world as a dichotomy of winners and losers. In fact, we seem to retreat into sport in order to deny the complexity and ambiguity that marks the political, social, and religious issues of our time.[34]

The article argued that Christian athletes needed to take seriously the conflation of sports and war in America and rethink Christian involvement in both. Deford noted that this critique was not well received in the Christian athletic community and implied that sports ministry was more comfortable with a sales-pitch mentality than with actual systemic change.

> While athletics does not appear to have been improved by the religious blitzkrieg, the religious people who work that side of the street seem to have been colored by some of the worst attitudes found in sport. The temper of athletic religion is competitive, full of coaches and cheerleaders, with an overriding sense of wins and losses, stars and recruiting, game plans and dugout chatter.[35]

Deford even goes so far as to suggest, "It might be a good idea right now to talk to the veteran GM in the sky about the possibility of a rebuilding year."[36]

Because winning is central to gaining cultural attention, Christian athletes tied their evangelistic potential to their win-loss record and understood winning as God's will. For example, Roger Staubach told the press after the 1972 Super Bowl, "I had promised that it would be for God's honor and glory, whether we won or lost. Of course the glory was better for God and me since we won, because victory gave me a greater platform from which to speak."[37] This sort of affiliation between winning and God's will was problematic for a number of reasons. It could not explain why Christian athletes might lose games. It did not take into account that there may be Christian athletes on opposing teams. And it elevated a win-at-all-costs mentality that eclipsed any discussion of the morality of athletic behavior. This infuriated Deford and led to his *Sports Illustrated* articles.

At the time that Deford leveled his critique of Christian involvement in sports, football had come under critique in the popular press for its emphasis on violence, particularly in the context of the Vietnam War. Coverage of Vince Lombardi in the 1960s openly admired his coaching cruelty, but by the 1970s, press coverage was more likely to embrace players like Joe Namath for their rebelliousness.[38] Michael Oriard argues that this shift in the NFL's cult of personality was directly connected to the rise of the counterculture youth movement in America: "Joe Namath had everything that Youth could want—Youth not marching for civil rights or against the war, that is."[39]

For those who were marching in protest of the war or inequality, football may have appeared more like Paul Hoch's Marxist description, an "opiate of the masses," distracting the population from "the illicit violence in today's society—riots, student uprisings, bombings, crime in the streets, and revolutionary deeds. . . . By contrast, the clean, hard violence of football is refreshing and reassuring, because it is done according to rules."[40] Hoch and other critics posited that America's sporting establishment worked to justify American involvement in Vietnam. "It goes without saying that a worker who is so busy rooting for the Yankees that he forgets that his real wages are declining is a good bet to be so busy rooting for the Yanks in Vietnam that he forgets his son might get killed there."[41] Along these lines, Deford's *Sports Illustrated* article quotes Episcopal priest Malcolm Boyd on the dangers of combining Christianity and sport in a time of war: "It is this kind of trying [to win], the kind that this athletic religion teaches, which is killing off so many men, leaving widows. It is very dangerous right now to be trying harder. It is making us more machinelike instead of more human. We'd do better to learn how not to try so."[42]

Contemporary press coverage has had to address a similar problem given US military involvement in Iraq and Afghanistan. Some reporters have conscientiously stopped using language of battle and warfare to describe football "because it disrespects the young American men and women who are actually engaged in combat everyday in Iraq and Afghanistan, or have put on the uniform and got shot at, or had to shoot somebody. Nobody is using bullets on an American football field."[43] Even those that choose to downplay overtly military metaphors tend to stick to established football narratives of coaches as visionaries and star athletes as examples of achievement through merit.

However, as Deford and other critics point out, sport seems to demonstrate not a foundation for moral training as these narratives suggest, but instead an area of moral ambiguity where some ethically questionable behaviors are tolerated, if not encouraged, in the quest for victory. Football is arguably America's most violent sport. Perhaps it is as ESPN's Paolantonio put it, "Being the most violent sport, football has always lent itself to . . . hyperbolic characterizations"—indulged and promoted in television coverage.[44] These hyperbolic characterizations made football an appealing avenue for evangelical Christians who were able to use the basic narratives of football and football's unquestioned masculinity to garner press coverage for Christian athletes. While Deford unashamedly critiqued this practice, contemporary news media not only tolerates but also often contributes to evangelicals' ability to mobilize the narrative possibilities of football.

Contemporary Evangelical Football Narratives and Masculinity

In Deford's critique of "Sportianity," he conjectured that religion is appealing to professional athletes because the sporting world is inherently uncertain. He writes, "The men who stay in sport, coaches who make it their career, tend to be conservative and conformist. In their most indefinite world, they seem to seek assurance and comfort in routine and order, and in religion."[45] While this may help explain why sports ministry appealed to athletes, it fails to address why evangelical Christians were motivated to elevate athletes as Christian spokespeople in the first place and why the media would cover these practices. Recognizing that sport is a domain of masculinity, and that it carries the pretense of being a domain of morality, can help explain the continued presence of Christian athletes in the media. It is masculinity, not just morality, that is integral to the evangelical project of athletic witnessing. But it is morality that remains appealing to the popular press as Christian athletes can serve as evidence that sport continues to fulfill the role of character building it was touted to have in the late nineteenth century.

Arguably, football is the most masculine of big-time sports. As sports scholar Mariah Burton Nelson notes, far more than other sports, football has resisted the participation of women whether as players, coaches, administrators, or reporters.[46] Football uniforms undergirded by protective pads emphasize the male physique by broadening the shoulders. And football relies almost entirely on upper body strength, a kind of strength more easily developed in men.[47] It is these qualities that make football an unquestionably male domain, explaining perhaps why evangelicals were drawn to football as a source of masculine authority. The combination of Christianity and football seems to be accepted in contemporary media coverage because it resonates with football's underlying narratives. This final section explores two contemporary phenomena as examples of this: the Promise Keepers, a men's ministry organization formed by a football coach in the 1990s, and the coverage of quarterback Tim Tebow's evangelical practices. These two examples demonstrate a connection to football narratives established in the popular press—the coach as visionary leader and the quarterback as admirable individual. The continued presence of these narratives in sports coverage, and in coverage of Christianity in football in particular, shows that it is not just morality but also masculinity that constitutes the appeal and effect of these kinds of Christian athletes.

Former football coach Bill McCartney formed the Promise Keepers in 1991 in Boulder, Colorado, in response to a vision he had of filling stadiums with Christian men. His first convention drew 4,200 men, and at its peak in 1996, more than a million men attended stadium gatherings nationwide. The Promise Keepers arranged the "Stand in the Gap" march in Washington, DC in 1997, attended by 700,000 to a million men. According to Promise Keepers' teachings, men are meant to be America's leaders and "moral depravity in our society is due to the lack of appropriate male leadership."[48] Promise Keepers generated significant press coverage in the 1990s, particularly surrounding the Stand in the Gap gathering on the mall in Washington, DC. The media coverage emphasized two aspects of the movement: its explicitly apolitical agenda for the event (praying, not protesting) and the backlash against Promise Keepers by women's groups like NOW that accused Promise Keepers of having a secret political agenda. All in all, media coverage was sympathetic to the Promise Keepers' event and critical of NOW's accusations that the group was antifeminist and antihomosexual.[49] For example, though CNN noted the conservative politics of founder Bill McCartney and NOW's concerns, the bulk of their coverage focused on McCartney's nonpolitical "message of spiritual unity."[50]

Part of the media's sympathy for the organization may have stemmed from the taken-for-granted connection between football coaches and grand vision. Religious studies scholar Becky Beal argues that football was used in Promise Keepers settings to conjure mental images of male superiority and to rally men around the idea of male superiority.[51] This collusion of masculinity and football went unexplored in the popular press. McCartney emerged from the Promise Keepers coverage as a good football coach, a man of grand vision dedicated to improving the moral character of his followers. Using the archetype of the coach as a mastermind and trainer of players long popular in football coverage, reporters described the group as a successful and well-organized project. Perhaps since McCartney's identity as a football coach aligned him with long-established popular press narratives, the media was more sympathetic toward his organization.

This also seems to be the case with football's other major narrative protagonist, the character of the All-American. As noted earlier, the figure of the All-American signified success through hard work and determination, as well as the idea of individual genius, most often cited in the position of the quarterback. This description brings to mind a quarterback famous for his evangelical outspokenness, Tim Tebow. Tebow has become one of the most celebrated and scrutinized players in college football history. Heisman winner and two-time national champion, Tebow is commercially appealing for his talent, but also for his clean-cut image. (For example, *NCAA Football 11*, an Electronic Arts video game, used Tebow as their cover boy.) It's worth noting that when the turn-of-the-century press established the football hero as a cultural icon, nearly all football players were white. In fact, football was seen as a game best suited to "white" skills like organization and coordination.[52] Whiteness continues to be an assumption in the character of the All-American, and Tebow's whiteness may be a factor in his popularity. Pictures of Tim Tebow in the press nearly always show his face (rather than his helmet), and prominently displayed on that face are usually Bible verses written in silver Sharpie over his eye-blacks. According to press coverage, after the 2009 BCS Championship Game, ninety-two million people Googled "John 3:16," the verse on Tebow's eye-blacks that game.[53] The NCAA later banned eye-black messages starting with the 2010 season in what the press called "The Tim Tebow Rule."[54] Coverage regarding this practice generally accepted Tebow's eye-black Bible references as part of his personality and evidence of his strong will and character.

USA Today quotes descriptions of Tebow as "the kind of guy you want your daughter to marry" and "one of the smartest quarterbacks."[55] As journalist Tom Krattenmaker puts it, "As anyone who has seen Tebow on television would know, broadcasters cannot find enough superlatives to describe him. What's not to admire? He plays with a rugged, infectious enthusiasm. He's a born leader."[56] This kind of characterization of Tebow aligns him with one of football's primary narratives, the All-American, and his overt evangelical identity gains more coverage because of the ways he already meshes with football narratives.

Perhaps the most controversial moment of Tim Tebow's career as a Christian athlete was his appearance in a 2010 Super Bowl ad funded by the conservative Christian organization Focus on the Family. Though the ad carried no explicit evangelical content, it generated controversy due to its insinuation that Tim Tebow is living proof that abortion is wrong. The commercial opens with Tim Tebow's mother holding a baby picture of the now-famous quarterback and saying, "I call him my miracle baby." Though the commercial did not mention Tebow's mother's rejection of her doctor's advice to abort the fetus for medical reasons, this story did receive a lot of press in the days and weeks leading up to the Super Bowl. Focus on the Family's decision not to release the commercial's content prior to the Super Bowl led to rampant media speculation as to how Focus on the Family would use Tebow's mother's decision to promote their pro-life stance. As Tom Krattenmaker, an oft quoted source in Tebow stories, put it, "I can't recall ever seeing so much (attention) around one athlete: both incredible respect, incredible accomplishment on the field, sterling character off the field, combined with this level of controversy and discussion and hoopla."[57] Part of what made Tim Tebow a viable candidate for this sort of commercial was not only his outspoken evangelical position but also his identity as a professional football star. The insinuation was that abortion would have prevented the existence of this impressive person, a moral and masculine model for today's youth.

Implicit in this message is the idea that men like Tim Tebow matter, and the answer to why these men matter can be found in the history of the relationship between Christianity, football, and the news. Turn-of-the-century muscular Christians successfully conflated sport and manliness with Christian morality, and the elevation of sporting celebrities through television in the 1950s and 1960s made athletes appealing candidates for evangelical witnesses. Additionally, football coverage narratives rely on particular sorts of protagonists, and evangelicals have been able to use this to their advantage. Because of their success in gaining media attention, it is likely that evangelicals will continue to recruit and promote professional athletes as Christian witnesses. And, so long as evangelical football players and coaches can continue to mobilize the long-established press narratives of the coach and the All-American, they will continue to have a presence in the popular press.

NOTES

1. Frank Deford, "Religion in Sport," *Sports Illustrated*, April 19, 1976, 102. The three-article story spanned three weeks of *Sports Illustrated* publications. Deford, "Religion and Sport," *Sports Illustrated*, April 19, 1976, 88–102; "The Word According to Tom," *Sports Illustrated*, April 26, 1976, 54–69; "Reaching for the Stars," *Sports Illustrated*, May 3, 1976, 42–60.

2. Deford, "The Word According to Tom," 55.

3. Some estimate that 35 to 40 percent of professional football players are evangelical Christians, as opposed to 20 to 25 percent in America generally. See David Plotz, "The God of the Gridiron," *Slate*, February 4, 2000, http://www.slate.com/id/74294/.

4. Christianbook, http://www.christianbook.com.

5. See Shirl Hoffman, "Evangelicalism and the Revitalization of Religious Ritual in Sport," in *Sport and Religion*, ed. Shirl Hoffman (Champaign, IL: Human Kinetics Books, 1992); William Baker, *Playing with God: Religion and Modern Sport* (Cambridge, MA: Harvard University Press, 2007), 217.

6. Within religious studies, there is an ongoing debate over how to define "evangelicalism." Scholars recognize that this term is not self-evident or simple, but in fact envelops a great variety of people and institutions. See Donald Dayton and Robert Johnson, eds., *The Variety of American Evangelicalism* (Knoxville: University of Tennessee Press, 1991). Religious studies scholars tend to cluster and delineate evangelicals in America either through self-identification and measurable behavior or through historical identification of institutions. On self-identification and measurable behavior, see Christian Smith, "Appendix B: On Religious Identities," in *American Evangelicalism: Embattled and Thriving* (Chicago: University of Chicago Press, 1998), 233–47; and Robert Wuthnow, *The Restructuring of American Religion: Society and Faith Since World War II* (Princeton: Princeton University Press, 1988). On historical and institutional identification, see Mark A. Noll, *American Evangelical Christianity: An Introduction* (Malden, MA: Blackwell Publishers, 2001); and George M. Marsden, *Understanding Fundamentalism and Evangelicalism* (Grand Rapids, MI: W. B. Eerdmans, 1991). My use of the term *evangelical* refers to shared core beliefs regarding salvation and witnessing, as well as the political history of Christian institutions that prioritize gospel outreach. As such, I see evangelicalism as an ideology and as a cultural relationship.

7. Micheal Oriard, *Reading Football: How the Popular Press Created an American Spectacle* (Chapel Hill: University of North Carolina Press, 1993), 37.

8. Ibid., 56.

9. By far, the most successful muscular Christian institution was the Young Men's Christian Association. For histories of the YMCA, see Margaret Spratt and Nina Mjagkij, eds., *Men and Women Adrift: The YMCA and the YWCA in the City* (New York: New York University Press, 1997); John Donald Gustav-Wrathall, *Take the Young Stranger by the Hand: Same-Sex Relations and the YMCA* (Chicago: University of Chicago Press, 1998); and Thomas Winter, *Making Men, Making Class: The YMCA and Workingmen, 1877–1920* (Chicago: University of Chicago Press, 2002).

10. William J. Baker, "Introduction," in *Basketball: Its Origin and Development*, by James Naismith (Lincoln: University of Nebraska Press, 1996), xii.

11. Quoted in Baker, "Introduction," xi.

12. Baker, *Playing with God*, 104. On sport and evangelicalism in the late-nineteenth-century American South, see Ted Ownby, *Subduing Satan: Religion, Recreation and Manhood in the Rural South, 1865–1920* (Chapel Hill: University of North Carolina Press, 1990).

13. Joshua Gamson, "The Assembly Line of Greatness: Celebrity in Twentieth-Century America," *Critical Studies in Mass Communication* 9, no. 1 (1992): 20 n.8.

14. Randy Roberts and James Olson, "The Impact of Roone Arledge on Televised Sports," in *Major Problems in American Sport History: Documents and Essays*, ed. Steven A. Riess (Boston: Houghton Mifflin, 1997), 423.

15. Quoted in Benjamin G. Rader, *In Its Own Image: How Television Has Transformed Sports* (New York: The Free Press, 1984), 106.

16. Michael Oriard, *Brand NFL: Making and Selling America's Favorite Sport* (Chapel Hill: University of North Carolina Press, 2007), 26–27.

17. Steven J. Jackson, David L. Andrews, and Jay Sherer, "Introduction," in *Sport, Culture and Advertising: Identities, Commodities and the Politics of Representation*, ed. Steven J, Jackson and David L. Andrews (New York: Routledge, 2005), 10.

18. Sociologist of religion Christian Smith describes this as "engaged orthodoxy." See Christian Smith, *Evangelicalism: Embattled and Thriving* (Chicago: University of Chicago Press, 1998).

19. Wayne Atcheson, *Impact for Christ: How FCA Has Influenced the Sports World* (Grand Island, NE: Cross Training Publishing, 1994), 158.

20. Joe Smalley, *More Than a Game* (San Bernardino, CA: Here's Life Publishers, Inc., 1981), 26, 31.

21. "About Us," Campus Crusade for Christ, http://www.campuscrusadeforchrist.com/aboutus/history.

22. Bill Bright's four spiritual laws are as follows: (1) God loves you and has a wonderful plan for your life, (2) humans are sinful and separated from God, (3) Jesus Christ provides the only avenue for humans to have meaningful access to God, and (4) humans must individually pray to receive Jesus in order to access God and salvation. The four spiritual laws are used around the world to communicate this message. For an exploration on how this is a departure from a traditional gospel message, see David Harrington Watt, *A Transforming Faith: Explorations of Twentieth-Century American Evangelicalism* (New Brunswick, NJ: Rutgers University Press, 1991), 22.

23. John G. Turner, *Bill Bright and Campus Crusade for Christ: The Renewal of Evangelicalism in Postwar America* (Chapel Hill: University of North Carolina Press, 2008), 102.

24. Cahn, *Coming on Strong*, 224.

25. Mariah Burton Nelson, *The Stronger Women Get, the More Men Love Football: Sexism and the American Culture of Sports* (New York: Harcourt Brace and Company, 1994), 53–54.

26. Sal Paolantonio, *How Football Explains America* (Chicago: Triumph Books, 2008), 163.

27. This premise is explored at length in Eric Bain-Selbo's *Game Day and God: Football, Faith, and Politics in the American South* (Macon, GA: Mercer University Press, 2009).

28. Robert Wuthnow, "The Political Rebirth of American Evangelicals," in *The New Christian Right*, ed. Robert C. Liebman, Robert Wuthnow, and James L. Guth (Hawthorne, NY: Aldine Publishing Co., 1983), 167–85.

29. Deford, "Religion and Sport," 100.

30. Ibid., 102.

31. Shirl Hoffman, "Sports Fanatics: How Christians Have Succumbed to the Sports Culture—and What Might Be Done About It," *Christianity Today*, February 2010, http://www.christianitytoday.com/ct/2010/february/3.20.html.

32. Deford, "Reaching for the Stars," 58.

33. Deford, "The Word According to Tom," 69.

34. Jerry Pile, "Sports and War," *Christian Athlete*, January 1972: 2–8.

35. Deford, "Reaching for the Stars," *Sports Illustrated*, May 3, 1976, 60.

36. Ibid.

37. Quoted in Hoffman, "Evangelicalism and the Revitalization of Religious Ritual in Sport," 121.

38. Oriard, *Brand NFL*, 28–54. For more on historical context, see Michael Oriard, *Bowled Over: Big-Time College Football from the Sixties to the BCS Era* (Chapel Hill: University of North Carolina Press, 2009).

39. Oriard, *Brand NFL*, 43.

40. Paul Hoch, *Rip Off the Big Game: The Exploitation of Sports by the Power Elite* (Garden City, NJ: Anchor Books, 1972), 22.

41. Ibid., 82.

42. Deford, "Religion and Sport," 100.

43. Paolantonio, *How Football Explains America*, xix.

44. Paolantonio, *How Football Explains America*, 165.

45. Frank Deford, "The Word According to Tom," 69.

46. Nelson, *The Stronger Women Get, The More Men Love Football*, 11.

47. Ibid., 55.

48. Becky Beal, "The Promise Keepers' Use of Sport in Defining 'Christ-like' Masculinity," in *The Promise Keepers: Essays on Masculinity and Christianity*, ed. Dane S. Claussen (Jefferson, NC, and London: McFarland and Company, Inc., 2000), 155.

49. For analysis of this press coverage, see Ken Waters, "Who Are These Guys? The Promise Keepers' Media Relations Strategy for 'Stand in the Gap,'" in *The Promise Keepers*, 255–68.

50. "Promise Keepers Fill Washington's Mall with Prayer," *CNN Interactive*, October 4, 1997, http://www.cnn.com/US/9710/04/promise.keepers.pm/index.html.

51. Ibid., 153–63.

52. Oriard, *Reading Football*, 229–47. Racial tensions in sport at the turn of the century have been well explored. See also Gail Bederman, *Manliness and Civilization: A Cultural History of Gender and Race in the United States, 1880–1917* (Chicago: University of Chicago Press, 1996).

53. Ben Volin, "NCAA Trying to Ban Messages on Eye Black Under the 'Tebow Rule,'" *Palm Beach Post*, February 12, 2010, http://www.palmbeachpost.com/sports/gators/ncaa-trying-to-ban-messages-on-eye-black-232356.html.

54. "NCAA Bans Eye-Black Messages and Will Implement Stiff Penalty for Taunting," *Florida Times Union*, April 15, 2010, http://jacksonville.com/sports/college/florida-gators/2010-04-15/story/ncaa-bans-eye-black-messages-and-will-implement stiff?utm_source=feedburner&utm_medium=feed&utm_campaign =Feed%3A+JacksonvillecomUfFootball+(Jacksonville.com%3A+UF+Sports). Tim Tebow was not the only player to display messages in his eye-blacks. Most notably Heisman Trophy winner Reggie Bush displayed his home area code in San Diego.

55. Jon Saraceno, "Tim Tebow: Is He a Miracle Worker or Just an Average QB?" *USA Today*, April 22, 2010, http://www.usatoday.com/cleanprint/?1287774221997.

56. Tom Krattenmaker, "And I'd Like to Thank God Almighty," *USA Today*, October 12, 2009. Krattenmaker is the author of a book addressing the intersection of Christianity and sports. The book, not surprisingly, features a picture of a praying football team on the cover. See *Onward Christian Athletes: Turning Ballparks into Pulpits and Players into Preachers* (Landham, MD: Rowman and Littlefield Publishers, 2010).

57. Quoted in Adelle M. Banks, "God and the Gridiron? Some Are Calling Foul," *Religion News Service*, February 3, 2010, http://www.religionnews.com/index.php?/rnstext/god_and_the_gridiron_some_are_calling_foul/.

REFERENCES

Atcheson, Wayne. 1994. *Impact for Christ: How FCA Has Influenced the Sports World.* Grand Island, NE: Cross Training Publishing.

Bain-Selbo, Eric. 2009. *Game Day and God: Football, Faith, and Politics in the American South.* Macon, GA: Mercer University Press.

Bederman, Gail. 1996. *Manliness and Civilization: A Cultural History of Gender and Race in the United States, 1880–1917.* Chicago: University of Chicago Press.

Claussen, Dane S., ed. 2000. *The Promise Keepers: Essays on Masculinity and Christianity.* Jefferson, NC: McFarland and Company, Inc.

Dayton, Donald, and Robert Johnson, eds. 1991. *The Variety of American Evangelicalism.* Knoxville, TN: University of Tennessee Press.

Hoch, Paul. 1972. *Rip Off the Big Game: The Exploitation of Sports by the Power Elite.* Garden City, NJ: Anchor Books.

Jackson, Steven J., and David L. Andrews, eds. 2005. *Sport, Culture and Advertising: Identities, Commodities and the Politics of Representation.* New York: Routledge.

Liebman, Robert C., Robert Wuthnow, and James L. Guth, eds. 1983. *The New Christian Right* (Hawthorne, NY: Aldine Publishing Co.).

Marsden, George M. 1991.*Understanding Fundamentalism and Evangelicalism.* Grand Rapids, MI: W.B. Eerdmans.

Nelson, Mariah Burton. 1994. *The Stronger Women Get, the More Men Love Football: Sexism and the American Culture of Sports.* New York: Harcourt Brace and Company.

Noll, Mark A. 2001. *American Evangelical Christianity: An Introduction.* Malden, MA: Blackwell Publishers.

Oriard, Michael. 1993. *Reading Football: How the Popular Press Created an American Spectacle.* Chapel Hill: University of North Carolina Press.

———. 2007. *Brand NFL: Making and Selling America's Favorite Sport.* Chapel Hill: University of North Carolina Press.

———. 2009. *Bowled Over: Big-Time College Football from the Sixties to the BCS Era.* Chapel Hill: University of North Carolina Press.

Ownby, Ted. 1990. *Subduing Satan: Religion, Recreation and Manhood in the Rural South, 1865–1920.* Chapel Hill: University of North Carolina Press.

Paolantonio, Sal. 2008. *How Football Explains America.* Chicago: Triumph Books.

Putney, Clifford. 2001. *Muscular Christianity: Manhood and Sports in Protestant America, 1880–1920.* Cambridge, MA: Harvard University Press.

Rader, Benjamin G. 1984. *In Its Own Image: How Television Has Transformed Sports.* New York: The Free Press.

Smart, Barry. 2005. *The Sport Star: Modern Sport and the Cultural Economy of Sporting Celebrity.* Thousand Oaks, CA: Sage.

Smith, Christian. 1998. *Evangelicalism: Embattled and Thriving.* Chicago: University of Chicago Press.

Turner, John G. 2008. *Bill Bright and Campus Crusade for Christ: The Renewal of Evangelicalism in Postwar America.* Chapel Hill: University of North Carolina Press.

Watt, David Harrington. 1991. *A Transforming Faith: Explorations of Twentieth-Century American Evangelicalism.* New Brunswick, NJ: Rutgers University Press.

Wuthnow, Robert. 1988. *The Restructuring of American Religion: Society and Faith Since World War II.* Princeton: Princeton University Press.

CHAPTER 28

THE CELEBRIFICATION OF RELIGION IN THE AGE OF INFOTAINMENT

KATHRYN LOFTON

Studying Celebrity and Religion

Studying celebrity and religion in concert requires parsing the multiple ways these terms have become increasingly interactive, overlapping, and co-constitutive in modern America. This chapter will explore how this has transpired, examining both the forms of news reporting that have succeeded in recent years and the changed way that religion is publically discussed. Its focus will be the national daily newspaper *USA Today* (*USAT*). With a circulation of nearly two million, *USAT* competes with the *Wall Street Journal* to be the most widely circulated US paper. One of the reasons *USAT* provides an excellent archive for the relationship between religion and celebrity in the news is its own oft-touted (and oft-satirized) synthetic style, including short articles, cheery cartoon graphics, and intentionally "easy to read" copy. The paper consists of four sections: News, Money, Sports, and Life. Though Life is the section where most stories concerning religion, celebrity, and combinations of those terms are located, there are also instances when these subjects slip into the News section, especially when market forces are at stake.

The abundance of celebrity news within the pages of *USAT* signals an editorial certitude of its universal appeal. "Celebrity culture is now ubiquitous, and establishes the main scripts, presentational props, conversational codes and other source materials through which cultural relations are constructed," Chris Rojek writes.

Rojek argues that celebrities have become the mythic scrim for quotidian lives. It seems impossible to avoid them; celebrities pervade every part of market, print, and artistic cultures. Scholars of celebrity have observed that their importance is heightened in an inverse relation to the importance of religious authority. Or, as Rojek notes, the circulation of celebrity has become "the milieu in which religious recognition and belonging are now enacted."[1]

Rojek's narrative fits the secularization thesis, which sketches the declension of religion through the many philosophical, scientific, and sociological shifts of modernity. In recent years such secularization narratives have been criticized, suggesting that the word *secular* is a problematic diagnosis for the contemporary condition. Given the available anthropological, demographic, and textual evidence, there seems no lack of social forms organizing relationships to superhuman powers. It cannot be useful to say that religion has diminished or been eradicated from the range of human expression. Rather, it seems more useful to specify how religion forms itself in the modern era, especially as it is articulated outside of institutionalized forms of religious ideation and practice.

Like *celebrity*, *religion* is a word that seems to be an encompassing whole but that actually articulates multiple things at once. A sociologist may ask "what religion are you?" and the respondent may provide single-word answers (i.e., Hindu, atheist, Lutheran). But it's not so easy to decide what makes someone Hindu, and it is even more difficult to name something neatly consistent across all "Hindu" practice. Tracking how religion has been received in the news requires a consciousness of the way it is wielded as a singular consolidation despite its relentless plurality and idiosyncratic articulations. *Celebrity* and *religion* are similar words, then, insofar as their very invocation communicates something iconic and singular while also calling forth vast, irreducible cultures.

The image of religion in the media has often been a relatively flat one reflective more of aberrant crises than a nuanced demography. For example, in the 1970s, religion often inferred *cult*. In the 1980s, religion often invoked *scandal*. These caricatures connect to redactions of individual personality gone awry and to the dangerous possibilities for the powerful. In *USAT*, the whisper of such condemnation continues, as the isolated compound cult or oversexed preacher seems likely to erupt onto the headlines.[2] Religion has also meant *simple-minded*, a trope of description familiar to celebrity coverage. "Celebrities have long had an affinity for mystical mishmash," writes one *USAT* reporter in a 2006 article. "Shirley MacLaine, joking about her many lives, is no longer news."[3] It isn't news because it's so obviously silly that nobody needs to report it. Yet one of the ways journalists mock religious belief is through the fame of figures like MacLaine. Rather than indict average citizens who claim to channel past lives, MacLaine is introduced in part to articulate a critique of faith. Like the adulterous pastor or the megalomaniacal minister, the free-spirit celebrity stands in for a broader secular suspicion of the power claimed by religious authority.

News reporters offer their own rationale for the conjunctions of religion and celebrity that they introduce time and again:

> The relationship between celebrities and religion can be mutually beneficial. "Religious groups clearly feel having a celebrity endorsement helps give pizzazz and credibility, just like any product that benefits from a celebrity endorsement," says Steve Waldman, editor of beliefnet.com, a multi-faith and spiritual web site.[4]

According to this description, celebrity involvement is advantageous to religions. But is it helpful for the celebrity to be religious? "It hurts celebrities," says media image consultant Michael Sands. "Celebrities should maintain separation of church and state. These people are not Billy Graham."[5] This language from *USAT* offers many of the reasons that the combination of religion and celebrity saturates the news. Celebrities present glamour (pizzazz) *and* familiarity (credibility). But they also present a test of what Americans want to be sacred (like Billy Graham) and what they want to be profane. Yet neither religions nor celebrity can be so controlled. Celebrities dramatize basic conceits about proper religion simply by participating in religions themselves and by provoking religious responses from their fans. Just as religious groups benefit from religious celebrity, so do newspapers benefit from religious celebrity and celebrity religion.[6]

In reportage about celebrities and religion, it is important to note that the reportage itself is rarely centrally motivated by religious exploration. Almost always, reportage that ties these two categories together arrives at religion through some form of celebrity promotion in which the celebrity seeks to connect the journalist, reader, and consumer to his or her new film, CD, or project. That religion appears in a form of press release to the advantage of the star's publicity and market circulation should not be overlooked. This genre of journalism invites the celebrity to open up, intimating that this is no mere product plug, but rather earnest disclosure. Hence, the consumer becomes complicit in a cycle of commodity, gossip, and investigation. "The game itself is the source of pleasure, as players scrutinize celebrity appearances and entertainment magazines, sharing their knowledge with one another as they peel away the never-ending layers of the proverbial onion," write David Croteau and William Hoynes.[7] The cycle begets itself, manifesting more products to satisfy the desire that cannot be sated since the unpeeling is simultaneous with obfuscation. Just as you think you begin to know the celebrity, he or she must disappear again into their mystery to propel your desire to know them. To maintain celebrity, the celebrity must be known as accessible and untouchable.

Such celebrity subjects emerge in certain rote modes in relation to religion. First, religion may be a subject *within* celebrity productions. Religion may then be mentioned in reviews of film or books, such as a review of a PBS documentary on James Baldwin, or a profile of outsider artist (and evangelical preacher) Howard Finster, whose art gained prominence through use on Talking Heads and R.E.M. album covers.[8] Second, religion may be a devotion or identity *of* celebrities. Athlete profiles, like those of Olympic medalist Carl Lewis, University of Utah quarterback Scott Mitchell, and Houston Rockets center Hakeem Olajuwon, often include descriptions of the motivational power of faith.[9] One might even claim that there are some celebrity *religions*, chief among them being the Church of Scientology (SCI). Few subjects appear as unrelentingly connected to celebrity as SCI, as illustrated by *USAT* headlines like "Cruising with Scientology," "Celebrities Celebrate Scientology," "Scientology's Stars," "Celebrities Denounce Anti-Scientology Stand," and "Church: A Hold over Travolta?"[10] More than any other religion in contemporary America, SCI carries the specter of cult accusation, a looming indictment that invites its allies to return to the media for its defense, thus reigniting its accusation through its endless disavowal.

Life cycle rituals connect celebrity with religion in a different mode of submission and personalization. Whether it is Mick Jagger defending the legitimacy of his Bali union to Jerry Hall (December 4, 1990), celebrities seeking to design remarriage rituals (June 21, 1991), Scientology rituals for baby delivery (the birth of Jett Travolta Preston, reported on April 14, 1992), or celebrities going to midnight masses (December 15, 1993), *USAT* tracks these events with an eye to the ritual needs of the famous. Even if burials at sea or expensive christening gowns are not accessible for the common reader, they are possible facets of his or her life, thus linking him or her to the ritualism, however excessive, of the reported celebrity. It isn't just you who are humbled by doctrine; the icon, too, must supplicate.[11] Third, and finally, religion emerges as a diagnosis *for* celebrity consumption itself. In *USAT*, this appears most frequently in updates about Elvis Presley, his estate, and his continuing celebrants as an icon producing relics and worshipful adherents.[12]

Distinguishing these three different forms of intersection between religion and celebrity may suggest a neat and tidy usage of these terms in *USAT* or the broader culture. This is certainly not the case. Perhaps no celebrity appears more often in conjunction with the term *religion* than Madonna, who seems to partake of every modal relation to that term, displaying the constant amalgamations and shifts of these terms even within one subject. There is religion in her productions, there are religions in which she is involved, and her celebrity itself inspires its own kind of devotion for her fans. Madonna may mark an arc of transitions that celebrity and religions have taken together over the last thirty years, and so she will reappear in this essay as a metonym for religious invocation, personal piety, and object of communal adulation.

Occluded in the forthcoming treatment will be the ways religions themselves deploy the language of celebrity in a positive and negative manner. For instance, the Church of Scientology publishes *Celebrity* magazine, while Amish communities condemn tabloids altogether. Likewise, this essay will not focus on celebrities *in* religions, such as evangelists Billy Graham or Rick Warren. Such celebrities of religion appear less often than the religious celebrities that most often populate *USAT*.[13] In *USAT*, religions appear as fads (i.e., Tibetan Buddhism) and as nemeses of certain subjects (i.e., Sinead O'Connor and the pope).[14] But what transfixes this research is the way that entertainment news deploys religious idiom to express something inexpressibly potent in its subject and to translate democratic moral agency in an increasingly privatized corporate media structure.

Infotainment and Celebrification

Infotainment is a portmanteau that emerged in the late 1980s to refer to a specific genre of news, as well as an overarching shift in the content of news. Specifically, it refers to a genre of news reporting in which the reporters themselves must reflect celebrity performances and in which those reporters, now cast also as entertainers, provide information about other entertainers.[15] More broadly, though, the invocation of *infotainment* is a category of critique, and it speaks to the changing patterns of ownership, structuring, and information distribution among current affairs programs and publications. In a similar lexical tone, the terms *militainment*, *charitainment*, and *politainment* have emerged to diagnose analogous shifts in portrayals of war (i.e., the Iraq War), charity fundraising (like the 9/11 telethon), and political candidacy (such as Sarah Palin) as formatted to serve an aesthetic more coordinate with the history of entertainment cultures than those of journalism. It would be wrong to imagine that entertainment and such ventures once had been in some easy binary, that prior to this particular moment wars weren't drawn as dramas (World War II news reel footage), that fundraising wasn't made fun (charity balls), or that politics weren't seeking sound-bite legibility (Theodore Roosevelt). But media scholars consistently draw attention to the media proliferation and consolidation over the last twenty years, empirical shifts that have created a different market culture for the news.

The proliferation of news outlets has led to increasing competition for audiences. "As television news has been commercialized, the need to make it entertaining has become a crucial priority for broadcasters, as they are forced to borrow and adapt characteristics from entertainment genres and modes of conversation that privilege an informal communicative style, with its emphasis on personalities, style, storytelling skills and spectacles," writes Daya Thussu. There are more networks, with more options, specified to a narrower audience share. Meanwhile, this multiplicity has not meant a diversification of ownership. Rather, news networks across the United States are increasingly owned by a small number of conglomerates. Not coincidentally, these conglomerates possess as their primary investment interest the *entertainment* business (e.g., Viacom-Paramount owns CBS News, ABC News is now a part of Disney). "This shift in ownership is reflected in the type of stories—about celebrities from the world of entertainment, for example, that often get prominence on news, thus strengthening corporate synergies," Thussu concludes.[16]

Despite its origins in an elaborate corporatism, infotainment articulates itself as a populism designed—to borrow from its idiom—to tell *you* the real stories behind their stories and the real stories that help *your* life. One scholar has described this as a transition from slogans espousing the "news you need" to networks arguing they offer "news about you."[17] From the news of CBS anchor Edward R. Murrow (1908–65), whose celebrated objectivity led to his eventual appointment as head of the US Information Agency, to the news of Fox journalist Bill O'Reilly (1949–), who performs a doggedly subjective conservatism, this transition in modern journalism might be witnessed through any number of documentary fronts.[18] However, within *USAT*, the complexity of this opposition continues as a form of secular surprise, as if every reporter approaching a religious subject is latter-day Murrow in an overwhelmingly O'Reilly world. Whenever a religiously intoned object appears materially successful, the editors at *USAT* seem temporarily floored, no matter the recurrence of the success. "Holy Bestsellers! Christian Mysteries Are Hot" headlines announced when Christian mysteries by Frank Peretti became blockbusters. "Spiritual Thriller Is an Unlikely Success" read the headline when *The Celestine Prophecy* became a bestseller.[19] Christian novels or hip-hop gospel, Catholics with Sirius radio stations or Jews using books describing *Kosher Sex*—the posture of surprise evinces the secular assumptions of the staring critic.[20]

None of this is precisely new. Journalists have had a complex relationship to the interpretation of religious materials; religious authorities have always maximized available media; and the journalistic enterprise has never been without its soliciting entertainments. Imagining some neat divide between old news and new news, between the news and infotainment, requires a dichotomy in which the news is critical, objective, rational, and investigative, whereas infotainment is amusing, personalized, superficial, and manufactured.[21] Obviously, such a divide is as impossible to draw as the attempt to distinguish religion from culture. "From one perspective, this sinking of religious performance into cultural entertainment might be seen as religion's decline into something more insipid, and thus as evidence of religion's weakening hold on American life," Amanda Porterfield has written. "From another perspective, however, this submergence of Christian religiosity into American culture, and its seepage into the land of entertainment, might be said to lend strength and vibrancy to American life."[22] Historians of religion wobble on a pivot of indecision as to which perspective possesses more archival credence. What is clear is that the news participates in a formation of religion that shifts our definition of what right, safe, and democratic religion is.

The medium of infotainment has increasingly shaped the message of religion in modern American society. Celebrities become the key characters in these unfolding changes. Rojek describes *celebrification* as the increased tendency to imagine every social encounter through the filter of media and its emphases on charisma, beauty, and fame. Thinking about the representation of religion among celebrities in the news is to think about how religion becomes formatted to such media standards. Insofar as celebrities "*humanize* desire," observing celebrification cannot be distinct from observing patterns in the history of religions, in which the effort to mediate human desire and social possibility has been a central feature.[23] This is not to say that the religions of celebrities become the religions of ordinary Americans. Rather, it is to say that infotainment regards religion as not merely a usable trope for celebrification, but also the stakes for its perpetuation. In the space remaining, a short history of the emergence of infotainment reportage and its corollary celebrification will be offered to illustrate the speed of these changes and the central characters through which the drama of celebrity religion has been played.

Religion and Celebrity, 1989–96

The end of the Cold War left a vacuum in the news. For nearly a half century, the Manichean terms of Cold War conflict held rapt a viewing audience uncertain of the outcome. Would *they* win, or would *we*? Its conclusion required the framing of a new nemesis. Perhaps an enemy could be named again in and through religious authority? In the same year that inaugurated the quick close to Cold War spectacle, a music video circulated that would not only begin a new stage in a single artist's celebrity but also become a signifier for the way religion might solve a certain narrative problem. The success of Madonna as an international pop star cannot be disconnected from the religious history she created through her relationship to a series of religious authorities—Catholic, Hindu, and Jewish—and who she incited to reply to her ostensible profanations. That these contestations did not take place through ecclesiastical courts but in the entertainment pages shows how religion became a usable post–Cold War enemy and also how its diminishing institutional authority encouraged the ascent of new forms of moral leadership.

Released in February 1989 by Sire Records, "Like a Prayer" was the first single from Madonna's fourth album, *Like a Prayer*. The single would go on to be one of Madonna's most successful, for many marking the emergence of her artistry from the shallow waters of eighties pop. Yet it is the video for the song that drew the most vitriol. In it, Madonna witnesses the murder of a white girl by white men. When a black man is arrested for the crime, she tries to intervene but is only then accused herself. The crux of the controversy emerges next, as Madonna flees to a church for safety where she prays to a statue of Saint Martin de Porres. In her worshipful state, she kisses him. He weeps and comes to life. The climax of the video includes Madonna testifying to free the falsely accused and her dancing amid a black gospel choir. Interspersed in the video are scenes of a cross burning and of Madonna developing stigmata.

USAT seized on the potent combination of sensuality and Catholic iconography as a subject newsworthy for its profaning spectacle. "Madonna's new 'Like a Prayer' video, a passion play melding sex and religion, delivers its moral message through an erotic medium," wrote a reporter. "The video is open to interpretation, but Madonna—who was raised a Catholic—says her intentions were pure." The reporter, Edna Gunderson, seeks to design a story in which anyone against the video must themselves be immoral. Madonna says she meant well, and the message of justice and racial redemption in the video fit certain liberal politics. It may bother some, but, the article suggests, nobody can stop something this popular. "Contrary to recent reports," it concludes, "'Like a Prayer' will air in Italy, despite the protests of Catholic groups."[24] The reportage moved from the Life to the News section when religious authorities—and not, it turned out, Catholic ones—threatened the economy of a Fortune 500 company, Pepsi, that had been using Madonna in an ad campaign. When Rev. Donald Wildmon of the American Family Association called for a Pepsi boycott, he did so because, he said, Madonna was "ridiculing Christianity."

Wildmon was identified by *USAT* as the man "who also organized boycotts of the movie *The Last Temptation of Christ*." In the necessary battle formats for infotainment reportage, *USAT* cast Wildmon as the threat to values, while casting Madonna as upholding values. The article on the boycott gives Pepsi's representative Tod MacKenzie the last word. "Why isn't [Wildmon] going after the video?" MacKenzie asks, "Why has he targeted really an innocent, wholesome commercial people have responded favorably to?"[25]

Why, asks MacKenzie, is Wildmon focusing on a wholesome commercial when there is a disturbing music video to target? Wildmon is cast as disconnected from the genre codes of consumer capitalism, as someone too tied to old institutions and ideas to participate productively in the political now. For Madonna, the medium of her productions insulates her from such old-fashioned final judgment by religious leaders. She isn't trying to serve *them*, she winks to her audience. She is just trying to serve *you*. As she does her pop star job, she will invariably incite formal religious reply to her creative religious articulations precisely because what *we* want and what *they* want is no longer the same thing. In a 1991 story placed on the *USAT* front page, rabbis accused her of insulting Jews in certain versions of "Justify My Love" by reading from Revelations 2:9.[26] Reports on such encounters between Madonna and religious authorities emphasized her irrepressible religious individualism and constitutional artistic freedom as the presumed values of the public to whom *USAT* reports. Madonna stands in for all of us who may not agree with her positions but believe she has the right to have them and to express herself however she pleases.[27] "True to her taboo-smashing instincts, Madonna turns sexual and religious conventions inside out, often fusing the two to heighten discomfort," explains a review of her Blond Ambition tour. "To the eastern strains of a slowed 'Like a Virgin,' she simulates sex on a velvet-draped bed, then cries, 'God?' In the presence of a priest, she partially disrobes and smashes a crucifix to the ground."[28] The description offers up the sacred to be smashed by Madonna's profane usage of it; yet, it also venerates Madonna in her particular celebrity as the brazen truth teller, the unstoppably free actor.

Just as Madonna seemed intrigued by the commodity her profanations might make, so did *USAT* seem intrigued by the inferred contrast between profane celebrity and sacred authority, like when Michael Jackson was kept away from the Wailing Wall. *USAT* reporter Jack Kelley framed the Orthodox Jewish rejection of Jackson as ultimately futile in the face of the 80,000 fans who filled one of his two sold-out concerts in Israel. The article concludes on these two notes:

> "Nobody can excite people like M.J.," says Tel Aviv University student David Eizenstadt. "Not Rabin, Peres or Arafat. Michael's so electrifying. We think he may even be the Messiah."
>
> Jackson, 35, has been accused of molesting a 13-year-old boy, a charge he denies.[29]

The article begins with the matter of one man's approach to, and rejection from, a sacred site. It finds a way to explode this transgression into an incident highlighting not the power of the rabbis but the power of the people. The people here are manifest in two senses: first, the public that chooses Jackson over political leaders; second, the public that makes up the juridical that is also his potential judgment and downfall. Although this era includes the emergence of mega-churches as a news story, as well as the rise of Tibetan Buddhism as a popular celebrity practice, it is this celebration of celebrity iconoclasm as an articulation of the public's preference that distinguishes the media moment.[30]

Religious Celebrity, 1997–2003

Midway through the Clinton two-term presidency, many of the established features of celebrity coverage in the news remained the same, and Madonna was still embodying all of them. There was still talk of Madonna stirring trouble when she wore Hindu facial markings at the MTV Video Music Awards, and there was still the translation of new religions through celebrity support of them. Madonna's turn to kabbalah inspired articles emphasizing her new spiritual enthusiasms, as well as the faddish success of red bracelets sold through her favorite kabbalah center.[31] Yet the tone of this reportage was not defamatory. It was, increasingly, correlating celebrity spiritual wellness with a broader social turn to health and redemption through individual seeking. Here again Madonna took the lead, declared by one agency as a positive force for sex education and declared by herself as on a new trajectory: "I've found a way of life I'd like to share. Despite the illusions I've been a slave to all my life, I feel a tremendous amount of hope for a life of fulfillment and happiness."[32] Such a sense of hope pervaded accounts of the positive role religion played in the life of certain hip-hop stars, like Mase, or raunchy comedienne Roseanne, or activist actor Jane Fonda.[33] If once the fourth estate looked upon religion with cynicism, it now named it as a force for transformation.

This spiritualization of celebrity was always a mutual process, with celebrities and entertainment reporters functioning in a complex dialectic of terms and tones. The late nineties may be seen as a turning point in the history of religion in news reporting, if only because it began to seem requisite to the terming of the subject itself. Was this because a liberal evangelical occupied the White House, legitimating a brand of religious authoritarianism as properly rational and democratic? Or was it because that same leader had so publicly collapsed in a squalid story of failed spirit? Reportage on Robert Duvall's *The Apostle* (1998) could not seem to avoid invoking evangelicalism as a format for wrestling with these immediate political dilemmas.[34] Portraying a charismatic preacher wrestling with the legacies of infidelity, Duvall visited the White House for a screening of the film in the midst of a strangely analogous trauma. On the verge of the millennium, there were no obvious solutions to what ailed the nation. The economy was booming, and media was exploding. Why, then, were individuals still collapsing under the weight of individual struggle?

It is perhaps no surprise that this era would be branded in its spiritualization by talk show host Oprah Winfrey. Unlike her original talk show competitors, Oprah's show seemed always to be predicated upon a higher power. This became an explicit program change in the mid-1990s. When Oprah went to Amarillo, Texas, to testify in her defense against the cattlemen who sued her for defaming the beef industry, she was asked a series of questions meant to imply that she had sensationalized the news. She explained later that this experience made her realize she must become a tool for good in the world. Her spiritual revelation was converted into a corporate makeover in which her show became "Change Your Life TV." Initial responses to the shift were largely negative, with some suggesting that her move to Change Your Life TV was "too evangelical." At the time, she replied, "It's a shame that we've evolved into the kind of society where evangelical is considered negative. I have come to believe that we are all, or at least most of us, searching for the assurance that good exists in our world, even in the midst of evil and evil abuse."[35]

For religious historians, Oprah's disavowal of critics is a familiar maneuver. Religious leaders often suggest that the words used to insult them are precisely the terms of their power. Rather than disagree with naysayers, Oprah merely asks why they aren't on board. Isn't everyone worried about evil? Doesn't everybody want the good? At a time when religion was increasingly portrayed as either idiotic or extremist, Oprah plotted a middle way allowing her viewers to be believers and critics, consumers and missionaries. She criticized religious institutions but she encouraged spiritual practices. She urged viewers to buy their favorite things but also to offer the gift of their lives to the world. *USAT* reportage described Winfrey's subsequent touring Live Your Best Life workshops in positive terms. "The workshop's biggest surprise, however, was the openness with which Winfrey talked about her spiritual beliefs," the reporter said, continuing:

> She ends the show on a guided meditation—lights are lowered; melodic, instrumental music plays, and Oprah instructs the audience to close their eyes, breathe deeply and open their souls as she recites her own personal mantra asking for guidance.
>
> Something the audience already feels it has received from Winfrey.[36]

Her spiritualization organized the expansion of her corporate empire and resonated with a public no longer willing to feel embarrassed by their hunger for it. Winfrey enshrined an American sensibility of choice and personalism as the form of acceptable religious ideation for the marketplace.

Winfrey formed a counterpublic to spiritual seekers who wanted religion without Religion and spirituality without restriction in a world where some religious authorities still lingered.[37] In 1999, *USAT* narrated a situation where a Lebanese pop star was the subject of attack for "Muslim fundamentalists" who "decreed she should be put to death for reportedly naming her pet dog after the prophet Mohammed." Described by *USAT* as a young Christian woman, Najwa Karam was known as one of the most popular singers in the Arab world. Because a rumor suggested she had given her dog the prophet's name, she was no longer safe. "In Qatar, Q-Tel, which controls the country's television, said it would stop playing her music," wrote Matthew Kalman, explaining that in Jordan and Lebanon, fundamentalist factions said she should be killed.[38] As the United States entered war against terrorists motivated by fundamentalist beliefs, soldiers were in no small way fighting to protect the right for Karam to live in an Oprah sort of world, a world where she might name her dogs whatever she likes, be good through whatever rites she chooses, and sing for whomever will listen.[39]

A Mission Emerges, 2004–10

The Cold War concluded and in its wake new ethnic and religious conflicts emerged around the world, events that ranged from minor skirmishes to major global conflicts. In the United States, the role of the celebrity seemed only to expand. In its democratization of fame, reality television programming enlarged the base numbers of potential celebrities. And with twenty-four-hour news coverage including paparazzi focused solely on tracking celebrity movements, cognizance of celebrity lifestyles became increasingly detailed and pervasive. News consumers could know not only what diamonds a starlet wore but also the brand of toilet paper she bought. The increasing numbers of ordinary reality stars and the increasing paparazzi attention to all celebrities suggested that the fame was more and more a quotidian fact of American life. Celebrities seemed caught in their own feedback loop: their artistry and activism led to media coverage, which then demanded even more activism and artistry to justify the attention.

In 2004, Mel Gibson released *The Passion of the Christ*, a film that depicts the passion play in real-time detail. With an explicitly religious subject and dialogue entirely reconstructed in Aramaic, Latin, and Hebrew with vernacular subtitles, the film seemed destined, by all market suppositions, to be a spectacular indulgence and an inevitable flop.[40] "After mainstream Hollywood studios and distributors spurned *The Passion of the Christ* because some thought it was too violent and included anti-Semitic themes, Gibson, who was forced to finance the film on his own, began discussing his fundamentalist views on Catholicism," reported one *USAT* journalist. "The movie would end up raking in more than $370 million in the USA alone, the most successful R-rated film ever."[41] Gibson claimed, time and again, that the film's production was a testimony of his faith, a gift to the religion that had given him all he had. Indeed, as *USAT* would track, Christ's passion offered a compensatory articulation for a star who could not control his own sins. Gibson offered *The Passion*, and he would also offer his mug shot after several arrests for drunken, disorderly, and violent behavior. Like the much-reported hysterical performance by Scientologist Tom Cruise on the *Oprah Winfrey Show* and the *Today* show, Gibson's fall only established the premises for an eventual resurrection.

Gibson's film offering—and his struggle to maintain its extreme moral aspirations—offers a fitting emblem for the opening years of the twenty-first century. Whatever spiritual sustenance was sought in Oprah Winfrey's late-1990s spiritual expansion became in the twenty-first century an unabashed certitude that things either had to change or come to an end. This is how "change you can believe in" could become such a powerful slogan of political promotion during the 2008 election. In that year, *USAT* reported that there was, perhaps, a "theological underpinning" to the enthusiasm espoused by Obama voters.[42] Obama could be interpreted as a climax to a patterned emergence of entertainment leaders as unequivocally confident in their abilities to assist, serve, and save. His resume was his personhood: his life story, his racial amalgamation, and his embodiment of the American Dream.

Just as politics seemed increasingly reflective of celebrity formats, so did celebrities seem increasingly complicit in the political process. The election of Barack Obama was attributed to many sources, including that of his own celebrity power, as well as the celebrity power gathered to him by Oprah Winfrey. When the *Oprah Winfrey Show* concluded in May 2011, it ended an era of self-help and self-validation.[43] When Oprah began, she succeeded in a time slot and format that spoke directly to millions of women who were staying at home or wondering if they should be. Proceeding with the kind of frank discussion of professional and domestic issues that was rare at the time, she instructed them on how to live their best lives. Over the course of twenty-five years, she hosted shows on every conceivable subject, from how to find love to how to save for retirement, and from how to decorate a kitchen to how to heal from childhood pain.

Like the media formats of which she was a master, Oprah increasingly sought not only to pervade the problems of your life but also to serve your happiness. Just as infotainment media articulates itself as organized in service to the individual, so do leading celebrities increasingly represent models of media usage for you to follow. Oprah concluded her show in a multimedia moment in which everyone with access to YouTube or a blog could be a mini-Oprah, broadcasting his or her first-person story or dispensing advice over the Internet. Time and again, this democratized media form is also interpreted as a political possibility. While revolutionaries might use Facebook to organize demonstrations, so do celebrities use their mastery of media mechanics to brand social problems with their faces. Now every celebrity must possess a mission to succeed as a global icon, with George Clooney and Angelina Jolie traipsing the world searching for suffering their attention can salve. As the political necessity of celebrity and the celebrity circulation in politics continue to expand, it will be useful to recall that such missionary projects do not merely have their origin in ideologies of secular reason. The power of celebrity to expand and contract, to fit the image of the given moment, and to belong in the crevice of every crisis is not because that image is denuded of meaningful religious authority. It is precisely because they possess such spectral power that they may direct attention to their causes. "As a rock star, I have two instincts," said Bono, the lead singer for U2. "I want to have fun, and I want to change the world. I have a chance to do both."[44]

This is what transports the celebrity from the Life pages to the News pages—practicing their spiritual ambitions with missionary zeal complicit with the new politics of global media and neoliberal power.

NOTES

1. Chris Rojek, *Celebrity* (London: Reaktion, 2001), 57, 58, 97.

2. Follow-up stories indicate the vestigial quality of such crises. See Jack Kelley, "Tammy Bakker to Return—When Bills Are Paid," *USA Today*, October 30, 1989; Lawrence McQuillan, "Ghosts of '93 Still Found at Waco," *USA Today*, August 31, 2001.

3. Cathy Lynn Grossman, "Hindu Lite," *USA Today*, February 16, 2006.

4. Gary Strauss, "Stars Unleash Their Passion," *USA Today*, July 5, 2005.

5. Ibid.

6. For a further elaboration of the role of celebrities in contemporary media, see Su Holmes and Sean Redmond, eds., *Framing Celebrity: New Directions in Celebrity Culture* (London: Routledge, 2006); Richard Schickel, *Intimate Strangers: The Culture of Celebrity in America* (Chicago: Ivan R. Dee, 2000).

7. David Croteau and William Hoynes, *Media Society: Industries, Images, and Audiences* (Thousand Oaks, CA: Pine Forge Press, 2003), 296.

8. Walter T. Middlebrook, "Baldwin's Journey Deserves Better Vehicle," *USA Today*, August 14, 1989, 3D; Elizabeth Snead, "Howard Finster, Evangelist with a Paintbrush," *USA Today*, August 7, 1991.

9. John Pitts, "Lewis Lifts Heart in Testimony, Song," *USA Today*, July 28, 1989; Steve Wieberg, "High Standards; Records Not Utah QB's Mission," *USA Today*, September 12, 1989; "Daily Prayers Are Ritual for Olajuwon," *USA Today*, June 10, 1994.

10. David Landis and Darren Summers, "Cruising with Scientology," *USA Today*, May 14, 1992; "Celebrities Celebrate Scientology," *USA Today*, August 1, 1994; Karen Thomas, "Scientology's Stars," *USA Today*, November 30, 1994; Kitty Bean Yancey, "Celebrities Denounce Anti-Scientology Stand," *USA Today*, January 10, 1997; Karen Thomas, "Church: A Hold over Travolta?" *USA Today*, April 29, 1991.

11. Paul Hoverstein, "More People Opting to Be Buried at Sea," *USA Today*, July 23, 1999; Cesar G. Soriano, "Celebs Know How to Throw a Good Christening," *USA Today*, December 27, 2004.

12. Deirdre Donahue, "Giving a Bow to the Sanctity of Elvis," *USA Today*, July 7, 1989; Arlene Vigoda, "King of Kings?" *USA Today*, April 29, 1993; Jerry Shriver, "Rites and Relics of Elvis," *USA Today*, August 15, 1997.

13. Cathy Lynn Grossman, "The Gospel of Billy Graham," *USA Today*, May 16, 2005; Cathy Lynn Grossman, "This Evangelist Has a 'Purpose,'" *USA Today*, July 21, 2003.

14. Jeannie Williams, "Sinead Has Christmas Spirit," *USA Today*, October 28, 1992.

15. Daya Kishan Thussu, *News as Entertainment: The Rise of Global Infotainment* (Los Angeles: Sage Publications, 2007), 7; Edward S. Herman and Robert W. McChesney, *The Global Media: The New Missionaries of Corporate Capitalism* (London and New York: Continuum, 1997), 144.

16. Thussu, *News as Entertainment*, 3.

17. Andie Tucher, "You News," *Columbia Journalism Review* 36 (May/June 1997): 26–31.

18. For just one example, see this description of the changes at the *Los Angeles Times*, Croteau and Hoynes *Media Society*, 171–74.

19. Anita Manning, "Holy Best Sellers! Christian Mysteries Are Hot," *USA Today*, November 28, 1989; Deirdre Donahue, "The 'Celestine Prophecy' Karma: Spiritual Thriller Is an Unlikely Success," *USA Today*, April 21, 1994.

20. Cathy Lynn Grossman, "Faith's Purchasing Power," *USA Today*, December 13, 2006; Tom Krattenmaker, "Faith Embraces Pop Culture, Technology," *USA Today*, October 9, 2006. On the relationship between journalism and religion, see Jay Rosen, "Journalism Is Itself a Religion: A Theological Investigation," *TheRevealer.org*, January 8, 2004, http://therevealer.org/archives/93.

21. Interestingly, such a dichotomy has been portrayed throughout US religious history as a profoundly gendered one, in which the Calvinist masculine leadership is poised against the sentimental evangelical readership; it is inviting to consider how this historical processing of the news might coordinate the historical processing of the religious twentieth century, as narratives describing the end of the mainline conclude with the rise of nondenominational Christianities.

22. Amanda Porterfield, *The Transformation of American Religion: The Story of a Late-Twentieth Century Awakening* (New York: Oxford University Press, 2001), 22.

23. Rojek, *Celebrity*, 186–87.

24. Edna Gunderson, "Madonna's Video 'Prayer' Is No Sin," *USA Today*, March 8, 1989.

25. James Cox, "Boycott Aim: Pepsi; Madonna 'Ridicules Christianity,'" *USA Today*, March 9, 1989.

26. "Madonna Still Justifying Her Song," *USA Today*, January 7, 1991.

27. Jeannie Williams, "Madonna: Catholicism Is 'Mean,'" *USA Today*, May 1, 1991.

28. Edna Gunderson, "Daring Madonna Is All Show," *USA Today*, May 7, 1990.

29. Jack Kelley, "Michael Jackson Kept Away from Wailing Wall," *USA Today*, September 20, 1993.

30. For an article typical of mega-church coverage, see Nanci Hellmich, "Kids Bringing Parents Back to the Faith," *USA Today*, March 24, 1989. Coverage of actor Richard Gere's comeback seems in part spirited by his new awareness as a Buddhist. See Ann Trebbe, "Gere Is Moving Back into Limelight," *USA Today*, November 24, 1989; "Gere Rebounds Without Baring All," *USA Today*, April 12, 1990; Jeannie William, "Richard Gere's World Beyond Camelot," *USA Today*, July 25, 1995.

31. Steve Jones, "Talent That Grabs Grammy's Attention Gospel's McClurkin Places Ministry First," *USA Today*, February 24, 1998; "Madonna Incarnation Offends," *USA Today*, September 14, 1998; Sue Factor, "Celebs Get Wrapped Up in Red String," *USA Today*, November 26, 2002; Edna Gunderson, "Madonna's Epiphany," *USA Today*, April 18, 2003.

32. Kim Painter, "Madonna Tops Chart as Positive Sex Voice," *USA Today*, April 5, 1999; Olivia Barker, "Madonna Has Faith on a String," *USA Today*, May 26, 2004.

33. Steve Jones, "Mase: Why I Chose God," *USA Today*, April 26, 1999; Matthew Kalman, "Roseanne's Mystic Journey," *USA Today*, June 24, 1999; Jeannie Williams, "Fonda's Not Fond of Born-Again Talk," *USA Today*, January 13, 2000.

34. Jeannie Williams, "'Apostle' Duvall Not Holier than Bill," *USA Today*, January 27, 1998; Mike Clark, "Duvall's Divine Performance," *USA Today*, January 20, 1998.

35. Ann Oldenburg and Kevin V. Johnson, "Oprah's Optimism Seems More Like Opportunism and Is Growing Oppressive, Opposition Says," *USA Today*, October 23, 1998.

36. Deirdre Donahue, "Live Your Best Life, with Oprah Workshop Connects with 1,600, and Me," *USA Today*, June 2, 2001.

37. She was the emblem of anti-Islam in her role as emcee and master of ceremonies for "A Prayer for America," an interfaith service for the families of 9/11 victims. Jill Liever and Traci Watson, "Interfaith Service Stresses Life, Hope," *USA Today*, September 24, 2001.

38. Matthew Kalman, "Arab Pop Star: Foes Barking Up Wrong Tree," *USA Today*, March 15, 1999.

39. Ann Oldenburg, "The Divine Miss Winfrey?" *USA Today*, May 11, 2006; see also Kathryn Lofton, *Oprah: The Gospel of an Icon* (Berkeley: University of California Press, 2011).

40. Michael Medved, "'Passion' Will Inspire Other Religious Films," *USA Today*, March 15, 2004.

41. Gary Strauss, "Stars Unleash Their Passion," *USA Today*, July 5, 2005.

42. Mary Zeiss Stange, "Obama's Believers," *USA Today*, April 7, 2008.

43. Ann Oldenburg, "'It Is Done,'" *USA Today*, May 20, 2011.

44. Edna Gunderson, "Bono: You Too Can Make Y2K Better for 3rd World," *USA Today*, October 7, 1999; Laura Ingraham, "U2's Bono Sells Relief Effort," *USA Today*, June 20, 2001; "Bono: Appeal to America's Greatness to Aid Africa," *USA Today*, September 16, 2003.

REFERENCES

Allitt, Patrick. 2003. *Religion in American Since 1945: A History*. New York: Columbia University Press.

Croteau, David, and William Hoynes. 2006. *The Business of Media: Corporate Media and the Public Interest*. Thousand Oaks, CA: Pine Forge Press.

———. 2003. *Media Society: Industries, Images, and Audiences*. Thousand Oaks, CA: Pine Forge Press.

Hendershot, Heather. 2004. *Shaking the World for Jesus: Media and Conservative Evangelical Culture*. Chicago: University of Chicago Press.

Herman, Edward S., and Robert W. McChesney. 1997. *The Global Media: The New Missionaries of Corporate Capitalism*. London and New York: Continuum.

Herwitz, Daniel. 2008. *The Star as Icon: Celebrity in the Age of Mass Consumption*. New York: Columbia University Press.

Holmes, Su, and Sean Redmond, eds. 2006. *Framing Celebrity: New Directions in Celebrity Culture*. London: Routledge.

Lofton, Kathryn. 2011. *Oprah: The Gospel of an Icon*. Berkeley: University of California Press.

Porterfield, Amanda. 2001. *The Transformation of American Religion: The Story of a Late-Twentieth Century Awakening*. New York: Oxford University Press.

Rojek, Chris. 2001. *Celebrity*. London: Reaktion.

Rosen, Jay. 2004. Journalism Is Itself a Religion: A Theological Investigation. *TheRevealer.org*, January 8. http://therevealer.org/archives/93.

Schickel, Richard. 2000. *Intimate Strangers: The Culture of Celebrity in America*. Chicago: Ivan R. Dee.

Thussu, Daya Kishan. 2007. *News as Entertainment: The Rise of Global Infotainment*. Los Angeles: Sage Publications.

Tucher, Andie. You News. *Columbia Journalism Review* 36 (May/June 1997): 26–31.

SECTION V

INTERNATIONAL COVERAGE

CHAPTER 29

LATIN AMERICAN RELIGION IN THE NEWS

MAGALI DO NASCIMENTO CUNHA

SIGNS OF AN EXCLUSIVIST UNDERSTANDING OF CHRISTIANITY

Despite the variety of spiritual expressions practiced in Latin America, American readers relying solely on the *New York Times* for information could be forgiven for thinking that Christianity, specifically institutionalized Roman Catholicism, is the continent's sole religion. During the period of study, between 1968 and 2007, news of other religions, as well as nonhistorical Christianity, is seldom presented. When these religious traditions are covered, they're likely to appear in travel articles among other exotica or in news stories as part of a strange setting for unusual situations, especially scandals.

This approach indicates American journalists' exclusivist understanding of Christianity and the role of religious leadership in the "civilized world." In philosophical and sociological terms, the exclusivist understanding is based on the position that only one group or ideology possesses the truth. Racism, for example, is an exclusivist understanding of society and human relations. Religious exclusivism is the position that only one religion is completely true.[1] To understand how this perspective is developed, it is important to first reflect on the configuration of the Latin American religious field and how it is related to the process of news construction. Moreover, it is essential to consider how news construction is related to a cultural process by which professional journalists and the larger society are shaped by the social imaginary.

A close reading of the letters of Christopher Columbus following his arrival on the continent provides a historical background for this social imaginary. An analysis of the coverage of papal visits to Latin America between 1968 and 2007 in *Time* and the *New York Times* demonstrates journalists' exclusivist understanding and how it is perpetuated in the modern US press.

Religion in Latin America: A Mosaic

In the fifteenth and sixteenth centuries, Spanish and Portuguese explorers first arrived on the continent that came to be christened Latin America. Here they encountered indigenous populations who had preceded them by thousands of years. These people had created various ways of life that reflected the diversity of their environments. They spoke a multitude of languages and had developed many forms of art, architecture, infrastructure, and commercial networks. Moreover, their religious practice was rich and diverse. But with the fierce colonial occupation, Roman Catholicism became "the" religion of the continent, and the indigenous faiths were demonized and marginalized.

The religious encounters between the colonizers and the indigenous people did not end with that experience. Soon the colonizers enslaved the natives to serve as the labor force that would keep their numerous plantations operating. Additionally, the arrival of millions of blacks, forcibly brought from Africa to the New World, initiated another encounter between different cultures and religious forms as they attempted to keep their traditions and religions alive in their new "home." The Roman Catholic Church, as the official religion of the colonial system, again promoted the demonization and marginalization of African religions just as it had with the continent's indigenous practices. However, similar to some indigenous groups, the African slaves found ways of keeping their traditions alive through underground practices or by adapting them to the dominant tradition. These were Latin America's first syncretic religious expressions.

The encounter between these different religious traditions and the practices consequently engendered was never distant from the ordinary expressions of life or culture, making it possible for Latin America to become a multicultural, religiously diverse continent. This mixture became even more complex in the nineteenth century with the arrival of Protestant missionaries, primarily from the United States, and the migration of Asians who replaced the emancipated slaves. From these myriad cultural encounters, myriad religious expressions emerged. These were the result of the mix between various institutionalized religions and the persistence of a rich, complex, noninstitutionalized religiosity within Latin America. This synergy has made it possible for Roman Catholicism to maintain its predominance through the power and strength inherited during colonial times. It also enables the existence of a popular Catholicism that keeps indigenous and African traditions alive, as well as the growth of a Catholic Charismatic Movement that brings together traditional Catholic practices with Pentecostal ones.

Pentecostalism and its diverse denominations found fertile ground in Latin America and have flourished as the most expressive religious phenomena on the continent since the beginning of the twentieth century. From the establishment of its first congregations in Chile (1909), Pentecostal Christianity has faced opposition and marginalization from the mainline churches. Nevertheless, it has been embraced and supported by millions of followers, especially among the poor. The Charismatic Movement in Catholicism and in Protestantism has been a search for synthesis between the traditional Christian approaches brought by missionaries in the past and the Pentecostal religion that promotes a re-encounter of these historical forms of Christianity (Catholicism and Protestantism) with the grassroots population.

Alongside the Christian denominations that dominate in Latin America are indigenous African and Asian religions. While the number of their adherents may be less significant, their presence is felt strongly in some regions.

Though Latin America is a predominantly Christian continent, a legacy of the colonial system that was supported by later governments, in recent years Catholicism has struggled to maintain its hegemony in the Christian religious field due to the growing strength of the Pentecostalism and other evangelical movements.

As Daniel H. Levine wrote:

> The bedrock of any discussion of change in religion, society, and politics has to be acknowledging the disappearance of the Catholic monopoly. Latin America is now approaching a state of religious pluralism (among Christian groups) for the first time in its history. . . . Religion in Latin America has been the scene of so much change in so little time that, to use a colloquial expression, there is a lot of shaking out to be done. . . . Managing religious pluralism and competition will not be easy, but it is clearly high on this century's agenda.[2]

North American Journalists and the Process of News Construction

At this point, it is important to examine the construction of news about religion in Latin America. News is not just a result of the technical work of writing texts; it also is the result of a process of construction that starts with the journalist's understanding of the social reality in which events happen.

The Spanish researcher on news and journalism theories Miquel Rodrigo Alsina points out some important aspects of this perspective:

> The social reality is the result of inter-subjective social actions. Reality cannot be completely different from the way actors interpret it, internalize it, rethink it and

define it historically and culturally. The construction of reality, therefore, is the production of meaning through productive practice and routines of the organization of the journalistic profession.[3]

This process is directly related to the place language holds in society; as an expression of reality, it is itself part of the social construction, with its worldview set, schema or stereotype, influencing our way of perceiving reality.

In producing a news story, a journalist draws on a worldview derived from the concepts built into the society and the social institutions with which he or she has interacted. These concepts help to construct an individual and collective imaginary. In reporting a story, the journalist brings the individual imaginary to the issues that in turn shape the writing of the story.[4]

When it comes to religion, a collection of social constructs determines individual knowledge. A journalist, as any other member of a society, relies on these assumptions. While concepts around religion may or may not be a result of a religious experience, they will be directly related to the journalist's understanding of God.[5]

There are many studies on the construction of the Protestant imaginary in the United States.[6] Most agree that its base is a Puritan-Pietist Christian exclusivism that has led to the belief in manifest destiny and in the superiority of the American way of life. Likewise, perspectives of Eurocentric ideology and of Christendom in the Middle Ages that have been resignified can be identified in the first news "stories" regarding Latin America produced in the fifteenth century.

Letters of Columbus: The First News on Latin America

Christopher Columbus wrote the first news about the "Mundus Novis" to his Spanish sponsors. As a result, the Spanish Crown claimed the territory. During the return trip to Spain, Columbus's letter, dated March 14, 1493, from the port of Lisbon, was sent to Raphael Sanchez, treasurer of the Spanish Crown.[7] The navigator's news excited the royal couple as well as Spain's political and financial leaders. His impressive narrative was immediately translated and disseminated throughout Spain, Italy, France, and Germany.

Although historians cite records dating as far back as 900 AD that indicate that the coast of the Americas had been visited previously by Scandinavians, Welsh, Venetians, Portuguese, and Arabs from the Spanish peninsula, the news contained in Columbus's first letter, along with other letters he wrote about the "New World," was the most elaborate and widely disseminated report of a "world" beyond Europe. These missives, together with news from travelers who described expeditions, as well as early settlements, helped form an imaginary of the New World. As mentioned earlier, there was nothing inherently "new" in that part of the world, but the novelty of these well-illustrated accounts, which spread across Europe from the late 1400s through the 1500s, helped cement images of the environment and its inhabitants and created a new way of imagining and understanding this world-changing discovery.

Among the first points to attract attention in these accounts was Columbus's decision to call the native people "Indians." He did so because he mistakenly believed he had reached the region of the Indies. This misnomer, which has remained attached to the native peoples of the American continent, resulted from the contemporary European belief that explorers might discover "lost paradises" or "Heaven on Earth." This imaginary served "to convey mythic-cultural traits belonging to a generic non-European 'Primitive Other,' an exemplary human living in an exemplary place, 'India,' situated on the very edge of the then-unknown world."[8] Paradoxically, Europeans, steeped in medieval travel narratives, also believed that these inaccessible lands were populated by monstrous creatures and cannibals.[9] Columbus's language reflects this understanding:

> They are very simple and honest, and exceedingly liberal with all they have; none of them refusing any thing he may possess when he is asked for it, but on the contrary, inviting us to ask them. They exhibit great love towards all others in preference to themselves: they also give objects of great value for trifles, and content themselves with very little or nothing in return. . . . I did not find, as some of us had expected, any cannibals amongst them but on the contrary, men of great defense and kindness.[10]

Columbus's narrative also attracted great interest because of its locale. His language suggested an image that paradise on earth, the biblical Eden, was a reality in this previously unknown world.

> [The land] is surrounded with many bays, spacious, very secure and surpassing any that I have ever seen; numerous large and healthful rivers intersect it and it also contains many very lofty mountains. All these islands are very beautiful, and distinguished by a diversity of scenery; they are filled with a great variety of trees of immense height, and which I believe to retain their foliage in all seasons; for when I saw them, they were as verdant and luxuriant as they usually are in the month of May. . . . The nightingale and various birds were singing in countless numbers, and that in November, the month in which I arrived there. There are . . . seven or eight kinds of palm tree, which, alike all the other trees, herbs and fruits, considerably surpass ours in height and beauty.[11]

It is not difficult to imagine the reaction of the literate population when they read this narrative. When they added their own context and imaginary—virgin wilderness, abundant land, inhabited by primitive/savage but good people—it seemed to represent the possibility of accessing paradise not in heaven, but here and now.

Hence, the references from Columbus that cast his conquest in a specifically religious Christian light are clearly stated in several passages but especially at the close of the letter:

> These great and marvelous results are not to be attributed to any merit of mine, but to the holy Christian faith, and to the piety and religion of our Sovereigns; for

> that which the unaided intellect of man could not compass, the spirit of God has granted to human exertions, for God is wont to hear the prayers of his servants who love his precepts even to the performance of apparent impossibilities. . . . Therefore, . . . render thanks to our Lord and Savior Jesus Christ, who has granted us so great a victory and such prosperity. Let processions be made and sacred feasts be held, and the temples be adorned with festive boughs.[12]

This statement reveals an exclusivist understanding of religion prevalent in the "civilized and saved" Europe: the Christian faith was the only faith and should be embraced by every man and woman for his or her own salvation. Violations were considered idolatry, which could only lead to damnation. Consequently, Columbus expressed concern regarding the salvation of the good people he had just met:

> Thus they bartered, like idiots, cotton and gold for fragments of bows, glasses, bottles, and jars; which I forbad as being unjust, and I myself gave them many beautiful and acceptable articles, . . . that I might the more easily conciliate them, that they might be led to become Christians. . . . They practice no kind of idolatry, but have a firm belief that all strength and power, and indeed all good things, are in heaven, and that I had descended from thence with these ships. . . . I conceive to be the principal wish of our most serene King, namely, the conversion of these people to the holy faith of Christ, to which indeed, as far as I can judge, they are very favorable and well-disposed.[13]

Columbus's assessment shows that he was unable to identify and consider the diversity of the already existing religious expressions among the peoples inhabiting the "New World." His European Christian upbringing, combined with the restrictive ordinances of the medieval Iberian Catholicism, compelled the silencing of other experiences. These religious presuppositions became the basis for European colonizers' intolerant and violent actions toward indigenous peoples. Whether Roman Catholics in the fifteenth century or Protestants in the nineteenth century, all were most likely inspired by the last words of Columbus's enthusiastic and popular first letter:

> Let Christ rejoice on earth, as he rejoices in heaven in the prospect of the salvation of the souls of so many nations hitherto lost. Let us also rejoice, as well on account of the exaltation of our faith, as on account of the increase of our temporal prosperity, of which not only Spain, but all Christendom will be partakers.[14]

US Journalists: The Contemporary Columbus

As mentioned at the beginning of this study, the American mainstream media have demonstrated by their reporting on Latin American religion that Columbus's colonial precepts have been rigorously maintained: this subcontinent has been chosen by God to be Christian, a faith that must continue to be exalted; the land is wonderful and worth visiting; inhabitants are friendly but naïve people who require the guidance of enlightened foreigners; and other religions need not be taken seriously. When transformed into news stories, these ideas, formed by the colonial ideology that was also part of US history, reveal that coverage of Latin American religion still predominantly expresses the fifteenth-century imaginary of the "civilized" Christians who came to save the "pagan" land. Therefore, Roman Catholicism is still shown as "the" religion of Latin America.

To provide evidence of this statement, a case study analyzed the coverage of papal visits from Pope Paul VI's trip in 1968 to Benedict XVI's 2007 visit (see Table 29.1). The periodicals studied were the *New York Times* (*NYT*) and *Time* magazine. The selection reflected the fact that the *NYT* has reporters in both Latin America and the Vatican, and *Time* features longer, more in-depth stories, as well as more analysis on the region. Only informational pieces, rather than analytical articles or editorials, were included in the study. A combined methodology that drew on content analysis and discourse analysis explored how an image of Latin American religion was constructed through these narratives.

The Coverage of Papal Visits to Latin America as a Reflection of the Continent's Religion: Trends Through the Content

By the first decade of the twenty-first century, there had been forty-five papal visits to Latin America: one by Pope Paul VI (1968), the first pope to visit the region; forty-three by Pope John Paul II, from 1979 to 2002; and one by Pope Benedict XVI (2007). Prior to the papacy of John Paul II, popes did not travel much. Pope Paul VI's sole visit to the continent was the first by any pope and only took place because of the Latin American Episcopal Conference (CELAM) in Medellín, Colombia.

Paul VI's visit, which took place from August 22 to August 24, 1968, garnered thirty-seven stories in the *NYT* during the period from May 9 to August 28; *Time* published two articles on August 23 and August 30. That year, the *NYT* published ten more stories about religion in Latin America: nine related to the Catholic Church (four on the reformation of the Catholic Church in different countries, two on the issue of contraception, three on the involvement of priests with political and social issues) and one on Mormon leaders being prevented from entering Argentina. *Time* did not publish other articles on religion on the continent.

Taking the numbers into account, the two publications gave plenty of space to the first papal visit to Latin America. When evaluating news about other religions or religious happenings on the continent that year, *Time* magazine published nothing and the *NYT* published just ten stories—nine of which exclusively concerned the Roman Catholic Church. The tenth reported on a negative event related to another religion.

This trend was consistent throughout the entire period of sampling: among all materials on religion in Latin America published by the *NYT* and *Time*, over 95

Table 29.1 Papal Visits to Latin America

The first	
1968	Paul VI in Colombia—Medellín—CELAM Conference
John Paul II—43 visits	
1979	The Dominican Republic and Mexico
1980	Brazil
1982	Argentina
1983	Costa Rica, Nicaragua, Panama, El Salvador, Guatemala, Honduras, Belize, and Haiti
1984	Santo Domingo (the Dominican Republic) and San Juan (Costa Rica)
1985	Venezuela, Ecuador, Peru, and Trinidad and Tobago
1986	Colombia and Santa Lucia
1987	Uruguay, Chile, and Argentina
1988	Uruguay, Bolivia, Paraguay, and Lima (Peru)
1990	Mexico and Curaçao
1991	Brazil
1992	Santo Domingo (the Dominican Republic)
1993	Jamaica and Merida (Mexico)
1996	Guatemala, Nicaragua, El Salvador, and Venezuela
1997	Brazil
1998	Cuba
1999	Mexico City
2002	Guatemala and Mexico
Benedict XVI—one visit until 2011	
2007	Brazil

percent refer to the Roman Catholic Church. The emphasis on the Catholic Church is even greater in years of papal visits. Coverage is broad and comprehensive at these times—albeit varying according to the perceived importance given to the country of destination.

The first visit of Pope John Paul II to Latin America, specifically to Mexico in 1979 for the CELAM in Puebla, resulted in twenty-one stories in the *NYT* and two in *Time*. In this case the trip was especially important, since Mexico has strong ties to the United States, and this was the first time that a newly elected pope had traveled to the continent. The second visit to Mexico (1990) received only ten *NYT* stories, an average maintained by the newspaper for visits to other countries considered important to US geopolitics in the 1980s: Brazil (1980) generated ten stories in the *NYT* and one story in *Time*; Argentina (1982) generated thirteen stories in the

NYT and two in *Time*. The visit to Central America (eight countries in 1983) generated twenty-two stories in the *NYT* and three articles in *Time*. This average only changed in 1998 when John Paul II visited Cuba. Given the historical tensions between the United States and Cuba, the pope's visit to the Communist nation generated a series of thirty-eight stories in the *NYT* and five articles in *Time*.

The coverage of Benedict XVI's first visit to Latin America, in 2007, did not receive the same attention as Paul VI's first visit or John Paul II's trips, revealing that despite the prominence of the Catholic Church as "the" religion in Latin America, the new pope did not receive the same support from the American press: there were only seven stories in the *NYT* and three articles in *Time*. Even with these variations related to geopolitics and the popularity of the papal figure, as well as the politics of the pope, in the years that papal visits took place in Latin America, only 5 percent of stories covered other religious expressions. Of these, 75 percent refer to religions of African origin, such as Voodoo, Candomblé, and Macumba, indicating that the "exotic stranger" has secured its place in the imaginary of journalists and readers from the "civilized world." That 50 percent of these stories appear in the travel and art (dance, crafts) sections is further evidence of this predisposition of the press.

The remaining 25 percent was primarily about Protestant/Evangelical/Pentecostal growth from the 1980s on, followed by articles on topics including the crisis of indigenous culture in Argentina, the Catholic-Jewish dialogue in Brazil, the respect achieved by the Unification Church, and the presence of Mormonism.

As the content analysis of religion coverage in the *NYT* and *Time* demonstrates, journalists saw and presented the Latin American continent as almost wholly Roman Catholic. A headline from an *NYT* story on October 17, 1990, the year of John Paul II's second visit to Mexico, illustrates how the press constructed a religious worldview that treated Catholicism as dominant: "Guatemalan Church Fights Evangelicals' Rise." The "Guatemalan Church" referred to here is the Roman Catholic Church; the discourse effectively silences all the other Christian churches present in Guatemala, the most Protestant country of Latin America.

Despite the fact that Roman Catholic hegemony has been put in check since the second half of the twentieth century, American news organizations continue to privilege its status. In the process they inhibit the dissemination of expressive stories on other religious forms that could reveal the true, complex picture of religious diversity in Latin America.

The Coverage of Papal Visits to Latin America as Means of Understanding of the Continent's Religion: Trends Through the Discourse

An article in *Time* magazine, written during the first papal visit to Latin America (Paul VI) in 1968, exemplifies how the American mainstream media treats Catholicism as "the" Latin American religion. In the lead paragraph, the pope's arrival invokes the advent of the colonizers, thus reinforcing the perception that religion in Latin America first appeared with the Spanish Conquest.

> In imitation of Columbus' first act when he landed in the New World, the frail figure in the scarlet cloak fell to his knees at the foot of the airplane ramp and kissed the concrete. With that dramatic gesture, Paul VI last week became the first Pope to set foot in South America, the only predominantly Roman Catholic continent.[15]

Although the article acknowledges that the Roman Catholic Church is divided in Latin America, *Time* makes it clear that Roman Catholicism maintains the same principles as Columbus did: do whatever is necessary to keep this region on the path of true Christianity. These principles are revealed in the discourse of the magazine itself. Another article on the 1968 papal visit acknowledges the crisis in the Roman Catholic Church, but instead of citing divisions among the leadership and declining membership, the magazine attributes the crisis to the Catholic Church's lack of competence in caring for its "flock." The language employed in the *Time* article reveals the Christian exclusivism that permeates the author's imaginary and hints of threats to Latin American Catholicism.

> Although 90% of Latin America is nominally Catholic, probably fewer than 10% of the people practice what the church preaches. Thousands turn out for such semi-religious spectaculars as Lima's festival honoring Our Lord of the Miracles, but grandmothers and schoolchildren are often about the only worshipers at Sunday Mass in the ancient, silent churches. In Brazil, perhaps 25 million people are devotees of a voodoo cult called macumba. Across the continent, the zealous, fundamentalist Pentecostal sects constitute the fastest-growing faith. Even worse, the church lacks the ecclesiastical manpower to serve the sheep still within the fold. The ratio of priests to laymen in Latin America is 1 to 5,600 (in the U.S. it is 1 to 785).[16]

Remarkably, the author labels popular religion as "semi-religious spectaculars." He likewise describes Brazil's Afro-religions as a "voodoo cult called macumba," and he terms Pentecostal churches "sects." The author classifies as "worse" the fact that the church is incapable of developing and maintaining "ecclesiastical manpower to serve the sheep." The article constructs an image of non-Catholic religions as being minor and deficient. It also defends traditional Catholicism as the true religion, slighting the stirrings of an indigenous social gospel (later called Liberation Theology):

> The talk of the Catholic left can sometimes sound like a message from Radio Havana. The best known of the continent's revolutionaries, Brazilian Archbishop Helder Camara of Recife, argues that "either the church will ally itself with progressive forces that demand social justice for the enslaved masses, or it will perish for lack of insight and social dynamism."[17]

By associating Catholics supportive of the social gospel with "the left" as well as with Cuba and its revolution, the article helps to construct a social imaginary of a divided church that is threatening the historical project of Christendom on the continent. The close of the article reinforces this conclusion: "To some observers, Latin

American Catholicism is heading toward something very like a schism—based not on dogma or theology, but on commitment to social principle."[18]

NYT coverage of the first papal visit was less critical. Stories positively described the pope's leadership while remaining silent about other religious expressions. Headlines set the tone: "Pontiff May Call for Latin Reform; 'Courageous' Statement Is Forecast by a Prelate" (Wednesday, August 21, 1968); "Pontiff Exhorts Latins on Reform; More Equitable Taxing and Agrarian Progress Urged in Address to Peasants" (Saturday, August 24, 1968); "Paul Electrifies Workers' Parish; 200,000 Hail Pontiff at Close of 3-Day Colombian Visit" (Sunday, August 25, 1968).

When comparing the coverage of the most recent papal visit, Benedict XVI's trip in 2007, the form of the language may have changed, but the discourse remains the same. *Time* dispenses with its previously critical and aggressive language in favor of a softer but ironic tone that conveys a critique of the Catholic Church's failures, including the growth of other religious expressions. At the same time, the magazine celebrates the revival brought about by the Charismatic Catholic Movement. The story suggests that despite questions about its practices, the movement guarantees the recovery of hegemony that was threatened in the 1980s:

> New figures show that the exodus of worshipers to Protestantism has stopped. Government census data show that in 2003 73.8% of Brazilians declared themselves Catholics, almost exactly the same number (73.9%) as three years earlier. The number of Protestants did rise to 17.9% from 16.2%, but those joining Protestant denominations, rather than disaffected Catholics, were unhappy followers of other religions or people who had previously declared themselves to have no religious faith. . . . No one knows whether the plateau means the Vatican's prayers have been answered or whether the numbers will continue to fall again later. But the Pope can be expected to welcome signs of a Catholic resurgence with open arms. Father Rossi might not be able to get Benedict dancing at the altar, but the numbers he has helped produce just might.[19]

In its coverage of Benedict XVI's 2007 trip, the *NYT* kept silent about other religious expressions, instead reinforcing the role of the Roman Catholic Church on the continent. In the story "Pope Denounces Capitalism and Marxism" (May 14, 2007), Benedict's voice dominates and his speech to the Latin American Catholic bishops who met in Brazil for the CELAM is heavily quoted. Although the content of the pope's words is seen as a reflection of his conservatism, his persona remains authoritative: "His personal style, praised often even by critics, remains pastoral and gentle." Ordinary citizens corroborate this estimation; a retired female postal worker says, "I like his zeal. . . . He was a loyal comrade of John Paul II, and it is good that he is here to defend the traditional values of the Catholic Church, which are under attack from all sides."[20]

The newspapers also quoted a Chilean priest who was critical of the pope:

> The Vatican is afraid of liberation theology, but it shouldn't be. . . . The church can't afford to retreat. We have to react and bear Christian witness by continuing

to speak out for the poor, the marginalized, the jailed, Indians and blacks, and in favor of human rights.[21]

By the story's end, such critiques are summarily dismissed as "some modern-day theologies." The pope has the last word, and he reiterates the perspective that has predominated among Europeans since Columbus's first letter:

> Some modern-day Latin American theologians have lamented the destruction of indigenous civilizations and sought to incorporate elements of those cultures into the Mass as one way of making amends. But in a statement likely to be controversial in countries with large Indian populations, including Mexico, Peru, and Ecuador, Benedict rejected that approach: 'In effect, the proclamation of Jesus and of his Gospel did not at any point involve an alienation of the pre-Columbus cultures, nor was it the imposition of a foreign culture,' he said. He added: 'The utopia of going back to breathe life into the pre-Columbus religions, separating them from Christ and from the universal church, would not be a step forward; indeed, it would be a step back' and 'a retreat towards a stage in history anchored in the past.'"[22]

Final Considerations for New Possibilities

This study is intended as a critical examination of how the US news media cover religion in Latin America. Rather than a demand for politically correct coverage, this approach seeks to provide journalists, students, and scholars concerned with Latin American religion with a broader perspective, one that is free of the stereotypes founded in the collective imaginary of the "civilized world." The first steps to a practice that goes beyond the perspective of the conquerors and considers life (and religion) in Latin America as a rich, authentic, and complex experience would be to consider the cultural dimension that permeates both the so-called relevant and the ordinary stories and to seek out plurality and diversity in identity in news narratives.

NOTES

1. William J. Wainwright, ed., *The Oxford Handbook of Philosophy of Religion* (New York: Oxford University Press, 2005), 345.
2. Daniel H. Levine, "The News About Religion in Latin America," in *Religion on the International News Agenda*, ed. Mark Silk (Hartford, CT: The Leonard E. Greenberg Center for the Study of Religion in Public Life), 123–24, 137.
3. Miquel Rodrigo Alsina, *La Construction Social de la Noticia* (Barcelona: Paidos Iberica, 2005), 48. [English version of the citation by the author of this article]. The classic

contribution by Peter Berger and Thomas Luckmann is fundamental to this approach: *The Social Construction of the Reality: A Treatise in Social Knowledge* (New York: Anchor Books, 1967).

4. Here, the approach of "imaginary" is based on the reflections of Cornelius Castoriadis, who explains that imaginary is the incessant and essentially undetermined (social-historical and psychological) creation of figures/forms/images, from which it is possible to discuss "something." What we call reality and rationality are its products. Thus, reality is composed of a complex fabric of meanings that pervade, guide, and direct the entire life of social groups and all individuals who constitute it. Social imaginary significations are embodied in the social group and also animate it. These interpretations are imaginary because they do not match or are depleted from being "rational" or "real" and they are introduced by a creation. They are social because they only exist while they are established and shared by an anonymous and impersonal collective. See *The Imaginary Institution of Society* (Cambridge, MA: MIT Press, 1987).

5. On this subject see Claire H. Badaracco, ed., *Quoting God. How Media Shape Ideas About Religion and Culture* (Waco, TX: Baylor University Press, 2005).

6. In Brazil the excellent work by Viola Sachs and others has been a reference: *Brasil & EUA: Religião e Identidade Nacional* (Rio de Janeiro: Graal, 1988).

7. R. H. Major, ed., *The Selected Letters of Christopher Columbus with Other Original Documents Relating to His Four Voyages to the New World* (London: Hakluyt Society, 1847).

8. John F. Moffit, "Why Are Native Americans (Still) Called 'Indians'? The Illuminating Example of Giovanni di Paolo's Quattrocento Mapamundi," in *Art and the Native American Perceptions, Reality and Influences*, Vol. X, ed. Mary Louise Krumrine (University Park: Pennsylvania State University, Papers in Art and History, 2001), 15.

9. Among them the works of Mandeville, popular throughout Europe from the midfourteenth to the late fifteenth centuries, and Marco Polo. See Peter Hulme, *Colonial Encounters: Europe and the Native Caribbean, 1492–1797* (London: Routledge, 1992), 33.

10. Major, *The Selected Letters of Christopher Columbus*, 7, 18.

11. Ibid., 4–5.

12. Ibid., 16–17.

13. Ibid., 8, 10.

14. Ibid., 17.

15. "The Pope in Latin America," *Time*, August 30, 1968, http://www.time.com/time/magazine/article/0,9171,844591-2,00.html.

16. "Latin America: A Divided Church," *Time*, August 23, 1968, http://www.time.com/time/magazine/article/0,9171,838615-4,00.html#ixzzowJI4amf1.

17. Ibid.

18. Ibid.

19. "Behind Brazil's Catholic Resurgence," *Time*, May 8, 2007, http://www.time.com/time/world/article/0,8599,1618439,00.html#ixzzowJb6E96x.

20. "The Pope Denounces Capitalism and Marxism," *New York Times*, May 14, 2007, http://www.nytimes.com/2007/05/14/world/americas/14pope.html?pagewanted=2&sq=pope brazil&st=nyt&scp=12.

21. Ibid.

22. Ibid.

REFERENCES

Alsina, Miquel Rodrigo. 2005. *La Construction Social de la Noticia*. Barcelona: Paidos Iberica.

Badaracco, Claire H., ed. 2005. *Quoting God. How Media Shape Ideas About Religion and Culture*. Waco, TX: Baylor University Press.

Berger, Peter, and Thomas Luckmann. 1967. *The Social Construction of the Reality: A Treatise in Social Knowledge*. New York: Anchor Books.

Buddenbaum, Judith, and Debora L. Mason. 2000. *Readings on Religion as News*. Ames: Iowa State University.

Calloway, Colin G. 1997. *New Worlds for All: Indians, Europeans and the Remaking of Early America*. Baltimore: The John Hopkins University Press.

Castoriadis, Cornelius. 1987. *The Imaginary Institution of Society*. Cambridge, MA: MIT Press.

Hulme, Peter. 1992. *Colonial Encounters: Europe and the Native Caribbean, 1492–1797*. London: Routledge.

Krumrine, Mary Louise, ed. 2001. *Art and the Native American. Perceptions, Reality and Influences*. Vol. X. University Park: Pennsylvania State University, Papers in Art and History, 15.

Major, R. H., ed. 1847. *The Selected Letters of Christopher Columbus with Other Original Documents Relating to His Four Voyages to the New World*. London: Hakluyt Society.

Sachs, Viola, and others. 1988. *Brasil & EUA: Religião e Identidade Nacional*. Rio de Janeiro: Graal.

Shaff, Adam. 1973. *Language and Cognition*. New York: McGraw-Hill.

Silk, Mark, ed. 2000. *Religion in the International News Agenda*. Hartford, CT: The Leonard E. Greenberg Center for the Study of Religion in Public Life.

CHAPTER 30

AMERICAN COVERAGE OF IMMIGRATION, ISLAM, AND IDENTITY IN THE UK AND THE NETHERLANDS

ELIZABETH POOLE

How do American journalists cover religion in Europe, where issues of faith and church-state relations lead to differing interpretations of religio-ethnic news events? To address the question, this chapter examines US newspaper coverage of the anti-Islamic Dutch MP Geert Wilders. This case is particularly useful as it allows for an examination of the kind of issues taking place in Europe that have resonance for American journalists. A focus on Geert Wilders incorporates both the Netherlands and Britain into the analysis but also Europe more generally given that the case prompted a wider discussion of immigration and the place of Islam in European societies.

After discussing the differing roles and perceptions of religion in the United States and Europe, which has had an obvious impact on the way these issues are reported, the chapter reports on the differing models of integration for immigrants on the two continents and demonstrates how this has played out in news coverage of Islam. An examination of the reporting of the Geert Wilders case shows how Islam in Europe is represented through a conflict frame that incorporates a discourse of immigration, cultural incompatibility, identity, liberalism, and freedom. However, while these issues have clear implications within a US setting, in this instance coverage was not domesticated but clearly delineated as a foreign problem. The case therefore provides US journalists with a safe context for expressing anxieties about Islam and immigration while disassociating them from domestic affairs.

Religion and Immigration Issues in Britain and the United States

There can be no doubt that religion has a different place in US and European societies, and this almost certainly has had an impact on American perceptions of religion in Europe. In their groundbreaking work *Religious America, Secular Europe*, authors Peter Berger, Grace Davie, and Effie Oakes identify several explanatory factors for the religiosity of America compared to a relatively secular Europe.[1] Their finding of greater US religiosity is based on the measurement of a number of indices such as institutional behavior and expressed opinion. The authors argue that the Americans' exaggerated responses and the Britons' downplayed responses demonstrate something equally important about the significance of religion within specific cultural contexts. The evidence has led to a notion of Euro-secularity with North America being the exception.[2]

However, the theory that Europe was ever really "secular" and is now entering a "postsecular" phase and the theory that the United States was exceptional in its religiosity[3] have both now been challenged. Given the growth of religious movements globally, particularly Islam and Christianity in southern and eastern continents, Davie suggests that it is Europe that should be seen as the exception rather than the United States.[4] According to Berger et al., the example of North America challenges the idea of an organic link between modernization and secularization.[5] Rather, they argue, it is due to historical, social, political, and religious evolution in specific contexts. The most prominent factor is the relationship between church and state. However, this alone cannot account for the difference in religiosity given the various models across Europe. Additional intervening factors include competition among churches in the American market system, differing forms of Enlightenment in various cultures, types of intellectual and institutional transmission of Enlightenment values in various cultures, the relationship between class and religion in the United States, and the importance of churches in immigrant settlement.

In the last half of the twentieth century and beyond, global upheaval and postwar politics have led to the mass movement of people, the accommodation of whom has presented a significant challenge to immigrant and host societies alike. Postwar boom economies and the need for new sources of labor led European nations to encourage immigration from former colonies. In Britain, immigration occurred from the West Indies and Indian subcontinent; in the Netherlands, from former territories Turkey and Morocco. But as these former migrant workers became settlers at a time of economic downturn, models of integration became an issue, with religion often at the center of the problem. The Dutch model for dealing with religious immigrants is based on "pillarization," whereby individual denominations (separate pillars) were entitled to exist alongside one another with equal access to state funding (as in the education system).[6] However, the policy of "multiculturalism," defined as the accommodation or acceptance of difference whereby all ethnic groups are afforded equal status, has been increasingly criticized on several fronts, one of these being that it encourages segregation.

As Muslim political agency has increased, the "failures" of multiculturalism have been used as an excuse to toughen integration policies, both in the UK and Netherlands, including citizenship tests aimed at more fully incorporating immigrants.[7] Postcolonial immigration and the resulting social, political, and legal resolutions were centered on race and ethnicity. Hence, Muslims have been particularly marginalized in the process of allocating resources and promoting equality. As Muslims have begun to assert themselves along their chosen identities (religious), this has created an ideological conflict for those who promote equality within a secular framework. This has led to a particularly tense situation for the Dutch, whose liberal society is struggling to adapt and is demonstrating significant illiberalism in its accommodation of its minorities, particularly since the assassinations of politician Pim Fortuyn (2002) and film director Theo van Gogh (2004).[*] Muslims in particular, with their public religiosity, have been perceived as a challenge to this secular liberal framework.

The United States, on the other hand, has constructed an identity as an immigrant society, alternately identifying itself as "a nation of immigrants" or, employing a metaphor more akin to assimilation, as a "melting pot." Religion has played a central part in the settling of immigrant communities, the structural context provoking a "religious response," which in turn reinforced the importance of religion and religious pluralism in American society.[8]

One possible reason for the difference between European/US reactions to Muslims could be that 70 percent of immigrants into the United States are Christian and only 10 percent are Muslim.[9] Yet reaction to Muslims has been similar, particularly since 9/11, when Muslims, who were previously accommodated within America's pluralist mentality, came under greater public scrutiny. Further, despite America's religious pluralism, Berger et al. suggest that Islam is more difficult to accommodate in that it is perceived to be resistant to the republican ideal.[10] This is one way in which US and European attitudes toward religion have more parity.

Hence, global and local politics have resulted in negative representations of Islam in the Western news media, including a conflict framework of news reporting as various groups struggle to establish hegemony in an unstable and changing multicultural environment. In Britain, studies show that post 9/11 and -7/7 (Lon-

* Fortuyn was a Dutch politician who was openly hostile to Muslim immigration in the Netherlands. Van Gogh was a film director who, with Ayaan Hirsi Ali, produced *Submission* about the treatment of women in Islam.

don bombings of July 7, 2005), there was a shift in mainstream news reporting from the availability of a relatively broad range of discourses that reflected the multiple identities of Muslims in Britain to a more homogenized output in line with international coverage of Islam that centered around violence, conflict, and terrorism.[11] D'Haenens and Bink have shown how this conflict plays out in the Dutch press with journalists emphasizing the differences between the Muslim world and the West rather than commonalities, which they argue gives "news value to those divergences."[12] However, while studies have found that there is an effort to provide more balance when discussing Muslims at a local level, there are also significant moments locally when this is disrupted (e.g., the 2004 murder of Theo van Gogh in Holland).

The negative representation of Muslims in the Canadian and American news media has also been well documented.[13] Karim's detailed study of the fanatical and violent associations through which Islam has been constructed as a nemesis of the West feeds misperceptions informed by historical stereotypes.[14] However, this type of reporting pales into insignificance compared with coverage after 9/11 and the start of the Iraq War, which Kellner argues can be equated to propaganda.[15] He contends that the media were manipulated through "spectacles of terror" by both Islamist jihadists and the Bush administration to further their own causes. In both cases, a "clash of civilizations" discourse prevailed, reinforcing binary opposing positions. Here is the paradox: despite the expectation that, given specific national histories, Islam would be represented differently in diverse contexts, it appears to be negatively constructed in a fairly uniform manner. The value of the work undertaken here, focusing on the representation of one country grappling with its domestic issues by reporting on another, provides an insight into how narratives and constructions of Islam are formulated.

The Case of Geert Wilders

Geert Wilders is a Dutch politician and leader of the Party for Freedom (PVV). He was previously a member of the conservative-liberal People's Party for Freedom and Democracy (VVD) but left to set up his own party in 2004 over differences on Turkey's accession to Europe. Well known internationally for his controversial anti-Islamic stance, Wilders's position has brought him some success (and popularity) in Dutch politics, increasing his seats in the 2010 Dutch election from nine to twenty-four, which was only seven fewer than the winning party.[16]

In 2008, Wilders produced *Fitna* (translated in the US press as "discord" and "strife"), a short film that juxtaposes violent images of extreme Islamism with verses from the Koran. The film was widely criticized. On February 13, 2009, Wilders was refused entry to Britain on public order grounds. Lord Pearson of the UK Independence Party had invited him to a screening of *Fitna* in the House of Lords. The home secretary deemed *Fitna*, in tandem with Wilders's presence, as "threatening community harmony and therefore public security" and denied him entry. Wilders flew to London, aware that he would be turned back at the airport, thus creating a huge publicity coup. Since then a tribunal has overturned the ruling, and Wilders entered the UK in October 2009 and January 2010 to protests from Islam4UK, an organization since banned under the UK's 2000 Terrorism Act. The following analysis focuses more on coverage around *Fitna* and the subsequent fallout than Wilders's political gains in the Netherlands.

Study Methodology

To investigate US coverage of religion in Europe, the study analyzed both the national and regional press. The newspapers chosen were based on their status and readership both in the United States and wider society. While there is evidence to show newspaper readership is in decline,[17] there remains a close relationship between elite opinion, newspaper coverage, and public policy in Western democracies.[18] In turn, this coverage is reproduced online on newspaper websites, which then becomes a source for other online publications. Analyzing press reporting, then, gives us an idea of the competing dominant discourses about an issue at a particular historical moment, as well as what solutions are preferred. Using the search terms "Geert Wilders," articles were retrieved with a combination of approaches based on accessibility (either from the Lexis-Nexis database or the newspapers' websites). The newspapers analyzed and the number and types of articles retrieved are shown in Table 30.1. As expected, those papers aimed at a national audience have more coverage of the case, while regional coverage is low. Taken together, though, and with a total of 113 articles analyzed, the study provides an overview of at least some of the dominant ideas circulating about Islam. While not claiming to be representative of wider issues, an analysis of this case provides some useful pointers and connections to other studies that demonstrate particular patterns of reporting (see previous section on studies that examine representations of Islam).

Analysis of Coverage

Two periodicals include coverage that supports Muslims and defends them from Wilders's attack (*Newsweek* and *New York Times*), four had coverage that is broadly balanced (*Boston Globe, Philadelphia Inquirer, Chicago Tribune*, and *Dallas News*), and seven are more sympathetic to Wilders's position, particularly in relation to

Table 30.1 Type of Articles by Newspaper

Newspaper	Articles Generated by Search	Articles Analyzed	News Articles	Commentary	Editorial	Feature	Letter	Review
Washington Times	30	21	5	12	2	1	1	—
Washington Post	21	12	8*	1	—	3	—	—
Wall Street Journal	34	21	—	7	—	1	13	—
New York Times	35	24	14	3	1	4	1	1
Newsweek	9	9	1	—	—	7	1	—
LA Times	5	5	1	4	—	—	—	—
Boston Globe	9	9	5	2	—	1	1	—
Chicago Tribune	2	2	2	—	—	—	—	—
Dallas News	2	2	2	—	—	—	—	—
Philadelphia Inquirer	4	4	2	1	—	—	1	—
Denver Post	1	1	—	1	—	—	—	—
USA Today	1	1	—	1	—	—	—	—
Daily News	2	2	2	—	—	—	—	—
Total no. of articles	155	113	42	32	3	17	18	1

*Seven of these being "News in Brief."

issues of freedom of speech and terrorism (with the *Washington Times* being the most outwardly anti-Islam). This section demonstrates the dominant discourses appearing in the articles with reference to how the story was largely formulated within the binaries of "culture clash" and freedom of speech vs. censorship, with Europe's struggle with its identity and immigration as a central focus. This largely reinforces the opinions of Wilders. The British press reaction to the story of Wilders's ban from Britain was to condemn it on the basis of free speech with a strong double-standards discourse: why should Wilders be banned when extreme Islamists are allowed entry to Britain? This theme also was evident in the US press, but the greater balance in the reporting of Wilders, particularly in some newspapers, is likely due to their distance from the story, the event being formulated as a "European problem" (particularly in relation to immigration and identity). Notably, initial coverage of Wilders, which largely reports on his political rise in Holland, is much more balanced than later stories focusing on *Fitna* and his ban from Britain. A point of clarification before starting: most of the articles cited (unless otherwise stated) are op-ed pieces chosen largely because they offer the most explicit quotes. While it cannot be explicitly said that these represent the editorial positions of the papers, the repeated use of the same commentators or commentators with similar opinions (while excluding an alternative construction) demonstrates a strong indication of the interpretation the newspaper prefers *in coverage of this case*. One example is the frequency with which the *Washington Times* asks Diana West, a right-wing analyst, to comment both in relation to this case and other stories regarding Islam. Having examined all articles on Wilders, it can also be said that the selected opinion pieces are representative of wider coverage *of this case*.

Wilders is afforded more credibility in the US press than in the British press, where he is constructed as an outsider, even an "oddball." In the US newspapers, he is merely a "critic of Islam"[19] with only a couple of articles negatively depicting him as a "dangerous extremist and self-promoter."[20] Wilders is even constructed positively in some pieces as "courageous," "heroic," and a victim of Muslim bullies.[21] While many of the papers take pains to point out that they do not agree with his views, coverage often suggests otherwise.

Craft and Waisbord's analysis of the Danish cartoons controversy[**] (which has obvious parallels with this story) found that there were two ways in which the story was framed.[22] First, a freedom-of-speech frame pitted absolutist and social responsibility positions on free speech against each other.[***] Elaborations of this frame often equated socially responsible speech with religious tolerance on one side and with submission or "appeasement" on the other. Second, a "clash of civilizations"

** In which the editor of the Danish newspaper, Jyllands-Posten, commissioned twelve cartoonists to depict Muhammad as a comment on Islam and censorship.

*** "Responsible speech" is speech that contributes to the common good by refraining from criticizing people's sacred values (in this case, religious beliefs) out of tolerance for diversity or strategic considerations.[81]

frame pitted "the West" against "the Muslim world." The Geert Wilders story produces coverage drawn largely from the absolutist position.

The assassinations of the anti-immigrationist Pim Fortuyn (2002) and Theo van Gogh (2004) were catalysts for media coverage, but *Fitna* sparked a new debate. While the story could have been framed as an attack on Muslims, many papers used a conflict framework that positions liberal freedoms against religious intolerance as demonstrated by David Harsanyi from the *Denver Post*: "The Brits proved Wilders's point about Islam's influence by suppressing his right to free expression."[23] When the ban is overturned, it is described by the *Wall Street Journal* as a "victory for free speech."[24] This position is also held by the *Washington Times* and *Los Angeles Times*. While the *Wall Street Journal* does admit that "There are of course limits to free speech, such as calls for violence," it adds, "[b]ut one doesn't need to agree with Mr. Wilders to acknowledge that he hasn't crossed that line."[25] Several editorials also use the Wilders case to oppose US support for the UN resolution on "negative and religious stereotyping." In *USA Today*, Jonathan Turley goes as far as reconstructing this as "blasphemy laws." In "Just Say No to Blasphemy Laws," he asserts, "This country should never sacrifice freedom of expression on the altar of religion."[26] The US Constitution and the First Amendment are referred to regularly to support this argument.[27] According to some commentators, European countries' liberal tolerance is to blame for the situation in which they find themselves, as in: "The Dutch, Too Tolerant for Their Own Good? A Country Caught Between Tradition and Terrorism."[28] Britain, "the motherland of parliamentary democracy," has also "surrendered to Islamists."[29] This commentary acts as an attack on leftist politics and political correctness, which has led to the self-censorship that Schwammenthal asserts is "in truth . . . no act of courtesy but the result of intimidation and fear."[30] The stereotype that Muslims are easily offended and quick to react ties into this discourse. Worldwide protests against the film are a central focus of coverage.[31] In "Preemptive Rage," Diana West speaks of the "widely anticipated Islamic outrage."[32] The most frequently occurring graphic used to accompany the articles, besides an image of Geert Wilders, are photographs of predominantly Muslim group protests, particularly in the *Washington Times*. As with the Danish cartoons controversy, it is the conflict rather than the cartoons or, as is the case here, *Fitna*, which is of most interest.[33] If Muslims are criticized, they become threatening: "other perceived insults to Islam in Europe have turned deadly."[34] Only the *Boston Globe* mentions protests by non-Muslims against Wilders.[35] For the more conservative publications, tolerance becomes submission or appeasement. In "Appeasing the Islamists: Craven Dutch Submit," Paul Belien of the *Washington Times* compares the censorship currently taking place to appease Muslims to that of Nazi intimidation in Germany in the 1930s.[36] Elsewhere in the paper this is equated to the totalitarianism of the USSR[37] and fascism.[38] In its concessions to Muslims, Europe is experiencing "Islamization"[39] and Britain has become "Londonistan."[40] Yet these governments are perceived as "selective in opposing extremism"[41]: "Just look at Britain. It is currently harboring a gaggle of non-British Muslim preachers who call for, among other things, the slaughter of Jews and the imposition of Sharia law in Britain. These people are accepted, sometimes even given welfare benefits, in the name of pluralism, multiculturalism and tolerance."[42]

The incompatibility of liberal Western ideals and intolerant Muslim values is a recurring framework in relation to Muslims in "the West," if not explicitly, then implicitly, whereby numerous events are used as illustration. This is evident in the "contextualizing" of this event to other examples of "conflict," such as the Danish cartoons controversy and the assassination of van Gogh and Fortuyn—"The latest twist in the clash between Western values and the Muslim world"—and in the self-segregation of a Muslim community who cannot accept Dutch values.[43]

Given these frameworks, it is no surprise that Muslims are categorized negatively in most of the reports and editorials discussed. References are made to "Islamic militants," "murderous fanatics," "Muslim radicals," "Islamofacism," "Islamic supremacism," and "Islam inspired violence."[44] If freedom of speech represents democracy, liberalism, and so forth, and Muslims appear to be opposed to it, this positions Muslims as antidemocratic, antifreedom, unlawful, and so forth. The threat of Islam is not just a cultural one. Many papers refer to the terror threat. In "The Case for Mistrusting Muslims," Dalrymple argues that in Britain "[t]here are reasonable grounds for suspicion. Surveys . . . show a . . . degree of sympathy . . . for the bombers on the part of the young Muslim population of Britain. They show a large number of Muslims in Britain want the implementation of Shariah law and think that murdering British Jews is justified simply because they are Jews, etc." To deny this is "to ignore sociological reality."[45]

The problem is seen as emanating from Muslims themselves: "The West and the world's solution to dealing with radical Islam lies not in banning or attacking Islam. The solution lies, ironically, in educating Muslims about their own religion."[46] However, there is also evidence of Muslim voices in news features, as in a *Washington Post* article that presents "one woman's experience" as a Muslim convert to illustrate "Europe's struggle with its identity"[47]; in letters, such as Mohammed Asmal's "Free Speech Aside, Paper Wrong to Grant Forum to Bigotry"[48]; and in sourcing that uses moderate Muslims for comments. Some of these voices support the paper's stance, as evidenced by Islamic reformer Tawfik Hamid's position that Wilders is merely exposing the activities of radical Islamists and should not be denounced for this.[49]

The US press treated this story as an indication that immigration (synonymous with Islam here) is extremely problematic within Europe. The situation is variously described as a "simmering cauldron of immigration issues,"[50] "discontent,"[51] and "problematic."[52] The problem is generalized (also a feature of coverage of the Danish cartoons), so Europe becomes homogenized: "An invisible front line runs through the quiet streets of many a European city or town where there is a significant Muslim population."[53]

But European tolerance is found to have resulted in a host of problems, including a European identity crisis and a terrorist threat (*Daily News, New York Times, Chicago Tribune, Los Angeles Times*). Again, freedom is perceived as central to a national identity now under threat: "The proud self image (of tolerance) has abruptly given way to an angst-filled identity crisis leaving the Dutch struggling to figure out how to deal with the very real risk of terrorism, wondering how to persuade Muslim immigrants to embrace their tradition of tolerance."[54] The *Washington Post* and *Wall Street Journal* adopt an anti-multicultural approach: "The successful integration of Muslims in the Netherlands and the rest of Europe will require that immigrants adapt to Western norms, not vice versa."[55] Neither American nor European newspapers show evidence of an open debate over what form multiculturalism should take in an ever-changing and complex situation. In the US case, however, "their [the Founding Fathers] most wondrous legacy was creating the foundations of a culture of religious diversity in which the secular and the religious could live in harmony, giving faith a role in the life of the nation in which it could shape us without strangling us."[56] In "Battleground Europe," an English commentator, Timothy Garton Ash, endorses the view that "All the evidence suggests that American Muslims are better integrated than those in Western Europe."[57] Western Europe, on the other hand, "is a post-Christian society with secularism as its state ideology. The secularists have created a religious vacuum in the heart of European society—which Islam is filling."[58] The distinctive challenge to Europe is that it has been forced to bring religion back out of the private sphere. What is evident in the discourse of the papers, then, is the construction of collective identity and nationhood.

The initial balance in articles such as "Tolerance Tested in Holland,"[59] which seek to show both that Holland's tolerant image may be a myth and that the tension is inflated, is later overtaken by a conservative framework. The balance to be found in the majority of news stories (as opposed to commentary) reflects the objectivity central to US journalists' values but also contributes to "distancing" from the story, since Americans position themselves as impartial observers of someone else's conflict.[60] However, only *Newsweek* and the *New York Times* come near to challenging the dominant framing of the story. Both publications ignored the provocation to construct the story within a free speech framework and chose instead to attack Wilders and his position. *Newsweek* is particularly forthright in challenging tropes about Muslims. It explores and then dismisses Wilders's and others' right-wing arguments, as well as criticizes other news outlets' coverage.[61] In pieces such as "Christian Rage and Muslim Moderation" by Christopher Dickey, the stereotype of Muslim fanaticism is displaced to the Christian Right.[62] In these articles, Wilders is cast as a "provocateur" and hypocritical while Muslims are "conciliatory." Tension is underplayed.[63] Interestingly (and absent from the British press), the writers suggest the current climate in Europe toward Muslims is comparable to the anti-Semitism in Europe's history.[64] Both *Newsweek* and the *New*

York Times use the coverage to attack what they perceive as a previously liberal Europe moving to the Right.[65]

The *New York Times* portrays Wilders as holding a double standard, advocating free speech while simultaneously wanting to ban the Koran. Also at fault are the Dutch, who tolerate only like-minded people.[66] The coverage also demonstrates a pro-immigration standpoint and commentators write passionately against racism and prejudice.[67] However, at certain moments the tension in Europe and the problem of integrating minorities in "polarized" communities is highlighted as in "Our Ally, Our Problem": "Here is the problem for the United States: Under our Visa Waiver Program, residents of Londonistan who hold a valid British passport can board a plane for the United States without an interview by an American consular official."[68] The newspaper also positions Islam as negative in its opposition to liberal values on women's rights, as in an interview with Ayaan Hirsi Ali, Theo van Gogh's coproducer. Ali is described as the "democracy campaigner" and "daughter of the Enlightenment," positioning that contributes further to the idea of "cultural clash."[69] In general, though, the majority of the *Times'* coverage runs against the dominant discourse present elsewhere in the American press. Liberal reaction to Islam reveals a level of intolerance not found in relation to other minority groups according to Casanova[70] and Modood[71] and is an example of "illiberal secularism."[72] A liberal hegemony among the "secular intelligentsia" has created a double standard whereby conservative religious groups have to accept behaviors they disagree with but secular liberals will not tolerate beliefs at odds with their liberal values.[73] This is justified by the liberal majority on the basis of "the secularist teleological assumption built into theories of modernization that one set of norms is reactionary, fundamentalist and anti-modern, while the other set is progressive, liberal and modern."[74] This is clearly at play in the case of Geert Wilders. In the hostility to Islam from the US press, Muslims clearly demonstrate a non-Christian other that is a threat to the values of a secular elite.

Conclusion

Despite the fact that all the countries covered here are multicultural liberal democracies with a Christian history and a significant Muslim population, US press coverage of the Wilders case clearly delineates this as a European problem. While this is obviously related to the fact that the specific event covered is based in Europe and fits with the cultural proximity aspect of news values, the event does have resonance within an American context. The few references to the domestic context demonstrate a discourse of superiority in dealing with immigration related to the separation of church and state and the myth of the United States as a "melting pot" with a long tradition of tolerance for immigration. This detachment is an example of how Europe plays the role of the "bad self" onto whom problems can be projected. Discussion about Europe allows anxieties about Muslim integration to be expressed without inflaming tensions at home.[75]

These findings are in keeping with Craft and Waisbord's analysis of the Danish cartoons coverage in America.[76] They argued that although the story was picked up as a typical international news story of drama and conflict, which could be framed within broader conflicts that have relevance for US audiences, "journalists drew clear national boundaries about whose conflict it was," placing it within a "European vs. Muslim" frame.[77] Most of the papers' response to this issue demonstrates the cultural consensus on Muslims suggested by studies cited earlier on in this chapter. However, this cannot be put down to the globalization of news production processes alone. As Craft and Waisbord's research demonstrates, journalists are key in deciding to "domesticize" a story based on its relevance to their own citizens. Yet their analysis suggests that the Danish cartoons controversy was not domesticated (as with the Wilders case) due to its sensitivity and concern that it may have significant repercussions at home.

The newspapers also represent the model of incorporation of Europe's minorities as particular to Europe based on the very differing histories of immigration and the development of religious pluralism on both continents. This allows them to keep their distance from the "problems." However, as is suggested by theory and made evident in the analysis of coverage here, the presence of Muslims (due to a complex mix of global and local politics) does threaten America's myth of itself as a model of immigrant incorporation.[78] In fact, the reality is both complex and fluid.**** The simplistic press portrayal of ethno-religious divisions in Europe and the reasons posited for the differing responses to immigration by Europe and the United States, as well as resorting to dualisms about where Muslim and secularists stand on different debates, only exacerbate the tension, maintain social relations in line with the status quo, and do not offer any positive solutions that current multicultural democracies require. Modood argues that the situation requires a "pragmatic case-by-case, negotiated approach to dealing with controversy and conflict: not an ideological 'drawing a line in the sand' mentality."[79] By seriously engaging with issues faced in Europe, the US press could open up a constructive debate about developing appropriately dynamic and pluralistic integration in the current context, how different societies could "widen and adapt the national culture and the public symbols of national membership" to incorporate minorities, a "difference affirming equality" or "political multiculturalism."[80]

**** Examples of "home-grown" Islamists would suggest otherwise. For example, Major Nidal Malik Hasan, an army psychiatrist from Virginia, killed twelve people and injured thirty-one others at Fort Hood, a US Army base in November 2009.

NOTES

1. Peter Berger, Grace Davie, and Effie Fokas, *Religious America, Secular Europe* (Surrey: Ashgate, 2008).

2. José Casanova, "Immigration and the New Religious Pluralism: A European Union-United States Comparison," in *Secularism, Religion and Multicultural Citizenship*, ed. Geoffrey Brahm Levey and Tariq Modood (Cambridge: Cambridge University Press, 2009), 139–63.

3. José Casanova, "Religion, Secular Identities, and European Integration," in *Religion in an Expanding Europe*, ed. Peter J. Katzenstein and Timothy A. Byrnes (Cambridge: Cambridge University Press, 2006), 66–90.

4. Davie, 2007, cited in Berger and others, *Religious America*.

5. Berger and others, *Religious America*.

6. Ibid.

7. Leen D' Haenens and Susan Bink, "Islam in the Dutch Press: With Special Attention to the Algemeen Dagblad," *Media, Culture and Society* 29 (2007): 135–49.

8. Casanova, "Immigration and the New Religious Pluralism," 150.

9. José Casanova, 2007, 79, cited in Berger and others, *Religious America*, 107.

10. Berger and others, *Religious America*.

11. Elizabeth Poole, *Reporting Islam: Media Representations of British Muslims* (London: I. B. Tauris, 2002); Elizabeth Poole, "The Effects of September 11 and the War in Iraq on British Newspaper Coverage," in *Muslims and the News Media*, ed. Elizabeth Poole and John Richardson (London: I. B. Tauris, 2006), 89–102.

12. D' Haenens and Bink, "Islam in the Dutch Press," 136.

13. Karim H. Karim, *Islamic Peril: Media and Global Violence* (Montréal: Black Rose Books, 2000); Karim H. Karim, "American Media's Coverage of Muslims: The Historical Roots of Contemporary Portrayals," in *Muslims and the News Media*, ed. Elizabeth Poole and John Richardson (London: I. B. Tauris, 2006), 116–27.

14. Ibid.

15. Douglas Kellner, "9/11 and the Discourse and Spectacles of Terror: A Critique of Jihadist and Bush Media Politics," *Critical Discourse Studies* 1 (2004): 41–64.

16. Ian Traynor, "Geert Wilders on Course for Dutch Cabinet Seat," *The Guardian*, June 10, 2009, http://www.guardian.co.uk/world/2010/jun/10/geert-wilders-cabinet-seat-election (accessed September 29, 2010).

17. Richard Pérez-Peña, "Newspaper Circulation Continues to Decline Rapidly," *New York Times*, October 27, 2008, http://www.nytimes.com/2008/10/28/business/media/28circ.html (accessed May 20, 2010).

18. Robert Entman, *Projections of Power: Framing News, Public Opinion, and U.S. Foreign Policy* (Chicago and London: University of Chicago Press, 2004).

19. "Britain Bans One of Islam's Critics," *Wall Street Journal Europe*, February 13, 2009, http://online.wsj.com/article/SB123447930283579567.html (accessed June 1, 2010).

20. Mark Hosenball, "The Flying Dutchman," *Newsweek*, February 17, 2009, http://www.newsweek.com/2009/02/16/the-flying-dutchman.html (accessed September 29, 2010).

21. Diana West, "Pre-Emptive Rage; Protestations of Dutch Film," *Washington Times*, March 28, 2008; "The Politics of Intimidation; Islamists Work to Silence Critics," July 11, 2008.

22. Stephanie Craft and Silvio Waisbord, "When Foreign News Remains Foreign. Cartoon Controversies in the U.S. and Argentine Press," in *Transnational Media Events:*

The Mohammed Cartoons and the Imagined Clash of Civilizations, ed. Elisabeth Eide, Risto Kunelius, and Angela Philips (Sweden: Nordicom, 2008): 133–50.

23. "The Right Not to Be Offended," *Denver Post*, February 25, 2009.

24. "Geert Wilders Comes to Britain," Opinion Europe, *Wall Street Journal*, October 18, 2009, http://online.wsj.com/article/SB10001424052748704322004574447 (accessed June 1, 2010).

25. "Silencing Islam's Critics," Opinion Europe, *Wall Street Journal*, January 22, 2009, http://online.wsj.com/article/SB123257047606303395.html (accessed June 1, 2010).

26. "Just Say No to Blasphemy Laws," *USA Today*, October 19, 2009.

27. For example, Wesley Pruden, "A Flying Dutchman in Pursuit of Speech," *Washington Times*, February 24, 2009.

28. Frida Ghitis, "The Dutch, Too Tolerant for Their Own Good?" *Washington Post*, October 30, 2005.

29. Daniel Schwammenthal, "Britain's Surrender to Islamists," *Wall Street Journal*, February 17, 2009, http://online.wsj.com/article/SB123482476050494869.html (accessed June 1, 2010).

30. West, "The Politics of Intimidation."

31. See News in Brief, *Washington Post*, March 29, March 31, April 7, and April 21, 2008.

32. West, "Preemptive Rage."

33. Craft and Waisbord, "When Foreign News Remains Foreign."

34. Leander Schaerlaeckens, "Dutch Film to Slam Islam," *Washington Times*, February 29, 2008.

35. "Thousands Protest Anti-Koran Film," *Boston Globe*, March 23, 2008, http://www.boston.com/news/world/europe/articles/2008/03/23/thousands_protest_anti_koran_film/ (accessed June 1, 2010).

36. "Appeasing the Islamists; Craven Dutch Politicians Submit," *Washington Times*, March 26, 2008.

37. Frank. J. Gaffney, Jr., "Islamists Catch-22," *Washington Times*, July 8, 2008.

38. Nat Hentoff, "The Cost of Criticizing Jihadists; UN Resolution Is Part of the Islamic Muzzle," *Washington Times*, February 9, 2009.

39. Arnaud de Borchgrave, "Switzerland Bans Minarets; A Deepening Chasm Between Cultures," *Washington Times*, December 1, 2009.

40. Daniel Schwammenthal, "Britain's Surrender to Islamists."

41. "Britain Bans One of Islam's Critics."

42. Jonah Goldberg, "The 'Truth to Power' Gap," *Los Angeles Times*, February 17, 2009, http://www.latimes.com/news/opinion/commentary/la-oe-goldberg17-2009feb17,0,7528745.column (accessed June 1, 2010).

43. "Silencing Islam's Critics."

44. West, "The Politics of Intimidation."

45. Theodore Dalrymple, "The Case for Mistrusting Muslims," *Los Angeles Times*, July 8, 2007, http://www.latimes.com/news/opinion/commentary/la-op-dalrymple-8jul08,0,6923090.story (accessed June 1, 2010).

46. Donald A. Jordan, "Letter," *Wall Street Journal*, December 10, 2008, http://online.wsj.com/article/SB122887126779093353.html (accessed June 1, 2010).

47. Molly Moore, "Dutch Convert to Islam: Veiled and Viewed as Traitor," *Washington Post*, March 19, 2006.

48. Mohammed Asmal, "Free Speech Aside, Paper Wrong to Grant Forum to Bigotry," *Boston Globe*, March 15, 2009, http://www.boston.com/bostonglobe/editorial_opinion/letters/articles/2009/03/15/free_speech_aside_paper_wrong_to_grant_forum_to_bigotry/ (accessed June 1, 2010).

49. "Islam Needs to Prove It's a Religion of Peace," *Wall Street Journal*, March 9, 2009, http://online.wsj.com/article/SB123654552575064501.html (accessed June 1, 2010).

50. Henry Chu, "Dutch City's Unity Falls to Muslim Mayor," *Los Angeles Times*, October 4, 2009 (also in *Chicago Tribune*).

51. Arthur Max, "In Netherlands, Anti Europe Attitude May Defeat Charter," *Philadelphia Inquirer*, May 27, 2005.

52. David R. Sands, "Anti-Islam Film Prompts Damage Control," *Washington Times*, March 22, 2008.

53. Timothy Garton Ash, "Battleground Europe," *Los Angeles Times*, September 13, 2007, http://www.latimes.com/news/printedition/asection/la-oe-garton13sep13,0,1482382.story (accessed June 1, 2010).

54. Ghitis, "The Dutch, Too Tolerant for Their Own Good?"

55. "Silencing Islam's Critics"; "Free Speech and Europeans," Editorial, *Washington Times*, December 26, 2008.

56. Jon Meacham, "The Religious Case for Church-State Separation," *Newsweek*, April 23, 2010, http://www.newsweek.com/2010/04/22/the-religious-case-for-church-state-separation.html (accessed June 1, 2010).

57. Garton-Ash, "Battleground Europe."

58. Belien, "Islamofascism in the Netherlands."

59. Tom Carter, "Tolerance Tested in Holland," *Washington Times*, December 20, 2004, A01.

60. Craft and Waisbord, "When Foreign News Remains Foreign."

61. See Hosenball, "The Flying Dutchman."

62. Christopher Dickey, "Christian Rage and Muslim Moderation," *Newsweek*, March 27, 2006, http://www.newsweek.com/2008/03/26/christian-rage-and-muslim-moderation.html (accessed June 1, 2010).

63. Friso Endt, "The Dutch Greet *Fitna* with a Yawn," *Newsweek*, March 29, 2008, http://blog.newsweek.com/blogs/ov/archive/2008/03/29/the-dutch-greet-fitna-with-a-yawn.html (accessed June 1, 2010).

64. See Denis MacShane, "Europe's New Politics of Fear," *Newsweek*, April 16, 2010, http://www.newsweek.com/2010/04/15/europe-s-new-politics-of-fear.html (accessed June 1, 2010).

65. Ibid.

66. Ian Burma, "Totally Tolerant, Up to a Point," *New York Times*, January 30, 2009, 29.

67. "Shame in Calais," Editorial, *New York Times*, May 2, 2008, 20.

68. Peter Bergen, "Our Ally, Our Problem," *New York Times*, July 8, 2005, http://www.nytimes.com/2005/07/08/opinion/08bergen.html?_r=1&scp=1&sq=our%20ally%20our%20problem&st=cse (accessed June 1, 2010).

69. Christopher Caldwell, "Daughter of the Enlightenment," *New York Times*, April 3, 2005.

70. Casanova, "Immigration and the New Religious Pluralism."

71. Tariq Modood, "Muslims, Religious Equality and Secularism," in *Secularism, Religion and Multicultural Citizenship*, ed. Geoffrey Brahm Levey and Tariq Modood (Cambridge: Cambridge University Press, 2009): 164–85.

72. Casanova, "Immigration and the New Religious Pluralism," 146.

73. Berger and others, *Religious America*.

74. Casanova, "Immigration and the New Religious Pluralism," 147.

75. Sander L. Gilman, *Difference and Pathology: Stereotypes of Sexuality, Race and Madness* (London: Cornell University Press, 1985).

76. Craft and Waisbord, "When Foreign News Remains Foreign."
77. Ibid., 142.
78. Casanova, "Immigration and the New Religious Pluralism."
79. Modood, "Muslims, Religious Equality and Secularism," 180.
80. Ibid., 169.
81. Craft and Waisbord, "When Foreign News Remains Foreign," 140.

REFERENCES

Karim, Karim H. 2000. *Islamic Peril: Media and Global Violence*. Montréal: Black Rose Books.

Poole, Elizabeth. 2002. *Reporting Islam: Media Representations of British Muslims*. London: I. B. Tauris.

Richardson, John. 2004. *(Mis) Representing Islam: The Racism and Rhetoric of British Broadsheet Newspapers*. Amsterdam: John Benjamins.

Said, Edward. 1981. *Covering Islam: How the Media and Experts Determine How We See the Rest of the World*. London: Routledge.

CHAPTER 31

AMERICAN NEWSPAPER COVERAGE OF ISLAM IN THE ARAB WORLD

PHILIP SEIB

GOING back to the earliest days of the American republic, the Muslim world, particularly the Arab Muslim world, has been described in most coverage by US newspapers as a vaguely menacing place, with values and cultures often depicted as antithetical to those of the United States. Islam itself has often been portrayed as an archaic religious and political force that has consigned the Arab world to backwardness.

Anti-Muslim sentiment developed early, as eighteenth-century American religious leaders such as Cotton Mather and Jonathan Edwards denounced Islam and the prophet Mohammed. An early American traveler to Egypt, John Ledyard, wrote in 1788 about many local afflictions that he discovered: "Poverty, rapine, murder, tumult, blind bigotry, cruel persecution, pestilence!"[1] A predisposition toward the negative has long continued to characterize many dispatches from the region.

News coverage and popular culture feed off each other. The Barbary Pirates' raids on American shipping in the late eighteenth and early nineteenth centuries fostered anger toward Arabs and one of the new American nation's first bellicose pronouncements: "Millions for defense, but not one cent for tribute." In the aftermath of World War I, the exploits of the likes of T. E. Lawrence—a quintessential Westerner leading Arabs—became the stuff of sensational journalism and cinema. American correspondent Lowell Thomas, author of *With Lawrence in Arabia* (1924), referred often to the "land of the Arabian nights" and wove condescending references to "the noble Arab" into his stories.

Compared with countries in Western Europe that have significant Muslim minorities (such as the roughly 6 percent in France and the Netherlands), the United States, with around 2 percent Muslim residents, has limited exposure to Islam in its daily life. Imam Dawud Walid, executive director of Michigan's Council on American-Islamic Relations, observed, "The media have significant influence because the majority of Americans don't know much about Islam or have general interaction with Muslims. All they know about Muslims are the images they see on TV, hear on the radio, or read in magazines or newspapers."[2] This pertains to coverage of Muslims in America but also to reporting about Islam more generally.

News organizations, like the entertainment media, grasp at stereotypes. Just as the nomadic, camel-borne Arab and later the "Muslim terrorist" have become stock characters in film, television, and novels, so too do the news media often reduce their coverage themes to simplistic formulae. This kind of coverage is the product of two principal factors: news managers do not believe the public is knowledgeable enough to expect much sophistication about the topic, and reporters in the field lack the background knowledge essential to meaningful journalism about this topic.

Simplified coverage is usually less expensive coverage, and this has considerable appeal to news executives. As long as news organizations do not encounter public pushback about this approach, relying on stereotypes and sensational aspects of complex stories is the path of least resistance. Of course, this approach to reporting can set up journalists to be manipulated. By the midtwentieth century, as the interests of the Arab world, Israel, and the United States became increasingly intertwined, news coverage reflected the politics of war and peace and the petroleum-dependent global economy.

An example of this could be seen in the US coverage of Saudi Arabia, which, as journalist Thomas W. Lippman observed, had long benefited from a "protective cocoon that American business interests and diplomats" had built around this essential oil supplier.[3] But the attacks on the United States on September 11, 2001, dramatically changed the American public's attitude toward Saudi Arabia, which was the homeland of most of the terrorists who participated in the attacks. As the *New York Times* reported, "The United States seeks to build a coalition against terror with the kingdom, long a Western business and military ally, and yet the country has revealed itself as the source of the very ideology confronting America in the battle against terrorism."[4]

Shaping news coverage of the Middle East and its political effects has become one of the contemporary "great games" in global affairs. In the contest to affect American journalism about the region, Israel has portrayed itself as a foil to Arab and Islamic extremism and as a reliable ally of the United States. The consistency and impact of this message are enhanced by the political sophistication of Israel's friends in the United States—ranging from American Jews to fundamentalist Christians—who can be counted on to complain loudly about news coverage that they consider critical of Israel. Coupled with intense lobbying of elected officials and other policymakers, this politics- and media-oriented Israeli strategy has long proved effective. The relatively tepid response of American news organizations and the US government to the Israeli attack on the "Gaza flotilla" in 2010 was evidence of this. Meanwhile, Arab nations' US constituencies are not nearly as well organized and so do not wield the kind of clout that news executives and politicians respond to.

Despite Israel's prominence, Judaism per se usually appears in news stories as only a secondary issue, if at all, behind political matters such as the Israeli role as American partner, while Islam as Islam receives relatively greater attention, and not often in complimentary ways. Everything from headscarves to Ramadan fasting seems to be depicted as somewhat bizarre, and stories about brutal acts such as the executions of hostages gravitate to Islamic linkages, however tenuous. The perpetrators of the most violent acts are often stateless terrorists, so in the absence of any other grounding, "Muslim" becomes their convenient identity.

Two decades prior to the 9/11 attacks, Edward Said wrote about Islam serving as "a kind of scapegoat for everything we do not happen to like about the world's new political, social, and economic patterns. For the right, Islam represents barbarism; for the left, medieval theocracy; for the center, a kind of distasteful exoticism. In all camps, however, there is agreement that even though little enough is known about the Islamic world there is not much to be approved of there."[5] Reflecting Said's point was Bernard Lewis's question at a later date about the Arab world, "What went wrong?" Lewis added, "Whatever the form and manner of the question and of the answers that it evokes, there is no mistaking the growing anguish, the mounting urgency, and of late the seething anger with which both question and answers are expressed."[6]

While academics pondered such matters, news consumers remained adrift. In terms of quantity and intellectual quality of news reports, Americans who wanted more substantive information about Islam's principles or history needed to search beyond the offerings of their daily newspapers.

With the events of 9/11, everything changed, at least for a while. The exotic, vaguely mysterious religion became an existential threat, and the theory of a devastating "clash of civilizations" seemed validated by news coverage of the aftermath of the terrorist attacks. Mainstream American newspapers featured headlines such as these: "This Is a Religious War"; "Yes, This Is About Islam"; "Muslim Rage"; "The Deep Intellectual Roots of Islamic Terror"; "Kipling Knew What the US May Now Learn"; "Jihad 101"; "The Revolt of Islam"; and so on. Several discussed the Crusades and were illustrated with pictures of Richard the Lion Heart.[7]

Coverage that rose above sensationalism was also available. A week after the attacks, a *Washington Post* story began, "The suspects in last week's attacks in New York and Washington are Muslims who adhered to a version of Islam that sanctions terrorist violence, but it is an interpretation of Islam that is rejected by most other Muslims around the world."[8] Later that month, *USA Today* published "Q&A on Islam and Arab-Americans," which concisely explained basic tenets of Islam. The response to the question "How does Islam view terrorism?" was "Islam does not support terrorism under any circumstances. Terrorism goes against every principle in Islam. If a Muslim engages in terrorism, he is not following Islam."[9] In October

2001, a *New York Times* article distinguished between mainstream Islam and the radical version of the religion embraced by Osama bin Laden: "Although many Muslims are horrified at the notion of their faith being used to justify terrorism, Mr. bin Laden's advocacy of jihad, or holy war, against the West is a natural extension of what some radical Islamists have been saying and doing since the 1930s."[10] A May 2010 *New York Times* article described the work of an Arab iman based in Germany who tried to counter calls to violence by Al Qaeda and other groups, saying that these violate the tenets of Islam and that "We cannot just sit down and let other people hijack our religion."[11]

These news stories about Islam have been particularly important because many Americans, seeking to understand the terrorist attacks and the resulting "War on Terror," have tried to comprehend who "the enemy" was. Although a military response targeted Afghanistan, that approach was unsatisfying because none of the September 11 hijackers were Afghans and the friendliness of the Taliban to Al Qaeda provided only a flimsy rationale for an invasion. There was no conventional state to be blamed for the terrorism and then to be attacked and conquered in the way that Germany and Japan had been dealt with by the United States in World War II. Even the Cold War featured a state, the Soviet Union, that could be vilified as needed. The "War on Terror," however, was a war on a strategy rather than against a nation, and the idea of nonstate actors was new to most people and hard to grasp. Islam became more prominent as the "other" and even as the "enemy" partly because it was more conceptually solid and identifiable in the vacuum that existed.

A *New York Times* piece by Andrew Sullivan reflected the complexity of these matters:

> The religious dimension of this conflict is central to its meaning. . . . The terrorists' strain of Islam is clearly not shared by most Muslims and is deeply unrepresentative of Islam's glorious, civilized and peaceful past. But it surely represents a part of Islam—a radical, fundamentalist part—that simply cannot be ignored or denied. In that sense, this surely is a religious war—but not Islam versus Christianity and Judaism. Rather, it is a war of fundamentalism against faiths of all kinds that are at peace with freedom and modernity.[12]

As Sullivan, among others, pointed out, the most significant conflict is not a "clash" between the Islamic and non-Islamic civilizations, but rather a struggle within Islam between those endorsing harsh fundamentalism and those desiring to make Islam compatible with the realities of the twenty-first century.

A *Christian Science Monitor* article in November 2001 discussed the idea that a Muslim "silent majority" needed to stand up to violent fundamentalists. That task had become far more challenging when the United States attacked Afghanistan in October 2001. The article quoted a moderate Egyptian journalist who said, "I'm afraid that people have mostly forgotten September 11, and now they are talking about October 7," which is when the US bombing of Afghanistan began. The article described the Muslim reaction this way: "Poor and powerless, most of them already resent America's sway over large parts of the world, and that resentment feeds a readiness to see Washington as the enemy when bombs start falling on fellow Muslims."[13]

As the George W. Bush administration built its case for going to war against Iraq, most policymakers were careful to avoid direct attacks on Islam, but a subtext of their argument was that the Muslim world is composed of a loose collection of dangerous adversaries (overlooking the fact that Saddam Hussein's government was one of the most secular regimes in the region). This theory received minimal critical analysis from the mainstream US press, which tended to follow the administration's lead. Responding to this, *New York Times* Public Editor Daniel Okrent wrote in May 2004 (fourteen months after the Iraq war began), "Some of the *Times's* coverage in the months leading up to the invasion of Iraq was credulous; much of it was inappropriately italicized by lavish front-page display and heavy-breathing headlines." Some stories, wrote Okrent, "pushed Pentagon assertions so aggressively you could almost sense epaulets sprouting on the shoulders of editors."[14]

After the invasion had begun, news coverage implicitly raised the question of whether war against Iraq was also a war against Islam, and whether Islam would fight back. "The call to jihad is rising in the streets of Europe, and is being answered," reported the *New York Times* in April 2004. The *Times* story quoted a Muslim cleric in Britain touting the "culture of martyrdom," an imam in Switzerland urging his followers to "impose the will of Islam on the godless society of the West," and another radical Islamist leader in Britain predicting that "our Muslim brothers from abroad will come one day and conquer here, and then we will live under Islam in dignity."[15]

Similar warnings appeared in a *Washington Post* op-ed column in January 2003 in which the author asked, "Can Islam and democracy coexist at all?" and argued, "Absent a true reformation within Islam itself (which seems increasingly unlikely), the frustration over the present and the dreams of past glory of the 7th century are manifested by a destructive effort to bring the rest of the world down to Islam's current level."[16] The message of such articles was that a reactionary and bellicose Islam was the new, post–Cold War "enemy" of the West.

This same line of reasoning was applied to coverage of possible political and cultural change in the Middle East. *New York Times* reporter Douglas Jehl wrote:

> Throughout most of the Muslim world, the tension between Islam and modernity remains profound. Indeed, some observers have suggested since September 11 that it is the absence of a Reformation in the history of Islam that helps explain why universities in the Arab world that were once the most advanced centers of learning have often turned inward and backward. It appears clear that some of the resonance of Osama bin Laden's appeal to the Arab masses lies in the very fact that those masses have little alternative means of political expression.[17]

Jehl also cited "the Koranic injunction to 'obey God, obey the prophet, and obey the ruler'" as the foundation of justifying absolute rule rather than democracy.

Washington Post columnist Fareed Zakaria, meanwhile, was cautiously optimistic in his appraisals of politics in the Muslim world, arguing that Islamic extremism, "in all its variations, has been unable to garner mass support in any Muslim country." He was also upbeat about prospects for political change, writing: "Arab elites remain enormously resistant to reform and will try to scuttle plans for change. But I sense that the dinosaurs are on the defensive. For the first time, other views are being aired." He added, "Perhaps this will forge a new Arab community, one created by the practical realities of contact, culture and commerce rather than war, rhetoric and politics."[18]

Part of the challenge of covering Islam is the change in the geopolitical environment fostered by globalization. Concerning the notion of a "global village," George Packer wrote that it is "not the utopian community promised by the boosters of globalization but a parochial place of manifold suspicions, rumors, resentments, and half-truths. If the world seems to be growing more, rather than less, nasty these days, it might have something to do with the images all of us now carry around in our heads."[19] Along similar lines, Thomas Friedman observed: "Maybe the Internet, fiber optics, and satellites really are, together, like a high-tech Tower of Babel. It's as though God suddenly gave us all the tools to communicate and none of the tools to understand."[20]

The related issue pertaining to coverage of Islam is the new tenacity of myth. Rumor, often hateful, has always been able to find its way into public discourse. The channels through which it could travel were limited, however, in number and reach. Established news media could enhance rumor by adopting it or could shoot it down. Today, rumor benefits from the plentitude of venues. Beyond false rumor, true but one-sided reporting also can gain unprecedented traction because it can reach so many people so quickly through Internet-based media. Websites exist today that are primarily devoted to translating into English outlandish statements by scattered Muslim clerics. The material may be true, but it is distorted by the emphasis it is given.

A case can be made that newspapers today have increased responsibility to offset this kind of reporting through their own broad-based, responsible coverage of Islam. Stereotypes and inaccuracies abound and should be countered by responsible news coverage. Part of the struggle to define the future of journalism is not about economic models but rather about commitment to in-depth reporting and renewed championing of truth in a world in which truth is assailed from many directions.

Globalization affects information purveyors and information consumers, with ripple effects touching diverse constituencies. Lebanese journalist Diana Mukkaled wrote in 2005 that Muslim leaders who used inflammatory rhetoric when speaking to Arabic media but were more circumspect when speaking English on international networks were increasingly surprised to find that English speakers had read translations of their earlier comments. Mukkaled noted that "the world is closely watching. There are Western institutions that specialize in translating material that is used by all forms of Arab media" and so extremist comments cause "Muslim and Arab immigrants and their children in the West to pay the price for such words."[21]

The Islamic world today also finds it much easier to monitor and critique stories from the West. In his online news story about American television coverage of the 2006 Israel-Hezbollah war, Al Jazeera's Habib Battah said that an MSNBC analysis featured "field reporters and pundits, many blatantly supportive of Israel's fight against 'terror acts' and the 'worldwide Islamic threat'—still no mention of the widespread devastation and human loss in Lebanon."[22] Although this case involved television coverage, similar instances were plentiful in print media. News stories from the Middle East attract constant scrutiny not only from other journalists but also from political organizations that recognize the importance of news reports in shaping public opinion. Pro-Israeli and pro-Palestinian "media watchdog" groups duel regularly about alleged bias (intentional or not) in coverage of the region. Addressing this is a thankless task for news organizations, as is reflected in "Letters to the Editor" that on any given day might have one letter alleging that a particular news story showed pro-Israel bias, while the following letter accuses the same story of featuring a pro-Palestinian slant. If the debate extends into "principles of Judaism" and "principles of Islam," it is likely to become even more complicated and more contentious.

Understanding Islam requires recognizing that the Arab states constitute just 20 percent of the world's Muslim population. The four most populous Muslim states are not Arab but East and South Asian: Indonesia, Pakistan, India, and Bangladesh. There are almost as many Muslims in China as there are in Saudi Arabia. And yet, US news coverage of Islam is disproportionately weighted toward Arab Muslims. This produces a misshapen context in which Islam is considered by the public.

The spectrum of misperception is extensive. A LifeWay Research survey of more than 1,000 Protestant pastors in the United States found in 2009 that 45 percent strongly agreed and 21 percent somewhat agreed with the proposition "Islam is a dangerous religion." A 2009 Pew Research Center survey found that 38 percent of Americans believed Islam was more likely than other religions to encourage violence, but the Gallup Muslim-West Dialogue Index reported that 70 percent of Americans said interaction between the West and the Islamic world was a benefit rather than a threat.[23]

On reviewing these and similar surveys, it becomes obvious that attitudes about Islam fluctuate considerably. For instance, in response to the Pew Research Center survey question "Is Islam more likely than other faiths to encourage violence?" in March 2002 (just six months after the 9/11 attacks), only 25 percent said "more likely." The numbers in the following years: July 2003, 44 percent; July 2004, 46 percent; July 2005, 36 percent; August 2007, 45 percent; and August 2009, 38 percent.[24] No solid cause-and-effect formula can be drawn from this, but it appears that the rise in "more likely" answers correlates with the often uncritical news coverage of the George W. Bush administration's march toward war with Iraq. During this time, the implicit message from the administration, relayed to the public by the press, reinforced the notion that a Muslim state was likely to be a friendly home for terrorists. The later figures reflect some of the bloodiest periods (and heaviest US casualties) of the war, and finally the arrival of the Obama administration.

That many in the news media accepted this link between Islam and violence is evidence of flawed journalism. The central story was missed: What exactly was the connection between terrorism and Islam? To what extent were they linked and, as a policy matter, how might the religion be pulled away from criminal acts? Dismissing the issue entirely would not have been the answer. There were Muslims, such as

Osama bin Laden, who made the case that Islam was under siege and was justified in declaring war on the United States and some other Western countries. But the vast majority of Muslims find terrorism reprehensible, and that deserves attention as well.

Although the Bush administration did not overtly label Muslims as the enemy, that was a subtext in much of the reporting about the war, particularly as intra-Islamic religious strife kept postinvasion Iraq in turmoil and contributed to the rising number of American military casualties. As the US news media delivered stories from the region about internecine conflict and presented images of the destructive force of car bombs, Muslims could be seen as, at best, crazy and, at worst, fundamentally murderous. Moderate voices were rarely heard, and they could not compete in the fast-moving news cycle with sensational depictions of violence.

News coverage that so relentlessly focuses on violence takes a toll over time. As Nicholas Kristof observed in the *New York Times* in late 2006: "There's a fatigue in the West with an Arab world that sometimes seems to put its creative juices mostly into building better bombs. Even open-minded people in the West sometimes feel a sense of resignation that maybe the bigots are right: maybe Islam just is intrinsically backward, misogynistic and violent." Kristof went on, however, to point out that such sweeping judgments are flawed. He noted, as have many others, that Islam is not monolithic—the Arab and non-Arab parts of the Muslim world differ considerably in the ways they integrate religious and political beliefs.[25]

That's an interesting, if hard-to-prove, point, just as Samuel Huntington's clash of civilizations hypothesis is easier to speculate about than to prove or disprove. Critics of the idea of homogeneity in this context can argue that diversity trumps commonality, but they must contend with the flow of mass media product that blurs differences. The fatigue that Kristof cited is attributable not just to real events but also to the mélange of fact and fiction that information consumers must deal with as it comes pouring in from news and other media sources. The exponential growth in the number of information providers, of which conventional news organizations are only a part, has produced information overload. Nuance does not fare well in the torrent of rumor-filled blogs, stereotype-dominated entertainment, and oversimplified news offerings.[26]

American journalists working around the world have consistently encountered skepticism, cynicism, and anger toward the United States—feelings exacerbated by the Iraq War but with deep roots that are growing deeper. At the American University of Beirut, the *Washington Post's* David Ignatius found that the students "don't believe that America is serious about its values. Suggest to them, for example, that America really wants to advance democracy and freedom in Iraq, rather than grab the country's oil, and you get smirks and guffaws."[27]

Many young Arabs see the United States as a bastion of hypocrisy and arrogance, showing no respect toward other people and cultures. American news coverage (which is widely read by educated elites in the Arab world) may reinforce this negative outlook. In Saudi Arabia, wrote Nicholas Kristof in the *New York Times*, "I kept asking women how they felt about being repressed, and they kept answering indignantly that they aren't repressed." When he asked about wearing *abayas*, one Saudi woman told him: "I cover up my body and my face, and I'm happy that I'm a religious girl obeying God's rules. I can swim and do sports and go to restaurants and wear what I want, but not in front of men. Why should I show my legs and breasts to men? Is that really freedom?" Other women made the same case to Kristof, "that Saudi women are the free ones—free from sexual harassment, free from pornography, free from seeing their bodies used to market cars and colas. It is Western women, they say, who have been manipulated into becoming the toys of men."[28]

Although the women's arguments were in line with conservative Islamic views, Kristof was not ready to fully accept this, and he asked why Saudi women were not at least given more of a choice about what to wear and other social issues. In a way he reflected an American characteristic that aggravates much of the rest of the world: the assumption that American standards are the best and should be embraced by everyone. Such paternalism imbues much of American journalism, affecting the substance and tone of coverage.

But some American news coverage of Islamic culture in the Middle East breaks away from this approach, examining and undercutting pernicious stereotypes. A *USA Today* article in 2006 examined the state of women's rights and took issue with Kristof's apparent assumption that the wearing of conservative attire reflects a widespread repression of Muslim women. Souheila al-Jadda reported on women's education, their role in politics, and the general changes in Arab Muslim culture that affect women. Making her point to her US audience, al-Jadda wrote: "It took American women more than 130 years after the signing of the constitution to gain the right to vote. . . . American women, perhaps more than most, understand that what a woman wears has nothing to do with having the same opportunities and rights as men."[29] Another article that debunked certain stereotypes was the *Christian Science Monitor*'s description of a trip through parts of the Muslim world by a group of young Americans who sought to "understand the nuances and complexities of Muslim society."[30]

As portrayed by the American news media, Islam remains a great, mystifying "other." Stories about terrorism and tales about eccentricities of religion, politics, and culture overshadow the essence of Muslim life and religious practice. The simplest description of this coverage is that it lacks appropriate seriousness and sophistication, and as such it does a disservice not only to the Muslim world but also to the American public that relies on journalism to provide an honest and comprehensive picture of the world.

NOTES

1. Michael Oren, *Power, Faith, and Fantasy: America in the Middle East 1776 to the Present* (New York: W. W. Norton, 2007), 42, 45.

2. Jennifer Hoewe, "Media Coverage of Muslims and Islam Still Open to Criticism," United Press International, October 22, 2009.

3. Thomas W. Lippman, *Inside the Mirage: America's Fragile Partnership with Saudi Arabia* (Boulder, CO: Westview, 2004), 325.

4. Neil Macfarquar, "Anti-Western and Extremist Views Pervade Saudi Schools," *New York Times*, October 19, 2001.

5. Edward Said, *Covering Islam* (New York: Pantheon, 1981), xv.

6. Bernard Lewis, *What Went Wrong?* (New York: Oxford University Press, 2002), 3.

7. Ervand Abrahamian, "The U.S. Media, Samuel Huntington, and September 11," *Middle East Report* 223 (Summer 2002): 62.

8. Caryle Murphy, "Bin Laden's Radical Form of Islam," *Washington Post*, September 18, 2001.

9. "Q&A on Islam and Arab-Americans," *USA Today*, September 30, 2001.

10. Robert Worth, "The Deep Intellectual Roots of Islamic Terror," *New York Times*, October 13, 2001.

11. Souad Mekhennet, "Munich Imam Tries to Dull Lure of Radical Islam," *New York Times*, May 17, 2010.

12. Andrew Sullivan, "This Is a Religious War," *New York Times*, October 7, 2001.

13. Peter Ford, "Listening for Islam's silent Majority," *Christian Science Monitor*, November 5, 2001.

14. Daniel Okrent, "Weapons of Mass Destruction? Or Mass Distraction?" *New York Times*, May 30, 2004.

15. Patrick E. Tyler and Don Van Natta, Jr., "Militants in Europe Openly Call for Jihad and Rule of Islam," *New York Times*, April 26, 2004.

16. Dennis Mullin, "Call It by Any Other Name, It Still Adds Up to a Crusade," *Washington Post*, January 5, 2003.

17. Douglas Jehl, "Democracy's Uneasy Steps in Islamic World," *New York Times*, November 23, 2001.

18. Fareed Zakaria, "Glimmers of Hope in the Arab World," *Washington Post*, December 21, 2004.

19. George Packer, "When Here Sees There," *New York Times*, April 21, 2002.

20. Thomas L. Friedman, *Longitudes and Attitudes* (New York: Anchor, 2003), 390.

21. Diana Mukkaled, "The World Is Closely Watching," *Asharq Alawsat*, August 30, 2005.

22. Habib Battah, "Watching American TV in Beirut," aljazeera.net, July 14, 2006, http://www.shunpiking.com/ol0306/0306-MC-HB-0731-watchingtv.htm.

23. "'Islam Is a Dangerous Religion,' Most American Pastors Say," *Christianpost*, December 14, 2009, http://www.christianpost.com/article/20091214/-islam-is-a-dangerous.

24. Pew Forum on Religion and Public Life and Pew Research Center for the People and the Press, "Muslims Widely Seen as Facing Discrimination" (results from the 2009 Annual Religion and Public Life Survey), 7.

25. Nicholas Kristof, "The Muslim Stereotype," *New York Times*, December 10, 2006.

26. Seib, *The Al Jazeera Effect*, 187.

27. David Ignatius, "America's Doubters in Beirut," *Washington Post*, June 6, 2003, A27.

28. Nicholas D. Kristof, "Saudis in Bikinis," *New York Times*, October 25, 2002.

29. Souheila al-Jadda, "A Veil Doesn't Mean 'Oppressed,'" *USA Today*, June 22, 2006.

30. Jane Lampman, "Students Tour Muslim World," *Christian Science Monitor*, April 19, 2007.

REFERENCES

Esposito, John L. 2002. *What Everyone Needs to Know About Islam.* New York: Oxford University Press.

Friedman, Thomas L. 2003. *Longitudes and Attitudes.* New York: Anchor.

Lewis, Bernard. 2002. *What Went Wrong?* New York: Oxford University Press.

Oren, Michael B. 2007. *Power, Faith, and Fantasy: America in the Middle East 1776 to the Present.* New York: W. W. Norton.

Said, Edward. 1981. *Covering Islam.* New York: Pantheon.

Seib, Philip. 2008. *The Al Jazeera Effect.* Dulles, VA: Potomac Books.

CHAPTER 32

AMERICAN NEWS COVERAGE OF CHINESE UIGHURS

DALIA HASHAD

IN an interview on PBS's investigative journalism series *Frontline*, journalist Laura Ling tells of reporting in "a province in Western China where people are afraid to speak. It's called Xinjang." Ominously, she adds, "Coming here would change my life."

Ling traveled to the region to cover Uighur life under Chinese rule and covertly arranged an interview with a Uighur man. Sitiwaldi "Dilkex" Tilivaldi wanted to speak but was "terrified." After several months and two trips to China, Tilivaldi gave Ling an interview in a hotel. As they left the hotel, the police detained them. Ling tells of her interrogation: "They asked me, why I wanted to talk with terrorists. Again and again, just conflating the words 'terrorists', 'Uighur', 'separatist.' In their minds, it was all one thing." The Uighur man disappeared into custody and has not been heard from since.[1]

This story, remarkable enough to turn the tables on a journalist and put her in the interviewee's seat, is both representative of and an explanation for the crushing silence surrounding the Uighur people's destruction. The following chapter will explore American press coverage of the Uighurs—a religiously and ethnically distinct Chinese Muslim community—before and after 9/11. Despite similarities to a well-known beleaguered Chinese community, Tibetan Buddhists, the Uighurs' plight has received very little media attention. Indeed, when their story has been told, it has been linked, however tenuously, to the specter of international Islamic terrorism. By looking at how and why this happened, the chapter aims to illuminate American press practices regarding the coverage both of religion in China and of Islam.

In the center of Asia, buffered by some of the world's highest peaks, sits Xinjiang, home of the Uighurs. Uighurs, who are largely Sunni Muslims, share more in common with their Central Asian neighbors, ethnically and culturally, than their Chinese rulers. They speak a different language, possess different physical characteristics, and maintain their own distinct way of life and traditions. Most Americans know nothing about the Uighurs or their dire situation. With few exceptions, major media outlets have underreported their struggles. The sparse coverage that has been done tells little of the daily oppression unfolding in Xinjiang. In fact, China's Uighur population is subject to religious monitoring and restrictions, forced abortion, detention, torture, secret trials, and even execution. But most of this is unreported in the American press.

The silence surrounding this decades-long drama shrouds violent oppression. Human rights groups are banned and individuals like Tilivaldi who tell their stories risk penalties ranging from imprisonment to death. Chinese authorities detain, arrest, torture, disappear, and even kill Uighurs who criticize their government or speak out in defense of basic human rights. Independent reporters are prohibited; instead, officials engineer infrequent government-sponsored journalistic tours that provide propaganda rather than the real story. Before 9/11, many outlets never carried so much as a mention of the Uighurs.

After the attacks on the Pentagon and the World Trade Center, Uighurs received new notice. The subsequent media spotlight on Muslims worldwide cast light on Xinjiang, but the news was not good in and of itself or for the Uighur people. Most of the Uighur-related coverage stemmed from an interest in uncovering hidden, but potentially threatening, Muslims. Instead of reporting on China's subjugation of the Uighurs, which in many ways is similar to what is happening to Buddhists in Tibet, journalists cast the shadow of Al Qaeda over the Muslim minority group. When Beijing folded Uighurs into the narrative of Muslims as terrorists with potential links to the Taliban, foreign journalists followed suit. Eager to uncover global terrorist threats, media coverage simplified the Uighur struggle, reducing complex history, traditions, culture, and context to a potential Islamic menace.

A Rich History

Xinjiang, or the Xinjiang Uighur Autonomous Region,[2] sits in remote northwestern China. It makes up approximately one-sixth of China's land mass. Xinjiang was an ancient world center that a thousand years ago was host to legendary adventurers and caravans of global traders traveling along this branch of the famed Silk Road.

Xinjiang's eight million Uighur inhabitants are a majority Muslim population that is ethnically, religiously, and visibly different from China's Han majority, often simply referred to as "Chinese." Uighurs share more in common with their neighbors in the central Asian countries along their border: Afghanistan, Mongolia, Kazakhstan, Kyrgyzstan, Tajikistan, India, Pakistan, and Russia. Notably, Xinjiang also borders

Tibet. In 1933 and again in 1944, Xinjiang declared independence and adopted the name East Turkestan. In 1949, the Chinese Communist Party annexed Xinjiang. Since then, the People's Republic has expressed constant worries of Uighur separatism. China maintains authority by maintaining tight economic and political control over Xinjiang.

China seeks control for various strategic reasons. The land of Xinjiang is home to some of China's greatest natural resources. In addition to enormous quantities of minerals ranging from gold to salt, Xinjiang holds 20 percent of China's proven oil reserves,[3] 40 percent of its coal reserves, and more than 20 percent of its natural gas.[4] Apart from China's southeast coast, Xinjiang's per capita income is the highest in China.[5] But while the Uighur land is rich, the Uighurs are among the most destitute of China's rural poor, as Xinjiang's great wealth is concentrated among nonnatives.[6]

Gross discrimination lies at the root of Uighur poverty. Beijing's state-owned companies control the oil and the many government jobs derived from that industry. Much of the employment sector in Xinjiang is either explicitly or implicitly reserved for Han Chinese. Job advertisements often stipulate "Han only."[7] In 2006, for example, Chinese officials designated 800 of the 840 available civil service jobs for Han only.[8] Uighurs who are able to acquire government employment find themselves limited in their ability to advance. Promotion often depends on joining the Communist Party and disavowing Islam, which excludes the vast majority of Uighurs. Most Uighurs barely eke out a living in agriculture or in unskilled labor. Attaining even the most unskilled jobs presents a challenge to many Turkic-speaking Uighurs, who do not know enough required Mandarin to survive in an economy controlled by Han. Those who do speak Mandarin often find themselves ridiculed for their accents.[9]

Han didn't always dominate Xinjiang. About sixty-five years ago, Uighurs populated 75 percent of Xinjiang, while Han Chinese accounted for only 5 percent. Recognizing an opportunity to tighten central control of Xinjiang by changing the demographics, Beijing has provided incentives for Han Chinese to move there.[10] The policy has been so successful that Han Chinese now make up approximately 40 percent of the population to Uighurs' 45 percent.[11] In Urumqui, Xinjiang's capital city, Han Chinese make up over 70 percent of the citizenry, making Uighurs a minority in the northern part of their province.

In addition to stifling political and social repression, the Han campaign to dilute the Uighurs' population and culture is a significant concern. China bans the publication of many books on Uighur history, literature, and poetry. Religious restrictions abound. Imams, Muslim religious leaders, must enroll in government "trainings," and China monitors all mosques. Additionally, Communist Party policy forbids students, government employees, and children younger than twelve years old from entering Islamic houses of worship. Frequent complaints charge China with pursuing policies designed to obliterate Uighurs' centuries-old way of life. One Uighur merchant lamented to a reporter, "Our traditions, our clothing, our language, they want us to get rid of it all."[12]

Aggressive Chinese government actions seem to verify the charge as Beijing seeks to destroy Uighur civilization through symbolic and actual stratagems. Often called the "heart of Uighur culture," Kashgar, the 2,000-year-old capital city of Xinjiang, is disappearing. Chinese government bulldozers systematically raze its ancient mud-brick structures to the ground. Centuries-old traditions are disrupted as Uighurs living in Kashgar are displaced from the Old City to its outskirts to make room for high-rise apartment dwellers and their attendant features of Han modernity. Since Western interest in the issue is minimal, China has been able to keep a relatively tight lid on the destruction. When the rare journalist does appear, China rigorously monitors his or her activity and allows only interviews that support official government policy. Conscious of potential retribution, Uighurs fear speaking to reporters and outsiders. If discovered, journalists who enter under the pretense of tourism find themselves tightly monitored or even summarily escorted out of cities like Kashgar.[13]

Missing the Uighurs in Pre-9/11 Coverage

Chinese government officials have long understood that the state of affairs in Xinjiang mirror many of the problems in adjacent Tibet. While attempting control by quietly tamping down on civil and political activities, Chinese officials publically downplay displays of dissatisfaction as the product of a few, solitary "ruffians" advocating for separatism. They claim that, in general, the larger Uighur community lives in contented harmony. Contrary to what China would assert after 9/11, in the early days of September 2001 the secretary of Xinjiang's Communist Party declared that "society is stable, and people are living and working in peace and contentment."[14]

Pre-9/11 US media coverage largely supported the official Chinese narrative that nothing newsworthy occurred in the northwestern corner of China. Despite the drama that regularly unfolded in Xinjiang, the executions, bombings, torture, and discrimination did not receive mention in most media outlets. Geographically and figuratively, Xinjiang was far removed from stories that captured world attention and the Uighurs' troubles went unnoticed by the mainstream media. Even papers that had every reason to cover the Uighurs ignored Xinjiang. In 2001, the *Los Angeles Times*, a large metropolitan daily striving to provide in-depth, contextualized international news coverage, stationed more than forty foreign correspondents around the globe, including in China.[15] Given Los Angeles's location on the Pacific Rim and that 13 percent of the county is Asian,[16] the *Times* tries to offers solid and reliable China coverage. However, Xinjiang was still ignored. Before 9/11, the *Los Angeles Times* did not run a single story mentioning Uighurs, let alone discuss their dramatic human rights struggle.

Time magazine, which has been covering China since the publication of its inaugural issue in 1923, was the originator of the modern newsmagazine. *Time* reports and analyzes each week's events. Over the course of its long history, for many readers, if it did not appear in *Time*, it did not happen. One of its founders, Henry Robinson Luce, was the child of American missionaries in China.[17] Luce maintained a lifelong involvement in China-related issues and in *Time's* first year, China made its way into the magazine 115 times. Despite China's mention in countless articles since, *Time* never provided a thorough piece on the Uighurs before 9/11. From its inception in 1923 through September 10, 2001, *Time* ran only six stories that mentioned Uighurs. (For comparison's sake, *Time* ran 586 stories mentioning Tibet during that same period.) Of the six stories, only a brief April 1997 piece centered on Uighurs. Titled "Crackdown in Western China,"[18] it included some contextualization but flubbed the facts. Reporting on a police crackdown on protestors, the story provides elementary background, elucidating only some of the root causes of Uighur unrest. It does not even identify the Uighurs as Muslims, something that would never occur again in *Time*, or most other news outlets, after 9/11. The article oversimplifies the complex state of affairs in Xinjiang and unadvisedly relies on Chinese authorities to convey key information. The writer allows China, with its proven record of deception on this issue,[19] to control the reports of the numbers of people killed, injured, and executed, as well as the depictions of Uighur protestors as "anti-government" and rioters: "A Chinese official confirmed Monday that police had opened fire on Uighur protesters in the Xinjiang region, killing two and injuring five. The shootings occurred Thursday as Uighurs were protesting the executions of three people for their part in anti-government rioting." These numbers are, in fact, disputed and there is evidence to indicate that as many as 100 Uighurs were killed while peacefully protesting the execution of thirty proponents of Uighur independence.[20]

Even when the article strays from the People's Republic's talking points, Chinese influence remains clear: "Uighurs, a Turkic speaking people with little cultural ties to the dominant ethnic Han minority, look to separatism as the only way out of increasingly desperate economic straits." Uighurs are depicted as universally pushing for separatism, a false oversimplification. Interestingly, with the phrase, "[t]he news further illustrates the unraveling of Xinjiang," *Time* reveals an understanding of a problem with some complexity that has both a history and a certain future, yet this brief article stands alone in their pre-9/11 coverage.

In August 1999, *Time* ran its next most significant but still brief item on the Uighur struggle. The stripped-down simplification present in the previous article prevailed again. Cushioned between marriage and death notices, the magazine ran a few sentences under their "Milestones" section:

> ARRESTED. REBIYA KADER (sic), 50, one of China's best-known businesswomen; on as yet undetermined charges; in Urumqi, China. The owner of a department store, Kader, a member of the Muslim Uighur minority, was detained while on her way to meet members of the U.S. Congressional Research Service—reportedly to deliver an account of police harassment.[21]

The opening description of Rebiya Kadeer as "one of China's best-known businesswomen" is telling. The brief leads with what makes her most significant, in the magazine's perspective. That she is a Muslim Uighur is secondary and used to identify her status as a member of a marginalized group as opposed to focusing on her as a representative of an oppressed Chinese minority. This misses the true significance of and, indeed, the motivation behind the arrest of the woman commonly known as "the mother of all Uighurs."

While it is true that Kadeer was well known for her business prowess, by 1999 her advocacy for Uighur human rights had made her an open target of the People's Republic. The piece fails to make clear that her detention was motivated by and symbolic of China's repression of her people. Key details that would complete the picture are absent. No mention is made of Kadeer's position as a leading Uighur human rights advocate or the fact that her husband had fled to the United States to avoid persecution for his criticism of Chinese repression. To keep Kadeer from following him, China revoked her passport.[22] To miss these details misses the story and the tragedy of the Uighur struggle.

Again, in this pre-9/11 era, *Time*'s Uighur reporting did not focus on religion. Here, Uighurs are qualified as Muslims, but the purpose is to further identify the Chinese minority group. This has a very different effect from the later depictions of Uighurs as Muslim militants, which would dominate media descriptions in the "War on Terror" era. *Time* would not find cause to mention Uighurs again until after 9/11.

With scant coverage in print media, Uighurs fared just as poorly on radio news programs where sparse, simplified coverage continued to be the rule. Between its inception in 1970 and 2001, the second largest radio group in America with over twenty-five million weekly listeners,[23] NPR, covered Uighurs only twice and once more just before the September attacks. Unlike post-9/11 reporting, there was generally no focus on Islam and coverage did not wrap Uighurs in the cloak of terrorism. Notably, there was one prescient exception. In a preview of how Xinjiang would be discovered and covered by media after the 9/11 attacks, NPR first reported on Uighurs in 1998, just months after the US embassy bombings in Dar es Salaam and Nairobi.[24] As the American public first learned the names of Osama bin Laden and Ayman al-Zawahiri, general anti-Muslim sentiment rose. The international attacks on American citizens and institutions by Al Qaeda drove attention and journalists toward reporting on global Islamic terrorist threats. In this atmosphere NPR explored Xinjiang for the first time.

The introduction to the segment summarizes the Uighur conflict for an audience in need of a primer. Using words like "volatile," it describes "periodic bus bombings, riots and other acts of terrorism by the Uighurs." Immediately identified as Muslims, Uighurs are portrayed as "frustrated," "traditionally resistant to central authority," "demanding," and refusing to "give up." The story's prevailing frame of China under attack presents Uighurs as petulant, dangerous children rather than a violently oppressed majority in their own province. This tenor of this account, strikingly similar to the structure of many post-9/11 stories, would be a solitary occurrence for NPR.

In the subsequent summer, NPR's flagship drive-time program, *All Things Considered*, ran a second piece on Uighurs. The story's title, "Uygur-Drama," was promising, but misleading for one looking for coverage on the human rights situation. The segment was not about Uighurs' daily struggle for economic, cultural, and political survival under the Chinese government's repressive thumb. Rather, it centered on a journalist's lunch experience in which he "finds the restaurant engrossed in a gross-out epic drama on the television, with medieval warriors, damsels in distress, and lots of blood. [The commentator] finds the whole scene as riveting as it was gruesome."[25] The depiction of Uighurs leans toward the primitive and there is no hint of the real-life drama actually occurring. Like most pre-9/11 coverage, religion assumes a noncentral role and, in fact, is not even mentioned here. In a post-9/11 context, the image of primitive Muslims thirsty for bloody entertainment in a remote corner of the world fit in nicely with the dominant media narrative of uncivilized Muslims thriving on violence.

In the week before 9/11, NPR's other flagship show, the popular weekday morning program *Morning Edition*, ran a piece on Uighurs that was part of the network's commentaries and coverage of the UN World Conference against Racism in Durban, South Africa.[26] The station's unfamiliarity with the Uighur people is immediately evident in the host's introduction. He consistently mispronounces Uighurs, calling them "Oy-Gers." Uighurs are identified as part of an ethnic minority group in China, but as with NPR's previous commentary on Uighurs, the host does not explain they are Muslim. Rather, they are introduced as part of a group of "people who have experienced racism." Even when he asserts that "Uighurs have carried out bombings and fought Chinese security forces," the post-9/11 obligatory accompanying words "Muslim" and "terrorist" are conspicuously absent. Instead, it is noted that "human rights groups have documented increased incidents of execution and torture of Uighur activists by the Chinese." Uighur commentator Akida Rouzi gives compelling testimony describing dual and vastly inequitable systems and services for ethnic Chinese and Uighurs. The segment echoes the *Time* "Milestone" piece in its lack of contextualization and striking demonstration of unfamiliarity with its subject by failing to identify the commentator as the daughter of the Uighurs' most prominent activist and political prisoner, Rebiya Kadeer.

After describing institutionalized segregation in public services, employment discrimination, political persecution, and religious repression, Rouzi provides the bright spot to her story: "I now live in America, home of freedom and justice, which all of us hungered for in my country. I will be strong because I've got America to help us. But my mom and the rest of my family still suffer in China." Strikingly, in the moments before the execution of the crime that would taint Muslims around the globe and subsequently launch of the War on Terror with all of its incidental casualties, America is the savior and Islam is barely worth a mention. That was September 6, 2001. Five days later, Islam was the headline.

Among the Ashes of 9/11

Immediately after 9/11, news organizations began to fold Uighurs into their War on Terror coverage. Previously invisible to most outlets, Uighurs suddenly began appearing in stories. But rather than covering repression in Xinjiang, most of the reporting on Uighurs inferred they were a domestic, if not global, terrorist hazard—even if no one really knew who they were.

Heightened sensitivities and increased fears of Islam generated new and amplified journalistic interest in Muslims around the world. The hysteria resulting from the 9/11 hijackers' success focused journalists and news consumers on uncovering other potential Muslim threats. Uighurs, however victimized and far removed from terrorist activities, were an unfamiliar people with two strikes against them: most of them were Muslims and they had a grievance.

The third strike came in the form of official Chinese propaganda. In a deliberately calculated move immediately following 9/11, China reassessed its public relations strategy and adjusted its portrayal of Uighurs. Exploiting worldwide anti-Muslim sentiment, China sought to win support for its repressive policies by recasting Uighurs as part of the global Islamic terrorist threat. The Chinese Foreign Ministry claimed that China, too, suffered as "a victim of international terrorism." The government crafted a report connecting Uighur resistance to Osama bin Laden.[27] China levied its influence in pursuit of a new goal: subsuming their suppression of Uighurs under the banner of America's war against Islamic radicals. China's efforts met with success. In exchange for China's cooperation in the globally unpopular War on Terror, the United States changed its position on a Uighur separatist group. Where it had previously declined to certify the Eastern Turkistan Islamic Movement (ETIM), as a terrorist organization, it now did so, acquiescing to China's assertions that the Uighur struggle was connected to a broader ideology of fundamentalist Islamic terrorism.[28]

For the most part, reporters unwittingly played along. In an environment of panic, journalists acquiesced to an ideology that defined almost any Muslim group as a presumptively terroristic threat. Anti-Islamic fervor brokered dramatic changes in reporting on Uighurs. Due, in part, to the dearth of pre-9/11 reporting on Xinjiang, simplistic journalistic observations on Uighurs often conveyed China's new characterizations with credibility. Terms such as "violent separatism," "jihadis," "Muslim fundamentalists," "terrorists," and "militant Muslim separatists" began to crop up in stories describing Uighurs.[29]

Despite the absence of any Uighur coverage pre-9/11, the *Los Angeles Times* quickly turned its attention to Uighurs, using a post-9/11 lens. Six weeks after 9/11, in an article titled "Bush Has Come a Long Way in World Eye," Uighurs made their *Los Angeles Times* debut.[30] While they were characteristically absent for most of the article, at the end, the paper shapes a preliminary approach to addressing the Uighur struggle in Xinjiang. After noting how President Bush's image as foreign policy leader had changed, the piece ends with another 9/11 transformation. It acknowledges that many countries were motivated to support Bush's War on Terror because of their own "long-standing" domestic fights against terrorism, and then attention turns to Chinese Uighurs:

> Many countries have signed on to the coalition partly because of their own domestic problems. Russia's most serious security challenge is from Muslim guerrillas in its republic of Chechnya, while China faces Uighur Muslim militants in the western province of Xinjiang. Though Washington concedes that some

> Chechens and Uighurs have engaged in terrorism, the U.S. also has traditionally viewed both problems as political issues that grew out of repression of minorities and human rights violations.

Before the article mentions the Uighurs, the reporter sets up the frame of a "serious security challenge . . . from Muslim guerrillas" and then describes the group as "Muslim militants" forcing China's hand. The description is presented as fact, not as China's newly developed characterizations. There is a subsequent nod to the reality that the situation has typically been considered one of Chinese political repression, but that is mitigated by the framing and use of words like "Muslim militants" and "terrorism." Given the political climate, the reader could believe that the problem is one of terrorism. Even if, as implied, that terrorism may have roots in political repression, the perception is damaging to the Uighurs. Once again, the Chinese narrative stands unquestioned.

A couple of weeks later, the *Los Angeles Times* came even closer to fully embracing the Chinese perspective on the Uighurs. Still so fresh to the paper as to require "(pronounced WEE-gur)" reading instructions, the group made their second-ever *Los Angeles Times* appearance in the bottom third of the article. The piece reported on China's recognition that 9/11 created an opportunity for closer relations with the United States.[31] The "thing that could draw the United States and China a bit closer is a new, shared enemy: Muslim extremists." With that introduction, a religious association, again, tainted the Uighurs with the sins of others. This oft-repeated media frame aligns China with the United States as victims of terrorist attacks and the Uighurs with the 9/11 hijackers.

The article roots China's quiet and uncharacteristic acquiescence to US military action in a reflection of "China's recognition of its own vulnerabilities as a rapidly developing country facing a Muslim separatist movement in its far northwest." This sentence signifies the emergence of a trend in the way American media would report on Chinese treatment of Uighurs in a post-9/11 world. With the loaded term "vulnerabilities," the article gives the impression that China is the victim, not the longtime aggressor. Furthermore, the article describes China as having recently recognized this situation, giving a false impression that belies the truth of decades of calculated repression.

Like many other articles, this one fails to adequately distinguish between Uighurs advocating for independence and the general Uighur population, leading the reader to incorrectly assume that they flow from and into each other. It also fails to make plain the length and breadth of the bitter relationship resulting from decades of brutal domination of an overwhelmingly peaceful people. There is no sense that mass arrests and executions of Uighur separatists were actually state-sanctioned tools that were regularly employed against everyday Uighurs who advocated for basic political, cultural, economic, and religious rights.

The story references the 1990s emergence of a "sometimes violent separatist movement," presumably the ETIM.[32] Yet, there is no mention that many experts considered the ETIM to have been long dormant, if not dead, and general agreement holds that the ETIM has no real connection to Al Qaeda.[33] Instead, the article presents the "movement" as an active force. Compounding the confusion, the article conflates the Chinese response to the ETIM with tactics that China has employed in their general repression of Uighurs, most of whom exercise no political objectives for severance: "Beijing has responded to the separatist movement with mass arrests and many executions, drawing heavy criticism from human rights advocates and other countries, including the United States."

The reporter could be forgiven for not adequately appreciating the extent of Chinese propaganda against the Uighur population, were it not for a brief acknowledgement of Beijing's PR aspirations. The end of the piece leaves readers with the clear misunderstanding that the Uighur concern in Xinjiang is not one of minority persecution, but of Muslim terrorism:

> Chinese officials claim Uighur militants have trained at camps in Afghanistan run by Osama bin Laden. Since the Sept. 11 attacks, Beijing has tried to link Uighur separatism with global terrorism. "We hope that our fight against the East Turkistan forces will become a part of the international effort against terrorism, and it should also win support and understanding," Foreign Ministry spokesman Sun Yuxi said last month.

With the quote from the government official echoing Chinese propaganda, the article's only source presented on Uighurs possesses clear bias. An opposing view isn't presented. Instead, the writer offers a generality from President Bush[34] and passes on providing specific examples that prompted the concern:

> Bush has cautioned China that the global campaign against terrorism "must never be an excuse to persecute minorities." But Beijing hopes Washington will be less apt to criticize China's handling of a Muslim-related terrorism problem now that the United States faces one of its own.[35]

This final paragraph concedes the existence of apprehension that China is using the War on Terror to mask its own repressive agenda. However, the concern is negated by the specter of 9/11. With a qualifier starting the last sentence of the article, the reporter directly conflates the Uighurs, "a Muslim-related terrorism problem," with those who attacked the United States.

After 9/11, a flood of articles in *Time* also mentioned Uighurs. In the months after the attacks, the magazine cited, discussed, or focused on Uighurs more often than it had in its previous seventy-eight-year history. In the first few instances, Uighurs made fleeting appearances in stories that focused on explaining the Taliban and describing different global perspectives of the War on Terror.[36] Unfortunately, even with Uighurs front and center, simplification of their story continued and appropriate background and contextualization were glaringly absent. In October, *Time*'s cover read "The Fear Factor." In bold print, the byline stated, "Anthrax letters. FBI warnings. Bin Laden's videotapes. Bombarded by threats, real and imagined, a nation on edge asks, what's next?"[37] The question was answered in an article about Uighurs, "China's Own Islamic 'Extremists.'"[38]

Despite the title's promise indicated by quotes around "Extremists," the article does not unpack China's identification of Uighurs as Muslim radicals. Instead, it provides select facts without contextual analysis or appropriate historical background. For example, the statement "It is definitely not a great time to be a Uighur" belies the truth of daily life in Xinjiang and gives the impression that, until recently, Uighurs lived in relative comfort. It fails to adequately explain the systematic repression and persecution in Xinjiang or hint at the inferior resources and vastly diminished rights of Uighurs. Instead, select details, like detentions and soldier deployments, present a picture of a people whose grievances are related to China's attempt to shield itself from domestic terrorism. There is no questioning of the fundamental premise that Uighurs actively employ violence for political gain and no examination of China's use of the War on Terror to shield itself from legitimate human rights critique.

Without citing a source, but presumably using the Chinese government statistic, the article claims that "300 Uighurs from China have trained in Afghan terrorist camps." Legitimizing Chinese propaganda, the article warns of future Uighur threats: The "trainees will someday bring their new skills home." In the oft-repeated theme, the magazine incorrectly aligns Uighurs with terrorism: "There are signs of religious radicalism in the region, especially the growth of Wahhabism, the creed of the Taliban."[39] Simplistic, rudimentary misunderstandings of Islam are revealed in the details used to flesh out the description of Uighurs' practice of their faith. Uighurs are portrayed as less threatening than other Muslims because "[t]heir women can drive. They wear colorful hats." Such statements, meant to reassure readers, reflects a general misunderstanding of Islam, as well as a simplification of a specific people.

After the initial post-9/11 burst of coverage, attention once again turned away from Xinjiang. But the War on Terror wasn't done with Uighurs. While not all news outlets immediately integrated Uighurs in their postattack coverage, such mentions became inevitable as the War on Terror stretched on.[40] In 2005, the group was back in the news. By then, it was becoming well known that a handful of Uighur men were stranded in the highly controversial Guantanamo Bay detention camp.

Most of the coverage of this chapter of the Uighur story is emblematic of the media's simplification of the group's struggle, as well as their disregard for facts on the ground in Xinjiang. In 2001, when Uighur refugees were living in Afghanistan, US forces bombed their camp. When the Uighurs tried to escape, Pakistanis turned them over to the United States in exchange for substantial bounties. Twenty-two Uighur detainees were transferred to the Guantanamo Bay detention camp in Cuba as "enemy combatants." Years later, they were all cleared of the designation and, in various stages, courts ordered their release. However, they still could not leave Guantanamo. Ironically, the United States would not return them to China for fear of persecution, and they could not find a third country willing to accept them. The US government simultaneously attempted to negotiate settling the Uighurs in third countries while rebuffing efforts to relocate the Uighurs inside the United States and fighting court cases brought by the Uighurs' attorneys.

The media largely reported this as a story of innocent Muslim men, still shackled in one of the world's most notorious detention camps because they had no home to which they could return. Headlines read "Chinese Detainees Are Men Without a Country: 15 Muslims, Cleared of Terrorism Charges, Remain at Guantanamo with Nowhere to Go."[41] While hundreds of other cleared detainees returned home from Guantanamo, Uighurs remained chained to their prison cell floors. As journalists followed the global ping pong game of attempts to settle them, stories related details of the Uighurs' confinement and possible new homes. Absent in these accounts were the reasons why these men could not be returned to their homeland. Instead, most stories gave a cursory explanation—"Returning them to China would probably mean torture"—but neglected to delve into the broader narrative of why this would be the case, or to describe the oppression Uighurs suffered in Xinjiang.[42] Once again, Uighurs made the headlines, but their story was nowhere to be found.

Back Where They Started

For years, many Uighurs believed that their subjugation would end once they captured world attention. But journalist Glenn Greenwald addressed the most significant hurdle for Uighurs in transmitting their story in a piece titled "What if the Uighurs Were Christian Rather Than Muslim?"

For all the serious analysis about the War on Terror, so much of it has been driven by nothing more complex or noble than sheer hostility toward Muslims. Muslims generally—not just Al Qaeda—replaced Communists as our new enemy and became the new enabling force for our endless state of war and never-ending expansions of executive power. Rather obviously, the Uighurs were swept into the enemy category solely by virtue of their status as Muslims.[43]

Disappointingly, post-9/11 reporting illustrated that few outlets were willing or able to see past Islamophobia to devote the time, energy, and resources into developing appropriate contextualization of the Uighur narrative. Worse yet, anti-Muslim sentiment frequently provided the basis for bringing Uighurs into skewed stories. Most media accounts presented Xinjiang as an outpost of Muslim terrorists. Ironically, when Uighurs attained their longtime goal of visibility, they were misrepresented. Uighurs at Guantanamo were thrust into the spotlight precisely because they were not a threat and their story, like the imprisoned men, had trouble leaving the Cuban island.

No doubt, reporting on the oppression of Uighurs in Xinjiang is extremely challenging. China severely restricts outside journalistic access to the region and its people. Uighurs understand that the penalty for speaking about their repression is severe. Prison, torture, disappearance, even execution follow defiance. In a perfect world, these factors would make the story even more attractive to journalists. However, in an era with increasingly competitive media markets, drastically shrinking news budgets, and trends of consolidating corporate ownership, outlets are hard pressed to invest the time, effort, expense, and in-depth knowledge required to properly tell the complicated, rich story of Muslim Uighurs. Instead, it becomes easier and more efficient to fold them into a larger narrative about Islamic terror and to believe that this narrative, somehow, provides truth.

NOTES

1. "China Silenced," *Frontline World*, PBS, http://www.pbs.org/frontlineworld/stories/china401/.
2. In China, autonomous regions are entities where the majority of the population is made up of a minority group. There are five autonomous regions in China: Xinjang; Ningxia, home to China's largest Muslim group, the Huis; Guangxi; Inner Mongolia; and Tibet.
3. China claims that Xinjiang may have up to 33 percent of Chinese oil reserves.
4. Matthew Teague, "The Other Tibet," *National Geographic*, December 2009, http://ngm.nationalgeographic.com/2009/12/uygurs/teague-text.
5. Preeti Bhattacharji, "Uighurs and China's Xinjiang Region," *Council on Foreign Relations*, July 6, 2009, http://www.cfr.org/china/uighurs-chinas-xinjiang-region/p16870.
6. Mark Coatney, "Crackdown in Western China," *Time*, April 28, 1997, http://www.time.com/time/nation/article/0,8599,8046,00.html
7. James Fallows, "No Uighurs Need Apply," *The Atlantic*, July 10, 2009, http://www.theatlantic.com/technology/archive/2009/07/-no-uighurs-need-apply/21071/.
8. Bhattacharji, "Uighurs and China's Xinjiang Region."
9. Jeffrey Hays, "Uighurs," *Facts and Details*, April 2010, http://factsanddetails.com/china.php?itemid=1036&catid=5&subcatid=89.
10. Teague, "The Other Tibet."
11. Bhattacharji, "Uighurs and China's Xinjiang Region."
12. Edward Wong, "Fuse of Fear, Lit in China, Has Victims on 2 Sides," *New York Times*, July 12, 2009, http://www.nytimes.com/2009/07/13/world/asia/13uighur.html.
13. Andrew Jacobs, "China Fears Ethnic Strife Could Agitate Uighur Oasis," *New York Times*, July 22, 2009, http://www.nytimes.com/2009/07/23/world/asia/23kashgar.html.
14. Teague, "The Other Tibet."
15. Christopher E. Beaudoin and Ester Thorson, "LA Times Offered as a Model for Foreign News Coverage," *Newspaper Research Journal* 22, no. 1, 80–93 (2001).
16. "State & County Quickfacts," US Census Bureau, November 4, 2010, http://quickfacts.census.gov/qfd/news.html.
17. "Luce, Henry R. 1898–1967," American Decades, *Encyclopedia.com*, http://www.encyclopedia.com/topic/Henry_Robinson_Luce.aspx.
18. Coatney, "Crackdown in Western China."
19. Robert Mackey, "Another Media Tour Goes Very, Very Badly for Chinese Authorities," The Lede, *New York Times*, July 7, 2009, http://thelede.blogs.nytimes.com/2009/07/07/media-tour-goes-very-very-badly-for-chinese-authorities/.
20. "Gulja Massacre," *YouTube*, http://www.youtube.com/watch?v=4RUCOrg2Pbo (accessed January 9, 2011).
21. Harriet Barrovick and others, "Milestones," *Time*, August 30, 1999. http://www.time.com/time/magazine/article/0,9171,991862,00.html
22. Paulette Chu Miniter, "Taking a Stand for China's Uighurs," *Far Eastern Economic Review*, March 2007, 27–29.

23. "About NPR," *NPR.org*, http://www.npr.org/about/aboutnpr/ (accessed December 10, 2010).

24. "China Unrest," *Weekend Edition*, NPR, November 29, 1998.

25. "Uygur-Drama," *All Things Considered*, NPR, July 27, 1999.

26. "Racism Conference Summary," *Morning Edition*, NPR, September 6, 2001.

27. Teague, "The Other Tibet."

28. At the time, many experts claim that the ETIM had long been dormant, if not defunct.

29. Charles Hutzler, "China, in Strategy to Fight Taliban, Cultivates Taliban," *Wall Street Journal*, September 13, 2001.

30. Robin Wright, "Bush Has Come a Long Way in World Eye," *Los Angeles Times*, October 22, 2001, http://articles.latimes.com/2001/oct/22/news/mn-60220.

31. Frank Langfitt, "After U.S. Strikes, China Shows Unusual Restraint," *Los Angeles Times*, November 9, 2001, http://www.latimes.com/news/nationworld/wire/sns-worldtrade-china-bal,0,4039576.story.

32. The World Uyghur Congress, founded in 2004, advocates for the human rights of the Uighur people. China labels it a terrorist organization, yet it receives funding from the National Endowment for Democracy, a nonprofit organization funded by the US Congress that gives money to groups to promote democracy worldwide.

33. Bhattacharji, "Uighurs and China's Xinjiang Region."

34. Alex Frew McMillan, "Cold Shoulder for Bush's China Comments," *CNN World*, October 20, 2001, http://edition.cnn.com/2001/WORLD/asiapcf/east/10/20/bush.shanghai/index.html

35. Langfitt, "After U.S. Strikes, China Shows Unusual Restraint."

36. Phil Zabriskie, "Many Voices," *Time*, October 8, 2001, http://www.time.com/time/magazine/article/0,9171,176993,00.html.

37. "The Fear Factor," *Time*, October 22, 2001.

38. Matthew Forney, "China's Own Islamic 'Extremists,'" *Time*, October 22, 2001, http://www.time.com/time/magazine/article/0,9171,179526,00.html.

39. Wahhabism is a school of thought, developed in the 1700s, that interprets Islam conservatively. The overwhelming majority of adherents are peaceful.

40. NPR did not carry a single post-9/11 story that mentioned Uighurs until their Guantanamo coverage in 2005.

41. Robin Wright, "Chinese Detainees Are Men Without a Country: 15 Muslims, Cleared of Terrorism Charges, Remain at Guantanamo, With Nowhere to Go," *Washington Post*, August 24, 2005.

42. "Uighur's Translator Reflects on Their Odyssey," *All Things Considered*, NPR, December 15, 2010, http://www.npr.org/templates/story/story.php?storyId=105490034.

43. Glenn Greenwald, "What if the Uighurs Were Christian Rather Than Muslim?" *Salon*, July 6, 2009, http://www.salon.com/news/opinion/glenn_greenwald/2009/07/06/uighurs.

REFERENCES

Fallows, James. 2009. No Uighurs Need Apply. *The Atlantic*, July 10.

Greenwald, Glenn. 2009. What if the Uighurs Were Christian Rather Than Muslim? *Salon*, July 6. http://www.salon.com/news/opinion/glenn_greenwald/2009/07/06/uighurs.

Teague, Matthew. 2009. The Other Tibet. *National Geographic*, December. http://ngm.nationalgeographic.com/2009/12/uygurs/teague-text.

CHAPTER 33

RELIGION AND REPORTING IN AFRICA

ANTHEA BUTLER

A 1990s article, with the spectacular title of "Penis Shrinkers in Africa," is as good an introduction as any to thinking analytically about religion and media in Africa. The article reported on Senegalese men who were fearful that sorcerers held the power to "steal" or shrink their genitalia. Over the last thirteen years, the occasional news story about penis shrinkers, or penis stealers, has come across the news wires, only to be debunked.[1] These stories function as attention grabbers, focusing on religion in Africa as exotic, replete with witch doctors and superstitious natives. But however frivolous the story may be, religion's role in Africa has always been a contentious, confusing, yet compelling tale.

Reporting on religion in Africa has been complicated for the American mainstream press because it is often filtered through the lens of US politics and interests. Moreover, covering religion's role in African political, cultural, and social life in the context of a single religious tradition would be difficult, but reporting these within the framework of the multitude of traditions active across the continent is even harder. Both the global and the local are important in the African context as many cultural issues in the continent's religious world are connected to other areas across the globe. For example, the struggle within the Anglican Communion over the issue of homosexuality is a global story with local ramifications in several African nations. Adequate coverage of religion's role in Africa means attentiveness not only to the domestic but also to the international scene.

With that in mind, two crucial moments in the past thirty years stand out as exemplars of religion reporting in Africa: apartheid in South Africa and the Rwandan genocide. These two cases illuminate how the American press corps has covered religion in Africa and provide a variety of stories that demonstrate the challenges of covering religion in Africa, as well as the myriad ways in which religion touches many aspects of life and political action in African countries.

Reporting on Religion's Role in South Africa's Apartheid Battle and Aftermath

From the 1980s forward, coverage of religion's role in both opposition to and support for apartheid in South Africa focused primarily on denominational organizations, parachurch organizations, and "men of the cloth." In some ways, the coverage mimicked reporting found in the Saturday religion section in most American newspapers of the period. Stories focused on churches, denominational issues, and charismatic clerics who were politically active, whether socially conservative campaigners or progressive agitators at odds with their denomination.

The Dutch Reformed Church (DRC) and its relationship to the apartheid government of South Africa was the logical starting point for many of the religion stories written in the 1980s. The church's role in upholding the apartheid system through its theological beliefs about racial separation, as well as the internal struggles within the church over apartheid, were an important and accessible way to examine the religious world of South Africa. In addition, the DRC's worldwide connections to the Reformed tradition, the World Council of Churches, and Reformed Churches in America made the story not just a local South African one, but also news that spanned the religious world.

"Apartheid Strains South Africa Church," a *Washington Post* article by Caryle Murphy, was reprinted in several major newspapers on July 1, 1980. It chronicled the break within the DRC between white members and the members of black, Indian, and mixed race Dutch Reformed Churches.[2] The colored churches' split from the white DRC represented "an internal crisis," according to the article. The Reverend Allan Boesak, who would become a major figure in the antiapartheid movement, was quoted, saying, "the parting of the ways has come." The story, aiming to show the racial divisions within the DRC, also highlighted how the white DRC conservatism had stymied South African Prime Minister P. W. Botha's attempts for changes in the apartheid law. P. W. Botha, along with many other whites in the apartheid government, was a member of the DRC and as such was held captive to the DRC beliefs. The DRC, solidly against integration and interracial marriage, was portrayed as leaving the white branch of the church "domestically isolated" because of their support of hard-line apartheid.

Later in March 1981, that trajectory was followed with a *Los Angeles Times* article titled "Rift over Apartheid Reaches South Africa's Most Powerful Pulpits."[3] Journalist Jack Fosie discussed the contradictions internal to the DRC, whose theological stance was part of the underpinnings of apartheid law. The article begins with the story of the Mbangs, a black African couple turned away from the funeral of the white man who they served as cook and gardener for thirteen years. When the couple arrived at the front doors of the DRC church, the pastor officiating at the funeral told them, "Go to the cemetery, you can observe the graveside service." The article explicated the fissures within the DRC, ranging from pastors who disagreed with P. W. Botha's seeming leniency on apartheid policy to both black and white clerics who had defied the denomination to support the antiapartheid movement and the African National Congress (ANC). Unlike other articles, this one discussed the role of the DRC's theology in supporting and legitimating the structures and beliefs of the apartheid system. Fosie also explored the problems some DRC theologians had in speaking out against the denomination's theology and profiled those within the DRC who opposed the church's support of apartheid.

Since many of South Africa's leaders and governmental officials were part of the DRC, journalists wrote religion stories about the major religious DRC leaders and denominations within South Africa. Since the DRC's Calvinist theology was understood to rank whites as superior to coloreds and blacks in South Africa, its popularity provided a lens by which the press could gauge the acceptance of conservative views of apartheid. Likewise, journalists also covered challenges to the DRC's theological beliefs.

But the straight-line coverage was complicated by internal conflicts that ultimately fractured the DRC. On June 10, the Associated Press carried a story that ran in most major American news outlets. The article reported that 123 white South African ministers had opposed the DRC's official racial segregation policy as "unscriptural" and had issued a call for racial equality.[4] The item underplayed the fact that this was not merely a statement, but rather the foundation for what became the Belhar Confession, a key factor in the World Council of Churches' (WCC) decision to expel the DRC from membership. The Belhar Confession also was the first in a series of theologically based statements against the apartheid regime. The theological maneuverings that allowed white South Africans to uphold a racist belief system sanctioned by their church would have been difficult for many American news consumers to follow. By focusing on white racism, American reporters skipped over many of the DRC's theological twists and turns. Yet their stories provided an effective theology lesson.

Statements, however, were not enough to gain traction with readers. The story only gained a strong narrative line—and greater reader interest—when reporters began writing about the religious leadership in South Africa. From the mid-1980s forward, the courageous stances of leaders such as DRC cleric and ANC Chair Allan Boesak, Anglican Bishop Desmond Tutu, and DRC cleric Rev. C. F. Beyers Naudé became the frames within which the story of apartheid was told. These public theologians, who vigorously opposed apartheid, became the voice of and vehicle for American coverage of religion and politics in South Africa. Other religious luminaries also carried the news forward; for example, Pope John Paul II denounced the apartheid church and government. Another crucial factor in facilitating the shift in coverage was the awarding of the 1984 Nobel Peace Prize to Bishop Desmond Tutu.

International recognition placed the black South African cleric at the center of the narrative about religion's role in the antiapartheid movement.

Shifting the focus from the role of the DRC in maintaining racial separation to the actions of individual religious leaders and groups unaffiliated with the DRC and against apartheid also changed the perception of the story. No longer a chronicle of one church's struggles, it now was one of individual and collective acts of valor. The new emphasis would prove important in swaying American public opinion against apartheid. The 1985 papal visit to Africa also was a major push in this direction. E. J. Dionne, reporting on Pope John Paul II's trip for the *New York Times*, started with the pope's condemnation of the South African policy of apartheid: "The church's repudiation of racial discrimination is forceful and total."[5] By placing apartheid at the beginning of the article, the rebuke to the South African government became the lead. John Paul's travels throughout the continent, covered farther down in the article, were relegated to second-tier status.

A few days after the pope issued his rebuke to South Africa's apartheid government, Rev. Allan Boesak, along with other clergy members, was arrested for attempting to attend a black teenager's funeral in Gugulethu, a township outside of Cape Town, South Africa. Once again, a funeral served to put forward the contradictions in the apartheid South African church. Funerals would become a meme in the American press coverage of apartheid and religion in South Africa. Stories like that of the Mbangs, covered in Fosie's *Los Angeles Times* article mentioned above, or of violence breaking out at funerals or police action at the funerals of black South Africans showed how deeply the apartheid regime reached into the worship lives of black and white South Africans. These stories, portraying life for everyday people, helped to humanize institutional struggles. They also showed how blacks, including their leaders, challenged an oppressive regime.

The switch to covering the major personalities in the antiapartheid struggle also allowed the press to create a narrative about religion's role in the movement. By placing Tutu, Boesak, and others in the role of charismatic leadership, the story, from the mid-1980s on, became a "big man" narrative, similar to the trope surrounding coverage of Martin Luther King, Jr. during the civil rights movement. That narrative, recognizable to Americans, would prove to be an effective means to disseminate the story. The addition of a familiar face would make the distinction even sharper, as Rev. Jerry Falwell's 1985 visit to South Africa demonstrated. His meetings with Prime Minster Botha along with his condemnation of Bishop Tutu as "phony" made headlines in newspapers across the United States.[6] As a result, another civil rights icon, Rev. Jesse Jackson, came forward to condemn the Lynchburg pastor. Likewise, Rev. Phillip Cousin, the head of the National Council of Churches, proclaimed that Falwell was "acting like a segregationist."[7]

As the tide started turning against the apartheid regime, American reporters turned to the United States and sought responses among its religious communities. One of the big stories in the 1980s was church divestment of funds invested in South Africa. A January 14, 1986, *Los Angeles Times* story was headlined "US Churches Will Launch Campaign Against Apartheid."[8] Citing the contributions of the civil rights movement and the Vietnam antiwar movement, a new group, the Churches Emergency Committee on South Africa, pledged to push for government sanctions, divestiture of US holdings, and boycotts against American companies investing in South Africa. This shift in coverage from South Africa to the United States placed American churches, politicians, and protesters into the story of apartheid South Africa, which became not only about the ongoing struggle of black South Africans but also an echo of the 1960s civil rights movement in the United States, as white religious communities sought to support black efforts for change.

Thus, for the most part, the American press coverage of religion in South Africa was reported and written through the lens of denominational institutions and was almost a redux—albeit updated and more sympathetic—of reportage on the American civil rights movement. Rather than looking for stories outside of denominational and church struggles, the narrative of apartheid's supporters and foes was written initially through the actions of the state church (DRC) and opposition to it. The expansion of that story to religious leaders fighting apartheid was made easier by the international recognition of figures like Bishop Tutu and Pope John Paul II. By the time coverage of South Africa and apartheid reached a peak in the early 1990s with the release of Nelson Mandela from prison, most stories had moved away from focusing only on the DRC to featuring individuals, like Mandela, and their religious activities in the apartheid struggle.

This focus on a few leaders and organizations also suggests that "on-the-ground stories" of the apartheid struggle may have been difficult to get because of racial prohibitions. After apartheid, a fuller story about religion in South Africa began to emerge, and these stories showed the diversity of religious traditions in the region. Subsequent US press coverage of the truth and reconciliation movement, Pentecostalism, and traditional religious practices, just to cite a few stories that appeared in the American press in the late 1990s and beyond, gave a refreshingly different picture of religion in South Africa. The polarized religious and racial environment that existed under apartheid stunted coverage of religious life in South Africa, sublimating all else to the struggle against an unjust regime.

Ethnic Conflicts and Religion

Media coverage surrounding war, ethnic conflicts, and religion in Africa were important worldwide stories of the late twentieth century. Conflicts in Somalia, Nigeria, Rwanda, and Ethiopia all contained religious elements that either incited or resulted in hostilities among faiths. One of the most compelling and harrowing clashes was the Rwandan genocide against the Tutsi people in an attempt to "cleanse" the country. Rwanda, a predominantly Christian country, is important because of the scope of religious leaders' complicity in the genocide. The genocide, rooted in historic conflicts between the Hutu and Tutsi people, was perpetuated by the Hutus' use of the media to incite and organize attacks. For weeks prior to the genocide, radio broadcasts on RTLM or Radio Rwanda discussed how to kill Tutsis, played songs that fueled the hatred, and, at the start of the conflict, reported on where Tutsis could be found. In an informative book, *The Media and the Rwandan Genocide*, the missteps of the worldwide media in coverage of the Rwandan genocide is discussed from various angles. As UN Lieutenant General Romeo Dallaire stated succinctly, "It was a strange dichotomy, watching the local media fueling the killing while the international media virtually ignored or misunderstood what was happening."[9] Put starkly, coverage of the double murder that precipitated the O. J. Simpson trial was much broader than that of a genocide that killed 800,000 people.[10] Worldwide media coverage of the genocide in Rwanda was actually less than the coverage of the war in Bosnia.[11] Yet for all of the detail of this volume and others, very few took up the task of reporting on how the media reported the religious element of the genocide. If the coverage of the genocide was slow and spotty, how did the religious aspect of the story fare in the American press?

Initially, the genocide received scarce attention because of a confluence of events. The violence was thought to be a continuation of the previous civil war, and journalists were leaving, rather than coming to, Rwanda. What reporting there was centered on Kigali, yet most of the killing took place outside of the city. Religion had not been a major topic in earlier reportage, in part because of the homogeneity of the religious space, with many Rwandans belonging to the Roman Catholic Church. In fact, the religious dimension of the tragedy did not surface until bodies were found in many churches. Then, stories began to leak out about the complicity of Hutu clergy in murdering Tutsis. One early story, however, from the *New York Times* focused on the violence through the lens of American missionaries who had been evacuated from Rwanda. The article, "Refugee Missionaries from Rwanda Speak of Their Terror, Grief and Guilt," chronicled the evacuation of Seventh Day Adventist missionaries who were brought from Rwanda into Burundi.[12] Their accounts hinted at the bloodshed that was occurring. "'The worst part,' says Phil Van Landen, 'was not the constant crackle of the gunfire around the house, or the trucks piled with corpses, or even the gangs of wild eyed young men who were always out there, somewhere. The worst part was fleeing Kigali, and leaving behind African friends and co-workers.'"

The thrust of this story was to show both the perilous conditions of the missionaries and their selflessness in trying to help Rwandans before and during the massacre. One of the missionaries, Dr. Per Hourmann, housed twenty-three escaping Tutsis in his home while his Hutu gardener went out into the streets to find and kill them. Still, most of the article recounted the horrors going on around the missionaries and concentrated on their rescue. It only hinted at the extent of the violence. Granted, the April 1994 story appeared very early on in the massacre. The true extent of the violence and its religious roots were yet to be revealed. At that moment in time, a story about American missionaries rescued from carnage in Africa would be recognizable to most readers and a good fit for the A1 page of the *New York Times*. The story was filtered through not only the voices of Americans but also a particular kind of American Christianity focused on saving foreign souls and offering selfless service. The takeaway from this article, if one did not know otherwise, was that Rwanda was not a predominantly Christian country, and that the sole purpose of the missionaries was to spread the Christian message. In reporting for a US audience, the "American" hook becomes important—a story about American missionaries rescued, with the backdrop of the Rwandan genocide, would likely garner a broader readership for a difficult foreign story.

The religion story would become very complicated as news slowly trickled out on the extent of the genocidal rampage in Rwanda. By June 1994, the narrative would change sharply. Within a week's time, the *New York Times* would run several articles on the Rwandan church and the genocide. The first, "Heart of Rwanda's Darkness: Slaughter at a Rural Church," described the gruesome scene of the bodies of more than 500 Tutsis hacked, shot, and bludgeoned to death discovered strewn across a Catholic church's grounds.[13] No overt reference was made to religion, other than the fact that the murders had occurred at the church, ostensibly at the hands of Hutu and extremist militia. What came to the forefront later was that Catholic priests, nuns, and others were murdered and that some of the Hutu clergy had participated in the slaughter of the Tutsis. A subsequent report on June 9 would still further confound the situation with its headline, "Insurgents Deplore Massacre of Catholic Prelates."[14] According to the article, two Catholic bishops and ten priests were massacred by soldiers in the Rwandan Patriot Front, a group predominately led by Tutsi tribesmen. The Tutsis murdered the Hutu clergy whom they were assigned to guard, believing the clergy were implicated in the murder of their families.

The article is important not only for reporting on the murders of the Catholic clergy but also for the inference that clergy had been involved in the massacres. Later in the piece, Alison Des Forges, an American working with the human rights organization Africa Watch, said that she had reports from Belgian Catholic contacts that the Hutu militia had presented the Rwandan archbishop with a list of sixteen priests, a nun, and a layperson whom they wished to take away. The archbishop gave his consent, and the people disappeared.[15] Later the same week, the *New York Times* would begin to chronicle the horror of the discovery that clergy had handed over other clergy members to be killed and had even participated in murders. The Catholic Church would become a focal point of the critique. In articles like "In Rwanda, Catholics in the Crossfire," the church was implicated in the racial hatred that pitted Hutus against Tutsis.[16] According to Domenico Del Rio, a veteran Vatican correspondent, "It is also Christian Africa that practices discrimination within the church itself. It was said that not only in state schools but also in diocesan seminaries, places were not given to Tutsi."[17]

The implication that the Catholic Church was complicit in the massacres because it had tolerated discriminatory practices within the Rwandan church was a source of consternation. It also was a cause for pushback from the Vatican, and the back and forth was played out in the media as well. As reports continued to flow out of Rwanda about clergy involvement in the massacres, Pope John Paul II took great pains to distance himself and the Roman Catholic Church from the scandal. During a 1995 mass in Nairobi, Kenya, he called for an end to the killings in Rwanda. A year later, he advocated for forgiveness and reconciliation as the only solution to the ethnic conflicts. By this time, however, the story of Catholic clergy's complicity in the massacres was public. A *New York Times* article cited the Reverend William Knipe, a Maryknoll priest, who said, "The church failed so miserably in Rwanda in 1994. Many Rwandans have in a sense written off the church. It no longer has any credibility."[18]

The Rwandan situation would prove to be far too complex for the simple remedy of forgiveness and reconciliation that the pope had prescribed. Because of the scope of the massacre and the conflicting stories, much of what had occurred would continue to bedevil the Catholic Church.[19] Despite Pope John Paul II's assertion that the church was not to blame in Rwanda, stories of the clergy's responsibility for the killings continued to surface. One egregious example was Father Athanase Seromba, who lured 2,000 people into his church with promises of protection, only to lead the Nygane parish massacre.[20] Later, when the strife ended, the tribunals and trials in The Hague showed many church officials had supported ethnic cleansing and helped to perpetrate the genocide. The participation, especially of Catholic Church officials, was predicated on the previous close ties of bishops and clerics to the Hutu government. But this story did not begin to emerge until after the genocide had been completed. Only then did the use of churches as killing grounds and the involvement of clergy and laity become apparent. Catholics were not the only ones implicated, however; Pentecostal pastors, Anglicans, even Seventh Day Adventists participated in the slaughter of Tutsis. Even more recently, arrests of clerics continue to make news, such as the July 2010 detention of Pentecostal Pastor Jean Bosco Uwinkindi. Authorities had offered a $5 million reward for Uwinkindi's capture.

However, the clergy's complicity in the Rwandan genocide was not as well covered as other aspects of the civil war. Occasional stories chronicling the progress of trials in The Hague made news, for instance, the 2001 trial of four nuns, including a mother superior, who had participated in the killing.[21] Although the clergy's role in both aiding the genocide and saving Tutsis from genocide had been featured in a number of important stories written by the American press, much more of the coverage was by African and European news outlets. In 2011, African news outlets continued to report on the arrests and trials of the leaders of the Rwandan genocide because of their parallel with tribunals investigating mass murders and prosecuting warlords in other African countries. The complete story of religion's role in the Rwandan genocide remains to be told—including the story of the press's role in not initially, or ever fully, reporting on the genocide.

One last Rwanda story mirroring the history of missionary activity in Africa and Christian media reporting on Africa can be traced through the work of Rick Warren and his book, *The Purpose Driven Life*. In 2005, the American press jumped on a story that Rwanda's leader, Paul Kagame, expressed an interest in Warren's book.[22] Warren, in partnership with President Kagame, brought "the purpose driven life" curriculum derived from his best-selling book to Rwandan schools and businesses with the goal of remaking Rwanda as a "purpose driven country." The story, followed closely for a time by American media outlets, is one that is embedded in the coverage of another story that was covered by both the mainstream media and religious media alike: the rise of HIV/AIDS on the continent of Africa. The use of the *Purpose Driven Life*, for the most part, was heralded as a success by many media outlets. Rather than interrogate what Christianity previously meant or had accomplished in Rwanda, the American press focused on the humanitarian or missionary aspects of Rick Warren's assistance.

The story of Rwanda's genocide has many of the elements that complicate coverage of religion and conflict on the African continent: ethnic conflict, a complicit clergy, and double speak from denominational leadership. Unlike South Africa, it was a story that did not have a definitive end but continues to play out in the courts.

Untapped Stories of Religion in Africa

Shifting social mores and religious affiliations are the source of a wide variety of religious stories that can be told about Africa. The rise of globalization has resulted in a continent more interconnected than before—resulting in some cases in an expansion of religious experience and in other cases in a return to traditions that include fundamentalism. Western media coverage of homosexual issues in Africa, for instance, usually begins and ends with articles on HIV/AIDS or papal pronouncements on condoms and abstinence. The continued struggle over homosexuality, especially with the introduction of Uganda's antihomosexual bill, known as the "Kill the Gays" bill for the provision for the execution of gays in some cases, promises to remain an important religion, as well as politics, story. Involvement of American Protestant clergy and politicians in encouraging the draconian persecution of lesbians and gays and their political intervention in assisting the introduction of laws forbidding homosexuality hearken back to some of the strategies employed by the religious Right in the United States in the 1970s and 1980s.

Sexuality will certainly have a place in future stories about the Anglican Communion. Africa's Anglican Church is much more conservative than its Western counterpart, and there is speculation as to whether or not the continent will remain part of the worldwide communion. If the communion splits, it will be divided by issues of gender and sexuality. The African Anglican opposition to female ordination, especially of bishops, and their opposition to homosexuality are nonnegotiable for many Africans who are in the Anglican Communion. Likewise, reporters will need to track how issues of gender and sexuality affect other denominations such as the Baptists, Presbyterians, and even Catholics on the continent. Women's roles and their place in African societies—both religious and secular—will continue to be in flux. The treatment of rape victims in the Democratic Republic of Congo and in other African states has been dealt with as a human rights issue, but few news reports have examined whether or not religious institutions have helped or harmed victimized women. Another poignant question is whether women's leadership will continue to be questioned in church traditions that arose out of American missionary outreach.

Another story that deserves more coverage is the ongoing violence between Muslims and Christians in Nigeria. Politics and religion have a very close connection in that country, and many Christian mega-church pastors are connected to political figures. Fundamentalist Islamic groups such as Boko Haram, which calls for Sharia law to be implemented nationwide, are important to the broader political and social context of Nigeria, one of the wealthiest nations on the continent. Without an understanding of the tensions between Muslims and Christians, especially in Northern Nigeria, American readers will see these conflicts as recent, rather than historic, divisions.

Nigeria, Ghana, South Africa, and other nations on the continent are also experiencing exponential growth among Pentecostal and nondenominational mega-churches. The rise of these groups has changed the landscape, both literally and figuratively, of Africa and has led to the creation of worldwide networks of adherents among African immigrants. Some religious leaders, like Matthew Ashimolowo, have connections to American mega-church pastors, like Bishop Eddie Long. These American pastors' movement of money, as well as their real estate dealings—replete with extensive building and land acquisition projects—is a story waiting to be written. Also ready to be reported is an investigation into the exponential membership growth in these pastors' vast global media network. Far from disconnected from the African continent, these far-flung churches with "home churches" in Africa then support immigrant communities in the United States and elsewhere. The African immigrant story, then, is not just about the yearning for jobs and a better life on another continent; it also is the story of a religious "migration" and new diasporas.

There are many other stories at the intersection of religion, politics, sexuality, money, and immigration on the African continent, and journalists should be aware that covering them can be a daunting task. But if religion had been focused on earlier in conflicts like Rwanda, perhaps the outcome would have been different, or at the very least, illuminated in a different way. More religion coverage, not less, is imperative for future reporting on the countries of the African continent.

NOTES

1. Joe Bavier, "Lynchings in Congo as Penis Theft Hits Capital," Reuters, April 22, 2008, http://uk.reuters.com/article/2008/04/22/oukoe-uk-congo-democratic-witchcraft-idUKL2290323220080422.

2. Caryle Murphy, "Internal Division: Apartheid Strains South African Church," *Los Angeles Times*, July 23, 1980.

3. Jack Fosie, "Rift over Apartheid Church Reaches South Africa's Most Powerful Pulpits," *Los Angeles Times*, April 18, 1981.

4. Associated Press, "Pretoria Clerics Attack Apartheid," *New York Times*, June 10, 1982.

5. E. J. Dionne, "John Paul on Eve of Trip to Africa, Speaks out Against Apartheid," *New York Times*, August 8, 1985.

6. "An Unholy Uproar," *Time*, September 2, 1985.

7. Robert Pear, "Falwell Denounces Tutu as a Phony," *New York Times*, August 21, 1985.

8. Sarah Fritz, "US Churches Will Launch Campaign Against Apartheid," *Los Angeles Times*, January 14, 1986.

9. Romero Dalliere, "The Media Dichotomy," in *The Media and the Rwanda Genocide*, ed. Allen Thompson (Ottawa, Canada: International Development Research Center, 2007), 12.

10. Steven Livingston, "Limited Vision: How the American Media and Government Failed Rwanda," International Development Research Center, http://www.idrc.ca/rwandagenocide/ev-108202-201-1-DO_TOPIC.html.

11. Ibid.

12. William E. Schmidt, "Refugee Missionaries from Rwanda Speak of Their Terror Greif and Guilt," *New York Times*, April 12, 1994.

13. Donatella Lorch, "Heart of Rwanda's Darkness: Slaughter at a Rural Church," *New York Times*, June 3, 1994.

14. Associated Press, "Insurgents Deplore Massacre of Catholic Prelates," *New York Times*, June 9, 1994.

15. Associated Press, "Rebels in Rwanda Said to Slay 3 Bishops and 10 Other Clerics," *New York Times*, June 10, 1994.

16. Allan Cowell, "In Rwanda, Catholics in the Crossfire: Killings Provoke a Sense of Failure," *New York Times*, June 12, 1994.

17. Ibid.

18. Donatella Lorch, "Pope Calls for End to Killings in Rwanda," *New York Times*, September 20, 1995.

19. Associated Press, "Pope Says Church Is Not to Blame in Rwanda," *New York Times*, March 21, 1996.

20. Marlise Simons, "Trials Test the Faith of Rwandans: 5 Clergymen Face Charges of Genocide in Slaughter of Tutsis," *New York Times*, May 12, 2002.

21. Marlise Simons, "Mother Superior's Role in Rwanda Horror Is Weighed: Belgian Court Tries 4 in 1994 Massacre," *New York Times*, June 6, 2001.

22. David Van Biema, "Warren of Rwanda," *Time*, August 15, 2005, http://www.time.com/time/magazine/article/0,9171,1093746,00.html.

REFERENCES

Dalliere, Romero. 2007. The Media Dichotomy. In *The Media and the Rwanda Genocide*, ed. Allen Thompson. Ottawa, Canada: International Development Research Center

Schraeder, Peter J., and Brian Endless. 1998. The Media and Africa: The Portrayal of Africa in *The New York Times*. *Issues: A Journal of Opinion* 26 (2): 29–35.

SECTION VI

THE RELIGIOUS PRESS

CHAPTER 34

THE INDEPENDENT CATHOLIC PRESS AND VATICAN II

DENISE P. FERGUSON

THE more than 600 publications that make up the Catholic Press Association serve over twenty-six million readers who look to the diocese-owned and independent newspapers, magazines, and online news outlets for information that strengthens their faith and promotes understanding of social, economic, and political issues and events from a Roman Catholic perspective. To appreciate the role of the Catholic press today in the life of the church, the laity, and their interaction with the world, one must understand (1) the history of the diocesan and independent publications, (2) the role of the press in coverage of Vatican II and post–Vatican II Catholic life, and (3) the role of Vatican II in the development of the Catholic press.

The first ongoing, weekly, distinctly Catholic publication, *United States Catholic Miscellany*, was founded in Charleston, South Carolina, in 1822 by Bishop John England, who believed "American Catholics needed a publication to inform and unite them."[1] It wasn't until the second provincial council, in 1833, that the US bishops first attempted to define the mission of the Catholic press to "explain our doctrines, to protect our feelings, and to increase our devotion."[2]

Milestones in early institutionalized Catholic press history included the establishment in 1911 of the Catholic Press Association to combine resources and support affiliated publications and the creation of the National Catholic War Council (NCWC), also in 1911, to support the war effort during World War I (which in 1919 became the National Catholic Welfare Conference News Service). The NCWC News Service (now known as the Catholic News Service) continues to be the principal Catholic source of national news, with its stated mission the same as the mission of the Church itself: "to spread the Gospel," in this case, ". . . through contemporary means of communication, which it attempts to accomplish by reporting the news which affects Catholics in their everyday lives."[3] The establishment of the Catholic News Service, which provided an increased number of ready news sources, along with an influx of journalists trained at secular papers, helped professionalize the press and enable it to "present information about the church and its activities, . . . serve as a medium for diocesan, parochial, and general announcements emanating from religious authorities, as well as to express editorial opinions in conformity with ecclesiastical judgment."[4]

Along with the development and increase of clergy- and lay-edited diocesan publications came a number of independent newspapers and magazines dedicated to publishing news from a Catholic perspective. *America* magazine, started by the Jesuits in the United States and Canada, called itself "A Catholic Review of the Week" when it was first published in 1909. Its stated purpose was to "meet the needs of the times,"[5] which included addressing social issues from a Christian standpoint, defending church doctrine, and providing a platform for the church to opine on modern life. Given its independent editorial philosophy and operation, *America* was considered a "radical departure from the Catholic journalism of the past."[6] It presents a moderate to liberal view on Catholicism and moral and social issues and takes positions contrary to official Catholic Church teaching on matters such as homosexuality, priestly celibacy, AIDS, and the roles of women in the church. Today, the magazine is still published weekly by American Jesuits and has a circulation of 45,000 readers and 600,000 monthly online readers.

Another innovator was *Our Sunday Visitor*, a nonprofit Catholic publishing company that began as a weekly newspaper in 1912. The editorial policy of founder Father John Noll was to "combat anti-Catholicism, work to educate Catholics in their faith, help them to preserve their Catholic identity in a sometimes hostile environment, and combat social and political trends contrary to their faith."[7] Today, *Our Sunday Visitor* has a circulation of nearly 66,000 and publishes over 500 products including religious books, tapes, periodicals, software, catechetical and educational materials, and over 800 million offering envelopes annually. A third upstart, *Commonweal*, began in 1924. The oldest independent lay Catholic magazine, it covers literature, the arts, religion, society, and politics and has a circulation of only 20,000. *Commonweal* was founded as a journal of opinion and focuses on ethics and social issues of interest to progressive Catholics.

By the end of World War II, the Catholic press was substantially different than it had been at the turn of the century. The loose network of independent lay-owned and -edited publications, which varied greatly in terms of quality and religiosity, had been replaced by a centralized Washington, DC-based news service and several large chains, with clergy holding high posts on both the editorial and business sides.[8]

The Second Vatican Council (1962–65), popularly known as Vatican II, changed the practice of Catholicism worldwide, and its impact on the American Catholic press was part of a sweeping change. One easily discernible effect was the establishment of two independent publications, *U.S. Catholic* and *National Catholic Reporter*

(*NCR*). *U.S. Catholic*, first published in October 1963, evolved from monthly magazine *The Voice of St. Jude* to reflect the publication's broadened scope and interests. Its editorial policy emphasized interpretive reporting to make "the world we live in more intelligible."[9] The *National Catholic Reporter* started as a diocesan newspaper in Kansas City-St. Joseph, Missouri, and evolved into an independent paper with a circulation today of 44,000. After analyzing 420 Catholic magazines and 118 diocesan newspapers, founding *NCR* editor Robert Hoyt developed eight "questions" or criticisms of policies and issues, including the following: content that focused on the church rather than on readers' everyday lives and social issues; a lack of truthful and objective reporting; financial ties to the diocese, which weakened quality; and a reliance on "cheap reasoning" and "rosy" public relations techniques.[10] These criticisms were the basis for his new publication, the *Reporter*, a national weekly that was published on October 24, 1964, during the third session of Vatican II.[11]

To illuminate the role and impact of the Catholic press on the church and on society, this chapter will focus on independent Catholic publications—committed to covering ecclesial matters, social issues, and world events—that matured through coverage of Vatican II and developed a post–Vatican II Catholic perspective. Vatican II, with its updated approaches to ecumenism and religious liberty, church governance and structure, liturgy and laity, brought profound changes to Catholics and to the Catholic press.

As house organs for the local church, diocesan papers tend to be more conservative in both reporting and opining on news and information relevant to Catholics. Oftentimes, the desire to provide interpretation of these events works at cross-purposes with journalistic ideals for a free and unbiased press. For example, Pittsburgh Diocese Editor John Deedy, Jr., also a contributor to *U.S. Catholic*, has been highly critical of diocesan newspapers, insisting that "unquestionably, if Catholic publications were sold wholly on their merits, and not on secondary grounds of loyalty or promoting an apostolate or supporting missions, Catholic press circulation figures would shrink considerably."[12] Readers, too, have held the Catholic diocesan press responsible for neglecting social and political coverage. In one reader survey, 80 percent of respondents agreed that Catholic newspapers that steer clear of controversial issues have contributed to the loss of credibility the Catholic Church has suffered in recent years.[13]

The stated missions, purposes, and editorial coverage of *America, U.S. Catholic*, and the *National Catholic Reporter* more closely reflect an "ideal" Catholic and were ranked the "best Catholic publications," according to a 2005 survey of *U.S. Catholic* readers.[14] In its first issue, *America* distinguished itself from newspapers under the auspices of the Catholic Church that "do not attempt to chronicle events of secular interest or to discuss questions of the day in the light of Christian principles" and are "circumscribed in territory."[15] A 2005 editorial in *America* stated its mission is to "serve educated Catholics and other readers interested in intelligent examination of church and world affairs, seen through the lens of the Catholic faith and with the eyes of catholic reason."[16]

U.S. Catholic, published monthly by the Claretians, states on its website that it is "the most award-winning religious general-interest magazine in the United States," a distinction earned by winning the top award from the Catholic Press Association for nine consecutive years.[17] Since its first issue in October 1963, it has been characterized as "a magazine that carries on a continuing conversation with its readers."[18] These surveys consistently reveal that the magazine's audience is "almost totally uninterested in Churchy subjects."[19] Instead, editors seek to "explore the wisdom of their faith tradition and to apply that faith to the challenges of life in the 21st century" in ways that are relevant to their own religious lives and in the "outreach of Christian love into the social political realm."[20]

Developed through the inspiration of the Second Vatican Council in 1964, *National Catholic Reporter* is a weekly newspaper and website that presents itself as "one of the few, if not the only truly independent, journalistic outlet for Catholics and others who struggle with the complex moral and societal issues of the day."[21]

These three national independent Catholic publications provided lengthy and substantive coverage, commentary, and dialogue about the major forces that shaped the role of the Catholic press in Catholic life and in social, economic, and political issues that was substantively different from and more extensive than most diocesan newspapers. To assess the impact, this chapter will look at coverage of Vatican II and liberation theology. The Catholic presses provided coverage of the planning and pre–Vatican II phase through the four years of the Vatican sessions, and continuing in the post–Vatican II years as the implementation of changes reverberated through Catholic life. A second and related news story was liberation theology, which was practiced by Catholic clergy and lay workers in Latin America during the 1970s and 1980s. An outgrowth of the council's call for involvement in the world's problems, liberation theology evidenced a professional and matured Catholic press that applied the church's post–Vatican II vision of enlarging the reach of Catholic faith in transforming the world. Together, these events illuminate the role of the Catholic press in setting the social, political, and economic agenda domestically and abroad for twentieth-century American Catholics.

Second Vatican Council

The twenty-first general council of the Catholic Church, which brought to Rome more than 3,000 bishops from around the world, met in four sessions: October 11–December 8, 1962; September 29–December 4, 1963; September 14–November 21, 1964; and September 14–December 8, 1965. Vatican II has been called "the watershed in modern Roman Catholic history" and "the greatest event in the life of the Church in this century."[22] Michael Novak, a Catholic journalist who covered Vatican II for *National Catholic Reporter* and later as a staff reporter for *Time* during the third session of the council, wrote at the time that "it was as though the world (or at least the history of the Church) were now to be divided into only two periods, pre-Vatican II and post-Vatican II."[23] Pope John XXIII called for a general ecumenical council of bishops to convene for an "*aggiornamento*, a bringing up to date of Catholic thought and practice," or an opening of doors and windows for a fresh wind to blow through the church.[24]

Starting with Pope John's announcement on January 25, 1959, of an ecumenical council and throughout all four sessions, *America* featured lengthy reportage and commentary; Vatican II was prominent in *U.S. Catholic* and *National Catholic Reporter* coverage after their founding in 1963 and 1964, respectively. The three independent publications presented a unified voice for unfettered access to sessions and documents and provided extensive articles detailing proposals and profiling the leading figures in the debates, all while advancing a transformative agenda for Catholic faith and its impact on society.

In a 1961 encyclical, Pope John addressed the importance of the religious press: "By the natural law every human being has the right . . . to freedom in searching for truth and in expressing and communicating his opinions . . . and he has the right to be informed truthfully about public events."[25] The pope's recognition of the individual's right to information and the church's need for free public opinion demanded thorough, accurate journalism over and against any controlled, secretive tendencies of official press councils.[26] An *America* editorial about the Central Preparatory Commission's work in developing press policy for Vatican II optimistically pointed out that in contrast to the secretive, rumor-laden atmosphere of the First Vatican Council (which ended in 1870), Pope John had initiated a "liberalized press policy," which, interestingly, was described by editors as "not a right extended to the Catholic press but an opportunity for it to serve the Church."[27]

However, the first two-month session in 1962 did not permit direct coverage by either the religious or secular press; rather, the press was expected to be satisfied with official distributions from the Vatican Press Council.[28] *America* editors acknowledged that "the press policy of the Vatican Council seems the weakest link in the chain of preparations," reflecting "a deep-seated distrust of secular (and even religious) journalism, no doubt based on sad experience."[29] In this framing the independent Catholic magazine seemed to excuse the attempts to obfuscate and control the dissemination of information that emanated from the Vatican Press Council. It acknowledged that the "danger of sensational, irresponsible and politically motivated journalism ever hangs over such a world assembly as an ecumenical council."[30] By the opening of the second session, "news flow[ed] freely out of the Council"[31] as a result of critical coverage and pressure by the independent Catholic press and secular media demanding full access to the proceedings and documents.

One week before Vatican II opened, independent Catholic press editors expressed optimism about the success of the council. The work of the ecumenical council touched on every aspect of Catholic life, including the liturgy, mass communications, church unity, the Eastern Catholic churches, the nature of revelation, church structure and governance, the use of mass media, celibacy, the role of bishops and priests, missionaries, diocese operations, laity, ecumenism, dogma, religious freedom, Catholic-Jewish relations, birth control, and the role of women in the church. Some of the most profound and controversial issues discussed, which gained the most attention in the Catholic press and resulted in decisions and documents, were the liturgy, church structure and authority, ecumenism and religious freedom, and Catholic-Jewish relations.

Liturgy

Pope John had issued repeated pronouncements that the first tasks of Vatican II would be internal renewal, adapting the organization and structure of the church to the world's changing conditions and equipping and involving the laity.[32] *America* editors commended the council for considering the liturgy first, viewing the choice as wise from both a political and organizational standpoint, as it "underscored the fact that internal renewal of the Church was the bishops' primary concern" and reflected the pope's conception of the Church as the People of God.[33] According to an *America* editorial, another reason for addressing the liturgy was the projected doubling of Latin America's Catholic population (to 400 million) over the next four decades. (This was directly relevant to the church's later involvement in liberation theology in that region.[34])

The bishops approved the schema on the liturgy on the last day of the second session, December 4, 1963. *America, U.S. Catholic*, and *National Catholic Reporter* continued to cover clergy and lay reaction and implementation of the changes and to provide commentary and analysis of its impact on the church throughout the next several years. The first issue of *National Catholic Reporter* in 1964 featured an article titled "How the Mass Will Change" that explained that "English was introduced into the audible parts of the Mass, except for the Canon; the laity were given fuller participation in the worship service by responding to prayers and singing hymns."[35] *U.S. Catholic* predicted that Catholics' "entire participation" in church life would be transformed.[36] During the council's fourth session, *U.S. Catholic* published the results of a survey that found "enthusiastic support for most of the Mass changes, 77 percent favoring English in the Mass and 67 percent favoring Mass facing the people."[37] Reports (e.g., in *U.S. Catholic*) of clergy who were resistant to the changes and of laymen ill-equipped for their expanding role were countered with editorials and articles urging acceptance of the church's liturgical renewal and forms.[38]

Collegiality in Organization and Structure

America's editorial at the conclusion of the first session characterized the proposed collaboration between bishops and "clarification or redefinition of relations between the bishops and Pope" as a "conciliar breakthrough."[39] In the interim, Pope John died and was succeeded by Pope Paul VI, who announced his four objectives for the second session of the council, which opened on September 29: (1) to more fully define the nature of the church and the role of the bishop; (2) to renew the church; (3) to restore unity among all Christians, including seeking pardon for Catholic contributions to separation; and (4) to start a dialogue with the contemporary world.[40]

De Ecclesia, which addressed church governance and structure, was anticipated for discussion early in the second session following approval of the schema on the liturgy, as well as those on ecumenism and religious liberty.[41] *America, U.S. Catholic*, and *National Catholic Reporter* opined that the "decisive problem" of Vatican II was the bishops' conferences and their authority,[42] and each carried extensive coverage and commentary supporting the establishment of a bishops' conference that would share governance and decision-making authority. An *NCR* editorial endorsed the creation of a " 'senate' or representative gathering of bishops chosen from sees to meet periodically, under the leadership of the bishop of Rome, to consider the state of the Church anew" as a practical arrangement that would make "real and operative the principle of collegiality."[43]

America editors predicted that collegiality could be the "most decisive issue of Vatican II." Likewise, *NCR* writers said, "the key to the significance of the Second Vatican Council"[44] was the decision to empower bishops and renew church governance. The debate on birth control, the schema on ecumenism, and the declaration on religious liberty were predicted to have deep and lasting importance. But to *NCR* editors the "practical implementation of collegiality will have much to do with the effective communication of council decisions on these matters to the faithful, and with their administration and interpretation in decades and centuries to come."[45]

Ecumenism and Religious Liberty

America editors expressed optimism based on "well-conceived and well-executed" schema and on the bishops' push for "a strong declaration of the rights of conscience and freedom of worship."[46] The schema on ecumenism for the first time, wrote *NCR* editors, "recognizes the Catholic share of guilt for Christian disunity and officially commits the Church to join in the work of repairing disunity."[47] Signaling a profound change in global involvement of Catholics, the schema "bluntly state[d] the way is open for cooperation in the duties for the common good of humanity which are demanded by every Christian conscience" and which promote social justice, declared *U.S. Catholic* editors.[48] The church must be in the world, they further asserted, cooperating and applying Christian principles to social problems, including poverty and war, as well as paving the way to Christian unity.[49] The third session of the Second Vatican Council closed on November 21, 1964, with Pope Paul's proclamation of the Constitution on the Church and the Decree on Ecumenism.

America editors called the documents discussed above the Decree on Ecumenism, the Dogmatic Constitution on the Church, the Constitution on the Sacred Liturgy—and the changes they entail the "Three Giant Steps" for the Catholic Church.[50] Coverage of the four years of Vatican II also brought profound changes in the Catholic press. Along with the Catholic Church, the Catholic press was renewed, which led to greater professionalization.[51] Catholic editors felt a mandate

> to inform the people, to provide a forum for public opinion, and to inspire action for justice. The purpose of the Catholic press was no longer just to report what the Church was telling the Catholic to do or not to do. It was no longer simply to guard the faith by withholding news considered disturbing or hurtful to it. Instead it was to enrich one's faith, to help it grow, and to help the maturing reader apply faith to the workplace so that he or she could help transform the world.[52]

The years during the sessions of Vatican Council II and the decade or two following yielded provocative copy for the Catholic press: the council documents updating and refreshing the church, advocacy for the poor and oppressed, attention to issues of social and economic justice, and peace activism in the United States and abroad. One such significant example that applied the post–Vatican II vision of enlarging the reach of Catholic faith in transforming the world was the church's involvement in liberation theology in Latin America.

Liberation Theology and the Catholic Church in Latin America

Pope John XXIII's plea to American priests to go as missionaries to Latin America expressed his belief that renewal in the post–Vatican II Church must involve Catholics in the problems of the world.[53] Coverage of liberation theology in Latin America in the 1970s and 1980s by these three Catholic publications reflected this increased focus on social justice and power inequities between the poor, government, the wealthy, and businesses.

Initially, American Catholic missionaries went to Central America to serve the church and the world, and the Catholic press covered their efforts. As reporters saw the poverty and injustice and began to understand the complexities of the region, coverage evolved from telling stories of missionaries to galvanizing opposition to policies that oppressed the poor. The Catholic press was an important and energized sector in the United States, and it was a source of support and resources for progressive Catholics in Nicaragua, El Salvador, and Guatemala.[54] Liberation theology encouraged Catholic workers to serve and advocate for the oppressed, sometimes risking physical and material danger to champion the multitudes of Latin America's needy.[55] Bishops who stood up to despotic governments on behalf of the poor and powerless in El Salvador, Nicaragua, Brazil, Chile, and Argentina in the late 1970s were described by *U.S. Catholic* as "selfless men [who] believe, evidently, that preaching the gospels without speaking out for the powerless would be hypocritical."[56]

America and *U.S. Catholic* published regular, detailed reports of Catholic clergy and workers in Latin America who, as they became more involved in social justice and spoke out against oppressive governments and policies, were forced to leave their work, targeted by enemies, and sometimes killed.[57] From the Sandinista priests' conflicts with the Nicaraguan hierarchy to the persecution of the church in El Salvador and the martyrdom of Archbishop Oscar Romero, the Central American story was of genuine interest to the readers of the Catholic press.[58]

San Salvador's Archbishop Oscar Romero was killed while saying mass, just days after sending a letter to U.S. President Jimmy Carter warning that military aid, "instead of favoring greater justice and peace in El Salvador, will undoubtedly sharpen repression."[59] The repressive Salvadoran government and its "political terrorism," *America* reported, killed dozens and injured hundreds with bombs and gunfire during Romero's funeral, adding to the total of 8,000 dead from January to October 1980.[60] The magazine charged that "the guns of right-wing assassins" were responsible for 3,000 deaths during 1980, including many clergy. According to *America*, these murders were part of the Salvadoran government's efforts to intimidate the church, a campaign that also saw death threats issued against fifty-two Guatemalan Jesuits and a threat to drive from the country all the foreign Jesuits for protesting social injustices and human rights abuses.[61]

The independent Catholic press was particularly influential in raising support for humanitarian and economic aid and in opposing US government aid for weapons during both the Carter and Reagan administrations. Coverage by *America, U.S. Catholic*, and *National Catholic Reporter* was a source of energy, support, and even resources for progressive Catholics in Nicaragua, El Salvador, and Guatemala.[62] *America* editors urged Congress to approve the Carter administration's request to Congress for $75 million to aid in rebuilding Nicaragua's economy after Sandinista revolutionaries overthrew dictator Anastasio Somoza in 1979.[63]

U.S. Catholic editors called the decision of the Carter administration, in its final days, to renew military aid to the government of El Salvador "a tragic blunder" and predicted that US military aid "can only feed the wasteful violence that threatens to consume the land and its people."[64] A 1981 editorial charged the US State Department under President Ronald Reagan, as well as the mainstream US media, with misrepresenting the positions of rightists and centrists representing the Salvadoran government and the leftists or Marxists who opposed them. The "ideological content" of the war, said the editors, "comes from outside, from cold-blooded men in Moscow and, I regret to say, from cold-blooded men in Washington."[65]

Catholic news coverage reflected a central fact of the post–Vatican II climate, engaging the church with a fundamental question: should it concern itself "chiefly with announcing the kingdom of God, or should it also attempt to bring about the kingdom?"[66] Until Vatican II, wrote a contributor to *America*, American bishops did not attempt to influence the foreign policy of the US government. The Latin American experience awakened them to the relationships between American multinational corporations, government, and military power in Latin America.[67] Through their experience in Latin America, the US Catholic Church and Catholic press became aware that they had the power to influence US policy.

In the decades since then the independent Catholic press has become more vocal in challenging church positions on celibacy of priests, birth control, abortion, the role of women, the priest shortage, and the clergy sex abuse scandals. The *National Catholic Reporter* is credited with publishing the first article about sexual abuse within the church in 1985. After the *Boston Globe* published a series of articles covering cases of sexual abuse in 2002 and the topic became its most intense, *NCR* devoted fully two-thirds (66.7 percent) of its Vatican coverage to the scandal, while Catholic News Service and the Catholic News Agency devoted only 44.8 percent and 33.3 percent of their coverage, respectively.[68] Independent Catholic publications, including *NCR, U.S. Catholic*, and *America*, urged the church to admit cases of sex abuse, extend compensation and healing to victims, and enforce punishment and prevention of future abuse.

While the diocesan press also has become more outspoken in its review and criticism of church policies and action, it has continued to be perceived as neglecting social and political coverage and avoiding controversial issues. For example, during the clergy sex abuse scandal, diocesan newspapers were more likely than independent Catholic publications to defend accused clergy and official church responses and accuse media of sensationalized and biased coverage. Still, readers of diocesan newspapers value these outlets for their local focus, providing news, identity with the larger Catholic community, commentary, and catechesis and faith formation.[69] Clearly, given the value Catholics place on news coverage that applies their faith to social and political issues and the perception that church-sponsored publications neglect controversial coverage, there continues to be an important role for independent Catholic publications and the kind of national and international coverage they provide.

Twenty-First Century Catholic Press

The twenty-first-century Catholic press is confronted with challenges related to the decline of newspapers as a business model and the enormous opportunities associated with media technology and global communication. With the advent of the Internet, some Catholics predicted that diocesan newspapers would migrate online.[70] The same market forces that drive secular publishers influence the Catholic press, including "the content of the editorial product, the rising cost of paper and postage, the ability to pay competitive salaries and provide adequate fees for manuscripts."[71]

The challenge and opportunity for both the diocesan and independent Catholic press is to take full advantage of new resources to serve readers who continue to demand professionalism and comprehensive coverage. At the same time, media technology affords opportunities to create spaces for dialogue on key issues that Catholics find relevant. Competition from electronic media and the Internet is forcing Catholic publications to creatively harness the technology and to find better ways to get out its message. For example, *National Catholic Reporter*, *America*, *Commonweal*, and *U.S. Catholic* have websites comparable to secular online media outlets, though their focus is on national and international issues, culture, and religion relevant to Catholics. They use multiple media platforms to provide content in text, audio, and video formats. Extensive archives and timely news gathering from other outlets provide a library of information to readers. These online media sites are taking advantage of cyberspace to create forums to interact on issues, through blogs, e-newsletter subscription, polls, comment boards, and e-mail exchanges.

At the 2010 annual gathering of the Catholic Press Association, Pope Benedict XVI offered a long-distance greeting, in which he said that "[i]f Catholic communicators are to use new media effectively, they must use it in ways that touch people's hearts and draw them to living faith communities."[72] The 2010 meeting focused on the theme "Spreading the Good News—Byte by Byte." This theme, said the pope, "highlights the extraordinary potential of the new media to bring the message of Christ and the teaching of his church to the attention of a wider public."[73] If online technology, news delivery, and communication "promote and encourage the flow of information that will enable Catholics to deepen and enrich their faith"[74] and to engage that faith with their world, these new media will likely further the renewal to the Catholic press that Vatican II brought to the church as a whole.

NOTES

1. Apollinaris Baumgartner, *Catholic Journalism: A Study of Its Development in the United States, 1789–1930* (New York: AMS Press, 1967), 7; John. P. Foley, Preface to *The Mission and Future of the Catholic Press* (Ronkonkoma, NY: Catholic Press Association, 1998), 17.
2. John F. Fink, Introduction to *The Mission and Future of the Catholic Press* (Ronkonkoma, NY: Catholic Press Association, 1998), 20.
3. "ABOUT CNS," Catholic News Service, http://www.catholicnews.com/aboutcns.htm.
4. Baumgartner, *Catholic Journalism*, viii.
5. "Editorial Announcement," *America*, April 17, 1909, 1.
6. Ibid., xi.
7. Ibid., 59.
8. Michael Real, "The *National Catholic Reporter:* Communications and Change in a Turbulent Era" (PhD dissertation, University of Illinois at Urbana-Champaign, 1972), 34.
9. "A Statement of Purpose," *U.S. Catholic*, September 1963, 3.
10. Real, "The *National Catholic Reporter*," 71.
11. Real, "The *National Catholic Reporter*," 72–77. See also Robert G. Hoyt, "Questions for Catholic Papers," *America*, January 31, 1960, 521–24; Robert G. Hoyt, "The Issue Is Greatness," *Commonweal*, February 15, 1963, 534–38.
12. John G. Deedy, Jr., "The Religious Press in America," *Oxford Journal of Church and State* 6, no. 3 (1964): 392–95.
13. "Feedback," *U.S. Catholic*, November 2005, 21.
14. Ibid.
15. "Editorial Announcement," *America*, April 17, 1909, 2.

16. "Speaking the Truth in Love," *America*, http://www.americamagazine.org/content/article.cfm?article_id=4242.

17. "U.S. Catholic: What We Think It Means," *U.S. Catholic*, May 1979, 2; "NCR Nets Top Press Award for Ninth Consecutive Year," *National Catholic Reporter*, June 13, 2008, 3.

18. Ibid.

19. "About Us," *U.S. Catholic*, http://uscatholic.org/about-us.

20. "U.S. Catholic: What We Think It Means," 2.

21. "Mission and Values," *National Catholic Reporter*, http://ncronline.org/mission-and-values.

22. Real, "The *National Catholic Reporter*," 40; "Vatican II: October 11, 1962," *America*, February 17, 1962, 637.

23. M. Novak, *The Open Door* (New Brunswick, NJ: Transaction Publishers, 2002), xix.

24. F. Murphy, "The Council Opens: Underlying Every Issue Is the Pontiff's Call for an 'Aggiornamento,'" *America*, October 20, 1962, 925.

25. Pope John XXIII, *Mater et Magistra* (Glen Rock, NJ: Paulist Press, 1961), no. 12.

26. Real, "The *National Catholic Reporter*," 39.

27. "Catholic Press at the Council," *America*, February 24, 1962, 676.

28. Real, "The *National Catholic Reporter*," 40.

29. "Secular Press at the Council," *America*, April 21, 1962, 71.

30. "Better Council Coverage," *America*, October 26, 1983, 473.

31. See, for instance, "Reporting the Council," *America*, September 22, 1962, 768.

32. See "Updating the Church," *America*, May 19, 1962, 259; "Pentecost and the Council," *America*, June 9, 1962, 373.

33. "Council and Liturgy," *America*, November 3, 1962, 977.

34. Ibid.

35. Real, "The *National Catholic Reporter*," 99.

36. Editorial, *U.S. Catholic*, March 1964, 55.

37. "The Examined Life," *U.S. Catholic*, September 1965, 2.

38. See "Church in the News, to Those Changes in Mass Pope Paul Asks Patience," *U.S. Catholic*, March 1965, 60; "The Church in the World, Pope Paul Urges Conservative Catholics to Cooperate with New Liturgy," *U.S. Catholic*, June 1965, 57.

39. "Conciliar Breakthrough," *America*, December 22, 1962, 1266.

40. "To the Council Fathers," *America*, October 19, 1963, 412.

41. "Vatican II: A Look Ahead," *America*, September 28, 1963, 348; "Council Jottings," *America*, October 12, 1963, 409; "To the Council Fathers," *America*, October 19, 1963, 412.

42. "Vatican II: A Look Ahead," *America*, September 28, 1963, 348; "Council Jottings," *America*, October 12, 1963, 409; "To the Council Fathers," *America*, October 19, 1963, 412.

43. "Church Government and Collegiality: Meaning of a 'Senate,'" Opinions, *National Catholic Reporter*, November 11, 1964, 3.

44. "How Is the Council Going," *America*, December 7, 1963, 732; Desmond O'Grady, "Collegiality: The Crucial Issue to 'the Old Firm' at the Vatican," *National Catholic Reporter*, November 11, 1964, 3.

45. O'Grady, "Collegiality," 59.

46. "Council Jottings," *America*, October 12, 1963, 410.

47. "'Ecclesia,' Ecumenism Pass; Mary Is 'Mother of Church,'" *National Catholic Reporter*, November 25, 1964, 1. See also "Council Jottings," *America*, December 14, 1963, 765.

48. Bishop Connare, "The Church and the World: Social Justice Is Ecumenism in Its Finest Form," *U.S. Catholic*, September 1965, 59.

49. "Church and the World," Opinions, *U.S. Catholic*, November 11, 1964, 3.

50. C. J. McNaspy, "Three Giant Steps," *America*, December 12, 1964, 778.

51. Ethel M. Gintoft, "The Catholic Press Faces Several Threats to Freedom of the Press," in *The Mission and Future of the Catholic Press*, ed. John F. Fink (Ronkonkoma, NY: Catholic Press Association, 1998), 73–74.

52. Ibid.

53. Edward T. Brett, *The U.S. Catholic Press on Central America: From Cold War Anticommunism to Social Justice* (Notre Dame, IN: University of Notre Dame Press, 2003).

54. Brett, *The U.S. Catholic Press on Central America*.

55. Gerald M. Costello, "Latin America: The Mission Transformed," *America*, January 20, 1979, 26.

56. "The Leadership You Follow May Be Your Own," *U.S. Catholic*, May 1979, 2.

57. See "Land Grabbing in Brazil," *America*, January 26, 1980, 50; John Garrison, "Democratization in Brazil?" *America*, February 2, 1980, 81.

58. See "Clouds over El Salvador," *U.S. Catholic*, January 19, 1980, 32; "Weapons in El Salvador," *America*, March 1, 1980, 160; Stephanie Russell, "Millions Mourn Slain Romero," *National Catholic Reporter*, April 4, 1980, 5; "Bishops Want 'Another Romero' for El Salvador," *National Catholic Reporter*, April 11, 1980, 3; "New Leader for San Salvador," *America*, April 26, 1980, 350.

59. See "Three Things North American Catholics Can Learn From Salvadoran Catholics," *U.S. Catholic*, July 1984, 26; June Carolyn Erlick, "El Salvador: 'Last Chance for Peace,'" *National Catholic Reporter*, February 22, 1980, 1; "Weapons in El Salvador," *America*, March 1, 1980, 160; "Romero Rites Erupt into Bloodshed," *National Catholic Reporter*, April 11, 1980, 18.

60. "Unfinished Task in El Salvador," *America*, April 19, 1980, 330; "Terror in El Salvador," *America*, October 25, 1980, 330.

61. "Death in Guatemala," *America*, February 16, 1980, 111; "Guns and Martyrs," *America*, August 8, 1981, 42–43.

62. "Death in Guatemala," *America*, February 16, 1980, 111; "Guns and Martyrs," *America*, August 8, 1981, 42–43; "The Salvadoran Tragedy," *America*, January 31, 1981, 74; "Senate on El Salvador," *America*, October 10, 1981, 190; "Human Rights Reconsidered," *America*, November 21, 1981; Brett, *The U.S. Catholic Press on Central America*.

63. See "The Sandinists Move In," *America*, February 2, 1980, 71; "Rebuilding Nicaragua," *America*, March 15, 1980, 201; "Nicaragua Aid May Fall to Budget Axe," *National Catholic Reporter*, March 30, 1980, 2; "Changes in Nicaragua," *America*, June 7, 1980, 470–71; "Aid to Nicaragua," *America*, September 20, 1980.

64. "The Salvadoran Tragedy," *U.S. Catholic*, January 31, 1981, 74; "Human Rights, Anyone," *America*, March 14, 1981, 191.

65. "The Examined Life: Red or Not, Bogeymen Are Just That," *U.S. Catholic*, May 1981, 2.

66. James R. Brockman, "Preparations for Puebla," *America*, January 27, 1979, 50.

67. Costello, "Latin America: The Mission Transformed," 28.

68. "The Pope Meets the Press: Media Coverage of the Clergy Abuse Scandal," June 11, 2010, http://pewforum.org/Christian/Catholic/The-Pope-Meets-the-Press—Media-Coverage-of-the-Clergy-Abuse-Scandal.aspx.

69. "Feedback," *U.S. Catholic*, November 2005, 21.

70. Ethel M. Gintoft, "The Catholic Press Faces Several Threats to Freedom of the Press," in *The Mission and Future of the Catholic Press*, ed. John F. Fink (Ronkonkoma, NY: Catholic Press Association, 1998), 79.

71. Mark Brummel, "New Challenges for Catholic Media," in *The Mission and Future of the Catholic Press*, ed. John F. Fink (Ronkonkoma, NY: Catholic Press Association, 1998), 47–48.

72. Carol Glatz, "Pope: New Media Must Touch People's Hearts," http://www.americancatholic.org/news/report.aspx?id=2682.

73. Ibid.

74. Mark Brummel, "New Challenges for Catholic Media," in *The Mission and Future of the Catholic Press*, ed. John F. Fink (Ronkonkoma, NY: Catholic Press Association, 1998), 50.

REFERENCES

Baumgartner, Apollinaris. 1967. *Catholic Journalism: A Study of its Development in the United States, 1789–1930*. New York: AMS Press.

Brett, Edward T. 2003. *The U.S. Catholic Press on Central America: From Cold War Anticommunism to Social Justice*. Notre Dame, IN: University of Notre Dame Press.

Deedy, Jr., John G. 1964. "The Religious Press in America," *Oxford Journal of Church and State* 6 (3): 392–95.

Fink, John F., ed. 1998. *The Mission and Future of the Catholic Press*. Ronkonkoma, NY: Catholic Press Association, 1998.

Hoyt, Robert G. 1960. Questions for Catholic Papers. *America*, January 31, 521–24.

U.S. Catholic. 1963. A Statement of Purpose. September, 3.

CHAPTER 35

THE MAINLINE PROTESTANT PRESS AND THE IDEA OF "DECLINING" LIBERAL RELIGION

MARK HULSETHER

SUPPOSE a bully approaches and asks, "Have you stopped battering your spouse? Are you still in denial?" Suppose the accused has never done any such thing. Shouldn't the response to the bully's premise be to turn the tables: "When will you stop slandering me? Are you doing this because you aren't listening or from conscious malice?" Unfortunately, if the accusation has long shaped media scripts, a simple report about the countercharge may not clear it up. The charge may take on its own life: "When will you admit that no one cares what you say, and it's your own fault because you're an abuser?" It may evolve: "Whatever became of that guy who was fired for battering? Is he still alive to ask?" Eventually, an accused batterer—all along minding his own business—could reach a point of absurdity reminiscent of Mark Twain's complaint that rumors of his death were exaggerated.

Such is the situation faced by anyone who approaches intersections between the mainline Protestant press and the news. This press has long done significant work and continues to do so. It is not dead, and there is limited need for it to apologize for past mistakes. Nevertheless, pundits routinely treat mainline intellectuals as naïve idealists who lost their constituents' confidence by veering into ultra-leftism (an offense as damning as battering for many pundits) and its institutions—including its journals—as approaching the bottom of a slippery slope leading to institutional death, greased by compromises with liberalism.

Pundits routinely contrast evangelicals who dominate the religious-political scene with a waning mainline. Liberal decline need not be argued; one can simply gesture at the idea to evoke a dismissive response. Even when a friendly observer, Jeff Sharlet, assessed speculations that religious left liberalism is reviving, he judged that

> the weak alliance of amiable evangelicals, well-intentioned mainline Protestants, old school social justice Catholics, and Michael Lerner that's currently heralded by mainstream media as a resurgent Religious Left is neither left nor surging. Rather, it's a centrist coalition of the willing that's reporting for duty—not to the task of prophetically challenging power but to a Democratic Party bent on peeling off undecided voters.[1]

For Sharlet, such "faith outreach" efforts are not especially democratic "nor particularly reaching anyone." And Sharlet gives more respect to left liberals from mainline denominations compared to other writers who discuss this trend he douses with cold water. Many narrow their attention to liberal Catholics and evangelicals, whereas Sharlet titles his article "Waiting for Lefty" and actually hopes that Lefty will return, presumably from groups that intersect, in part, with the mainline Left.

Undoubtedly, there is much for the mainline to be pessimistic about, which might make a skeptic wonder how much its journals matter. Still, it is not the case that the mainline's cup is 90 percent empty and leaking, as opposed to some idealized past such as the 1950s or 1800s when it was full. Nor is it a given that observers must discuss "exactly how empty is it?" Largely due to the mainline's historical resources, its cup remains perhaps a third full—well above levels often assumed. And this cup has never been full to the brim. In fact, the sort of cultural work highlighted in this article—public interventions by its best journals—has always spoken for a minority, even during purported golden years. The question is not whether mainline groups are failing to surge (for the record, the answer has always been yes), but whether the institutional and communications networks of liberal Protestantism provide a tradition and infrastructure that allows them to continue doing important work. Despite the mainline's serious problems, its decline has been exaggerated, often by people with malicious intent. "Everyone knows" that the mainline is irrelevant—but if such knowledge is based on half truths and tendentious analysis, then anyone oriented by it may be launched down a street in the wrong direction.

Accordingly, this article focuses on assumptions that frame media discourses about the mainline, treating cases related to its press as it proceeds. Its goal is not to retread the ground of demonstrating that the mainline and its communications networks remain significant, but rather to presuppose this significance and reflect, first, on how media scripts about liberal decline obscure the situation, and second, on how mainline journals' internal discourses are shaped by debates about how to respond to such scripts.

I

Depending on where one sets a threshold at which mere newsletters and promotional publications cross a boundary and become "real" newspapers or journals, it would be possible to track thousands of mainline Protestant periodicals. In the nineteenth century, there were dozens of religious newspapers and countless journals. Although hundreds of such journals folded across the twentieth century, denominations continue to sponsor a wide array of publications. For example, the Evangelical Lutheran Church in America has the *Lutheran*, *Lutheran Women Today*, the *Little Lutheran* and numerous regional and/or specialized publications. This is before one considers many other Lutheran denominations past and present, then moves on to *Presbyterian Outlook*, *Presbyterians Today*—and so on ad infinitum. Intersecting with such periodicals and partly balancing the loss of print journals are religious websites and blogs—so many that it is hard to imagine how to count them.

Despite the great historical interest of this enterprise—scholars have demonstrated its centrality to the foundations of US journalism and popular culture—most such publications are fairly unimportant for religion and the news on the contemporary scene. Typically they do not aspire to general coverage or circulation; rather, "they are instruments of religious institutional promotion and of the development and informing of the faithful."[2] Often they center on human interest stories, least-common-denominator devotional writing, and announcements about people from their sponsoring groups, alongside commentaries relevant to the news.

Insofar as such journals relate to public issues, their influence is typically indirect. Their readerships "may help form a movement or direct an impulse that 'makes news,' and the secular media may pick it up." For example, Protestant periodicals during the civil rights era were "gatekeeper[s] to a world larger than the parish, [helping] form a cohort to support [Martin Luther] King or a force that opposed him"—even though average citizens "would not know how the constituencies had been formed by a press that was, to them, invisible."[3]

There is another threshold question to consider when assessing the scope of this topic. When do periodicals like the *Atlantic Monthly* or *Chicago Tribune* cross a line beyond which they are no longer mentionable as part of the historic Protestant establishment? The point of this question is easier to grasp if one considers the *Christian Science Monitor* (with its obvious linkages to Christian Science) or *Commentary* (with a Jewish character well understood by readers). "Normal" journals are often no less grounded in liberal Protestantism than these journals are rooted in their own faith traditions. Did not *Bill Moyers' Journal* reflect liberal Protestant values as clearly as *Commentary* reflects Jewish ones? The more one explores the roots of mainstream journalism—institutional genealogies, the ethos of investigative reporters, or what Mark Silk calls "topoi" of news reports (i.e., characteristic narrative themes and associated values that repeatedly structure stories)—the harder it becomes to sustain strong narratives of a mainstream changing from religious autonomy to antireligious forms of secularization.[4] True, things changed.

Newspapers and broadcasting evolved in ways that transformed an earlier ecology of journalism with many niches for religious newspapers into another ecology dominated by large "secular" city newspapers, which was later radically reshaped by the Internet. Nevertheless, the term *secularization* actually signals, in large part, ways that establishment Protestants came to understand themselves and/or inflect movements into which they poured their energies. Moreover, it is often hard to disentangle a "secularism" that conservatives love to hate from simple conflict over religious priorities and/or an ethos of pluralism. If one's own religion presupposes pluralism and/or other priorities that conservatives disapprove of—as liberal Protestants typically do—then positing zero-sum conflict between "religion" (someone else's) and "secularization" (which includes one's own religious values) makes limited sense.

The more one pursues such analyses, the more a liberal Protestant ethos seems like an inescapable net covering our culture—an ironic result for those who begin by assuming liberalism's fatal decline. In fact, critics sometimes have trouble deciding whether they disdain liberal Protestantism for being all-pervasive or irrelevant. Insofar as it is pervasive, it carries forward Protestant hegemony, but there seems to be nothing "distinctly religious" about it. Insofar as one focuses only on its distinctive aspects (note well, not its most significant ones), it seems trivial. Yet there it is, a key component of the air we breathe.

Turning from threshold questions to the matter of religious periodicals influencing the news indirectly, this idea applies best to interdenominational journals with national readerships—especially the Chicago-based *Christian Century* (*Century*), which was founded by Charles Clayton Morrison from complicated roots around the turn of the twentieth century and is still alive today, and the Manhattan-based *Christianity and Crisis* (*C&C*), which was founded by Reinhold Niebuhr in 1941 and ran until 1993. Although other denominational and/or movement-oriented periodicals have done important work (*The Liberator*, *The Outlook*, *The World Tomorrow*, and many more), for simplicity this article focuses on the *Century* and *C&C*. For many decades, commentary on public issues in mainline magazines often overlapped with these journals, unless inflected by denominational concerns beyond the scope of this chapter.

By the 1920s, the *Century* had become the top interdenominational forum for liberal Protestants, publishing a wide spectrum of mainline intellectuals. Before and after *C&C*'s run, the *Century* was the mainline's default forum, and during most of the 1950s and 1960s the two journals overlapped—both were invested in civil rights, anti–Vietnam War lobbying, and rapprochement with Vatican II–style Catholics (reversing decades of anti-Catholicism). In these years their key difference was that *C&C* was smaller and more focused, with a higher proportion of academic writers, so that *C&C* was more often the forum for hashing out emergent controversies.

The journals' differences were sharper in the 1940s—when the *Century* was dragged reluctantly into support for US military policies while *C&C* hammered on the "responsible" inevitability of such policies—and, importantly for this chapter, from the mid-1960s until *C&C*'s 1993 death, when *C&C* continued on a left-liberal course and broke with neoconservatives while the *Century* trimmed its sails. The *Century* maintained a big tent that welcomed the center Right, although not what it considered the far Left, and bemoaned an erosion of the common good. Meanwhile, *C&C* became decentered, with similar breadth as the *Century* but a more leftward center of gravity and deeper concerns about racial and sex/gender injustices. Since certain academic subfields that used *C&C* as a forum established specialized publications, there is a sense in which *C&C*'s internal development continued on a similar trajectory after it folded. By no means did *C&C*'s sensibilities disappear in mainline communication networks; there was simply less of a journalistic focal point and a growing sense of drift. Thus, one can use the term "*C&C*-style" as shorthand for an ongoing set of positions on the mainline's spectrum—perhaps finding a niche under the *Century*'s big tent, popularizing in the *Lutheran*, or moving online to *Religion Dispatches*.

Reinhold Niebuhr—who wrote prolifically for the *Century* before becoming *C&C*'s leader from the 1940s into the 1960s—is a classic example of overlaps between Protestant and "general" journalism that make it risky to claim sweeping secularization. Niebuhr launched his career in the *Atlantic* and published in the *Nation*, *Commentary*, *Foreign Affairs*, and many others. His public writing, floating between Protestant academia and an international stage, won him a cohort of elite colleagues known as "atheists for Niebuhr." One Niebuhr article of the 1940s—advocating bolder moves toward a Cold War military economy—appeared in both *C&C* and *Life*. Importantly, news about "religious" stances toward public issues often trickled down from *C&C* editorials, through *New York Times* reports, to the wider world. After Niebuhr's 1971 death, interviews with Martin Marty (the *Century*'s longtime public voice) sometimes played a loosely comparable role—although by then everyone understood that liberal Protestants held no monopoly on US religion.

In some respects, the Niebuhr and Marty models are passé. Protestants are deeply divided, and even considered as one group they have not monopolized US culture since the mid-1800s. Some mainline institutions are in trouble, and even in thriving ones the decline discourse takes its toll. Today's mainline intellectuals negotiate scholarly careers amid a historic shift of resources away from Protestant divinity schools—key institutional matrices for the *Century* and *C&C*. Nevertheless, shortly after voicing doubts about "Lefty," Sharlet described Cornel West—who makes no secret of his liberal Protestant roots, and whose early rise was based largely on writing in *C&C*—as "the preeminent intellectual of our generation, no qualifiers."[5] Although West is the best example of public intellectuals grounded in the mainline, one could easily extend the list with figures such as Krista Tippet of NPR's *On Being* (educated at Yale Divinity School), authors like Chris Hedges (educated at Harvard Divinity School), and Moyers, a long-standing leader among left-liberal journalists.

True, the book sales of all these writers combined may not match one volume of *Left Behind*. Still, few would judge the importance of musicians based solely on album sales, lest the latest teen pop star outrank a revered innovator whose influence trickles down to thousands of artists. Few would extrapolate from the demographic footprint of American Jews (smaller than the mainline's and declining at a comparable rate, in both cases due largely to birthrates) and assume that this translates into a dearth of Jewish cultural influence. Measuring "importance" requires exercising judgment about whether people have important things to say.

II

Reflecting on media frames for interpreting Protestants from the 1925 *Scopes* Trial to the present, Diane Winston notes that after 1980,

> Mainline denominations lost control of the news narrative and were trapped by the stories being told about them. The dominant post-Scopes caricature—religious conservatives as buffoons—was replaced by the depiction of religious liberals as bleeding hearts or commie shills. Adding to the portrait of liberal ineptitude and irrelevancy was coverage of the "graying" mainline, its attendant membership losses, and its financial woes. Even when mainline Protestants took action—objecting to budget cuts for the poor, campaigning to secure debt forgiveness for developing nations, or seeking corporate responsibility—their activities were virtually unnoticed.[6]

If there were no truth to this image, it could not have become common wisdom. Mainline churches did lose demographic power—although this was primarily a decline from a baseline of strength in the nineteenth century to a clear minority status by the 1950s, when they supposedly were still an establishment. Stereotypes shifted from an image of ignorant rural fundamentalists versus polished mainline elites to one of well-connected evangelicals versus pathetic "old-liners." Budgets shrank, so that it became routine to read of such things as a 13 percent cut at the Presbyterian national offices on the heels of five cuts in the previous seven years—with the latest round killing *Ideas* magazine and reducing subsidies for *Presbyterians Today*.[7] Although mainline leaders continued to pursue goals related to the news, these increasingly went unremarked. All this is well known.

Still, the portrait remains a caricature, just as Winston implies. It distorts as much as it illuminates, and to a disturbing degree it recycles conservative talking points about what counts as religion, how to interpret demographic trends, and what activities deserve to be reported respectfully rather than trivialized. Speaking of neoconservatives centered on *First Things* magazine and the Institute for Religion and Democracy (IRD), Winston notes their success—"as much due to skillful manipulation as to world events"—at encoding hostility toward the Left into standard narratives.

> What made it possible for the Religious Right's ideological frame to shape news coverage of religion and politics? The simple answer is that many journalists could not comprehend what unfolded before their eyes. . . . Even when repeating the Right's religious formulas . . . reporters never doubted their own objectivity. . . .

> [They] rarely mention [their] own role in the Right's purposeful campaign to marginalize religious moderates and progressives.[8]

Winston is tactful compared to Cornel West, who states bluntly that

> [g]roups like the World Council of Churches [WCC], the National Council of Churches [NCC], and liberal mainline denominations . . . [that] spoke out in defense of the rights of people of color, workers, women, gays, and lesbians . . . were targeted. Christian fundamentalists (with big money behind them) lashed out with vicious attacks against the prophetic Christian voices . . . and worked to discredit voices of moderation. . . . They equated the liberation theology movement, which put a limelight on the plight of the poor, with Soviet Communism. They cast liberal seminaries . . . [as] havens of freaks, gays, lesbians, black radicals, and guilty white wimps. Such slanderous tactics have largely cowed the Christian Left, nearly erasing it off the public map.[9]

West and Winston underline defeats that have rendered the mainline's cup two-thirds empty, whereas this article puts more stress on the remaining third. Whatever the spin, to emerge weaker after being "erased" by bullying is not the same as fading from ineptitude. The image is more like being shot or unjustly jailed (which, of course, actually happened to King). One must not conflate a sober appreciation of the forces deployed against the mainline with the most pernicious image propounded by its enemies: that its foot soldiers simply lost confidence in its leaders and defected to the Right, causing liberals to be overwhelmed by evangelicals.

This is the "big lie" in punditry about the mainline. Let's recall some key points. First, the bulk of mainline demographic declines are the result of a long-term shift to minority status—largely complete by the 1950s—and/or lower birthrates. Just as few use comparable Jewish declines to posit the irrelevance of Jewish voices, no one doubts that the mainline had ample numbers for strength during the 1950s—although it could no more speak for Catholics, evangelicals, or racial minorities then than it can today. Second, insofar as declines have continued since the 1950s, a crux issue is whether the mainline can retain the loyalty of upcoming generations. Most defections are not toward the Right, but either toward the Left or a half-engaged stance of apathy. Such defectors constitute a swing group that may be counted as "liberal religious" or not, depending on how pollsters frame questions. The same person who was shaped by a Methodist upbringing, is currently inactive in a congregation, and is "spiritual but nonreligious" might be counted as Methodist, "none," or new-age "seeker" in three different datasets. This swing group includes many potential recruits for mainline initiatives—but candidates likely to shun the conservative end of the mainline spectrum.

Meanwhile, there is another swing group, related to a historic trend of liberal churches gaining more converts who "switch in" from conservatism compared to those who "switch out" toward conservatism. Such replenishment is becoming less significant—but not because all evangelicals are conservative and its youth have stopped liberalizing. Rather, more youth who earlier might have abandoned evangelicalism are moving to moderate evangelicalism. This results in a group that may be counted as evangelical or liberal by different pollsters—a group that may account for a third of all evangelicals.

These two swing groups—people one could count as either mainline or "spiritual" and the liberal end of an evangelical spectrum—represent an overall liberal shift, not a stampede to the Right. Nevertheless, pundits routinely use low-ball estimates for a liberal Protestant share of these groups to generate stories with a "decline" topos. Often such stories appeal to theories about a need for strong moral boundary maintenance—although, inconveniently, the same theories predict the futility of building evangelical mega-churches.

So what *was* leaking from the Left to the Right? Winston and West have the main story right—it was elite allies and money. Mainline leaders were part of a New Deal coalition that came under sustained attack. Their enemies have been able to cripple them and then, as victors do, write a history of the battle. Much of the rest of the story—the spinning of poll data, the defunding of mainline institutions, the sense that if one were to tell a pollster that one is Protestant this would be reported as endorsing Republicanism—can be understood as ripple effects.

Turning to how this story applies specifically to *C&C*—the journalistic leader of the mainline Left—its goal after 1970 was to nurture its constituency on the leftward end of its spectrum to compensate for losses on the conservative end. It sought to retain its core liberal constituency while appealing to younger readers abandoning it on the Left. This path proved difficult because it was off-message from mainline centrists and it unfolded in a context of dwindling institutional support. Even so, *C&C* could have survived if it had embraced different institutional trade-offs, primarily related to its historic sponsorship by academia.

Mainline leaders have made their share of mistakes—especially related to cultivating youth—in the spaces where they have been pressed to maneuver. They have not always shown the backbone that critics desire; this is why West calls them "cowed" and Sharlet waits for Lefty. The cumulative weight of numerical losses is heavy. Nevertheless, if one measures liberal Protestantism in ways that include a reasonable share of the above-mentioned swing groups, it continues to have rough parity in resources, numbers, and long-term historical momentum with evangelicals who receive massively more attention. Rather than the story of pathetic decline, a more apt narrative is the mainline being trapped by a hostile media frame.

III

Having discussed, first, how a battering accusation can be leveraged into silencing its victim, and second, why paradigmatic narratives of liberal Protestant decline are misleading, this chapter arrives at a crossroads that may feel familiar to anyone who follows media scripts about Democrats. Consider how John Kerry was smeared for turning against the Vietnam War, Bill Clinton was impeached on frivolous charges, and Fox News incessantly attacks Barack Obama. How should Democrats respond? Should they engage Fox in debate, conceding them victory in setting the terms of discussion? Or should they ignore Fox as disreputable propaganda—and if forced to engage with it, do so solely within a frame that identifies it as such? If Fox reports that Obama is a socialist Muslim, one need not acknowledge this as a serious truth claim, as opposed to a talking point for attack politics.

Journalists have learned to see through this dynamic, far more consistently than they see through a similar dynamic related to liberal Protestants. Often they fail to appreciate that, just as there are times to deny that Fox is a legitimate dialogue partner, so also there are times to tune out charges that mainline Protestants are irrelevant liberal dinosaurs.

However, rather than end the discussion at this point, it is critical to note three nuances that complicate this matter. Adopting a critical stance toward them, one can perceive more accurately both the internal complexities of the "decline" discourse, as well as what journals like the *Century* and *C&C* seek to accomplish in response to this discourse.

First, just as there are times and places for Democrats to dialogue with sincere conservatives who, for example, might be persuaded that Obama is a US citizen or that national health insurance is good policy, so also one could patiently rebut smears against mainline activities or insinuations that liberal religion is not really religious. In fact, much of the day-to-day work in mainline journalism consists of precisely such dialogue—frequently in forms cautious enough to alienate a generation of activists. *C&C* worked hard at such dialogue for decades—debating both with emerging neoconservatives among its readers and with people from the *Century* who flirted with similar ideas—although it eventually concluded that most neoconservatives who engaged with it were uninterested in honest debate.

The *Century* has been more patient in keeping dialogues limping along in the territory from center Right to center Left. Often it deploys a discourse of tolerance against the Right's limitations in this area. The benefits of such work are obvious, despite its downside trade-off of allowing conservatives to set the terms of debate while neglecting the priorities of *C&C*-types. However, one result is that the mainline often saps its energy treading water, going nowhere in an ongoing gridlock. The none-too-inspiring question becomes whether all other alternatives represent greater evils.

This leads toward a second nuance complicating this discussion—the disagreements about mainline strategies that often structure discussions among its journalists. Here it is useful to recall the conventional lesson learned from George McGovern's 1972 campaign—the idea that Democrats cannot succeed by mobilizing their base, but only by swinging right to co-opt swing voters. By extension, Hubert Humphrey was a lesser evil in 1968 and radicals who refused to support him enabled Nixon's victory, Al Gore's 2000 campaign was sound while Ralph Nader's third-party candidacy enabled George W. Bush's success, Clinton's neoliberal policies were the best hope for anyone besides naïve idealists, and so on.

Similar logic is pervasive among mainline Protestants, and a similar prescription—put the brakes on the Left to stop voters from defecting on the Right—often informs its strategy. Just as critical observers must grasp the difference between principled left-liberal stances and mere "triangulation" between last year's Democratic values and whatever the Republicans are proposing this year, so also one must distinguish between the mainline's centrists (including the *Century* and many denominational leaders) and its unrepentant progressive cohort that reads Cornel West (formerly centered on *C&C*, now lacking journalistic focus). Nancy Ammerman calls the moderates "Golden Rule Protestants"; she presents them as pluralistic, committed to social service but rather apolitical, and "the dominant form of religiosity among middle-class suburban Americans."[10] This is the group that accounts for the mainline's rough parity with evangelicals. It is also a good place to find the wishy-washy voices that West and Sharlet bemoan. However, the mainline's progressive cohort shades off from this matrix—sometimes seamlessly, sometimes with bitter conflicts about wedge issues like LGBT rights. In historical perspective, the mainline remains one coherent tradition, albeit with deep internal differences.

Although the Right loves to hate left liberals of all stripes—pragmatic or otherwise—the Democrats' pragmatic strategy has worked out well for Republicans. Even during the Clinton and Obama presidencies, it boxed Democrats into lose-lose situations and allowed Republicans to move the political center of gravity rightward. Years of tax cuts for the wealthy, out-of-control military spending, and neoliberal deregulation have forced old-school New Dealers and socialists into the absurd position of being nostalgic for how relatively less skewed the wealth was during the 1980s. Today, anyone proposing a return to Reagan-era wealth distribution (which was understood at the time as dismantling the New Deal) would be dismissed as an outrageous radical. Such is the sense in which mainline intellectuals are "bleeding hearts and commie shills"—they wish to revitalize the New Deal and extend its logic. Within the Right's narrative frame, this creates a scenario of "heads I win, tails you lose." Moderates are dragged inexorably rightward, alienating their core constituencies (who defect on the Left), while radicals are attacked for supposedly causing people to defect on the Right.

In this context, for both Democrats and the mainline, healthy diversity devolves into squabbles about the priority of catering to swing voters, LGBT politics, antiracism, or issues of economic justice and empire. Centrists see leftism and identity politics fragmenting their coalition; leftists ask how centrists expect to thrive by appeasing the Right more than their own base. Often it is difficult to judge which arguments are strongest from case to case.

A third complication is equally critical. There are obvious differences between overt promoters of conservative religious propaganda like *First Things*, the IRD, or Pat Robertson's *CBN News*—groups that deserve respect comparable to Fox News (or, in the case of *First Things*, perhaps a think tank like the Heritage Foundation)—and centrist journalists who report on such groups within their own critical frames. When Heritage rolls out another proposal to shred the social safety net, competent journalists grasp where it is coming from. Likewise, many religion reporters grasp the agenda of *First Things*, even if all too many are not confident on this turf. This opens space for complex combinations among three broad perspectives in play—the Right's, the Left's, and journalists reporting on both.

For example, there is no doubt that Peter Steinfels—a longtime religion reporter at the *New York Times* and former editor at *Commonweal*—understands the Right's agenda well. In 1982, he penned a scathing critique of IRD for *C&C*. At this time Richard John Neuhaus (later of *First Things*) was a rising neoconservative star, and he had persuaded *60 Minutes* to attack the ecumenical Left. *C&C* was leading a countercharge. When Neuhaus responded to Steinfels's attack, insisting that he "didn't get a penny" for working with IRD and did not intend to be an apologist for Reaganism—only an impartial champion of democracy and the gospel—Steinfels replied that whether or not Neuhaus *intended* to baptize Reaganism, he clearly *did* baptize it; moreover, it was "ridiculous to believe that money has nothing to do with [this] intellectual offensive." Steinfels pointed to Neuhaus's "public air of studied innocence" while showing readers that this was either hypocritical or remarkably devoid of self-criticism.[11]

At the same time, although Steinfels sees through the Right's game plan, to some degree he agrees with the Right that the Protestant Left is sick unto death. Although he is friendlier to the centrist parts of the mainline, his *New York Times* obituary for *C&C* drew heavily on the decline topos, with a key quotation calling the later *C&C* "boring, predictable, and filled with empty leftish clichés."[12]

Silk provides another variation on a similar theme. He writes lucidly about religious values encoded in news, refuting conservative complaints that the news is "naked" of religion. Yet when speaking about mainline Protestants, he is an example of the problem of measuring swing groups in ways that generate low numbers for left-liberal Protestants compared to "nones" and evangelicals.[13] In *Unsecular Media*, he writes that "this is hardly the place to evaluate the merits" of an argument about liberal decline—but then goes on to assume such decline provisionally, even while showing how it fits a topos that may take on a life of its own.[14]

A suggestive example of a topos shaping evidence (rather than vice versa) is Silk's discussion of the neoconservative worldview in which the United States is "a war zone divided between orthodox believers of all faiths and New Class humanistic liberals." (Note the lose-lose choice this offers religious liberals.) Silk calls this "demonstrably a point of view that the religious public at large embraced" and offers as evidence a 1986 survey in which only 19 percent of Catholic priests agreed that news stories were "fair, honest, or objective."[15] In fact, it is unlikely that all the other 81 percent endorsed a neoconservative worldview, and almost certain that some sizable percentage worried about other issues that loomed large at the time, notably Reagan's arms buildup (vigorously criticized by Catholic bishops) and the thousands of Catholics then being murdered by Central American armies in a war that the mainstream media often defended using propaganda readers of the Catholic press knew to be false. Such priests—rendered invisible by Silk's topos—mistrusted the news because they had learned that it was a mouthpiece for neoconservatives, not because they agreed with neoconservatives.

Drawing these three nuances together—virtues of dialogue, debates about strategy, and the complex ways that journalists like Steinfels and Silk critique conservative scripts while also carrying forward certain aspects of their worldview—it is clear that not all narratives about mainline decline are driven by right-wing machinations or intentionally slanted arguments, as West's harsh imagery might suggest. The discourse is immensely murky, with much sincere and well-intentioned analysis all around.

Nevertheless, one must not lose sight of two things. First, the dynamic stated starkly by West remains part of the mix. Second, the overall discourse remains captured by a logic that favors the Right. Even sincere disagreements about strategy and demographics perpetuate this problem if they distract from critically analyzing the interpretive frame.

IV

The mainline's "triangulating" pragmatists and "principled" leftists blame each other for their group's travails, while the Right benefits from the resulting weakness. This is the historic problem from which the mainline must escape in order to thrive—to minimize zero-sum conflicts between its strategies, spend less time on infighting and more on contesting conservative attacks, and rediscover a morale commensurate with the resources it still commands. The health of its journals—the *Century*, whatever emerges in *C&C*'s former space, and hundreds more—will depend largely upon how well it succeeds.

Such efforts matter for a wider group than the mainline alone, because mainstream news coverage is limited to a disturbingly narrow range of issues and sources. To sustain a democratic public sphere, there is a need for various "alternative" analyses that are rooted outside of mainstream business models and circuits of information while remaining in dialogue with them. The *Century* and *C&C* are solid models in this regard. For example, they offered critical perspectives on policy toward Vietnam and Israel-Palestine—in part due to their independence and distinctive priorities, and not least because they were a forum for missionaries with contacts on the ground outside the United States. Likewise, the religious press was a key communications network for critics of Central America policy. Because religious journals have a mandate to care about suffering people and are less dependent on advertising, they often give more attention than other sectors of the media to issues like homelessness, international debt, and the mixed benefits of consumerism. Again, questions arise about how to judge "importance," but there is no reason for mainline journalists to be modest about such work.

The common wisdom about liberal Protestant decline runs in deep ruts and commands huge resources. But before inertia reasserts itself—accompanied, perhaps, by suspicions that any defense of liberalism represents the protestations of a batterer in denial—consider one last thought. Even if one prefers to stress that the mainline's cup is two-thirds empty, and even if conservatives continue to box left-liberal Protestants into lose-lose choices and mock any resulting weakness—even so, to describe the remaining one-third as dying and irrelevant represents, at best, a half truth that distorts as much as it illuminates. Embracing this interpretation is akin to accepting the analysis of a Fox pundit about the prospects for liberal victory in a contested electoral campaign. By extension, to accept a conventional analysis of why mainline journals are struggling for respect (they have swung too far to the Left, etc.) is akin to embracing Fox's analysis of how much Democratic politicians should compromise with the latest Republican policy proposal.

NOTES

1. Jeff Sharlet, "Waiting for Lefty," *The Revealer*, November 20, 2008, http://www.therevealer.org/archives/main_story_003127.php
2. Martin Marty, "The Religious Press," in *Encyclopedia of the American Religious Experience*, ed. Charles Lippy and Peter Williams (New York: Scribnerss, 1988), 1697.
3. Marty, "Religious Press," 1698.
4. Mark Silk, *Unsecular Media: Making News of Religion in America* (Urbana: University of Illinois Press, 1995).
5. Jeff Sharlet, "The Supreme Love and Revolutionary Funk of Dr. Cornel West, Philosopher of the Blues," *Rolling Stone*, May 28, 2009.
6. Diane Winston, "Back to the Future: Religion, Politics, and the Media," *American Quarterly* 59, no. 3 (2007): 98.
7. Leslie Scanlon, "Budgets Approved; Staff Positions, Work Areas Cut," *Presbyterian Outlook*, June 14, 2010, 19–20.
8. Winston, "Back to the Future," 970, 977. See also Frederick Clarkson, "Battle for the Mainline Churches," *Public Eye*, Spring 2006, http://www.publiceye.org/magazine/v20n1/clarkson_battle.html.
9. Cornel West, *Democracy Matters: Winning the Fight Against Imperialism* (New York: Penguin, 2004), 165–66.
10. Nancy Ammerman, "Golden Rule Christianity: Lived Religion in the American Mainstream," in *Lived Religion in America: Toward a History of Practice*, ed. David Hall (Princeton: Princeton University Press, 1997), 199.
11. Peter Steinfels, "Christianity and Democracy: Baptizing Reaganism," *C&C*, March 29, 1982, 80–85; Peter Steinfels and Richard John Neuhaus, "Continuing the Discussion," *C&C*, May 10, 1982, 135, 136.
12. Peter Steinfels, "Influential Christian Journal Prints Last Issue," *New York Times*, April 4, 1993, citing Max Stackhouse.
13. For more discussion see Mark Hulsether, "Protestant Liberalism," in *Blackwell Companion to Religion in America*, ed. Philip Goff (Malden, MA: Wiley-Blackwell Publishing, 2010), 658–62.
14. Silk, *Unsecular Media*, 134.
15. Ibid., 38.

REFERENCES

Fackler, Mark, and Charles Lippy, eds. 1995. *Popular Religious Magazines of the United States*. Westport, CT: Greenwood Press.

Hulsether, Mark. 1999. *Building a Protestant Left:* Christianity and Crisis *Magazine*. Knoxville: University of Tennessee Press.

Hutchison, William, ed. 1989. *Between the Times: The Travail of the Protestant Establishment in America, 1900–1960*. New York: Cambridge University Press.

McChesney, Robert. 2004. *The Problem of the Media: U.S. Communication Politics in the 21st Century*. New York: Monthly Review Press.

Nord, David Paul. 2001. *Communities of Journalism: A History of American Newspapers and Their Readers*. Urbana: University of Illinois Press.

Schultze, Quentin. 2003. *Christianity and the Mass Media in America: Toward a Democratic Accommodation*. East Lansing: Michigan State University Press.

Toulouse, Mark. 1993. The *Christian Century* and American Public Life. In *New Dimensions in American Religious History*, ed. Jay Dolan and James Wind, 44–83. Grand Rapids, MI: Eerdmans.

CHAPTER 36

THE AMERICAN JEWISH PRESS

JONATHAN D. SARNA

"JEWISH newspapers," reporter Debra Nussbaum Cohen once observed, "are the Rodney Dangerfields of journalism. Not getting any respect but providing an incredible service that everybody depends on."[1] Since their emergence in the first half of the nineteenth century, Jewish newspapers have helped to shape religious community, tied far-flung American Jews together, and kept them informed. Indeed, the establishment of Jewish newspapers marked a critical turning point in the community's history. Subsequently, at key moments in the community's evolution, new "must read" periodicals regularly appeared. Yet, the history of Jewish journalism in the United States also represents, for long stretches of time, a sad saga of decline. As independent newspapers became dependent and critical voices were silenced, Jewish newspapers became harder to respect—more indeed like Rodney Dangerfield.

Like newspapers generally, the Jewish press both shapes and reflects its times. It serves as a barometer of communal highs and lows, of aspirations and insecurities alike. This is an opportune moment to take the measure of American Jewish journalism, for the field stands at something of a crossroads. On the one hand, the economic crisis has hit the American Jewish press with particular force, closing some newspapers entirely and resulting in painful cutbacks to others. On the other hand, the quality of Jewish journalism has markedly improved in recent decades, and thanks to new technologies more people are reading the fruits of Jewish journalism than could in the past. For American Jewish journalists, this is, at once, the best of times and the worst of times. For a historian, it is a propitious time to look back.[2]

The Beginnings of Jewish Journalism

The history of Jewish journalism dates back to seventeenth-century Amsterdam, then a center of Jewish printing. Traditionally, the *Gazeta de Amsterdam* (1675) was considered the first Jewish newspaper; more recently it has been argued that the paper was only printed *by* a Jew, and that the first paper published *for* Jews was Amsterdam's *Dinshtagishe un Fraytagishe Kurant*, published in Yiddish in 1686–87.[3] From its earliest beginnings, then, Jewish journalism has never been easy to define. What is it that makes a newspaper Jewish? Though some would point to the religion of the publisher, insisting that the *New York Times* and the *Washington Post* are Jewish, and others insist that to be Jewish a newspaper must appear in a Jewish language (Hebrew, Yiddish, Ladino, etc.), here we define a Jewish newspaper by its intended audience. A Jewish newspaper centrally addresses Jewish readers and their interests.

In the United States, the earliest newspaper with a Jewish name was not, by this definition, a Jewish newspaper. *Cohen's Gazette and Lottery Register* (1814–30), published by Jacob I. Cohen, Jr., was published by a Jew and may have been read by Jews, but it primarily addressed those who invested in lottery tickets. It was, in essence, a gambling sheet.[4]

A journal of a different sort, the *Jew* (1823–25) is more difficult to characterize. It carried a subtitle explaining that it was "a defense of Judaism against all Adversaries" and took aim, principally, at the American Society for Meliorating the Condition of the Jews, a Protestant missionary group. While the *Jew* presaged one of the major functions of every vernacular Jewish newspaper—defending Jews—it did not principally address Jewish readers and their interests. Notwithstanding its title, it was more of an antimissionary sheet than a Jewish newspaper.[5]

Jewish newspapers that truly addressed Jewish readers and their interests emerged in the 1840s—not only in the United States but also in England, France, Germany, and elsewhere. Some seventy new Jewish periodicals emerged worldwide during that decade. Jewish scholars often explain this simultaneous worldwide emergence of Jewish newspapers on the basis of the 1840 Damascus Affair, when Jews in that city were falsely charged with ritual murder. Persecution, they contend, brought home to Jews the importance of sharing information and working together to defend Jewish rights at home and abroad.[6] Technological changes that drastically cut the cost of both printing and paper, however, also strongly stimulated the emergence of Jewish newspapers. The family newspaper, the Christian religious press, the Penny Press, and the semipornographic so-called flash press ("male weeklies") all emerged at about the same time as the Jewish press, and all responded to the same technological changes and possibilities. Where previously newspapers were expensive and focused on the business and political elite, beginning in the 1830s more affordable mass journalism emerged.[7]

The appearance of the *Occident* in April 1843 serves as an appropriate starting date for this new kind of Jewish journalism in the United States. Focused squarely on Jewish readers and their interests, the *Occident* was edited by Isaac Leeser, reader (*hazzan*) of Congregation Mikveh Israel in Philadelphia and the most significant Jewish traditionalist religious leader of his day. Leeser understood the power of the printing press—he published some 100 titles of various kinds—and sought to harness that power to strengthen Jewish life. He was influenced by a range of factors, including the development of national Jewish periodicals in Europe, the desire to unify far-flung American Jewish communities, the emergence of newspapers as instruments of Jewish enlightenment, and, most immediately, the need to respond to a missionary journal published in New York titled the *Jewish Chronicle* (not to be confused with the distinguished London Jewish newspaper of the same name).

Publicly, Leeser described his journal as an "advocate" for Jewish interests (the full title was the *Occident and American Jewish Advocate*), and its announced aim was "diffusion of knowledge on Jewish literature and religion"—in other words, communal defense and Jewish education, two principal aims of Jewish journalism forever after.[8] To carry out these aims, the *Occident* published news from American Jewish communities and from abroad (often reprinted from foreign Jewish publications), as well as sermons, editorials, historical articles, book reviews, innovative policy proposals, religious philosophy, and controversial (or apologetic) articles leveled against missionaries and other enemies of the Jewish people. He admitted into his paper many writers with whom he disagreed, sometimes debating with them in footnotes, and he also published many invaluable primary documents. Especially in its early years, he saw his as the newspaper of record for the American Jewish community, and he opened its pages to a wide range of contributors, including non-Jews interested in Jewish matters. In effect, he created a Jewish "print community," an antecedent of today's "virtual community." He informed Jews, defended Jews, and linked them one to another.[9]

The *Occident* was a high-quality, well-designed publication, and it remains a magnificent historical source, one of the finest journals that the American Jewish community has ever produced. Nevertheless, there were significant limits to what it was prepared to print. "On no account can our pages become the vehicle for violent denunciation or unfounded aspersion," Leeser wrote in his introductory remarks, and he naively urged readers "never to send us any thing which may require contradiction or amendment in a future number."[10] Although he understood that controversy and error were unavoidable, he hoped to project an image of Jewish consensus—a projection of the community as he wished it to be, rather than as it was. In this, he adumbrated a problem that has long plagued the field: a tension between the Jewish journalist as a reporter of news and the Jewish journalist as a shaper of community. In Leeser's case, this explains why he mostly closed his columns to divisive debates over slavery and the Civil War. He feared that such debates would be harmful to Jewish consensus. But, as events demonstrated, self-censorship comes at a price: Jews who sought to debate the hotly contested issues of slavery and union had no regular Jewish forum in which to do so.

Alternative Models of Jewish Journalism

The success of the *Occident* generated a spate of new journals on the American scene, published in diverse locations including New York, New Orleans, Cincinnati, and San Francisco.[11] Already by the 1850s, the movement in American Jewish journalism, as in American journalism generally, was away from all-embracing national newspapers and toward local or regional papers that were more narrowly focused and more circumscribed in their ambitions and aims. Most of these newspapers were weeklies, not monthlies like the *Occident*, and were modeled on American religious and family newspapers, rather than highbrow journals. As a result, their format was different from the *Occident*'s. They looked like broadsheet daily newspapers and they aimed to entertain, as well as inform; one, for example, published chapters from a serial novel weekly on its front page.

In New York, the first significant Jewish newspaper to be published was the *Asmonean*, edited on business principles by a (failed) New York Jewish businessman named Robert Lyon. The *Asmonean*, America's first Jewish weekly, was livelier, bolder, and much more diverse in its subject matter than other nineteenth-century American Jewish newspapers. It billed itself as "a family journal of commerce, politics, religion and literature devoted to the interests of the American Israelites." It represents a model of American Jewish journalism not seen again, at least in English, until contemporary times: a journal for American Jews but by no means limited to Jewish subject matter.[12]

The *Asmonean* lasted for nine years (1849–58), until Lyon's death, but the absence of a follow-up suggests that most English-speaking American Jews conceived of Jewish journalism in more restrictive terms. Just as American Jews compartmentalized their lives into secular and Jewish realms, so too did their newspapers.

A quite different direction was followed by the first Jewish newspaper in Cincinnati, now the oldest continuous Jewish newspaper in the United States. The *Israelite*, founded in 1854 and renamed the *American Israelite* in 1874, was published by the pioneer of American Reform Judaism, Rabbi Isaac Mayer Wise. It was the first American Jewish newspaper committed to advancing a particular ideology and unafraid of controversy in defense of that ideology. Wise wrote with a lively pen and cultivated an engaging, often biting, journalistic style. From his first issue, he waged war against "error, superstition, prejudice, ignorance, arrogance, hypocrisy and bigotry in whatever shape or form they may fall under our notice."[13] This made his newspaper much more entertaining than the *Occident* and gained it a wide national readership. As long as Wise was alive, it was recognized as his semiofficial organ representing the Reform Movement in American Judaism.[14] Although the *American Israelite* lost this mantle after Wise's death and steadily deteriorated into a run-of-the-mill local newspaper, a pattern had been set. Many subsequent, movement-sponsored periodicals followed, representing different streams of Judaism, as well as political movements such as socialism and Zionism. In the best cases, the same idealism, energy, and commitment that underlay a movement found reflection in its journal.

The Foreign-Language Jewish Press

Another model beginning in this period was the foreign-language Jewish newspaper. Several appeared even before the Civil War, *Sinai* and *Die Deborah* being the most famous, both published in German. Later, the Yiddish daily *Forward*, edited by Abraham Cahan, became one of the most influential and widely read foreign-language newspapers in the United States, one of no fewer than 104 Yiddish periodicals of different sorts to appear in the United States prior to 1905. Significant Jewish newspapers were also published in Hebrew, Ladino, and, more recently, Russian.[15]

Some foreign-language newspapers aimed at a highbrow readership, drawing chiefly upon intellectual émigrés, while others catered to a more popular readership, women in particular. Either way, the foreign-language Jewish press was generally far less compartmentalized than its English counterpart. It offered its readers both secular and Jewish news, as well as features. The foreign-language press was also much more focused on issues of immigration, Americanization, and developments in the old country than the Anglo-Jewish press. Several nineteenth-century American Jewish newspapers, notably the *Jewish Record*, published in Philadelphia, actually printed foreign news in German and domestic news in English.

Foreign-language Jewish newspapers tended to be bolder and more critical of America and American Jewish life than their English-language counterparts. Immigrants were understandably more comfortable protesting against America's ills in their native tongue and likely enjoyed the security of knowing that their words would impact only a select and sympathetic audience: those with whom they shared a common language. Hebrew-language journals, written for the elite who studied the "holy tongue," were particularly prone to be critical. Their writers could assume that they wrote for "Jewish eyes only," unlike writers for the Anglo or German-Jewish press who might be read by non-Jews as well.

The *American Hebrew*

By the late nineteenth century, a large native-born generation of American Jews had come of age, many of them the children of Central European immigrants. Raised on American newspapers, this "rising generation" had a different journalistic standard than its predecessor—its English prose was livelier and less Germanic, its interests broader, its journalism (like that of the *New York Times*) less personal and more highbrow. In addition, some of these young people differed ideologically from their parents. They sought to revitalize and deepen the religious and spiritual lives of American Jews, to strengthen Jewish education, and to promote pride in being members of the Jewish people.[16] In November 1879, nine of these young Jewish revivalists, maintaining strict anonymity, probably because none of them had yet reached the age of thirty, established a New York newspaper titled the *American Hebrew*. "Our work," they explained in their first issue, "shall consist of untiring endeavors to stir up our brethren to pride in our time-honored faith."[17] Since the paper sought both to "serve the future historian" and "to be sought by the best classes of non-Jews," it took pride in its broad coverage of Jewish life and in the amount of original material that it published. It set new standards in American Jewish journalism and reached out to a broad range of Jewish and non-Jewish writers. For decades, long after it had passed out of the original owners' hands, the *American Hebrew* stood as the foremost Jewish newspaper in the United States.[18]

Downward Slide

Even as the *American Hebrew* set a new standard, Jewish journalism as a whole, particularly during the interwar years, deteriorated. Many, including the well-known Jewish leader Rabbi Stephen S. Wise, began to deride them as "weaklies." The proliferation of local Jewish newspapers across the United States was partly responsible for this downward slide. While probably unavoidable given the local character of American journalism generally, local Jewish newspapers, especially those outside of major population centers, could not attract the kinds of contributors that a national newspaper could, and their goals became proportionately more modest and consensus oriented. Primarily, they sought to convey information, promote local communal involvement, and if necessary defend Jews against their enemies. This changed the focus of much of Jewish journalism away from the national issues that dominated the leading Jewish newspapers and toward a much narrower local-oriented journalism with a strong component of boosterism.

In addition, financial pressures led to the deterioration of Jewish newspapers. Most proved unable to break even, especially in smaller population centers, and they came to depend on financial backers. Beginning in the 1940s, in cities like Philadelphia, the local Jewish Federation stepped in to cover the annual deficit. Inevitably, this financial dependence affected the ability of local Jewish newspapers to remain independent. In Philadelphia, according to one study, criticism of federation-supported Jewish agencies, and even widely available negative news concerning these agencies, stopped appearing in the Jewish newspaper once it became subsidized (or in some cases, found mention only long after news was widely available elsewhere).[19] In smaller communities, even independent editors found that they dared not alienate subscribers, investors, or advertisers, so they played it safe. "There is not one editor of a quality Jewish newspaper that has not had a serious clash with a Federation director," Neil Rubin, editor of the *Baltimore Jewish Times*, wrote in 2004. "In Atlanta, I was regularly threatened with withdrawal of Federation advertising funds—some $50,000 a year—were coverage not favorable."[20] Faced with the choice of having a bland Jewish newspaper or no Jewish newspaper, most editors understandably chose the former. They justified their journalistic compromises as necessary to keep their local Jewish newspapers alive.

Finally, anti-Semitism, particularly in the period between the wars, had a chilling effect on the Anglo-Jewish press. As fear stalked the Jewish community and conditions for Jews deteriorated domestically and abroad, newspapers became frightened of controversy, scandal, or other news that reflected badly on the Jewish people, and they worked all the harder to promote an image of consensus and sobriety, lest they unintentionally play into the hands of Israel's enemies. While there was no shortage of intracommunal controversy or scandal during this era—witness the fierce debates over Zionism, the tactical debates over how best to respond to anti-Semitism, or the many scandals connected with Prohibition violations—these were not by and large reflected in the Jewish weeklies. Even anti-Jewish violence, such as regularly occurred in Boston in the 1930s and early 1940s, only rarely found mention in the press. Jewish leaders apparently persuaded the publisher of Boston's *Jewish Advocate* that writing about such violence would stir up trouble and make the situation worse.[21]

Other Sources of Jewish News

Once again, then, the press exercised considerable self-censorship. It did so with the best of intentions, believing that it served the larger interests of the Jewish people. The result, however, was a loss of credibility. Those who sought accurate and reliable Jewish news increasingly turned elsewhere. For years, many Jews read the Yiddish Press or in some cases the Hebrew Press, which, as noted, felt less constrained than the English-language weeklies; they were a much better and more accurate source of news. Other Jews subscribed to national Jewish magazines, which displayed more vibrancy than the local weeklies and did open their pages to debate. One thinks of *Menorah Journal*, the *Reconstructionist*, *Jewish Frontier*, the *Contemporary Jewish Record*, *Commentary*, *Midstream*, and many others.

Indeed, the number of English-language national periodicals proliferated in the twentieth century. There were a grand total of four such periodicals in 1900: one for "Young People" (*Young Israel*), one for "the Jewish Religious School and Home" (*Helpful Thoughts*), one for Hebrew Union College students and alumni (*Hebrew Union College Journal*), and one, the *Menorah*, the official organ of the Jewish fraternal organization, B'nai B'rith. A century later, by contrast, more than sixty such periodicals regularly appeared, in addition to magazines for schoolchildren, catering to the widest array of ideologies and interests. Jews dissatisfied with local Jewish newspapers, who wanted more serious and in-depth analyses, had, as a result of this exponential growth, many alternative publications.[22]

American Jews also turned to other sources for reliable news, including the Jewish Telegraphic Agency (JTA), founded by Jacob Landau in 1917, to provide world Jewry with news from the European war fronts from a Jewish point of view. Its cable service, set up in the 1920s, soon became the dominant provider of worldwide Jewish news for most American Jewish weeklies, improving the quality and range of their coverage. More than 400 newspapers (Jewish and general) subscribed to the JTA by 1925. Later, during World War II, JTA distinguished itself with revelations concerning the fate of European Jewry under Hitler during what is now known as the Holocaust. Following the war, it broke trailblazing stories concerning the persecution of Jews living behind the Iron Curtain. JTA greatly improved the Jewish press's coverage of international and national events. Given their growing reliance upon this source, however, Jewish newspapers came to share a certain uniformity of perspective: what the JTA produced, they published. This was especially true of news from Israel. Moreover, as a Jewish-sponsored agency, the JTA faced some of the same tensions that local weeklies faced: its commitment to journalistic *detachment* on the one hand and its very strong *attachment* to the Jewish community on the other hand.[23]

The *New York Times* also became increasingly influential within the American Jewish community. Purchased by Adolph Ochs, the son-in-law of Rabbi Isaac Mayer Wise, in 1896, it consciously paid special attention to news of Jewish interest both because of its Jewish ownership and because Jews made up a substantial percentage of its New York readership. In return, Jews rightly or wrongly came to perceive the *New York Times* as the ultimate authority on substantial news stories of Jewish interest. The *New York Times*, in reporting such stories, generally sought to project an air of objectivity. Its owners deeply feared being perceived as "too Jewish." During the Holocaust, partly for these reasons, it played down reports of anti-Jewish atrocities. Influenced, some believe, by the assimilationist tendencies of its owners, the paper also opposed the creation of the state of Israel.[24]

American Jewish Journalism's Golden Age

The last third of the twentieth century witnessed tremendous improvements in American Jewish journalism. The best newspapers became bolder, more probing, and more critical. Their coverage of Jewish life broadened. More journalists in the Jewish press boasted degrees from journalism school and sought to bring the lessons they had learned there to religious and community papers. Beginning in 1980, the professional organization of Jewish journalists, the American Jewish Press Association (founded in 1944), encouraged these advances through a program of competitive Rockower Awards for Excellence in Journalism (the "Pulitzer Prizes" of American Jewish journalism), which came to include such categories as "excellence in commentary" and "excellence in comprehensive coverage or investigative reporting."[25]

The aftermath of the Watergate scandal in the United States (1972–74), which raised the status of journalists and crowned them as guardians of American values, encouraged these developments. Jewish students, like their non-Jewish counterparts, were also influenced by the era's crusading "new journalists" who integrated literary techniques, passion, and advocacy into their writing. Jewish student newspapers, beginning in the late 1960s, ventured into subjects ignored by the mainstream press (such as the priorities and economics of the Jewish community) and, in 1970, established the Jewish Student Press Service (JSPS) to share and disseminate their "underground" work. Many JSPS writers eventually made their way into mainstream Jewish media, which they proceeded to transform. But publications like *New Voices*, founded by JSPS in 1991, as well as *Zeek* and *Heeb* and the website "Jewlicious," offered young outsiders in the Jewish community continued opportunities to make their voices heard.[26]

The rising affluence of America's Jews also helped journalism in this era. Advertisers seeking to appeal to the upscale Jewish market brought new funding to some Jewish newspapers, notably the *Baltimore Jewish Times*, allowing them to hire more and better journalists, to publish in-depth and investigative stories, and to become bolder and more independent. The field of Jewish journalism, as a result, looked more promising than at any time since World War I.

In 1990, the association that had produced the famed Yiddish-language *Forward* established an English-language weekly, the *Forward*, as an independent national Jewish newspaper under the editorship of Seth Lipsky, formerly a distinguished editor at the *Wall Street Journal*. The paper set new standards in Jewish journalism and pioneered extensive critical coverage of Jewish culture and the arts. It quickly won respect in mainstream journalistic circles, and many of its young reporters went on to achieve fame (and in some cases fortune) in the mainstream press—continuing a long tradition of the Jewish press serving as a "minor league" for excellent journalists (Daniel Schorr is a prime example, and more recently Jeffrey Goldberg) who later graduated into the "major leagues." Three years later, partly in an effort to compete, New York's long-running newspaper, the *Jewish Week*, hired editor Gary Rosenblatt away from the *Baltimore Jewish Times* with a mandate to improve the paper's quality. The revamped paper promised "to build and strengthen Jewish community while championing an aggressive and independent press" and declared that its "first loyalty is to the truth."[27] Between them, these two newspapers in America's largest Jewish community broke many significant stories in the 1990s, providing coverage of such formerly taboo subjects as the compensation packages of Jewish communal leaders and sexual abuse by rabbis. The JTA, emboldened by these developments, likewise became edgier in this period, introducing more critical coverage into local Jewish newspapers across the country that carried its stories.

The Best of Times, the Worst of Times—Recent Developments

Yet just as hopes for a new "golden age" of American Jewish journalism rose, technology—the same force that made possible mass journalism in the first place—now conspired to shatter those hopes. With the rise of the web, the circulation of traditional newspapers (general and Jewish alike) fell precipitously. Young people increasingly looked online for the news they wanted. As a result, the average age of Jewish newspaper readers rose—so much so that one editor quipped that the average age of his readers was now "dead."

In addition, and even more seriously, advertising declined. Indeed, some of the traditional profit centers of the Jewish newspaper, such as classified ads and singles ads, migrated almost completely to the web. Why pay to sell used items in the Jewish press when one can sell them for free on eBay? Why advertise publicly for a mate when membership in J-Date (or one of its clones) is so much cheaper, more private, and more efficient? Large-scale advertisers, too, shifted their attention to the web; increasingly, they discovered, that was where their prime customers were. As a result, Jewish newspapers, like their secular counterparts, watched their revenues plummet.

In time, many Jewish newspapers developed websites of their own. Most sites made their stories available to the public without charge, the industry mantra being that "information wants to be free." This increased the readership of Jewish newspapers and opened them up to young readers, but at a cost that was difficult to recoup. Even if they brought in new online ads and paid subscriptions, websites could not make good the losses in overall circulation and advertising.

The economic downturn of 2008 further battered Jewish newspapers. Many that had received subsidies from Jewish federations saw those funds reduced. Revenue from advertising and circulation declined even further than before. As a result, several Jewish newspapers either shifted to the web or, as in the case of the *Las Vegas Jewish Reporter*, went out of business entirely. Others, following the lead of the Boston *Jewish Advocate*, dispensed with paid national and international content from the JTA and focused exclusively on local community news, hoping thereby to pare costs and to draw in readers interested primarily in reading about themselves and their neighbors.

The impact of online technology also has had some highly positive implications for Jewish journalism. For one thing, Jewish journalists have never enjoyed so many readers as they currently do. Even a local story can "go viral" and reach millions of people. The offerings available to consumers of Jewish journalism have, in addition, become far more diverse. Readers no longer need to confine themselves to their local Jewish newspaper. Now the online reader can easily peruse a range of Israeli news websites, religious and antireligious Jewish websites, and websites of Jewish newspapers and organizations across the globe.

Significant online newsletters and magazines also bring Jewish news daily to the inboxes of those who want them. The Jewish Telegraphic Agency, reborn as JTA: The Global News Service of the Jewish People, sends out a free daily newsletter read by thousands of subscribers. It also aggregates articles from other sources that it believes informed Jews should read. The Jerusalem Center for Public Affairs similarly distributes an online "daily briefing" focused on Israel and the Middle East, aggregating news and opinion from many sources. An online daily Jewish magazine named *Tablet* is among the most exciting developments in Jewish journalism in recent years. Handsomely subsidized by Keren Keshet, it employs state-of-the art graphics and some of the finest young Jewish journalists and writers currently at work and produces a daily fare of provocative features and widely read cultural articles on Jewish life. Another subsidized web publication, *Jewish Ideas Daily*, aims at a higher-brow level with a focused daily essay and additional links for those who seek to learn more.

Whether these online Jewish journals ultimately crowd out their print cousins remains to be seen. Currently, the most prestigious of them, *Tablet*, is heavily subsidized, while those that are independent, like JTA, live hand to mouth. The *Jewish Journal of Greater Los Angeles*, the largest Jewish newspaper outside of New York City, is experimenting with a mixed model, influenced by studies of "niche journalism," that is attracting attention. It produces a lively newspaper, featuring multiple conflicting voices on controversial issues and racy lifestyle articles ("Tiger Wood's #1 Whore, Rachel Uchitel, Is Jewish. So What? And Heading to Playboy. Maybe."[28]), as well as a website with blogs and other features not found in the print publication and a glossy monthly magazine that extends the newspaper's reach. It expects to cover the bulk of its budget through advertising and looks to philanthropic donations to cover the rest. Should the model succeed, editors of other Jewish journals seem sure to follow suit.[29]

Critical Questions

In the meantime, journalists in the Jewish press face central questions that will shape the field's future.

First, what is the mission of Jewish journalism? Is its mission primarily to inform? To educate? To defend? To entertain? To support one or another Jewish ideology? To promote community and continuity? Or something else? To insist, as many do, that its mission embraces all of the above is to beg the question, what happens when two or more of these missions come into conflict?

Second, what are the responsibilities of Jewish journalism? Should the "good of the Jewish people" (or of the local Jewish community, or of the state of Israel) be the highest goal? Or should "truth" be the highest goal? What should be done when, as happens all too often, these goals come into conflict? Which should be sacrificed for the other?

Third, what are the community's responsibilities toward the Jewish press? Should it subsidize it? Control it? Set the bounds of who may and who may not be heard? In an era of scarce resources, should a Jewish newspaper (print or online) be a community priority at all? Or should communities simply encourage individuals who want Jewish news to go out and pay for it on their own?

Finally, what compromises should a Jewish journal be prepared to make to ensure its survival? Should it seek private or communal support? How much independence should it be prepared to sacrifice in return for such support? What red lines must it refuse at all times to cross?

These are not easy questions. Nor are Jews alone in confronting them. Parallel questions, indeed, face religious and ethnic-based journals of every kind. Yet for Jewish journalists to escape being known as the "Rodney Dangerfields of journalism," these issues, even if not fully resolvable, cannot be avoided. They define both what Jewish journalism is and what it might become.

NOTES

1. Luke Ford, "Debra Nussbaum Cohen," http://www.lukeford.net/profiles/profiles/debra_nussbaum.htm (accessed July 19, 2010).

2. The literature on this subject to 1983 is reviewed in Robert Singerman, "The American Jewish Press, 1823–1983: A Bibliographic Survey of Research and Studies," *American Jewish History* 73 (June 1984): 422–44; see also Robert Singerman, *Jewish Serials of the World: A Research Bibliography of Secondary Sources* (New York: Greenwood Press, 1986); and Robert Singerman, *Jewish Serials of the World: A Supplement to the Research Bibliography of Secondary Sources* (New York: Greenwood Press, 2001).

3. Joel Cahen, "Amsterdam, Cradle of the Jewish Press?" *Proceedings of the Symposium on the Jewish Press: Why? Past, Present, Future* (Amsterdam: Nieuw Israelietisch Weekblad, 1985), 17–23.

4. Extant numbers of this journal are available in the American Periodical Series, reel 93. On Cohen, see Isaac M. Fein, *The Making of an American Jewish Community: The History of Baltimore Jewry from 1773 to 1920* (Philadelphia: Jewish Publication Society, 1971), 22–24.

5. The *Jew* is now available on Google books, http://books.google.com/books?id=fx4AAAAAQAAJ&printsec=frontcover&dq=jackson+the+jew#v=onepage&q&;f=false (accessed July 19, 2010). For its history, see George L. Berlin, "Solomon Jackson's the Jew: An Early American Jewish Response to the Missionaries," *American Jewish History* 71 (September 1981): 10–28.

6. Baruch Mevorah, "'Ikvoteha shel 'alilat Damesek behitpathuta shel ha'itonut hayehudit bashanim 1840–1846, ['Effect of the Damascus Affair Upon the Development of the Jewish Press']," *Zion* 23–24 (1958): 46–65; Jonathan Frankel, *The Damascus Affair: "Ritual Murder," Politics and the Jews in 1840* (New York: Cambridge University Press, 1997), 404–5.

7. Frank L. Mott, *American Journalism: A History of Newspapers in the United States Through 260 Years: 1690–1950* (New York: Macmillan, 1950), 206, 215–326; William E. Huntzicker, *The History of American Journalism*, Vol. 3, *The Popular Press 1833–1865* (Westport, CT: Greenwood, 1999); Nathan O. Hatch, *The Democratization of American Christianity* (New Haven, CT: Yale University Press, 1989), 125–33; Patricia Cline Cohen

and others, *The Flash Press: Sporting Male Weeklies in 1840s New York* (Chicago: University of Chicago Press, 2008).

8. Naomi W. Cohen describes early American Jewish newspapers as "Pioneers of American Jewish Defense." See her article by that title in *American Jewish Archives* 29 (November 1977): 116–50.

9. The best study of Leeser, including his newspaper, is Lance J. Sussman's *Isaac Leeser and the Making of American Judaism* (Detroit: Wayne State University Press, 1995). On the origins of the *Occident*, see Jonathan D. Sarna, "The Impact of Nineteenth-Century Christian Missions on American Jews," in *Jewish Apostasy in the Modern World*, ed. Todd Endelman (New York: Holmes & Meier, 1987), 242–43. The journal's first number is reprinted with an introduction in Abraham J. Karp, *Beginnings: Early American Judaica* (Philadelphia: Jewish Publication Society, 1975).

10. *Occident* 1 (April 1843): 5.

11. Listings of nineteenth-century American Jewish periodicals may be found in *American Jewish Year Book* 1 (1899–1900): 271–82; *Jewish Encyclopedia* 9: 616–40; and Robert Singerman, *Judaica Americana: A Bibliography of Publications to 1900* (New York: Greenwood, 1990): 931–1070.

12. Cohen, "Pioneers of American Jewish Defense," 133–40; Barbara S. Reed, "Unity, Not Absorption: Robert Lyon and the *Asmonean*," *American Journalism* 7 (March 1990), 77–95; H. B. Grinstein, "The 'Asmonean': The First Jewish Weekly in New York," *Journal of Jewish Bibliography* 1 (1939), 67–71; Henry S. Morais, "Robert Lyon," *Eminent Israelites of the Nineteenth Century* (Philadelphia: Edward Stern & Co., 1880), 221–22.

13. *Israelite* 1 (July 15, 1854): 4. Wise's writings in the *Israelite* are available online from the Isaac Mayer Wise Digital Archive of the Jacob Rader Marcus Center of the American Jewish Archives: http://www.americanjewisharchives.org/wise/home.php.

14. Cohen, "Pioneers of American Jewish Defense," 140–49; Sefton D. Temkin, *Isaac Mayer Wise* (Oxford: Oxford University Press, 1992), 112–24.

15. Key articles include Arthur A. Goren, "The Jewish Press," in *The Ethnic Press in the United States*, ed. Sally M. Miller (New York: Greenwood, 1987), 203–28; Ida C. Selavan's bibliography in *The Immigrant Labor Press in North America, 1840s–1970s: An Annotated Bibliography*, ed. Dirk Hoerder and Christiane Harzig (New York: Greenwood Press, 1987); Tony Michels, "Speaking to Moyshe: The Early Socialist Yiddish Press and its Readers," *Jewish History* 14 (2000): 51–82; Fannie M. Brody, "The Hebrew Periodical Press in America 1871–1931: A Bibliographical Survey," *Publications of the American Jewish Historical Society* 33 (1934), 127–70; Michael Brown, "All, All Alone: The Hebrew Press in America," *American Jewish Historical Quarterly* 59 (1969): 139–78; Shai Nechushtai, "The American Hebrew Language Press 1871–1914," *Qesher* 4 (November 1988), 31–49; and Aviva Ben Ur, "The Ladino (Judeo-Spanish) Press in the United States, 1910–1948," *Multilingual America*, ed. Werner Sollors (New York: NYU Press, 1998), 64–77.

16. Jonathan D. Sarna, *A Great Awakening: The Transformation That Shaped Twentieth Century American Judaism and Its Implications for Today* (New York: Council for Initiatives in Jewish Education, 1995).

17. *American Hebrew*, November 21, 1879, 3.

18. Philip Cowen, *Memories of an American Jew* (New York: The International Press, 1932), 40–111; Charles Wyszkowski, *A Community in Conflict: American Jewry During the Great European Immigration* (New York: University Press of America, 1991), xiii–xvii.

19. Maxwell Whiteman, "A Century of Jewish Journalism: The Jewish Exponent, 1887–1987," in *A People in Print: Jewish Journalism in America* (Philadelphia: National Museum of American Jewish History, 1987), 19–20.

20. Neil Rubin, "Show Me the Money: The Economics of Jewish Journalism in North America," http://www.lukeford.net/profiles/profiles/neil_rubin.htm (accessed July 19, 2010); see Neil Rubin, "The Economics of Jewish Journalism in North America," *Qesher* 29 (2001): 89–97.

21. Jenny Goldstein, "Transcending Boundaries: Boston's Catholics and Jews, 1929–1965" (senior honors thesis, Brandeis University, 2001), http://www.bc.edu/research/cjl/cjrelations/resources/articles.html#history (accessed July 19, 2010) details the story of anti-Semitism during those years; little appeared in the *Jewish Advocate*; for the national situation, see Jonathan D. Sarna, *American Judaism: A History* (New Haven, CT: Yale University Press, 2004), 214–23.

22. *American Jewish Year Book* 2 (1900–1901): 636–37; 101 (2001): 650–62.

23. Verena Dohm, "Diplomacy in the Diaspora: The Jewish Telegraphic Agency in Berlin (1922–1933)," *Leo Baeck Institute Yearbook* 54 (2009): 219–41; Murray Zuckoff, "The Jewish Telegraphic Agency: 'Eyes and Ears of the Jewish People,'" *The Jewish Directory and Almanac*, ed. Ivan Tillem (New York: Pacific Press, 1984), 282–90; Boris Smolar, *In the Service of My People* (Baltimore: Baltimore Hebrew College, 1982).

24. Lauerel Leff, *Buried by The Times: The Holocaust and America's Most Important Newspaper* (New York: Cambridge, 2005); Susan E. Tifft and Alex S. Jones, *The Trust: The Private and Powerful Family Behind The New York Times* (New York: Little Brown, 1999).

25. See the American Jewish Press Association's website, http://www.ajpa.org/ (accessed July 20, 2010).

26. Donald Altschiller, "The American Jewish Press," in *Encyclopedia of American Jewish History*, ed. Stephen H. Norwood and Eunice G. Pollack (Santa Barbara, CA: ACB-Clio, 2008), I, 275, http://findingaids.cjh.org//JewishStudentPressService.pdf (accessed July 20, 2010).

27. Luke Ford, "Gary Rosenblatt," http://www.lukeford.net/profiles/profiles/gary_rosenblatt.htm (accessed July 20 2010).

28. http://www.jewishjournal.com/keepingthefaith/item/tiger_woods_1_whore_rachel_uchitel_is_jewish_and_heading_to_playboy_20100051/ (accessed July 20, 2010).

29. James Rainey, "On the Media: Jewish Journal of Greater Los Angeles Adapts to Changing Media Market," latimes.com, May 12, 2010, http://articles.latimes.com/2010/may/12/entertainment/la-et-onthemedia-20100512 (accessed July 20, 2010).

REFERENCES

Goren, Arthur A. 1987. The Jewish Press. In *The Ethnic Press in the United States*, ed. Sally M. Miller, 203–28. New York: Greenwood.

Mott, Frank L. 1950. *American Journalism: A History of Newspapers in the United States Through 260 Years: 1690–1950*. New York: Macmillan.

Sarna, Jonathan D. 1987. The Impact of Nineteenth-Century Christian Missions on American Jews. In *Jewish Apostasy in the Modern World*, ed. Todd Endelman, 242–43. New York: Holmes & Meier.

Singerman, Robert. 1984. The American Jewish Press, 1823–1983: A Bibliographic Survey of Research and Studies. *American Jewish History* 73 (June): 422–44.

CHAPTER 37

THE EVANGELICAL PRESS

KEN WATERS

MAINSTREAM media often depict the religious Right as a monolithic force dominated by televangelists dictating orders to millions of religious conservatives who are often called evangelicals. Yet even a casual reader of evangelical magazines and newspapers finds those periodicals facilitating vigorous dialogue about spiritual, emotional, lifestyle, and public policy issues. Research asserts that evangelical publications not only help readers form their personal identity but also are an important influence on the voting decisions of evangelicals. While evangelicals remain steadfastly conservative in their political and cultural tastes, voting patterns in the election of 2008 show a slight crack in the rock-solid marriage between conservative politicians and evangelicals. This shift was already a topic of conversation on the pages of evangelical periodicals months before the election. This chapter argues that to fully comprehend the influence of evangelicals on American culture and current events, one must study the vibrant but often overlooked dialogue evident on the pages of evangelical periodicals.

Historically, "[i]n the United States the religious press has been one of the most important vehicles for bringing people of faith into a shared public space to converse about the broader society."[1] The publications help believers recapture the power of their own symbols and narratives, which are lost when the dominant media communicate them to the wider culture.[2] Austin asserts that "the secular press is often blind to or simply ignores the role that religion plays in newsworthy events; and it is incumbent upon the church-related press to fill in this gap."[3] On the pages of evangelical publications, an astute mainstream journalist or columnist might find prophetic religious voices debating theology and doctrine or sharing information that encourages its readers to form new social and cultural movements. In keeping with the populist bent of the evangelical movement, its periodicals are written in a conversational tone and illustrated with photos, drawings, charts, graphs, and other visual elements that reinforce the written word. Because periodicals reach across space and time, editors, readers, and contributors can "engage clergy and lay members of churches in vigorous conversations about important events, ideas and artistic expressions that are shaping culture far beyond the boundaries of the ecclesiastical channels."[4]

Evangelical publications tend to reflect American values of individual agency, fairness, justice, and capitalism, with a strong entrepreneurial bent. Christian periodicals have been published since the early days of the American colonies. Protestants were early adopters of the new technology of mass printing to publish evangelistic tracts for wide distribution.[5] Whenever a new religious movement began or a denominational split occurred, a new magazine or newspaper arose to help its readers form their new identity. The Church of Christ, whose members number in the millions, was nurtured in the mid-nineteenth century through its newspaper editors and today is still united more through dialogue in its denominational periodicals than through any formal ecclesiastical structure.

Educated estimates put the number of publications currently targeted to evangelicals at around 400, with readership numbering in the millions. Few of the publications boast readership numbers equal to those of mainstream news and advocacy publications, but what they lack in individual circulation, they make up for in aggregate readership. As the twenty-first century began, readership suffered the challenges of a prolonged recession coupled with technological changes moving people away from print as a primary source of information. The history of media use by evangelicals suggests that some of these publications will survive and new ones will arise—in print, online, and eventually on wireless devices such as phones and tablet devices. Already, many evangelical publications are attracting more readers through their websites than through paid subscriptions or controlled circulation.

The content in religious magazines has focused on the reader—on providing biblical commentary for use in personal studies, personal testimonies on how God changes lives, and explanations about how a particular news event or trend should be understood when viewed through a Christian worldview. Through much of their history, but not all, evangelical publications have encouraged believers to be constructive and influential forces in the cultural and political life of the nation. Put another way, evangelical publications play a critical role in helping evangelicals create, maintain, and transform their personal identities as Christians and their corporate identity as members of a democratic society.[6] The influence of these publications, while subtle, is thus an overlooked area of the interplay between religion and culture.

History of Evangelical Publications

A survey of early publications finds most editors were pastors desiring to use the printed word to spread their message. The first of these was *Christian History*, published from 1743 to 1745. Although short-lived, the publication shared with colonists important information on the Great Awakening, helping readers understand how the movement's "pious Principles and Spirit are at this Day revived, and may also guard against all Extreams (*sic*)."[7] Other publications such as *En Geistliches Magazien* (A Religious Magazine) knit together non-English-speaking ethnic communities by providing religious information, as well as insights into American culture. Later, African American publications would serve a similar function for their communities. In 1837, the Reverend Samuel Cornish founded the *Weekly Advocate* to provide African Americans with "lessons of instruction on religion and morals, lessons on industry and economy—until our entire people are of one heart and of one mind, in all the means of their salvation, both temporal and spiritual."[8] (See John Giggie's chapter for more on the African American religious press.) Another publication was the first to link Christian belief with a particular vocation. *Christian Scholar's and Farmer's Magazine* stated its purpose as promoting religion, and "to diffuse useful knowledge and to help farmers in their work."[9] By the mid-1800s, evangelical publications had linked together new denominations and helped raise awareness and funds for missionary activities, orphanages, and women's causes.[10] Voskuil notes: "The Protestant perspective, at this time pervasively evangelical, reached to the very center of national life; and Protestant journalists took all of society to be their 'beat.'"[11]

During the second half of the nineteenth century, changes in immigration patterns, industrialization, the growth of cities, and the rise of Darwinism and the scientific method undercut the hegemony of Protestantism over American society and culture. The evangelical dominance of American society declined, as did the readership for religious publications, as many Protestants moved away from a belief in the infallibility of the Bible, the virgin birth, and the death and resurrection of Christ as historical facts. In response to these developments, during the 1920s to 1940s, conservative Protestants quietly opened more than 250 Bible colleges to train conservative religious leaders. New magazines played an important role in keeping culturally marginalized evangelicals tied together across time and space. They gave their journals "militant-sounding names: *The Conflict*, *The Crusader's Champion*, *Dynamite*, and *The Defender*." Among these was *Sword of the Lord*, which facilitated evangelism and exhorted believers to "earnestly avoid compromise in doctrine or yoking up with unbelievers."[12]

The post–World War II period saw a growth of the once-defensive fundamentalists into a new force to be reckoned with: white suburban Christians who no longer subscribed to a separatist mentality. Instead, they challenged mainstream denominational leaders' lax doctrines and started nondenominational churches or moved their denominational affiliation to congregations that taught biblical inerrancy and conservative doctrine. In time, the Moral Majority and its successor, the religious Right, advanced the notion that evangelicals had a biblical mandate to influence every aspect of politics and culture. These fundamentalists gradually became known by today's moniker, evangelicals. Evangelistic groups like Youth for Christ played key roles in launching Billy Graham's ministry and in founding the international aid organization World Vision. Graham's own denomination, the Southern

Baptists, saw their membership swell as they began publishing a host of specialized magazines for Baptist families, single adults, and youth. During this same period, the number of independent niche publications significantly increased because anyone with a message could use inexpensive desktop publishing programs to produce a magazine or newspaper. New magazines were targeted to Christian doctors, nurses, athletes, motorsport enthusiasts, choir directors, youth, singles, women, men, and supporters of myriad missionary efforts, with mixed success.[13] To provide further credibility to the burgeoning number of evangelical publications, like-minded editors formed the Evangelical Press Association in 1949. Today the membership is about 300 publications. Many are public relations magazines from parachurch organizations, seminaries, and colleges, but others are dynamic venues for vigorous discussion among evangelicals still striving to better understand how to incorporate their beliefs into the changing nature of their culture.

Magazines and Evangelical Identity

Evangelical publications that play a crucial role in helping believers shape their identity are patterned on mainstream newsmagazines like *Time* and *Newsweek* and opinion publications like *National Review* and *Atlantic Monthly*. These periodicals are independent of denominational or organizational control and can thus set editorial policies consistent with the audience interests and informational needs. The editorial content in three of the most influential—*Christianity Today*, *WORLD* magazine, and *Sojourners*—reflects the varied nature of evangelical thinking on a variety of political, cultural, and doctrinal issues. With paid circulation of around 140,000, both *Christianity Today* and *WORLD* outpace the paid circulation of *Sojourners*, which has trended downward over the years to around 35,000. Readers of all three publications are highly educated. *Christianity Today* and *Sojourners* report that around half of their readers have graduate degrees. Where they differ, though, is in political orientation. *WORLD*, at one extreme, says its readers are 51 percent male and that 91 percent are registered Republicans; *Sojourners*, on the other extreme, reports that 55 percent are female and 72 percent of its readers identify themselves as progressive or liberal.

Christianity Today

Christianity Today was founded in 1956. It arose from a need expressed best by evangelist Billy Graham: "I feel that there is needed in Protestantism today a magazine that is the counterpart to the *Christian Century*. Something that will be evangelical, theologically oriented, and will commend itself to the Protestant ministers of America. I feel it is desperately needed."[14] Graham's aversion to *Christian Century*, now more than 100 years old, is because, as one researcher noted, "There were no conservative magazines that carried the cross-denominational, national impact of this liberal standard bearer, which gave the false impression that liberalism was both the majority and an irrefutable position."[15] Pastors and lay leaders loyal to evangelical doctrines made up *Christianity Today*'s primary audience. While theologically dense writing and a distrust of mainline Protestants and Roman Catholics characterized founding editor Carl Henry's leadership, he was not averse to using the magazine's pages to dialogue with Protestant leaders with whom he differed. Early editions of the magazine featured articles by Charles Morrison, the long-time editor of *Christian Century*, and Eugene Blake, the head of the liberal National Council of Churches. That changed in 1968 under Harold Lindsell's editorship. Lindsell introduced more practical and readable articles, sprinkled with personality features and testimonies. This helped keep readership around 150,000; but more was needed to ensure the magazine's survival. To reduce costs, its board voted in 1976 to move the magazine from Washington, DC to the Chicago suburbs. By then the magazine had become recognized as the nation's leading evangelical magazine.[16] Since that move, *Christianity Today* has become a publishing conglomerate, spinning off or taking over niche publications such as *Marriage Partnership*, *Books & Culture*, *Today's Christian Woman*, and *Leadership*. Today *Christianity Today* calls itself "A Magazine of Evangelical Conviction." News and commentaries are written to the highest journalistic standards so that content is accurate and factual and presented in a dispassionate manner befitting a benevolent mentor. Rarely does the publication launch an investigation of other evangelical organizations or Christian leaders. Once the shortcomings of such a leader become public knowledge, the magazine will usually provide additional news reporting and commentary. The magazine's founder, Billy Graham, was a master at reaching large audiences through innovative uses of media. Thus, it is no surprise that while the editorial content and philosophy of the magazine are fixed, its marketing activities are innovative and flexible. Beginning in the 1990s, the company created a highly accessible, interactive, and well-respected website that serves as a portal for all of its publications.

Sojourners

Sojourners began in 1971 when a disgruntled group of seminary students founded the People's Christian Coalition, which later became the Sojourners movement. The students were troubled by the inconsistency between their understanding of biblical values and the support given by their parents and other evangelicals for America's involvement in the Vietnam War. Led by Jim Wallis, the students asserted that evangelicals were ignoring issues of injustice, human rights, and care for God's creation. These youthful dissenters used the magazine to exhort evangelicals to rethink their priorities and become more involved in social justice issues. Theirs was a message of transformation, of changing the political identity of their fellow believers. The group originally attempted to live communally, but after moving from Chicago to Washington, DC in the late 1970s, they gradually dispersed to separate housing in the area. Their modest lifestyle and selective use of civil disobedience (Wallis has been arrested numerous times for staging sit-ins to protest nuclear weapons and such) has gained the editors begrudging respect from evangelicals who may disagree with *Sojourner's* insistence on seeking common ground with people of all political and cultural persuasions.

Today the magazine's mission is similar to that of its founding principles: "... to articulate the biblical call to social justice, inspiring hope and building a movement to transform individuals, communities, the church, and the world." Through workshops and symposia *Sojourners* has hosted and then profiled in its magazine's pages, the movement has largely succeeded in nudging evangelicals to a broader understanding of their role in society. Wallis, who also is a prolific author, is often consulted by political leaders desiring to court progressive evangelicals. Over the past decade, the magazine's extensive website with daily blogs and news feeds has expanded its readership and facilitated an active dialogue between the magazine's writers and its readers.

WORLD

In January of 1995, newly elected Speaker of the House Newt Gingrich unleashed a firestorm with his remarks on welfare reform. Reporters and pundits pressed the brash congressman to cite the sources of his charges that public welfare begat more welfare and that only private, voluntary aid programs restored the dignity of people and brought them economic relief. During the months that followed his proclamations, Gingrich repeatedly cited a little-known book by Marvin Olasky, called *The Tragedy of American Compassion* (re-released 2008), which discussed why the welfare system needed a complete overhaul. Gingrich later said the book "is one of the great works of our time."[17] That book and Olasky's relationship with then-Texas Gov. George W. Bush led to Bush adopting Olasky's catch phrase "compassionate conservatism" for his presidential campaign in 2000. As reporters zeroed in on Olasky, they discovered an outspoken scholar and Jewish convert to Christianity touting an editorial philosophy called "directed reporting" or "biblical journalism."

Like *Christianity Today* and to a lesser degree *Sojourners, WORLD* provides insightful reviews of movies, books, and plays and analyses of issues in the world of sports that attract the attention of mainstream readers. *WORLD* embraced the possibilities of the Internet early on and all issues are available and searchable on its website. The online content is updated daily to facilitate ongoing discussion between writers and readers. Its editorial philosophy is aimed at repairing and transforming the evangelical movement. Using controversial reporting methods reminiscent of the muckrakers, *WORLD*, published in Asheville, North Carolina, has succeeded in provoking discussion on local, national, and international topics. While its ideological stance is closely aligned with the religious Right, *WORLD* is not shy about criticizing actions of Republicans who violate biblical morality, and it regularly investigates and exposes the actions of fellow Christians, churches, and large parachurch organizations. Olasky explains his philosophy in this way:

"Directed reporting is designed to show readers the salient facts in bible-based contextualization, and allow them to agree or disagree with the conclusions reached."[18] Thus, "A solidly Christian news publication should not be balanced. Its goal should be provocative and evocative, colorful and gripping, Bible-based news analysis."[19]

A good example of biblical journalism in action can be found in a series of articles in 1997 that pitted the magazine against the world's largest publisher of Bibles, Zondervan Publishing House, a division of NewsCorp. "Femme Fatale" by Susan Olasky (Marvin's wife) charged that Zondervan and a well-respected translation committee were quietly making plans to introduce a gender-neutral version of the New International Version of the Bible. This, Susan Olasky charged, signaled that the "feminist seduction of the evangelical church" was close to undermining traditional understandings of the gender roles God had created.[20] Zondervan immediately protested what it felt was unfair reporting techniques. That led to more *WORLD* stories and a challenge that Zondervan refute the general truth of the articles. Zondervan eventually filed an ethics complaint with the Evangelical Press Association (EPA). At face value, the articles were true, an ad hoc committee of the EPA concluded, even if the inferences drawn from the facts were sensationalized. *WORLD*'s article and the concern expressed by its more influential evangelical readers forced Zondervan to delay plans for the translation's release. The dialogue about the proposed translation spread out from *WORLD* to other publications like *Christianity Today*, which ran a series of articles about the difficulties of translating Bibles.

Evangelical Publications and the Abortion Debate

No issue has caused evangelicals more angst and unleashed their resolve to redeem the sinful slide of society than that of the legalization of abortion in the United States. Since the 1973 Supreme Court ruling in *Roe v. Wade* that overturned state bans on abortion, evangelical publications have reported on lobbying efforts to change federal and state laws, elect pro-life candidates, defeat pro-choice politicians, and create and nurture privately funded programs to assist women facing unwanted pregnancies. Occasionally evangelical magazines have used their editorial space to condemn violence against abortion providers while exploring the effectiveness of demonstrations held outside abortion clinics. The magazines also report on and debate the latest pronouncements from evangelical leaders, especially when those proclamations are directed at political leaders and public policy decisions that appear to increase the availability of abortions. The excitable rhetoric of the religious Right may get ink, but the tone of most evangelical periodicals is less inflammatory and judgmental.

A study of hundreds of articles in the three influential publications reveals both the unity and the diversity within the evangelical movement. *Christianity Today*, *Sojourners*, and *WORLD* magazine all regard abortion as a form of murder. All report on major developments involving legislative and legal maneuverings to ban abortion and feature commentary from either their editors or recognized evangelical leaders. But the stories also reveal a spectrum of strategies popular among evangelicals for reducing or eliminating abortion in America.

When the Supreme Court's decision was first announced, *Christianity Today* said the court "clearly decided for paganism, and against Christianity, and this in disregard even of democratic sentiment, which in this case appears to follow Christian tradition and to reject permissive abortion legislation." To further educate its readers, the magazine's editors also noted that the court's claim that ancient religions did not bar abortion was patently false, that Judaism and Christianity did bar abortion. It concluded: "Christians should accustom themselves to the thought that the American state no longer supports, in any meaningful sense, the laws of God, and prepare themselves spiritually for the prospect that it may one day formally repudiate them and turn against those who seek to live by them."[21]

The harsh tone of that first salvo has softened. Two years later, writer Nancy Barcus, an assistant professor at Houghton College, called on Christians to lessen the confrontational rhetoric: ". . . sometimes, especially on an issue we care a great deal about, we have a bad way of explaining ourselves." She goes on to suggest that using logical arguments based on medical evidence and seeking a common ground for discussion with abortion adherents would be more successful strategies. She also suggests that evangelicals "activate our adoption and counseling services to do more to encourage unwed mothers to bear these children."[22] Gradually the magazine began educating readers about the variety of reasons why women seek abortion. It also gave an inside look at the activities of crisis pregnancy centers, counseling dilemmas faced by male pastors, how churches can support pregnant women, counseling available for women experiencing postabortion guilt, and how to help guilt-ridden fathers. Thus, the coverage has been comprehensive and continues to be so. It is, of course, presented in a context that assumes readers and editors agree that abortion is wrong.[23]

Sojourners states on its website that its editors are opposed to abortion, but its editorial content is primarily focused on how Christians can work with one another and with pro-abortion forces to lessen the need for abortions. The magazine is more ambivalent about attempts to overturn *Roe v. Wade*. Articles explicate the magazine's contention that all life is sacred; thus, capital punishment or any other action by individuals, government, or industry that deprives people of a healthy life is biblically wrong. Finding "common ground" is a central theme running through articles that discuss how poverty, oppression, and a lack of viable options lead women to abort. One staff member said "that energy, outrage and passion to protect all life are desperately needed in the form of thoughtful engagement with our cultural dialogue on the meaning and costs of abortion, and in creating a society where no one thinks abortion is the only choice."[24] The credibility gained by Jim Wallis through his books advocating dialogue on cultural and political disagreement, plus *Sojourners'* coverage of Christian humanitarianism, impressed Democrats courting religious conservatives. In 2008, Wallis and other *Sojourners* writers helped the party frame portions of its platform and the magazine hosted several debates and symposia that provided a supportive audience for candidates such as Barack Obama to explain their positions on abortion and other issues of interest to progressive Christians. That's quite a change from the day a group of seminary students decided to start a countercultural Christian magazine.

As would be expected, *WORLD*'s coverage of abortion mirrors its editorial philosophy. Editor Olasky and Publisher Joel Belz strongly side with evangelicals who have no doubts that abortion is biblically and socially wrong. The abortion issue is so important to *WORLD* that each January (the month *Roe v. Wade* was handed down) the magazine devotes a major portion of its editorial coverage to the subject. The editorial strategy of its news and analysis, while not readily apparent, is to report on legal battles to limit or eliminate abortion while spotlighting successful strategies of the antiabortion movement. Olasky uses his column and news-analysis articles to debunk culturally accepted statements about abortion, especially commonly held beliefs about its history and prevalence in the past.[25] Trends in popular culture also receive attention. In 2008, a story notes an increase in movies (*Knocked Up*, *Juno*, and others are cited) in which the heroine decides to keep her baby even as her friends and family counsel her to abort. Writer Lynn Vincent provides the biblical journalism comment that "Some peg the change to ultrasound technology, others to a changing of the guard among filmmakers. But all agree that Hollywood has awakened to this fact: Abortion is not only unarguably un-sexy, but also un-heroic."[26]

Some of the more nuanced or conciliatory rhetoric found in *Christianity Today* and *Sojourners* is absent in *WORLD*'s coverage. Dialogue with abortion supporters is cautioned. The subhead of one article asks, "how far should pro-life advocates go in working with 'abortion grays' to reduce the number of abortions?"[27] The article focuses on legislation introduced by antiabortion Sen. Sam Brownback (R-Kan.) and abortion-rights proponent Sen. Edward Kennedy (D-Mass.). The duo wanted to establish a national registry of people willing to adopt children with Down syndrome. The legislation was proposed after Brownback learned that "80 to 90 percent of parents who learn their unborn children have Down syndrome choose abortion." Also in that article a well-known pastor, Joel Hunter, defended his alliance with an "abortion gray" group. "We can save babies here—that's the bottom line. The question isn't what's your ideology? It's are you saving babies?" Later he is quoted, "I think evangelicals have to ask: Can I go step by step instead of having the whole thing at one time?"

Groups seeking incremental change or dialogue with pro-choice forces frustrate *WORLD* Publisher Joel Belz.[28] In a commentary piece he asserted the following:

"Abortion and same-sex marriage are uniquely heinous sins. They rattle the foundations of a civilized society. They take a culture in a dreadful direction. We haven't been wrong to do so [oppose abortion]. We aren't fanatics."

"It's hard to see how anyone can claim to be a protector of the environment and not put a high priority on the preservation of human babies."

Abortion is "one of the most racist of all social causes in history" because so many abortion clinics are situated in poor, predominantly non-white neighborhoods.

He also notes that fifty million abortions had been performed since *Roe v. Wade*. "No economist can look at the loss of 50 million babies over the past 45 years and not wince at the impact of such a drain on the economic vitality of our society." He also says that "tomorrow's elderly will worry about Social Security more than they would have with 50 million more contributors to the system."

The 2008 Election

The differences among evangelical publications are evident when reviewing their reporting on the 2008 presidential election. *Sojourners* stopped short of endorsing Barack Obama for president, but its coverage attempted to paint Obama and Democrats as people who struggle daily with how to integrate faith and politics, not misguided or morally blind as the religious Right would claim. *WORLD* used its news pages to educate readers about the major issues of the presidential election using the biblical journalism approach of analyzing those issues through the lens of conservative evangelical doctrine. The publication, which had sometimes been accused of being a shill for the religious Right, had previously criticized John McCain's policies as senator, provoking an outcry from national columnist William Safire.[29] In its coverage of the buildup to the 2008 presidential election, the magazine does not salute Republican Party politics like other evangelical media. Rather, the publication is true to its mission statement of analyzing news and presenting commentary. That commentary compliments Republicans more than Democrats for espousing biblical values, but readers did not find a ringing endorsement for McCain's presidential aspirations. The *Christianity Today* analysis of candidate Barack Obama is even-keeled, even sympathetic, while the analysis of the McCain campaign notes that the Arizona senator is playing catch-up in terms of articulating his Baptist faith.[30] Perhaps a January 2008 editorial best sums up the conundrum faced by the candidates: "There isn't an evangelical vote. We are not some pious voting bloc up for grabs. Regardless of how pollsters might pigeonhole us, evangelicals come from across a broad spectrum of society—pragmatics, purists and in-between."

THE FUTURE

Early into the twenty-first century, both religious and secular periodicals struggle to adapt to technology that threatens the continued existence of paper and ink as a major communication source. The history of evangelicals' use of the mass media and their early adoption of new technology bode well for their survival. Already evangelical publications have strategically presented themselves as news and advocacy "brands" delivered through a variety of mediated platforms. It is likely that the strong websites like those of *Christianity Today*, *WORLD*, and *Sojourners* (which features an array of educational guides and notes from symposia it hosts) will continue to attract more readers than its printed versions. New uses for the web will arise and more web-only publications are likely to appear, flourish, and perhaps replace publications that don't adapt. This certainly appears to be the case with some of the parachurch publications like *World Vision*. Its magazine is still sent to 400,000 donors on a quarterly basis (in the 1980s it was monthly), but its website and e-mail alerts provide a more diverse and immediate form of communication. That may be true of other printed periodicals as well.

Still, the urge to give credibility to a movement by publishing a magazine is a strong feature of evangelical history, and as recently as 2000, that impetus was still strong. One example is *RELEVANT Magazine*, which started as a website that later added a print magazine. Founding Editor Cameron Strang grew up in a household where daily discussions revolved around the family's ownership of Strang Communications. The company publishes *Charisma and Christian Life*, a magazine for evangelicals who believe that miraculous manifestations of God's Holy Spirit (miraculous healing, speaking in tongues, and the like) persist today.

As a student at Oral Roberts University, Cameron found that few of his classmates read *Charisma* or any Christian periodical. After graduation, he created an online Christian discussion venue called RELEVANTMagazine.com. Nine months later the online community had attracted 100,000 participants. A year later, they started a print edition of *RELEVANT Magazine*. Within a few years the magazine had 80,000 paid subscribers. The writing in *RELEVANT Magazine* reflects the conversational and personal tone of the website, a contrast from the reportorial and essay style found in publications shepherded by older evangelicals. The magazine attracts Christians from a variety of denominations, including those that are generally classified as Pentecostal and those that are not. Public policy issues and political events are not heavily covered in print, but lively discussions take place on the website. "Over the last 20 years, the religious right has tried to legislate Christianity back into American society. Do I want a nation that stands for godly values? Of course. But do I want to deflect that responsibility onto our elected officials and rely on them to enact change in society? No. That's the Church's responsibility. That's our responsibility."[31] Later Strang explained: "We're not afraid of talking about issues head-on or taking a stand, but the issues and importance of them may be different from my parents' generation." The magazine interviews non-Christian celebrities who have commented publicly on Christianity and their own spirituality. Strang believes the periodical attracts people of all ages who question some Christian traditionalism and desire to see the Gospel related to contemporary culture. "We don't want to be finger pointing," he says. "But we do want to examine situations and ask, 'How could this be? Here is something challenging and here is how we could fix it.'"[32] Although Cameron Strang turned thirty a few years after *RELEVANT*'s debut, the magazine and its online following provide a hint as to how the next generation of evangelicals will approach the use of technology.

Historically, evangelical publications have targeted white, middle-class readers. African Americans tend to be more socially conservative than whites but also much less likely to feel at home in movements like historical evangelicalism or the religious Right.[33] The growth of web-based communication may encourage African Americans, as well as believers who speak Spanish, Korean, and a host of other languages, to participate in the evangelical dialogue. More evangelicals are already entering the dialogue through existing publications. ChristianityToday.com reports 2.1 million unique visitors monthly to its website that serves as a portal for its twenty-four online publications, while Sojourners' Sojo.net reports more than 100,000 unique visitors per month.

Given its history of innovation and the diversity of its content, it is likely that evangelical publications will continue to fill an important role for believers. A day may arrive when those messages are not communicated through paper, but electronically. It is also likely that the publications attracting the most eyeballs will be those carrying on a tradition of measured advocacy on behalf of what will still be a powerful movement in American culture.

NOTES

1. Quentin J. Schultze, *Christianity and the Mass Media in America: Toward a Democratic Accommodation* (East Lansing: Michigan State University Press, 2003), 100.
2. Stewart M. Hoover, *Religion in the News* (Thousand Oaks, CA: Sage, 1998), 151.
3. Charles Austin, "The History and Role of the Protestant Press," in *Reporting Religion: Facts and Faith*, ed. B. J. Hubbard (Sonoma, CA: Polebridge Press, 1990), 115.
4. Schultze, *Christianity and the Mass Media in America*, 91.
5. Paul David Nord, "The Evangelical Origins of the Mass Media in America, 1815–1835," *Journalism Monographs* 88 (1984).
6. James Carey, *Communication as Culture: Essays on Media and Society* (Boston: Unwin Hyman, 1989), 23.
7. Roberta Moore, "Development of Protestant Journalism in the United States, 1743–1850," (PhD dissertation, Syracuse University, 1968), 19.
8. Bernell Tripp, "Origins of the Black Press in America," in *The Media and Religion in American History*, ed. W. David Sloan (Northport, AL: Vision Press, 2000), 95.
9. Moore, "Development of Protestant Journalism in the United States, 1743–1850," 8.
10. See, for instance, Teresa Lueck, "Women's Moral Reform Periodicals of the 19th Century: A Cultural Feminist Analysis of the Advocate," *American Journalism* 16 (1999): 37–52.

11. Dennis N. Voskuil, "Reaching Out: Mainline Protestantism and the Media," in *Between the Times: The Travail of the Protestant Establishment in America, 1900–1960*, ed. William R. Hutchison (Cambridge: Cambridge University Press, 1989), 73.

12. W. Russell Congleton, "Sword of the Lord," in *Popular Religious Magazines of the United States*, ed. Mark Fackler and Charles Lippy (Westport, CT: Greenwood Press, 1995), 457.

13. See, for instance, Martin Marty, "Not of this World . . . but Like It," *Christian Century*, June 1998, 663.

14. J. C. Pollock, *A Foreign Devil in China* (Minneapolis, MN: World Wide Publications, 1971), 238.

15. Daryl Alan Porter, "Christianity Today: Its History and Development, 1956–1978," (MA thesis, Dallas Theological Seminary, 1978), 4.

16. See, for instance, Kenneth Woodward and Jane Whitmore, "Capital Flight," *Time*, February 7, 1977, 77.

17. E. Freda, "Mr. Speaker," *Atlanta Journal and Constitution*, March 20, 1995, 6A.

18. Marvin Olasky, *Telling the Truth: How to Revitalize Christian Journalism* (Wheaton, IL: Crossway Books, 1996), 33.

19. Ibid., 25.

20. Susan Olasky, "Femme Fatale," *WORLD* 12, no. 2 (March 29, 1997), http://www.worldmag.com/articles/229 (accessed May 25, 2010). For more information on the Stealth Bible controversy, see Ken Waters, "Competing Moral Visions: Ethics and the Stealth Bible," *Journal of Mass Media Ethics* 16, no. 1 (2001): 48–61.

21. "Abortion and the Court," *Christianity Today*, March 1973, 32–33.

22. Nancy B. Barcus, "Think Straight About Abortion," *Christianity Today*, January 17, 1975, 8.

23. For a sampling of these articles, see: Ted Olsen, "The Art of Abortion Politics," *Christianity Today* 50, no. 3 (March 2006): 73; Stan Guthrie, "Don't Cede the High Ground," *Christianity Today* 51, no. 5 (May 2007): 60; "Abortion Overreach," *Christianity Today* 51, no. 5 (May 2007): 23; Frederica Mathewes-Greene, "Wanted: A New Pro-Life Strategy," *Christianity Today* 42, no. 1 (January 12, 1998): 26–31; Guy M. Condon, "You Say Choice, I Say Murder," *Christianity Today* 35, no. 7 (June 24, 1991): 20–23; and Frederica Mathewes-Green, "The Dilemmas of a Pro-Life Pastor," *Christianity Today* 41, no. 4 (April 7, 1997): 27–31.

24. Julie Polter, "Outrage Over the Abortion Veto," *Sojourners* 24, no. 4 (July–August 1996): 9–10.

25. See Marvin Olasky, "Lessons from the Past," *WORLD* 24, no. 1 (January 17, 2009): 32–35; Marvin Olasky, "Selling Abortion," *WORLD* 24, no. 1 (January 17, 2009): 40–42; Marvin Olasky, "Back to the Present," *WORLD* 24, no. 1 (January 17, 2009): 30–31.

26. Lynn Vincent, "The Plots Thicken," *WORLD* 23, no. 1 (January 12, 2008): 58.

27. Jamie Dean, "Life Decisions," *WORLD* 22, no. 41 (November 10, 2007): 27.

28. Joel Belz, "Stop Apologizing," *WORLD* 23, no. 14 (July 12, 2008): 6.

29. See William Safire, "Bush Campaign Stoops to Sleaze," *Ventura County Star*, February 20, 2000, B-11.

30. See, for instance, John W. Kennedy, "Preach and Reach," *Christianity Today* 52, no. 10 (October 6, 2008): 26–30; and Tony Carnes, "Talking the Walk," *Christianity Today* 52, no. 10 (October 7, 2008): 32–36.

31. Cameron Strang, "The Politics of Faith," *RELEVANT Magazine*, November–December 2004, 14.

32. Cameron Strang, e-mail message to the author, June 12, 2007.

33. Carin Robinson, "From Every Tribe and Nation? Blacks and the Christian Right," *Social Science Quarterly* 87, no. 3 (2006): 595.

REFERENCES

Austin, Charles. 1990. The History and Role of the Protestant Press. In *Reporting Religion: Facts and Faith*, ed. B. J. Hubbard, 108–17. Sonoma, CA: Polebridge Press.

Congleton, W. Russell. 1995. Sword of the Lord. In *Popular Religious Magazines of the United States*, ed. Mark Fackler and Charles Lippy, 457–62. Westport, CT: Greenwood Press.

Hoover, Stewart M. 1998. *Religion in the News*. Thousand Oaks, CA: Sage.

Schultze, Quentin J. 2003. *Christianity and the Mass Media in America: Toward a Democratic Accommodation*. East Lansing: Michigan State University Press.

CHAPTER 38

ONE NATION, MANY VOICES: THE MUSLIM PRESS IN THE UNITED STATES

FAIZA HIRJI

"Read: And thy Lord is the Most Bounteous,
Who teacheth by the pen,
Teacheth man that which he knew not."

—The Quran, Surah 96, The Clot

THE story of the Muslim press in the United States is a story of struggle: the struggle for justice, identity, and the ability to be heard. It is also a story of the evolution of the extraordinarily diverse Muslim population in the United States and American Muslims' desire to forge identities that balance the various influences in their lives. This chapter helps provide insight into the development of the Muslim press and the challenges it faces as American Muslims enter a new era.

Islam has its very origins in reading: on the night that Muhammad became a prophet, he received his first revelations in written form. Though illiterate, Muhammad was visited by the angel Gabriel and ordered to read. Perplexed, Muhammad discovered in response to the angel's insistent command that he had miraculously been granted this ability. The passages that he read on that night, which Muslims commemorate every year as a sacred occasion, are the first ones revealed from the Quran. For that reason, the idea of books, of print, and of knowledge remains sacred within Islam.

Centuries later, Muslims around the world, including American Muslims, take up the pen to continue the work of Allah and his prophet. The Muslim press in the United States is no exception, and like Muslim communities in that country, it is diverse, ever changing, and responsive to contemporary realities. The United States is home both to a variegated immigrant Muslim population and to a significant population of native-born African American Muslims who either adopted Islam or returned to it in response to the social, economic, and political obstacles that have faced their community.

Tracing the story of the Muslim press, then, helps to trace the story of Islam in the United States. Beginning as a way to promote a positive image of Islam and to fight inequity, the Muslim press has served at various times as a vehicle for bonding communities, creating identity, offering imprisoned populations redemption and purpose, and countering negative representations of Islam in the mainstream media. At the same time, the Muslim press has been riddled with controversy and differences of opinion. It has been plagued by the economic challenges that affect many ethnic and religious media. Finally, in its most contemporary manifestation, it is giving rise to commercialized ventures that may inhibit the kinds of intellectual and philosophical engagement that marked the press's early years. Yet, despite these challenges, the Muslim press has survived for more than a century, providing the disparate Muslim American community with a venue through which its members may speak.

Born in the USA: The Beginnings of the American Muslim Press

While ethnic media and religious media often address the issues of integration in a host society or offer news from "back home,"[1] the Muslim press in the United States has historically fulfilled more varied functions. Indeed, the earliest American Muslim newspaper was founded by Alexander Russell Webb, a white convert to Islam. The former US consul to the Philippines and journalist founded his publication, the *Moslem World*, in 1893 in conjunction with the American Islamic Propaganda mission to the United States, a venture financed through Indian connections. The intent was to project a positive image of Islam to the American public, and the newspaper prompted the production of related papers, including one or two short-lived newsletters stemming from the original. The *Moslem World* began publication with the following statement from Webb:

> Briefly stated, the purpose of *The Moslem World* is to spread abroad among the independent thinkers of America a knowledge of the character and teachings of Mohammed, and to correct those errors into which the masses have fallen, through the false history and misconceptions published by prejudiced and ignorant followers of other systems, who have written about Islam and its inspired founder.[2]

To achieve his hope of projecting positive perceptions of Islam and building connections between Muslims and the country's intellectual elite, Webb used high-quality materials and a range of scholarly contributions, attracting the attention of newspapers such as the *New York Times* and the *Boston Globe*.[3] Excerpts from Islamic texts, including the Quran, were translated into English. Feedback was mixed, but Webb did succeed in reaching a broad audience: Americans of different backgrounds used the paper as a forum to debate immigration, Prohibition, and the relative superiority of Christianity versus Islam.

Webb also included a section of the paper that featured stories of crime and bigotry, including lynchings. In some cases, Webb drew not-so-subtle links between crime and Christianity. He argued that opponents of Islam used similar tactics, highlighting a handful of crimes committed by Muslims in order to make sweeping generalizations about the religion.[4] Webb had limited opportunity to judge the effectiveness of these tactics, however, as lack of funding resulted in the paper's cessation mere months after its launch. As Singleton concludes, "Although ultimately an ephemeral venture, *The Moslem World* gained international recognition as a unique, well-produced newspaper, and it spurred religious discourse in the press of the United States."[5]

Islam was an undercurrent in other influential newspapers that had a strong political bent, such as the *Negro World*, but the specific work of shaping the American Muslim press was taken up in the 1920s by Prophet Noble Drew Ali. Founder of the Moorish Science Temple of America Inc., Drew Ali published the *Moorish Guide*. Drew Ali's religion, referred to as Islamism and incorporating elements of other religious practices, spoke to the need among African Americans to forge an identity during a time of widespread segregation and inequality. The Moorish Science Temple movement gave rise to a number of competing factions, such as the Nation of Islam (NOI), which was even savvier in its use of media. The NOI's beliefs and practices markedly differed from those found within the two main branches of Islam, Sunni and Shia. Indeed, as NOI continued to grow, a number of American Muslims voiced their opposition, suggesting that the organization was political, extremist, and hate driven, rather than religious. Others expressed their resistance in different terms, describing NOI practitioners as heretics who did not adhere to the pillars of Islam. Nonetheless, NOI's strict principles and nationalist identity proved to be a powerful draw for its mostly urban, African American followers.

Under the leadership of Elijah Muhammad, the NOI founded a newspaper in the 1930s called the *Final Call to Islam*, which by the 1960s had evolved into *Muhammad Speaks*. *Muhammad Speaks* was a notable success, providing high-quality journalism[6] to a readership of as many as 500,000 subscribers. Elijah Muhammad used the press to great advantage, promoting the NOI as a way to positively transform African Americans and to inspire their struggle for justice. In addition to *Muhammad Speaks*, Muhammad demonstrated a willingness to experiment with various print formats, including pamphlets and *Salaam*, a magazine modeled on the popular African American publication *Jet*.

After the death of Elijah Muhammad in the 1970s, the NOI splintered into different factions. Competing leaders founded new newspapers—*Bilalian News*, the *Final Call*, a new version of *Muhammad Speaks*, and the *Muslim Journal*—all advocating what they understood to be Islamic principles. Given the complex mechanics of creating, publishing, and maintaining ethnic newspapers and magazines, it is no surprise that there are conflicting stories about the founding of these newspapers. Ethnic newspapers and magazines are often founded on minimal budgets with uncertain sources of funding, fueled at times by a political cause whose popularity may not last. For these reasons, as well as the difficulty of securing distribution outlets and maintaining their underpaid or unpaid staff, such newspapers often have a short shelf life and their histories are rarely well documented.

A Place of Their Own: New Americans and the Muslim Press

In addition to American-born converts to Islam, Muslim immigrants also played a significant role in the evolution of the Muslim press. Muslim Albanians, Turks, and Arabs founded their own newspapers in the early 1900s, all with slightly different purposes: several had a strongly nationalist bent and were engaged in the politics of their homelands, while others focused on promoting a sense of community among new arrivals. Over time, Lebanese, Syrian, Bosnian, Iranian, Yugoslavian, Pakistani, and Indian Muslims also started newspapers with similar goals.

For many Muslims on the margins of American society, the press represented an opportunity to find a voice. This is true for new immigrants struggling to integrate into American life, but also for those Muslims who are marginalized within Islam itself, such as Ahmadiyya Muslims or Ahmadis. Ahmadis belong to a movement founded in 1889 that is based on a belief that the Messiah came in the person of Mirza Ghulam Ahmad (1835–1908). Condemned and sometimes persecuted by Muslims who do not accept their beliefs, Ahmadis have found numerous ways to express their identity. In the United States, they have engaged in vigorous use of the media to address misperceptions about their religion and, interestingly, developed some relationships with the media-savvy NOI. Sulayman Nyang identifies the *Muslim Sunrise*, founded in the 1920s by Ahmadis and still in existence, as the longest-running Muslim publication in the United States.[7] Richard Brent Turner suggests that this journal may well be the Ahmadis' greatest contribution to the American Muslim community.[8] Ahmadiyya Muslims have developed other newspapers, magazines, and websites whose professional appearance and clear message belie their marginal status.

Shia Muslims are less numerous than Sunnis, who make up the majority of Muslims around the world and within the United States. American Shi'ites, estimated to compose between 10 and 15 percent of the US Muslim population, publish the *Islamic Review*, founded by the Shia Association of North America (SANA), and *Islamic Affairs*. Within the Shia minority, Ismailis constitute a smaller group. Ismailis are followers of an imam who traces his ancestry to Prophet Muhammad, and members adhere to his interpretation of the Quran. In keeping with the guidance of the current imam, His Highness the Aga Khan, Ismailis seek to integrate into their host societies, and substantial numbers have settled in the United States. A national magazine, the *Ismaili USA*, is published three times a year and is distributed to the majority of American Ismaili households, as well as to non-Ismailis. The magazine keeps American Ismailis informed of events and activities taking place among coreligionists in the United States and updates them on the work of His Highness, who heads an international development network.

The media presence of so many Muslim communities supports the findings of scholars of diaspora[9] who suggest that groups that have experienced persecution, or that have found it difficult to achieve acceptance, seek out creative ways to express themselves. They may use the media to reframe or clarify messages and disseminate these among themselves and to external audiences. Diaspora communities are often swift to adopt new technologies, an essential requirement in the current media landscape, where many smaller media outlets have found a place online. The Ahmadiyya Muslim community has done just that, using media to enhance its place within diaspora and to give its children a sense of identity, as with the use of the magazine *Al Hilal* (*The New Moon*). Although the magazine is intended for Ahmadi Muslims, the topics tackled are ones that are raised by any number of young Muslims, from love of Allah to why some Muslims do not celebrate Halloween.

Building or Burning Bridges? Challenges to the Islamic Press

Notwithstanding the accomplishments listed above, a number of fissures have affected the functioning of major Islamic groups. The diverse composition of the American Muslim community has led to recurring tension between and among American-born Muslims and immigrants, whose goals are not always the same and whose practice of Islam may be different. As Yvonne Haddad and Jane Smith[10] note, the struggles faced by these groups may vary significantly. Depending on their country of origin, the branch of Islam with which they identify, their politics, and their leadership, they may understand their faith in divergent ways and may even question the piety of their copractitioners. This has become more complicated as the number of South Asian Muslims in the United States continues to rise, potentially shifting leadership toward that community.[11] Thus, the Muslim press has the potential to be a community builder, but it has not succeeded in uniting the highly diverse Muslims who live in the United States.

Other fissures exist. Websites such as the now-defunct Muslim WakeUp! (2003–09) highlight the tension between Muslims who consider themselves to be traditional and those who classify themselves as progressive. Muslim WakeUp!, edited by supporters in the United States and Canada, was associated with the Progressive Muslim Union of North America, which has advocated a more prominent role for women and has reached out to marginalized groups, such as homosexuals. While Muslim WakeUp! and similar publications speak for some Muslims, especially those who are uncomfortable with practices that are exclusionary, other Muslims are troubled by liberal perspectives that may not reflect a foundation in Islamic scholarship, as well as definitions of "progressive" that may be slippery or judgmental.

Although the Muslim press has played and still plays a key role in explaining Islamic practice to others, as well as in fostering community, there are a number of ongoing struggles that have been exacerbated by events such as the first and second Gulf wars and September 11 attacks. If the early Muslim press fought a social and political battle for racial equality, current outlets fight a variety of battles: some speak out against perceived Islamophobia in the United States; others criticize policies that negatively affect citizens in predominantly Muslim countries. In turn, non-Muslim organizations such as the Militant Islam Monitor scrutinize websites, newsletters, and speeches of Islamic groups to find evidence of an Islamist threat to the United States.

Even established organizations and their publications draw the critical scrutiny of those groups that question the role of Muslims in North American society. In some minor publications, there may well be signs of anti-Semitism or racism or other extreme points of view. In other publications, the desire to create a cohesive Muslim community, to establish it more firmly in the United States, or to support political causes such as a state for Palestine may all attract negative attention. Magazines and newspapers critical of Israel have been named on the website of the Anti-Defamation League. A number of outlets clearly understand these pressures and defy them, publishing articles that criticize Zionism, imperialism, and media stereotypes of Islam.

The Contemporary Muslim Press: The End of Struggle?

On university and college campuses across North America, Muslim students have been integral to fostering and maintaining a sense of Islamic community while resisting racism. This effort has been advanced by an active publishing regime. In the 1980s, Muslim students at UCLA founded the first Muslim student newsmagazine in the United States, *Al-Talib* (*The Student*). In 2010, the magazine reached a reported 56,000 readers in thirty-seven states. Muslim students seek ways to articulate their faith: as minorities on university campuses and as educated individuals, they want to explain their religion to others and many have the intellectual capital to do so. Moreover, students engaged in such an enterprise are growing increasingly younger. *Al Hilal*, mentioned previously, was started as a magazine for children but is also a magazine by children, who write articles and provide other contributions. Similarly, the *Muslim Link* began as a high school project in 1998 and is now regularly distributed throughout the Washington-Baltimore area while maintaining a well-developed online presence.

The tradition of the Muslim press is entrenched in the United States. Less well established is the notion of a unified Muslim press, due to the fact that American Muslims are not ethnically, spiritually, or politically homogenous. Some Muslim journalists advocate for the creation of a strong community voice through a high-quality, high-circulation media outlet. However, the continued settlement and establishment of Muslims in the United States poses a challenge to unifying the community, much less defining what constitutes successful American Muslim media projects.

Nevertheless, various groups do make attempts to represent the whole community. The Islamic Circle of North America (ICNA), a relatively conservative Muslim organization that has been cited in the past for national meetings segregated by gender, has published the *Message International* since 1989 with the intention of creating a successful publication that represents all North American Muslims. This is a laudable goal, but it is difficult to judge the success of ICNA's mission to create a quality magazine for the entire American Muslim community with all of its diverse voices and needs. Moreover, at a time when prominent mainstream publications are struggling to adapt to a changed media environment, its future is uncertain.

Some Islamic publications that seek a broad audience have shown considerable growth. *Al Jumuah Magazine*, internationally distributed by the American Islamic Revival Association to approximately 100,000 readers, is one example. *Al Jumuah* is a fifty-two-page full-color publication that began as a one-page pamphlet in 1991. It describes itself as a Muslim lifestyle publication, which might seem to imply that it is less engaged with theological or intellectual issues than some of its competitors. However, the content of *Al Jumuah* addresses issues of morality, Islamic education, and jurisprudence, as well as health, finances, family relationships, and the environment.

The *American Muslim* is an outlet that has used new technologies and a changing media environment to reestablish itself. The magazine started as a quarterly journal in 1989, ceased publication in 1995, and was brought back as an online publication under the auspices of founding editor Sheila Musaji. Shortly after September 11, 2001, Musaji recounts, she became concerned about the lack of a moderate Muslim voice in the public sphere. In response, she revived the *American Muslim* as a forum for discussion and the exchange of ideas. Another success is Muslim Media Network, which covers a variety of online, print, and broadcasting platforms. iViews.com, also a popular website, was started by board members from the Council on American-Islamic Relations, a national advocacy group seeking to educate media outlets and the general public about Islam.

An interesting feature of the contemporary Muslim press is a change in its focus: for example, gender is far more central to current media outlets than in the past. Whereas some of the older publications spoke explicitly to issues of gender, they did so in ways that reflected traditional perspectives of a woman's role. Moreover, they did not always ask women to articulate these viewpoints, nor were they aimed specifically at Muslim women. In contrast, *Azizah Magazine*, founded in 2002, was launched by two Muslim women and is published by a private company held by Muslim women. The magazine covers a wide range of issues, some general interest (politics, financial planning) and some gender specific (inspirational female figures, finding religious identity as a Muslim woman). With its frequent positive references to assertive women, the magazine's intended readership cannot be in doubt.

Azizah Magazine's focus on the female audience seems logical, since many women are ardent consumers of books and magazines. But this focus also addresses the overwhelming amount of negative attention that the mainstream media devote to Muslim women, often branding them as objects of oppression. Additionally, *Azizah* speaks to the competing challenges that Muslim women face as minorities in American society; as individuals balancing spiritual, personal, and professional lives; and as females who, at times, may confront sexism or attempts at control within their cultural communities.[12]

Moreover, *Azizah* is not the only magazine targeting the female Muslim market. *Muslimette Magazine*, founded in 2009, is directed at women, but its scope is narrower than that of *Azizah*. Primarily addressing issues of fashion, relationships, and beauty, *Muslimette* pursues a youthful Muslim audience, with no apparent dogmatism about how "Muslim woman" is defined. Although some stories address the challenges of maintaining one's style within the confines of a hijab, a picture of a woman posted on the magazine's website shows her unveiled. The content is not wholly devoted to beauty and fashion; some of the stories and links are on prayer and religious festivals. Yet, in its conception, even in its playful name, *Muslimette* seems to represent a lifestyle publication rather than a serious sociopolitical voice.

In 2009, Omar Haq created a similar venue for Muslim men, founding *Muslim Quarterly* or *MQ*, with a mission to assist men in managing everyday issues in accordance with the teachings of the Quran and the example of the Prophet Muhammad. Given the mainstream media's proclivity to treat Muslim men as terrorists or violent oppressors, Haq's desire to provide an alternative voice is understandable. Like *Azizah*, *MQ* tackles myriad questions and issues, ranging from current court cases against accused terrorists to finding a proper Muslim wife, and from stress management to maintaining one's beard in accordance with Islamic teachings. On the one hand, this could be seen as a response to the numerous focal points that form the contemporary American Muslim identity. Another view is to consider the current publishing landscape and ask whether *MQ*, as its *GQ*-evoking moniker implies, is trying to emulate popular lifestyle magazines, which often prioritize stories on relationships, personal care, and fashion. In fact, that aim is not surprising. As Haq, *MQ*'s editor-in-chief, points out, today's American Muslims are exposed to a variety of media influences, many depicting a consumerist, superficial lifestyle that is not consonant with Muslim values. The content of *MQ* may seem superficial in comparison to that of newspapers advocating political activism, but Muslims growing up in the United States, which has the largest, most powerful popular culture machine in the world, are confronted constantly by competing images of what they should buy and how they should behave. *MQ* may be superficial, but it is still more Islamic than the mainstream alternative. The approaches of magazines such as *Azizah* and *Muslim Quarterly*, despite their different agendas, suggest that the purpose of the American Muslim press is changing.

In the postsegregation era, the Muslim press still has important battles to fight. Racism against African Americans and new immigrants remains, existing alongside anti-Islam sentiment. Some expressions of prejudice are more veiled now than in the time of Alexander Webb or Noble Drew Ali, and responses from the press may be correspondingly diplomatic. Moreover, some members of the Muslim press are not especially interested in this work. Instead, at a time when numerous Muslim immigrants have joined the African American Muslim population, some of the community's media outlets focus on everyday life, addressing ways to make it easier by suggesting there is no conflict between one's faith and one's American citizenship. The narratives that dominate the Muslim press have changed in the decades since Alexander Webb criticized lynching and prejudice in his newspaper's pages, or since African American groups used their print platforms to rail against unjust laws or oppression by white Americans. Indeed, while the African American presence is not absent from the current American Muslim press, it is certainly diminished, supplanted by the voices of first-, second-, and third-generation immigrants. The notion of struggle has not been lost—indeed, it is reasserted in a way that links it fundamentally to a spiritual quest—but it has been reconfigured in some outlets and eroded in others.

In the wake of September 11, 2001, the struggle for many Muslims is to explain their faith and to speak out against what they see as Islamophobia, colonialism, and the problem of the Palestine-Israel conflict. This struggle for acceptance and understanding at a time when Muslims are seen as inherently different, if not inferior, is as critical as that of the African American Muslims who linked their own political conflicts to the strength provided by faith. In this case, the cause may be less clear, and the tensions around Islam and American Muslims may be further complicated by the transnational implications and geopolitical realities of conflict in places like Pakistan, Afghanistan, and Iraq. Moreover, there is also an internal challenge, because Muslim immigrants, as well as their children and their grandchildren, face the strong force of assimilation. In an environment where Islam seems unwelcome and under suspicion, young American Muslims of various ethnicities may be especially tempted to consume mainstream culture, even if it only acknowledges them in a negative way. American Muslims belong to a faith community, a cultural community, and a national one, and although these identities need not compete, they sometimes do. When this occurs, second-generation and third-generation Muslim immigrants seek to reconcile competing influences on their sense of self.

Some magazines aimed at youth, or founded by university students, were started with these issues of integration and belonging in mind. *Al Hilal* seeks to provide a strong religious foundation for children and an understanding of how to articulate difference so that they are equipped to answer questions about their faith. Similarly, *Azizah Magazine* addresses questions of faith or religious debate, even though its tone is distinctly contemporary. One article, published in 2010, explores the documentary *New Muslim Cool*, a film built around a young Puerto Rican Muslim involved in community activism and hip hop. The young man addresses some of the same problems that are raised in Muslim publications: the incarcerated population that embraces Islam, intermingling between different Muslim communities, and contemporary artistic forms that Muslim youth use to express their faith.

Likewise, *America's Muslim Family Magazine* speaks to the challenges of keeping families together, practicing the faith, and understanding Islam. Its tone, however, resembles the matter-of-fact voice found in mainstream magazines like *Today's Parent*. Though some community members may indeed be passionately invested in the fight for Palestine or debating points of theology, those who read *America's Muslim Family Magazine* may simply wish to live their lives as "normal" Americans, raising their children in the best way possible.

While media outlets come and go, exhibiting varying degrees of distinction along the way, several high-quality Muslim newspapers and magazines have established themselves on the journalistic landscape. The goal of *Illume Magazine*, founded in 2006, was to be the leading Muslim American media organization. Judging by the number of awards that its writers have earned for journalistic excellence, including an Emmy award, several George Foster Peabody Awards, and an Edward R. Murrow Award, it appears to have succeeded. While individual articles may vary in quality, the range of topics, from movie reviews to global banking to the politics of beauty pageants, indicates the broad audience that *Illume* seeks to reach. It is also a reminder that the Muslim community is diverse and has wide-ranging interests.

Illume also demonstrates a change in mindset for the Muslim press: in some ways, it remains a venue for combating oppression and mounting political activism, but it goes beyond that. The publication frames its proactive goals in terms of its distinctive abilities, including "[t]elling stories mainstream media does not have the ability to" and "[p]roviding opportunities for journalists, writers and other media professionals by offering a place to get their works published." While there may be a desire to balance the scales, offering coverage that is more equitable and nuanced, this objective is framed in a different context than the writings of the NOI. Undoubtedly, this change may be due to the different beliefs endorsed by NOI, but the greatest factor is likely the change in the status, composition, and integration of the American Muslim community. American Muslims may well be marginalized and even stigmatized in the post-9/11 world, but their issues are complex and wide-ranging in a different way. Like black Americans when the NOI first rose to power, current Muslim communities are concerned with justice, but they are also concerned with basic issues of survival, success, and integration in American society.

These changes are due to the passage of time, as well as the spread of Islam in the United States. The African Americans who converted to Islam, at least initially, often did so in response to the extraordinary pressures faced by their community. Islam provided a way forward, one that gave hope, faith, and guidance to the oppressed and downtrodden. The tone of the Muslim press founded by these practitioners is more explicitly political and, in some ways, more angry than is found in the immigrant-sponsored papers. The Muslim immigrants to the United States have had their own struggles: undoubtedly, many of them also faced injustice, cruelty, and marginalization. The early immigrant newspapers, however, project the desire to maintain community and strengthen identity. If the African American Muslim battle was to change the course of history, the Muslim immigrants struggled to keep their identity while finding ways to peacefully coexist with mainstream America.

The diverse and sometimes confusing nature of the contemporary Muslim press stems from these varied, though not necessarily divergent, purposes. Across the spectrum of race and ethnicity, however, the Muslim press offers a platform for those who seek social justice. Similarly, it provides a way to stay connected to distant homelands, forge a sense of community, and wrestle with theological questions.

At the same time, American Muslims' social position has changed in recent decades. They may be minorities, but they are integrated into the fabric of the United States. Some of them are no longer new to the country: *Illume*'s choice of "Muslim-American" as the chief designation for its audience is a strategic reminder that its readers can balance their religious identity and their national one. Like *Azizah*, *Illume* speaks to both historical and contemporary issues, wrestling with the complexity of belonging to the United States, to Islam, to families, and to peer groups. This struggle to forge a multilayered identity was once shelved in favor of basic survival, but today, media outlets attempt to speak to the plurality that is Islam in America.

The new generation of Muslim editors, publishers, and writers is even more diverse and media savvy than the first. Unlike the pioneers, however, American Muslims now have the benefit of a longer view. Having seen firsthand the consequences of remaining voiceless and allowing others to tell their stories, American Muslims now seek to create a platform for themselves. Rather than dwelling on the dearth of Muslims in mainstream media, *Illume,* for example, provides a training ground for Muslim journalists, as well as an alternative to extreme voices.

A number of the Muslim media outlets that currently exist were founded in recognition of the power of media, a knowledge that stemmed from years of reading, watching, or listening to reports that painted Muslims as extremists, terrorists, oppressors, or, in the case of women, victims. Many of the media organizations that make up the Muslim press implicitly and explicitly rebut such stereotypes, a task still relevant in the United States. After the Iranian Revolution, two Gulf wars, and a war in Afghanistan, the spotlight remains on Islam, both globally and domestically. For American Muslims, the search for identity remains complex. Within this diverse community, there are few points of agreement and few rallying points around which all American Muslims may coalesce. Today's struggle is less about a specific political movement and more about an ongoing campaign for education and acceptance.

Some of the current outlets lobby ferociously against policies and actions that they consider discriminatory. Others view their work through a different lens, refusing to criticize defamation or prejudice. Instead, their work is to present an Islam that is peaceful and committed to social justice. Still others treat the practice of Islam as a fact of life that affects a variety of everyday decisions, without necessarily requiring a political stance. In every case, journalists and publishers must walk a fine line. Newer outlets that try to foster conciliation and dialogue must contend with anti-Islam sentiment and community divisions. Magazines that speak of beauty and fashion run the risk of emphasizing consumerism and vanity, rather than Islamic values. The struggle of the Muslim press is very far from over. It takes place internally and externally, facing division within the community, as well as hostility from Islamophobic forces. This struggle changes depending on the political and social circumstances of American Muslims at any given time. Today's fight is that of a community that has developed roots in the United States and that seeks acknowledgement of Muslims as productive, diverse citizens with variegated identities, similar to many other Americans. The Muslim press has fostered social progress and community building in the United States, and the newest generation of that press continues that essential work.

ACKNOWLEDGMENTS

I would like to express sincere gratitude to my research assistant, Christine Larabie, whose diligence and hard work were invaluable in the completion of this chapter.

NOTES

1. Karim H. Karim, *From Ethnic Media to Global Media: Transnational Communication Networks Among Diasporic Communities* (Ottawa, Ontario: Department of Canadian Heritage, 1998).
2. Brent D. Singleton, "The Moslem World: A History of America's Earliest Islamic Newspaper and Its Successors," *Journal of Muslim Minority Affairs* 27, no. 2 (2007): 298–99.
3. Ibid., 299.
4. Ibid., 301.
5. Ibid., 305.
6. Richard Brent Turner, *Islam in the African-American Experience* (Bloomington and Indianapolis: Indiana University Press, 1997), 199.
7. Sulayman S. Nyang, *Islam in the United States of America* (Chicago: ABC International Group, Inc., 1999), 105.
8. Turner, *Islam in the African-American Experience,* 121.
9. Robin Cohen, *Global Diasporas: An Introduction* (Seattle: University of Washington Press, 1997), 175; Karim H. Karim, "Mapping Diasporic Landscapes," in *The Media of*

Diaspora, ed. Karim H. Karim (London: Routledge, 2003), 12; Peter Mandaville, *Transnational Muslim Politics: Reimagining the Umma* (London: Routledge, 2001).

10. Yvonne Y. Haddad and Jane I. Smith, "Introduction," in *Muslim Communities in North America*, ed. Yvonne Y. Haddad and Jane I. Smith (Albany: State University of New York Press, 1994).

11. Karen Leonard, "South Asian Leadership of American Muslims," in *Muslims in the West: From Sojourners to Citizens*, ed. Yvonne Y. Haddad (New York: Oxford University Press, 2002).

12. For examples, see Homa Hoodfar, "More Than Clothing: Veiling as an Adaptive Strategy," in *The Muslim Veil in North America: Issues and Debates*, ed. Sajida Alvi, Homa Hoodfar, and Sheila McDonough (Toronto: Women's Press, 2003); and Shahnaz Khan, *Muslim Women: Crafting a North American Identity* (Muslim Women: Crafting a North American Identity, 2000).

REFERENCES

Aijian, M. M. 1919. The Mohammedans in the United States. *Muslim World* 10:30–35.

The American Muslim. http://www.theamericanmuslim.org.

Azizah Magazine. http://www.azizahmagazine.com.

Cohen, Robin. 1997. *Global Diasporas: An Introduction*. Seattle: University of Washington Press.

Curtis, Edward E. 2006. *Black Muslim Religion in the Nation of Islam, 1960–1975*. Chapel Hill: University of North Carolina Press.

Gardell, Mattias. 1999. North America. In *Islam Outside the Arab World*, ed. David Westerlund and Ingvar Svanberg, 420–42. New York: St. Martin's Press.

Haddad, Yvonne Y., and Jane I. Smith. 1994. Introduction. In *Muslim Communities in North America*, ed. Yvonne Y. Haddad and Jane I. Smith, xvii–xxx. Albany: State University of New York Press.

Hoodfar, Homa. 2003. More Than Clothing: Veiling as an Adaptive Strategy. In *The Muslim Veil in North America: Issues and Debates*, ed. Sajida Alvi, Homa Hoodfar, and Sheila McDonough, 3–40. Toronto: Women's Press.

Illume Magazine. http://www.illumemag.com.

Islamic Circle of North America. http://www.onlineislamicstore.com.

Karim, Karim H. 1998. *From Ethnic Media to Global Media: Transnational Communication Networks among Diasporic Communities*. Ottawa, Ontario: Department of Canadian Heritage.

Karim, Karim H. 2003. Mapping Diasporic Landscapes. In *The Media of Diaspora*, ed. Karim H. Karim, 1–17. London: Routledge.

Khan, Shahnaz. 2000. *Muslim Women: Crafting a North American Identity*. Gainesville: University of Florida Press.

Leonard, Karen. 2002. South Asian Leadership of American Muslims. In *Muslims in the West: From Sojourners to Citizens*, ed. Yvonne Y. Haddad, 233–49. New York: Oxford University Press.

Lincoln, Charles E. 1994. *The Black Muslims in America*, 3rd ed. Grand Rapids, MI: William B. Eerdmans Publishing Co.

Lotfi, Abdul H. 2002. Spreading the Word: Communicating Islam in America. In *Muslim Minorities in the West: Visible and Invisible*, ed. Yvonne Y. Haddad and Jane I. Smith, 3–24. Walnut Creek, CA: Altamira Press.

Mandaville, Peter. 2001. *Transnational Muslim Politics: Reimagining the Umma.* London: Routledge.
Mukhtar Curtis, R. M. 1994. Urban Muslims: The Formation of the Dar ul-Islam Movement. In *Muslim Communities in North America*, ed. Yvonne Y. Haddad and Jane I. Smith, 51–74. Albany: State University of New York Press.
Muslimette Magazine. http://www.muslimette.com.
Nyang, Sulayman S. 1999. *Islam in the United States of America.* Chicago: ABC International Group, Inc.
Singleton, Brent D. 2007. The Moslem World: A History of America's Earliest Islamic Newspaper and its Successors. *Journal of Muslim Minority Affairs* 27:297–307.
Smith, Jane I. 1999. *Islam in America.* New York: Columbia University Press.
Smith, Jane I. 2002. Introduction. In *Muslims in the West: From Sojourners to Citizens*, ed. Yvonne Y. Haddad, 3–16. New York: Oxford University Press.
Turner, Richard B. 1997. *Islam in the African-American Experience.* Bloomington: Indiana University Press.

CHAPTER 39

THE AFRICAN AMERICAN RELIGIOUS PRESS

JOHN M. GIGGIE

TODAY's consumers of black religious news and newspapers have never had it better. They can quickly satisfy their interests by turning on a computer, searching the Internet by denomination or dogma, and scrolling through an endless stream of articles and hotlinks. Most newspapers are online and bloggers regularly report on and tweet about breaking stories, making it easy to keep up with happenings in faith communities around the country and the globe.

The literary luxuries of the present, however, are a far cry from the historical realities of the past. Readers should not be lulled into a belief that news about African American sacred life has always been readily and amply available, as nothing could be further from the truth. Indeed, the history of the modern black religious press is more a chronicle of failed endeavors than long-running successes, of aborted efforts than sustained publications. Since the birth of black newspapers in the nineteenth century, only a few denominational organs have avoided bankruptcy and lasted beyond a few months. That notable list includes the *Christian Recorder*, the *Christian Index*, the *Baptist Vanguard*, and the *Southwestern Christian Advocate*.

This chapter takes up the question of how this small group of African American sacred presses beat the odds and survived in the heyday of black newspapers, which was during the decades after the Civil War. Although black newspapers as a whole trace their origins to *Freedom's Journal*, a weekly published in New York City from 1827 to 1829, it wasn't until the end of slavery that they surged in number. Former slaves closely tied their newly won freedom to their ability to read and write their own works and especially create their own newspapers, which they did by the hundreds. For African American Baptists and Methodists in particular, local and national newspapers emerged as the most important way of disseminating and publicizing religious and political issues, as well as building up their churches, districts, and regional and national associations. But while many newspapers sprang up during Reconstruction and its immediate aftermath, only a few ever celebrated anything more than a two-year anniversary.

The topic of black religious newspapers is one that has received scant attention from scholars of religion and the media, who prefer wider stories on the rise of the institution of the black press in general or narrower ones on a famous secular press, such as *Freedom's Journal* or Frederick Douglass's *North Star*. When scholars turn their attention to black newspapers sponsored by faith communities, they tend to lump them with those backed by nonspiritual groups and treat them as an undifferentiated collective. The problem with such an intellectual grouping lies not in the formulation of its historical meaning. Scholars rightly point out that African Americans founded and sustained newspapers both sacred and secular as a means to control the public representation of their culture and history, attract notice to their struggles and accomplishments, nurture their communities, and expand African American entrepreneurialism. What is typically missing from current scholarship, however, is a careful consideration of black religious presses themselves. What distinguished them as a form of black printed voice and, more important, why did certain ones endure while nearly all others—including the secular ones—failed?[1]

The *Christian Recorder*, the *Christian Index*, the *Baptist Vanguard*, and the *Southwestern Christian Advocate* persisted far longer than their peers because they shared a range of editorial themes, advertising strategies, and marketing tactics that set them apart from their competitors and, in the minds of many blacks, made them essential to their daily lives. In particular, these editors—young ministers eager to grow their newspapers and careers—survived by creating a spacious "Letters to the Editor" section and establishing their press as a critical public resource for a wide range of information about segregation and the consumer market. Of the four black religious newspapers under consideration here, all but one—the *Southwestern Christian Advocate*—is still being published in some form.

The *Southwestern Christian Advocate* was the voice of the black church embedded within the Methodist Episcopal Church from 1876 to 1929. Founded in 1876 in New Orleans, Louisiana, it reached congregants scattered across the southeastern states. The newspaper closed after a fifty-three-year run because of declining black membership within the Methodist Episcopal Church. Also regional in scope, the *Baptist Vanguard*, the newspaper of the Arkansas Baptists, was founded in 1893 in Little Rock, Arkansas. Extant records are spotty, but they clearly indicate a strong publishing run between 1893 and 1897 and then again between 1921 and 1951. During these decades, it enjoyed a broad readership that stretched into Mississippi and up and down the Mississippi River, from counties in southern Missouri to parishes in eastern Louisiana. Today, the *Baptist Vanguard* survives under the aegis of Arkansas Baptist College; sports a new name, the *Baptist Vanguard Today*; and appears quarterly. The other two newspapers are more national in scope. The African Methodist Episcopal Church has published the *Christian Recorder* continuously since 1854 in Philadelphia, Pennsylvania. The *Christian Index* is the official mouthpiece of the Christian (formerly "Colored") Methodist Episcopal Church. Its first copy rolled off the presses in 1868 in Memphis, Tennessee. It moved its headquarters to Jackson several years later and since has reestablished its offices in Memphis and added new ones in Birmingham, Alabama.

The black denominations historically connected to these presses—the black conferences of the Methodist Episcopal (ME) Church to the *Southwestern Christian Advocate*, the National Baptist Convention to the *Baptist Vanguard*, the African Methodist Episcopal (AME) Church to the *Christian Recorder*, and the Colored Methodist Episcopal (CME) Church to the *Christian Index*—represent some of the most popular and powerful black religious bodies in the nation.[2] They constitute a diverse sample of African American Protestantism. Two began in the North. The ME Church convened its first General Conference in Baltimore in 1784, though it traced its North American origins to the 1730s and John and Charles Wesley's successful effort to import Methodism from England to the colonies. White bishops directed the ME Church, but they successfully recruited black congregants after the Civil War with invitations to join a church without racial boundaries. They never built such a community, but instead they organized segregated conferences. The AME Church held its first General Conference at Bethel Church in Philadelphia in 1816 as part of the growing free black community in that city. The other two denominations were southern based. The CME Church originated in 1870 as an all-black offshoot of the Methodist Episcopal Church, South. The black Baptist churches were loosely modeled, both theologically and organizationally, on white Baptist churches. Their popularity rested largely in their decentralized denominational structure, which allowed local communities a great deal of freedom to form their own churches, select their ministers, and design and implement their by-laws. Answering the question of how the newspapers sponsored by these celebrated black denominations endured, then, ultimately will shed new light on the multiple ways that the media and African American spiritual life historically intersected.

Editorial Themes

As editors for black religious newspapers took stock of their chances for continued existence in the post–Civil War era, not many could find reason for sustained optimism. While hundreds of churches and denominational associations announced the formation of a new press during this era, only a few would ever last. For example, hardly any of the approximately forty-one black religious newspapers founded between 1880 and 1897 across Mississippi survived very long. Nearly every one collapsed within twenty-four months of publishing their first edition.[3] Success rates were no better in Arkansas; only the *Baptist Vanguard* survived more than three years. Typical was the story of the *South-East Advocate*, the short-lived newspaper of the Southeastern Baptist District Association in Arkansas. As reported by the district's president, Rev. Isaac Bailey, "[t]his paper was doing fairly well and was keeping the people informed about the work of the District, but a great many of the subscribers got behind and the editor of the paper began to cry out for help but failed to get relief."[4]

Under enormous pressure to find ways of recruiting and retaining patrons, editors of the *Christian Recorder*, the *Christian Index*, the *Baptist Vanguard*, and the *Southwestern Christian Advocate* thought hard about what they published. One key to their achievement was the extraordinary diversity of their coverage. They published, of course, on religious topics—local church news, obituaries, bishops' travels, creedal dos and don'ts. But unlike their competitors, they also devoted considerable copy to regional and national politics, the activities of different denominations, short stories and poems by black authors, train schedules, crime reports, and the fluctuating price of cotton and corn, as well as news bulletins of fraternal orders and women's organizations. As a result, they garnered support not only from their denominational faithful but also from African Americans of every Christian stripe and even blacks with little interest in organized religion. They further broadened their audience through the use of visuals. Illiterate blacks enjoyed these newspapers in part because their pages were filled with pictures of black heroes, maps, and vivid fliers for clothes, shoes, dishes, books, magazines, bicycles, and landscape prints.

Besides offering a greater variety of news stories, popular interest features, and illustrations and photographs than other sacred newspapers, those at the top of the masthead at the *Christian Recorder*, the *Christian Index*, the *Baptist Vanguard*, and the *Southwestern Christian Advocate* gave their presses an added dimension that touched a chord of popular fascination. They lavished attention on the "Letters to the Editor" section of their papers, regularly devoting full-length columns to it. Typically, at least one letter to the editor began on the front page and ended by directing the reader's attention to a fuller complement found on page two or three. Hugely popular, the section became a staple for readers. It was not uncommon for any single issue to feature a dozen letters to the editor, which ranged in length from a twenty-word blurb to a half-page missive and usually included the name and address of the author. By contrast, unsuccessful religious newspapers included only one or two brief letters per edition and buried them on the back pages.

Editors at the *Christian Recorder*, the *Christian Index*, the *Baptist Vanguard*, and the *Southwestern Christian Advocate* grasped that African Americans found in the "Letters to the Editor" section much of what they demanded from a newspaper: a selection of contemporary topics drawn from the warp and woof of everyday life usually written by their peers. Editors certainly censored the letters that landed on their desks, weeding out those broadcasting harsh sentiments. But beyond these obvious cases, there was little reason to limit what was published.

Authors frequently discussed the tensions of living with the color line and the threats to black spiritual communities. The most popular subject was segregation, especially in travel and public accommodations, and how the indignities suffered by black rail passengers symbolized the broader crisis of the steady erosion of African American liberties. Railroad segregation laws, one writer warned in 1890, demonstrated that "[o]ne by one all the results of the war, secured at such tremendous cost in life and property, are being frittered way. . . ."[5] Another took pen in hand after South Carolina passed separate coach legislation in 1898 and scratched out a lament: "the further we get away from the day of our emancipation, the higher we climb in the scales of knowledge, wealth and moral sentives [*sic*], . . . something transpires to make the impression that the Negro is 'not so much after all.'"[6] Other letters focused on the stresses dividing black religious communities, such as the threat that fraternal orders posed to churches as the dominant institution in African American life. As fraternal orders surged in popularity among black men, a reverend with the AME Church in 1883 complained that lodges are "leading many who before have been true and tried adherents and supporters of the church, to . . . diminish their contributions, in order to be regular in attendance upon 'lodge meetings,' and remain 'financial.'"[7] Another popular issue of interest was the emergence of the African American Holiness-Pentecostal movement in the late 1800s, which attracted thousands of converts from traditional churches and extensive criticism from denominational ministers. A main point of contention was the character of the new church's service, which openly encouraged members to sing, dance, twirl with outstretched arms, and call out words of praise as the Holy Spirit moved them. Reverend R. T. Thomas, in a letter about the Holiness movement in Mississippi printed in the *Southwestern Christian Advocate*, mocked members' propensity for outward displays of emotion and belief in the supernatural.

> I do not believe in nor can I tolerate the idea of . . . howling at the mercy seat, falling out prostrate, dead an hour to two; meantime the sinner's spirit leaps out and descends to hell, has a time with the devil, and overcomes him, all hell combined; from thence ascends to heaven and views the situation, gets on a crown, wings, and a heavenly suit and flies to all parts of heaven, sings and is sung to and eventually comes back to earth. . . .[8]

These letters to the editor are a reminder that leaders of successful black religious newspapers understood that a large part of the public dimension to religion was epistolary, especially in the rural South. Many isolated church communities had a key existence in the form of letters: people isolated by geographic distance knew each other's travails, values, apprehensions, and wishes through their missives.[9] In print, preachers detailed the topic and content of their sermons, the look and decoration of their churches, the size and history of their congregations, and the reasons members were disciplined. Male and female congregants described their hopes and dreams, what they read, how they spent their money, what social issues demanded their attention, and what they thought about their church. These letters, then, effectively functioned as an accessible site of public testimony and correspondence and one deeply valued by black readers.

Advertising Strategies

While the "Letters to the Editors" section helped to popularize the *Christian Recorder*, the *Christian Index*, the *Baptist Vanguard*, and the *Southwestern Christian Advocate*, it didn't secure their financial futures. Editors and the bishops they worked under needed to compel blacks to subscribe on a yearly basis and donate money to meet their financial needs and compete with rival newspapers, both religious and secular. It was a high-stakes competition in which they endured only by experimenting with different tactics until they found a formula that worked.

As an early strategy of shoring up their denominational associations, church officials ordered ministers and congregants to sacrifice financially. In 1878, AME elders alerted its southern clerics "that they will not be able to get their licenses renewed if they do not take the CHRISTIAN RECORDER and read it."[10] That same year, CME bishops, seeking to relieve the burden of debt threatening the livelihood of the *Christian Index*, mandated preachers to subscribe. Those who refused risked being publicly sanctioned.[11] In 1892, African Americans from the all-black Upper Mississippi Conference of the ME gave money both to their local college, Rust, in Holly Springs, Mississippi, and their regional newspaper, the *Southwest Christian Advocate*, in accordance with a new resolution that stated "we as a Conference rejoice in the success of establishing institutions of higher learning in the Southern States . . . [and] work for the interest of that grand and noble cause."[12] As a result, churches organized special events like "Rust Day," when congregants offered special prayers for the success of the college and took up a collection whose final tally was publicly reported at the annual state conference the following winter.[13]

But merely asking or even browbeating blacks to subscribe fell far short of the mark required by any editor to run his newspaper comfortably. Appealing to sympathetic white churches and religious organizations for small amounts of aid and material assistance was a distant possibility. Certainly one editor of a start-up black press tried it. When Richard Boyd worked to open the doors of his National Baptist Publishing House in 1896, he begged his white counterparts with the American Baptist Publishing Society to lend him printing and book plates. When they turned him down for fear of increased competition in the selling of religious literature, he asked another white organization, the Southern Baptist Convention, and got what he wanted.[14] Still, editors of the *Christian Recorder*, the *Christian Index*, the *Baptist Vanguard*, and the *Southwestern Christian Advocate* seemed to agree that blacks, regardless of their denomination, could never completely depend on a steady stream of aid from white benefactors. To ensure the health and longevity of their institutions, they had to rely primarily on their own wherewithal.

The pressure to raise money and public support forced editors to experiment with new techniques of advertising and tap a rapidly developing sector of southern society, the consumer economy. Grasping the shifts in the regional economy and the historical importance of the consumer market to black ideas of liberty, editors moved swiftly to exploit both. During the late 1800s, the rise of mass-produced, inexpensive domestic and literary goods; improvements in the national and regional transportation infrastructure; the expansion of the US Postal Service; and the growing density of commercial stores across the South enabled white and black southerners to view and sample the market's goods and services more easily. To be sure, black interest in the market was hardly new. Since slavery, African Americans, when they had the time and money, often had bought new clothes, tools, or reading materials. Many sought to own literary and consumer goods, transgressing the cultural spaces where they were exchanged because such activities resonated with the thrill of emancipation. They evidenced a notion of identity that integrated citizenship and consumption: to be free meant to be able to buy what they wanted and could afford. Emancipation only intensified this link.

Starting in the 1880s, editors at the *Christian Recorder*, the *Christian Index*, the *Baptist Vanguard*, and the *Southwestern Christian Advocate* began to treat their constituents as consumers who gave money or subscribed to their newspaper only when given something tangible in return. Reverend Joseph Booker, the president of Arkansas Baptist College and the editor of the *Baptist Vanguard* in the 1880s, organized alumni to sell pencils stamped with the name of their alma mater. Booker hoped to sell hundreds, delivering them either in person, through a colleague, or through the mail. He believed that the pencils held symbolic significance for sharecroppers and tenant farmers without any formal education, as well as for all black people who, "when they buy these pencils, . . . give and yet get something back—that's the only way the majority of our people care to give."[15] Whether Booker's campaign netted the desired amount of cash is uncertain, but his philosophy of rewarding patrons with a small commodity signaled a subtle shift in how editors developed new marketing techniques built on the evolving relationship between faith and consumption in the late nineteenth century. Even though Rev. Booker sold only pencils, his fundraising campaign indicated that his role as a fundraiser, subscription pitchman, and preacher was beginning to encompass a new level of involvement with the commercial market—in this case, the distribution of small manufactured items in return for patronage of the *Baptist Vanguard*.

Like Booker in the late 1800s, other black spiritual leaders charged with raising money for the *Christian Recorder*, the *Christian Index*, the *Baptist Vanguard*, or the *Southwestern Christian Advocate* quickly began rewarding supporters with small, mass-produced items sometimes marked with recognizable emblems of African American history. Although other presses followed suit, none were more aggressive in their attempt to exploit the consumer market for ways to impress these newspapers ever more deeply into the daily lives of black readers. In 1896, editors of the *Southwestern Christian Advocate* gave new subscribers a free set of communion implements; two years later, they offered a calendar that recalled their Methodist heritage by featuring a different scene each month from the life of John Wesley.[16] During subscription drives, editors presented the most industrious agents with a new Epworth organ or "fine $75 Mead Bicycle."[17] In 1896, men and women scanning the *Baptist Vanguard* learned that a new, leather-bound Bible could be theirs for free if they subscribed.[18] Or if they preferred, they could receive an "Emancipation Chart," a two-foot-high reproduction of the Emancipation Proclamation framed by winged angels and a series of elaborate sketches of blacks progressing from slavery to freedom.[19]

Through this new effort to reward support for these four denominational presses with consumer goods, blacks began to discover access to a narrow range of commodities. Indeed, they saw that an act of consumption performed through a black religious institution carried distinctive social meanings. They witnessed how their financial support for a newspaper brought new products into their homes—products that were otherwise difficult, if not impossible, to obtain—and which, in their physical makeup (as in the case of the stylized reproduction of the Emancipation Proclamation), often represented a proud moment in their history. Equally important, they joined a distinctive campaign that cleverly connected black political and racial identity, rising popular interest in domestic goods, and support for the *Christian Recorder*, the *Christian Index*, the *Baptist Vanguard*, or the *Southwestern Christian Advocate*.

Similar to their effort to tie support for their presses to popular interest in the consumer market and its goods, editors began to advise readers directly how to minimize the problem of racism that they frequently experienced in the marketplace. It was another way for them to interest readers and strengthen bonds with them. Editors alerted readers about merchants who treated blacks unfairly because of their skin color. In 1894, for example, church leaders listed on the masthead of the *Baptist Vanguard* urged constituents to avoid reading any Arkansas white newspaper or patronizing its advertisers if it failed to oppose lynching or the recent expulsion of local blacks from the ranks of postal employees.[20]

Selling Consumer Goods

Building on their roles as guides to the marketplace, editors of black religious presses also transformed sections of their newspapers into mail-order catalogs. They guaranteed the quality and fair price of most items advertised in their pages and backed the buyer's full satisfaction with a money-back guarantee. Sometimes they even promised to secure fair terms of credit backed by the manufacturer. Interested readers mailed back an order with payment to the editors, who then contacted the wholesaler or manufacturer, arranged for delivery via an itinerant minister or the postal service, and sometimes pocketed a small commission on the sale.

Leading the way were the editors at the *Southwestern Christian Advocate*, who forged a series of relationships with local and national white manufacturers interested in finding new avenues to reach black consumers. They openly pitched their press as one of the most sensible and economical ways to shop. Subscribers learned that they could buy a twelve-volume encyclopedia at half-off the normal price and with no shipping cost if they placed an order through the newspaper.[21] If they wanted a new bell for their church, they could entrust their order to an editor who worked closely with a maker in New Orleans.[22] To quell any apprehensions about buying an item advertised through their paper, editors inserted a comforting pledge: "Our readers will please bear in mind that every organ, piano, bell or book purchased through us, helps to swell the profits of the Book Concern; and, furthermore, we can and do give purchasers better articles at lower prices than if sent elsewhere.[23] One 1894 pitch, which simultaneously underscored the newspaper's role as a purveyor of domestic commodities and reminded readers that items purchased through the paper helped it to survive and supported the overall cause of black Methodism, offered a Singer Sewer machine at a steeply discounted price with the word "Advocate" boldly stenciled in big white letters on both sides of its metal casing.[24]

In these examples, black religious newspaper editors offered a fresh opportunity for their constituents to simultaneously participate in the consumer economy and shore up the financial future of their spiritual organizations. Other religious presses failed to follow suit or did so only intermittently. A few peers at secular papers played a similar role as mediator between the market and their readers, but never to the same degree. And none matched the entrepreneurialism of the religious editors who took a more personal interest in selling by following the lead of itinerant black ministers who peddled consumer goods. Following established preaching circuits or establishing new ones, they turned their pastoral visits into occasions both to save souls and to sell a narrow range of literary and consumer goods usually produced by northern white manufacturers.

In contrast to their peers at secular presses in particular, the editors at black sacred newspapers benefited directly from their status as men of the cloth and from dense networks of contacts with African American spiritual communities. When recruiting black agents to sell for them, white manufacturers prized black ministers above all others. The Union Book and Bible House of Philadelphia and the John Hertel Company of Chicago solicited preachers across the South, offering them a small commission of a few cents for every Bible and religious storybook sold.[25] Companies like these viewed African American religious leaders as uniquely positioned to advise members of their race about matters of consumption.[26] Black ministers, because of their status as religious leaders sworn to lead an honest, virtuous, and God-fearing life, enjoyed an unparalleled level of public confidence among African Americans. After the mid-1880s, they also traveled for free or at a greatly reduced rate on the railroad, thereby making them more mobile and better able to visit plantations and rural towns than most black travelers.

Throughout the 1890s, Rev. Booker knocked on the doors of African American churches, homes, and schools across Arkansas to raise money for the two Little Rock institutions under his leadership, Arkansas Baptist College and the *Baptist Vanguard*. During his travels, Booker regularly solicited financial pledges to the college, subscriptions to the newspaper, and mail orders for a wide selection of consumer goods. In person and as editor of the *Baptist Vanguard*, Booker advertised Bibles, pencils, church bells, and organs produced by white manufacturers. Like Booker, Rev. Henry Bullock, a CME missionary and an editor with the *Christian Index* in the late 1890s, was a salesman who dutifully attended to blacks curious about new manufactured products. Whether working on the road or at his desk, he fielded questions about the value and price of different market items and filled orders for those advertised in his paper. In a letter titled "From the Agent to the Church," Bullock told readers that "[m]any of the patrons write to me for goods we do not carry, and we feel it our duty to get it for them. . . . We have a force of nice workmen and think we can give satisfaction."[27]

Sometimes religious newspapers enlisted the preachers who wrote regularly for their papers to sell subscriptions for them while riding their circuits and peddling goods. In 1895, Rev. James H. Hoke, an Arkansas Baptist and the general missionary for the state, searched far and wide for converts, subscribers to the *Baptist Vanguard*, and donors to Arkansas Baptist College. Although Hoke was ultimately disappointed with the fruits of his labors, it was not for want of effort. By his own account, he covered 1,270 miles, visited forty-one churches, preached fifty-six sermons, delivered twenty-five lectures, attended twenty prayer meetings, and organized six Sunday schools and one church. Despite his grumbling, he raised $106.70 and sold hundreds of single issues of the *Baptist Vanguard*, several six-month and year-long subscriptions to the newspaper, and one hundred "Bibles, Testaments & Books."[28]

In addition to drawing on the pastoral and commercial networks spun by themselves and their allies, editors further bolstered the viability of their presses by making use of the organizational activities of churchwomen. They turned to them as another spiritual resource to make their newspapers successful. Similar to black ministers, some leading southern black churchwomen developed a limited commercial role for themselves as peddlers of consumer goods, though of a far more restricted nature. They were typically presidents of women's associations and young people's unions, as well as the wives of ministers, all prominent social roles that defined them as responsible public figures and brought them into close contact with a wide range of churchgoers. Organizing rural black women into "Bible bands," they created small, interlocking networks of women's religious organizations that promoted literacy, scriptural study, and religious publications. As part of their missionary efforts, they sold subscriptions to their denominational presses and regularly published columns about how women should lead "holy" lives. They also served as limited literary agents for northern white religious organizations eager to promote Christianity among African American southerners, such as the American Women's Baptist Home Missionary Society.[29]

Formulas for Success, Yesterday and Today

Like their secular counterparts, most black religious presses rarely lasted more than several years. Competition between them was fierce, while public support was marginal. Those that lasted the longest deserve special notice because they offer a rare glimpse at the particular ways that the media and black religion overlapped and interacted. Black sacred presses endured because they practiced a formula that bought them publishing success. They provided readers with an extraordinary variety of stories, a mélange of religious and nonreligious topics, and a range of visual images. Success also turned on editors' ability to employ different advertising and marketing techniques adapted from the emerging consumer market. Making their newspapers into indispensible sources of advice about commodities for the black public and themselves into vehicles for the sale and delivery of a host of small domestic goods, editors established their presses as essential to the livelihood of their readers. To be sure, this formula was not perfect. The *Southwestern Christian Advocate* eventually failed and the *Baptist Vanguard* has surged and sputtered during its history. But even in these cases, the ability of black sacred presses to survive for any significant duration turned on whether they followed the rough outline of this formula.

It is a formula, moreover, that still bears fruit. Indeed, the story of the modern black sacred press continues through the present day. It arcs forward from the late nineteenth century, a reminder that the practices employed by African American religious newspapers to maximize their chances for publishing success still work. Pick up any edition of the *Christian Recorder* or the *Christian Index* and note the mix of denominational news with current events and local tidbits, such as obituaries and graduations.[30] See, too, how eagerly and completely the editors address readers' inquiries. Now much of the communications between editors and readers occurs electronically through each press's online publication site. But the notion of creating something similar to the "Letters to the Editor" section begun in the late nineteenth century still persists. In the online version of the *Christian Recorder* published on May 27, 2010, for example, Rev. Dr. Calvin H. Sydnor III, the twentieth editor of the newspaper, published a thank-you note for prayers and blessings for a loved one recently stricken ill, as well as letters describing what books the faithful are reading, women's spiritual awakenings in Nashville, Tennessee, and—not surprisingly—an appeal to subscribe to and closely read his newspaper.[31] Similarly, these two newspapers continue to experiment with ways to harness the marketplace to strengthen ties with readers, as well as to squeeze revenue by facilitating the buying and selling of consumer goods with their constituents. Readers of the main webpage for the AME Church can link directly to the "AME Storehouse," which is hosted on the "Amennetwork" website. On the top half of the page, viewers can read breaking denominational and political news, or they can click on one of several advertisements at the bottom. Interested parties can purchase Magic Cabin toys for children, an antioxidant shake called "Vemma," or Limoges Jewelry.[32] A small portion of the proceeds directly benefits the church and its newspaper.

While the *Christian Recorder* and the *Christian Index* currently publish in print and electronic form and tap the power of the Internet to sell a variety of personal and household goods, they share a time-tested blueprint of success. As did their predecessors in the late nineteenth century, they are far more than a staid accounting of national and local happenings. Through their radical editorial, marketing, and advertising practices, they are a vital means of communication among African Americans and between them and the larger world of racial politics, consumption, and domesticity. Indeed, these black sacred newspapers, as they have been for generations, are critical expressions of black identity that connect readers to denominational and racial histories even as they help them navigate the shoals of contemporary culture.

NOTES

1. Henry Lewis Suggs, ed., *The Black Press in the South, 1865–1979* (Westport, CT: Greenwood, 1983); Frankie Hutton, *The Early Black Press in America, 1827 to 1860* (Westport, CT: Greenwood, 1982); Armistead S. Pride, *A History of the Black Press* (Washington, DC: Howard University Press, 1987); Bernell E. Tripp, "The Origins of the Black Press," in *Media and Religion in American History,* ed. William David Sloan (Northport, AL: Vision Press, 2000): 93–107; Todd Vogel, *The Black Press: New Literary and Historical Essays* (New Brunswick, NJ: Rutgers University Press, 2001); Patrick Washburn, *The African American Newspaper: Voice of Freedom* (Evanston, IL: Northwestern University Press, 2006); and Jacqueline Bacon, *Freedom's Journal: The First African American Newspaper* (Lanham, MD: Lexington Books, 2007).

2. J. William Harris, *Deep Souths: Delta, Piedmont, and Sea Island Society in the Age of Segregation* (Baltimore: Johns Hopkins Press, 2001), 366; US Bureau of the Census, *Census of Religious Bodies,* Vol. II (Washington, DC: Government Printing Office, 1919), 240–42, 278–79.

3. Julius Thompson, *Black Life in Mississippi: Essays on Political, Social, and Cultural Studies in a Deep South State* (New York: University Press of America), 14, 40 n.3; appendix 1, 150–89; Vernon Lane Wharton, *The Negro In Mississippi, 1865–1890* (Chapel Hill: University of North Carolina Press), 272–73; and Neil McMillen, *Dark Journey: Black Mississippians in the Age of Jim Crow* (Urbana: University of Illinois Press, 1989), 72–108.

4. Rev. Isaac Bailey, "Moderator's Report" (typescript, November 3, 1909. Box 4. F. 23. Bailey-Thurman Papers, Special Collections, Emory University).

5. Editorial, "Separating the Races on the Cars," *Southwestern Christian Advocate,* March 13, 1890.

6. Editorial, Untitled, *Christian Index,* March 19, 1898.

7. H. T. Kealing, "Secret Societies Among the Negroes," *Christian Recorder,* April 12, 1883.

8. Rev. R. T. Thomas, "'Feeling Not Religion', but Religion and Feeling Combine," *Southwestern Christian Advocate,* October 19, 1902.

9. On the creation of community and identity through the publication and exchange of letters, see Walter Johnson, *Soul to Soul: Life Inside the Antebellum Slave Market* (Cambridge: Harvard University Press, 1999), 13; Richard Bushman, *The Refinement of America: Persons, Buildings, Cities* (New York: Vintage, 1992), esp. 215.

10. Rev. J. B. Webb, "Encouragement," *Christian Recorder,* December 5, 1878.

11. Phillips, *History of the Colored Methodist Episcopal Church,* 113, 127. See also F. M. Hamilton, "An Earnest Appeal to the Presiding Elders and Pastors of the CME Church," Christian Index, January 15, 1887.

12. *Journal of the Second Session of the Upper Mississippi Annual Conference of the Methodist Episcopal Church, Held at Columbus, Mississippi, February 3–8, 1892* (Columbus, MI: Excelsior Book and Job Printing Establishment, 1892), 18, 20. Cain Archives. Millsaps College. Jackson, MI.

13. *Journal of the Ninth session of the Upper Mississippi Annual Conference of the Methodist Episcopal Church, Held at West Point, Miss., January 11 to 16, 189[9]* (Jackson, MI: Press of the Mississippi Sentinel, 1899), 37. Cain Archives.

14. Sally G. McMillan, *To Raise up the South: Sunday Schools in Black and White Churches, 1865–1915* (Baton Rouge: Louisiana University Press, 2001), 113–14, 190–91.

15. Jos[eph] Booker, "An Open Letter to Our Students," *Baptist Vanguard,* June 25, 1896. Two years later, anyone raising ten cash subscribers for the *Christian Recorder* earned a fourteen-karat gold "Christian Recorder Fountain Pen," April 14, 1898, and also March 30, 1900, *Christian Recorder.*

16. Subscription advertisement featuring communion implements, *Southwestern Christian Advocate,* April 21, 1896.

17. Advertisement, "Prizes . . . Prizes," *Southwestern Christian Advocate,* September 23, 1897. See also "Further Inducements," *Southwestern Christian Advocate,* November 23, 1893.

18. Subscription advertisement featuring bible, *Baptist Vanguard,* July 30, 1896 and October 8, 1896. In earlier years, editors offered new subscribers a copy of Webster's Dictionary for one dollar. "Do You Want a Dictionary," *Baptist Vanguard,* February 16, 1893.

19. Subscription advertisement featuring "Emancipation Chart," *Baptist Vanguard,* April 6, 1896.

20. Editorial, "The Press and the Colored People," *Baptist Vanguard,* July 14, 1894.

21. Advertisement for Chamber's American Encyclopedia, *Southwestern Christian Advocate,* July 20, 1893.

22. Advertisement for Church Bell, *Southwestern Christian Advocate,* October 29, 1891.

23. Editorial announcement, *Southwestern Christian Advocate,* June 20, 1895.

24. Advertisement for Singer Sewing Machine, *Southwestern Christian Advocate,* April 12, 1894.

25. Henry T. and Mary Ann Harris Papers (no. 4360, Box 1, Series 3, F. 8, Southern Historical Collection, University of North Carolina, Chapel Hill).

26. McMillan, *To Raise up the South,* 26–31; Harvey, *Redeeming the South,* 20–22.

27. H. Bullock, "From the Agent to the Entire Church," *Christian Index,* August 20, 1898. See also "Wynne District [Arkansas]," *Christian Index,* January 11, 1892.

28. J. H. Hoke, "From the Field," *Baptist Vanguard,* April 19, 1895. For a short biography of Hoke, see Clark, *History of Negro Baptists in Arkansas,* 43.

29. *Price List of Hope, Bibles, Fireside School Books, Etc.* (Nashville: np, nd). Box 1. F. 4. Bailey-Thurman Papers (Emory). On southern women working as literary agents, see McMillan, *To Raise Up the South,* 118.

30. See, for example, the online version of the *Christian Index,* May 27, 2010, http://thechristianindexonline.blogspot.com/ (accessed May 30, 2010).

31. See, for example, the online version of the *Christian Recorder,* May 28, 2010, http://tcr-online.blogspot.com/ (accessed May 30, 2010).

32. See http://www.ame-church.com/links/index.php and http://www.amennetwork.com/ (both accessed May 30, 2010).

REFERENCES

Hutton, Frankie. 1982. *The Early Black Press in America, 1827 to 1860*. Westport, CT: Greenwood.
Pride, Armistead S. 1987. *A History of the Black Press*. Washington, DC: Howard University Press.
Tripp, Bernell E. 2000. *The Origins of the Black Press*. In *Media and Religion in American History*, ed. David Sloan, 93–107. Northport, AL: Vision Press.
Vogel, Todd. 2001. *The Black Press: New Literary and Historical Essays*. New Brunswick, NJ: Rutgers University Press.
Washburn, Patrick. 2006. *The African American Newspaper: Voice of Freedom*. Evanston, IL: Northwestern University Press.

Index